MAN AND WOMAN, WAR AND PEACE

Frontispiece - Final home of Robert and Elizabeth, built in 1979, photographed 2 April 2002, three years after Elizabeth's death. We are pictured 9 March 1980, joyful a our success, the turmoil of our early years behind us, as we welcome the challenges an beauty of our land.

MAN AND WOMAN, WAR AND PEACE 1941–1951

A Dual Autobiography, Verbatim from Their Letters and Diary

Robert W. Doty
and
Elizabeth N. Doty[†]

[†]Posthumous

VANTAGE PRESS
New York

Published by Vantage Press, Inc.
516 West 34th Street, New York, New York 10001

Manufactured in the United States of America
ISBN: 0-533-14331-4

Library of Congress Catalog Card No.: 2002091905

0 9 8 7 6 5 4 3 2 1

CONTENTS

MAN AND WOMAN,
WAR AND PEACE

INTRODUCTION

Mon 21 July 1941

I place my hand tenderly upon the pliant waves of your hair, encircle the warmth of your body and taste the tang of life's mystery on your loving lips. May our kisses always distill the sweetness from life's enigmas, that we may answer each other's thirst after the unknowable, with the perfection of attainable beauty.

- Bob

Midnite Fri 13 Feb 42

Just enough space to tell you I love you as only woman can love her mate, now and forever.

- Elizabeth

10:45pm Tue 24 Feb 1942

Nothing could ever exceed the joy of being mated to you, that I can love so completely and unreservedly. To kiss you is to be in ecstasy, but to realize that you are my wife, my eternal love, so kind, so beautiful, sweet, sincere - the emotion that such thots bring can only be profaned by words. Only when I look into your radiant face can I know that you receive and cherish my love and return it thru the channels of the inexpressible. What an overawing experience this is to feel your soul meet and convey its love in the mystic world of intangible knowledge.

- Robert

10pm Sunday 18 Apr 43

Robert, I shall never never ever forget some of the kisses you have indelibly imprinted on my lips, on my heart; and as for loving you, it is an eternal thing, something that existed before I met you (hoarded carefully until that fateful time), and will con-

1

tinue to grow in intensity no matter whether we are apart in time or space. Love you beyond earthly expression.

Always,
Elizabeth

Sat 19 Aug 44
Oh, how constantly thankful & joyful I am to be your husband, your mate thru all of life, boundlessly beautiful, serene, complete & richly satisfying always.
- Robert

These fervent expressions, consistently distributed throughout the years, encapsulate the bliss they obviously anticipate, "Always", "Forever", "Eternally" . Would that it were perpetually so, save that these lines were written by two human beings; actually, two subpecies, man and woman. While neither faltered throughout some 58 years in fundamental adoration, there were, none the less, seemingly inevitable days of stony silence, each feeling betrayed by the stubbornness of the other. These were episodes of utter misery, thankfully few, but painfully threatening to the bond that each held sacred. It is forcefully evident from the statistics of today that such bonds are, indeed, all too frequently severed by the incapacity of firmly mated pairs to resolve such mutually destructive behavior. Since the above subjects, Elizabeth and Robert, did succeed, there may be merit in reviewing the togetherness of their lives, to seek some understanding of their ultimate achievement. This opportunity is happily enhanced by their having committed their acts and emotions to a written record, four years of nearly daily letters exchanged throughout most of World War II, and the faithfully recorded daily diary of Elizabeth.

Their first 10 years offer sufficient examples that the full 58 are not required; the bliss and quarrels of the ensuing 58 were fully adumbrated in the initial 10. Those years, 1941 through 1951, involved a brief and intense courtship, a year of mated life before war intruded with its chaos and adventure, then children and the postwar struggle to make up the "lost years". The story is not without romance and literary appeal, travelogue and social history of the times. The written record alone constitutes some

2

1.25 million words and has thus been culled for "representative passages" that will convey the focal points of the relationship, the character of the participants, the background and setting of the critical events, and yet evoke some continuity in the unfolding history. The chosen and veridically presented happenings will here be augmented by brief synopses and explanatory detail; followed finally by analyses that seek to extract clues from this record as to how this truly rapturous marriage survived those human lapses that, from time to time, so grievously assaulted it.

A sad fact must be faced, that this retrospective emanates from but one of the pair, Robert, who herewith undeniably seeks to memorialize his precious Elizabeth; but who, also undeniably, brings but the male's view of the proceedings to the arguments to be deduced. How unbiased this analysis may be can be judged only by the reader. Of much greater concern to me is how Elizabeth might have perceived such public revelation of our very private lives. My motivation to do so springs, primarily, from my ever-revisiting the joy of our wedded state, and my perception that therein resides an example others might come to value. This book is urged not by the futility of mourning, but by the celebration of the beauty with which life can be endowed, can the course but be presciently discerned.

Elizabeth faithfully kept her diary, and we each preserved the other's letters. They have heretofore been but dormant family treasures, a history of our trials and triumphs, receiving little interest in the busy 50 years. Yet it must also be admitted that, as the volume of our exchanges grew, we were not wholly oblivious to the drama they contained. And while considerations for posterity played no role whatever in our scribblings, we both commented from time to time on the uniqueness of our history, and the possibility that it, and the manner of its telling, might merit publication. I thus have confidence that Elizabeth would have joined me, not only in the process of publishing our past, but in analyzing it as well. She had at the time assembled my attempted poetry; for during my long days of idle sea duty, I had contemplated a career as an author. Science, however, intervened to offer greater assurance of success; and so the letters,

3

and the earlier diaries, have languished in the closets and attics of our homes.

There seems no way out of the difficulty posed by having three sources of material, the diaries and the two sets of letters, all necessarily truncated mercilessly. There is thus an unavoidable demand upon the reader to distinguish just whose words are being read; and to forgive the resulting discontinuities. The turnaround time for mail within the States was of a week or so for each of us answering the other's letter; but, of course, there is no resulting valid order as to which should be the "preceding" letter, since each contains both "answers" and "questions". Where it seemed necessary, notation has been inserted in the body of the letter to clarify a particular passage. For mail to the theaters of war there was essentially no "turnaround" possible, so these letters are generally presented en masse. When we were together, of course, the diary is the only record that exists. Occasionally, for emphasis, I have included her diaried observations on events or opinions not dealt with in her letters.

As can be seen at the start above, the two writers are distinguished by setting their material each in a different font which, in turn, differs from that of the comments. All of the entries are dated as per the originals. Original spellings have been retained, characterized by our common, but desultory, usage of what Chicagoans came to call "Chicago Tribune" spelling, a noble but seemingly futile effort to make English orthography more rational. I have even thought that it might be of interest to see on what occasions we used Tribune versus conventional spelling, the latter being followed for all commentary.

I am indebted to Dr Jacqueline A. Liederman, one of my former students, now Director of the Brain, Behavior and Cognition Program at Boston University, for patiently reading the draft of this book. She, as I, recognized several of the irremediable faults of this presentation, but her encouragement has been uniquely helpful. I am deeply grateful also for the rare talent of Dorothy Roberts in translating historical materials written in Pitman shorthand (see, e.g., **Neurology 55:** 289-293, 2000). It was she who brilliantly rescued Elizabeth's diary of 29 Aug 1941 - 8 January 1942, a treasure otherwise lost to the Pitman code of that era. That work constitutes **Chapter IV**, that is perhaps the most unique record in this series.

Finally, I must thank my daughter, Cheryl A. Joyce, whose skilled secretarial eye, like her Mother's, descried my lapses in orthography or grammar; and whose discernment has been most reassuring, that the frank story of her parents' marriage is of sufficient interest and value as to excuse its violation of family privacy.

RWD
Rush, New York
23 August 2002

15 Nov Move from RW's rooming house to 3-room apartment, having bought furniture
7 Dec Pearl Harbor

CHAPTER V

17 Jan 1942 EN begins 6-day week with Corps of Engineers
2 Feb - 1 Mar EN on duty in Cleveland, Ohio; habit of daily correspondence between EN and RW initiated
20-26 Apr Vacation, Ann Arbor, Detroit, Smoky Mountains
1 Jul RW to 2nd shift, 6-day week, foreman of screw machines making machine gun bullets

CHAPTER VI

25 Sep RW, drafted, leaves for Ft Custer, Michigan
2 Oct RW begins basic training at Camp Lee, Virginia
12 Nov RW passes Regimental examination for Officers' Candidate School (OCS)
4-8 Dec Rapturous hours snatched from RW's Army routine, EN making 33-hour train trip between Chicago and Camp Lee
9 Dec RW passes Post Board Exam for OCS

CHAPTER VII

2 Jan 1943 RW begins OCS

CHAPTER VIII

3 Apr RW commissioned 2nd Lieutenant, Quartermaster Corps
14 Apr RW reports to Ft Warren, Wyoming - Bitter quarrel begins as to his insistence that EN join him
1 Jun EN surrenders, stores furniture, quits hard-won job, and joins RW as an army wife

CHAPTER IX

19 Jun RW ordered to New York Port of Embarkation (NYPOE - Brooklyn Army Base) and transferred to Transportation Corps

21 Jun Arrive New York City together

1 Jul Rent apartment in Brooklyn Heights, RW departs for duty aboard ship

2-4 Jul Together in Baltimore prior to sailing

15-20 Jul Together again, Newport News, Virginia, awaiting assembly of convoy- RW departs as Transport Commander of 335 troops

26 Jul - 6 Aug EN has temporary work with news agency

14 Aug RW arrives Oran, Algeria

9 Aug - 13 Sep EN works for Electric Advisers

15 Sep RW returns to New York with 700 Afrikakorps prisoners of war

5 Oct EN returns to her parents' home in Chicago

10 Oct RW departs NYPOE on SS Wm S. Rosecrans for Mediterranean Theater

21 Oct EN transfers our first $1000 to Savings and Loan account in Chicago

30 Oct RW arrives Gibraltar

11 Nov RW in bombing attack south of Cagliari, Sardinia; 6 ships sunk

20 Nov - 13 Dec RW in Palermo, Sicily

16 Dec RW arrives in Naples harbor.

28 Dec RW visits front line at San Pietro (Battle of Cassino)

6 Jan 1944 Wm S. Rosecrans sunk at Isle of Capri, brief illness keeping RW from his tweendeck office where first torpedo hit - EN takes job with Royce Publishing in Chicago

20 -26 Jan Air flight: Sicily, Algiers, Casablanca, Marrakech, Dakar, Fortaleza, Georgetown, Puerto Rico, Washington, DC

CHAPTER X

27 Jan EN leaves to join RW in Brooklyn

10 Mar RW leaves NYPOE with Meteorology Company for Alexandria, Egypt; fighter planes for Karachi, India - EN returns to Chicago

27 Mar EN takes position as Civil Service Commission Examiner

1 May RW's convoy attacked south of Crete

26 Apr - 2 May RW in Karachi

21-23 May RW in Perth, Australia

6 Jun D-Day RW in mid Pacific

26 Jun RW arrives Los Angeles

CHAPTER XI

30 Jun RW joins EN in Chicago

3 Jul They arrive in New York, room in Brooklyn

10-14 Jul Both in Philadelphia as RW assumes assignment to another ship

15 Jul EN returns to Chicago and to Civil Service Commission job

2 Aug RW arrives Belfast, Ireland

14 Aug RW unloads ship at Stranraer, Scotland

18-26 Aug RW in Glasgow, Edinburg, Loch Lomond

29 Aug EN resigns from Civil Service Commission job

1 Sep EN arrives New York, returns to room in Brooklyn

5 Sep RW arrives New York

28 Sep EN returns to Chicago, RW assigned to ship going to Bristol, England

2 Oct EN resumes her job with War Department, Corps of Engineers, now termed "Manhattan Project"

10 Nov RW promoted to 1st Lieutenant, begins shore duty at NYPOE

15 Nov RW gets apartment in Flatbush section of Brooklyn

CHAPTER XII

19 Nov EN joins him, transferred to New York office of Manhattan Project
12 Apr 1945 President Roosevelt dies, EN becomes pregnant
8 May VE Day
6 Aug EN: "Our Secret is Out! The Atomic Bomb!"
14 Aug VJ Day
18 Aug EN resigns from Manhattan Project, awarded Medal of Merit
15 Sep With RW EN, quite pregnant, returns to parents in Chicago

CHAPTER XIII

24 Sep RW back to Brooklyn apartment
2-11 Oct RW in Boston, assigned to SS Josiah Bartlett
18 Oct - 2 Nov SS Josiah Bartlett loading grain in New Orleans
10-13 Nov SS Josiah Bartlett puts in to Norfolk for repairs
19 Nov RW arrives Antwerp
2-4 Dec RW visits Paris
7 Dec RW promoted to Captain, Transportation Corps
11 Dec SS Josiah Bartlett leaves Antwerp with 676 US Army troops
27 Dec SS Josiah Bartlett, troops and RW stranded in Azores by inadequate fuel in violent storm; RW, Jr born in Chicago, 05:40 AM, EN unsure whether RW has survived the storm, being incommunicado and with false announcement of his ship's arrival
30 Dec RW arranges with Portugese authoritics for troops to have shore lcave
5 Jan 1946 EN returns to parents' home from hospital with new baby
9 Jan SS Josiah Bartlett arrives NYPOE

CHAPTER XIV

12-17 Jan RW visits wife and son

18 Jan RW assigned shore duty NYPOE, quartered at Fort Hamilton

26 Jan RW applies for admission to University of Chicago

30 Jan RW buys 35-mm camera for $90, begins serious hobby of photography

31 Jan, 5 & 14 Feb RW takes examinations (Army General Education Development Exam) for admission/placement at U of Chicago

4 Apr RW sails from NYPOE as Transport Commander of USAT Jarrett M. Huddleston, hospital ship converted for "war bride" transport

20 Apr Huddleston leaves Southampton, England with 471 women, infants and children

3 May Huddleston arrives NYPOE

17 May RW leaves for Fort Sheridan, Illinois and terminal leave

CHAPTER XV

19 May RW home with EN and son, living with her parents

23 May Buy 5-room bungalow with finished attic, $6000 down, $5000 mortgage, presently rented

27 May Scarcity of cars for sale, buy 1939 Graham Paige for $752

31 May Car doesn't run

14 Jun Take another entrance exam for U of Chicago

21 Jun First paycheck for job as night fireman, 3rd shift, 32 hours, $30.72

22 Jun Under "GI Bill" enroll for Summer Quarter: Physiology, Chemistry and Psychology at U of Chicago

1 Sep RW walks out on EN and in-laws (sleeps in car), returns next day

6 Sep Tenants finally leave our house

7 Sep We move in, begin month (and years) of repairing and refurbishing, sand floors, washing and painting ceilings, etc. - 4 tons of coal arrives

28 Sep EN and RW wallpapering until 5AM

1 Oct Fall quarter begins (Analytic Geometry, Physics, Chemistry, Biology), start job on 2nd shift as electrician on calrod testing line

3 Jan 1947 Another quarter (Biology, Anatomy, Chemistry, Physics)

15 Feb - 7 Mar EN and RW have miserable "subterranean" quarrel, i.e., normal behavior in presence of others, stony silence when alone

5 Apr Flooded basement

10-14 Apr RW repairs washing machine, electric water heater arrives

5-14 Jul Quarrel

28 Jul EN begins deep and lasting commitment to flower gardening

25 Aug RW takes exam for admission to U of Chicago Medical School

3 Nov RW passes French (foreign language) exam after 5 intense days of study

5 Dec EN finally gets her sewing machine

19 Dec Another car catapults over concrete curb to strike ours, EN sustains multiple bruises but protects RW, Jr cradled in her arms - $552 repairs to our car

24 Jan 1948 Get back our repaired car

23 Feb $1000 accident settlement to us, $500 to attorney

24 Feb RW declines offered admission to U of Chicago Medical School

19 Mar RW receives Bachelor of Science degree in Physiology

CHAPTER XVI

25 Mar - 1 Apr RW resigns factory job, starts as Teaching Assistant at U of Chicago and graduate student on stipend from Office of Naval Research (Professor Ralph W. Gerard), $166/month

22 Apr EN records: "RW brot 100 exam papers home and was up till 3AM grading them"

1 May EN "Irritated by RW's absorption in his studies these days. He takes no interest in the house or his family."

8-15 May Quarrel (precipitated by RW not taking ashes out of furnace)

1 Jul Quarrel (over behavior of RW, Jr) EN cuts RW's lip with hurled slide rule (This was the only instance of physical assault in any of our quarrels.)

20 Aug "RW not home till 11 PM tonight. I am alone so much. If I didn't like reading and my plants."

19 Oct Miscarriage - EN ill until mid November

3 Jan 1949 EN types Abstract for RW's first scientific paper/presentation

26 Jan We buy new Hudson automobile, $2540 after trading in the junky Graham

25 - 26 Feb EN types RW's Masters Thesis, finishing 4:30AM, 50 pages

1 Mar Crisis for RW that protocol of Thesis circulating to Faculty not observed

8 Mar Faculty votes to waive rules in case of RW's faulty procedure

18 Mar RW granted Masters Degree in Physiology by U of Chicago for work on metabolism of nerve conduction

22 Apr RW's first scientific presentation, at Detroit Meeting of American Physiological Society

21 May RW takes written Preliminary Examination for admission to PhD candidacy

15 Jun Quarrel, EN's threshold crossed over RW's neglecting family

18 Jun EN takes RW, Jr and leaves RW, goes home to mother

22 Jun EN visits our house, "finds signs of RW's continued habitation. Watered plants, fed goldfish."

25 Jun EN returns home, reconciliation

2 Aug RW passes PhD Comprehensive exam in French

25 Aug RW passes oral German exam for PhD

30 Aug 8th Wedding Anniversary, RW visits in-laws for first time since June quarrel

2 Jan 1950 RW prepares report on failure of his PhD thesis research to confirm previous research in Prof Gerard's laboratory; must seek new PhD research problem

17 Jan Makes new PhD research proposal, on neural control of swallowing

17 Feb RW and EN visit the Jerome Lettvin (pupil of Prof Warren S. McCulloch) family at Manteno State Psychiatric Hospital, exploring possibility of Postdoctoral Fellowship with McCulloch

17 Mar EN and RW work until 5AM typing RW's papers on kidney and on carbohydrate metabolism for his graduate courses

4 Apr RW visits McCulloch at Illinois Neuropsychiatric Institute, Chicago, re Fellowship

5-17 Apr Another "subterranean" quarrel

30 May RW starts writing PhD Thesis

5 Jun EN starts typing it

16 Jun US Public Health Service Fellowship approved for work with McCulloch

25 Jun EN believes she is pregnant

10 & 20 Jul 20,000 drafted, Reserves being called up for war in Korea, could RW be recalled?

27 Jul 3 copies of EN's typing of RW's PhD Thesis delivered to Chairman of Physiology Dept

2 Aug EN begins prenatal care at U of Chicago Clinic

8 Aug Delivered final copy of Thesis to University's Dissertation Secretary

18 Aug RW passes his Thesis defense

30 Aug Ninth Wedding Anniversary, RW does all day and night experiment

1 Sep With EN in attendance this time, RW receives PhD for defining "neural code" for initiation of swallowing

4 Sep RW begins Fellowship at Illinois Neuropsychiatric Institute, begins experiments on recovery of vision in kittens after neonatal lesions of cerebral cortex

13-18 Sep EN and RW drive to Columbus, Ohio where RW presents paper at meeting of American Physiological Society; home via Turkey Run, Indiana

15

28 Sep - 7 Dec (!) Subterranean quarrel

13 Dec RW finishes typing paper on swallowing

1 Jan 1951 RW home at midnight after all day experiment at INI

2 Jan EN and RW wrestle with decision whether to take job at U of Utah or Philadelphia Naval Research Section

28 Feb Mary Elizabeth born 2:02 PM at Lying In Hospital, U of Chicago

1-9 Mar RW painting and wall papering home preparatory to sale

2 Mar Paper for American Journal of Physiology too long, must be revised

3 Mar Navy pay too little, we accept position as Assistant Professor of Physiology, U of Utah College of Medicine, $6,000/year

8 Mar We buy 20 shares of GM stock at $50/share

9 Mar EN and ME come home

CHAPTER XVII

13 Mar EN types RW's application to United Cerebral Palsy Fndn for Research on vision following neonatal cortical lesions

26 Mar EN types RW's revision of paper on swallowing

11 Apr Truman relieves MacArthur of command

29 Apr-2 May RW in Cleveland to present paper to Amer Physiological Society

13 May Advertise our house for sale, only two responses

17 May First customer to look at house

6 Jun RW corrects proofs for Amer J Physiol paper

7 Jul Testing kittens' vision at home, demonstrated to Dr and Mrs Arnold Scheibel; last bottle of Azores champagne consumed

19 Jul Sell house, net $9959 after mortgage paid

6 Aug Start packing

22 Aug Moving day

16

23-27 Aug En route to Salt Lake City, via Rocky Mountain National Park

30 Aug 10th Wedding Anniversary, Apt #3, Stadium Village, Salt Lake City, Utah

7 Sep RW, Jr's first day in kindergarten

19 Sep Buy new 5½ room house on 140x120 ft lot, with view of Mt Olympus from picture window, and irrigation rights: $20,000 with $10,000 mortgage

4 Oct Move in, mud and all

31 Oct - 3 Nov Quarrel

5 Nov Plant lilacs

9 Nov EN finishes sewing second pair of drapes

10 Nov Start planting lawn

15 Nov Buy lumber for fence

move to Mount Vernon, New York, where I was born, they rapidly acquired friends, for my "baby book" notes gifts from 43 people other than relatives. When I was 14 months old, I was enrolled in the Sunday School of the Baptist Church of Mt Vernon, i.e., my parents were very active members of their church. They enjoyed singing, and one of my earliest memories is of my mother playing the piano and their singing "'Tis a long, long trail a'winding, into the land of my dreams", a melancholy, turn of the century piece so popular in parlors of that time. We soon moved on to Chicago and, my father's fortunes steadily improving, in 1926 they built their "dream house" in River Forest, Illinois. My mother died in surgery for her "goitre", 13 Nov 1926, some 10 weeks after they moved in.

She lay now lifeless in our parlor, the trail to the land of dreams forever vanished into the void. My father pressed a funereal rosebud to her lips, placed it in her bible, and presented me with this mournful token of life's impermanence. The blow was heightened by the taunting of several thoughtless schoolmates, not over my name, but over my lack of a mother. I am sure those experiences have had a compelling influence on my perception of mankind, and the vacuity of the common mind.

The house was sold, and I lived in Oak Park with my two grandmothers for a while; then to Camp Penlock in Michigan for a horribly homesick summer. I survived it, came to enjoy swimming and camp activities, and the "initiations" that revealed boys less inured to "hardship" and discomfort; shades of my future in the army. My father married Helen McMahon, who had lost her husband, Patrick Quinn to tuberculosis in Santa Fe, New Mexico, as well as her baby daughter, Shirley Jean, of whom she always spoke so longingly. Clearly, they both shared a recent grief, if not much else. She was Catholic, and the "contract" extracted was that any children of the marriage must be raised in the faith, as was then the case with my half-brother, Richard Earle, born 17 March 1929 in Macomb, Illinois. My father's venture in owning the Macomb Mfg Co soon foundered, and we returned to a rather nomadic life in Chicago, summing to the fact that, in all, I attended nine different schools before graduating from high school.

We were barely scraping by during those depression years, 3-day workweek for my now accountant father, lucky to have it. I delivered morning newspapers, spent an educational week or two at age 14 in the Cook County Contagious Disease Hospital with fellow patients, a drunk, a one-legged bum and a gangster, all of us with scarlet fever. Happier but equally educational episodes were two summers spent helping with farm chores with my cousins in Plymouth, Indiana, where my mother had been particularly beloved. I had the grueling test of endurance on the second summer, riding my bicycle, into the wind of course, the 120 miles from Chicago to Plymouth. I recently came across a letter I wrote describing a bit of life on the farm:

Sunday, July 5, 1936

Dear Grandma: [My 94-year-old paternal grandmother]
I pitched hay Monday morning and shocked rye Tuesday morning. Have been swimming every day but couldn't stand the heat in the fields to do an awful lot of work. However I water the pigs & calves every noon and night. We have to pump most of the water for there is no breeze to run the windmill. . . .

In 8th grade I had fallen hopelessly in love with Marjorie Mae Gintz, but though she thought I would make a great doctor, I never seemed to touch that vital chord in her. When I did on one occasion get her to a party at our house, my father commented on the remarkable resemblance she bore to my mother. It was she who first stirred in me an interest in "the arts", and had a further influence, by attending the University of Chicago for a few semesters, alerting me to the attraction of that institution.

I graduated from high school in Feb 1937 with a totally impractical degree in "history". As had earlier been Elizabeth's experience, I too had just turned 17, and with financial prospects not much better. I quit my job as a clerk at National Tea Co (having paid my first 3¢ Social Security tax there on 2 Jan 1937), since my father was able to get me a job on the assembly line, making electric ranges at Hotpoint, where he worked. With this little income I was to alleviate our family's lack of transportation by contributing to the purchase of a new Plymouth car; only I was not to be allowed to drive it. This provoked a very surly argu-

Sun 18 May - M - Slept till 2PM. Then settled down to do some serious studying of philosophy. Made up rough draft for Rationalism & Empiricism for Humanities. Boy, I'll be glad when school is over & the house is all settled. Feel like a zygani [Wow, note the Slavic/European word!] living the way I have for the past month.

Mon 19 May - M - Becoming more & more convinced that I like our Lt Chase. He's got the most leisurely way of moving & the nicest smile. And he smiles back at me! Wonder which of our 2nd Lts I'll be daydreaming about a week from now? Out to school to hear Carter read T.S. Eliot on modern poetry. [Another night of Carter that I remember!]

Tue 20 May - Out to school to hear a very good lecture on biochemistry by a doctor from U of C, introduced by Mr Shapiro. - Mr Swanson of Civil Serv Comm over to see Col Hayden about the shenanigans about hiring girls. About time something was done.

Thu 22 May - More people coming into the office today. I must confess I got a bit flustered when Capt Mackenzie & Capt Peck from Wash DC came in, to be joined by Gen Ramsey of Rock Island, then Col Parker, lots of other people. I'm beginning to see what the receptionist's job will be when we really get going. I worked on Lt. Chase's personality interviews. His spelling is atrocious.

Fri 23 May - God, our office is a madhouse. They're getting out the specifications for construction at the Savannah Ord Depot. Col Hayden & Col Parker (from Col Grove's office in Wash DC) [Note "atom bomb" Groves only a Col at this point.] went out to Rock Island. Lt Chase & I engaging in a bit of conversation when he asked me to type up his offer to accept foreign service to the QMC. I jokingly tried to discourage him. He told me he liked my smile when I talk to people. He is a very nice person. Johnnie Rizzi called me at 8. Date with him for 7:30 Sun to go to O'Henry Park dancing.

Sun 25 May - Johnnie Rizzi called for me at 7:30 in a swanky grey Plymouth deluxe coupe. Taking a long ride out to O'Henry Park. Wonderful dancing. Johnnie is 25, home in Aurora. Has been working at Inland Steel for 3-4 years, earns about $2000.

Apparently can manage his money, because he appears well-dressed, car paid for. Talking in his car until one or so. He works shift nights. Fairly interesting person, even tho not an intellectual.

Mon 26 May - Lots of new people reporting for work today, keeping me busy notarizing their oaths of office. Got an "A" on my philosophy theme.

Tue 27 May - Out to school to Biology. Mr Burdine tried to coach us in dihybrid crosses, but it made absolutely no impression on me. Pres Roosevelt on air as I got out of the building, broadcasting his much heralded & much discussed "unlimited emergency" speech.

CHAPTER III
Courtship

Synopsis - In the preceding Chapter, as "Charlie" receded in importance, Elizabeth was casting a wider net, Lt Chase, Mr Shaw, "Brother Flaherty", Trainor (15 Apr), "Tom" (26 Apr), Ed Falhaber (4 May), Marty Kearn (12 May), Johnnie Rizzi (25 May); and, on 6, 11, 27 March, 17 and 22 April, Robert Doty. The evidence is clear that she had her eye on me, as I did on her. I so clearly recall the luscious girl, enticing in her orange mohair sweater; but oh, how was I ever to meet her? Fortunately, sitting beside her one day sufficed since she, so utterly unbeknownst to me, had set getting acquainted with me as one of her goals. At first I did not seem to measure up (22 Apr!); but then, on 15 May, I got reasonably high marks. Perhaps she liked watching me eat.

But it was 28 May, that I have taken to mark the beginning of our courtship, where we had more of a chance to get acquainted; and two days later (30 May), after an intense 15 hours together, we were ensnared. It was clear to each of us, without the confirmation of our grades on10 June, that we were closely kindred spirits intellectually. However, I naively misjudged the situation. Perceiving that she was a "modern" woman, who smoked and drank and had a free-thinking philosophy akin to mine, I eagerly leapt to the conclusion that we might simply start living together. Thus, on 14 June, I "propositioned" her. As she wrote, "this did and yet did not shock me", and she "never heard a word of it." In later years I came to be deeply grateful for her level headedness in this regard; but it was not to be the end of the sexual sparring. As she notes, this "bugaboo" reared its head on several occasions during the ensuing weeks, as male urgency sought to shorten the route to connubial bliss. My bizarre letter of 17 July ridiculously sought to bury the issue with asceticism, which neither of us, least of all she, desired. Although I was by far the most demonstrative, it can frequently be perceived that I was not alone in these feelings. Yet, wisely, she resisted; hoping, in her rather opaque and baffling letter (not delivered) of 14 August, that I would not give way to "empty-phrased argument of practicality and sane behavior", but would carry her off to my pagan way of life!

Whatever, the pace of romance and its many problems moved swiftly, the lines of the diary ever more closely spaced as events and emotions followed their tumultuous course. By 22 June it was already clear that we were going to marry, the detail was the draft. Finally, against uniformly negative opinion, we had the courage to follow our own perception, that our love was an enduring, sacred bond, that we should never abandon what merciful fate so irresistibly offered. Our confidence was supreme, and correct. It had taken 94 days, 28 May to 30 August, to cast our lot irrevocably together [Fig 8].

A year or so later, while these doings were still fresh in mind, we exchanged thoughts on our precipitate action, and I have appended these excerpts at the end of this Chapter.

Wed 28 May - Out to school by 6:30, taking the Bi-Sci Comprehensive & finding some of it very stiff, including practically all of the essay. So Robt Doty & I went to a tavern for 3 beers & 3 cokes, cigs, much conversation, the "give & take" kind that I like. So I didn't get home until past midnite. Have a date for Fri at 2:30 to study for our humanities exam.

Fri 30 May [Memorial Day Holiday] - Robt Doty called for me at 3. I took along several of my books. We drove out to Garfield Park where we studied quite intensively for several hours, until 7:30 or so. Hungry, so we drove out to the restaurant he patronizes. Having a sandwich apiece & reading a T.S. Eliot play in between bites. Then I went up with him to his room (dear, dear!) and he played Beethoven's Fifth & several other recordings. Left at 10. We then drove out around Harrison High & parked on a side street where we listened to the Music Lover's Program. Then we talked until 1 AM. He is more than my equal in intellectual attainment. I just wonder how old he is. Home, but we did get acquainted.

Sat 31 May - Pay Day - Noting Lt Chase all dressed up in his tan suit. 's too bad he's leaving for Ft Custer. I sat & lay on my bed with books on all sides of me reading until midnite & then went to bed with a sensuous pleasure as I settled down for the night. Hope I pass both my exams.

Sun 1 Jun 1941 - Listening to the Columbia Symphony. Am going to spend the entire day studying, the last time I sacrifice my weekend to the cause of knowledge. So I studied, reviewed everything in the whole darned Humanities course. Finally called it quits at 11. Went to bed & all kinds of greater ideas & thots running thru my mind. Really feel like I've been transported back to the days of Homer or the Medieval ages. Well, tomorrow's the day.

Mon 2 Jun - Oh, what an exam in Humanities. All dates & crazy connections that had one baffled. So after 3 hours of that, Doty & I drove out to a lounge where we rationalized that we'd gotten a lot out of the course as is & I had 2 Rum & cokes. Got home at 11:30. Says he'll call me Thurs re seeing "Citizen Kane" perhaps this Saturday.

Tue 3 Jun - INDIGO BLUES - Boy, do I feel down in the dumps today! It never rains, but it pours. Uncertainty about my job. Doing elementary stuff thus far & the feeling that both Mrs Mac & Mrs Fohr resent my Civil Service status. Without Capt. Jensen I don't know what I'd do. Then, my school studies. I'll bet this marks the end of my academic career. I'll really be surprised if I passed either one of the exams. The international situation, our house still in an uproar, the state of my own physical being, my wardrobe, all this conspires me to feel a deep indigo blue: clouds roll away, and let the sun shine through!

Thu 5 Jun - Home to eat ad lib and to wait expectantly for my call from Robt Doty. So I made a date to meet him at 1pm Sat & will spend the aft together.

Fri 6 Jun - So I went to bed kind of tired of the way things are dragging. Wish I'd get settled at work. Wish the house would get all done too. Wonder how my date tomorrow will turn out? [Marriage!!! What life forbids us to foresee!]

Sat 7 Jun - Met Doty at one. He was all dressed up. We ate at The Hut. Went to Field's where I bot a black suit for 8.15 in the basement. Wore it. Seeing "Citizen Kane" with Orson Welles, very stirring spectacle of a newspaper magnate's life. Afterwards at 5&10 having cokes. Home at 7:30. I took a bath, changed. He called for me at 9. We drove Sis to Casino, then to — [illegible] on Madison St, where two of his friends, one Fred S, play. Sitting thru a sordid floorshow, an obscene MC. Drinking cokes, smoking cigs & discussing mystical subjects with Fred. Leaving at 1:30. Parking in front of the house. He put his arm around me & kissed me so boyishly. He is very sweet & he said he could see a lot of pleasure ahead for us two. Perhaps?

Sun 8 Jun - Typical boresome Sunday. I do aim to change things, tho. I hope to get out & play some golf, perhaps with Doty. Says he has golf clubs, too, & is an amateur. Doty said he'd call me Mon about 8 to see if our refunds are in, as well as our grades. I swear I'll study up on both subjects (if I flunked them) & take the Comprehensives come next semester & really pass the damn things. It's a blow to my pride to fail so miserably.

Tue 10 Jun - Red Letter Day - [Passed her exams!] - Strolling into Biology at 8:15, Doty not there yet. Mr Burdine gave me my 5.00 refund, also my grade, a "B". Oh! Blessed relief! Doty came in about 8:30. He got an "A"; only 2 "A"s & 3 "B"s given, 3 "C"s, rest "D"s & 2 "F"s, out of 18! So we left at 9. Stopped at office & found out our Humanities grades. Doty got another "A", I got a "B". So we had a coke. Out at his music store listening to records. I bot some cactus needles (12 for 35 cents). Listening to Music Lover's Program parked on St Louis Ave. Doty telling me he's gonna see a lot of me this summer if he may. Right now I'm perfectly willing to do that. He's so versatile & what a memory! He's going to call me Friday & it's up to me to find out where Fantasia is playing.

Wed 11 Jun - M - My GE radio came. I played my album of records. In the evening trying out our shortwave reception.

Fri 13 Jun - M - Unlucky day [Fri 13th] **- I wonder? -** Bob came over with Oscar Wilde & a record (Richard Crooks in Manon) for me (for keeps). We drove out to the Alex to see "Gone With the Wind", and enjoyed it all over again. So did he. A cup of coffee afterwards, then parking across the street until 3 AM. Asked me if I thought I could "give him what men call love" and I said I could try. Said his heart was mine, etc. & I told him not to be so blunt. But he is a darling, and we parted reluctantly. Am to see him tomorrow at 8. So here I sit, not a bit sleepy, trying to figure out just what I'm in for. Someone very much akin to me in intellectual attainments, likes & dislikes & so sweet. I wonder just how much younger he is than I?

Sat 14 Jun - M - Doty over at 8:30. We played Tschaikovsky's Fourth, then listened to the NBC Summer Symphony. Let him read some of my scribblings in English & Social Science. Left home 9:30, going to one of his old hangouts where we drank 15¢ drinks and philosophized. He tried to teach me German. We left at one or so. We parked, and he made me a proposal which did (& yet did not) shock me. I told him I hadn't heard a word of it. So we talked ourselves out of it somehow. I got home at 4. Oh, Lord, I am really a "goner", heart, body & soul. Why, oh why, did it have to happen?

Sun 15 June - M - Bob told me he was going to betray Doty and get married - and of course, the implication was unmistakable - and I felt another one of those exquisitely poignant tugs on my heart - Oh, Betty, do try to keep your head even though you're emotionally and spiritually beyond salvation. Awakened by Doty's phone call at 2:30. Sleepily, when he asked "how's the intermission?" I answered "fine", & then realized I was supposed to be listening to the Columbia Symphonic program. He'll be over at 8. I should be ironing, but instead I sit listening to the radio & just daydreaming. It's like a fantastic idealistic dream this affair of mine with Doty. It seems all I need do is pinch myself & awake to find that's all it is. I'm convinced that it'll be indelibly impressed on my memory. I'll never be able to forget his high ideals, his courageous, unconventional outlook on life. Enough! So he came over at 8. We stayed home & read excerpts from books. He brot over Moussorsky's "Nite on Bare Mountain". Listening to music. I "bared my soul" & let him read my own anthology of poems & stuff; this until about one. Then he didn't leave till 2, and we indulged in some innocuous necking.

Mon 16 Jun - M - Getting to sleep after 2am last nite with Doty's words indelibly inscribed on my memory "You're everything that is woman, no wonder man is jealous, all eyes staring at you."

Maybe he's a crackpot, but I love it right now. Read over Doty's attempts at philosophical essays. Rather immature and utterly lacking in organization. [As an excuse, these were possibly just jotted notes?]

Wed 18 Jun - I got home to find a strange letter from Doty. Full of beautiful romantic thoughts & yet, not strange, but so much like him. It really thrilled me to my very core. [This letter does not seem to have survived.] He called at 8. Orlando [Narduli] (his violinist friend who plays at the Camelia Room at the Drake) with him. We went up to his room & Orlando made recordings of Pagannini's Caprice & Bach's "Chaconne", Turkish Street Song. Picking up "Life of Nijinsky" at O's house. I didn't get in until 1:30 AM and we exchanged mutual vows of adoration, etc.

Sat 21 Jun - Dressing, just finishing when Bob came at 7:30, all dressed up in his palm beach suit. We sat & listened to Tschaikowsky's 5th, the NBC until 9 or so. Then we drove out to Robert's where we had a drink. Parking in Palos Park listening to WCFL pillowed in his arms. Parking across the street from home until 4 AM. Bob told me first 'if he was the marrying kind, I'd be the girl he'd want to marry', and when I laughed at the 'if' part of it, he said he wanted to marry me. So I said he paid me a beautiful compliment. So we finally disengaged ourselves from one another's arms and said au revoir in the dawn.

Sun 22 Jun - About 2 PM I was very much startled to hear that Hitler had declared war on Russia, heard Churchill's speech in which he promised all aid to Russia. So I composed very bad poetry all afternoon listening to one symphonic broadcast after another. Bob over at 7:30 promptly. We sat & discussed the latest war development. Then he suggested going to Bughouse Square [An area where various nuts and activists made rabid speeches.] to hear what the soap box orators had to say on this Russian invasion. We spent an hour or two listening to a colored fellow give an interpretation of the events similar to my own views. Parking in Douglas Park until 2 AM and somehow we both have fallen into the mannerisms and intimacy of two who plan on spending our lives together. I truly confess I could see my way to marriage with Bob even tho I suspect he is several years my junior. It is uncanny how well suited we seem to be by temperament, and our minds seem to function so much alike. 'You're too good to be true', says he, and I echo back the same sentiment.

Mon 23 Jun - Going to Goldblatt's & becoming very much attached to a White Rotary automatic [sewing] machine in a maple cabinet for 89.50, a maple bench thrown in without charge. So I let a Mr Joffe sell me one. Have resolved to take advantage of their Sat aft sewing classes & really learn how to use the machine & perhaps make my own clothes. Appeals to the creative instinct in me. I told Marcella I thought it was the "real thing" for Bob and me.

Tues 24 Jun - I went to lunch with Marcella at Triangle & we discussed our respective "Bob's" & bared our hearts. Her advice is to "make the catch while the catching is good." Playing Bob's records once more. God! The man really has captured my mind and heart. It seems my every thought turns to him, and this longing to be with him. Either I'm an awful fool or this is destiny that has brought us together. I feel as though I would follow him to the ends of the world if he asked me to. With him by my side I would be courageous enough to defy anything, dare anything. Oh, fate, if this is all just an illusion, what sorrow lies in wait for me! I wonder if he's thinking of me even as I do sitting here by the fading light and listening to tango music? Bittersweet ecstasy.

Wed 25 Jun - Oh, wotta day! - Absent-mindedly and dreamily thinking of Bob all day. He came over at 8:40 , brought along a disk on which he had recorded the beginning of his play. He certainly sounds very dramatic, his voice to me sounds ideal for radio. So I returned his records & stuff. We drove out, way out northwest somewhere and parked near a babbling brook; and for about 2 hours we just talked intellectual-like. Then he kissed me, more intimately than ever before; and I told him 'because I love you'. And then that horrid bugaboo again. So I told him of my ideals in retaining my virginity; and we seriously discussed marriage and he had thought of all the objections: his job, the draft, the fact that he had only $125 saved, had only a car, a radio, his mother's diamond ring. I can't decide yet what decision we arrived at. I'm almost frightened at the turn things have taken. So I got in at 2:30 and I'm to see him Friday.

Thu 26 Jun - So my 'beloved' is out with his friends satiating his lust for that which I deny him. I think it's contemptible! - Mom, Sis, and all the family have discussed the idea of my marrying Bob. Mom says do as I please but puts forth the war and draft as one real objection. I wonder what Bob and I will have to say to one another tomorrow. Shall I rush in blindly, or sit back calmly and rationalize my way out entirely?

Fri 27 Jun - Bob came all exhausted. Said he got in at 3:30 AM last night. Said he had reconsidered, now convinced that I was right and he was wrong. Parking in front of our house, listening to Beethoven's Eroica. He's so sweet, my darling, even at his very worst, which he was tonite. Rather laconic and what not. So we parted at 12:30.

Sat 28 Jun - Saw "The Great Dictator". Thence out to Forest Preserve where we read modern poetry, Ezra Pound and T.S. Eliot with his car light on. Then just necking for hours until 4 AM. Told me he's so full of love he's afraid to release it. His reference to me as 'Mrs Doty' made my heart turn somersaults. Yes, I think it's the real thing. Each meeting seems to make me more and more certain of it. His mind compels my admiration, his physical appeal I never have denied, but above all there seems to be a spiritual bond between us that grows stronger and stronger.

Sun 29 Jun - Awakened from my dreams by Doty's call at 2:30. Listening to Bob's "La Traviata", also Scriabin's Études. Read some Indian love lyrics to Bob, pure unadulterated passion in verse. We parked in Columbus Park until 1 when an "ossifer" routed us. We talked about our love of travel and how we'd like to get around. Bob thinks his music points the way. I don't know. I'm beginning to have my doubts as to the eventual outcome.

Mon 30 Jun - Somehow I can't think any more without Doty appearing somewhere. Which is very wrong because he is so sweet and I don't know whether I could be happy with him.

Tue 1 July 1941 - I can't concentrate on anything but Bob; and the thought worries me, his being several years my junior. I'm going to have it out with him on that point. This is terrible, can't read, can't settle down to do anything. This must be settled one way or another. I'd rather pluck it out of my mind and heart right now than watch it die a slow lingering death. Yes, must make some definite decision tomorrow.

Wed 2 Jul - Bob brot 6 red rosebuds for me. Looked very handsome in his tweed suit. We sat and listened to Beethoven's 5th which I'd gotten from the library today. Bob asked me "when will we get married?" once again. I finally asked him how old he was. He'll be 22 in January. Said he knew all along I was about 4 years older than he. Meant to tell me soon. Almost convinced me (as I have always maintained) that age does not count.

Thu 3 Jul - He came at 7:30. We drove down to St Luke's to see his b.f., Gus [Psouras], a pianist, there for a double rupture. Liked him. Visiting until 9:30, then out to the Capitol Bar where we sat at the bar listening to knocked out rhythm by Roco & the four Mills Bros. Parking in front. I fell asleep in his arms for a half hour or so. He is so sweet and I seem to just belong to him. Coming in at 3:30. This gets worse and worse. I fall more deeply into the unfathomable well of love or something.

Fri 4 Jul - Decided to go to Brookfield Zoo . He came over at 4. We had a wonderful time tramping all over the grounds until closing time, 7. Home. Reading Omar Khayam, then necking; and when he tells me his past was but a preparation for me, his present just being with me, and the future something glorious to look forward to, and words in similar vein, I wonder if it is reality or just a dream. He left reluctantly at 2:30. We're to go picnicking tomorrow at Starved Rock. Oh, pleasurable existence.

Sat 5 Jul - M - We rode the 90 miles, at Starved Rock at 2 PM. Finding a grand spot just off one of the trails, the Illinois River 200 feet below. Eating with relish, sunning ourselves. Bob practicing on his cornet. Then we went off to explore, miniature Grand Canyon; winding trails, ferns, mosses, lagoons, steep cliffs. Being dared to climb an 80° hill with little vegetation to hold onto & I can't understand how I did it, but I did with Bob's aid. Felt grand to do it if a bit foolish. Oh, I just loved the whole day. We left at 9:30. Parking to 3:30 or so. Bob's caresses become more and more touching. We talked about marriage again and came to no definite conclusion.

Sun 6 Jul - M - Before I knew it Bob was over at 7:45 with Brahm's 2nd Symphony. I read him my sociological theme on marriage and divorce (masterpiece for my English 102 class). Thot he might like to know the hazards attendant thereto. We listened to Brahms, and Pirates of Penzance, following the libretto in my Gilbert & Sullivan book. Mom retiring at 11. We just sat without touching or talking to one another until almost 1 AM. Oh, I just seem to melt in his arms, our bodies just seem to dovetail into one. Mom's discreet coughing at 1:15 or so made it necessary for me to send him on his way. Lord! What can I do when every cell of me craves him, yet craven-like I put obstacles in the way?

Tue 8 Jul - M - Meeting Marie at 7. Out to Grant Park to hear Chgo Opera Orch. Much talk about me & Bob & sex & feminine hygiene. She thinks I'm still young & that it wouldn't hurt to have Bob wait for me. But I don't know, I might lose him if I do, so I guess the decision will be up to me in the final analysis. Perhaps what I need is a "new attitude" as Marie puts it to get me out of this romantic trance.

Wed 9 Jul - M - Leaving office at 5 with keen anticipation of seeing Bob tonite. I was ready & waiting at 7. Listening to Scriabin's études over & over again. Reading poetry until he came at 7:30. Brought me <u>House of Dust</u> by Conrad Aiken to read. Out to Grant Park to hear Rudolf Ganz & the Chicago Women's Symphony. So now Bob has decided to wait until he gets his classification before doing anything about us. So we parted reluctantly then in the dawn.

Thu 10 Jul - M - We went riding way out north to park by our babbling brook (what a sweet memory it brings to mind!), and we listened to the radio. We didn't do much necking, he was rather aloof & the mosquitoes were biting, so we turned homeward very early. We've lapsed into the habit of discussing our forthcoming marriage very nonchalantly. Just being together seems to be the only thing that counts. Bob wants me to get a student's driving license so he can teach me how to drive his car. Said he'd give me his car if he ever got drafted. That should be sufficient incentive for me to learn how to drive.

Fri 11 Jul - We drove out to Grant Park to hear Jerzy Bojanowski conduct a so-called "Paderewski Memorial" program. Bob is so passionate, and I know it's difficult for him to hold himself in check. He's remarked about my restraint. Hope he never doubts the sincerity of my affection for him.

Sat 12 Jul - At 12:45 he picked me up & we parked the car under Wacker Drive. Had a bite to eat at The Hut (where we ate our first Sat date in the Loop). To library returning records & getting Franck's D Minor & Beethoven's Eighth, respectively, lui et moi. Taking out various books of poetry, one on ballet. Loaded thusly we went to the playhouse to see a French movie, Chas Boyer in "Les Animaux", not bad at all. Home at 6:30 to sit down to a good meal Mom had ready for us. He waited while I had a bath, changed to fresh clothes. Parking in the Forest Preserve all night. Indulging in some necking, talking about us. Bob glosses over objectionable angles with such ease! Money is the only angle that is rather a sticker. So we greeted the dawn at 5:45 AM, also reading poetry, Louis Untermeyer's 'Eve Speaks'. He showed me the erstwhile Doty domicile in River Forest which his Dad sold for $50,000 in 1930 or so.

Sun 13 Jul - We drove out to Grant Park to hear some very good music by Chgo Women's Symphony. Delightfully cool out there, me wrapped in blanket. We left at 9:30. Parking in front of my house listening to WEDC symphonic hour until 11. Bob started just gently kissing me, but he just can't restrain himself. Says it seems so natural for him to make love to me, so shameless. I feel the same way about him. Crazy people; and when he tells me he can't wait until 'we both go in the house together', my heart skips a beat. So, I told him to start making up a list of stuff and things we need before we do set up housekeeping. Says he intends to go to school all his life. Wants a PhD in Biology, also music. So I got in at 1:30 AM. Oh, he's so sweet.

Mon 14 Jul - I've never felt so blissful and at peace with the world as I am now. Mom is reconciled to things as they stand but keeps telling me that if he should change his mind and we don't get married, I shouldn't feel bad about it. I'd rather he did that before rather than after we take the fatal step. Bob asked me the other day $10.00 would be enough? I said yes, but we should have a reserve to start out with. Well, I'll be all thru paying for things by the end of August and then I could save probably 400.00 by the end of the year. Maybe if he doesn't get drafted we can be married on Thanksgiving Day or thereabouts.

Tue 15 Jul - Nazis and Russians battling around Kiev. Churchill calls the Russians 'Britain's Allies'. Talk of retaining Selective Service draftees for more than a year. Should I marry Bob soon before he leaves. I'm afraid if he leaves I won't want him when he returns. Gad! I'm bored with life today. Nothing seems to hold my interest. I do know this, if I don't take this opportunity to get away from home, I'll be doomed to an old maid's existence. Think I'll talk to Bob about it tomorrow.

Wed 16 Jul - Driving out West to get my 1st try at the wheel. I don't think I did so good, but Bob says I shift fine. I just can't handle the wheel. Bob told me of telling his folks about me. Their reaction, it's his life, etc. He was very different today. Rather cynical, and when I questioned him further, the old bugaboo. His attitude rather repelled me. Made me wonder if it was his way of 'beginning the end'. He said no; said his solution would be to seek satiety elsewhere. I said I would not insist on abstinence, which he agreed was a half-way solution. So I came in at 4:30, but I feel very much troubled, and the seeds of doubt are sown in my mind.

Thu 17 Jul - I got up at 6:45, down early at 8:15. Reading Walt Whitman's lustful poems enroute. Came home with strife and turmoil raging within me. Bob called and spoke to me about 9, said he'd be delayed as he wanted to write me a letter before coming out. A vague fear took hold of me and I waited like a caged tigress until he came out at 9:30. Said he hadn't eaten yet and we set out for the Rex restaurant in Austin. While he ate his meal, I read MacLeish's poetry, also his letter, a passionate presentation of his less pleasant side and his repudiation of the solution we arrived at yesterday; and his decision that we try to be ascetic. I was surprised and relieved at this turn of events. We parted without a kiss or embrace.

[The Letter:]

To my future serenity and my present happiness
To my personification of the ideals of life
In short, to Betty

Hastily written, but turned over in the mind throughout the entire day.

Lust, sex, desire, libido, animal urge, instinct, copulation or co-itus, call them what you may, it is a powerful influence in the web of life. Let us generalize it under the name of Libidines. Libidines dances thru the streets of life robed in gaudy attire with beer on his breath, quick puns on his tongue and dirty jokes in the back of his mind. The clothing that Libidines appears in is all that we care to dis-tinguish him by. There are a few people that have minds capable of dressing him in stars and jewels. Then he is healthy, clean and desir-able. Beneath these clothes is his skeleton comparable to the raw pigments and stark white canvas of the painter. If we are true art-ists, we may blend these raw materials into a thing of beauty and clothe the skeleton with the perfection of our minds.

Last nite we rather tore the shirt of Libidines. He came out showing an ugly nature in spots. But the analogy, my darling, has gone far enough. Last nite we raised a problem (or was it I who raised it?). The solution temporarily accepted is one I find too dis-tasteful to hold to. The disgust which I would feel on solving the thing in this fashion can be read and felt as I wrote today.

The bull treads the soggy earth
Insensate hooves in the sow's urine, the
    damp straw, the cow dung.
My love has bathed in the water of the
Andes' melted snow
         Her satin body
Glows with a diffuse distillation of suave
      rose sweetness.
The bull places its ponderous dung caked claw
In the valley of her breasts.
Hide, monstrosity! Desecrate not the shrine
Of virgin passion.
Slink from her house into the dark filled alley,
Hide your Minotaur hands in the trash,
Cleanse them of the harlot's flesh.

Let us attempt to deny ourselves, then, the passion of our love. Let us spend ascetic evenings without kisses and blend not our eyes in flame. I could not suggest it were it not for the disgust of the other "solution". When the clouds clear from the future and our marriage can be realized, our passion and emotion will be easier to control. A blank future leads one to desire a too happy present.

Time does not permit more - my tongue will say what the pencil has omitted.

Till we have climbed the steep hill, seen the verdant valley or the parched desert. Till the bottom of the pit is lighted - and we have seen the jewels on velvet or the yellowed skull - Till the uncertain hand of fate has erased the question mark from time's blackboard - The volcano smolders, and waits for the princess to sheath the dagger - by her own hand.

Love, flames, love
By nite
By day
From now till I blend with time
BoB.

*　　*　　*　　*　　*

Fri 18 Jul - Bob over at 8:30. I gave him my new poetry book. He told me he had drawn No 5 in his draft board lottery. We set out heavy hearted for a ride in the country. He suggested going to O'Henry Park and there we went. Baron Elliott's orchestra, very sentimental and smooth. Surprised at my ability to enjoy his dancing. Leaving at 12:30. Deliciously tired and yet so relaxed. He refused to kiss me good night. I left him with an airy 'good nite' and slammed the door in his face; and heard him start his motor and roar off into the night with a sickening sensation. Went to bed feeling bruised and broken hearted.

Sat 19 Jul - He had gotten a German and French grammar, the latter for me. Walked to the Art Institute to see an exhibit of International water colors. Home at 6 with a watermelon in tow. He practiced his cornet while I helped Mom prepare supper. We sat and read and listened to the radio until 10. Then the restraint grew unbearable and we both broke down. Yesterday's farewell, the prospects of his leaving soon, Bill Beamish's marriage the 25th, the idea of making it a double wedding, these were all covered. Until 3 AM in his arms within a world filled with sheer ecstasy. I finally disengaged myself and shooed him home. I fall in love with him every time he embraces me.

Sun 20 Jul - Having a nice talk with Mom about Bob & me & she agreed that on the one hand life was so trivial there was no point in postponing things; on the other hand, there was no sense in being rash & impractical. We went out to Grant Park to hear Ganz conduct the Chgo Opera in Beethoven's 1st. Parking on roadside until 3 AM. Just 'loving like gods and goddesses' as Bob put it. I do enjoy it, and he keeps referring to me as his 'wife'. Rather ironic when we can't even visualize our future. With my coat spread around us like a rug or blanket, clasped in each other's arms, we stayed in a delicious half-waking state. 'Like nestling beneath clean bed sheets, my wife', said Doty, and I nodded a rapturous assent. Bestirring ourselves, finally. Home at 3:30, but I didn't get in until 4 AM. Our last embrace Bob said he never kissed anyone like that, and I believed him. He's going away until next Friday to go to his folk's [rented] cottage. Promised to write me a letter.

Mon 21 Jul - Mom and I talked about Bob and agreed he is a rather unusual person. His personality, his good nature, his impeccable appearance, all these find favor in Mom's eyes. To me he is the synthesis of all I have admired in men I have known. If I should lose him it'll be as though the earth should slip out from under my feet and leave me dangling in midair. But somehow I can't believe that fate will play such a dirty trick on me. And I can't believe that Bob would ever change so that I couldn't find the happiness I seem to see in the future with him.

Tue 22 Jul - Mom & Dad got started on one of their rampages, and it's so disgusting. Bob dropped me a postal card from Plymouth, Indiana. Asked me to write him too. I don't know what to write, so I wrote rather perkily. To bed about midnite, reading "The Prophet" by Gilbran.

ELIZABETH'S LETTER

Tuesday evening [22 July 1941]
(on account of you don't remember
dates, my dear!)

My darling -

Your post card announcing your safe arrival gratefully received, and I hasten to comply with your not-so-subtle hint.

I took myself in hand and got myself over to the beauty parlor this evening and had myself shorn of my locks. Vanity just had to give way before comfort and practicality. But as I viewed myself in the mirror, I'm still recognizable and the effect is rather pleasing.

Someone wrote

If you can love me for what I am
  We shall be the happier
If you cannot, I will seek
  To deserve that you should

And so I've been listening to music, and reading (to improve my mind, mon serieux) and I came across the enclosed. Who would have thought "Mumbo Jumbo" and this were creations of the same man? Nevertheless, it expresses my views on the subject more aptly than I ever could. I think I'd like to have it back after your perusal, inasmuch as I laboriously copied it, and I do hate to write.

Seriously, though, I do hope you are enjoying your vacation. Even more do I hope that you look forward to your return to our tres belle ville. I haven't had time to forget you yet, but I guess it's only because I haven't tried very hard.

Oh, yes, I got my temporary driver's license permit yesterday, which expires October 15, 1941, so now I've just got to learn how to drive before then. I know I can count on your patience and perseverance on that point, n'est ce pas?

The rain drops are dashing themselves against the window panes with wild abandon, I find myself sinking into a languorous half-waking state, and so I'll mail this out tomorrow.

Bon soir, mon ami
Betty

The Perfect Marriage - Vachel Lindsay
I hate this yoke; for the world's sake put it on:
Knowing 'twill weigh as much on you till life is gone.
Knowing you love your freedom dear, as I love mine -
Knowing that love unchained has been our life's great wine:

66

Our one great wine (yet spent too soon, and serving none;
Of the two cups free love at last the deadly one).

We grant our meetings will be tame, not honey-sweet,
No longer turning to the tryst with flying feet.
We know the toil that now must come will spoil the bloom
And tenderness of passion's touch, and in its room
Will come tame habit, deadly calm, sorrow and gloom.
Oh, how the battle scars the best who enter life!
Each soldier comes out blind or lame from the black strife.
Mad or diseased or damned of soul the best may come -
It matters not how merrily now rolls the drum,
The fife shrills high, the horn sings loud, till no steps lag -
And all adore that silken flame, Desire's great flag.

We will build strong our tiny fort, strong as we can
Holding one inner room beyond the sword of man.
Love is too wide, it seems today, to hide it there
It seems to flood the fields of corn, and gild the air -
It seems to breathe from every brook, from flowers to sigh
It seems a cataract poured down from the great sky
It seems a tenderness so vast no bush but shows
Its haunting and transfiguring light where wonder glows
It wraps us in a silken snare by shadowy streams,
And wildering sweet and stung with joy your white soul seems
A flame, a flame, conquering day, conquering night,
Brought from our God, a holy thing, a mad delight.
But love when all things beat it down, leaves the wild air,
The heavens are gray, and men turn wolves, lean with despair
Oh, when we need love most, and weep, when all is dark,
Love is a pinch of ashes gray with one live spark -
Yet on the hope to keep alive that treasure strange
Hangs all earth's struggle, strife and scorn, and desperate
     change.
Love?. . . we will scarcely love our babes full many a time -
Knowing their souls and ours too well, and all our grime -
And there beside our holy hearth will hide our eyes -
Lest we should flush what seems disdain without disguise.

Yet there shall be no wavering there in that deep trial
And no false fire or stranger hand or traitor vile -
We'll fight the gloom and fight the world with strong
    sword-play
Entrenched within our blockhouse small, ever at bay
As fellow warriors underpaid, wounded and wild,
True to their battered flag, their faith still undefiled!

*   *   *   *   *

ROBERT'S LETTER

[In pencil on lined dictation pad:]

Monday July 21, 1941 11PM
As I commence this all words seem empty, meaningless, impotent - Picture a thick darkness, a deep lake, gentle breeze, a boat and the brilliant heavens of a cloudless nite. The Spirit of the wind pushes noiselessly against the boat and I drift beneath the awesome ocean of the sky, drinking infinity with every moment. Thousands, millions of years ago the star's pulse beat and some of its life blood was launched into the void. Thru the cold nothingness it cut a scintillating path, plowing sedulously across unthinkable distances, preserving its separateness from time - all to spend its energy on the retina of a dreamer lying on his back in a boat in Indiana. Stars, I thank you for your luminescent blood, but it is surely not for me you die. Why do the stars die? For whom? For what. Embrace this beauty of the perishing universe, clasp infinity to your breast. Send your soul soaring into the fire of Sirius - you are one with them - the same stuff - the same mystery.

What are you and I on this blood soaked earth? Do we matter - does Antares care if our love is loved? Will not the unknown planets of an unseen sun continue to brew another seething pot of life after our love is loved and the worms have been fattened?

Such questions I murmured into the ear of God and the stars twinkled naively down, the plastic waters laughingly lapped the boat, the whispering wind did not understand. No one knew the answers.

I place my hand tenderly upon the pliant waves of your hair, encircle the warmth of your body and taste the tang of life's mystery on your loving lips. May our kisses always distill the sweetness from life's enigmas, that we may answer each other's thirst after the unknowable, with the perfection of attainable beauty.

For the nite I must despair of conveying my emotions to you by words and rely instead upon the similarity of our minds to create the thots of the mystery of cosmic infinity and the blending of our lives with it.

Today has been perfect for vacationing. I slept till noon. Got up and practised and then lay in the sun for 2 hrs. Very much surprised to find that I could still swim across the lake with ease (about 3/4 mile). Sun, fresh air, rowing, swimming and good books, Here is a bit of MacLeish (Pot of Earth) that somewhat fits my mood:

"I tell you the generations
Are a ripple of thin fire burning
Over a meadow, breeding out of itself
Itself, a momentary incandescence
Lasting a long time, and we that blaze
Now, we are not the fire, for it leaves us.

I tell you we are the shape of a word in the air
Uttered from silence behind us into silence
Far beyond, and now between two strokes
Of the word's passing have become the word -
That jars on through the night;
         and the stirred air
Deadens,
      is still -"

This French and Shorthand are hard to study alone. You taught me more French in 20 min than I can learn in 2 hrs by myself.

Midnite is just about here and dokes is really tired after all that exercise.

Please forgive me for leaving you so early, but then I can only see you in thot anyway, so the dream world can take over. I thot that being down here with so many things to do that I would get off easier than you when it came to being lonely. That isn't true. Tonite has been a constant, of one beautiful person in the world that I long to see. Thinking of last nite and Friday and couldn't resist a few pivoting capers in the solitude of the room. You haunt me darling, but you're such a precious ghost. Good nite. I'll write more in the morning.

Tuesday

Good morning! Up at 9 (the unappreciated luxury of sleeping late) and a pre-breakfast swim. This is almost the perfect life for a while.

Mom says that we might be able to get a cottage down here for a weekend. Maybe Bess and Max and you and I could spend a couple of days down here. It's worth considering. I sure wish you were here right now. Then life would be perfect.

I'm afraid that this is a horrible example of what a letter should be, but it will have to make that 11 AM mail as is.

Despite all the enjoyment I am getting in being here, I find myself looking forward to leaving Friday. You will most likely get this Wednesday nite, so may I make a date. At 11PM I'll lay [sic] out on the lake and send my thots up into those myriad specks of lite. Will you meet me there on the periphery of space - we will glide easily across the Milky Way, the river of the sky, locked in an embrace of thot.

Amor omnia vincit! even time and space.
I leave you with this letter and my heart to keep you till the
    appointed hour

Love riding high on a wind of Time
Captures an atom from Orion's belt
Stoops to pick a treasured fragrance
From a jungle flower
And lays a living thot
Upon the bosom of my
Soul's delight.

BoB

*   *   *   *   *

Wed 23 Jul - Home at 7, reading Bob's letter, philosophical, romantic, chatty. Oh, he is everything I've ever wanted in a friend, a lover, a mate. Must hurry! Cause I have a 'date' with Bob, tonite at 11 when, his letter states, he'll try to meet me in thought; a rather mystic idea. I can't wait until Friday when my darling will come back to me. I'm going to ask him for a tangible token of our love; and I'm not being mercenary, either.

70

Thu 24 Jul - Home to find another letter from Doty. I think if our only contacts were to be by correspondence, my love would grow & flourish, a sort of idealistic love. Thinking of Bob & his ideas as expressed in his letter. Somehow I feel that they are sincere & a part of him. Well, I'll see him tomorrow night. I go to bed to linger in a half-waking stage with my thoughts of Bob, and attempt in my helpless fashion to probe into the future and try to glimpse a hint of what it may hold in store for us both. I can't believe Fate will be unkind to us. We're too real for her to betray us.

ROBERT'S SECOND LETTER

Wed. July 23 1941 10 AM

Last nite I had a great longing to write, but my sunburn was a bit uncomfortable. I fell asleep reading Point Counter Point. Huxley has a marvelous command of his conversational style, but I am rather bothered by the utter lack of plot, just a series of slightly connected scenes. The stuff also has a rather poisonous effect in presenting the picture of our warped modern life. I surely would hate to think myself a character of the Huxley fashion. It cannot be denied, tho, that the book is a true exposé of much of our inner emotional life.

At times this vacation isn't all it could be. I miss someone that I can talk to and be understood. The reception on the radio is so poor that there isn't even the consolation of music.

You must have had an awful day with that 94° and no swimming. I kept thinking of that all day yesterday till I almost felt criminal being down here enjoying cool breezes while you suffocated over a typewriter.

You know sometimes I think Wordsworth was right when he said that good poetry came from "emotion recollected in tranquility". There are many beautiful bits of nature around here, but somehow I just can't put them into words as well as when I am away from it; reconstructing or creating the scene in my imagination. How did Keats say it: "Heard melodies are sweet - but those unheard are sweeter" That the thing imagined is often more beautiful than the thing itself.

The beauty that one is capable of experiencing is determined

71

by the beauty of the mind. A flower to an ordinary person is "pretty", to an artist or a botanist it is a thing of perfection. Its texture, coloring, purpose, symmetry, organization, balance, are all blended into his enjoyment of it. There is a beauty in everything that exists if we will only find it.

To me a spider is a very repulsive creature, yet I can watch it, becoming completely carried away in contemplation of its agility, coordinated movement and the mystery of its living.

I believe that some such idea may be behind all these drab paintings of slum districts, Arizona gas stations and Main Street Hokum, Ohio. Many of them have a so-called social purpose, but perhaps some artists are actually trying to present the beauty that may be found on North Clark St. They have set themselves a very difficult task (if such is the case), for tho they may experience an emotion of depth on such subjects, it is very difficult to convey, or arouse a similar emotion in one that sees only ugliness in the sordid squalor of the slums.

As usual, the time is flying and the mailman will soon be here. The end is near. I'll have seen you in the stars tonite and when you get this there will be only about 24 hrs to go.

Did I ever tell you this before
As I love life so I love thee
For you mean all in life to me

It is true. All my hopes for accomplishment in art or science revolve in the vortex of your being. You symbolize life in all its beauty, its essence of sheer joy in living. You stand for the history of man and life itself, my rare specimen of mind and body. Let us stand for each other as personification of what life should be, what art should create and science understand. Love then becomes a thing eternal and the passion of youth a mere sideline in its expression. Loving and thinking in this manner we will be something sure to last.

Your kisses are still warm on my lips.

The kiss of soul and flesh, and I carry them thru my quick moving life till my mind is nil and the earth has claimed them with a kiss of death.

BoB

*   *   *   *   *

Fri 25 Jul - He came at 7:30 with 2 dozen roses for me. Kissed me at the door. Mom fixed a mess of eggs and bacon for him. He ate til 9 or so. Then we drove out to the Forest Preserves. Oh, it was good to feel his arms around me again, to have him kiss me tenderly at first, and with the heat of passion and desire. I went to bed feeling ecstatically happy.

Sat 26 Jul - Home for supper, both of us taking baths, etc. Parked in River Forest until 5 AM, alternately dozing off in one another's arms, and I can truly say 'twas one of the happiest nights of my life. Home at 6 AM.

Sun 27 Jul - We drove out to the Forest Preserves, Palos Park. Tramped about a bit, but it was too hot, so we sat in the car & Bob read me poetry by MacLeish & Hart Crane. Home at 7 to have supper. Rode out west to a Forest Preserve. Listening to Music Lover's Program till 11:40. Interrupted by John Law. Coming home at one, but we parked in front of the house & talked about us. Bob wants to get married right away, take a furnished apartment until such time as we know definitely where he stands with the Army. It's intriguing, to be married to Bob not knowing for how long or how it will all turn out. If he leaves, then I return to Mom. I don't know what to do. It bothers me to think that he accepts my working so nonchalantly and doesn't want any children. Is it purely for sex convenience that he wants to marry me?

Mon 28 Jul - 98 F - Before I marry Bob there is so much I must do. Trying to visualize life with Bob, even if for a short time. If we ever got our own house, then I could get my books and other things. Yes, this intrigues me. Marry Bob and enjoy the best of married bliss (the first few months would be) and then if he left, I'd be left to myself. When he returned, we could begin all over again, on my terms. I'm awfully scared of motherhood tho. Wish I knew enough about sex hygiene to deal with that problem. I'm going to arbitrarily set myself some objectives and when I attain them (and I hope to by Sept 1st then I may marry Bob). Tired of being sensible all the time.

Tue 29 Jul - He got his questionnaire from the War Dept, which had to be returned by Aug 5th. So now he expects to leave before the end of August. So, sorrowfully, we drove over to our driving grounds and I went thru the paces of starting, stopping, making right hand turns until 8:30 or so. Parking in a secluded spot without lights. The North Riverside police making Bob follow them to police station and gave him a ticket for Aug 14th. So we parked near home talking. Bob says he'll give me his car, his books and records, but will not marry me now, because he doesn't want to just sleep with me, as he put it, but to live with me, eat breakfast with me, wash dishes, etc. So, I agreed he was very sensible, but I don't know, to me it seems like the beginning of the end.

Wed 30 Jul - Somehow I don't feel all broken up about Bob's leaving. I accept it fatalistically, as something predestined to be. Mom says I should refuse the car, try to forget all about Bob. I'll see when he comes tonite. When he came, he was very morose. I didn't help things any by playing mournful music and being rather perky. We decided to go to Armanetti's where we had 4 or 5 setups of sauterne and port, which made me very reckless at first and I reminisced about former affairs, MS [Maurice Shapiro], RHD. Bob didn't seem to mind. Told me about Felicia. Then I got sick. I got into the car, and for an hour or so, blank. I awoke in front of our house, Bob apologizing for having me drink such a conglomeration, very much concerned about my welfare; and as he put it, another episode in our bond of memories to link us together, our first drunk together.

Thu 31 Jul - Bob called about noon to find out how I felt, and to tell me his Dad would join us at the concert tonite. Oh! I got home in a dither. Tried to dress my very nicest, etc. Wore my black sheen. Bob called at 7:30. So I met Mr Doty Sr. Typical senior executive type, rather commanding and overbearing, but we got on all right. At Parkside Lounge having soft drink apiece while Mr Doty reminisced and told stories which were very interesting. I finally had to suggest leaving at 12:30. He said he hoped to see me again soon, etc. I think I made a good impression, at least Bob thot so. Why else did Mr Doty spend 2 hours talking to us?

Fri 1 Aug 1941 - Bob came over in a squirrely mood. We sat in for an hour or so, and he demonstrated ballet steps, etc. Talking about us again and stuff. Planning on buying a piano perhaps jointly. I think I really want to learn to play well. One of my secret suppressed ambitions.

Sat 2 Aug - We set off for Indiana Dunes State Park. Bob took a

10 min swim while I sat me down for a sunbath on top of a dune. Reading Maupassant, MacLeish. Bob practicing his horn. Hot sun, cool breeze, Heavenly, and so much fun to go coasting down the hills. In Bob's sweater and our blanket back up to our dune. Moonlight, Bob looking as handsome as a Greek god on Mt Olympus. I never wanted to surrender as much as I did then, but sanity intervened and I demurred. And he told me he thot I was afraid he wouldn't marry me and was holding that back as a come on. Well, maybe I am. We finally left reluctantly at 11.

Sun 3 Aug - M - I had about an hour's driving. Improving, but traffic scares me. Talking, necking. Bob says he never knew it was possible to love like this. He's so boyishly sweet. We talk about getting me a piano to keep me in nights while he's away in the army.

Tue 5 Aug - Bob startled me when he said maybe we better get married even if for a couple weeks. Asked me to think it over. Said this Sun we are going to Plymouth for family reunion. I'm to drive us out there.

Wed, 6 Aug - Thinking of Bob all day. Turning over in my mind idea of marrying him now, seeing pros & cons. Congress rejected 1 yr extension for draftees. Bob over at 8 all dressed up. Said he received notice for medical exam this Friday. Home at 12:30, but parking till 2. Bob again suggested getting married, living together for a few weeks; but rejected it as being something two barflies would do. I don't know. He was in a very 'moody' mood when he left me. Perhaps the right choice is to do nothing. I bow to omnipotent Fate.

Thur 7 Aug - Talking to Mom about Bob & me, & she seemed to agree that we could get married if we really wanted to. Bob over at 8:45. I drove around for a half hour or so without any serious mishap. Parking. He was in a 'mood'. So we threshed it out and I told him we were both cowards in not having the courage of our convictions and so after he gets his classification we'll do something about becoming Mr and Mrs Doty. Sweet necking and stuff.

Fri 8 Aug - Bob is to have his medical exam tonight. He came at 9, talking of going apartment hunting. He passed the medical, but the doc said no men were sent from his draft board since last April. So now he doesn't know what to expect.

Sun 10 Aug - As soon as we were out of the city Bob made me get behind the wheel and I was going along fine until around Dyer at a stop light cross road I banged into a new Buick fender [scratched it]. So the Runds called a copper and he made a report and I didn't have my driver's license which was bad. But we promised to pay them and got on our way. At Pretty Lake, liking the spot very much. Mrs Doty very friendly. I enjoyed the Family Reunion dinner, meeting his grandmother. Climbing to a forest, scrambling down; rowing a boat quite satisfactorily. Taking a ride with the Dotys to Culver (about 16 miles away) and seeing the military grounds. About 9:30 Bob and I went out on the lake in the row boat and lay flat on our backs looking up to the clouded skies. Glad to have the day end, altho I did enjoy the surroundings at Pretty Lake.

Mon 11 Aug - We went to visit a friend of his at 9300 Sheridan Road, one Harry. I had wanted to go to Grant Park to hear Benny Goodman; mad because Harry wasn't there when we got out. When he did come we just sat around smoking my cigarettes. Home at 12 or so, Bob saying he wouldn't see me tomorrow. I got a bit peeved and told him he needn't bother seeing me Wed either. I don't care, I was never so bored in my life as I was tonight, when we could have read or listened to music, or necked. Mom and the family riding me about Bob, to forget him, etc. [This episode needs a bit of background about Harry. He worked on the assembly line with me, and clearly had some connection to the upper crust, as per the Sheridan Road address. He was also an entertaining sort of guy, but wholly unreliable, as the above episode typifies. However, on occasion his braggadocio turned out actually to be true. His sister was Bertie McCormick's secretary (infamous publisher of the Chicago Tribune), and he showed his "pull" one time by getting me and my date front row seats on short notice for a radio broadcast featuring a famous tenor on the "Tribune Hour" (or whatever it was called). On another occasion we attended a small soirée with a soprano of some note, who was leaving to give a concert in Vienna; a memorable experience to hear such singing in the intimate surroundings of a home. Elizabeth's reaction to that evening, however, was entirely justified!!]

Tues 12 Aug - Saw JG [Jaffe & Green, the attorneys for whom she previously worked.] who advised me to "stay single". Marie over to see me tonight. We sat & talked & psychoanalyzed Bob from all an-

76

gles. She thinks I should be wary of getting married. Bob called me at 8:40 to tell me he talked to Rund & the bill for the fender is 6.00; so it's just 4.00 more. That's a relief. Congress passed the 18 mo extension of draft, by one vote, 203-202! What irony! Now I suspect that precludes any further developments of my relations with Bob. Somehow I don't care. Is all this negative advice of my friends finally having its effect?

Wed 13 Aug - Had quite a talk with Miss Cohen about sex & she's going to try to get me a book of her sister's on sane sex & stuff. Bob came over about 9 with Beethoven's 'Apassionata' album. Uneasy at Bob's reticence. We finally got us out in front of our house. I asked Bob questioningly what was wrong and he gave me my own casual remark of Sunday, 'No point in getting excited unnecessarily'. So we talked about the draft. 2½ years is so long; and when I lamented his denying me the comfort of his arms, he said it was better than the frustration of excitement; and asked if I'd mind if he didn't see me until Friday. What could I say? So I got in at 1 with this clue to my despondency and doubting. Circumstances have destroyed the romantic element in our love.

[The following letter, 14 August, not dated as to year, is unequivocally from Thursday 14 August 1941, when we were struggling so desperately to cope with our intense passion for each other within the confines of the "circumstances", as she puts it, in which we found ourselves. That evening, as she notes in her diary, she consulted a book on sexual matters; and the following day, when we met again, Friday 15 August 1941, I proposed the solution that we ultimately took, getting married and living in my room until we could do better. There is, however, no indication in the diary that she ever showed me this letter. She indicates at its start that she might not deliver it. I do not remember it from our courtship days. It was rediscovered, among other letters that had been returned from "Overseas Postoffice", still sealed when I read them for the first time as I was struggling for a reconciliation in one of our quarrels, 14 May 1948. - Her letter here is typewritten, 1.8 pages.

This is deep stuff. Obviously (or perhaps not so obviously), she is struggling with herself to accept the unconventionality of our personalities and the solution we both so eagerly but fearfully desired, marriage.]

August 14....[1941]

Robert, dear—

'Tisn't the things that are said that are always important, too many times it's what is left unsaid that counts. Yet, thoughts are so transitory and fleeting, so I try to detain them, at least till our next meeting. Somehow I rarely succeed, and once gone, I can never recapture them. So I'm letting my thoughts flow out through my fingertips, as it were, in an attempt to analyze them and clarify them for myself, and for you, although I don't know if I'll let you see this. Perhaps I shall, I don't know.

As I told you last night, my dear, I've been in a muddle. My mind has been like a garden overrun with weeds these past few days. I've been bewildered at my reactions to your most innocent remarks, your most casual statement left me wondering what you didn't say, it seemed incomplete; but today, somehow, I seem to have gotten out of this maze and I feel at peace with myself, with the world, and so contrite that it should have been otherwise.

Viewed in retrospect, it seems it all started Sunday. [10 August, when she had the minor car accident driving to Indiana, and had as well to meet a large crowd of my relatives at a family reunion.] The events of that day put quite a strain on my nervous system, I guess. Meeting so many strange people, the shock of the "collision", trying to overcome my phobias and inhibitions during the day, and then out there on the lake. How could I ever think that you were "trying to mold me into your ideal, even at the expense of destroying my individuality"? Momentarily, my ego rebelled at the thought, even as I knew that your "ideal" was what I wanted to entertain for myself anyway, and with your inspiration and encouragement and guidance how much more easily would I reach that goal! But you seemed to loom so big and strong there in that idyllic outdoor setting, and I found myself doubting my ability to measure up to your expectations. Forgive me.

Then Monday night, but I need not go into that. Why did I feel so hurt when you suggested not seeing me Tuesday? [She was justifiably angry at the disastrously boring evening we had spent visiting a boorish friend of mine on the near North Side, and I had perhaps reacted to her anger by saying I wouldn't see her Tuesday, to which she replied, "Fine, nor Wednesday either!" Then a further diary note: "Mom and the

78

family riding me to forget about Bob".] And why did I stare so long into my mirror at the dry-eyed, tired, drawn face? It seemed as though I were seeing a ghost from the past, when as a little girl, high strung and sensitive, after a rebuke from Mother, after loss of a favorite toy, the denial of something I wanted, I would climb onto a chair to stand looking into the mirror of the tall dresser in Mother's room. There I would stand, staring at my reflection, a dazed, wondering little girl, incapable of understanding why or how it was that that which we loved could cause such pain and suffering. I felt that way Monday night, my face white, my lips trembling, a questioning, haunted look in my eyes. I remained sleepless all night, and the hours went by so slowly.

I've tried to shake off this feeling. I lunched with Dorth. [The diary also notes "saw JG (her former employer, an attorney) who advised me to stay single".] I went to the dentist. Happily, Marie came to visit me in the evening. [And she noted that Marie "thinks I should be wary of getting married".] I managed to sleep Tuesday, because of sheer necessity, I guess. And then I had Wednesday night to look forward to.

The weather conspired to keep me in my melancholia, and when you came last night I felt so ill at ease, you didn't make it any easier when you denied me the comfort of your arms. Of course, I understand your reason. ["no point in getting excited unnecessarily".]

It was only when we parked in front of my house that my misgivings, vague and nebulous though they were, seemed to take wing and leave me. Do you remember what you said about circumstances taking all the romance out of our love, but that one could still love without romance, or something to that effect? Whatever you said, it conveyed to me a clue, and I feel that I can understand your reticence, my bewilderment. Of course, darling, some people need romance as an indispensable part of their love; but if it's denied us, I shan't shed any tears over it. [??? impenetrable!?]

I have always firmly believed that one can rise above circumstances if one but have the courage of one's own convictions. Then circumstances, obstacles, space and time, all these can be overcome. I feel that I know the decision of my soul, a decision not to be overruled by the logic of the mind, by the fickle inclinations of my heart; and having made such decision, I know the course I would follow, unfaltering, unhesitating, until I reached my goal. Everything seems to fade away into nothingness, so insignificant do the objections and arguments of cold logic seem to me, when I put them alongside the innermost convictions of my soul. The so-called "sane and practical solutions" seem superficial and incompatible with my resolution.

It's been difficult to phrase the foregoing thoughts into words, even now I wonder if I have conveyed to you just what I mean? To me, the touch of your hand, a look in your eyes, they speak sentences of meaning.

Darling, don't disappoint me by reacting like any normal person, with the appropriate empty-phrased arguments of practicality and sane behavior. I thought we were both pagans, you perhaps more so outwardly, but I have great possibilities and potentialities if only the opportunity presents itself and I find myself stimulated to do so. [These are the defining sentences of the searching thoughts of this letter!]

I've always been accused of writing so no one could understand me. Perhaps you'll present that plaint, too. In the event it needs embellishment and elaboration, I shall be only too glad to do so.

B

[The "pagan" and the "mold to an ideal" show how desperately she wishes to break out of the confines of her previous, rather dull and pedestrian life style and seek romance (sex) and adventure with a kindred "pagan" spirit, despite family and friends warning against it; "forget Bob", "stay single", "be wary of getting married", all echos of her logically defensible past caution and restraint. This was a day of decision, of self-analysis, ending with a plea that I, too, not give way to practicality and "sane behavior!"]

Thu 14 Aug - Meeting between Roosevelt and Churchill - Sis came home with a book on feminine sex hygiene, which treats rather fully douches and sex cleanliness. Odd, but I find myself curious and eager to enter into sex relations with Bob. Can I do it safely and with no loss of face with him? If I could be sure, I would have no hesitation. It would make him happy and gratify my own desire. I must tell him about it. Listening to comments on

80

meeting between Churchill & Roosevelt whereby they outlined 8 points of their peace aims. Can't wait till I see Bob tomorrow, the darling. I'll never meet anyone so thoroly desirable to me I guess. Oh, to be able to hold him close to me always, my love is so fiercely possessive. [Note the transformation in mood, once the sexual impasse has come into full consciousness as a possibly soluble problem.]

Fri 15 Aug - I felt angry when Bob told me he'd been at the concert yesterday with Orlando. Parking outside his house. Out of nowhere he asked me if I still wanted to marry him even if he was going to be in the army for 2½ years. I took a deep breath and said yes. So he told me of his plans to establish me in his room at the Larson's, to buy a studio couch, a piano and with the car [Figs 10, 12] and all he thot I could be busy until he came back. I demurred a bit at this arrangement, recalling my bedroom days in Springfield. Said he'd get his father to borrow $200 from Hotpoint so that we could go away for a short honeymoon. We sat and talked about this until 2 or so. I came home half gloriously happy, half doubting this could be true. Could it happen that I'd be getting married and with Bob away, within 30 days. I suggested he go to the draft board tomorrow to find when he could expect to go.

Sat 16 Aug - I broke the news to mother of our plans to get married and that I live at Bob's place. Mom in tears, said she thot it selfish of Bob to go away and leave me alone. Bob picking me up at one. Driving out West to look at studio couch. I told Bob of Mom's opposition to my leaving her. He didn't like it. We 'walked' it out in Garfield Park for hours. He finally agreed in a half-hearted way. Home for supper in tense atmosphere. Max [Gentsch, Bess' boyfriend] and Sis scoffed at our plans to get married. About 10 Mom gave Bob a fierce cross examination about our ages, our plans for the future, etc. Bob quiet and non-committal. We sat in the living room until 2 or so. I dozed off in his arms as I am wont to do. He's very sweet and I am so sorry all these unpleasant things have to interfere.

Sun 17 Aug - Mom suddenly had a change of heart and told me she disapproved of my marriage, mostly because of Bob's age and the fact that he might change his mind. I could probably 'do better', and the like. Bob came out at 3:30. We drove to P.A.

Stark piano warehouse and looked at spinets. For $165 we saw a piano that would do nicely. We parked in Columbus Park, sat by the waters edge, this dark dreary afternoon with a few scattered rain drops, until 8:30, discussing things pro and con and trying to convince Bob that I should stay with Mom instead of trying to live by myself. Parking in front of his house, Bob telling me a bedtime story he made up as he went along, this until 1:30 or so. Bob is going to break the news to his father tomorrow and get the loan, we hope. So I came home feeling deliciously satisfied because Bob was in a very tender and affectionate mood and I do feel happy if a bit scared at the prospect of things to come.

Mon 18 Aug - Mom all changed again. She says go ahead and get married. She's worried about our unorthodox manner of going about it, tho. Bob's father had given him a calling down when he told him of our plans; said we were both crazy. So we parked in front of my house until midnight talking it over pro and con, con and pro, and still Bob was the more optimistic. He refuses to let anything come between us. His father is going to get $200.00 for us. We'll pay off his debts and go on a honeymoon somewhere. This Thursday we're to go to his doctor for our medical exams.

Tue 19 Aug - Mom thinks I should have a trousseau. She also wants to write relatives out East. Parked on North Avenue listening to music until the 'Law' suggested we move on. We both felt rather tired. This intensive courtship period is certainly wearing us both out.

Wed 20 Aug - Altho I was jittery and nervous as a cat, Bob insisted I take another driving lesson. I did my best for about 15 minutes and then I just refused to 'carry on'. He climbed out, climbed into the driver's seat and drove in silence for about 5 min until we got to Armanetti's. Said it was as tho I slapped him when I wouldn't drive. He said someone as sweet as me could be nervous. So we made up and Bob said we were going to see his Dr Belding tomorrow for our premarital exams. I must confess I would have let him walk out of my life if he insisted that I drive when I didn't feel like it. Why?

Thu 21 Aug - Out to Dr Belding's. The doc was very sweet. Said all he asked the people who wanted to marry 'Are you in love', if so, he saw no reason for sidestepping the issues of life; the first encouraging word we've gotten so far. The exam consisted of blood test and smears. Bob broached the subject of birth control and Dr Belding said I could come in later for all that, checking fitting of diaphragm (all so nonchalantly). Bob told me in all sincerity that he'd be patient and considerate, and after the first few times it would be pleasurable, referring to our relations.

Sat 23 Aug - Met Bob at 12:30. He told me of his exam at the hospital, thinks he'll get 1B. Then, oh fatal step, we went to PA Starck & Co where somehow or another we bought for 300.00 a Louis XVI walnut spinet. Pd 10.00 down, 40.00 COD, delivery chez moi Monday. We both signed the contract to pay 10.00 a mo commencing Oct 15. Came home rather sobered up. Mom scolded us, of course, for everything. Bot a ring for 10.00, gold band with orange blossom design. Bob and I tried to park in Forest Preserve with no success cause we were all routed by the Law.

Sun 24 Aug - Getting a severe scolding from Mom about the piano, about my marriage plans, that we're so unorthodox. Robt [trying out a more formal appellation, now that I am to be her husband! - For as long as I can now remember she always called me "Robert". Also notable that this evening evidenced acceptance into the Jusewich clan!] calling about 1pm. Invited him to supper. Bob over, eating ad lib, washing dishes, then playing pinochle and poker, at both of which the 'Dotys' were quite successful. I never knew Bob could be so sociable and entertaining. Bob and I occupied the sofa til 1:30 or so. I don't know why we just seem to melt in one another's arms, but the fact remains that with Bob's arms about me the rest of the world does not exist.

Mon 25 Aug - Out to Dr Belding's picking up our marital exam certificates. We discussed postponing marriage pro and con and Bob said he was afraid one of us might change his mind. So we decided to go thru with it next Sat. Tomorrow to get our license. The piano came today. Bob gave me 40.00 for it. It's beautiful; receipt for piano made out to 'Robt & Eliz. Doty.

Tue 26 Aug - Feeling rather silly and kittenish as I met Bob at 12:30 today and we went down to the County Bldg for our license. Surrendered our premarital exams. Felt rather embarrassed at our ages, but we got the license for 3.00. We drove out to pick up the ring, engraved with the date '8-30-41'. Mom likes the ring.

Reading Dr Long's 'Sane sex and sane living', and necking until 2 AM on our sofa. Really feel like I'm married to Bob. He was so sweet tonite, so different from last night.

Wed 27 Aug - We went apartment hunting with no success at all. In Bob's room while he practiced his horn. His room does seem rather gloomy but I guess it will do.

Thu 28 Aug - During lunch I went over to the Fair and perhaps foolishly bot a black hat with veil (5.95), green velveteen suit (10.20) and silver grey satin blouse (2.95). June and Miss Mann found notice of license issued to Bob and me, and so I had to own up that I was getting married this weekend [Fig 8]; now it's out! Mom admired my purchases, but Bob's face fell when I showed them to him. Sis and I coaxed Bob into going with us on 26th Street for odds and ends shopping. He didn't like that either. I felt peeved. When we got home I heard a very good lecture on extravagance in buying clothes, etc. But Bob and I had a long session in the hallway and discussed it pro and con. He agreed it was all right so far but I'd have to stop it. Said I had a technique for getting my way. We necked a bit. Bob tells me he feels like a little boy waiting expectantly for Xmas, said he felt 'purified' by my love. Thinks I am so pure and innocent. I really feel that there is something almost sacred about our love. I feel unabashed by my emotions and so eager to share everything I am or have with Bob.

Fri 29 Aug - Came down to the office with the green velveteen suit in a box under my arm. Decided to return it for credit seeing as Bob does not like it.

*   *   *   *   *

Ex post facto analysis by those involved, 1.3 years later

10PM, Wednesday December 30, 1942

My darling wife:

Am so happy loving you yet a bit sad, longing impatiently to be back ready to spend the rest of life as your husband. Was it you, long ago, that used to wonder if we got married could we stand each other's constant company as well as we did as "lovers". And all our worries then. Should we? Were we sure? I think we both got married 'cause we didn't want to hurt the other's feelings by backing down. We were scared, but passionately curious, adventurous, romantically in love. We still are all that darling, except we are no longer scared, and we have found in marriage a love far more beautiful, serene, full, than anything we had imagined. We still have that healthy, lustful love of sex, a strong possessive bond between us. Always there was that, but marriage has brot also a love that means living together, building, dreaming together, - teasing about your girdle, making pancakes on Sunday morn, breasts caressed with naked thighs against the washstand, arguing over window washing and bottles to basement and sleeping with your nose against damp hair in curlers. The feeling built on love as experienced that way is intensely deeper, more subtle in perfection, completion, than even the godlust passion of hot lips welded in moonlight, buttocked in cool sand. Marriage has opened a love, limitless, unimagined in the days of singleness, our matelessness. Somehow, tho, we must have known or sensed this, to brave so surely, with such happy face the desperate decisions of those humid August evenings -

*   *   *   *   *

Saturday, January 2, 1943

Robert, my dearest -

. . . .To get back to your letter, my dear husband - it is an amusing thought to recall our very serious discussions and my personal qualms as to whether marriage would wear well for us two! About getting married - well, I was ready to call the whole thing off at the slightest signs of encouragement from you, but I didn't want to "disillusion" you about women and I guess you felt the same way. So we got married and I've never once questioned our compatibility. Everything you say, dear, I agree with you. I was scared, not of you, but afraid that I would not measure up to your expectations, Robert; and certainly I have lived a more full, richer life than I ever imagined possible, and gladly, eagerly I look forward to devoting myself, my whole life to us, building, dreaming, loving together. Sweetheart, little did we know what momentous decisions we were making in the August of 1941! I don't even want to think of what would have happened if either one of us hesitated. If we had deferred our marriage then, what a

85

glorious year would have been lost! That was one time when I'm glad I let my heart get the best of my head; with everything against us, we still went ahead. I'm so glad, so very glad . . . .

*   *   *   *   *

CHAPTER IV
The Bride's Diary

Synopsis - This unique and vivid document records a woman's response when first encountering the full sexual ardor of the man she loves, and begins to share life's private moments with one who, in that regard, is at first a stranger. The cross currents of emotion surrounding these events run deep, dramatized both physically and psychologically by the sacrifice of virginity. Few, if any, veridical accounts of these crucial transformations have made it into public view, yet such are among the most profound experiences of women. The case at hand is probably, and happily, in most respects prototypical.

Some appreciation of the delicacy surrounding these experiences can be seen in the fact that Elizabeth, beginning with her marriage, abruptly switched from recording her diary in plain English script to encrypting it in Pitman shorthand. Clearly, her intent thereby was not that these nuptial scenes be forever secret, for she returned to plain script 4 months later with her 1942 diary. Rather, this "encryption" was dictated by the prudence of a level-headed young woman realistically recognizing the vast change in her life that would ensue, with all its deep uncertainties, as she took up life with a man she had known for a scant 3 months. Preservation of some shred of privacy in her diary was a reassuring caution; and the encryption guarantees that her reactions presented here were recorded with unvarnished frankness.

As married life unfolded, the inherent proclivities of man and woman began to exert themselves. Most evident, of course, was the contrast of the ever-eager male with the female, for whom sexual engagement fluctuated from time to time between ecstasy and duty, or refusal, to the male's annoyance. But there were more subtle things. For instance, she writes (15 November) "my dishes", naturally and without thinking, as we established our home, where my term, of course, would have been "our dishes"; yet it would have been "my tools", if I had enough to mention. In other words, gender oriented spheres of influence came unbidden into place. The amount of effort to be exerted in "keeping house" remained a point of contention between us for years.

While these pages are pervaded with a sense of bliss and contentment, such moments were necessarily interpolated between the rigors of work and school, shortage of money, fear of unintended pregnancy, petulant outbursts on both our parts, and the insistent threat of war. All the more blessed then those moments of togetherness, that make the married state the pinnacle of life's delights.

Fri 29 Aug - M - The Day Before - Came down to the office with the green velveteen suit in a box under my arm. Decided to return it seeing as Bob does not like it. Marie called this evening and tried to dissuade me from going thru with my marriage unless I was absolutely sure that I wouldn't regret it. Tried several times to reach Bob with no success and was getting rather disgusted, what with Mother scolding me and Sis setting my hair, and noise and stuff. And then he called me about 9:30 and everything seemed all right. So I decided to pack just a light supply of clothing, took a bath, and got to bed about midnight. I am worried about menstruating. Mother kissed me goodnite, and said this was the last nite I was going to spend in her house as her "dziewica" [Polish, "dzyeVItsa", wholesome, unmarried little girl], and I almost cried.

Sat 30 Aug - M - M Day - Awakened at 7:45 and had breakfast. Robert came. Somehow I got dressed in my plaid suit, and at 10:30 we set out for the County Building. Bought corsages for Sis and me. The judge performed the marriage ceremony and he really made it very impressive with his kind looks and words about cleaving to one another - in adversity, prosperity, and forsaking all others until death. Robert kissed me, and then we were married. Had Tom Collins [a gin drink] at Gibbs. Mom had made a luscious chicken dinner. Then taking pictures. [As I remember, it was with a camera I borrowed from a friend at work, and I knew nothing of photography. All the honeymoon pictures were thus dreadfully out of focus.] Weather clouding up and when we finally left at 5 o'clock, the rain was pouring. We drove on to Milwaukee where we found clearer weather. Registering at Hotel Schroeder, $6 corner room on the 19th floor. I very shyly told Robert of my plight [menstruating] and he said he preferred it that way because he did not want to jump into things right away. So we dressed and went out to eat, and strolled along the main street, Robert buying me candy at Mrs Stevens. Back to our room and I got dressed in my eggshell negligée and then I really felt like a bride. Robert was very considerate and sweet, and I didn't feel a bit embarrassed to lie there in bed with him and feel his hands lightly stroking my body. I'm not a bit sorry I married him. Robert and I watched a beautiful orange moon from our window. Robert fell asleep about 2:30. I got up and put my hair up which had become messed up. Rather a strange feeling, I suppose, but it all seems so natural for me to be married to Robert; and as I look back on events, everything seems to have pointed to our doing just this very thing! [What a remarkable insight into a relation that had a history of a bare 3 months, and was to endure for our entire lives.]

Sun 31 Aug - M - Winona - Woke up at 9 o'clock and just lingered in bed until 10:30 or so. Dressing to go out to breakfast. Taking our pictures on automatic machine in lobby. [Fig 8] Pulled up stakes about noon and started out for LaCrosse. Ran into some fine country around Camp McCoy, and beautiful country around LaCrosse. Pushed on to Winona and so drove across into Minnesota, along the banks of the Mississippi. A very beautiful and inspiring sight even in the dark. Reached Winona about 8:30 and got a beautiful room for $5 with two beds. Everything a modern blend of furniture, roomy, with a real fireplace and "atmosphere". So we went to bed and Robert introduced me to the mysteries of his body, and I found it a rather new sensation. He really needed it I guess, but I had to help to induce an orgasm. I cried just like any silly schoolgirl and felt rather shaken up by the event. I suppose I'll feel that way with every new step we take. Robert took pictures of me in my negligée with his super-sensitive film, but I doubt whether they will turn out. Wish we had had this room for our bridal suite last nite.

Mon 1 Sep 1941 - M - Lake Chetek - We had a leisurely breakfast in the hotel and addressed cards to various people, getting started about noon again. Running into unquestionably beautiful country around Lake Pepin. Driving into the "Lakes of Wisconsin", getting to St Croix Falls about 5 o'clock. Took a short exploration along the river. Finally got to Lake Chetek and got a cabin by the lake for 2.50, with inside toilet and all the comforts of a hotel room, and with the addition of a screened porch and beautiful view. My first nite lying in bed entranced with Robert's flesh along mine and setting us both quivering. I am still menstruating, but Robert tells me it is all for the best, that we won't jump into this thing so quickly. - So Robert started playing his horn but, when he failed at something, cursed and threw it on the bed. His anger alarmed me. He said he would not do that anymore because now his actions affected not only himself but me too. And so we went to sleep under two blankets, as the nite was really cold. Beautiful lake spread out before us. This seems almost too good to be true. An ideal honeymoon, Robert and I both agree. We couldn't ask for a more lovely trip; and we do believe as much in love as we two seem to be, is, and could be true!

Tue 2 Sep - M - Enroute Home - Had a 50-cent breakfast at the hotel, fruit, cereal, bacon, ham, eggs, everything. Wonderful! Taking motor boat trip on the lake, 180 miles of shoreline they say; evergreens along the banks. Finally managed to tear ourselves away and started for home about noon. Driving at a terrific pace. We had about 400 miles to go. Driving thru some beautiful country, rather wild and monotonous; but we had seen the best along the banks of the Mississippi and in the Lake Pepin region. Had fine, clear weather, Robert driving 70-75 [miles per hour] all along. Finally got to Chicago about 11:30. Unpacking our clothes, taking a bath. Robert so tired he fell asleep almost immediately and I rather resented it. Well, honeymoon's over and we've got to settle down to just ordinary living. But I guess I was just as tired; and we really had a fine trip all the way around. [Fig 12]

Wed 3 Sep - M - Resting - I guess the honeymoon is over. I got me awakened this morning to find Bob will leave for work, and asking me what time I wanted the alarm set. Up at 10:30 all by myself. Called Mother, and she told me to come over for lunch, which I did. Taking some soiled blouses. Telling Mom all about our trip, washing my hair, playing scales on the piano, just resting all day. Robert called about 4 to say he had to work a little late and couldn't be out until 9. He came to eat. My big Pullman case handle broke, but somehow we got our things up to our room. [Fig 7] Robert thot we had better wait before entering into married life. As much as this was the last day of my menstruation I agreed, but I am just as anxious as he is to explore further into this new path that marriage has for me. Mom was very pleased when I told her how kind and considerate and sweet Robert was. Tomorrow I go back to work, and I somewhat dread the remarks that will be passed at me. But I suppose every new bride has the same reaction.

Thu 4 Sep - Back to Work - Was sweet to be awakened by Robert's arms around me and his lips on mine. Met Miss Cohen on my way to the office and we had breakfast together. She told me of the excitement my marriage caused at the office, being about romance . . . So I faced innumerable congratulations from people at the office. I think I stood up pretty well under the deluge. Cashed my check at Fields, as we are rather short on money. Home to find Robert home as well. We ate at Farmer's, which I didn't care much for, and then drove out to the Oak Park Library, getting scads of books. Gave Bob $22 to pay back Jay [Loan, at usurious interest, to finance our honeymoon.] and $45 to put away. I think it will work out all right. We are paying only $5/week for the room. Robert tried very hard to break thru the remainder of my virginity tonight, but it pained me so that he just couldn't. Said he couldn't bear to see me suffer. Every new stress we undergo seems to bring us both so much closer to one another. Robert does seem to crave affection as much as I do. I think we will be very happy together.

Fri 5 Sep - I'll never forget this day - Awakened as usual by Robert's good morning kiss before he leaves for work. Coming home to find Robert not home yet. So I settled down to figure up my expenses over the months of July and August. Bob came home and started to play his horn. He got rather self-abusive when he couldn't get the notes just right. This went on until 7 o'clock and I was getting a bit peeved. But we went out to eat at Rex's Restaurant and had a fine fillet of sole for 50 cents apiece, and read poetry while eating. A full moon out tonite but we returned to our room. Robert read a bit and fell asleep over his book. So we retired about 10:30. We were both moved by one another's nearness. Well, it finally happened and I am glad. Very glad, even tho I cried and trembled all over, quivering more with anticipation than with fear or pain; and with tears running down my cheeks. I felt a keen joy in being able to give Robert some pleasure, if only with my body. And so gradually I came to fall asleep in Robert's arms, into sweet, dreamless slumber. - Robert says we will have to look for another place, because altho this serves the purpose of a place to sleep and store our clothes, we lack the privacy that we would like; and I would love to have some of my personal effects here, including my records.

Sat 6 Sep - One Week Today - Up at 6:45 and Robert and I had breakfast together at Farmer's. At office showing Capt Jensen snapshots that we took, and he agreed that they were pretty good. [Very generous of him, for he himself took excellent photos, e.g., Fig 11. This shows our utter naiveté at the time re photography.] So, the morning passed with numerous congratulations from people in the office in as much as notice of my marriage appeared in the newspaper. Bob picked me up at 12:45, to library to return records and renew books. Went over to Mom's about 6:30 for supper. Tried on my winter coats, and Mom promised to fix them up for me. Playing the piano, Robert showing me the way to play the scales better. Dad gave Robert two pipes [I affected a tobacco habit at the time as a mark of sophistication, but gave it up for good a few months later.] and Mom said she would fix up some of his work trousers. We left about midnite. To bed, and Robert only kissed, he couldn't get as passionate as he would like to. But I am satisfied with just his kisses and his caresses, even if he did give only one to me and fell asleep in a hurry.

Sun 7 Sep - We Look at Houses - We didn't get up until noon, and then I was annoyed at Robert because he didn't kiss me good morning but instead started playing his horn. Looked at model homes in Elmwood Park. Beautiful but very expensive, a six-room house that I would like very much, but cost more than $10,000. So, we thanked the man very kindly and decided to draw up our own plans and save up enuf money to qualify for the FHA loan. In the meantime we will live in our $5 a week room. Back home and going to sleep. So ended all thot of becoming a home owner.

Mon 8 Sep - . . . . After supper we went to Austin College and registered. Robert for English 102 and Social Science 102. I have Psychology and Music Appreciation with Mr. Rapoport. [Anatol Rapoport, not only a brilliant pianist, but also a mathematician/philosopher. Our paths were to cross again in the late 1950s, when he was one of the founding professors of the Mental Health Research Institute at the University of Michigan. See: Rapoport (1957) Scientific approach to ethics. *Science 125*: 796-799.] So we paid out $12. Talked to Mom today on the phone and told her of our desire to buy a home. I still have not told Robert of my $800 in the bank and I don't think I will for awhile. [I can't recall that she ever did, although our future finances were such that it didn't matter.] Then I will surprise him with it some day. I am even thinking of trying to save money on the sly if I possibly can so as to have a thousand dollars some day. So much to buy. So much we want to do. It is a problem, but Robert is so sweet. I don't mind enduring some inconveniences with him.

Tue 9 Sep - Robert got up at 6:15 this morning so that he could get in a half-hour's practice. In as much as this was the last day before school starts, I wanted to get out to the dentist to get my teeth fixed. Made arrangements for Robert to go over to Mom's for supper. Had one tooth filled. Got a very nice reception from both Mom and Dad. Played the piano. Home, took a bath, got to bed. I am still rather tender when it comes to intercourse and Robert very kindly consented to wait until I am in the mood and physically healed.

Wed 10 Sep - First Day in My Music Class. I am Going to Like it - Robert very much rushed trying to get his music lesson in and still make his early class in typing. His knowledge is remarkable. During lunch I bought a book on "Marriage of John" [?] by Verrey for only 50 cents and it seems to be pretty good and comprehensive.

Thu 11 Sep - This morning we had something rather unusual. Had intercourse. We both woke at 5:30 for no reason at all and I guess mischief comes to tempt us. I still dread that after because I feel so down inside. Apparently all virgin brides undergo the same stress. Home to find Robert practicing with unusual vim, vigor and persistence. I was peeved because I had to eat by myself.

Fri 12 Sep - Late in getting up this morning but Robert doesn't leave for work until I am out of bed. Thank goodness for that! Ran into Dorothy and told her I was very happy and I really am. Except when I permit myself to recall with nostalgia some of the benefits of my home life; overlooking, I guess, that I was bored to death most of the time and had to seek deeper relation in school and such. After work got my last tooth filled and paid $12. Listening to Roosevelt's speech. He said our Navy would shoot on sight any hostile submarines. Robert at draft board.

Sat 13 Sep - White Pines - Had intended getting up early. Instead we stayed in bed and didn't get up until 10 or so. As usual we were proceeding with caressing and fondling. Robert is the perfect lover, because he does try to give me as much pleasure as he derives from it. He penetrated into the vagina, and I suppose we will have to go see Dr Belding, because it hurts so much when he tries to unite us. I despair of perfecting the technique, and think so much seems to be missing when we can't really have intercourse. I am still scared of becoming pregnant. . . . . About 2 o'clock we set off for White Pines, 91 miles from Chicago. Got there about 4. Took some snapshots with the pines in background and then it started to rain slightly. So we set out for home. Home by 8 o'clock. Robert practicing while I comb out my hair. Going out to eat in a few minutes.

Sun 14 Sep - Lazy Day - Woke at 9:30 or so. Bob went out and got sweet rolls, a quart of milk and four peaches, and we breakfasted thusly. . . . Drove out west and parked beside the Brookfield Zoo. Watching the sunset; and just like our courtship days, just necking, talking. This for an hour or two. Well, it was a fine weekend even tho we did not do very much. We are not spending much, the only expenses being for gas, rent and food. Robert has not had a drink since the one we had after our marriage. Tomorrow I get my check and pay up all my bills and then Robert wants to save about $100 a month. I think we can do it if we watch our daily expenses.

Mon 15 Sep - After work I went over to The Fair and paid my bill, 30.07 in full, and to Rothschilds to pay 25.50 for my plaid suit. Home at 6 pm to find Robert practicing. We rushed about getting ready for school. . . . Home. I took a bath while Robert practiced; says he is determined to get a PhD in Biology and then to get a professorship somewhere and also a Doctor's degree in music. Wonderful, but will he be able to get there? Will I be content to wait for him to get on? Question. Question!

Tue 16 Sep - This going to school at night is getting to be pretty hard to get used to. Getting up in the morning is really hard for both of us. It was a rush to get home to find Robert practicing. I was hungry and wanted to eat, but waited until he was ready to leave for school. We both had a milk shake. Got home about 11; and before we are ready to go to bed there is another mating. And so to bed. What worries me now more than anything is that somehow or another I might be pregnant, altho Robert claims it is impossible. Wish I could find out definitely. My class in Psychology should be fairly interesting. Somehow my interest in school work is lagging. What to do to revive it?

Wed 17 Sep - Robert woke me from sleep last night and I complied. I have no complaint about his affection for me. . . . I am very much in love with my music class; I think Mr. Rapoport is just grand and I really feel that I am learning much about music. We flew after school for pleasure at home. My stomach has been acting up all day, again I wonder if it can be pregnancy - it would be just my luck!

Thu 18 Sep - Aurora Borealis - A beautiful sight. Pale green shimmering light illuminating the heavens toward the north. So we sat for about half an hour watching it. Splendid! In shape and form and color, a marvelous spectacle and one we shall remember for all time. . . . We're going to Mom's for dinner tomorrow and I am glad because I have quite a bit of laundry to be done and Mom, the darling, said she would do it.

Sat 20 Sep - . . . . Met Robert at 1 o'clock, going to the library to return records. I got some books on interior decorating. Then to

Music Appreciation store and buying Beethoven's Fifth and Eighth, and Tschaikowsky's Fourth (cost was almost $6). We bought me a douche syringe for 2.50, and some spermicide and prophylactics for Robert. [i.e., condoms, an appellation not prevalent among young women of the time. The designation as "prophylactics", emphasized their relevance to Public Health, and served as a shield against their being banned by ever-present fanatics who fought their use for birth control, as was the case in Nazi Germany and, until 1965, the law of Connecticut.] . . . . Robert fell asleep with his clothes on and I couldn't budge him. I woke about 6 and he was still in the same position. Thus we spent our third-week anniversary, and I must confess I grow more and more attached to my husband. What a thrill it gives me.

Tue Sep 23 - Out to class for my Psychology lecture. Fairly interesting, discussing human minds and interpretations of the various Schools of Psychology. I really enjoy both my courses at school. I only wish Robert and I could have more time together because this idea of just sleeping with one another is a bit disappointing. But he is so energetic and so ambitious and wants to carry such a formidable program of study, his music too. I wonder just what the future holds in store for us. The situation in Russia is getting serious and perhaps we will be in the war before long. And then will Robert have to go and fight and if so when will he be back to me. I sort of hate to think of going back to Mother, although I know she will welcome me back.

Wed 24 Sep - Went out to Mom's after work and had supper there. She gave me advice as to how Robert and I should invest our money; be sure to have it in a joint account, etc. I agree we should have a joint account and I have talked to him about it. I got to school just in time. A wonderful session of piano music and lecture. Back home. Robert drove to a park to practice on his horn for about a half hour or so.

Thu 25 Sep - M - Last night I told Bob that I felt like I was nothing more than a "bed partner". He didn't like that and explained to me that the reason we were sitting here was because we were trying to save money etc. We both talked about getting an unfurnished apartment of three rooms, buying our furniture and staying there for about a year or so until we can see our way clear to get a home. Well, I don't know; it sort of frightens me. I don't know just what furniture to get or how much to pay for it. . . . Started menstruating and, boy! I've had the cramps all day. . . .

Sat 27 Sep - M - . . . . Met him at 1:30. We looked at several places that were just awful. Looked at furniture at various stores. Furniture is very expensive. . . . I am determined not to eat so much, none of those over-priced dinners for me. I'll stick to lettuce and tomato sandwiches until I diet down to 130 lbs. [Clothed - a fantasy, of course, that occasionally crossed her mind. She remained a stable 140 until in her 80s.]

Tue 30 Sep - M - . . . . Fairly interesting session in Psychology on endocrine glands and their effect on the body. . . . We have decided to look for an unfurnished apartment somewhere; take a six-month lease and get the minimum furniture necessary and then in the Spring look for a home or something. (I still have not told Bob of the money that I have and I won't until I decide what is best for us.)

Fri 3 Oct 1941 - . . . . Robert was very passionate tonight and said he would try to make up for the week of misery in menstruation. It is indeed comforting to have his arms about me.

Sat 4 Oct - Off work- Our fifth-week wedding anniversary. I took the day off from work. Raining out. A right sort of morning to stay in bed and just caress one another. This until afternoon. Robert wanted me to play with him this morning but I just kept on sleeping. . . . Looking at furniture, particularly modern furniture. Out to Starck's and paid 10.10 on piano. Then going to Mom's where I washed five blouses and pressed all of them. Came home and we both looked at some designs for homes in the paper. . . . Had a most wonderful experience. I really think Robert induced me to have an orgasm. It is the most intense feeling I have ever experienced. And so we didn't fall asleep until 4:30 or so; but then Robert says it is due to the fact that we didn't indulge in anything during the week.

Sun 5 Oct - Robert got up and went out for some rolls, chocolate cup cakes, grapes and milk and we had our breakfast. Then both felt we should indulge in some fine love-play, and we enjoy it now. This went on until 3:30. . . . We took a nice drive out west in bright moonlight with the radio turned on low. Got home about

10 or so. Looked over "Better Home and Gardens" magazines and clipped out coupons for "Modern Ideas on Homes and Home Construction." We didn't fall asleep until rather late. Robert was in a very romantic mood tonight and so was I. A day devoted to ourselves, it was perfect!

Mon 6 Oct - The one redeeming feature of the day was a piano recital by Mr. Rapoport in lieu of class tonight. Robert joined me by cutting his class and we really enjoyed the program, which started out with Beethoven's Moonlight Sonata, 4 selections from Chopin, etc. Came home and indulged in much caressing and volumes of attention. Robert is so sweet about us. I almost feel more contented than I ever have in my life . Then again, I feel a sinking sensation as I think of our being united for life; I don't know. [Strange. Fear of the uncertainties of the future?]

Thu 9 Oct - During lunch I went over to The Fair and looked at their Oakmaster modern furniture, which I like very much. Reading "Happy Family" and enjoying the frank discussion of marital problems in a very readable style. Robert is such a darling. He was so romantic last night and I think I will find him in the same mood tonite. I am glad to know that Robert is rather anxious to get us settled in an apartment. I am too in a way, altho I do think we should try to save up some money first.

Fri 10 Oct - Came home to find Robert very much excited about an apartment his father had told him about. We drove out and looked at the place. Four rooms with one bedroom for $45 a month. A corner apartment on the first floor [Fig 9]. The Whites are sub- leasing it until May 1st. So we made arrangements to sign the lease. Now we will have to worry about getting our furniture, but it will be fine to have our own place.

Sun 12 Oct - Getting up late and indulging in some fancy necking until 11:30 or so when Robert's mother called and invited us over for dinner. . . . Robert's mother suggested that his Dad give us one of his mother's rings, a diamond solitaire in a fine plain gold setting which looks very nice with my gold wedding band. I was very much interested to hear her remark about Robert coming from "good stock" and that he wouldn't shirk his responsibilities. Home and getting ready for bed. Robert disappointed because I wouldn't indulge in any more loveplay, but I think once a day is enough. So we went to bed both rather disconsolate.

Mon 13 Oct - I called Mother and told her about Robert's folks yesterday and she said I should try to be on good terms with his mother. . . . Back up in our room. Robert writing his Grandmother while I darned several pairs of hose and sewed buttons on my suit jackets. Should be studying for my Psychology class tomorrow but I am in no mood - thinking how being married alters one's outlook on things. I think Robert would be glad to settle down at just plain housekeeping too even if he wouldn't admit it.

Tue 14 Oct - A rather busy day at the office and Captain Jensen and I had a pseudo- quarrel about the CIO [Congress of Industrial Organizations, a powerful group of labor unions.] and that led to rather strained relations all day; but I was glad when he made a friendly overture and we forgot about it. Over at Mandel's during lunch looking at their selection of furniture and I don't think I like what they have. That is quite a problem - what kind of furniture - new or used - modern or period - and how to buy it - on terms or cash as we could do. . . . At the Psychology class I got 44 out of 50 right so I didn't feel so bad about it.

Wed 15 Oct - Checks came just before lunch so I went over to Mandel's and paid the last of my bills there. . . . Went out to Mom's for supper. Met Robert after school and eating at Central Plaza (it is our favorite eating place now), and then coming home. Both of us felt rather romantic and so we didn't get to bed until 1:30 or so.

Thu 16 Oct - I was rather morbid all day and I told Robert I have a rather ambitious and grasping nature. He refuses to get alarmed about it but I am. I would never be content until I have more than I have now. Oh well, let us leave off today and let tomorrow take care of itself.

Fri 17 Oct - I went over to The Fair to look at furniture during my lunch hour. . . . looked at Spiegel's catalog and picked out tableware. We had a slight quarrel whether to get the cheapest or most expensive, and Robert went deliberately for the cheapest. I thought nothing about that and we came home feeling pretty good. Didn't get to bed until 2:30 or so. I have never seen Robert so passionate as he was tonight.

Sat 18 Oct - I had a heart-to-heart talk with Robert about being niggardly about the things we buy. (Mom had called me this morning and scolded me for giving in on the tableware deal and so I told Robert I wanted the more expensive kind and he gave in.) . . . . We got back to our room and I felt so tired that I fell asleep before Robert came back from his bath. I think he was a bit peeved about it but I couldn't help it.

Mon 20 Oct - I called Mom before leaving the office and Dick answered the phone and said she was in bed. I think her heart hurt her. So I came home and felt blue about it. . . . I started feeling very melancholic about things in general; the thought that Mom was feeling ill and I thought of how worried father might be. So when we got home I really broke down and had a good cry. Fell asleep sobbing in Robert's arms. He is a darling though and very understanding and considerate.

Wed 22 Oct - My First Ballet Russe - . . . . Feeling rather low about things. Guess it is because I am going to be menstruating soon. Saw Chopin's Les Sylphides, Francesca da Rimini, all of which I enjoyed very much. . . . Am beginning to worry about my menstruating which I feel should be due now, but Robert is very reassuring.

Thu 23 Oct - Out to school. We took the intelligence test in Psychology and I was very much gratified to find that I placed in the upper 10% of the scores for students in various grades of college. After school we came straight home, having eaten our supper before class. Robert pleaded to have intercourse with me, as it is the last time before we go for a week or so. So I consented, but somehow I am not in the mood just before menstruating.

Sat 25 Oct - M - Ballet Russe - Buying Furniture - Married 8 Weeks Today - We bought a four-piece sectional sofa to be covered in turquoise, for about $200, a rose beige Wilton rug for the living room for $122, and a lime oak three-piece bedroom suite for about $100. . . . Saw La Carnaval, Paganini, etc. I really enjoyed all of it. Now we will have to worry about paying $370 or so for the furniture before December 15 in order to save $37 interest.

Sun 26 Oct - M - Out to Doty's. We had a delicious dinner, told them of our purchases and they seemed to approve of them. We discussed ways and means of paying for stuff and they said they would buy us a lamp and give us some cooking utensils. It seems we will have to buy appliances too; darn it anyway. Robert showed me his "baby book" and it really touched me to see the photographs and various notes made by his father and mother.

Tue 28 Oct - M - A very interesting lecture in Psychology tonight on courtship and marriage problems and I was rather surprised to learn that the odds are in favor of a marriage where the woman is several years older than the man; perhaps Robert and I are well-suited to one another. . . . Going to bed and really having nightmares about furniture and bills, but we are agreed that Robert needs a suit and we are going to get one for him this Saturday; also going to buy our dining room furniture and a rug and as much of our other things as we can. (The thought that I have some money in reserve gives me courage to do these things whereas otherwise I would be very hesitant about buying all this stuff on a deferred payment plan! Of course, Robert doesn't know about it and I do want us to work this out by ourselves.)

Fri 31 Oct - . . . . It started pouring in dead earnest about supper time and we really had ourselves in a fine mess trying to eat supper and get out to Beamish's house around 8. Visited there, listening to his tales of life in the army, and then left for Congo club where we had a drink or two. Came home and took my bath. We indulged in some loveplay which was rather unsatisfactory to me but then, as Robert puts it, it is rather difficult for two people to react at the same time. Oh well.

Sat 1 Nov 1941 - We splurge on DR and suit for RWD - Met Bob at 12:45. Went over to The Fair and bought Oakmaster drop-leaf table and four side chairs and two armchairs, a china closet totalling $210. Also a blue fleece rug for $61. We will make arrangements to have it transferred to a budget account. Then Bob got himself a $35 suit (a light grey) which was put on my charge. Robert had wanted to go over to Bill's house this evening but I protested firmly and he consented to call him up and call the date off.

Sun 2 Nov - Woke up about 9 o'clock but I stayed in bed and dozed on and off until one. Robert insisted on having intercourse with me and I acquiesced although I must confess I didn't enjoy it very much. Went to the Art Institute exhibit of American Painting and Sculpture. . . . At Mom's about 8 seeing our stainless steel tableware which I think will be very nice. Talking to Mom about things. She made some remarks about our paying which made Robert annoyed and irked me a bit too. We left at 11 o'clock. A perfect day except when Robert made a remark about wanting to see Felicia again and I found myself very annoyed about my husband still wanting to be friendly with a woman whom he had found lacking the passion and emotion which he seems to have found in me. Oh, well, I suppose I do think she will always make life interesting.

Mon 3 Nov - . . . . At school having mid-term exam in Music and it was one big headache. I know I failed miserably in the practical application part. I just couldn't seem to identify any of the tunes he played. But Robert was very understanding and I fell asleep in his arms. Feeling much better with all my cares and worries forgotten.

Tue 4 Nov - . . . . Indulging in sex relations tonight with Robert. Somehow I find it very soothing after a hard day at the office. Going to sleep after one o'clock and without my pajamas!

Wed 5 Nov - . . . . Coming home in a slight drizzle. Decided not to go to Mom's today, it tires me out so much to go out there and then right back home. . . . Very much gratified to find I got a B in music. My mistakes in recognizing pieces were logical ones and I don't feel so very bad about it. Home, listening to the radio, and again I feel the urge to have Robert. This is really terrible; perhaps it is just my over-wrought condition.

Thu 6 Nov - Came home in the rain to find Robert practicing. His music means so much to him. I tried very hard to "cram" for my Psychology exam tonight but I don't know just how I made out. The exam was fair enough, but as always I found my words leaving me as I looked at the exam questions. . . . We received a memo from Montgomery Wards that our monthly payments would be about $22.75; but we are going to try to pay for the rug before the end of this month if Robert's loan comes through. Not having any equipment [condoms] on hand, we went to sleep with only our usual nightly embraces.

Fri 7 Nov - . . . . Going out to eat at the Tea Room. Home and indulging in lovers antics until 10 or so. Seems wonderful to think that in another 8 days we will move into our own apartment. I am determined to get as much fun out of life while I can. Wars and stuff seem so remote when I am in Robert's arms.

Sun 9 Nov - . . . . Robert doesn't like the idea of borrowing money from my folks and in a way I don't blame him; but if we plan on paying things off in six months, I can't think how better we could do it than to save the 10% carrying charge.

Thu 13 Nov - I find it rather hard to concentrate on my work with the apartment in my mind all the time. After school we drove out by the apartment and stopped in to look the place over. Electricity was turned on. Thank God! We picked up scrubbing brush and mops and pails and things and left them overnight in the car.

Fri 14 Nov - I already made a start packing up our things. Robert had said he would stop by the apartment and wash the windows. He came about 7 and helped me pack too. The Doty's came about 7:30 and moved a great deal of stuff including Robert's radio. Without their help it would have been a lot more work trying to move things in our car. . . .

Sat 15 Nov - We were so tired that we didn't get up until 8:30. Managed to get all our clothing and books that we have amassed into our car about 9 o'clock and over to the apartment. Then I started in working without even having breakfast. Robert drove out to get Dick and I washed the cabinets and the refrigerator all over. By afternoon we had hung the curtains, the dining room all fixed up, my dishes all put away, my linens, etc.

Sun 16 Nov - . . . . So I got some dishes from Mrs. Doty and when we got home I got energetic and ironed a couple of blouses and slips, and it was about 1 o'clock before I got to bed. I know Robert doesn't like my ironing and washing but it has got to be done. I wonder how it will all work out going to work tomorrow from this new location. Anyway, we're moved. So good to snuggle into bed with Robert!

Mon 17 Nov - Getting up rather tired for breakfast which Robert had prepared - grapefruit and toast and coffee. Got my check and during lunch went over to The Fair and paid $53.07 for the mattress and springs and the dishes. . . . Going to the Illinois

Symphony concert tonight and hearing some Bach and Sibelius, and a new Russian composer's first symphony - Khrennikoff, which I enjoyed.

Tue 18 Nov - . . . . Took two tests in Psychology. Coming home and having a bite to eat, and I was innocently chatting about menus and other household material and Robert didn't like it. So I had quite a crying spell (he wasn't to know it was due to my nervous attitude right before my menstrual period) and told Robert that I was trying to be a housewife for his sake, that I didn't enjoy it any more than he did, having to worry about dishes and stuff. And so it all ended up with a loving session, and I fell asleep with tear-stained face and a relieved feeling.

Wed 19 Nov - . . . . After school coming home and Robert insisted on having me although I demurred, and so now I am two days behind schedule in my menstruation. Took a hot bath and went to bed feeling just awful.

Fri 21 Nov - M - . . . . There was a package from his Grandmother Mack with a hand-made quilt and six knives and forks (silver plated) as a wedding gift for us. I got all ready to make wheat cakes when Robert came home with a pint of Chinese chop suey, which made me rather peeved. After supper I washed my hair while Robert did the dishes. Then I went over my old letters and decided to discard all of it. Feel I am married and all that stuff merely brings a feeling of nostalgia for my days of single blessedness!

Sun 23 Nov - My Birthday - M - So Robert gave me a bottle of Yankee Clover cologne and a blue-flowered housecoat for my birthday - the darling! . . . . I hope Robert is always such a darling as he has been today, nice to our company and so sweet to me.

Tue 25 Nov - I ended my menstrual period which was rather painful this time. More uneasiness in the office about the Engineers. I really think that it would be ironic if I did lose my job. We all have bills we have to pay. Came home to find my income tax bill for about $23 due December 1st. So I told Robert the good news that eventually I might be out of a job, and he took it very nicely - said I could probably get another one easily, etc. Out at school very much gratified that I got an A = 90, my score for our mid-term in Psychology. Getting home and we had done the dishes before going to school and so we indulged in some very romantic love-making before going to bed. Robert is a darling!

Thu 27 Nov - . . . . Late to Psychology today but I was very much gratified to find that Robert has an IQ of 145 or 175 [?] which is an indication of very superior intelligence. In the genius ranks no less! This evening indulging in our loveplay and such, we had an accident and the sheath came off inside me. We were both frightened and I immediately injected some of the spermicide, but I am going to be uneasy until my menstrual period. Of course this happened during my so-called free period, but I don't know.

Fri 28 Nov - . . . . I think Robert was annoyed because I refused to have intercourse with him tonight, but I am a bit frightened at last night's events to tell the truth.

Sun 30 Nov - Got up about 11:30 - Robert annoyed because I was too sleepy to accept his embraces. While Robert prepared breakfast I got my veal roast together. In my absurd way I managed to get it really well done. So we finally sat down to our second dinner in the dining room, veal roast which Robert said was the best he had ever tasted. Afterwards Robert washed the dishes while I straightened up things. . . . Wrote up my diary and now about midnight and we are still up and active. I do so enjoy passion in our own apartment. - Ominous note, Japan and the U.S. are apparently on the brink of breaking off cordial relations. I do hope nothing happens to spoil our happiness, at least not for a year or two.

Tue 2 Dec 1941 - . . . . Rather disconcerting to get home and find the dishes waiting to be done, but Robert has been a darling by helping me. It is fun to have this apartment, really very spacious. Finding a letter from Bill Beamish, guess he's lonesome back in camp. Putting in the back of my mind this fear that Robert may have to go into the army. If he does, I hope it won't be until we have paid for all this furniture.

Wed 3 Dec - The whole office in a furor. This job has been a big headache to me, perhaps this is one reason I got married. Who knows. I came home feeling very stiff and Robert gave me a good rubdown. It felt so good to have one's husband administer to one's wants! He is really very loving and affectionate and I do en-

105

joy it all so much. I never imagined that married life would be like this.

Thu 4 Dec - Home - I did stay home and slept until 1 o'clock. I had a pretty good supper fixed and we got to school on time for a change. Drove out to Mom's after school. We got home about midnight and sleepily went to bed, indulging in some loveplay as usual. There seems to be no satiation point either. If everything goes well for a couple of months, we shall be very much in the clear with practically all of our bills.

Fri 5 Dec - Came home to find Robert's "instructions" for supper, which I proceeded to follow. He came home rather jubilant because his bonds had been cashed. He had paid the loan in full and had $105 left. We went to bed rather early, and of course it wasn't until midnight before we did go to sleep. But it was such a nice comfortable feeling to be together snuggled in bed with Robert by my side! All my vague fears seem to disappear into nothingness when I am with him like that.

Sat 6 Dec - Robert picked me up in front of the building at 12:45. He had just returned from paying for the living room rug and bedroom set and gotten the cash discount; so we have only $169 left to pay for the living room furniture. . . . This evening I managed to get all my scrap-book notes pasted in and caught up on my diary. This is a fine way to spend a Saturday evening, right in our own home doing things that interest us and not spending to get some night-life!

Sun 7 Dec - Japan declares war on US and Britain! - Robert was practicing his horn in the living room and I had started to prepare our dinner when the news came over the radio that Japan had attacked Pearl Harbor in Hawaii and had declared war on us. We listened dumbfounded as news came that the Japanese had bombed and set fire to ships etc in Pearl Harbor and Manila. An interruption came at 3 when Mother and Bess and Max Gensch came to see our furniture. We ate. Then we played the piano and Robert played his horn for Mom. Took her home about 7:30 and stayed for supper, listening to the radio and discussing things. President Roosevelt is asking Congress to declare war tomorrow. All military personnel are ordered to report for duty. How is all this going to affect Robert and me? And Max? - We got

106

quite a scare when Mother told me she was menstruating again after, I think, a ten months lapse. We had left the house on our way home when I mentioned it to Robert and he insisted that we go back and tell Mom to go and see Dr. Proud tomorrow because it might be a tumor or cancer! Which we did and she is going tomorrow.

Mon 8 Dec - War declared on Japan - Got down to the office with a vague fear. Captain Jensen and all the other officers are in uniform today, and the office has an entirely different atmosphere about it. The Corps of Engineers are to take over December 16 and how will it affect all of us? Colonel Hayden had his radio going all day listening to reports, and it seems that our navy and air force were really caught off guard in Hawaii and the Philippines. War was declared by Congress this afternoon. . . . Robert feels that he may be called to the army in several weeks, and if he goes, what will I do? Turn to my family, of course.

Tue 9 Dec - . . . . In spite of fears about the future and all sorts of things that I can worry about, I can truly say that I am very fatalistic about it all. I only know I love Robert more and more everyday.

Wed 10 Dec - . . . . discovered that we are certainly spending an awful lot, almost the exact amount of what we make! Of course there are special expenses like furniture and stuff. But if Robert has to go, I am going to really try to cut down our expenses.

Thu 11 Dec - Germany and Italy declare war on U.S. . . . . Went to Psychology and we had a reading comprehension test to my surprise. . . . . Well, we are just going home as if nothing startling is happening. Robert is so affectionate and sweet. We are becoming more and more the perfect lovers.

Mon 15 Dec - M - . . . . Rather nice not having to go to school, just being able to relax and do things about the apartment. I do wish I could retire and be a housewife, if only for a little while. I think I would enjoy it so much.

Tues 16 Dec - M - Captain Jensen making ready to leave for Washington this morning and I was quite busy getting last minute stuff out for him. Flaherty received word that his brother, an ensign at Pearl Harbor, was killed in action.

Sun 21 Dec - Getting up at 11:30 and having a leisurely break-

107

fast. Put our ham in to bake and mixed up two cherry pies etc.
Cleaned up the place a bit while dinner was cooking. Stopped
menstruating too. We ate a rather late dinner and then loafed
around all day, Robert reading his books while I addressed some
Christmas cards and took a leisurely bath. After a late snack
about 9 o'clock we went out for a walk and called his folks. Came
home and now I am ready to go to bed again. Robert was so sweet
and such a darling all day, so affectionate and considerate.

Mon 22 Dec - . . . . Came home and ate and Robert went shopping. We received several cards, and $2 from Grandma Mack
with the remark to buy ourselves something for the kitchen. Robert came home about 9 o'clock having spent almost $10 for gifts,
and told me that about 2000 men had been laid off in his place
and that he would only work 2½ days this week. That sort of puts
a crimp in my budget scheme.

Tue Dec 23 - . . . . I am just trying to figure out whether or not to
go back to school after the holidays. I can't seem to get any of my
assignments done and I find myself losing interest in things academic. I would like to get into the social whirl for awhile and really do some night-clubbing and stuff. Of course, there is the
searing thought that we still owe something on our furniture. Oh,
heck, wish I had never gotten married.

Wed 24 Dec - Christmas Eve - . . . . Came home to find Robert
still at the library; he wasn't working today. . . . We drove out to
the Doty's and gave them their gifts . . . . and then out to Mom's.
We had more fun unwrapping all the gifts. Then the liquor ran
freely and Mom and Dad and Robert really drank up about a
quart and a half. Robert was high but we got home safely and he
did a lot of funny things before I got him to bed, but he was very
good-natured about the whole thing. So ended Christmas Eve!

Fri 26 Dec - . . . . Out to Mom's for supper and Robert came
about 6 o'clock and we had a really delicious turkey dinner.
Robert ate much, I guess, because he was grumpy and insisting
on my going home. . . . . Took one of my bubble baths and we
were very pungent and sweet and didn't fall asleep until 1:30.
Why is it that he is so sweet sometimes and such a grouch at other
times? I can't figure it out.

Sat 27 Dec - . . . . I came to Mom's. In the meantime Aunt Kate and Uncle Iggy came over, so I called Bob at Masefield's phone and asked him to pick me up. He was annoyed, and when he came he refused to come in and meet the folks and then went back to the car without waiting for me to put on my coat and hat. So I waited until Edward (Sis' current beau) came over and they drove me home. It is 10 o'clock now. I have washed my hair and Robert is just sitting in the living room, not speaking. He really mortified me before all the folks by his action. Perhaps I was wrong in getting married.

Sun 28 Dec - Well, we made up last night and went to bed past midnight. But woke up about 10 this morning and after breakfast really started to clean house. Dick came over at 2:30, then Mom and Bess. They were very much interested to know the outcome of our little tiff last night. When I reassured them that it was all right they calmed down a bit. . . . We went to the Ballet Russe and saw a really fine program: "Serenade" by Tchaikovsky, "Spectre de la Rose" and the final ballet, "Prince Igor". I enjoyed it all very much. I really enjoy going out this way with Robert.

Mon 29 Dec - . . . . We had a phone put in this morning and now I will be able to contact Mom and some of my friends. I really felt isolated without a phone. Felt very much stimulated or something and so I sat up until midnight and got my book review for Psychology pretty well lined up. Robert appeared bored.

Tue 30 Dec - The day was uneventful as far as I can remember, and I managed to type up a rough draft of my Psychology review and went over to the library and got myself three books on Beethoven. Finally decided I might as well see if I can't get a theme written for music and try to get some credit for my music course. . . . Our forces in the Philippines are getting the worst of it with the Japs.

Wed 31 Dec - New Year's Eve - Got down to the office to find that the Secretary of War had issued a telegram to the effect that all War Department offices would work tomorrow. . . . Robert said he would do the dishes and I let him. I put my laundry away and then ironed most of my washing and took a bath; then we settled down for three very good drinks of gin and grenadine, and we went to bed feeling rather high, both of us.

Thu 1 Jan 1942 - Had to go to work today; the Loop was deserted and only a few places are open where we can get food. I got home to find Robert had prepared some stuffed green peppers which were very good considering the materials he worked with. After we ate I settled down to reading and Robert worked on his thesis. I felt very tired and went to bed before he did. He very sweetly tucked me in, kissed me goodnight, and returned to his studies.

Fri Jan 2 - . . . . I managed to get my Psychology book review all written up ready to hand in; sort of neat to go back to school after a three-week vacation.

Sun 4 Jan - . . . . We almost had a fight about Robert not eating his dinner but preferring to sit and listen to the music. I resolved not to make any fuss about dinner on Sundays hereafter.

Tue 6 Jan - . . . . Came home and found that Robert hadn't gone to the dentist because he couldn't get the car started again. We didn't go to school either, stayed home instead and necked and I helped Robert with his cancer research paper. It seems that I shall have to typewrite it for him. Cripes, can't he do anything by himself!? Men always have to be prodded along.

Thu 8 Jan - No one in the office today and I really was busy, trying to get the material assembled and the Field Reports all written up. Miss Cohen wasn't much help either; the responsibilities of my position really weigh heavy on me. . . . Just sitting this evening listening to the radio, getting the latest war news. This war is sure getting to be a serious thing.

CHAPTER V

The Cleveland Episode - The First Protracted Loneliness

Synopsis - At the beginning of 1942 we had been married 4 months, and had finally established a blissful routine in our newly acquired apartment, now fully furnished, although yet to be paid for. We were both still going to Evening College; I continued work as an electric range assemblyman, and she had had a year on the job at the War Department. The crisis arose when the Washington powers, in the confusion of organizing the nation's response to war, decided to move headquarters of the Great Lakes Division of the Corps of Engineers to Cleveland from Chicago. Elizabeth was "ordered" to Cleveland to help her "protector", Captain Jensen, organize the Labor Relations Office there. This, of course, meant separation for the newlyweds. It was made uniquely painful by the realization that we might soon be separated for the duration of the war, every moment together thus being all the more precious. So it was a difficult decision, between love, and the money we sorely needed.

In selecting from the diary, now in conventional script, and the daily letters that ensued, I have endeavored to convey both the stress of our loneliness and the decisions attendant thereto, as well as a smattering of the background within which this little drama was being played.

Sat 10 Jan - M - Came out to Mom's after work and started typing Bob's thesis on cancer. I typed and he dictated and I copied from his notes. Our car frozen up [Fig 10]. We had to ride home via street car, but it was fun - anything is fun with him. He's such a darling.
Wed 21 Jan - Bob was to have his Social Science exam tonight at

6:45, so I decided to have supper downtown. Capt. Jensen tried to coax me to have a drink with him. I demurred..... Got down to my music class to face an oral quiz on music theory.

Thu 22 Jan - Thinking of Mrs Hasse leaving yesterday, how grand to be able to retire because your husband can support you! Very stiff exam in psychology, but I came out second so that was fine. Almost makes me feel I should go on further in the study of psychology. Bob taking his final in English, and we both came home feeling very good at the thought that this was the end. Robert very sweet and affectionate tonite.

Fri 23 Jan - Rather angry when he told me his mother had told him she thought we should have a maid to do our housekeeping. I told him we were not going to live beyond our means. Very tired and I went to bed at 8:30 or so. I know Robert was angry at me, but I just couldn't keep my eyes open.

Sat 24 Jan - His specialist told him pulling the four impacted wisdom teeth would cost $40. He was in the midst of house cleaning when I got home at 5:45. Went to bed at 10:30. Bob angry at me and got up and read until 2 AM. Frankly I am getting fed up just working and not having any fun whatsoever. Being a wife certainly does curtail one's enjoyment of things previously done.

Sun 25 Jan - Robert angry at me this morning because I was sleepy. We breakfasted separately, but by lunch we had made up.

Wed 28 Jan - Got an "A" in my music appreciation class tonite. Something I most certainly did not expect. Crazy office, making arrangements to move to Cleveland. Jensen has asked me on innumerable occasions to transfer to Cleveland with him. But of course I demur, and then he points out that if I were not married, I'd be free to do as I please.

Thu 29 Jan - Surprise of my life when Capt. Jensen told me about 4 PM that Col. Hayden said I should go with him to Cleveland for two weeks or so and get the Labor Relations branch setup. Came home to tell Bob about my trip and he said you won't be back in two weeks. On to school to get my "A" in psychology. Called Mom to tell her of my proposed trip to Cleveland. She seemed acquiescent.

Sun 1 Feb 1942 - Leaving at 5:30 to go to the Dotys to say good bye. His mother telling me she'd look after him. Then to Mom's.

At 10 leaving for the Lasalle Street station, with $23 in my purse and my government transportation request. Fond farewells etc. Robert kissing me desperately and loath to leave until last call for visitors was made.

*   *   *   *   *

THE ALLERTON

EAST 13TH STREET AND CHESTER AVE

CLEVELAND, OHIO

[Penny Postcard!]
February 2, 1942

Dear Bob -
    Arrived safely - Made arrangements to stay here with Marcella. We merely reported to the office this morning - Looked up hotels.
Love,
Betty
P.S. You can write me here - as <u>Miss J.</u>

*   *   *   *   *

[On Allerton Hotel Stationery]
February 2, 1942

Dear Robert -
    So far, my sweet, nothing much has happened, but I knew you'd expect a letter, so I'll not disappoint you.
    We decided to take a room with twin beds, washstand and toilet and only a few doors away from the showers, for 3.50 per day. All the other conveniences (including a lobby of traveling men who ogle and "eye" every gal that goes by).
    Frankly, I'm a wee bit homesick even now and just writing to you seems to put me in <u>rapport</u> with you.

113

(Here I get a bit philosophical:)

   To get all there is out of living we must use our time wisely, never being in too much of a hurry to stop and sip life; but never losing our sense of the enormous value of a minute and, when I return to Chicago, I am going to put it to good use. I feel as though this separation is but a short interim of preparation to enter upon a more stimulating and more productive phase of our married life. I never realized what it would mean to leave you and our apartment. I think the realization will become more and more keen with every moment that I'm away. I'm selfish enough to hope that you will be eagerly awaiting my return.

Love, my darlin'

Betty

*   *   *   *   *

Tuesday, Feb 3, 1942, 10 PM

To my darling
   my sweetheart
   and my wife

   How I wish that I could begin as well as the Steinway Symphonic hour is being begun. Remember? Mozart #35, and now Mendelsohn's Italian Symphony. Music in many ways would be so appropriate for conveying all the strange, elusive emotions that your absence brings.

   As I started down the steps leading to the lobby of the station last Sunday, a pang of loneliness struck me. I missed you already. So many little things keep reminding me constantly that you are far away.

   Registered in Chemistry 200 for T & Th 6:45 to 9:45. Have some misgivings about the teacher, but the subject should be interesting.

   The Paris Conservatory Orch is now playing Debussy's suite "Printemps". (If I interpret the pronunciation correctly, that should be "Spring"?) At times Debussy's music seems to be weak, lacking fire, possessing that typical French super-refined grace. It is delicate, comparable to the work of Renoir (his light, soft brushwork). But yet there is a depth to it. Subtle, serene, his music establishes a mood of vague remembrances; one tries to clutch the misty "spirit of life" he seems to be seeking. That, I believe, is one of the chief weaknesses of the Impressionists, their indefiniteness. Monet is merely pleasing, soft, flowing pastels beautifully blended, but lack-

114

ing any backbone. He seems to shy from making a bold, powerful stroke of such definite line as to give the painting more zest than its naive complacency permits.

I love you and so desire to see you again. Kiss you, hold you, and just drink life from the beauty of my beloved's eyes. For 10 more days I love you thus by mail and thot.

Robert

*   *   *   *   *

WAR DEPARTMENT

OFFICE OF DIVISION ENGINEER, GREAT LAKES DIVISION

CLEVELAND, OHIO

ROOM 500 FEDERAL RESERVE BANK BUILDING

February 4, 1942
2:50 p.m. (EST)

Robert darling:

I know you're going to sigh with relief upon receipt of this letter and the discovery that it is <u>typewritten</u> — I do hope I find a letter from you when I get back to our hotel tonight.

[Now handwritten] 8:45 PM

Found your airmail letter, darling, and it was sweet of you to send me a note. I'll be home in a week or so, my dear (I hope) so you go ahead and enjoy your "bachelorhood" 'cause it will end before you get well on your way. I can't afford to let you find out that I'm not indispensable to you, m'love.

Love,
Betty

115

*   *   *   *   *

9:40 Wed Feb 4, 1942

Events: Got a little card with my check today that said $1685.60 was my total income for 1941. This is scheduled for $78 tax. Our total tax will be $167 - 1st payment $41.75.

But what are these trivial and trite details? They are not what I want to say or what I want to do. I want to see you, watch your smile, enjoy every pose and attitude that is you. I want to hear your voice, bicker over the method of making the gravy, hear you ask if I won't finish the potatoes, hear your sweet mumbles in the morning. I want to kiss you mischievously, tenderly, passionately, playfully, caress you, squeeze you and tell you that it will take a lifetime to express my complete devotion and love for you.

Such moods and thots can only bring on poetry or music, however poor -

Wrapped in a mist of lonely revery
I summon memory to sing
Our symphony of love
Playing body to body, mind upon mind
The counterpoint of souls in harmony
Weaves present joy
From the fabric of the past.
Crescendoing with chords of integrated being
Into the uncertain rhythms of the future,
Creating from the dissonant scales of life
A symphony, Intrepid. -
Distilled from crystal passion, to rise
And peril, the vacuity of time.

With this attempt I must leave and seek your company in the land of disconnected dreams. It is bewildering to attempt to catch my beloved in those fast-shifting scenes of sleep, but my arms are around you and my heart is in you for now and forevermore.

LOVE Robert

*   *   *   *   *

Thursday, February 5th 11:45PM

Darlin' - I just finished rereading your letter of the 2nd and I relented and decided to write you tonight instead of waiting until tomorrow. You're the darlingest darling to write me such a delightful letter and it sounds so much like you.

Am m———-g since yesterday and so it's been quite an effort to keep on going during the day, when all I wanted to do was to lie in my bed and dream of you. In the meantime I have made an effort to get the office set up, but all the personnel are new (up to 30 days ago the Division office force consisted of about 6 people, we now have about 30.)

If you go to the dentist Saturday, do take care of yourself; and darling, don't fall asleep on the couch any more than you can help. Would you mind calling my mother to say hello for me? I've written her daily but received no response. Tell her I'm well, etc. - and wish her a very happy birthday.

Love,
Betty

P. S. can't wait to be back and get tucked into bed a la Doty.

*　　*　　*　　*　　*

February 6, 1942

Dear Robert-

I await expectantly your letters. Darling you're the most marvelous husband a girl ever had. Your latest left me in a most delicious state of mind.

Capt Jensen came in this morning and he says he'd appreciate it very much if I did stay for three weeks in toto, and pointed out the fact that I was getting 5.00 per day while I'm here.

Don't think I'll be home in two weeks. Probably will at end of 3 weeks. You won't mind that, darling, will you? I'll be getting my per diem while here and besides I can't afford to antagonize my dear old Cap'n.

Room is costing us 3.15 per day for the two of us, which is only $1.50 odd cents for each one of us.

I'm kinda tickled at the thought that Capt Jensen spent close to 20.00 today on our steaks, wine, and café royales, a small token of his appreciation of the fact that I consented to come down to Cleveland even temporarily.

You keep on writing me your precious letters, sweetheart, and I'll keep falling in love with you every day all over again.

117

This separation might be termed a romantic interlude of post-marital courtship via the correspondence route.

With love and wifely affections,

Betty

*   *   *   *   *

February 7, 1942 - 9:45PM

My darling -

Sad but true, I fall in love with you all over again with every letter I get from you. I read the readable parts to Marcella and she just sighs and says "It's wonderful!" And it really is wonderful of you, darling, to be so faithful in keeping our "pen and ink" dates.

But first to settle a few mundane matters:

[Very detailed projections follow, the sum of which =]

If I only stay 2 weeks profit equals 28.00

If I stay 3 weeks net profit equals 45.00

And if I stay 30 days (as per my <u>orders</u>) and return to Chicago Monday March 2: net profit equals 80.00.

Isn't it marvelous? Unless there's some flaw in my reasoning, I should be able to come back with our income tax payment and enough money for an Easter bonnet for me and one for you! I told Capt Jensen I would get your husbandly approval before I committed myself beyond the two or three weeks that we had expected.

Robert, I find myself thinking of you constantly throughout the day and looking forward to your letters in the evening in much the same manner that I awaited with increasingly heightened expectation seeing you nightly before we were married. And now that we have these months of highly satisfying marital life, how much more keenly do I miss being with you! I miss your practicing, your "grouches" when crossed, your stubby beard against my cheeks, your strong capable hands so gentle when they caress me, and sleeping en seul just is no fun, but if I keep on this way I will feel like taking the first train home to you.

And I think, my sweet, this separation will make me realize

118

even more deeply what a prize I got in a husband. I fell in love with you with my mind long before you possessed my heart and soul, and your letters are so much <u>you</u>. It's comparable to almost being near you, reading the crystallized, set thoughts of your mind, without the distracting influence of matter.

*   *   *   *   *

7PM Sat Feb 7 1942

My most beloved sweetheart
Darling

Your letter came this morning and oh how glad I was to get it.

Last night I came expectantly home from work hoping to find a card from you at least. The box was empty. From then on I suffered first a disconsolate blue mood and then an angry one at your "neglect". Please forgive me. I almost phoned you about 11:30 (your time) but thot that you would be out perhaps. Your letter this morning was a blessing (I started looking for it at 8:30 AM). It completely dispelled all my lazily gathered moods.

To begin at the beginning. I arrived at the dentist's [To have impacted wisdom teeth removed.] actually quite scared and nervous. A double shot of novacaine didn't help my empty stomach any, but after lying down a while my calmness returned and I nonchalantly and curiously faced the operation. He made a mistake and tackled the most difficult tooth 1st. He had meant to remove this one on my 2nd trip.

He began on my lower left side and I experienced no pain at all except for the strain sometimes on the muscles of my jaw. The tooth lay on its side embedded in the bone. The bone was chiseled away by means of an automatic "stone crusher" resembling a drill in appearance. He then cracked the tooth into 3 pieces, removed them, and then bored into the bone for the roots. The upper tooth was removed comparatively easily by a little cutting and pulling. It's a real horse tooth, tho.

I drove home and lay down with an ice pack and listened to "Tosca". The pain increased greatly as the local wore off and was not helped any by hunger pangs. Can you imagine me with a whole egg held between my left cheek and teeth? Well, that is exactly the way I look now.

Next Wed I'll send you 25.00. Stop eating those hamburgher suppers.

I love you darling with all my heart and soul. That love has helped me today. When the pain became intense, I would think of you and the pain you suffer every month and the pain that you will someday suffer to provide joy for us both. Mine is very slight, and with such beautiful thots of you it is nothing. My mood tonite almost approaches an ecstasy in the martyrdom of being without you. Eugene O'Neill's "Strange Interlude" is adding to my mood and also the pain.

All the love of my life I give to you, my beloved wife. Your husband and lover.

ROBERT

* * * * *

Sunday, February 8th (after our phone conversation) My dear husband -

Really, I wish I could hire me a ghost writer to compose letters that would compare favorably with yours, but I doubt if I could find one who could adequately translate into words my thoughts and emotions where you are concerned.

My sweet, I appreciate how you feel about coming out here, I don't think it's feasible. First, round-trip coach fare would be 9.95. Secondly, you'd have to travel 8 hrs or so each way. Please, sweetheart, don't do anything rash like driving here. I'm enclosing herewith memo of my daily expenses, also memo of my meals during the week, just to prove that I have not been eating hamburgers for supper every nite. [Enclosed, on a densely detailed page, is list of almost every bite eaten, and every penny spent!] I just wish you were eating as well as I am, sweetheart, and I feel very contrite when I enjoy a meal and think of you having to endure makeshift meals all by yourself.

Well, I'll be expecting your letter tomorrow, my sweet, and I guess you'll have two from me.

Can't begin to tell you how I feel
Since I've been away
I think of you at every meal
You're on my mind all day

120

And when the day is done
That's when I'm really blue
The evening drags - until at one
I go to sleep and dream of you

In my dreams all night,
On my mind all day,
Nothing's been quite right
Since I've been away

's bad, I know, but it's so true - my "torch" song to you
Love & Kisses
From one who misses
Betty

P.S. have any of the neighbors asked you if I deserted you? If they do, just show 'em one of my letters -

*　　*　　*　　*　　*

2:10 PM Sunday Feb 8, 1942

Sweetheart:

The Philharmonic was just leaving the air and I was coming back to this letter when you called. Oh so near - I could hear you, almost see you, yet miles away. It seems so strange. I am adamant though about seeing you. Two weeks are enough, in fact it has only been one and I miss you terribly; but a month without seeing you. Not while it can be helped. Our time together may be short enough without taking an entire month away. All the $150 or even $1800 could never compensate for this, the happiness that prefaces the storm! Don't worry about Capt Jensen. He is a wily old fox in his paternalistic way that has wormed you into 2 weeks, now a month, and then what? We had the courage to snatch our happiness while we could and it has been everything, I believe, that we hoped for. You realize tho as well as I that the sword of war hangs over our heads, ready to separate us when it pleases. Its uncertainty makes it all the more imperative that we grasp the elusive dream of happiness while we may. So I say to hell with the money my sweet, I will hold you and love you till the moment that our happiness is sacrificed at the altar of WAR! I also vow that if such a thing comes to pass I will bear a relentless enmity to all persons and things that aid and support such butchery. To kill, destroy, and eradicate, forcibly or subtly all the damnable institutions, customs, beliefs, and persons concerned with the efficient and enduring prosecution of war. But more gently my love (and oh I do love you beyond belief), if you are going to stay away a month, I'm coming to see you, either next weekend or the following. You take Saturday off and we will have 2 days of constant company. I must leave for your mother's now but will write again tonite.

Love Forever, Robert.

*   *   *   *   *

Monday, Feb 9, 1942

Robert, darling -

I'm still all thrilled about my phone call to you yesterday. So thrilled that you want to come out here to see me, <u>but please don't</u>! I may only be here this week in spite of all that's been said before. This govt of ours doesn't know what it's doing. So let's conserve our cash and our energy and when I get back, darling, we'll have a real bang up welcome affair, yes?

As I meander about this hotel and overhear snatches of conversation here and there, I can't help thinking how shallow must be the lives of these traveling men. Salesmen discussing prospective customers and "big accounts", and stuff. Gals of assorted ages and sizes coming down to dinner in the hotel restaurant all primped up with side-wise glances at the men, or later sitting in the hotel lobby just staring as the people go by. I feel so sorry for them in a pitying sort of way. "I'm gonna make the 12:28, was gonna make the 7:45 but- two salesmen - Chicago men" - I can't help recording another bit of conversation emanating from behind my right shoulder from a group of salesmen. Oblivious of them all, I sit here and write to you letters which you may or may not find interesting, but after writing to you for an hour or two, somehow I feel that I can go to sleep in peace. It's a sort of mental exercise that does me no end of good; and as I write I seem to be in such close communion with you, darling. I almost wish it would never end, but four pages is about the limit of my penmanship and I do find myself a bit at a loss for words.

I do think, Robert, that you should do something about seriously getting down to work in the way of creative writing. You have such powerful, moving ideas and such an original way of expressing yourself. I'm going to save all your letters, darling, for publication among my memoirs when you get famous, sweetheart. [I had forgotten this comment when I wrote the Introduction hereto!]

'Tis easy to see where my thoughts turn. Do you know, I've had an irrepressible desire to make me a fine dish of slightly scrambled eggs the moment I get back to the apartment.

The wind is blowing - I hear its roar,
It's really blustering outdoors
But let it storm and let it blow
Makes no difference - rain or snow.

I sit indoors, warm and dry,
Try to be cheerful, but I don't know why
I should even bother to try -
If anything, I want to have a good cry -

Oh, I've got those lonesome, home-sick blues
And an awfully empty feeling
There's no use concealing
The fact that I'm missing you -

Tho I keep telling my heart
It's only for a short little while
That we'll be apart, sweetheart
It won't take heed and smile -

I never thought it would be so
That I'd miss you night and day -
Now I'm glad that I do know
How I feel when you're away -

I could go on for hours, but I take myself in hand and say "that's enough Tin Pan Alley stuff, my dear", and so I'll close this and hie me up to my room for another night of toss and toss and wait for another day. Hope you write me a good stiff note so I'll act my age and write you very formalized social notes with smart comments on what the shops are showing in the way of spring suits and how perfectly dowdy the women in this burg are.

With all love that a "one-man woman" can bestow upon the "one man" in her life, darling. I leave you until tomorrow

Betty

*   *   *   *   *

8:45 Monday Feb 9, 1942

To the sweetest wife
that a man ever wed

There is one thing though that still needs a lot more discussion, your staying a month. Sunday I let my emotions go. I hope I didn't hurt you, but I think that you felt that way too. In a calmer mood now I guess that you should stay the month if absolutely necessary. But, if you stay, I do insist on coming to see you week end of the 21st. At the most extravagant estimate the cost would not exceed $30, most likely about $22 (55 cents an hr sweetheart).

Your mother is really looking much better. You as a little girl came into the conversation several times. How you used to play a little harp, calling yourself "Lily", etc. It brought strange subtle emotions to me picturing you as a little girl, your environment, all the years of childhood, growing up to be the woman that I should love and devote my life to. How awesome and wonderful life can be.

Perhaps the mood of "Strange Interlude" [Eugene O'Neill] hadn't left me. It is a remarkably penetrating work. His depiction of character is so exact, perfect, that you can't help but live their emotions. It left me rather emotionally thotful, anxious to avoid enacting in life the unhealthy mental quirks that his people portrayed.

*   *   *   *   *

[Written on sheet headed: War Department, Sixth Construction Zone, Office of the Zone Constructing Quartermaster, 20 North Wacker Drive, Chicago, Illinois - which is lined thru and "FOO!" printed above it. Then, "In reply refer to:" is followed by "LOVE"]

Personal Bulletin
No 8

Subject: Same as bulletins #1-8 - the conduct of R.W.D. during separation from wife.

¶ 1. <u>Type of food</u>. Supper for 2/10/42. Remainder of buckwheat pancake flour mixed with 2 eggs, cup of sour cream, and teaspoon of butter. Perfect results - texture, thickness as specified in Bulletin 69 para 9A "Musicians as Cooks" (not crooks).

¶ 2. <u>Education</u> Books returned to library and card secured for E.N.J. Chemistry - no book - left half hour early - have an excellent lab partner, an intelligent lad.

¶ 3. <u>Music</u>. Practise resumed rather painfully but still able to play.

¶ 4. <u>Mail</u>. I've got to stop this nonsense now. Sweetheart, I found your Monday letter in the box tonite. What a wonderful surprise.

DAWN (a series of associations)

'Tis the dawn, timidly creeping
Thru the city's tapestry of smoke
As if ashamed to lay its gentle hand
Upon the tombs of toiling folk.

*　　*　　*　　*　　*

Gloriously bursting shaft of flame,
Dawn's light ignites the snow clad hill
Rolling brilliantly across the open plain.
Bold, proud dawn,
Happy to renew
Its service to beauty
In a troubled world.

*　　*　　*　　*　　*

Dawn pounces joyously across
Our spinning sphere
Relentlessly pursuing
Night's dismal shades

Dispelling darkness to its den
and in triumph calling
"Oh life, let's live again!"

      *   *   *   *   *

But in my heart dawn enters not,
My sun is absent, but not soon forgot;
Night's heavy sorrow shrouds the soul
Dissolving what once was whole.
Memory alone pervades the mind
Feebly kindling, tho remaining blind.

      *   *   *   *   *

Reflected glory of the missing one,
Taunting imitation of my smiling sun;
Oh, when will she return
To flood my soul once more;
To turn sorrow's shadows
Into sparkling day,
Convert existence
Into the joy we knew before?

Too much trouble with meter and rhyme. The alliteration and
word combination are natural, but it is difficult to combine all these
necessities of poetry and still express the desired thots. However, I
feel that there is improvement (in spots) in the rhyme and meter
end of things. Really the greatest good resulting from your being
away seems to be the goad that it supplies to make me try to write
such things. Your encouragement, criticism and praise are very
dear to me. I love you for that and so many many other things.

      *   *   *   *   *

Wednesday, February 11th

Oh, Darlin' -

Worked veree hard this afternoon on some wage rate re-
quests. Quite a touching scene when Capt. Aldis (our real estate
officer) made his adieus to the Chicago bunch. He received confidential orders to report to Washington prior to leaving for an unknown destination (I'm told in confidence that it's for Iceland to

acquire real estate for the govt, just between you and me). He came up to me to shake hands and I said to him, "good luck to you, Capt. Aldis." He squeezed my hand firmly and said with a catch in his voice, "and good luck to you <u>always</u>." A funny answer, I thought. He's always been very cordial to me - remember my telling you about the rivalry between Captains Aldis and Jensen for my services about six or eight months ago? Gee, maybe if I worked for him, they'd want to send me to Iceland as confidential secretary. Funny, what fate has in store for us.

It was interesting to read your comments on the birthday party [her mother's]. Darling, my parents are so different from any of my relatives, just as I differ from any of my cousins. Just have nothing in common with them. My mother, Robert, deserves the credit for trying to bring us up so that we would amount to something. You'd really love her if you knew how good and kind and self-sacrificing she has been for our sake and especially to me. Darling, I think she'd love it so much if you'd call her up this weekend and just ask her how she is, etc. Give her my love. I'm going to send her a valentine card for Valentine's Day. Why don't you send your mother one, too? Oh, yes, I dropped a card to Grandma Mack [Fig 14], telling her how much I missed you and stuff.

I just <u>loved</u> your letter of Monday night. Marcella walked in as I was reading it and she said my face just glowed. It was so <u>wonderful</u> after the last two I got from you, my love. You are undoubtedly the world's most romantic husband to keep on sending me these daily epistles of our mutual love and devotion.

*   *   *   *   *

Thursday, February 12th 1942

Dearest -

Lincoln's birthday, but we who are engaged in the war effort worked like Trojans all day.

'Tis wonderful what a magical effect a few pages from you will do to my drooping spirits. Your Tuesday letter is very good. I like the poem, too; you do pay me such wonderful compliments, darling, no wonder my hat seems to be getting too small for my head, and all while I thought it was my hair at fault!

To return to your letter, darling:

LOVE - RECIPROCATED 1st Ind. enj

E.N.J.D., c/o The Allerton Hotel, Cleveland, Ohio, 2/12/42

TO: R.W.D. Chicago, Ill.

1. With reference to Personal Bulletin No. 8, dated 10 PM, Tuesday, Feb 10, 1942 the following comments are made:

a. With reference to Par 1, thereof, approved. It is felt such a diet contains sufficient variety to ensure the maintenance of general health and well-being.

b. Reference Par 2, noted and approved.

c. Reference Par 3, it is felt that resuming practice should be delayed until such time as no dire results can ensue therefrom. [Consequent to my extracted wisdom teeth.]

d. Reference Par 4, the remainder thereof is devoted to the subject thereof (mail).

(1) You are so clever.

(2) You are such a darling.

(3) You ought to be scolded for not getting up on time. You can't use the alibi that you don't want to get out of bed because I'm in it. And I know you are not experiencing any of those "morning after the night before" effects.

(4) The poem has been read and comments are withheld for fear of making you pop the remaining buttons on your shirts. Information is requested concerning the interpretation that it was inspired and dedicated to the undersigned. (Don't you dare deny that it wasn't!)

(5) Your comments concerning communications from the undersigned are noted. It is appreciated that they are an indispensable remedy for the attacks of heart sickness.

(6) Information at the earliest practicable moment is requested concerning several vague references, "laundryman hasn't come yet". It is the belief of the undersigned that one Mrs Earle B. Doty may have telephoned said laundry not to call for any bundles during the absence of the mistress of the house. It is recommended that this matter receive your attention before supplies are wholly exhausted.

(7) Comments on closing paragraphs your communication are not considered necessary, as it is the belief of the undersigned

that they are reciprocal, mutual and natural on the part of two who have been separated.

For and on behalf of myself and no one else

ENDoty

Your wife always

*　　*　　*　　*　　*

9 PM Thursday Feb 12, 1942

To my precious wife
Darling

But darling, we must be serious for a while. If you promise not to worry the least bit, I have to tell you something (a probability) which you should know. Promise? It seems our dear gov't has issued orders to wit: Range production must cease come April 1st. This means so far that Hotpoint will practically close down until enough defense orders are secured to start work again. The foremen have, however, been ordered to hold all employees that they possibly can because it would be a great loss to lose the established personnel.

The probability must be faced tho that I may be out of work for an indefinite period. I would not burden you with this only that it may have to be a factor in any course of action that you might face.

I have considered the advisability of possibly moving to Cleveland. Pro: Your classification would be sustained and future advancement made more probable. The gov't (I believe you said) would pay transportation and moving costs. I might be able to secure a job there? (big question) (What does Herr Jensen know about getting jobs in nearby defense projects?) Rent is being raised here.

*　　*　　*　　*　　*

10 PM Friday, Feb 13, 1942

My darling:

Once more I seek solace in communing with my only goddess, you. It really approaches that sort of worship at times. You seem so distant and, except for your faithful letters, so unreal; a dream that came to me in the past and changed my life, only to flee and leave behind but half my soul. I have been trying to write poetry, but my subject requires a deft delicacy.

129

Mount Pleasure
Clasp arms to tender flesh
The warmth of spring,
Imprisoned in each beguiling breast,
Calls loving hands,
Silently, to caress.
Beauty of body - goddess formed.
Play lip to lip,
Passion aching,
Thrusting daggers of delight
With fingers gentle as the night;
Washed by a rushing tide
Too delicious to abide.

Astarte's succubus subsumed
In every tingling cell
Demands obeisance,
Immaculate oblation, body
Within body, union at love's altar;
Mind swept with ecstasy
The apogee of sense,
Elysian bliss exultant,
Love met with love intense;
The spring is sprung,
Pleasure coils
To permeate and possess.

Skin sinks to meet
Smooth, throbbing skin;
Soft whispers, mouth to ear,
Heads mingled, bodies one.
Hours sifting to eternity,
A Destiny desired, and won,
A Life, so lived, so loved;
Astarte's deed is done.

*   *   *   *   *

Inspired, my darling, by you. It is an attempt, as you can no
doubt see, to capture the mood of some of our more intimate, mutual experiences. It is possibly obscured in spots by symbolism and
by words chosen for their associational value. Astarte is an ancient

oriental goddess of love, the Aphrodite of the Greeks. I have employed her as a succubus invading every cell to give it the lust for reproduction. The association involved at that point is quite extensive. Many lines are far from giving the exact image and mood I wanted, but it's good practise. "Elysian bliss" is particularly bad, trite and flowery. Euphuism I think they call it. I particularly admire the couplet "Thrusting daggers" and hope that is entirely original since it sounds too good for me. I don't believe that anyone was plagiarized. Was tempted by E.E. Cummings "Orientale" (remember "Your lips are as Chords of crimson music" etc), but didn't use any of it. (Couldn't recall more than those lines anyway.) I did overdo the "to" stuff also.

Right now your man is going to sort of ooze into the tub and pile into his very empty bed. I would give anything for a glimpse of you setting the alarm in your baggy flannels, shiny nose and blue hair net. Sweetheart that is the way I love you when you are really my intimate wife. When to all the rest of the world you would be but a funny looking gal in pajamas, you are to me the perfection of woman's natural beauty. It makes me so sure that you are my wife and not just the beautiful romantic girl friend of a few months ago. I could just revel in the plain fact of living with you.

I love you
Robert

*　　*　　*　　*　　*

[Typewritten on pink (!) onion skin]
CLEVELAND , OHIO - Saturday, 2 p.m. 2/14/42

Dearest:

'Tis quite fitting me thinks that on this Valentine Day I should send you a letter on this lovely feminine pink paper. Do you know that it takes me about an hour and a half each night writing four pages to you, an hour and a half which I wouldn't miss for the world, an hour and a half when I become detached from my immediate surroundings and just lose myself in thoughts of you and home.

Dear ole Capt. Jensen has invited me to have dinner with him again tonight and I think we'll take in another movie. There is no reason, says he, why he and I should sit in all by ourselves tonight in our respective rooms bemoaning our loneliness, and so I accept.....it'll make the time go by faster if I see a movie.

131

About 4AM

Sweetheart -

The day dragged. I met Capt. Jensen at 7 PM and we proceeded to Fischer-Rohr's (Cleveland's outstanding seafood restaurant) and I really had me a meal, to wit: Pensacola Pompano sauté a beurre, parsleyed potatoes, turnips hashed in cream.

I've definitely told everyone I was leaving this Saturday. So start the fatted calf going for a welcome to your "prodigal wife".

Even as your poetry fails you and you turn to prose, so words fail me and thus I close my letter with love and kisses and lots more of love eternal to the man I adore.

<u>Lisbeth</u> (?) or do you prefer Betty (?)

* * * * *

1:30 PM Sunday Feb 15, 1942

Darling

Last nite was a rather enjoyable one in a sad strange way. After going to the library I drove out to the Chicago Ave forest preserves. Stirring memories came at the sight of the familiar spot. I thot of our many happy hours spent here wrapped in each other's arms and the plans we made that have since been so perfectly realized. It was a dark mysterious night with a dull gray mist that made the dim light of the snow quite eerie. The only sound was the crunching of the snow as I walked. A stifling quietness. The tangled branches of the trees had a ghostly uncertainty in this hazy lite. A rather mystic experience, being completely alone with nature's vastness. It was like being alone in the middle of the lake on a dark summer nite. The clean purity of freshly fallen snow, the oak's silent grandeur and the awareness that you and I are one and part of all this, framed my thots of you, and desire for you, in a complete mood of ecstatic mysticism. I hope that we can experience this together soon.

Words are futile at this moment. You have just called me and I heard your soft musical voice echo my love. Sweetheart I have desperately hastened the finishing of this poem; up to the line "Ensconced . . . " when you called. The sudden confusing change is due to your influence and the haste to the fact that I want you to get this tomorrow.

132

God's misty breath bestrews the night
And slumbering silence as of dormant death
Stalks the wintry forest in a shroud of white.
Cold hands have clad once barren boughs
Sculptured snow upon their tangled arms of bark.
Network of tortured growth outlined
Against the whispering, all pervading dark
Impressed alike into the winding channels
Of my mind, they find this eager thot.

Here in the sheltered stillness of deep sleeping life
I'll drink from memory's polished, peaceful glass
And drown my incubus of lonely sorrow
With dreams of that which was, and which is for tomorrow.

Ensconced beneath the forest's snow-knit dome
I'll feel a music of serene delight,
Pass to a revery of joy.
Lift now the iridescent gloom
And in the quiet twilight
Let my gladness bloom;
For sudden gaiety
Greets the night -
MY LOVE IS COMING HOME!

There is not enough room left on the page to tell you how I miss you and how happy I am at the thot that this time next Sunday we will be together. Darling, please don't let anything disappoint us. You will be back then. I'll meet you at the depot and if I can stop kissing you long enough bring you back to our brite clean home (it will be by then). Till that day I can exist in only the thot of you. With all my love, body and soul.

Robert, your husband.

* * * * *

Sunday nite - about 1am [15 Feb 42]

Robert, Sweetheart -

This has been such a wonderful day for me. Let me tell you the day's events to be sure I cover all the points. Met Capt.

133

Jensen in the lobby at 12:30. Found the art museum, a combination of our Art Institute and the Field Museum, including one room with potted plants (like a conservatory). So we looked at pictures until 5 PM (EST) when I called you from the public telephone booth in the museum.

I picked up your letter, sweetheart, upon our return to the hotel and parted for the night. I read your letter, reread the poetry, and think it is a wonderful way to bring the day to an end. Sweetheart, you are precious - and I see right through your symbolism, just restrain and retain all your emotion, my sweet, until my return. I'm just dying to feel your arms about me, your lips upon mine, to surrender myself to the emotions bottled up within me these past weeks, even as you have.

Singapore may fall, governments come and go, as long as you feel the way you do about me, life to me will continue to be a glorious adventure to be met with all the courage and ambition and determination we can muster between us to claim for ourselves that which we want. I feel that I know you so much better because of the fact that you have been so faithful to me in your daily letters, and because you have put your expressions of devotion upon such a high intellectually romantic plane. If we can but retain that spark of romance, we shall truly be eternal lovers.

I can't help feeling very much honored and highly flattered by your statement about my flannel pajamas and shiny nose and blue hair net, because darling I, too, have found such real satisfaction in just living with you. So many people lose their appeal upon close intimate contact, but in your case "familiarity did not breed contempt," on the contrary, it has been and will continue to be the source of constantly increasing satisfaction as time goes on.

*   *   *   *   *

11:45 Sunday Feb 15, 1942

My Sweet

When you get this it will be only about 4½ days more to go. For me right now it is 6½ days but I feel much better knowing just when you'll be back.

Sometimes when I stop and think of us, it just seems unbeliev-

134

able. So happy in each other, so deeply in love, married, and with a bright and well furnished home, darling, and we haven't known each other a year yet. How fast our wheel of fortune spins and so true to life's desires. I hope that we may always live so much, so fully in so little time that when we draw the curtain on our play we may say "well done, not one moment has been lost." Even separated as we are now we live rapidly in each other, building mutual experience and love upon the very sadness of our separation.

*　　*　　*　　*　　*

Monday nite - 2/16/42

Dearest -

I do think, Robert, my absence from you has had its good points, making you pour out some of that latent literary ability you neglected to exploit heretofore. You amaze Marcella (I only read portions of your letters to me) with your ability to just sit down and compose a poem to incorporate in your letter. I'm worried though, darling, if my being away hasn't led you to idealize me to a certain extent. When I return in flesh and blood you won't be disappointed, will you, if I fall short of your idealized notions.

*　　*　　*　　*　　*

10:30 PM Tuesday Feb 17, 1942

To my dearest darling wife:

I got your wonderful, heart satisfying letter of Sunday nite this afternoon. I just can't read of your love for me without feeling a wave of exultation and happiness. Your letters, so faithfully written, have greatly lightened the hours of being without you and, just think, only about 4 more days till Sunday morn. It will be like a second honeymoon to have my sweet wife home once more.

You know, your very slight suggestion of writing for money rather intrigued me. I don't know what I would write or for whom, but it would be fine sport. Have never tried to write short stories but if I did I would strive for the E. Allen Poe style. Maupassant is also a classical short story model but I fear that my conception or ability in plot forming is not up to that standard. Perhaps you are good at that and we could collaborate as we would anyway. There are so many fields of writing, historical fiction, plays, social plays, travel stories, essays, poetry; that any one with some ability should be able to acquire the knack of writing in one of them.

*   *   *   *   *

[Now pink onion skin again]

Cleveland, Ohio - February 17, 1942

Dear Darling:

I hate myself for having to write this letter to you, especially after my letter to you written late last night which you will probably receive about the same time you get this, but it's got to be done.

I don't know what is up. I can only tell you what has happened. Capt Jensen handed me his newspaper with a cryptic remark, "You may want to read this, my dear." His usual smile and cordiality were missing, and we piled into the station wagon in silence. We got to the Forum cafeteria and got our breakfast in marked contrast to the spirit of camaraderie that usually prevails.... "Well, what are you going to do?" he asked me in a tone of voice I have never heard him use in addressing me. "Why," I replied, "I thought we had decided yesterday that I was going to leave this Saturday." "Well, suit yourself," said he, with a shrug of shoulders, "but I think that in this time of war that personal considerations and personal selfishness should not be permitted to influence our actions, etc, etc, and I would like very much to be back with my wife and family, but here I am, etc." Well, I was stunned, no less! When Marcella remarked that after all Lt McGurn may not permit her to stay on longer, "After all, Miss Goldberg, this is not a New Year's Holiday," Capt. Jensen soberly observed that perhaps he "should have treated Lisbeth here that way." And so our meal was eaten in that sort of atmosphere. In the meantime I had my eyes immediately drawn to the column headlined "84,566 Sign In County Draft".

Robert, darling, I am really frightened. Darling, if you should get drafted into the Army this spring, what am I to do? Not that it would matter very much what I did, because as I have written you before and as I shall continue to reiterate, life without you is but an existence. But even to exist, darling, I must go

136

through the motions of eating and sleeping and working. SO, darling, I have consented to remain for the duration of the month! PHOOEY! But I think we can bear it, my sweet, and I think you were marvelously clairvoyant or something when you said to me, back in Chicago before I left— "You'll be away longer than two weeks." The fact remains, Robert, my sweet, that my orders read for 30 days only and so I've got to remain, and return to Chicago at the end of said 30 days in order to comply with them.

*　　*　　*　　*　　*

10:30 PM Wed Feb 18, 1942

My darling:

I have just tried to reach you by phone and undoubtedly will before the nite is over. On finding two letters in the box tonite I was immediately suspicious. The large envelope seemed particularly ominous. Upon reading it my first reaction was extreme rage. Almost cracked our solid oak table in lieu of your precious Jensen's head. That son of a bitch- Please pardon, but

[Arrow insert here points to]→

"The moving finger writes and having writ
Moves on: nor all your piety nor wit
Shall lure it back to cancel half a line
Nor all your tears wash out a word of it"

[From Fitzgerald's *Omar Khayam,* in reference to my not erasing the fact that I called Jensen an s.o.b.]

has a lot of nerve talking about sacrifice as he sits smugly in his office while soldiers are out dying. Selfishness, he and his kind epitomize it! If it were not that you will need a job while I am gone, I would say hang Jensen and the whole damn war department on the nearest tree and come home. However, I agree that we must be a bit sensible in view of future contingencies.

I am not in the least angry at you darling. I know it makes you as miserable as it does me to have to stay away another week.

As I hope to tell you in a few minutes, I am coming to see you. Any financial difficulty involved will be easily straightened out if I am so fortunate as to avoid the army for a few months more. But if

137

we were to be separated soon, we will know that we have seized all the happiness we could.

*   *   *   *   *

I feel immensely relieved and a bit elated after our call (Charge was $2.00). Sweetheart it makes me proud to think that you have such ability and may get the job you so well deserve. If you are able to get that position, it is certainly the thing to do. With the army an eventual certainty for me it is surely the most logical thing to have you situated so well financially during my absence. It can't help but give you a great deal of personal satisfaction at "making good" and materializing another step in your one time anticipated "career". Your happiness is inevitably reflected by me, darling, and I can't help being proud of your accomplishments.

From your letter:

My beautiful ideal of womanhood, I don't think we have to worry about over idealizing each other. We both are equipped with a flexible understanding of the human aspects entering our relations. The very fact that such possibilities are foreseen illustrates the point. We understand the psychology of over idealization and anticipation and should therefore be able to ward off any disappointment that would result from it.

We can endure each other's moods, and tho we may be peeved or worked up about it, we should be able to view the situation in an unbiased perspective so that no permanent anger is possible.

In all, the toleration of our moods binds us more closely by the knowledge gained. The more I really get to know you, the real you that can be cross, happy, passionate, angry, sick, sad, sleepy; the more I love you for being the sweet loving woman that you are.

Oh, darling, life is so full, wholesome and happy shared with you. Marriage has really been an introduction to life; for never did I experience the beauty of living as I have with you. It is a new world, and despite our moments of sorrow the fact that we are one, inseparably and eternally, makes life so worthwhile.

*   *   *   *   *

Wednesday, 2/18/42

Dear Husband -

This is going to be short and precise. As per our phone conversation I shall stay on another week. In the meantime Capt J. is going to see if he can't have me put on as his assistant at say $2600 per year, which would make it possible, for me to return to Chicago at least twice a month. It's a bit frightening, but I think I can do it. Lovelace, as I said, knows nothing about labor relations except what I have taught him these past few days. He told me himself he expects to be called for active service within a year, which would not warrant the trouble of teaching him only to lose him. I would be the logical one for the position (provided prejudice at my being a woman can be overcome).

I felt in loyalty bound to tell Capt J his assistant's shortcomings and so he asked me point-blank, "How much would it take to bring you out here as my assistant?" Without hesitation I replied, "Robert's permission", that I wouldn't do anything until I had talked to you and also gotten Mom's viewpoint. "After all," said I, "what you're asking me to do is to break up my home and perhaps alter the entire course of my life!" He agreed that was so, and said well, he had hesitated when Capt. Kempe told him to put me on as his assistant because he knew I wanted to return to Chicago.

I feel a thousand times better since talking to you.

$*$ $*$ $*$ $*$ $*$

[After our reunion]

10:45 PM Tuesday Feb 24, 1942

My darling:

As I was riding the L home Monday morning, an irrepressible feeling of disgust came over me as I rode through the backyards of "civilization". I felt akin to Rousseau, and Gaugin in wanting to demolish the last ugly trace of man's mercenary achievements and take refuge in the "natural" life. To leave all the dirty skyscrapers, neon signs and street cars and find life's purpose and pleasure in wresting an existence from the nourishing earth. I could paint an idyllic picture of life with you far "from the madding crowd's ignoble strife", living simply and wholesomely with hard labor, hearty meals, lustful sex; and watch our flesh and blood grow in our image. Primitive family, the uncomplicated fundamental of all real happiness. But, alas, it's not so simple. We have the civilized refinement, aesthetic taste and zest for knowledge, and beauty in art, that is too closely bound to the sordid machinery of modern living. At present we are dependent upon this world of trash, but I do dream of a day when we can leave it to run its own futile, trivial course while we seek to build a better world of our own.

Dreams, darling, but when shared with you even they are slightly satisfying. I know, tho, that wherever I am on earth it will be a paradise just to have you at my side. Nothing could ever exceed the joy of being mated to you, that I can love so completely and un-reservedly. To kiss you is to be in ecstasy, but to realize that you are my wife, my eternal love, so kind, so beautiful, sweet, sincere - the emotion that such thots bring can only be profaned by words. Only when I look into your radiant face can I know that you receive and cherish my love and return it thru the channels of the inexpressible. What an overawing experience this is to feel your soul meet and convey its love in the mystic world of intangible knowledge.

I despair of making this logically intelligible; words are mean-ingless and reason futile when I attempt to explain or convey such thots as these, but you know what I am saying, for your love has its own unspoken voice, a voice for which no words have been made.

*   *   *   *   *

[Typewritten pink onion skin to start]

Cleveland, Ohio
February 23, 1942

Darling:

And now I'm back at the office and assuming my female ver-sion of the Simon Legree role as far as Mrs. A is concerned. She must think I'm a bolt of lightning the way I can think of things for her to do and I must admit she does not comply fast enough. I'm really sorry for dear ole Jens if he has to get along with her, and there's so much that should be done and I can't hope to get things really going during the remainder of my stay here.

But to return to more cheerful things. Darling, I hope you felt as refreshed and as reinvigorated as I do today (if a bit sad) after our weekend together. Your coming out here made it the most exciting event of these past three weeks and I really felt like a bride on her honeymoon. Your kisses are still warm on my lips, it seems, and my body still tingles as it did when you caressed me.

140

This morning I looked at me (au naturel) in the mirror and just had to give myself a nice big hug, and then another for you by proxy.

This is going to be the longest week for me, until I can return to you - Robert, and every minute will seem an endless eternity. I love you, my sweet -

Your "Bunny Rabbit" - Betty

*   *   *   *   *

Tuesday, 11:30AM 2/26/42

Dearest -

I just reread your letter, darling, and it left me with that comfortable, all pervading warmth and glow that thoughts of you always bring me. I'm so glad to hear that your job is secure; somehow, darling, as I wrote you before, I can't believe that Fate will ever really give us a "raw deal". We're both so sincere and real in our strivings that it would be a cruel and heartless Fate to disregard us. I'm so glad, Robert, that I am what I am, that I can call forth your love, and merit respect and admiration in other people's eyes, too. And to feel that I can be a source of inspiration and aid to you, darling, what more can I ask of life?

So now I shall have to leave you, darling, but believe you me, I'm looking forward with badly concealed enthusiasm to leaving my "room 1344" existence to return to you and our apartment. This is probably the last letter I write you from here. I'll be in on the 7:15 AM, the train you took, on the Nickel Plate Sunday morning. Darling, I do return your "trusting kiss" via mail and stand ready, willing and eager to deliver a real one in person the moment I arrive in Chicago.

Until then -
Love
Betty

*   *   *   *   *

141

CHAPTER VI
Basic Training

Synopsis - As I once put it, it was with "malevolent timing" that I received notice, on our wedding anniversary, that I was to be inducted into the army. I found the fateful letter just after having made arrangements, by phone, to take the entrance examinations to the University of Chicago. We recognized, however, and were deeply grateful, that fortune had allowed us such a blessed year to establish our married life. We had endured the separation of her month in Cleveland, but now the duration was beyond reckoning. Indeed, had we fully appreciated that it would last for almost 4 years, we would have been desperately despondent. But we both turned to making the best of the situation and, again, fortune ultimately smiled, although not without first threatening my future ambitions with a classification as a bugle boy.

We quickly adopted the routine of daily letters which, while ruthlessly edited here, give a reasonably exact rendition of the first 3 months of army life and the lonesome days in Chicago.

Friday Evening 9/25/42

Dearest Darling

I'm going to start a letter and keep adding to it until I hear from you; and then, with a few finishing touches, I'll have a letter all ready to be mailed to you;

Well, you've probably been initiated into the ways and means of army life by now. You'll be glad to hear that I'm still holding back the tears. Oh, but I do miss you darling. So, so much!

Do you know you left without a picture of me, you lug! Well,

142

you'll get some with this letter, and you better keep it close to your heart, my sweet!

Saturday, 9/26/42

Hello, again, darling!Incidentally, I got a card from DePaul U today telling me to come in for a personal interview next week before I am accepted for the courses. At present they inform me I have been tentatively accepted.

Stalingrad still standing after 33 days of Nazi attacks. I feel more kindly towards Wilkie. He has just come out for an immediate second front to aid Russia.

Oh, darling, it was so-so good to hear your voice, so clear, so cheerful. I was so happy to hear you like it. Darling, I'm proud of that "130" score. You genius! Glad to hear you like the food. Do you know we talked for 18 minutes. The cost, only 2.10! Wonderful. My spirits soared sky-high and they've been up there all day.

Your name, my hero, will be placed on the service men's plaque to be dedicated next Saturday on Mayfield and Roosevelt Road. No objections from you, either, 'cause the deed is done!

Monday 9/28/42

My dearest darling -

Came down to the office expectantly, and your letter was there. 'Twas grand to read my favorite selectee's first impressions of army life. Incidentally, the clipping about Lt. Richard Pfohl, is that your old pal, "Dick"? I would think so from the address and the fact that he has a brother Frank in the Medical Corps. If he can get thru Officer's Training, why can't you? [He used to pay me to write his High School themes.]

*   *   *   *   *

4:30 PM 9/26/42

Sweetheart:

Leaning on my upper berth bunk while a crap game is starting. Pvt Doty is putting his time to better use. From the beginning: Arrived at Ft. Custer [Michigan] at 2:30. Were then given a brief physical and assigned to barracks, 116 men per. At about 6:30 we're marched over to theatre and given intelligence tests and mechanical aptitude test. Every one under same disadvantage, writing on knee boards, hot, close quarters, etc. Then listened to the Articles of War. A #* ^ @*%#*!! Army Chaplain. Then a spiel about allotments

143

and insurance and back to barracks exhausted by 10:30. Got to sleep finally about 1 AM Chicago time. We were up at 5:30 AM this morning. Got about 10 min practise with mute after breakfast. Ran thru the rain to clothing warehouse and there were given a barracks bag into which all civies save underwear are dumped. Barefoot on the muddy floor for about 20 min until shoes and socks fitted. Best shoes I ever had, big 10½ D brogans with rubber and leather soles (2 prs). This man's army really gives you the best clothes made. Really felt like a soldier with fine warm uniform and a barracks bag full of equipment. Field manual and skillet, razor, shave brush, 2 pr summer and winter pants and shirts, 2 pr fatigue clothes, 3 hats, overcoat, uniform jacket, 6 pr sox to name the majority of items. Carried the bagful of stuff back to the barracks and then over to receiving station. Got you my $10,000 insurance at $6.60 per mo. And a $50 allotment for you at $22/mo.

Got as far as the classification booths when lunch rolled around. Went back to where we left off. Asked all about work, hobbies, education, preferences, etc. Got a glimpse of my last nite's I.Q, 130. Not bad for the conditions under which taken.

Love
Robert

*   *   *   *   *

Monday Sept 28, 1942

My Darling

It was a marvelous feeling to call you up, just like you were only a mile away. It left me rather blue and lonely tho.

Sunday nite walk 1¼ mile down to the theatre but they wouldn't let me in because I didn't have my "O.D.s" (olive drab - "dress uniform") on. So I waltzed back in the wind and sleet and put them on like a good boy and came back because there was nothing else to do. To get in condition I walked back to the barracks as fast as I could hike. Kept up a grueling pace and left everyone far behind. Up at 5:30 this morn. 200 of us went out for drill. Had a good sergeant for our bunch. Pvt Doty went to the head of the class and was soon drilling with a group of sergeants and corporals who were showing off for the 1st Lieut. Kept right up to them every day of the week. [I had been in "picked squad competition" at the Armory while in High School ROTC {Fig 6}.] We then played games, two men, one on top of the other, had wrestling matches in mid air. I was always the horse with about a 160 lb rider. Fun. This is really a green bunch.

144

Even the barracks leader who has had his basic training is a drip of a soldier. Tells the new men that a "Lieutenant Major" has a silver leaf, etc. Does about face with his arms flopping like a windmill, and he has to be our instructor. I am writing this last at 6 AM Tues morn. We have to have lites out at 9 PM and be in bed by 11 PM.

Love and oh so many kisses

Robert

*   *   *   *   *

Tuesday, 9/29/42 (10:30PM)

Darling Dear -

I just dropped a five page letter to you at Ft Custer. Hope you'll forgive me for inclosing the snapshots of yours truly. I'll feel so much nearer to you if you keep my "pic" close to you, darling.

Oh, darling, when I told you to hurry up and become an officer, I meant it. I might be able to be near you if you get a permanent station here in the USA. I'm just a great big baby, I guess, cause I miss you so much. That constant anguish that nothing can quiet for very long. You don't know how much your letter meant to me - Your phone calls transport me to seventh heaven. Just love, I guess. The sound of your voice seemed to re-establish for a few minutes that bond that was so abruptly severed last Friday. I'm looking forward to your letter tomorrow, dearest, and if you are fortunate enough to come home this weekend, Grand, but I can take it if you don't come. I'm going to try to emulate the fine spirit which my parents' countrymen and country women are showing in Russia. We'll both be good soldiers, sweetheart!

Wednesday, 9/30/42

Hello, Sweetheart -

Dearest, if you're good enough to drill with the "non-coms," I'm sure you'll have little difficulty in "coming up from the ranks." I hope so, cause then you'll avoid all those menial tasks; and, darling, do make inquiry about Officers Training in the administrative branches. (I love you)

Frisco called this pm to ask about you and I gave him all the dope. Boy, he sure knows his army lingo - He told me "O.D." meant "ordinary dress" - Course I know it means "olive drab."

145

Today I got 14 prints (7 pictures) and all very good for 32 cents! They didn't print the one of me outstretched on the bed, too risque maybe?

I have been accepted for DePaul. Start Oct 2 (Friday) 6 P.M.

Thursday, Oct 1, 1942

Robert dear -

Miss Sloan called my attention to a passage in Lin Yutang's "Moment in Peking" which was something like this:

"Love is an immortal wound - which never completely heals. And if you should lose the object of your love, you feel that something has gone from you, and you never feel completely satisfied until it is restored"

Something like that has happened to me these past 6 days. It seems like six weeks since last Friday when we parted at the station. Getting your pictures seemed to restore something of you to me. But I shall not feel completely satisfied until you return to me, or I can join you.

They're dedicating the service men's plaque Sat nite and your name will be inscribed, too. I'll get a thrill every time I pass by Mayfield and Roosevelt [Road]! Behave yourself, so I can come see you after your period of basic training is over. Let's start a tradition of Dotys (you and me) as good soldiers, yes?

*   *   *   *   *

8:30 PM Wednesday Sept 30. 1942

My sweetheart

It seems like months since I left home. So much has happened and civilian life left so far behind. It would be marvelous to see you again and I almost hope I'm here this weekend so that I can come home.

Worked all day today in the clothing warehouse where all the new recruits are outfitted. They start at one end with their underwear on and a barracks bag in their hand and come out at the other a uniformed soldier with a bag of equipment. I was the overcoat fitter and disher outer. I could qualify in any store for a coat salesman after fitting 900 men today. It wasn't hard work, but I'd rather be outside. Went off over the hill tonite again for practise. The mosquitos were horrific. I killed 2 at a swat every 6 measures. Get going

146

on the piano so you can catch me. How's that DePaul deal? I don't like the business of writing letters in bed with about 38 other guys around. The lites have gone out at 9 PM now, so I'm across the street in the latrine to finish this up. I love you.

Robert.

*   *   *   *   *

Friday, October 2nd [1942]

Sweetheart -

To pick up the thread of my existence: Got out early this eve from school and got home by 8 P.M. Found letter from you dated last Wed mailed from Ft Custer. I see you feel the way I do about the time that has elapsed since you left home. Seems like weeks or months instead of just a week. All I can say you are getting experience of all sorts. Did you really fit 900 men? Boy, I'll bet your arms felt sore after that!

Your letters convey your moods and feelings so clearly, at least to me. You are irked by the "jerks" in the army aren't you? Try to be charitable, my sweet, they can't help being what they are, and if you ever become an officer, you'll be in a position to tell them how to correct their faults, in a nice brotherly sort of way, you know.

The DePaul deal is OK - Got a copy of Illinois State laws to study for Tuesday's class - You might make a note of the fact that I'll be going to school Tuesdays and Fridays.

*   *   *   *   *

Friday morning, Oct 2, 1942

Dearest:

Just a week ago that I bid you goodby, seems so much longer ago. I try not to think how much longer it will be before you come back and take me in your arms again, when I can sit on your knees and hug you oh, so tightly.

7:30

Now it can be told. Let out early from class. About 20 people, about 6 women, all dopey looking (except me) and composed of women in the State Dept of Unemployment Compensation, some DePaul law grads. But the course will treat Federal labor

147

legislation (National Labor Relations Act, the Fair Labor Standards Act, the War Labor Board) which will be useful. Classes Tues and Friday 6 to 7:40.

*   *   *   *   *

Saturday, Oct 3rd

Darling

Fairly busy all day. Maj Jensen may be in for a short while next Monday. [He had been hospitalized for a month or so at Ft Sheridan with jaundice, a sequel to yellow fever.] I bought a box of stationery so I can write you nice letters in the future. Do you want them scented with any particular brand of perfume? I'm serious.

Tonight is the dedication of the servicemen's plaque on Mayfield and Roosevelt Rd. I'm going to go take a look to see that your name is really on. Feel so proud of you.

I'll wake each morning and I'll promise to laugh
I'll say good morning to your old photograph (I want a new
    one, quick)
Then I'll speak to you dear
Just as though you were here

*   *   *   *   *

Don't be afraid that distance and time
Can ever tear us apart
The further you go, the longer you stay
The deeper you grow in my heart

Each night, before I wander off to sleep,
I might shed a few tears I've buried so deep
And I'll send you a kiss, dear,
Just as tho you were here

Kinda icky, maybe, but that's how I feel darling. Dedication ceremonies going on but I better wait for your folks to bring me groceries they said they would. I just mixed me and Sis a drink of gin

148

and stuff, a very mild one; a concession to Saturday night. . . .
Your folks just left. Your Dad shopped for me this week.

Sweetheart -

Mom called me about 6 pm to say Dick had taken a call from Western Union and she had read him your telegram. Dick had taken the address down as "Company K, 7th QM Training , Regiment C 498," so that's how this is going to be addressed.

I get a thrill seeing your name inscribed on the servicemen's plaque - Along with about 100 others - all from this immediate neighborhood.

I understand that the I.Q. requirements for officer training are a minimum of 110 - so you are eligible methinks.

And now, reluctantly, goodbye for the moment

Love as ever

Betty

*   *   *   *   *

Tuesday - October 6, 1942

Hi Soldier!

How's everything? Was hoping to hear from you before this. What's wrong? Don't you have any time at all for a bit of correspondence? Army vs wife, I can't win!

School tonight and we had a fairly interesting session on the Illlinois Workmen's Compensation Act -

The Major [Jensen was promoted] was in for about a half hour this a.m. with Mrs J along to see that he didn't tire himself out. It'll be 3 weeks or so before he returns for full time duty. He saw the Colonel today. I hope I get a raise soon.

Do you know school will be a fine diversion.

*   *   *   *   *

[On stationery with "seal" of Camp Lee, Virginia]

9PM Saturday Oct 2, 1942

My Darling Wife:

Where to begin. It seems so long since I have held and kissed you. The atmosphere here is so different from home.

149

We left Fort Custer at 5 PM after waiting all day for the train. There were 49 of us and about 500 colored troops. We had the 2 end cars and there were 23 cars in all. Made myself the best bunk on the train by sleeping on top of the barracks bags. Slept a lot better than the poor jerks that slept in their seats. Rode all day thru that beautiful Smoky Mt country in W. Va and Virginia following the New River. Beautiful scenery most of the way. We arrived in Petersburg Va at 11 PM Fri nite after 30 hrs on the train. I am now in the Quartermaster Corps and will receive here 4 weeks of basic training and then 4 weeks of technical training. We had the choice of 3 things in the Q.M. Mine were 1. Band, 2. Mechanic, 3. Admin & Supply (clerical). I may not make the band but I'm a cinch for the 2nd. Will have a chance to apply for Officer Training after 4 weeks basic, which I shall do.

We are housed in 2-story barracks that hold about 150 men. Every other bed is a double decker. I grabbed a single bed in the front corner. There are 36 men in the 6 tents in front of the barracks, but I didn't volunteer for that. Went over to the P.X. to call you last nite, but it was jammed, and thot I'd have better luck getting you home Sunday. Sometimes I miss you terribly, sweetheart, but there's not much hope of my seeing you for at least 2 more months. No furloughs during training and it is a very long trip for you to make down here to see me Sat aft and Sunday maybe.

I start training tomorrow and will write as often as I can to let you know what happens. I love you so much darling, and will really be ready to settle down and just live with you when we're free again. Try to keep busy and don't lament the inevitable. We have enough sweet dreams of the last year to keep us happy for a while.

Longing for your caresses

Robert

*   *   *   *   *

OFFICE OF THE DIVISION ENGINEER

GREAT LAKES DIVISION

#663 - 332 SOUTH MICHIGAN AVE,

CHICAGO, ILLINOIS

October 7, 1942
(immediately after receipt of your letter—9 a.m.)
Dearest Darling:

Was blue last night when I found no letter from you and wrote you a letter about it. But what a difference a letter makes! It's a beautiful sunny day and I think the radiance of my face just now outrivals the sun in its brilliance! I guess I do love you, when a few pages of hieroglyphics a la Doty can do that! Just can't wait till tonight to get home and start drawing some hieroglyphics of my own.

Your itinerary en route to Camp Lee brings a twinge of nostalgia to your reader, as it must have to you; or were you asleep? [We had been to the Smoky Mts earlier in the year {Fig 15}.]

Glad to note your aptitude ratings were very superior! I do so hope you can get into whatever you like best. The Mechanics part of it sounds good, and if you can get into Officers' Training! I'd love to be Mrs. Lieutenant Doty. Who knows maybe we could be together then.

*   *   *   *   *

Thursday - At midnite Oct. 8, 1942
My Dearest Darling -

The Colonel invited me to a discussion he was having with a man from the State Labor Dept and introduced me as "Miss J, who is pinch hitting for my Labor Relations Officer while he's getting over the jaundice"; made me feel good!

I'll be content if you remain a Buck Private for the duration

151

so long as you remain my dearest darling. Don't let anything make you bitter or disillusioned. You'd be betraying both of us and our hopes and dreams for the future. And now I'm getting myself in a sobbing mood. Please write me as often as you can -

Lovingly,
Betty

*   *   *   *   *

9 PM Tues. Oct 6, 1942

My darling.

Up at 5:45. We fall in for roll call at 6 and come back and clean up the barracks, make the bed, etc before chow. Drilled all morning. Had a corporal that didn't know beans about instructing. The lieutenant taught the men more in 5 min than the corporal did all morn. On the whole tho the sergeants and looies are very good and are really whipping this pack of rookies into shape. I was appointed guidon this afternoon for the 2nd platoon. The guidon sets the step, guides the platoon and keeps the men in line generally. A sergeant or corporal is guidon in regular formation, so Doty is going to town. The food here is O.K. if you can get enough of it. Always have to go back for seconds, grab your butter fast and get dessert before the others eat it all. After supper in T498 got hold of brushes, mops, broom, water, soap and stuff and scrubbed out the whole barracks. Surprising the way most of the men pitched right in with a will. A few gold bricks, of course, but the guys have fine spirit for the most. The corporal put pops here in charge again when he left. I'm getting there. We're going to make this the best platoon in the Co and the best Co in the Regiment. Lites will go out in a few min and I have to dig up a couple pairs of socks to wash for tomorrow. I love you and always think of you as the most ideal wife and woman in the world. Lites out.

Love you so much.

Robert

*   *   *   *   *

9PM Wed. Oct 6 (?) 1942

Sweetheart

Was called over to 12th Reg Band with 3 other fellows for tryout with the band. Didn't do so well or rather it wasn't bad, but not good enough I think. Just as well, am deciding I'd rather be an offi-

152

cer anyhow. The other guys didn't do well either and they have played a lot longer than I have. Afternoon 1st part spent on bonds. I was the only one in the Co. that didn't want to sign up for $3.75 deduction. All the other sheep let themselves be bull dozed into signing. The 2nd in command of the Co. called me in the office for a little chat on the bond issue (good publicity for Doty, you know, get acquainted.) He showed me how with my deductions I would still have $20 left, whereas when he came in on $21, after deductions he had $12 left. I countered "Wife? sir", and he rather condescendingly admitted "no, not then". Told him I was quite willing to sign for $1.25 per mo to keep the Co. 100%, so we agreed.

Good night sweetheart and Love x x x o o o Robert

*　　*　　*　　*　　*

[Starts typewritten]

Friday morning - 10:30 A.M. October 9, 1942

Dear Darling:

At about this time two weeks ago, we were saying farewell, and now you're a full fledged Private, USA. Gives me a funny sensation to look back, and I almost don't dare look into the future. So I'm going to adopt (as I've often resolved to do) a "day-by-day" philosophy and look back only at the dear memories and let the future unfold itself as decreed by Fate.

[Handwritten from here on]

but you think I'm worth my weight in gold, darling, don't you? Well, it's depreciating dear, I feel myself shedding avoirdupois every day you are away; and now I must leave for class, more later.

So class convened, a discourse on the 10th Amendment and the constitutionality of various labor laws was discussed and finally 7:40 PM.

Dearest, I repeat again: you remain a buck private (which you won't) for the rest of the duration so long as you return the same ole Doty that came, saw and conquered this meek female's

153

heart; and she is still thanking her lucky stars for the happy coincidence that made us both enroll in Bi Sci and Humanities that semester in school.

*   *   *   *   *

[Typewritten]

Saturday - Oct. 10, 1942

My dearest, dearest darling

Time certainly is a psychological thing. One day it seems to creep by at a snail's pace, other days it soars (as today) on the wings of song. I guess it can all be explained in terms of relativity of the rate at which certain events or activities occur. I often think of this: Up until May 30, 1941, you were a stranger (interesting person, but still a stranger) to me, and now it seems as though I've known you forever and that my love for you is an eternal thing which existed before you came along and which will endure forever. I feel so like a heroine, carrying on with the next scene in the plot of this little drama of life, even though my leading man has been taken away for an indefinite period. It's a unique sort of plot, no one, not even I know what the next scene will be, neither the locale nor the subject matter, sort of groping around in the dark, ad libbing as the occasions call for it, and always presenting (at least to the spectators) the appropriate lines and gestures which often belie the true state of my moods and emotions suppressed within me. Only in my letters to you do I achieve the catharsis so necessary for me to carry on, by letting you in on my innermost thoughts and feelings.

Love you so much, precious - Can't wait to get home and read your letter.

Love,
Betty

*   *   *   *   *

Thurs. 9:25PM Oct 8, 1942

Sweetheart:

Promise you a longie tomorrow if we don't have to scrub the

154

barracks down. They are really giving us the works here. Drill, lecture, drill, lecture, dust, sweat, heat, and drill. Saw two motion pictures tonite. Sex hygiene and Weapons of the Infantry Division, their use and how to recognize their fire.

I love you and want to be the best soldier out for your sake. Love, good nite, and a thousand kisses.

Robert

* * * * *

8 PM Friday Oct 9, 1942

My darling wife:

Have just finished reading your letter for about the 3rd time and absorbing your picture for hours. I sure would like to have a fine enlargement of you at your best.

TODAY

Up as usual at 5:45. Fall out at 6:00 for 5 min, sweep, make bed, mop up and eat about 6:45. March out for calisthenics ½ hr or more. Back for lecture on military courtesy. The officers here are real guys. They've been thru it too and haven't forgotten it. It's just like a big high school R.O.T.C. 24 hours a day. This afternoon we had shots in the arm, my 2nd for typhoid. Arm pretty sore now but not bad. Had a dress parade of 7th regiment for retreat tonite. 2700 men with feet striking the ground the same instant. A thrilling site [sic] somehow and it feels good to be a part of it. Must be akin to the feeling salmon get when they run, or when the birds group and fly south. I believe this is an original hypothesis as it just occurred to me now and haven't seen it anywhere's before.

* * * * *

9 AM Sunday Oct 11, 1942

Dearest sweetheart

I love you. The picture of you is almost alive. Looking at it I can feel myself squeezing you in your plaid suit, feel my lips on yours so perfectly. Just sitting here and dreaming all morning which is quite a luxury in army life. I just want to hold you, kiss you, feel your cheek on mine, your hair, look into your eyes, hear you speak, what heaven life would be then. That is what I'll work for here to be able to have you with me, but it takes so long. Each day is like a month without you, and there must be so many months till we can be to-

155

gether again. They can never stop our loving, tho, sweetheart, and we will always have love to keep us going.

Your letters are the apogee of happiness in this present existence, and your picture, Darling let's have more pictures of you, all kinds, shapes, poses, costumes. They are (it is) almost a savage fetish to me. A reality of you. At this point I have stopped for a little composition intended to convey the picture of lover versus selectee from board #55

Out of the muddled brain of
FALL OUT! tents pack a mile Hup
Hup Hup hupp 4 hats
OfF salute mop 10000 carrots and
fur crystsake shut up Swims
in the swirl of orange red sand
That grits between the molar teeth like powdered glass
Like picture, dream illusion of the past how
Soft flesh yielding - oh, warm
Woman of the graceful, squeezable
How your hands long for the
Feel of fingers tangled in flesh. Long
Uninterrupted staring of eyes, love
into eyes...brown framed spatially
aligned with the front sight on the target
Breath held, warm breath that
Sighs saying an oak leaf for a MAJOR
saying in the middle of the nite fer
Crist sake shut UP!

Does it convey the idea? It might look better in print with an E.E. Cummings set up. It looks pretty good to me right now because that's the way I feel.

Yesterday was quite an ordeal, KP. It's no cinch. Among my duties during the hours of 6AM to 7:30 PM (we were lucky in having a short day) were mop the floor 3 times, wash those 10 gallon pots and pans 3 times, clean and wipe the 2 monster ice boxes twice, trim a crate of lettuce, fill about 30 salt shakers, cut up gallons of carrots and potatoes and about 58 other things like dumping garbage, cutting bread, carrying in meat, etc. All in all it was a long, hot, hard day. We had one fellow sent to K.P. for not shaving and 2 more for moving while at attention. That will not be counted on their K.P. service and their name will come up again.

Forgot to mention that lites are out and am down in the latrine again. It's pretty crowded now so I'll stop. Too noisy to concentrate.

Love and dreams of love

Robert

*   *   *   *   *

8:30 PM. Monday Oct 12, 1942

My darling wife. I love you

It has been raining since 10 AM and this place is a mess of gooey yellow clay.

Received your letter of Fri 9th. We seem to be falling into that habit of writing daily despite all our saying we wouldn't. Still think it shouldn't be done even tho it does overjoy me every time I hear from you. Glad to hear your overtime extended and finances so well under control. Don't you dare skimp on anything, tho. Get all the clothes and stuff you can while they are still being made. Don't know how you stand that course of yours taking 10th Amendment stuff, but if you like it, fine.

Am down in the latrine again. We charter members are thinking of calling this the writer's club. They took us over for tetanus shots right after supper. Felt like someone inserted a flat iron between the triceps and biceps for a few min.

*   *   *   *   *

Wednesday 8:30 PM October 14, 1942

Dearest -

You have undoubtedly heard Secy Stimson's disclosure that there are 4,250,000 men under arms right now and by the end of 1943 there will be 7,500,000 under arms! These 18 and 19 year olds they intend to take in will be trained for a year before going into combat service. I imagine they'll need lots more officers. Who knows? Maybe you can be an officer or instructor here in the good ole USA.

Well, this is the 20th day since you left, precious, and there still remains that constant gnawing feeling inside me. On radio the duet "Ah, Mimi, Thou False One"; accidentally tuned in on stream-lined version of La Bohème. Nevair! shall that epithet be applied to me! I am yours and yours alone "till death do us part". I've been recalling our past year. Oh, darling, I'm so happy that

157

we didn't have any really unpleasant scenes. I've resolved never to permit myself the opportunity of repeating any of my past mistakes either. I'll really be the model wife you tell me I've been. This period of separation can only serve to deepen and enrich our mutual love. My devotion to you increases daily as I recall some little incident of the past. I miss your strong capable arms and the ecstasy of your warm embrace, the precious little nothings you used to murmur in my ear. Oh, how every ounce of me yearns to be near you; that's why writing letters to you, and reading your letters to me is a sort of communion between you and me. Darling, stay as sweet as you are.

Devotedly,
Your wife

*   *   *   *   *

10 PM Tuesday Oct 13, 1942

My darling

Details of the day. Went thru the obstacle course this morning. Greatest obstacle was the <u>mud</u>. Broke my belt sliding down a 15-ft rope net, but fixed it up again OK. The obstacles aren't so hard, it's the running from one to the other that gets your wind. Raining and drizzling intermittently. Had a Sodom and Gomorrah rendering for ½ hr by the chaplain. Disgusting. Almost forgot, they wanted me to be in the drum and bugle corps, but I refused. Figure this basic training will be of more value for O.C.S. than playing the bugle.

*   *   *   *   *

5PM Wed. Oct 14, 1942

Darling

May write later tonite but want you to get started on this immediately. Applications for O.C.S. will be taken Oct 15 and they must be accompanied by birth certificate and transcript of college credits.

My birth certificate and credits from Walton [School of Commerce, that I attended evenings] are in left middle drawer of the desk, I think. Get after the Board of Ed. and Austin Evening College to dust off the string of "A"s Doty has accumulated there. Should come in handy now. I'll have to leave it up to you to get them down here or

158

to the Company Commander (if the B of E won't send them to me?) but fast.

*　　*　　*　　*　　*

My sweet

Filled out my application for O.C.S. About 2 mos from now I might be called before the board of examiners and then before another board of examiners and may finally get in. It's no overnite snap.

We had to scrub the barracks down tonite. A lot of good it does with the mush outside. You can sweep out half the state of Virginia after the platoon goes in and out once. Am still holding the position of right guide and making out OK in general. Just moved down to the latrine as usual.

*　　*　　*　　*　　*

My beloved darling

I hope you'll forgive, but last nite was the 1st that I didn't write you. It's very difficult to write or even do anything except be a cog in the army. There is nothing but your knee or a board to write on in the barracks, the light is poor, and the place is noisy. This morning I am over in the day room. So here I sit writing a letter in the middle of 3 ping pong tables, a piano player and a guy at the radio trying to drown out the piano and some s.b. across the table giving off a fine example of smoke screening.

Saturday is inspection day. Had to display our equipment on our bunk (as shown in the field manual) with everything in exact place, bed made just so, clothes hung just so. Our lieutenant then inspected us and came back and gave us a training exam. Each man stands by his bunk and the officer comes by and asks him a question covering some point of the past week's training. When he came to me, I came to such a snappy, heel clicking attention without moving my eyes that he just passed on. The sergeant gave me a wink and signified his approval. Doty was not questioned just because he looked like he could answer any of them. The only man on the floor unquestioned. At the end of the inspection Lt. Luzopuone broke down and congratulated us with enthusiasm for the fine job we had

159

done. He's a swell egg. A young curly headed lad from Brooklyn just out of OCS. He's got a lot of snap and humor and the men like him.

Next we were marched over to the theatre to hear some jerk give a propagandized history and theory of Japan. You didn't know it but the Japs are a primitive, subhuman race.

*　　*　　*　　*　　*

9PM Sunday Oct 18, 1942

My darling:

Walked up to the library tonite. Looked up saltpetre out of curiosity as you here [sic] so much about it in the army. Legend has it that the army puts it in the food to keep the men sexually inactive as it affects the erection of the penis. (The legend is founded in fact as saltpetre is a nitrite and nitrites have a relaxing effect on the involuntary muscles. It is used in inhalators as relief for asthma. It is not however administered internally anymore.) Looked up chemical warfare too. Found an interesting fact which will be duly brought to the Lt's attention. Is an effective weapon as far as casualties go but it is not so deadly. 27% American casualties were from gas but only 2% died, whereas 24% of the usual battle casualties died. In other words gas is not to be feared so much by the individual as it only incapacitates him temporarily.

Also read some interesting articles on the gaseous composition of comets, the experimental stages of hibernation applied to schizophrenia, electronic distribution in iron alloy as explanation for alloy effect, etc.

*　　*　　*　　*　　*

Saturday 10 a.m. Oct 17, 1942

Dear Bob:

As soon as your letter arrived I called the Board of Education and found out I must go in person to Austin and request the transcript and they will send it out to the Commanding Officer, they will not send it to you nor to me. I'll get the birth certificate and Walton credits if I have to go thru everything in the house.

Darling, I'm so thrilled at the thought that you might get in OCS. Oh, oh, the Lieutenant Colonel [Another promotion for Jensen.] just walked in.

160

2:30 p.m. He just left, I got a letter of recommendation from him, written on office stationery, you can use it or not, as you please. I think that "Lt. Col." deal might mean something, and he told me with a smile that he was doing this "all for Robert", so I guess it's all right.

Come to think of it, I'll inclose Lt. Col Jensen's letter of recommendation herewith so that you'll have it right away. Jensen's home address is 244 Frank Avenue, Racine Wisconsin. He was a former Field Artillery Officer.....then was in the Quartermaster Corps while serving 8 years as Company Commander CCC duty in Wisconsin (Sparta, LaCrosse, etc) and then Corps of Engineers as of December 1941. This in case they question your acquaintance with him.

With all my devotion,
Betty

*　　*　　*　　*　　*

9:30 PM Oct 19, 1942 Monday

To my wife

Army routine is not half as stiff as I imagined; in fact it is very easy. Obstacle course and antiaircraft for noncombats? Non-combatants is meaningless in the Q.M. It is non-combatant no longer since the primary objective of modern war is to cut and destroy the enemy's supply line and the Q.M. is the supply line. Did not get hurt on obstacle course. It's fun. Don't ever worry about me getting hurt or anything here. Too wiry and supple for that. Don't have to go to church and you need not worry that I ever will. We had the chaplain as I said on Tues for an anti sex, anti clap talk. Hiking does not wear me out. Hiked 8 miles yesterday with my pack (which is as far as our longest hike in training here) and could have gone 20 more.

Your Sat letter. Darling I have to thank the Colonel very sincerely and I do for his letter. It should mean a lot to me and you and he can be sure I'll live up to all the fine stuff he says in it. Thank him for me will you my sweet. You must not however expect to see me in OCS next week. It takes several months usually to get in. It will be OK to have my credits sent to the C.O. of Co.K 7th Q.M. Training Reg.

*　　*　　*　　*　　*

161

My darling:

What a day! They really laid it on but good. Started off the morn with a little run over the obstacle course with light packs. Back to barracks. Fall out and fall in immediately with full equip. March over to the drill field for a surprise inspection. That's where the trouble started. The Major was tearing his hair because we were late. The C.O. brought the company in bassackwards and the Major almost bit his head off. We got organized finally about 15 min later and had to pitch tents and display equipment. Some of the men hadn't brot it all and none of us had ever done it before. What a mess. Just got everything set, tents up and equipment displayed properly when, "Strike tents, roll full pack on the double!" Then hell really let loose. The Major wouldn't even look at the stuff. Marched back dumped off the pack and right out again for more drill. No rest all day. Food in a rush. There is a rumor around that they are going to line us up a squad at a time and shoot the food into us with grease guns. Didn't have my OD hat for the parade retreat because its over having the QM braid put on it. Therefore had to put up tents outside for an hour. "Fall out at 5:50 with full field equip." Marched out again to see if we could get the inspection OK this time. Major Peabody bawled the hell out of our C.O. for letting two lieutenants off. Told him if he'd done it right the 1st time, etc. So at about 7 PM the Major gets him a flashlight and goes thru for inspection. Pvt Doty was very lucky. He had lost his comb on the obstacle course, but the old war horse didn't notice it was missing. He got about 15 guys in our platoon for missing handkerchiefs, soap, shave brush, etc. They really catch it; KP on Sunday or something.

Think I'll really go to bed tonite. Got to bed 11:15 last nite which is 15 min later than the limit. Can't get caught doing that. Keep up the letter writing, it's my greatest joy. It seems like years since I've held and kissed you my sweet beautiful wife. It is happiness tho to recall all of the perfection of our marriage. Could squeeze you now my little taffy apple

With so much love
Robert

*　　*　　*　　*　　*

Tuesday eve - Oct 20, 1942

Dearest Darling-

I called my Mom and told her of your constant progress in

the Army, and she said, "Happy girl, aren't you?" and I told her I sure was, and she agreed it was fine!

What about saltpeter? Do they really give it to you? I thought the physical exercise would curb any unnatural desires in that direction.

*　　*　　*　　*　　*

Saturday - Midnite Oct 24, 1942

My Precious One -

The oddest thing happened to me riding home on the L tonight. All of a sudden there came to my mind that night in the Forest Preserves when I first realized I could love you, dearest. Remember, there was the sound of a babbling brook, that you wanted to investigate? That was the night you and I started thinking of marriage. As I recalled the warmth and passion of your embraces, darling, I could feel my heart beating faster and a flush rising in my cheeks; and as the train sped on, I just let my thoughts wander back to those glorious days and those heavenly nights that summer before our marriage. Oh, to relive them again in reality with you, my love, that is all I ask of life! Do you remember, Robert, how quickly time went by when we were together? How impatiently I awaited your coming each evening? I couldn't help smiling, too, as I thought of your return from your vacation in the country, with a handful of roses for me! Oh, sweet reminiscing, that makes the present more bearable!

And darling, when I got home I found your letter (Wed-Thurs) and I find you beginning your letter with rambling along the same lines. I like that "Past pressed rapidly into future from behind memory rich with the rose tint of remembered warmth" (I love you, honest I do!)

Under separate cover I am mailing you a 8x10 enlargement of me [Fig 17]. You will please notice that it has been hand colored; and really is a lifelike reproduction of the original. Now don't pick any flaws in the workmanship, 'cause I did it myself. Had more fun this evening figuring the thing out. I used several saucers, a little water, tooth picks, cotton, face powder, rouge, eyebrow pencil, mascara, and green ink. I thought you'd like me in green, that's the only artistic license I exercised [I had com-

163

pletely forgotten this manifestation of artistic skill! The picture still exists, and is a lovely example of the retoucher's art, fully professional in quality. It also bespeaks a remarkable confidence in undertaking such an endeavor on a singularly precious picture!]

Reluctantly good nite and sweet dreams
*Elizabeth

*In lieu of Betty - I feel like an Elizabeth now that you are gone -

*   *   *   *   *

8:30 P.M. Monday Oct 26, 1942

My precious picture

Sitting here dreaming with my gallery of love spread out before me. Such tantalizing reminders of the you so far away. Sweet torture remembering the thrilling feeling of my arm slipping around my wife's slim satin waist, to squeeze the breath out of her in her big plaid suit. To snuggle nose to nose and smooth the delicate hair around her ears. Funny how all the little intimate thots, feelings and emotions can be bound up in a bit of black and white celluloid. That is wrong; nothing is on the celluloid but outline, the rest is in the mind. That is love.

*   *   *   *   *

8PM Wed Oct 28, 1942

My beloved

. . . . No rest in the army. Just get the above written when "Everyone downstairs!" - Announcement about our going on the range tomorrow. Changes, etc. Doty will coach on target 10. Another feather! (but I hope it doesn't mean more work.) The best marksmen (or in this case potential marksmen) are picked along with the officers and noncoms to coach the men firing. One coach to each target. Enough of that for a while.

Today was almost like Xmas. 2 letters from my darling and on top of that a picture of her. Darling your [sic] beautiful (and by this time it's not just one man's opinion) and I'll have you in front of me every chance I get. And what a genius you are. Didn't know that was a homemade color job until I read your letter. And now for your letters, all 8 pages of them which I have already read twice. Don't think for one minute that your letters are chit chat to me. They are the most precious things in the world for me now. The bread of each day's life as it were. My little Lizbeth is feeling like a big girl

164

now, Elizabeth. How I love you darling in any name as long as it is you behind it. If you feel like an Elizabeth, why just be one, sweetheart, but you will always be just a sweet caressable wife to me forever.

Had a physical inspection at 6 PM. Poetically termed "peter parade" or "short arm inspection". All men line up naked at their bunks and "milk" the penis as the medical officer walks by. Any cases of gonorrhea will be found thus. All army personnel must undergo this inspection once a month and it would be a good thing if the whole civilian world had to do the same. There is advantage of sort in regimentation.

To Elizabeth my wife
I love you
Robert your husband

*   *   *   *   *

Wednesday - 9:30PM. Oct 28, 1942

My Dearest Darling -

About 9:30 Maj Nelson (Army Specialist Corps) brings in Maj Striegl of Milwaukee and a Mr Gumz for the "conference" - "What conference", says I? I suspected it was on draft deferments, so I contacted Col Ralston of State Sel. Service and got the dope. He, Col R, had just been informed by the Sec'y of War's office that it would be in our office at 10 am. Col J not in yet so I had to go in his stead. Too informal to go in just in my sweater (yellow) and skirt (black), so I borrowed Mercedes' black jacket. I got roped in to take notes on the meeting. So there I sat, wedged in by the Administrative Assistant to the Secy of War, a bilious looking guy by the name of Billings, and two Colonels on either side of me; Majors and Captains galore, about 20 guys all told, from 10:15 to 1:30 PM taking shorthand notes. Phooey!

Sweetheart, when this is over and we face the "brave new world" together, this period of separation will be but another sweet memory for both of us; and when "Junior" climbs upon your right knee, and "Mary Elizabeth" [Remarkable that the names of our first two children were already chosen, by her!!] clambers onto your left knee, to hear you tell for the umpteenth time all about your soldiering, you will remember to tell them how "Mother" wrote "Daddy" every day he was away and how "Daddy" wrote

165

"Mother" that he "loved her beyond expression", won't you? 'Cause if you don't, I will. Oh, I love you, sweetheart. Keep that body of yours safe and sound, if only for my sake.

Love and kisses (so many saved up for you)
Elizabeth - Your wife

*　　*　　*　　*　　*

9:45 PM Thursday Oct 29, 1942

My darling wife:

Tonight we had field practise in night reconnaisance, scouting, patroling, defense, etc. The 2nd and 4th platoons were to defend a gasoline dump and the 1st and 3rd attack or reconnoiter it. Blackened all faces with burnt cork very thoroly commando style. Moved off into the woods with packs, gas masks and rifles. I was sent out on a reconnaissance patrol. We penetrated the enemy lines and discovered their pass word, etc and I was sent back with 2 men to bring the information to our H.Q. Ran into one of our outposts and we captured a couple men trying to penetrate our lines. Sent the prisoners back with the other guys and I took over the outpost. Soon left for more excitement and penetrated deep into the enemy territory and was just feeling around for their H.Q. when the game ended. Back to barracks by 8:30 PM and thus ended a long hard day. Fun tho.

*　　*　　*　　*　　*

8PM Friday Oct 30, 1942

My dream of a smile set in happy eyes

I love you. Beautiful contour of that smiling face familiar to my hands as well as eyes. So full of sparkling life and gentle womanhood. Oh glorious female, gracefully sculptured, to be held close, that her breasts may press firm against my yearning chest, hips meet thighs to blend as one body; my thumbs gently smooth your eyebrows, fingers twined in hair to lift mouth to lips, kissing, knowing pure delight.

We are really training intensively now. Rifle marksmanship all day; bolt manipulation, rapid fire loading, position. We go on the range early Sunday and will finish firing Tues. We fire 120 shots (rounds) in groups of 40. The final 40 for our record.

That "I'm not afraid of tomorrow - I lived thru yesterday" is a fine idea. - Mon letter - Booby traps, ask the Colonel, it's a very interesting subject. A fine example of booby trap as used by Russians. Upon retreating from a town they wire a bomb to a picture of Stalin in the finest house in town. The Germans use this for their H.Q. and someone spotting Stalin on the wall moves the picture and poof! booby traps, savvy?

Darling, every one here does envy me having such a beautiful and faithful wife writing to me every day. There aren't many that get that daily note of love, but then also there aren't many that deserve it. People marry in kind usually and most people are not like us. I love you sweetheart.

Your husband loving forever
Robert

*   *   *   *   *

8PM Saturday Oct 31, 1942

My beloved:

Company K started the day with a fine nourishing breakfast. One slice of greasy scrap baloney, one tablespoon plain potatoes, a crust of dry bread and an apple. For lunch we got a break: 2 slices of the same baloney, a piece of cheese, potato salad, an apricot and bread pudding. I don't know if the whole army is fed like this or if our mess sergeant wants to buy a '42 Buick.

The mention of your girdle reminded me of the gov't pamphlet on the care of girdles, quote: "It should be removed by a good strong yank". "This is preferable to its being taken off by a couple of jerks". Great language American, no. - My little one really talks army rank. Colonels, Majors, etc, but her C.O. is just a private.

Love to my sweetest wife, My Elizabeth beloved,
Her husband- Robert

*   *   *   *   *

Wednesday - 11:30PM. Nov 4, 1942

My Beloved C.O. - [Sealed with a lipstick kiss at the start, labeled "Kiss for You!"]

Us logical Doty's do start at the beginning of things, don't we? So I'll tell you all about me and then I'll comment on your letters line by line. Well, sweet, the Republicans got in by a landslide according to latest election return, Curley Brooks and Ham

167

Fish and stuff. The G.O.P.s! But I can't get excited about politics very much.

"Us Dotys" is OK with me. At first I wanted it "Jusewich and Doty," but it's progressed beyond the partnership stage and I do feel so much a part of you, dear, I want me definitely and unmistakably identified with you!

Dearest, I'm always "pleasantly surprised" by the "curse." It's my way of saying that I don't like it. Such a waste of function always makes me a bit angry. Guess it's my way of reacting to my repressed mother instinct or something. Robert, I do want to be a **mother**!!

You don't know the hold you've got on my heart, darling. It reacts so violently to your letters; what will it do when you come back and claim me physically? Soon I shall be taking my bath and as I loll in the warm scented water (à la RWDoty) I shall let myself really relax and let myself dream, and recall the days when you'd sit on the towel beside the tub and kibitz ('member?), and maybe give me a rubdown after I got out of the tub! Oh, poignantly sweet memories that I can call up just any ole time! "Thanks for the memories" springs both from my heart and soul, and my mind counters with "We Did It Before - We'll Do It Again!" So I'll tuck me into bed, put my arms behind my head and just start thinking of other nights when I could thus await my darling's joining me; and get those so, so pleasant little prickles up and down me that I used to experience while listening to you splashing in the tub. "Robert, hurry up darling, or I'll fall asleep on you!" Remember, sweetheart?

Love to my Dearest Robert,
Elizabeth

*   *   *   *   *

8:30 PM Saturday Nov 7, 1942

My beloved:

Marched for 4 hours and then pitched tents in a large wooded area. Put my raincoat down 1st then blanket. Donned my long underwear, O.D. shirt and pants, field jacket and gloves and the other blanket. Slept till about 3AM in fair comfort, but from then on the problem was to get up and go thru the damp, black forest to the latrine or stay uncomfortably in "bed". Finally got up and fought my way heroically thru the underbrush and mist and 2 other tents. Got lost on the way back and spent 10 min looking for the very vague outline of our tent in the blackness. Up at 5AM rolled packs had chow and marched 4 hours back (about 11-12 miles). [Fig 19]

Letter Love The impression of your lips carried such poignant longings. A strange sensuous thrill crept over me on seeing that red smudge. I could feel almost the moist firm flesh that fashioned that tempting pattern.

*   *   *   *   *

6PM Monday Nov 9, 1942

My darling, my wife

Was kind of disgusted today but will try not to let the letter echo my thots because they are only a passing cloud. Went over to the band barracks with high expectations but they didn't last long. I was classified already as a <u>bugler</u>! Same story after I told them 3 times I didn't want it. Sat around all morning and listened to the band. Can understand why I didn't make it. The 1st trumpet man from the Minneapolis Symphony. 1st clarinet from Indianapolis Symphony, etc. All experienced professionals and they are really good. The cream of the crop. Well I talked to the sarge about chances of me graduating from bugler to band in the future but he said couldn't be done. Therefore turned in my resignation and instituted immediate action to get my classification changed to mechanic.

*   *   *   *   *

Wed 9:30PM Nov11, 1942

Darling:

This is one letter I'm not going to enjoy writing. I wasn't going to tell you but it just isn't natural for me to withhold anything from my darling. To be short, the worst has happened, my classification as bugler will not be changed. With that news my whole outlook on the army changed. If that isn't about the dirtiest kick in the face I've ever gotten, to be stuck with a bunch of slow joes as a brainless bugler. I would like to start my fighting in this war by bayoneting a few classification "experts".

Got your long Sunday letter today. It's marvelous to get your letters sweetheart. Mine won't be much good for a couple of days till I get over this. I shouldn't write like this but is it better than none

169

at all? Don't mind the bugle job as such. What were you in the army? Oh I blew the bugle. Knew 20 calls. What a line to hand an employment manager after the war. However, it has its good points. I have 6 weeks to learn what I already know, 6 weeks of boondoggling, reading and practising. I'll dream of my pretty little girl too

*   *   *   *   *

9PM Thursday November 12, 1942

Dearest my darling -

The suspense of fear of something that might happen often keeps you on edge. Tonight my fear is of a worse type, the doubt of the outcome of what has already happened. In other words I've been before the OCS board. Will be in a state of agitated suspense till I know the outcome.

Started off the day as usual except somehow I'd polished my extra shoes very meticulously. Was in the mess hall at noon when they told me that I had to be before the regimental board for OCS at 1:15 PM. Was I thankful then that my uniform was all fixed, pressed, etc. Fortunate luck and forsight. Hope it is indicative of the outcome. Appearance was good I believe. There were about 50 men in our company to go over in groups of 10 or so. I was the 3rd one to go in and will give a blow by blow description.

The board consisted of 2 Captains and a 1st Lieut. I knocked on the door and was told to come in. Did so very clumsily. The room was about the size of a closet and didn't give you a chance to recover from closing the door before saluting and saying "Pvt Doty reporting as ordered sir". Was not given at ease so stayed at "relaxed" attention. "22?" yes sir. "Married?" yes sir. "How long?" 1 yr 3 mo sir. "From N.Y.?" "Originally sir" "What do you mean by that?" "Born there but didn't see much of it, spent most of life in Chicago" "Why do you want to be an officer?" That was one that I really missed, totally unprepared. Gave him the baloney 1st about being of more service to country, etc. Then told him my wife was counting on it and also that the higher standard of living attained by officers was attractive. He remarked that my motives were purely selfish (as he also told all the others I found out later) and I said No. Was then asked about my work, school etc. What did I have to offer that I should be made an officer? What was the name of the rifle I used on the range? Name the parts of the rifle in order starting from the muzzle. (Did well on that, got to the stacking swivel and

170

he said that's enough). How many men to make a double shelter and why? (I screwed up the "why" end of it) Did I know that France had declared war on the U.S.? No sir. Well, had she? "No sir" "Sure?" "Yes sir" Where was the Volga? Who was the commander of U.S. forces in Africa? Gen Eisenhower (I knew that from my darling's letters. You saved me sweetheart.) Who was the Allied comander in Egypt? Who and where was Doolittle? "Did my wife like my moustache?" "Not at first sir but she does now" (right?) (Test for humor I guess so he got a good laugh) "Is that why you raised it?" "No sir for my cornet" etc. That's about all of them I recall. Am not over confident of the results because some of the answers on my work and school and why I wanted to be an officer didn't come out so fluently. I hope I make it because if I don't I'm doomed as a bugler.

The food here is improving, altho we had some rice pudding with raisins the other day that brought forth some remarks like "Do raisins have legs" or "What do you do when the raisins get up and walk off".

*   *   *   *   *

Thurs. 9 P.M. Nov. 12, 1942

My Sweetheart -

Sis spent the night with me, perhaps for the last time - I got mad at her this morning and we had "words". So I came down to the office with a chip on my shoulders and boy, I got it but good. More phone calls, more trouble brewing all over the damn Division. No exaggeration. Had 20-25 phone calls before the day was done. All of which results in a hoarse throat, jangled nerves, indigestion and a general feeling of much talk, much ado about nothing! Why does everything have to happen when dear ole Jens is away?

I turned to Marie's letter and found two bulky questionaires Dr Burgess of U of C [see References] is circulating to determine "Attitudes on Marriage in War Time". Apparently she considers us good subjects for this survey. I'm sending you one of them, identical with mine, under separate cover. Look it over and if you decide to fill it out and return it (by Thanksgiving) let me know so I can send mine on. I think we ought to cooperate, don't you?

Darling, don't you question my wisdom in trying to build up

our nest egg! I've got a selfish motive in mind, in addition to our mutual welfare. 'Cause when you get back, sweetheart, and start being the breadwinner, I want to take necessary action for a blessed event. Promise me, darling, you won't deny me that privilege?

I just grope around and decide this emotion I feel is beyond expression; and then I get a letter from you and you've plagiarized my thoughts! I love you for what you are, what you will be, always the man I love, the one closest to my mind and heart. I can only concur in your statement that we must be patient and save our pent up love during this separation and spread it thru a lifetime. We will, Robert - I know it -

With All My Love,
Elizabeth

*　　*　　*　　*　　*

Sun 6:30PM Nov. 15, 1942

Dearly Beloved -

Dearest, I've counted your letters to me, 42 in all. Isn't it marvelous? How many have you gotten from me? What do you do with them after you read them? Someday you may have to dispose of them darling. Either by returning them to me or by destroying them! They are rather intimate, aren't they, sweet, tokens of my love. Your letters are precious to me. I wonder if you could write them in ink, dearest, so they'll be more legible. I don't mean to inconvenience you, darling, but I do want them preserved for posterity.

*　　*　　*　　*　　*

2:30PM Friday November 13, 1942

My darling wife

that I could hug so closely this afternoon. To see, to hear, to feel, to sense in every particle of self the mutual adoration and blending of our lives in love. Longing so to run my hands across the smooth naked stomach, over the sturdiness of the chest, and fondle your woman's breasts feeling the nipples pucker with pleasure. To experience that uncontainable delight, of grasping between her satin thighs the warm furry female flesh, and read ecstasy in glis-

172

tening eyes, as my fingers slip within the moist tantalizing folds. The portals of our future lives. To thrust gently, sturdy male flesh into the awaiting, loving female and couple body to body, mouth to mouth, inseparable symbol of our eternal attachment, our oneness and union from which will someday come the ultimate and complete blending of our lives into one being. How I worship and adore you my everloving wife and how happy I am that we symbolize our love in ritual. I will never forget the thots and feeling and emotion with which I placed the ring on your eager finger, our minds realizing at the same instant the significance of this ceremony. Oh my beautiful precious sweetheart I miss you so! -

4PM. You know maybe this bugle business which I detested at first so violently may not be so bad. It is really a racket and I wouldn't mind spending the rest of the war doing what I pleased. At 8:30 the others rush off to school while I take my time packing up my handbag with candy, fruit and books for the day to come. Walk across the "front yard" to the band room and sit around talking, "warming up" or reading. Play a couple of calls for the sergeant. Then walk about 1/4 mile out in the woods. Read "Ulysses" this morn and practised. This goes on for 6 weeks and then I'm a bugler and have to loaf with the drum and bugle corps.

7:15PM Friday November 13, 1942

Bella figlia del amore [Start of the famous quartet from last act of Rigoletto] Ich liebe dich. Don't ask me how I got started this way; just singing it, so it went into the pencil too.

My darling's letter. The war news peps you up too! It is very encouraging especially if Tobruk has really fallen and we can squeeze off Tunisia. Money's in the bank. Good but I want to make sure you're not pinching pennies. Don't do that. While I think of it how is the piano coming? I'll bet you haven't even touched it. Your forgiven and we'll wait for the day when there is more time for it. Rereading what I wrote this afternoon. Beloved just writing to you like that allows some of that pent up emotion to be spent. Am also struck by the similarities of my writing and that of James Joyce. I seem to have an unconscious tendency to imitate the author or poet with whom I am at the time engrossed. "Ulysses" is a marvelous tho difficult book. It is a psychological novel of a sort. Not the surface psychology of Flaubert but the workings and associations, and feelings, of the inner mind of his characters. His descriptive power is eerie; it comes so close to making you experience the same events as the character. His prose is beautiful and poetic. The book is very difficult to unravel, however; seems to be a jumble of events, thots, conversation, description, mixed inseparably. Have only read 217 of the 767 pages tho and the structure seems to be unfolding or resolving into a more intelligible picture. I'll send the book back to you when I've read it. Here are a couple of representative passages: "Bag of corpsegas sopping in foul brine. A quiver of minnow, fat of a spongy titbit, flash thru the slits of his button trouserfly. God becomes man becomes fish becomes barnacle goose becomes featherbed mountain. Dead breaths I living breathe, tread dead dust, devour a urinous offal from all dead. Hauled stack over the gunwale he breathes upward stench of his green grave, his leprous nosehole snoring to the sun."

Here is a description of a bath, and altho a male one, can't you almost feel the water on your body?

"Enjoy bath now: clean trough of water, cool enamel, the gentle tepid stream. This is my body.

He foresaw his pale body reclined in it at full, naked, in a womb of warmth, oiled by scented melting soap, softly laved. He saw his trunk and limbs rippippled over and sustained, buoyed lightly upward lemonyellow: his navel, bud of flesh: and saw the dark tangled curls of his bush floating, floating hair of the stream around the limp father of thousands, a languid floating flower."

That's what I call using language to perfection! Before you read it darling I should give you a good course in "vulgarities," altho in the hands of Joyce's genius all touch with vulgarity is lost. My little sweetheart tho I'm afraid would miss the meaning of such phrases as "the scrotum tightening sea", etc.

Well enough of "Ulysses", we'll analyze it together some nite snuggled close on our cozy couch.

How I long to be buttock to groin with a husbandly hand toying the warm silken bulges in your wifely nightie. My little jelly bean, I love you

Robert

*   *   *   *   *

Monday Eve - 9:30PM Nov 16th 1942

Robert, My Dearest -

<u>Friday letter</u> - Oh, marvelous letter! You made me blush, dearest, as I read your beautiful expression of your love for me; and I trembled, too, as you awakened my passion for you, sweetheart!

Darling, you are psychic. I haven't been doing everything you wanted me to do and I plead leniency on your part because it has been a full time job going to work, keep the apartment going, and corresponding with you. Writing to you is such a pleasure, I make it a one-two hour affair nightly, as I read and reread your letters and sort of dream while writing to you. That James Joyce sounds fascinating and smacks very much of my Robert W. Doty! Frankly, his vocabulary baffles me! Will have to wait until we can both analyze it together.

Ich liebe dich! Je t'aime trés beaucoup! I love you. Oh, so much. Dearest, love like ours seems like an end in itself. Never knew it could be so intense, so much a part of me, like living and breathing! Oh, darling, your letters intoxicate me with their ardor and their passionate appeal! We do need each other and if only for a little while and it will be ecstasy to know your love in reality once more

I adore you, sweetheart
Elizabeth

* * * * *

9PM Saturday November 14, 1942

My darling wife:

Headlines tonite 1.) <u>Passed</u> regimental O.C.S. board! 2.) Check enclosed for $169.06. 3.) Moved to Co. F Barracks T-472.

Had a nice long gab fest with the concert master violist of the Pittsburg symphony telling some of his experiences. Played under Reiner for years. He plays the cymbals in the band here. One thing I might pass on was how Enesco came to write his Rhapsody that you like so well. This violist happened to be playing on a borrowed Stradivarius the time Enesco was guest conductor in Pittsburg and they were playing the Rumanian Rhapsody. Enesco complimented him on the way he played the solo passages and told how he came to write the piece. The idea came to him on a Sunday morning in a little Rumanian village. He was watching the people come out of church. Out came this drunken peasant reeling and staggering down the street singing and picking up old cronies on his way. Now next time you hear this piece notice how perfectly it depicts this scene of the reeling peasant and his gathering of cronies as the various instruments join in the broken, staggering opening theme.

My busy little business bug just wait till I can keep you busy someday answering phone calls on how junior is doing!

Love
Robert

P.S. I'll leave the enclosed $169.06 up to you. C.U. or else save it for the trip down here and put part away. I love you

R.

*　　*　　*　　*　　*

8:15PM Sunday November 15, 1942

To my voice of sweetness -

Darling you sounded so sweet and lovable on the phone this morning, so squeezably soft and silken, the whole picture of your beauty conveyed by the gladness of your voice. It made me so happy those few moments. We will always love and appreciate each other more after this is over for we have learned to cherish the preciousness of a few fleeting moments together. And togetherness is what is uppermost in my mind now. You can get a week off! I'm impatiently awaiting your letter with the pros and cons but we know it will be pro. Already my darling has the date and the correct one chosen. About Dec 5th.

Filled out original and duplicate of a 6 page life history deal for OCS today and turned in 3 letters (from Jensen, Byler and my school teacher (Kempes), Birth Certificate and Walton and college credits. Noticed my General Classification Test was 134 and that my old Company Commander had recommended me and said I was an excellent leader. The Colonel's letter should be of great help now too. If I pass, why you as my proxy must buy him a couple extra potent thank you kindly's at the Blackhawk or sumthin!

For the while now we part by letter but never actually. We are made inseparable by love, souls intermingled so that minds and body have but one purpose, the living and enjoying of love, love as meant by a lifetime spent in perfect marriage. Wedded in passion, lived in wholesome happiness and leaving a small but eternal ember of life beautifully lived for history to forget. May we be counted as one of the multitudinous steps toward the far distant and elusive happiness of mankind. With strong clean bodies and minds we contribute our bit of beauty to make more perfect the perfection of the cosmos. My wife and idol of Perfect Beauty I worship and adore you, giving my whole life and love to you, only to be pervaded and surrounded by your life and love returned. Impatiently awaiting our

176

planned reunion with all the love a husband can give the dearest wife a man ever had

Love
Robert

*   *   *   *   *

10PM Monday November 16, 1942

Darling:

Have just spent over ½ hour filling out that questionaire on marriage. Very complete and interesting.

Another thing, if I don't make OCS, I have only 5 weeks before I'm ready for active duty anywhere. We should therefore see each other while we're sure we can. Petersburg is about 4 miles from camp. You'll stay at Petersburg and I'll take care of finding the place. Don't think I'd be able to get nites off but wrote you all about that last nite. Have drawn KP for this Sunday so that should be out of the way for a couple of weeks.

*   *   *   *   *

Thursday - Nov. 19, 1942 10 pm

Dearest Darling.......I love you:

Well, my mind is made up: I'm coming down to see you regardless of anything.

Think I'll come down to work in the morning 12/3 to save 4 hrs leave. That should give us 5 nights together, darling.

I feel sick at the idea of having to skimp on time with you, but rules and regulations are such. Will try to chizzle [sic] more time, but I don't know. Oh, hell. This idea of having to toady to people for favors.

Just ache with desire to look at you, hug you, kiss you and feel your arms about me. You will restrain your ardor at first, won't you dear? Will write more fully tomorrow.

Oh, so much love
Elizabeth

*   *   *   *   *

177

Friday - Nov 20, 1942 - 10PM

My Dearest -

This has been another one of those days that just flew by - Went to the Liaison Officers of Manpower Branch SOS Conference at Palmer House [A famous hotel in downtown Chicago.] at 9am with Jensen. There were about 100 officers and men there, me the only woman! Mr Mitchell (Thomas Mitchell of movies' brother - looks lot like him) shook hands with me. Lots of people there I knew. Col Wyman, Area Liaison Officer, who presided at meeting, said for the 1st time in 25 years in addressing this War Dept conference, he had to address the conference as "Lady and Gentlemen". Mr Mitchell acknowledged my presence by stating he noticed the Engineers had recognized the manpower problem and had taken steps to remedy labor supply by employing a woman in a field traditionally for men only. All of which really put me on a spot and I was under constant surveillance. Frankly, I was bored with all the talk about manpower mobilization to be done, persuasively, because there is no National Service Act as yet to give us legal authority. I shall have to go tomorrow morning, however - Phooey! You know what they say about conferences - a slightly organized method of wasting time.

Your letter - Don't you worry about my handling of the Doty Exchequer. We've got $519.06 in C.U. and 255.00 in P.O. Maybe a beginning for a home of our own some day.

*   *   *   *   *

8:30PM Wednesday November 18, 1942

My most beloved warmsoft

whose pastel scent is rising seductively from Sunday's scribbled page of love, tenderly redolent, carrying airborne thot, mind of body bearing on her rose beautiful bosom the smell of skin bathed, coiled, temptingly ensconced, clean, cool, a dream carved gardenia on red ruffled silk.

Don't know how many of my darling's letters I have but every one is saved. When they get too heavy I'll send them home. Maybe we can make excerpts from the love letters of the Dotys some day. I think we have marvelous material.

My darling sweetheart and the most lovable wife. Knowing that at this moment you too are feeling that thrill of intangible contact, as I mentally

squeeze you and place
a firm husbandlovingwife
kiss upon moist lips that say
so softly you are mine love

Robert

10:30AM Sunday November 22, 1942

Oh loneliness
Gentle and sad,
Aching for the warmth
of foregone kisses.
Awaiting the embrace,
Reunion, bursting flamelike
With radiant life, burning briefly,
Beautiful in passion,
Tolled by the hour.
Now fading, rutilant ember,
Vivid in memory,
Relapsing into the womb
of "has been" and "to be".
Oh, drear monotony of longing,
Broken only by dreams.
Sleepshut eyes, lids laden
with silver tears, gliding in silence
thru Time's haunted valley.
Whispered echo of a distant kiss. -

In free flowing thot, darling, a partial picture of us. Can't seem to write easily this morn. We love deeply and eternally as only a man and wife can, beautiful experience! Re-reading your letters mildly Intoxicated by the scent, the writing, the words, the kiss, all of which means you. Always my sweet innocent little bride, happy, naive yet also having the "knowingness", wisdom and judgement of the woman my wife. Makes me so happy to realize this. I promise not to be "smarty pants" any more.

9:45PM

I love you darling and now I am also beginning to attach to you the love of home, decent food, freedom, and common comfort. My

symbol not merely of my deepest love, but of the very life I want to lead. We are but soulless shadows carrying out the actions necessary to existence while our real selves live in an intangible paradise of hope, the future. Thirsting for your loving kisses soon!
Robert

*   *   *   *   *

Mon. Nov 23, 1942 - 10:30 PM.
My precious darling_
Oh, so much to tell you on this, my birthday.
About 10:30 A.M. I really got a thrill, you know why, too, you dear ole darling, you! That was a lovely, lovely surprise! At first I was nonplussed, nothing whatsoever in the package to tell me who from. So Marie got busy on phone to check with Lyon & Healey's and I wasn't surprised to learn my gift came from one Pvt Robt Doty! How did you do it by remote control? You are a remarkable person and I guess I'll never cease marveling at your unexpected delightful doings! I do so love you, and <u>Les Sylphides</u> is a perfect gift. I really love the waltzes, and the mazurka has such a cheerful lilt to it! Recalls to me our seeing that ballet performed by Ballet Russe last year!
Love and Affections Always
Elizabeth

*   *   *   *   *

8:45PM Monday November 23, 1942
My darling wife:
Hope that today has been a happy birthday for you. Makes me happy to read about my little jelly bean being such a successful career woman with Colonels, Palmer House, etc; but it is dull and silly stuff isn't it.

*   *   *   *   *

[Thanksgiving Day]

Thursday, Nov 26. 1942 10PM.
My Dearly Beloved -
Odd sensation to go to work with the streets deserted and the holiday atmosphere pervading the Loop - A travesty on justice to

180

make us come down to work because frankly very little was accomplished.

You're right about this career woman stuff being dull. I've given up the Labor Legislation class at DePaul, too. All I want to do, dearest, after this is over is apply my business knowledge to the household budget and really be the best wife and mother possible. Clean and scrub the house and take care of the little Dotys and cook good nourishing meals for Papa Doty and greet him with open arms every evening and just live, dearest; and help you in your career, that's all I want. This other stuff is so hollow, so empty, the thought of leading the life I led before I married you frightens me! I really began to live, Robert, when I began to love you.

*   *   *   *   *

9:30PM Tuesday November 24, 1942

My dearest:

Got all dressed up before retreat and went over to sign out at 5:30 sharp. Foiled again. Everyone had to be in mess hall to hear a lecture by the Captain. So while in the mess hall decided to kill two birds and ate the chili we had for supper while the C.O. gave his spiel. The damn cook makes everything black with pepper. Am not sure whether we'll have turkey and pepper or pepper and turkey for Thanksgiving.

Any hoo catches a cab for a quick trip to town (25 cents) and went straight to the USO travelers aid and asked for the best place they had. After making several phone calls she found a vacancy in a home out in Colonial Heights, the newer part of town. So I took a bus out to look the place over. It's not bad, not fancy but clean and with 50,000 soldiers here you can't get much more. All the hotels are reserved a month ahead. We lived at the Larsen's, darling, and this will bring back those happy days of honeymooning. Mr. Harrison is an old railroad man and he and I had quite a long talk. They have one boy in the navy and 1 in the army. Mrs Harrison is OK, a little deaf.

*   *   *   *   *

181

My darling:

Spent most of the evening in the barracks reading your letters from the start of this episode with the idea in mind of excerpts of the Dotys' letters. Noted in red pencil all passages that I thot should be included. When you come down I'll give you most of them to take home and save. They will be as precious to us 20 years from now as they are when we receive them. Part of our love - immortal.

Tomorrow is Thanksgiving so we'll have turkey. What a build up that turkey deal gets. Bet the public doesn't know that you eat baloney for three solid days so that you can get that turkey. That's the truth, too. Since Sunday nite we've had baloney 7 times, beans twice and chlorinated hot dogs tonite. At least we get 3 qts milk per 12 men for breakfast.

*   *   *   *   *

8PM Thursday November 26, 1942

To my cause for Thanksgiving:

I love you and might even permit myself the liberty of a kiss were you here. I'll go even further and promise that upon your arrival I will make very sure I kiss you. Getting bolder, perhaps put an arm around you and hear my little teddy bear squeak with delight as the squeeze becomes more oh so ummm squoze.

So full of a really good supper. Real Thanksgiving dinner, but afterwards had to go mop, sweep, dust etc the regimental HQ. Of course I "volunteered" for the job. You always volunteer in the army. "Need 10 volunteers, you, you, you etc." Was finished by 7:30 PM. - Your Mon letter - Happy that you got and like Les Sylphides. It is something you can become perfectly entranced in listening to, those pensive moonsilk melodies that make the soul dance, captured in enchanted rhythm. Joyous, sad, brilliant, mysterious, carefree, lonely, no word that includes, or adjectives that apply, except Chopin. Chopin is a word, a meaning, an emotion; there is no other way to say it.

Started menstruating on your birthday. In perfect time with life. I have wondered at times about that. Joyce has his main character Bloom wonder about it in Ulysses. Uncanny the exactitude with which Joyce discloses the human mind. The book is painstakingly written with every phrase, word, idiom worked in to give the maximum effect. In reading the book you also must be constantly alert and remember all previous passages, words and associations or you will miss much of the closely knit, astonishingly real depiction of human character which the book attempts. It is easy to see why it took 7 years to write it. I believe that I am capable of such a work except for one character fault which will always keep me down but also keep me happy. In 7 years I would have started 3 plays, 2 books, a symphony, a painting, studied Italian, and a 1,000 various other things without completing any. I am a man of tremendous beginnings but there are too many things to begin. Too many things to taste the enjoyment of doing to be bothered completing any one thing. Variety surcease monotony! Beauty of a fragment.

Oh dream dappled smoothness
Slipping silently into thot's
Coral caverns. Choking the motley
Half forms of the unanswered. Ugly cloud
Caught, bottled evil, ensnared genie-like in
Anfractuous bypaths of brain by
Dream dappled smoothness I mean dream beam
Seem sheen of starlight seen dream beam
Of moon caught curving noiselessly its
Pale sensitive fingers over the nude breast
Cold breast of white marble. Venus curved
Carved caught in the garden and the slim
Million fingered poplars gracefully nodded
Moonshadow.

How's that for a poetic variation on the theme that came to me out of nowhere, "Dream dappled smoothness". Don't know. It came to me so I started writing. Must mean you. All vague mist beautiful phrases mean you to me. Love you so. How would my poetry look in print or am I crazy by R. Doty. Waiting for you beloved with all the body and soul I have given you before.

Love
Robert

*   *   *   *   *

Saturday - 7:45PM Nov 28, 1942

My precious darling -

    I wondered what disposition you intended to make of all my

183

letters. I'll be very happy to take them back with me, and you're right, dearest, they are precious and will remain a testimonial of our love forever. I like to reread some of your previous letters, and always do that if a day goes by and I don't get a new one from you. I suppose some unimaginative people would wonder whence comes the inspiration for daily letters to one another. Still, I don't seem to run out of material to write you about, manage to fill all pages of the letters.

I remember what a terrific thrill it was to be in your arms back in February in Cleveland after an absence of only three weeks, and that was before I got to love you as much as I do now. So it's going to be collosal! There! That's the biggest word I could think up offhand to describe it. But I guess I'll react something like this - "Oh, Robert, darling - It's so good to see you" and end up with sobs and tears. I warn you, I'll be so happy, I'll cry! And I can just picture you, with a pained look on your face, putting your arms around me and patting my shoulders and saying "There, there, darling, It's nothing to cry about!" Gosh darn, I'm on the verge of tears already. But I'll try to be very stoic and greet you with a smile and snuggle up to my HERO and try to crowd in as much joy and happiness for us both as we possibly can during my stay. Oh, Robert darling, how can I live thru the next two days. Dearest, I do love you so much and I'm so impatient to get to you

Always with Love
Elizabeth

*   *   *   *   *

[Homeward bound, after a rapturous 5 days of togetherness, she scrawled the following notes in pencil on 3x6-inch notebook paper, summarizing the 33-hour journey.]

2:30AM Wed 12/9/42

Unable to sleep, my mind filled with impressions of the past twenty four hours. Kaleidescopic impressions whirling round and round in my mind.

With my darling's firm kisses still moist on my lips. Pulling away from Petersburg, Coach crowded. Soldiers, soldier's wives

184

or sweethearts, and sailors standing or sitting on suitcases in the aisles. I settled down in my seat. Contrite and angry at myself for not having snatched another loving embrace, or taken another long look at my darling's beloved face before the train left. - Felt very lonely. Like one suddenly bereft of one's most prized possession. So I gazed ruefully out the window; the imprint of my darling's kisses seem to linger, as if to console and comfort me.

The coach was noisy as we sped into the night. We made stops and people got off and people got on and finally by morning Things had balanced themselves, and all those remaining had a seat. The colored boy came by with sandwiches and coffee. I was hungry and I waited for him to come by me, holding my silver in my hand. But his supply was gone very quickly, and he left and came not.

So I went into the diner And was pleasantly greeted and seated at a table. There was a vase with flowers on the table. A colored boy handed me the menu. I studied it closely and ordered. Poached eggs on toast and coffee. And lit a cigaret and watched the scenery roll by my eyes. Sloping hills with scrubby pines perched on top. Some slopes had smooth snow on them. Others looked barren by contrast. My breakfast came. I ate; and felt warmed and nourished. The colored boy handed me a newspaper to read And I read "Tank Battle Rages in Tunisia" Only the headlines Was all I had time for And when I had eaten the colored boy served me a finger bowl And I felt flattered As I moistened my fingertips and dried them on my napkin. One of the niceties of our culture, I thought, as I returned to my seat.

"Next car ahead for Cincinnati" said the conductor, and I dutifully moved My belongings and me to the forward car And I sat by a sailor, a very young lad of 17, Six months service First class seaman Enroute to St Louis Ten day furlough Back from North Africa Casablanca He wished he hadn't joined Had seen his buddy killed While they manned the guns They were bombed by their own airmen. Why? Communications were bad at that stage of the game. Were many killed? Yes, but he had been lucky He reminded me of my kid brother, just 16; as we talked, he grew more confidential Showed me a bottle of Arabian perfume, For his mother. He proudly displayed it, holding the flacon [French

185

spelling] in his grubby stubby fingers that had dealt destruction not so long ago. "I'm bringing back a French rifle", he pointed to the package rack. Such an adorable youngster. Six feet tall, nice boyish features, only the slightest trace of fuzz on his upper lip.

I turned to the scenery. - Monotony of hills and valleys and lakes and frame shacks. Constant reference to my time table when we made a stop. We kept losing time. The colored boy came by "Sandwiches Hot Coffee!" I bought a sandwich and coffee and munched it hungrily altho I had been eating candy all the while.

Impatiently waiting for Cincinnati. People coming and going. Soldiers across the aisle discussing their lieutenant. They didn't like him. Planned to send him a Christmas present to prove it.

Thinking of my Robert. Would he be an officer? Did I want him an officer? Did it matter except That he return to me as he left, Sweet and considerate The man I vowed to Love, Honor and Cherish?

There was a woman Just one seat ahead Going to San Francisco To see her husband Had not seen him for 8 mos They had been evacuated from Pearl Harbor. Didn't know what she would do in San Francisco Only knew she wanted to see him For 8 months I waited to see him.

We got to Cincinnati The sailor, a soldier's wife and I ate dinner in the Railroad Station Restaurant Coffee Shop. The dining room was reserved for troops We watched them file in. Others file out.

There were 2 soldiers Sitting at the counter Drinking whiskey and beer Air Corps privates. The waitress refused to wait on them Said she was tired of being patriotic, and another girl could have them. So they kept on ordering from the other girl.

A Master Sergeant came in The privates spoke to him He was going to have a steak and then he was going to get drunk. Reason? He was bringing back the body of a boy to his mother. "Hell of an assignment!" "All in the line of duty", I consoled him. He was Irish and said a bit of liquor would see him through. Dinner eaten we three left, To repair our complexions, To check on trains. I wrote a short note to my darling. Mailed it at the station Sat and waited for my train.

186

Talked to strangers casually Everyone does it now. Old lady returning to Richmond. Had left her daughter-in-law with her son. Ruefully complained that she, the mother, had not seen much of her boy. One old man asked me where I was going. Said he'd make sure I got a seat. Railroad man. Put me on the coach before the gates were opened.

Train late in leaving Many soldiers on this train Same ones I rode with all day. All tired, Many drunk. I couldn't sleep. Tried to, but the train lurched and swayed and stopped so often I gave up.

Shall I go home? Shall I go home and go to work in the afternoon? Shall I go home and sleep Will see how late the train is.

Wondering how my darling is Is he missing me as I am missing him? Today's his Post Board Interview I wish him luck. Let Fate decide. I love him - so much.

Wed - 9PM 12/9/42

Dearest -

Enclosed scribbling gives you my thoughts en route home - Got into Chicago 6 AM - Home by 7:30 - Waiting for baggage, having roll and coffee, etc. So I called up the office. Took a bath, changed clothes and got down there at 10am.

Dopey day, tired, etc. So home. Finding bills, income tax - phooey.

Love you very much - Will write you longie tomorrow - How did today come out re OCS?

Love
- With all my Love
Elizabeth

*   *   *   *   *

9:15PM Wed December 9, 1942

My darling wife:

Today was my interview with the O.C.S. post board. Took a shower, washed hair, shaved etc and donned my brightly polished shoes and my almost pressed uniform. Looked pretty good. Got over there at 2:15 and waited till 4:15 before getting called in. Was 3rd from the last. Blow by blow account: This was a room this time and not a closet. Closed the door according to plan and proceeding across the room saluted the Major (and 3 1st Lts) and jumbled up

187

something about Pvt. Doty reporting. The 1st Lt on the right administered the oath to tell the truth etc and jumbled it up too so I felt better. Then right up my alley "Give a command so that a company of men could hear" Pvt Doty gave out with a Companee Tensh hut! that blew the roof off. It felt good, sounded good and I knew it was. Was then ordered to take a chair placed in the middle of the room in front of them. Had to explain a bit about my education, my work but was confident and really spoke well. Asked me about my R.O.T.C. and did I like it? Told him emphatically yes! Had a little discussion of my being a bugler. Asked me if I thot I had been misclassified and explain why. Told them yes etc and got them chuckling a bit (good sign). The Major asked me who the Chief Justice of the Supreme Court was and having just learned that this noon luckily I spit out "Justice Sloan, sir" but luckily also remembered a second later that it was Stone so I corrected it. Thinking he had found my weakness we did a little rapid fire work on who is chief of O.P.A., the W.P.B. the O.W.I. Ten minutes before I went in that room I was all messed up on that stuff but the answers came out easily, confidently and correctly somehow, so he relented. Then comes some military law - asked me to name the 3 courts martial. Out of thin air of memory I magically produced them tho I couldn't have remembered what they were ½hr before. Then asked me difference between marshal law and military law and what punitive article of war was. Got the answers fairly correct. Name two military highways - The Alaskan road and any of the highways in the U.S. such as Route 30 or route 6. "What is the Atlantic Charter?" "I don't know, sir" "Any idea?" "I believe, sir" - and so wandered confidently off onto the wrong answer about prewar agreement between U.S. and G.B. and he says that's close enough. "How do you fold the flag at retreat?" "I don't know, sir" Then Pvt Doty had to give out a bit on the grand war strategy of materials and territory. The last question was "What qualities do you think an officer should have?" The ability to lead men, not because the men have to obey but because they want to - and the ability to deal with situations out of the ordinary course of events by the application of native intelligence. The Major then returned all my letters, credits, etc and I gave out with a snappy salute, a crisp heel clicking about face and strode out with the feeling that I had made a fine showing. Sure hope so. Felt like a sick fish when I left the regimental board but I passed despite all my stammering there. Hope my confidence in this post board trial is not betrayed. Really, darling, I think I should make it, at least the sureness I feel helps to relieve the lonesomeness caused by your leaving. Everything seems to be proceeding just like your trip, perfectly timed, according to plan, etc. It must have been, in fact I know it was your recent kisses that enabled me to come off so well this aft. Here it is getting near closing time again and I've not taken time to say how much I love you. Our brief reunion resulted naturally in missing you terribly but sweetheart it has restored us to a reality once more. For awhile now the memory of you will be so vivid, so close that you will be actually here with me, before gradually fading off into a beautiful dream. You know what I mean. After being able to convey love to you by just looking into your radiant face or caress so tenderly your lovely body - it is so hard to get back to saying "I love you" on paper. Good nite darling.

Love
Robert

*   *   *   *   *

6:30PM Thursday December 10, 1942

Am still anxiously waiting for news from OCS, but it may be a week before I know, so we'll have to be patient.

Got your Cincinnati letter tonight you darling. I hope you have taken enough rest to recover from the rigors of that 33 hr trip. Your coming just seemed to do things to me. Hard to explain but I feel refreshed, reassured, happier, everything seems to be going right. I know we were both rejuvenated mentally, and the physical passion seems also to have been a body tonic. How marvelous, how beautiful my wife, our marriage. We have added another chapter of memories to our lives in love. Stored up enough happiness to last a while. I'll dream of just one little moment of your being here each nite, in that way making it last a long while. Love you always my dearest and will never forget that flannel nightie!

*   *   *   *   *

WESTERN UNION

C154 7 COLLECT=TDPT CAMPLEE VIR 11 508PM 42 DEC 11 PM 4 51

MRS ELIZABETH N DOTY=

1001 SO MAYFIELD

PASSED THE OCS POST BOARD. LOVE=

ROBERT.

* * * * *

My beloved -

    my life music of eternal joy always I marvel at the beauty of you and what you mean to me, what happiness the crossing and mating of our lives has made. Listening to soft music in an unusually quiet day room I interpret every note, each chord and melody to recreate some part of you now light, quick, gay then pensive, sad, soft, gentle, arousing, powerful, ruling, submissive intangibly lovely to the soul. Am in a happy elated mood tonight, touched a bit with lonesomeness that we are not together sharing it.

    Sent you a telegram (collect) telling you that I had passed the OCS post board. Knew you wanted to know and hope you were home to get it. Would have phoned but the telegram is faster, cheaper and easier. What happens now? Well Tues. at 8:30 AM go up to the hospital for physical exam and passing that I am in OCS and will have no more KP, guard duty etc till actually in school. Don't know how long it will be before I get into school, but while waiting will be part of the cadre in this company.

    They really eliminated a bunch of men. Out of 50 men that went before the regimental board with me 21 passed. Of these 21 there were only 6 to get past the post board. Some lads like Fendara with 6 yrs military experience (who washed out of flying school) had their papers returned without even going before the board. (He was too much of a spoiled brat I believe). And then there is B, secretary to the president of Chrysler Corp for years and a very capable man whom the board turned down? Possibly lack of forcefulness in his character?

    I am so happy to have passed but was confident this time. Now if I can only get into school and get thru it OK. Darling your coming here just seems to have set the whole thing right. Everything has been rolling our way ever since.

    I have about a dozen letters to write now to various people thanking them for letters.

Love to my sweetest wife
From her husband
Robert

* * * * *

Dearest -

Listening to the haunting strains of Valse Triste and every muscle and fiber of me just thrills and quivers as I recall the evenings when I used to play that record waiting for my "date" to arrive, and those halcyon nights when we would listen to the Music Lovers Program cuddled close together in your coupe! Oh, sweetheart, I couldn't ever forget you if I tried, what with a constant reminder to be found in every note of music I hear. <u>I love you</u> -

Sun. 4 PM. Dec 13, 1942

Precious -

I was <u>so</u> busy yesterday I just couldn't get to write and mail your letter as I have been doing, but you will forgive me, won't you? So much I want to say, and doing it by letter seems so inadequate after being able to talk to you and look at you sweet.

Hurried home confident there'd be a letter from you, and there was! A very wonderful letter giving me an account of your interview before the Post Board! I felt so proud reading your detailed description; I could just visualize you, well-poised, successfully undergoing the ordeal. Having received your telegram telling me you had passed, I enjoyed the letter very much and was glad your optimistic outlook as to the outcome was not in error!

Our brief reunion affected me like it did you, made me come back here missing you terribly! But as you say, it did restore us to reality, our love did become more vivid, revived from being a beautiful dreamlike memory, not that it had ever become less intense, but being together did make it a living, flesh and blood thing. I feel as though all of me underwent a revitalization. Ah, sweet memories! I'll never forget those 5 A.M. episodes, kissing you at the door in my nightie as you left for camp.

Oh, dearest, good luck always and always my love

Elizabeth

* * * * *

[The Camp Lee letterhead is augmented by a beautiful kiss. Puzzled at first, it then dawned on me that this was imprinted *after* the letter was received!]

191

10:30 PM Wed December 16, 1942

Beloved:

Won't have time to really answer your letters as I'd like to. Your "Freudian" error "someday you'll make it impossible for me to really devote myself to the things I want to do" is quite interesting. [In her letter she had commented on this writing of "impossible" when she intended "possible"] A development coming right in line with me wanting you to practise the piano which you <u>don't</u> want to do. A very natural expression of the fear that I will dominate your life. Haven't time to go into a lengthy discussion but that is one of the finest examples of the psychology of error that I've seen.

Dreaming of a soft sweet smile given to be kissed. Love night cuddled in flannel next to bare skin so warm and smooth

My roseblush so silken
I love you
Robert

*   *   *   *   *

8PM Thursday December 17, 1942

I think of you, and love;
I dream of you, and remember
Beauty; the moon splash,
Silver on the leaping fish,
The glitter of starlight,
Diamond in rippling waters
Propelled to unseen shores.

And I caressed your face,
Vague in the darkness,
Moist on a summer night.
The rhythm of the waves,
Languid, effortless - drifting
Beneath untold suns,
Buoyed by liquid blackness,
Noiseless with seething life.
We, bonded in Eternity,
One together, folded in time,
Between cool water
And the rim of space.

All for and about you my darling but it took a while to write tonight.

Needs a lot of revision [To say the least!!] but haven't time now. Got your Mon letter today and it made me just want to write poetry to you and about you all nite.

I want my little girl to stop worrying about bills, money etc. We are very well off in that direction and you know it.

Love my sweet
your husband
Robert

*   *   *   *   *

Sat - 10PM 12/19/42

Darling -

Your letter of Wednesday. Darling, you do say the most beautiful things, like "roseblush so silken", that I just glow with self pride to think I mean so much to you dearest. All these skeptics and scoffers who can't visualize two people being as much in love as we are. I feel so sorry for them. Darling, whatever happens in our future life, we'll keep our love as strong and beautiful as it has been in the past, won't we?

*   *   *   *   *

8:30PM Sunday December 20, 1942

My wife:

Got into my leggings, wool cap, etc and set out in 5 or 6 inches of snow. Crisp clean woods and walking a bit of an exertion, tramping thru drifts and over uneven ground. Acres of unbroken snow and forest, a real paradise for me. Startled a rabbit, came within a yard of its nest before it took off lickety split thru the woods. Decided it would be interesting to follow its trail in the fresh snow so I took off and it wove around thru all sorts of underbrush. Learned a lot about rabbit tactics. Also responded to curiosity about the olfactory sense of man. The tracks had wound around maybe ½ mile already when I got down and stuck my nose in one of the tracks. Was very surprised to find that I could actually detect the rabbit smell of those tracks! A fresh spoor. I never knew that man could do this, but I have smelled rabbits many times and know their odor and was definitely able to detect it in those tracks. Remarkable how brutish we are.

*   *   *   *   *

My sweetest wife:

Your letters sounded happier today. Church? For me? You know better for my part, and should also know better for your own. Religion is one of the basic factors making war, this senseless rampage of slaughter possible. And you would ask me to uphold and participate in such a rotten hypocritical practise. There is not a history of religion in any part of the world that is not a record of the foulest most underhanded crimes in history. I point to Mohammed, to Joshua, to the Crusades, the Inquisition, to cannibalism, to witchcraft, Cromwell, butchery of the Huguenots, the Nazis, the Japs, to the Ku Klux Klan, the priest begging a $500,000 church from the factory slaves and richer gangsters, the babbling Baptist ostracizing from his narrow mind all progress, thwarting science and the health and happiness of man at every step - suffer! woman bearing child, "God" meant it thus - examine not the corpse lest we learn to save a million lives. The indictment written in blood from the 1st priest to the last, from cannibal, to Hindu to Pope, and all based on the dirty mouthed lie of immortality. And strange to see how they put filth on man's only means of immortality, Reproduction; cursed act but admittedly necessary for continuance of the world wide racket. This one fact alone, the suppression of man's sexual-emotional life has caused more insanity, physical and mental suffering than could ever be undone by 10 billion prating happy self-righteous John Prayalways. - So please don't support them; curse them and remember their crimes always. Christmas cards are perhaps pretty but quite trite and add a million dollars to the Field Estate in the name of a poor misunderstood man, Jesus Christ.

I love you dearest and hate to hurt your ingrained childhood memories by writing such things, but you know it for the truth. You know also that my feeling of nature, love, philosophy is keen and deep, and that I hate to see the tawdry mercenary "simplified editions" of God passed off for religion. Religion is not contained on an altar. It is in the Milky Way on a summer night when you look up in awe and think that you are one with it. It is when you kill a cockroach and think how its life stopped and that fundamentally you and the roach are one. Religion is the coupling of warm naked bodies and knowing they are one, that you are living, and functioning perfectly, beautifully in a chain of life unbroken.

My mate, our oneness, eternal love

Robert

Sunday, Dec. 27, 1942 2:30PM

Darling -

    I was going to argue with you about church and religion, but I'm not in the mood today. In fact, I agree with you in your diatribe against formalized religion; but surely Christmas carols and Christmas music and the birthday of Christ should not be included. Oh, well, I didn't go to church myself, so let's drop the subject, yes? I think I understood your philosophy of life, so much akin to mine, and I do love you for your courage in your convictions, I sometimes waiver in mine.

*   *   *   *   *

Sat. 7:00PM. Dec 26, 1942

My Sweetheart -

    But to get to your letters. Sat. Dec 19 - First I shall point out glaring mistakes in spelling and grammar (don't take offense, but I got a bang out of your teasing your brother for his good "spelling" - you should talk!)

1) "Your itching for an explanation" - should be "you're" (you are) itching; otherwise you intimate that I am itching - contraction of you are; not possessive pronoun.

2) "nowhere's" should be "nowheres" minus the apostrophe - that's no contraction. [*Modern American Usage* lists "nowheres" as dialectical]

3) "mutual happy surprise" - mutually happy surprise.

4) "to be under its affect" should be effect - affect is never a noun [before the days of the psychiatrists!]; it's always a verb transitive, meaning to produce an effect upon. This puzzled me and I verified my suspicions in Webster's. Same goes for "alcoholic affects" - should be "effects"

5) "to be lieing on the couch" - Hm, you have trouble with "laying" and "lying" [Wrong! - in this case I merely had trouble with spelling! Pronunciation is correct word, but spelling implies telling a falsehood while sitting on the couch!?? However, she is absolutely correct in her accusation that I, at that stage of life, often shared with modern America the consistent confusion of "lay" and "lie", as she then notes and as is fre-

quently evident herein.] Should be "lying" meaning to <u>recline</u> - Simple, when you know how.

(You're not getting angry, are you? If you get to be an officer and spell like that, I'll feel it's my fault for not correcting you while there still was time, and hope.)

Spelling boners

1) <u>carress</u> - should be <u>caress</u>

2) <u>rythm</u> - " rhythm

3) crescendoes " crescendo (a noun; not a verb [Before the era of jargonization of the language!]

4) ectsasies " ecstasies

5) irresitible " irresistible

6) nacreous " no, that's right - had to look this up - "mother of pearl". hm?

I hate calling those errors to you, darling, but perhaps you'll appreciate it! Your thoughts are so beautiful, why mar them with misspelled words, says I?

*　　*　　*　　*　　*

1:30AM Friday December 25, 1942

My darling:

. . . . Like your Christmas card too, just something about those shy, coy little blue pastel lambs that remind me of you; and seeing that precious little "ME" on them. Love you my lambfleece soft as moonglow on silent heaps of cloud.

Have passed my physical exam I guess. They don't let you know unless you fail and there is nothing on which I would fail, so now you can concentrate your little worries on when school starts.

Love
Robert

*　　*　　*　　*　　*

Merry Christmas

10:30PM Friday Dec 25, 1942

My precious love

Rereading your letter of Mon. Don't start back for any more of

196

that labor legislation schooling. It's a very boring waste of time. If you want to go to school, why not take up something like Russian, Chemistry, Anatomy, Literature, Music (PIANO), Sculpturing, anything that has some life, some interest to it.

The day was spent studying Ulysses. Finished the book and am annotating it, noting the poetically beautiful passages, the psychological truths, and cross annotation of some of the thot relationships. I think that you would gain a great deal from this book not only as a work of art but also as a vicarious experience in the general mind. Somehow you seem to have escaped the commonplace experiences of most people. That is the way at least you appear to me, tho I can't figure out how you could live in the middle of an environment yet admit no traces of it. I will arm you with the necessary vocabulary, explanations, summary, etc, and you should be able to enjoy the greatest literary work of our century. Besides the vulgarities with which you are unfamiliar, Joyce, as one of the greatest masters of English, employs a startling vocabulary. Reading Ulysses I have come across 50 words I couldn't fathom, but they're in the Oxford dict. - Am enclosing a bit of nonsense I typed out in the orderly room. Playing with words. Even nonsense looks good when typed up. Like E.E. Cummings. Could you type out some of my better attempts sometime just to see what they look like. With perhaps a little revision I could be a poet. No? Yes? (Check in proper space) I love you so much my darling.

Longingly
Robert

SPRING IN the HEART of AKYAB

Blossoming in wimby-pamby wavelets
over lutulent beautulent rutilance
cascading in silver
    R
      ipp
        let
           s
           to splash dripplehappy
in mirror perfect pools
Oh, see the dappled fluid
    dripped in little droplets

coil in Liquid
        Per
      i
            stal
                sis?!

*   *   *   *   *

Dear Mrs Doty:
    Am up at the library listening to Rachmaninoff's Concerto #2. This Farnsworth radio and phonograph reproduces it just like the concert hall, marvelous.
    Sibelius #1 E Minor

I

Weird black flame
Formless flowing
Of visible thunder.
Night cloud, opaque,
Sullenly diffusing,
Thickening slowly,
Slowly thru the glittering ice,
Ponderous upon
Diaphanous diamond frost.
Crackling contact of crisp snow
Brushed with black flame.

II

Ominous whirr of wings,
Giant flight of evilshape.
The bat's heart heard beating
Eerie rhythms
Of Satanic power. POWER! unleashed,
Surging, fear filling, rumbling to
Irruption; avalanched in liquid fire,
Hot massive scourge, whipped,
Down plunging to the bottomless. . . .

III

And from the pit
An echo flowering,
Swiftly blossoming, in graceful
Pirouettes, dances on rosewarm toes
Across the ruby tinted snow, daintily

198

And with love, like the quiet
Moonkiss on deep green waters.

*   *   *   *   *

And now back from the library, hasty impression of Sibelius being finished, I'll answer my darling's letter. This lost one of Tues.

Dreaming on the L. I dream a lot, too, sweetheart, remembering all our past, trying to picture the future. Usually stick to the past; it is so much clearer, is beautifully behind us and free from worry. Our glorious enchanted summer and the Sunday mornings we spent inseparable in our cozy coupe. Starved Rock, the afternoon before we were married spent in deliberation (scared, both of us) in Columbus Park, the nervous happy tom collins after the ceremony and getting mad downtown cause my little girl wouldn't cross the streets.

Vividly remember the first time we kissed, your round full breasts enticing beneath your fuzzy orange sweater, lovely face and hair framed in soft fur, deep souled eyes set in Slavic cheeks, all this beauty building to the climactic ecstasy of passion kissed firmly, longing lips seeking for their mate, now found.

And never to be left beloved. I feel them kiss me every nite so tenderly, lovingly, as only such a sweet wife could kiss her husband.

Good nite my dream, snuggled caressably in sheets, so lonely the other hollow in the mattress

Love
Robert

*   *   *   *   *

[Begun with a kiss]

Monday - Dec 28, 1942 - 9PM

Dearest: - I LOVE YOU -

Am experimenting with sweet potatoes. [Her first attempt at "gardening", an endeavor in which she subsequently became extraordinarily adept.] Somebody told me ½ potato put in jar of water will grow into beautiful vines which will last all winter. So I quartered the "spuds" and time will tell.

Sweet - I do so miss you - Just ache for the love and warmth of your arms, your caresses. Worse some days than others - So

199

good to have you write that you feel that way, too - Best of luck re
OCS

Lovingly and Longingly
Elizabeth, Your wife

* * * * *

Tuesday, Dec. 29, 1942 9PM

Dearest Darling -

Two of my gals not down today — enjoying a bit of vacation
until Jan 4. I didn't dare take any time off although the Colonel
said I could. Huh! I should jeopardize my chances of leave in the
future as if and when you get a furlough or somethin — maybe
graduation from OCS!

Another item under Phooey Column! I had to "fish" out my
sweet potato halves from the mason jar, jam jar and vases, and
eat 'em today! Discovered I should suspend a whole potato with
toothpicks in a jar, with root end just touching the water in order
to produce my beeootiful green vines. Oh, the trials and tribulations of an amateur horticulturiste (feminine).

Darling, how my whole life revolves about you! And wotta
thrill to have me addressed as "Mrs. Doty". So happy we had the
courage to get married when we did. How empty life would seem.
I would feel I had been cheated of so much, if we had just let our
"courtship" drag on. Dearest, I hope I continue to be of cheer
and consolation to you during this separation, as much as you
have been to me.

* * * * *

10:45PM Thursday December 31, 1942

My most adorable swak: [She had initiated this acronym, Sealed With
A Kiss, on one of her letters with a lipstick sealed kiss.]

Loved, and how I could swak you now, pretty willing lips greasy
from eating savage broiled steak with butter hair mussed breasts
loose and playful in old housecoat sitting warm on my thighs so
heavy shall we relax.

Am anticipating that copy of "Impressions" or stuff by R.W.D.,
typed lovingly by Mrs R.W.D., the subject of most of them.

Your coming to see me, darling, seems miraculously to have

200

turned the world in our favor. Going to school so soon is really a break. It is 11:30 now so I must stop. All the poor "trainees" have been in bed for an hour or so. It will be hard in a way to become a trainee again at school after these few weeks of freedom, but I'll be a good one. I know I'll never fail because I'm not good enough, but let's not count too heavily on that commission till I get it. The army plays some odd tricks sometimes. And on the bottom of my sweetheart's letter "Best of luck re OCS" - Together, always, my prophetess

Love
Robert

*   *   *   *   *

WESTERN UNION

CAF308 11 COLLECT=TDPT CAMPLEE VIR 31 737P 1942 DEC 31 PM 7:45
MRS ELIZABETH N DOTY=
1001 SOUTH MAYFIELD AVE=
STARTING SCHOOL SATURDAY. KEEP WRITING. FORTUNE SMILES. LOVE=
ROBERT.

*   *   *   *   *

CHAPTER VII
Officer Candidate School

Synopsis - These were three months of intense pressure, for both of us. Elizabeth had to follow hopefully, but helplessly, the distant strivings of her so dearly beloved partner. As will be evident in some of her letters, the stress was, indeed, severe for her as well as for myself. She worked 6 full days a week, managing the Labor Relations Office of the Great Lakes Division of the Corps of Engineers; with two girls to supervise, and shoulder the responsibilities in the frequent absence of the Lt Col (Jensen) in charge. Despite all, we maintained our daily correspondence, often 8 pages from her.

In editing this voluminous correspondence, however, from 160,000 to a mere 32,000 words, I have given considerable precedence to descriptions of the life of an embryo officer, a "90-day wonder", as the epithet goes. Still, there are many revealing passages as to our marital relation, including small yet potentially pernicious tensions between us. While she manifests a much more muted argument than did I (as was also true in our expressions of passion), she nevertheless holds her own, and is not about to be dominated by my perception of things, regardless of my overextended vehemence. The seeds of our great crisis (Chapter VIII) are also sown, as we begin to face the problem of our possible togetherness following my graduation.

Finally, as graduation and its attendant leave approaches, expressions of craving for each other come to occupy much of the correspondence, a sexual melody of incrementing intensity.

Cadet R.W.Doty
Co. F 4th QMS Regiment
TR 026
Camp Lee, Va
4:30PM Saturday January 2, 1943

My Darling:

Here I am at school at last. I am now a Cadet with grade of corporal. Quartered in a one room tar paper shack with a cement floor and 40 beds. The 40 beds are being filled up spasmodically this afternoon with various 1st sergeants, Tech 4th grd, staff sergeants, as they arrive from Oregon, Florida, etc. This is the same type of barracks I had at Fort Custer. Stove heated with the latrine across the street. The lights are very few so I don't know where I'll do my writing (if I have time).

Master sergeant from Arizona arrives, another with 6 years infantry and 2 overseas stripes. This is going to be tough competition. They are chosen for companys according to size. I'm sure in with a bunch of bruisers. The negro lad next to me, Mitchum is 6'4" 220 lbs. Every man in this Company is 6' or over. Was surprised to find some real men after the droops I'd seen picked from the Q.M. Many of these lads are from Ordnance, Artillery, Armored Force, Signal Corps, etc.

*   *   *   *   *

8PM Sunday January 3, 1943

My dearest wife:

The Co. Com. is Capt. Hoff, a short redhead, snappy, business like and a swell guy. Can really bite off the orders but he's not one of those "ramrods". The assistants, Lt. Knox and 1st Sarg Oliver, come in the same category. All seem very competent, strict, but human. We cleaned up our classroom this morn. Same type of bldg as our barracks. 64 desks, a junky, but very usable imitation of the office desk. I have desk #26 so that I can see and hear OK. #64 is about 40 yards from the instructor.

The whole atmosphere is better here. No hillbillys or morons and all the boys are really trying, under constant surveillance.

It's a pleasure to march in the 6-ft. F Co, and seems almost miraculous to march blocks without anyone counting cadence and have everyone stay in step. Back in basic, cadence had to be counted constantly and still half the jerks would joggle along as they damn well pleased. No chow hounds in the mess hall and the

203

atmosphere actually makes the food taste better. Before it used to be like a bunch of pigs at the slop trough, your food heaped all on one plate. This is a long ways from West Point, but we have a few pine trees around the grounds and an earnest intelligent bunch of men. We have cadet battalion, company and platoon commanders that change weekly. Everybody gets a chance to practise this stuff. You can be company commander one day and KP the next. There is a compulsory study period from 6:30 to 8:30 PM every nite except Sat and Sun. Lites go out at 9:30 PM and the usual 11 PM bed check. Took a shower in ice cold water in a large cold shower room last nite. Envigorating [sic] if you live thru it.

9:10PM Monday January 4, 1943

My beloved:

I studied army regulations for two hours. That is my weak point because I've never had any of it. These regular military subjects like map reading, tactics, field operations, will be fairly easy for me. It is going to be a hard grind tho. Just the nervous tension of knowing you are constantly watched in everything you do and can be gigged for the least deviation from the straight and narrow, is tough to stand up under. They expect to flunk out about 20-30 out of a company of 150.

Love you so much but I'm afraid there won't be much time to say so for 3 months. I've been in the army only 3 months and it seems like that many years. Most likely able to see you after the 90 days terror is over, but certainly not before. It is a feeling of progress in life tho, which will compensate us for this even greater separation. I'll try to write daily, but it looks like the letters will be very hurried affairs.

*   *   *   *   *

Friday, Jan 1, 1943 9PM

Robert Darling -

Oh, I must relate this remark of Maj McElroy's re Miss Mack's date with Maj Wilhelm (just back from the Solomon Islands, he used to be in the zone office) last nite. "Purely Platonic", says Maj M. in his New Yorker accent in commenting thereon, "Play for her, and tonic for him!" Now I know why I could never maintain such a friendship!

*   *   *   *   *

My dearest:

I had a very happy coincidence occur, too. We were out "policing" the area for butts, etc. when whom do I meet but Gaffney. He's in the 2nd Platoon, too. To him I perhaps owe part of my being in OCS. At least he was one of the first links in the chain that landed me here. Way back in October, me a rookie in Co K, was recognized by Sgt Gaffney as an exceptional rookie. It was he who appointed me to the right guide position and that helped immensely for me to strut my stuff. That led the way for that "excellent leadership" recommendation by Capt Murch, a big factor in considering OCS applicants. Gaffney left for OCS last November and I remember thinking then he'd make a damn good lieutenant. (He was the other man I had in mind that could polish shoes better than I could.) Well, he landed in the hospital for 6 weeks, and so here we are in the same class same platoon; and I've been able to repay him for that right guide position by giving him instruction in all 3 days of school he missed. I think we'll do a lot of studying together.

Have another good partner too, Ray Brown. He sleeps next to me and our desks are together so naturally we collaborate a bit. He's 27, not handsome but quite intelligent and intellectual. From N.Y. and has gone to NY City College which is somewhat like our U of C. We had a couple interesting discussions all ready [sic] on Petroushka, Fantasia, psychoanalysis, traumatic neurosis, etc. He's the first person I've met in the army really able and qualified to participate in such discussions.

Might say a word about our instructors. They are lieuts and if their class doesn't come out with good grades they are activated; therefore they really are interested in putting the stuff across. Our Military Law instructor is a dandy. A former whiz of a lawyer he looks and acts every bit the part. He paces the platform just like he were talking to a jury with all the gestures etc. The Map Reading teacher is a dope and has the whole class confused because all he can do is read the lesson from the book. No analogies, or simplification. You can't teach that way. He can't confuse me tho because I've read the book too, and have simplified it for myself by explaining it to the poor cadets he has bewildered.

*   *   *   *   *

Monday January 4, 1943

Roraty, the "would-be mature savant", doesn't he go to

OCS with you? How were you 36 from the 7th QM chosen? Do you know? More laurels for you? Do you revert to KP and stuff? I should think you'd be busy enough with your studies. I think that you "elites" would be spared those ignominious tasks! Don't think you are considered a trainee, darling. You're an OCS Cadet! I know how you feel about not wanting to identify yourself with anyone like Roraty or Oscarson. I'm that way, too, darling an incorrigible individualist. Turrible, we'll probably never belong to any organizations or groups or anything! [Her prediction was remarkably accurate.] Maybe we'll mellow out, tho, before we're old and gray.

*   *   *   *   *

9 PM Saturday January 9, 1943

Woman memory my
life joy always

Have been wallowing in the delight of your letters, soaking up each precious word; as you say, a part of you. We are both black skies awaiting the glory of the coming morn, but the glittering stars of your letters must suffice for present promise. Am so happy to know that my little one is starting the piano again. Please do, so that I may spend the rest of my life listening to you. Music, too, is such a far superior companion compared to most people. Don't let people intrude on your time sweetheart. I suppose you have "Ulysses" by now and it too will take up quite a bit of time. Huxley [an author she liked] and Joyce are not to be mentioned in the same breath. Huxley writes of nonexistent people, continental type play characters. They probe some of life's problems but are abnormal, thinly disguised puppets for plotless rhetoric. Huxley is good but Joyce is one of the greatest. After reading Ulysses I think you will see what I mean. Joyce builds a balanced concrete image of man and his mind using with perfect mastery and skill all the means of literature. Studying Ulysses and the piano, and writing, and listening to music, should fill up a Sunday perfectly darling. (Perfect for these days) Your mention of other books. I think we should, must have all of Shakespeare's Sonnets, and the complete works of Conrad Aiken. Their [sic] is also a book by Farrell I believe called "Studs Lonigan" which has quite a reputation as a character study of man, especially man and youth of the 20th century. It is particularly interesting as its locale is Chicago right in our neighborhood

206

around Chicago and Cicero Aves. That might prove worth getting. I was reading Thomas Wolfe's "Look Homeward Angel" before coming to OCS but had to give it up here. It was an autobiographical book, very good and worth reading. There seems to be an opening in the field of literature for some woman to write a "woman mind" and "mental life" book. I'm sure that a man cannot depict perfectly the inner experience of a girl growing into a woman. There is no substitute for actual experience upon which to base such a work. I can by studying, discussing, living with, and the common fact of humanness, come close to expressing "woman," but yet never having been thru the life long experience of living it, my writing of woman mind could not be as true a picture as that written by a woman.

. . . then had lecture on guard duty and a surprise evacuation. After we stood in the woods about 20 min and the Colonel drove by in his jeep, we were released for chow of beans, cabbage, apple slice and lemonade; the usual Saturday evening policy of driving the men into town for food. I went straight to the woods after chow and got in about 1 hr practise. That always puts me in a good mood.

You are right darling. I think I will be able to take school in an easy going stride. These other lads are worrying and bewildering themselves, but so far it's been duck soup for me. Even the Company Administration with which I expected trouble. I'll wait for a couple exams before I start buying officer's clothes. Am not the least afraid of flunking out, but I do fear the habit the army has of changing its mind.

*　　*　　*　　*　　*

9PM Sunday January 10, 1943

Got your Thurs letter today precious. Your birthday kisses fondly impressed. I love you my luscious little swak and when this 3 mos is over I think I'll be able to swak and squeeze you hours on end.

You mention about KP. We not only have to do KP, we are graded on it too! The Colonel says any man who can't do a good KP can't be a good officer. He's right in a way. - I sure hope the Russians take Rostov and fast. That will be one of the greatest victories of the war.

. . . darling I do actually dream of you so much. The other nite I had a very intense erotic dream; we were making you a mother, my sweetest wife. How happy will be the day when we can peacefully start our family. May they all be so lovely as their mother.

Their loving father,
Robert

*   *   *   *   *

9:45PM Monday Janurary 11, 1943

My sweetest wife:

A hasty note tonite written in the mobbed latrine.

Took a shower last nite in the ice cold water in a room where I could easily see my breath, about 35 for room and 32 for water, and will most likely have to do a repeat tonite. The "polar bears" have nothing on me and it's good toughening if a bit rough at first.

Usual morning of law, map reading, morning report, methods of instruction, etc.

Longing to be snuggling up to you
Robert

*   *   *   *   *

9PM Tuesday January 12, 1943

And listen, no big head from you. That social take off stuff doesn't appeal to me at all, Major or Private is all the same as far as I'm concerned, so soft pedal that "wives of the OCS men" stuff. It's disgusting. You've got too much Army in your head working for that damn war dept. Rank, social scale, caste system, Major and Mrs Doty. Forget it sweetheart. These "hand picked men from millions", there are plenty not so hot.

Take it easy on that housecleaning business. You're no scrub maid, don't cover the furniture with gooey wax. You could put your time to better use than washing and scrubbing floors so don't!

You're [sic] letters are important dearest. They are the happiest and most important event of my day. So much more than idle chit chat.

Don't let my lecturing to you make you angry (for long). I get mad when you tell me off in some letters but just for an instant. Have to have some substitute for our particular type of family brawl. Such precious memories darling, our home and married life.

*   *   *   *   *

10:30 PM Thursday January 15 [=14th!], 1943

My dearest:

This will be very short. Have just finished 18 hours KP 4:30 a.m. to 10:30 PM. Very tired, sticky, sick feeling, etc. They really give you hell here just for the hell of it I guess. All day long I anticipated getting back to the barracks to find a letter from you. And I wasn't disappointed. You're so sweet darling. How I would appreciate falling quickly to sleep in your arms tonight.

*   *   *   *   *

9:15 PM Friday January 15, 1943

Darling my wife:

Cleanup over, both the barracks and me. Took my shower early in a futile effort to avoid the cold water. Still dopey this morn from that dishwashing grind yesterday. Studied organization of field army and corps. Have an exam on that stuff tomorrow, and I missed three hours of it while on KP. Had squad drill this aft. I had squad for 15 min or so and did fairly well though a bit rough in spots. Hard to drill men around about 50 square feet of coal pile, telephone poles, and barracks when you haven't done it for 6 years. Turned them over to Gaffney tho and he did a fine job.

*   *   *   *   *

7:30 PM Saturday January 16, 1943

My precious

Got two beautiful letters from you today. Love you so much my sweetness. How I wish I had been there to make you squeal as I slapped the Vicks on your chest, lovingly doctoring my little girl. Sounds tho like you are doing a good job for you for me so you should be better now. Hope so that you are, even if you are back to work. I'm glad you stayed home, for the change and rest did you good despite the bodily sickness. And my sweetheart is really going after the piano this time! I'm so glad. — That poem "Love Songs" by Mina Loy (who is she or he?) is _very_ good. Not much to explain about it. It is a symbolic-mind-poem of 20th-century tainted sex-love. Instead of writing the dreamy romantic love poem, she has presented the philosophized love act, culminated drunkenly in the back seat of a roadster. (Not actually, just typically.) The beauty of the act is played against its vulgarity. "Pig Cupid" "erotic garbage" "wild oats sown in mucous membrane" "daily news printed in

209

blood" "there are suspect places". What fine metaphors in Part II "skin sack" "wanton duplicity" (God and devil) "A God's door mat" (hair). The triple word meaning in "bed-ridden," "broken flesh with one another". It is a kaleidoscopic word picture, a mental impression of cheapened love; yet in a philosophical vein.

To look for a plot or description of action in such a poem is futile. It is an abstraction and must be taken by its word, symbolic and associational affects [sic!]. Here is one somewhat like it which I wrote long ago:

Who flew past me in the night
What wing brushed my hair
Wandering in silence
Like snakes in darkness
On a winding stair
Cool bellies slithering close.
Smooth marble cold.

*   *   *   *   *

Quiet as a thot it came
Turquoise drops in the pool of mind
Leaving; gone.
A ripple of azure cloud sinks,
Spreading, diffuse in crystal pool.
O cloud of memory, we cannot
Condense the nite, brush nor dream
In stone. Did I kiss Undine
Or Anubis?

I believe it gives a different impression like a dazed awakening from an erotic nightmare, but both poems are similar in abstract form of word impression. I like hers better, tho, it's more understandable.

What beautiful memories we do share my darling; never to be forgotten those summer moments lying close in young passion on your mother's couch. Crushed sweatily together, earnestly desiring, fearing finalities, but locked mouths together in desperate sensuous kisses.

And what beauty has resulted! From two dabblers in the thrills of youth-love a man and woman mated, eternally bound in union, a living whole, a separateness become one. And some day from the glorious fierceness of that possessive passion there will blossom from darkness in pain the culminating oneness, union of two souls in one being, blending of bodies mind seed to become flower, giving eternity. Love needed and found, enraptured music of pure beauty.

wrapped in dreams and music, for the moment oblivious of world horror, we say how good to live beauty and life. Some day we will feel this to ourselves, nestled together, thrilling to love and music in the happy darkness of our home. Our home darling us one roof, one bed, one purpose, one love, and all sprung brilliantly coruscating from a rain squall. Oh marvelous life. [This, of course, refers to the fact that we first met when I volunteered to drive her home during a rain squall after evening school!]

I must say goodnight once more and leave you with so many kisses dreamed upon your eager loving lips. I blow a kiss and caress to the moon to place gently on your eyes.

Tenderly my love -
Robert

*　　*　　*　　*　　*

Wednesday - 9PM - Jan 20 '43

Precious, My Darling -

I thought you'd like Mina Loy's "Love Songs". Frankly I was a bit embarrassed to find it included in the anthology of poems I gave Sis for Xmas. Thanks for the explanation, it's not a very pleasant presentation, though? I suppose I'm an old-fashioned romanticist, but my thoughts on sex are such glorious, ecstatic ones, I prefer to cloud them all in a rosy glow, emphasize the effects rather than the actual physical aspects.

Darling, your poem, "Who flew past me in the night," etc? Didn't you write that while I was in Cleveland? So familiar.

We do have such lovely memories. I put myself to sleep at night recalling some little incident between us since our meeting. Am doing it more or less chronologically. Last night I got to us in Winona Minnesota in our "bridal suite" that night when you initiated me into the mysteries of connubial bliss. Quite a tearful bride I was then! How sweet and understanding you were, darling! Fess up, my dear it was a trial, wasn't it? I mean to restrain your ardor, and it was so fiercely passionate. Oh, halcyon days, full of little trials and tribulations a secret between us forever. So

211

happy we did go through that, instead of being worldly wise and blasé.

Darling, by now you've received my Saturday letter. Notice the coincidence? Both of us writing at 7:30 PM, and I, too, was listening to Strauss' "Don Quixote" as I wrote to you and was reminded of you so much, darling! Music to me is so identified with you, a symbol of our love.

I put an hour on piano playing tonight, and systematically going through finger exercises, learning a lot as I go along. Coordination is difficult, dear. I can read music faster than I can play, sometimes and vice versa other times! Playing the keyboard certainly involves use of muscles never before utilized. I will develop me a good strong hand. I am really fascinated by the thing. Have no illusions of my musical ability, but trying to "make music" certainly gives you a greater appreciation of music as a whole; and it is a fine pastime (and inexpensive now that the piano is paid for!) Think this is much better than stuffy labor legislation at DePaul. Get 'nuff of that at work!
(Radio notes - just heard "Bewitched, Bothered and Bewondered", how well that describes me since first I set eyes on you.) So now I've got some Hungarian dance, tarantella-like rhythm that starts a warm glow flowing through your veins. I shouldn't be bothered with rhythm in my piano playing, heaven knows I'm very susceptible and responsive to it; savage reaction, I guess. Maybe it's the Tartar blood in me. But I love my rhythm!

I promise not to scold or philosophize, 'cause I know you don't like it. The beauty of the letter, no backtalk while it's being written. Seriously, I reciprocate your devoted adoration wholeheartedly, and bodily, and every which way, my loved one
Elizabeth

*　　*　　*　　*　　*

Dearest sun song, smile glittering,
Fresh blown from the clean mouth of morning
Eyes so keen, lovely, being JOY
To look deep into them, seeing trust,
And sweetness, Happy as the sun darts,
Dancing on ever moving waters. -

- And I look and love always darling so beautiful your picture, your letters, you and all our life together.

Today has been a day of leisure, spring and warmth, and I gave in to "spring fever". Spent the morning reading the paper and Life and cleaning up the latrine since I was on the latrine squad.

* * * * *

8:45PM Thursday January 21, 1943

Sweetest wife

Hardly seems like tomorrow is Friday, almost 3 weeks gone. Time is moving fast here, the faster the better. Have my full schedule made out. Regular army hours and my practising (5:45 - 6:30PM) and my writing my darling after study hours, and then shower and bed at 11. It is no fuller than the program I have followed for years; in fact I don't even read a book at meals now as I did in civilian life. If and when this accursed war ends and we get back together again, darling, I have 3 constant aims, one a family for us, an M.D. (even at 50) for me, and music (horn and piano) for us too [two??]. We can do it. After this anything will be possible, the more so when we're together. Dreaming always of us, my wife, our love -

Robert

* * * * *

9PM Saturday January 23, 1943

Photo Section 1

1 - Left to right: "Iggy" Radzun (just returned from World War I), Marinya Radzun Jusewich, Basilia, "Lily" (the only one smiling), Michael Jusewich - 1920.

2 - Lisaveta Natalya, 3 years old, defiant to demands of the world - 1918.

3 - Elizabeth makes her confirmation, unsmiling as unbelieving - 1929.

4. - House at 2115 South Trumbull, Chicago, owned by Elizabeth's parents, who occupied the first floor and rented out the upstairs. This is where Elizabeth lived when we met, where she lived for several interludes during the war; and where, from May through August 1946, we and our new son shared these quarters with the Jusewich family. Photo taken 25 October 2001.

5 - Robert and his mother - 1920.

6 - High school Reserve Officer Training Corps - 1936. This experience was of inestimable value to the draftee 6 years later.

7 - 5820 Race, Chicago, where Robert roomed, on the second floor front, and where he brought his bride, September, 1941. Photographed 25 October 2001.

8A and B - The bride and groom, taken at automatic photo machine, Hotel Schroeder, Milwaukee, Wisconsin, 30 August 1941. Other pictures of the occasion were even more out of focus.

9 - 1001 South Mayfield, Chicago, our apartment, first floor, left, from 15 Nov 1941 until Elizabeth surrendered it, 1 June 1943, to join Lt Doty at Fort Warren. Photographed 25 October 2001.

10 - In front of 5820 Race, September 1941, the car that was the womb of our love.

11 - 1942, Elizabeth at work, Corps of Engineers. Photograph by Lt Col Jens Peter Jensen.

12 - Elizabeth the bride, in our car, September 1941.

13 - 30 April 1942, last day of vacation, along the Desplaines River, Illinois.

14 - Elizabeth and Eva Madora Mack, Robert's maternal grandmother, Ann Arbor, Michigan, 22 April 1942, starting our vacation after the Cleveland episode.

15 - Laurel Falls, Smoky Mountains, 25 April 1942.

16 - The trumpet player, 24 September 1942, ready for the army.

17 - 24 September 1942. This is the picture she hand colored and which I kept, in one version or another, throughout my army life.

18 - 24 September 1942, the draftee, leaving the next day.

19 - Basic training, 7 November 1942, after 12 mile march returning from bivouac.

20 - January 1943, in the coat she wore when she visited Robert in Petersburg.

21 - Barracks at OCS, my bunk (with the footlocker) untidy because it is Sunday (24 January 1943).

22 - March, 1943 - foolishness, but also serious, that the QMC should pay more attention to training for combat.

23 - March, 1943 - following training exercise in kneading 150 lbs of bread dough.

24 - 4 April 1943, Elizabeth, proud of her Lieutenant husband, at my parent's home.

25 - 8 April 1943, the brand new Lieutenant.

26 - 4 April 1943, a miserable picture, to show my sentimentality for the "old" army, a Sam Browne belt (for carrying one's sword!) and a fancy hat. Both, rather thankfully, went down with my ship.

27 - 12 April 1943, just before Robert's departure, alone, for Fort Warren, Wyoming. Happy to be together, uncertain about the future.

28 - 20 June 1943, an ebullient moment during our few hours in Chicago, enroute from Ft Warren to New York Port of Embarkation, both of us happy that I had prevailed in our fierce argument about her surrendering job and apartment to join me.

29 - 27 June 1943, visiting Elizabeth's uncle, John Zielinski, in Brooklyn prior to ship assignment.

30 - 20 July 1943, Newport News, Virginia, while awaiting convoy formation. Elizabeth is dressed for our dinner with Lt Patterson and his wife at Old Point Comfort.

31 - September, 1943, Atlantic convoy, showing a sister ship also transporting German POWs. Note how high the "unloaded" ship rides out of the water.

32 - 6 January 1944, the sinking Wm S. Rosecrans, taken from lifeboat and out of focus in my excitement and the heavy seas. Note, compared to Fig 31, how low in the water she has settled in these few minutes; my starboard, below deck office undoubtedly flooded by then.

33 - January, 1944, stopover in Oran on one of my numerous flights to return to the USA from Italy after the Rosecrans was sunk.

34 - 16 April 1944, fighter plane deck cargo on Nathan B. Forrest, taken during brief stop at Aden.

35 - 28 April 1944, in Karachi, India (at that time) showing that Americans make little point of dignity.

36 - 30 June 1944, Mrs Doty acting up as her AWOL husband makes a brief stopover in Chicago, enroute from Los Angeles to Brooklyn Army Base.

37 - 11 February 1945, on a visit to one of Elizabeth's co-workers in the Bronx.

38 - 1 April 1945, Elizabeth just before she became pregnant.

39 - 18 February 1945, one of our evening pastimes in our Brooklyn apartment.

40 - 1168 Brooklyn Ave, Brooklyn, where we lived in a basement apartment from 15 November 1944 to 30 October 1945; in which of these houses is no longer remembered.

41 - April 1945, another evening in our Brooklyn home.

42 - Room of RWD on the Josiah Bartlett from 2 October 1945 to 18 January 1946, for voyage to New Orleans, Antwerp, and Azores with 676 troops after furious Atlantic storm. Note Elizabeth's picture beside the upper bunk in which I slept.

43 - 30 January 1946, the $90 35-mm camera. From that time on all black and white photos were developed and printed, and now also digitized, by RWD.

44 - Experimenting with "still life" with the new camera.

45 - "Shore duty", Spring 1946, here posing with a ship's screw (propeller) at Todd Shipyards, after inspecting conversion of a ship to accommodate war brides.

46 - The former hospital ship, Huddleston, converted for "war bride duty", of which I became the Transport Commander, 4 April 1946. Note the painter above the port anchor.

47 - Self-portrait with the new camera aboard the Huddleston, with my photographic "art" in the background.

48 - April, 1946, poem and photography, awaiting reunion with my beloved.

49 - 3506 West 66th Place, Chicago, the home we bought and lived in from 7 September 1946 to 22 August 1951. Photographed 25 October 2001.

50 - Our infamous Graham Paige, with Robert Jr in the driver's seat.

51 - 30 May 1946, mother and 5-month-old Robert Jr.

52 - January 1947, ambitious parent, introducing offspring to books.

53 - June 1946, happy mother, quizzical Robert Jr.

2

4

5

6

7

8a

8b

13

14

15

16

7

18

9

20

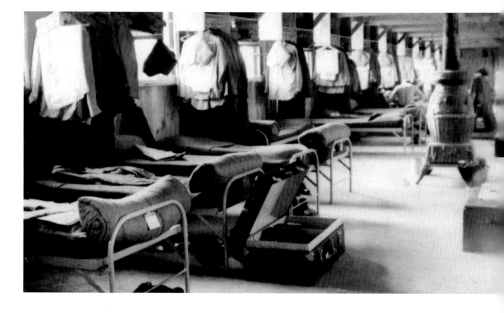

21

22

23

24

25

26

27

29

30

31

32

33

34

35

36

37

39

40

41

42

43

44

45

46

47

And as the swollen tide
Doth gently overtake the sand,
Importunate, with foamsoft hand
So too, slowly, insistent in demand
My mouth your lips will soon Command!

48

49

50

51

53

52

PERPETUATION [The first lines refer to her picture, Fig 20, recently received.]

My smiling bundle of squeeze tight
Wooly warm woman beauty muffled in lamb fur,
Cold puppy nose puckering playfully,
And a face to fit two firm hands drawing
Forward the willing lips,
Eagerly, for the flesh welded kiss.
Oh never cease, be forever thus,
Mouths mated, molding love,
Current of a thousand lives
Flowing in swift ecstasy
From soul to soul.
Passing the keen spark of mystery,
Energy exultant,
Muscles flexed, expectant;
Unleash the lightning of delight
Into a world forever bright.
Oh this is perpetuation!
This is to throb with life,
To plunge united,
Like two flaming suns,
Bursting, glorious inferno;
Subsiding into fertile quiet;
Nourishing the severed flesh,
That it may grow.
TO KISS —- TO PERPETUATE.

Looking at your pictures darling you so sweet and lusciously hidden in your bulky coat. I started to write you. My imagination kept working, building, remembering the past until an orgasm of words seemed to gush from my pen to give the foregoing. Just couldn't stop. It has lifted the mood of sadness from me remarkably. Somehow purged me of the emotion of beauty craving, a longing, loneliness, which the evening had built up within me.

Reading your Wednesday letter made me so happy in that respect. — Those radio programs really do get you all riled up about Japs and stuff. — That other poem I sent you "Who flew etc." was of the Cleveland period but was unpublished to my most appreciative audience. — Don't give me that you "have to work like a Trojan to

217

get Sunday off". Time after time I've told you to forget about all this fool cleanup business. Let the apartment get dirty and it can't get very bad with just you there for a few hours a day.

Darling, I love every word you say, your scoldings, your philosophizing, your daily picture of you. It is the next best thing to living with you and being exposed to it all firsthand. So happy we will be when we can argue across the supper table about this and that. Don't ever think that I haven't enjoyed every minute of life with you darling, squabbles and all, for it is such an integral part of the beauty of our marriage, our lives together. Let's not cease, even by the woefully inferior letter, to carry on our pleasant little chidings, bickerings, etc. as well as all the spontaneous, exuberant kisses and hugs. It's all a part of our home beloved.

*   *   *   *   *

10 AM Sunday January 24, 1943

Darling:

Yesterday was inspection day and we had the Major look us over this time. Not many got gigged on the inspection in the barracks but when we went outside for the usual personnel [? sic] inspection he really laid it on. I've had 3 minor gigs so far and got none yesterday and believe me there were plenty that caught up with me yesterday. Not only were they gigged but they are sentenced to Sunday KP on top of it! We wear our overcoats every day, to eat, to school, roll them up and put them on the ground for calisthenics, and then on Saturday the Major comes around and passes out KP to those with dirty overcoats. That's the army. We also have no material to clean our rifle bores so about 20 guys got gigged for dirty bores. Fortunately the rifle issued to me is broken and scheduled for ordnance department so that I avoided that risk.

*   *   *   *   *

Thursday - 10PM Jan 21, 1943

Darling -

Well, my beloved, one of my sweet potatoes has repaid my loving care and attention by sprouting some beautiful long slender roots. The other one still refuses to react and so I've "planted" a third one. Fun this experimenting. I suppose in these days of food shortage I ought to eat the darn things; but I do want vines in the apartment. Someday I want oodles and oodles of

218

plants in my windows. [Two years after her death in 1999 I count 80 still remaining in our house.] Wish I could plant a Victory garden, too. Am going to try to get Mom to have one in her backyard.

* * * * *

9PM Tuesday January 26, 1943

My sweetest "frustrated female"

I love you with your letter just oozing with beautiful fiery temper; seeming to be a tantrum well becoming a Mrs R.W.D. Love you so much darling and I'm sure the hammer is in the kitchen table drawer because I salvaged it, I know, when I sold the car. What radio tubes blew out? Wouldn't we have had a fine "growl and bawl" session together my lovely, and could have kissed, resolved and comforted all day Sunday. Hope that you did spend the day sleeping mostly, precious, for I think you need it. This is as much or more of a strain for you as for me.

It makes me more than phooey to have you cleaning, washing etc. Do only the barest essentials of that stuff and then forget about them except once a month or so. When I do get home finally, dearest, there will be no beds made, floors or windows washed or any similar disgusting tasks for at least a year.

* * * * *

9:15PM Wed. January 27, 1943

My beloved:

Are you my darling wife or a laundress? I insist that you throw every one of those damn blouses in the fire or give them to some scrub woman that has nothing more important to do in her few hours of spare time than to wash and iron each tedious inch of foolishness. You should have more sense than to spend six laborious hours futilely frittering your time and energy on such stuff. There would sure be a big squawk if the W.D. asked you to put in six hours manual labor for NOTHING! So lay off that stuff at home, because if you aren't ingenious enough to figure out a way to avoid that nonsense you should go around dirty. I mean it too, and if the situation doesn't come under control, why when I do get home, we'll dispose of the iron permanently and buy no laundry soap or flakes at anytime. It burns me up. You haven't got time for this or that, you're tired, etc. etc., too much to be done etc., yet insist on that inane debauchery of common sense, money, time, nervous energy,

219

and indulge yourself in menially scrubbing and sweating away at a Chinaman's trade. That's hardly being smart or fair to yourself or to me. So no more!

Hard to get out of that angry mood now and settle down and write a letter to my sweetheart.

So much I wanted to write besides that lecture to you dearest. Sweeter things but you know that I am thinking them always, remembering and wishing and dreaming of the beautiful days to be as I did last night. Dreamed of caressing your breasts, full with mother's milk my wife mother of our children our fulfillment of love eternally

ROBERT

*   *   *   *   *

Tues. Jan 26, 1943 11PM

My Dearest Husband –

Have just come back from a soirée with Miss Balcomb (Ph.D. in Social Sciences, I wrote you about her) and now I must hurry to give you the day's developments which should be interesting.

We drove out to Ida Noyes Hall at U of C Campus. Longtime no see same; consequently nostalgia set in upon seeing the Gothic structures.

Well, about 300 people were in attendance at this affair, marking the 13th anniversary of India's Independence Day. Seems in 1930 the National Congress Party declared its aims for India's independence. A Miss Fowler (related to McCormick of Trib) and various other gals dressed in Indian costumes (what do they call those wrap around toga like affairs?) proceeded to dish out on plates cafeteria style a typical Indian meal. We were fortunate in having seats against the wall. Lots of people sat on rugs on floor, Indian fashion eating their food. For dessert gals passed around tangerines. The gastronomic treat over, we turned to the intellectual. First to speak was professor Maynard of U of C, Socialist candidate for alderman of 6th Ward. Then a Dr. Fall, negro physician, who spoke of our racial prejudices. Then a Dr. Sohr, Indian missionary who spoke of dear ole India. The final and best talk was by an Indian, a close friend of Nehru, leader of the National Congress Party. The theme of all the speeches was

220

to the effect that India should be given immediate independence as a prelude to freedom for all the peoples in Asia and elsewhere. Almost convinced me that British propaganda alone is responsible for our lack of enthusiasm or knowledge of India and her affairs. Very interesting and rather thought-provoking.

We left at 9:30 and Miss B. and I drove leisurely homeward. It's been 10 years since I had her for a teacher. We agreed it was a mutual pleasure to visit again and I invited her to come see me when we could really sit down and talk. Of course, she was very much interested in you, the man I married, and I really told her you were everything I had wanted in a husband.

Well, Indian meals don't satisfy my healthy appetite, so I proceeded to have me 2 good Dagwood type sandwiches in my own kitchen, relishing them and your Sat. letter. — Perpetuation, so spontaneous, so beautiful in its thought! Just how I feel when I'm near you darling; good phrases like "swift ecstasy","keen spark of mystery".

*   *   *   *   *

Wed - Jan 27, 1943 11PM

(Short letter - with apologies) [Opened with a ruby kiss]

Dearest Darling -

Music is such a bond between us, and it's not just a coincidence that all my letters are written to you with a musical background. Somehow I find it puts me in the mood for letter writing. To suggestions that I "type you a letter each day at the office, to save time," I turn a deaf ear. I think the environment, at least for me, is so important. Let's see what would happen if I were to answer your Sat. letter in the atmosphere of the office.

1st Indorsement

Elizabeth N. Jusewich (Doty), Office, G.L.D., Chicago, Ill.

27 January 1943

To: Cadet Robert W. Doty, Co. F, 4th QMSR, T-20 26, Camp Lee, Va.

1. With reference to basic communication, the following comments are noted for your information:

a. A critical analysis of poem contained in par. 1 thereof

221

cannot be rendered at this time due to the fact that no personnel with necessary qualifications are available at this station.

<u>b</u>. Regarding remarks concerning music, it is believed same are substantially correct.

Oh, heck, The above is a grande exaggeration, but that's about the mood I'd be in. But chez moi, I am a transformed individual, and give vent uninhibited thusly. The poem is beautiful, dearest; music is and will ever be a bond between us. I love to clean up the apartment;'course it tires me out but I like to feel that I, as well as you, dearest, can stand a surprise inspection any ole time! Besides, I am a trainee at present, preparing for the time when I, like you, can order some one else to do the work (maid maybe someday?) and how can I be a good mistress unless I know how to do the work myself (a la remark re KP by your Major?)

Joyce is OK, but right now I crave "escape" literature, war news.

Usual reluctance to crawl out of bed. I've dubbed the alarm "General Tyrant", so mercilessly disturbing my peaceful slumbers day after day!

Hope you get through this week OK. I know you will! Doc Anderson wrote me on receipt "I'll bet your hubby comes out of the army a Captain"; I bet you will, too.

*　　*　　*　　*　　*

Thursday - 9:30PM Jan 28, 1943

My Beloved Husband -

You call me "wonderful womanhood" and other things that cause something within me to tremble like a leaf. In reply I can only say this: when I think of you, I think of the beauty of muscular strength, the stream of energy that seems to flow from your body to mine, in a synchronized smooth rhythm; and how naturally I identify myself with you, my mate, with life itself!

Your Monday letter. Strange that both of us found ourselves in a "funk" last Friday; all of which proves what I've always claimed, we are so much alike in so many ways, Robert.

*　　*　　*　　*　　*

222

My most lovely

There is some keen competition in our platoon. We are not only the highest standing platoon in the class in scholastics, we are <u>10%</u> above the next one. In the returns on 4 exams there have been only 4 "U's" in toto whereas most platoons average 3 - 7 "U's" on each exam. However, if ours is the best I'd sure hate to see the worst, or have them for officers, for though there are some real men and a lot of them in our platoon, there is a very generous sprinkling of these GFUs that you wonder how they ever got past the first board and still they pass somehow.

*　　*　　*　　*　　*

7PM Saturday January 30, 1943

My always

Eight men from our company were taken out and sent to a two weeks basic training course. Then they come back and go in class two weeks behind us. They were men weak in their military. They do that to every class in an attempt to avoid letting out these "civilian" type officers. Doesn't do much good tho from some of the droops I've seen walking around with bars and Q.M. insignia.

*　　*　　*　　*　　*

8:30 PM Sunday January 31, 1943

My beloved:

Have spent all afternoon writing for you. Please find results enclosed and after three or four readings maybe it will clear up. It is supposed to present three emotional states and then there [sic] blending into one in the fourth panel, showing how all experiences may be blended into love; "molded on the apogee" of life's moments. It should be set up in the Sandburg prose poem style. Does it show the rugged fierceness, the inner poetry and outer tenderness of love?

KITTEN SONG SNOW WOMAN

I

Have you ever held a kitten
Ball of fragile FUR warmluscious
And felt the power of your hand curling
Could stifle crush this trust
But no, caressed softness with delighted fingers
Purring.

II

Have you ever lain under the stars
Listening to Tchaikovsky, intoxicated
With sound, tensing with power, quivering
With loneliness and your soul is mated to music
Saying mactation! Burn me, that I may be
Pure emotion in the sphere of Eternity.

III

Have you ever taken a heavy axe and buried its
Whistling steel deep into chip spitting wood or
Lashed a brutal leather fisted hand into a
Sweating face or trudged pack laden thru new
Snow and felt the joy of conquest as you
Tramped heedless across its Virgin Beauty.

IV

But oh completeness, summation of being
Lying crushed in moist kisses
Steeled muscles circled in mating
Knowing the sumptuous smoothness of
Woman body grasped in greedy tenderness,
Feeling the power surge of brute;
Tempted to crush her softness,
To bring tears to her recumbent smile,
But the leather fisted axe hand toys
Boyishly with eager flesh
And two souls quiver, vibrating a
LOVELIFESONG - a music echoing FOREVER
Have you culminated instants past
To span the future? The alloy of experience
Forged from what you have have you
Molded on apogee?

224

*   *   *   *   *

Mon 10PM Feb 1, 1943

My dearest darling precious husband!

Your darlin' is a very, very contrite little gal tonight - so, so sorry for those two polly-annish letters I wrote you Sat and Sunday. I am such a baby, to get hurt by your well-meant scolding in your Wednesday letter. I know I deserved it. Oh, sweetheart, forgive me!

*   *   *   *   *

Wed. Feb 3, 1943 - 10PM

Dearest -

I've got your Sunday letter before me. Say, that KITTEN SONG SNOW WOMAN masterpiece is everything you say it should be. Why 3 or 4 readings? I understood what you meant right away, but darling, panel IV almost scares me! It's such a vivid description of love. You do have the ability of choosing your words to really convey your ideas, Robert. Would you say I'm partly responsible, as an inspiration?

*   *   *   *   *

10PM Tuesday February 2, 1943

My beloved:

Had a very interesting hour, field-stripping of a .30 cal machine gun by Capt. Hoff. Secret: they are arming every 4th QM truck with a 50 cal m.g. Every man has a carbine or a rifle and each platoon has a couple rocket launchers. These rocket launchers are very secret weapons so I won't say anymore than that they are very effective against tanks. After seeing that British picture on disclosing Military Information it was brought forcefully home to me how rife this crime is. I came back from the theater to find a letter from my Dad telling all about how Eddie Ross had just finished convoying his 2nd trip to Africa etc. etc. Don't think that the info isn't just what the enemy wants, for just one little clue as to movement, armament, may be enough to start the massing of fact which will defeat the most perfectly timed operations.

*   *   *   *   *

225

My Wife:

This is an afternoon letter in reply to your two of Sat and Sun. It has come to a fine point when you have to tear up letters and circumvent events in order to send me "an innocuous and pleasant letter". Never have I asked or desired any such silly patter. You deliberately misinterpreted my Wed letter and you know it. It had nothing whatever to do with the type of letter you were writing. It was about what you were DOING at HOME that aggravated me. I said then, meant it, and still mean it, that I don't want you making a laundress out of yourself. To turn around and read it that I didn't want you to write me about it makes me MAD! "No more mention of tiredness or housework or laundry in any of my future letters". It is (I hope) perfectly obvious, that I had no reference to that aspect of it at all. You should know that if you know me at all. Avoid mentioning it **NO!** Avoid **DOING** it! A petty, nicey, "innocuous" letter would certainly not "relax" me. Would most likely not be worth reading so don't write or attempt to write any of that stuff.

I want YOU, what you're doing, what you're thinking good bad or indifferent, but I don't want you to sit down and compose some "innocuous" hodgepodge to cover up any actions or thots you may have that you think are distasteful to me. I don't live that way and I don't write that way, so no more tearing up letters. 4 <u>attempts</u> to write a letter. The 5th one which I got must really be an expurgated edition of you tho it still sounds okay, but if you are going to take time to write 4 letters I'd like to get them regardless of what you said. Had I been home I would undoubtedly have heard all about it and just because I'm 1200 miles away is no reason I don't want to know your mind as intimately as ever. The glorious success of our marriage has resulted largely from our accepting each other as human animals and appreciating and knowing each other's thots and emotions. Separation is no reason for us becoming angels. I still get angry at you down here just as well as I could when you bought lisle hose and I have no intention of writing about the snow and what I did in school etc. until I've had my say on what I don't like. So you do the same and stop the feminine strategy of misinterpreting my meaning for your convenience. I have never objected to a single thing in the contents or wording of your <u>letters</u> but I have very definite responses on the action or contemplated actions on your part of which you write. You "haven't any interesting things to say". I'll bet all the "interesting" things were in the letters you tore up.

226

*   *   *   *   *

10PM Friday February 5, 1943

My beloved:

    Am writing this in the guardhouse. Have just finished a 2-hour stroll in the rain from 6:30 to 8:30 when relieved. It is really pouring outside. What a night to walk guard. I go on again from 1 AM to 3 AM. Only one compensation, got out of Friday night cleanup, but I'm tired already from dragging these overshoes and 9.67 pounds of rifle and bayonet around for 2 hours. My teeth feel funny and have a big canker sore deep in my gums, all of which with the dampness makes me feel rather irritable.

3:15AM

    Have just come off my two hours, taken off my shoes, poured the water out of them, wrung out my socks, cussed the dirty **%@#! who stole my comforter and now with my bare feet near the stove I can relax until the next relief goes out at 4:30 when maybe I can get a bed. Just couldn't write before so I lay down and slept a couple of hours. Now I come back and there are no beds and someone has helped themselves to my comforter.

7 AM

Darling —

    Have eaten breakfast after getting about 2 hours sleep. Feel kind of knocked out, but okay. Have to stop now and get set for inspection in the guardhouse. Damn this army. I love you eternally my sweetest wife

Robert

*   *   *   *   *

Friday, Feb. 5, 1943 - 9:30PM

Dearest -

    Do I remember our hurried kisses after breakfast? I'll never forget your "Dagwood Bumpstead" take off every morning, with me at front door ready to give you my wifely kiss! Seems just yesterday that you were going around in overalls held together with safety pins, and here you are buying an officer's uniform! [Fig 26]

*   *   *   *   *

227

My Dearest Darling -

Your Dad and I also discussed you dear, and your Dad thinks your Army experience should fit you for something worthwhile in civilian life. He envisions you as a sales executive or personnel administration head. I think you could be most anything you want, dear. You've always been interested in psychology and P.A. sure requires one versed in human psychology. "Postwar plans for RWD", but you're the final determining one, so it was purely academic, I assure you.

Oh, my dearest, you can't begin to realize how much I think about you and this army deal, and how every bit of news is appreciated, how avidly my eyes devour your words as I get a letter. First reading to assure myself everything is under control. Second, more leisurely reading to digest each phrase and sentence. Third reading, I give myself over to just enjoyment of the literary feast.

My dearest, we haven't missed writing each other every day; that, I'm sure, won't be duplicated by many other couples! Oh, so happy in my love for you! Want to comment on your Wednesday Eve letter some more. (After another reading of your Wednesday afternoon letter, I shan't reply to it, just say "comments noted and action in accordance therewith will be taken (will be taken into consideration) in the future correspondence."

*   *   *   *   *

9:45PM Sunday February 7, 1943

My precious darling:

Wednesday letter, you are completely responsible for my poetry darling. You were the first woman I ever wrote to like that; remember that first letter I wrote you almost immediately after our first kiss. I think it has been lost, but it was the first verbal impression I ever captured of you. Somehow darling you are the essence of poetry to me, radiant with beauty and life, which I try futilely to record. Strange that tho I loved (or thought I loved not knowing what it was) other women before you, none ever moved me to expression like you. From the beginning there must have been an unknown bond between us which drew us inevitably into oneness.

Mitch's background. Don't know exactly. He's been to college in Memphis. Been in the army 13 months. Was a corporal in colored training regiment here at Lee. Surprising how these boys, from Alabama and Louisiana with those Southern drawls, like him, respect him and really pal with him just as they would anyone. That's the way it should be, and I'll say I'd rather have Mitch to pal with than most any other lads I've seen in this army.

The Russians are taking Rostov it looks like, Stalingrad, Leningrad, Tripoli and now Rostov. May it continue! Most soldiers think Russia is okay, but there are a few "Tribunists" in the army too.

*   *   *   *   *

9:30PM Tuesday February 9, 1943

Darling:

Studying real hard tonight. Spent 3 solid hours digging out this stuff on depot and post supply system. We will be allowed to use our books, which portends a tough exam. Digested AR 35-6560, OQMG15 and OQMG Circ. 1-4 upon which a lot of it will be based. I'll really be able to give even you a lot of pointers on AR's, contracts, organization etc. Am writing in the study hall now, the boys are kidding me about my "daily telegram". Extra happy tonight on the news "Japs evacuate Guadalcanal". As far as I'm concerned that's the best news of the war to date, an armistice for Bill.

*   *   *   *   *

9:50PM Wednesday February 9 [sic - misdated, = 10th], 1943

Dearest beloved:

Starting late tonight. Very busy all day, in fact so much so that I just got to read your Sunday letter an hour ago. Exam on Post and Depot Supply which covered all the depot procedures for the receipt, storage, and issuance of supplies. Sixty questions with 40 of them true/false. The trouble with T.F. questions is that if you get one wrong it is also <u>deducted</u> from your score (double penalty). Half of the stuff you have never heard of and have to thumb rapidly through the text trying to find it. Think I came out okay. A tougher one yet is this Fiscal exam coming on Friday, covers all the appropriation, authorization, allotment and suballotment all the way from the operating agency's estimate of funds needed, thru Congress, Bureau of Budget, Gen A/c Office, Finance Dept, OQMG, Responsible Dept, Purchase and Contract Officers, Agent Officers. To know all the ins and outs of Fiscal procedure in 8 hours of lecture and ?

hours cramming. I know all about the Walsh Healy Davis Bacon Copeland acts from you but that is only an infinitesimal part of it. Form 23's T99's W.D. Circ 206 for open allotments.

So much more to say but it is too late now for my shower and I'll have to hurry to even make bed check. Was very silly of me to waste time on that Fiscal bunk. Will try to write a letter tomorrow darling instead of a Finance circular. Love you my sweetheart my wife

Robert

* * * * *

10:15PM Thursday February 10, 1943 [= 11th]

My beloved wife:

I can hardly write tonite with my hands all messed up from being in G.I. soap and water for 10 solid hours. Pretty rough today. At reveille the 1st Sergeant informs me that I'm to take someone's place on KP today. The guy is in the hospital and I was next on the list for next week so I was the victim. Of the whole day the only break I got was that I didn't get to the mess hall till 7 AM instead of 5 AM. However I got stuck on pots and pans and scrubbed hundreds of those damned 15 gallon pots, pans, and trays etc. etc. from 7 AM to 8:30 PM. That is one hell of a job. After about two hours and that soap and water your fingernails begin to feel like they are falling off and you sweat into a greasy gum. Scummy.

As I write this my arm is limp from scrubbing and the pen doesn't want to stay in my softened hands. On top of all the hardship of KP there is the fact that I've missed the final lecture in Fiscal and must take the exam tomorrow without studying for it. I'll be lucky not to flunk this one. However I am clever enough to make a little study time. Got off KP at 8:45 and headed for the shower pronto. Hair and me all washed and dressed in clean clothes I feel a bit better, so I put my overcoat, comforter roll and helmet under my blanket in bed to look like me and well, here I am in the theater for the rest of the night if I want to stay. The C. Q. will flash the light on my bed and see me with the covers up over my head, but here I'll be studying Fiscal too. It remains to be seen tho if I can stay awake enough to get any good out of it. — Got your Monday letter too darling and you're in pretty bad shape with me. Still haven't had time to answer your Sunday letter. However darling do you notice how we answer things we write each other so often before we even get the letter about it.

I've written you about the lease already. We'll wait on that till after April 2. — Postwar plans for R.W.D. are still an M.D. or PhD at 35 or 50 I'll still make it. Must get across the street now without being halted by the sentry, but since I walked this post I know how to avoid him. Sleepily and lovingly goodnight my dearest wife -

Love you always
Robert x x x

6:15 AM — P. S. it worked. Everything okay. Love you — Robert

*   *   *   *   *

Chez Nous

8:10PM Tues. Feb 9, 1943

My Precious One -

Darlin', can I fess up somep'n; you know the first letter I got from you, dearest, sort of frightened me. That was before I got to know you very well and I thought you were being too emotionally frank. You know me, I was rather blasé and disillusioned before you came along. That is, I thought I was a super sophisticate, what with two broken engagements and many turned down proposals of marriage, you know. And when I "fell" for you, Robert, it was with a very sinking sensation, and I discovered I was just a very naive innocent when I ran up against the ardor and passion of your love. Dearest, so fiercely wonderful and yet so sweet and tender, your love. I go spinning around in circles, my head just swims when I recall some of our first kisses!

I'm listening to a very sober analysis of Byrne's speech, that this is in preparation for a mobilization of manpower and all forces on a greater scale than ever; as a prelude to an all-out invasion of Europe. Oh, dearest, I hope you can stay here, dearest darling. Fate be kind!

Now, my husband, I leave you, with the usual poignant regret that I feel at this daily literary farewell. Spartan-like I shall endure this enforced separation, but I can't wait till you're back again, and for now, I await eagerly your next letter.

With so much loving thots to my darling,

Always
Elizabeth

*   *   *   *   *

My precious:

So faithful. I did get 2 letters from her today. I love you so. My Darling's two letters. It seems that either she or the Colonel have to be late to make it a normal day.

All our instructors are commissioned. However in our military each man is given the opportunity to show how he can instruct. They are liable to call you out of ranks at anytime and have you explain something like the manual of arms, or call on you to prepare a talk on treatment of burns. We have had some good and lousy cadet instructors. Mitch is the old reliable for basic. He gave 1 hr of the rifle today.

*   *   *   *   *

9:20PM Tuesday February 16, 1943

My dearest darling:

Sitting here making all sorts of little "ummms" and "how I could squeeze you" noises, as I look at your picture, my little mouthful of hot biscuits and honey, so sweet I could gobble you all up deliciously warm and sparkling. To look at you I can just feel my arms tight around you, my hands into the small of your graceful back, dipping into the warm silk smoothness of your slip beneath your sweater at the forbidding stiffness of your girdle armor. My lovable, kissable darling. Sweet armful of wife that I want to hold close to me forever. I love you so. Every day I experience such an intense longing to be near you again, to talk, to kiss, to play, to cook, to sleep, just to be with you always and love you, and every moment to thrill at the way you look fixing supper, taking your bath, my rosy little bubble, soap happy and wet; my trim tailored wife in her high heels and hair combed, attractive temptation; my beautiful tantalizing mate, woman glorious, naked in love on cool clean sheets irresistible possession; my snuggle puppy flannel cuddled cozy together in sleep with my hand feathered tenderly in the luxuriant cove of your nightie, the ecstasy of your breasts. Every moment spent with you darling was an eternity of happiness, my lips remember yours so vividly and ache for the return of kisses. We are so different from others my beloved. Just looking at your picture I feel how deeply and completely you are my wife, I your husband. No superficiality, no doubt, no desire of other affections, no halfway, no game or joke, just complete desperate love, lives welded to one destiny, we live for and in each other, our lives and our loves being one identity, one eternity. You have absorbed me forever and I must always feel myself an actual part of you my dearest.

Unless something very drastic happens I should be a commissioned officer on Friday, April 2nd. Won't know till then what I've been assigned to, where I'm going or how much delay or leave I'll be able to get. No telling or planning that part of it, but the odds are almost certain that I'll at least be in the US, and I think we should definitely count on your being with me then. Give up the apartment on May 1st, sell the piano if you're not playing it, and store the furniture or have the gov't ship it to my post if it looks at all permanent. The only certainty darling is that we should be together. That is the only happiness for us and the one reality for which we live. Therefore we must do all that we can to accomplish it. It will all work out smoothly my beloved. I dream, impatient for your caresses, sweetheart. All my life I will.

Your husband
Robert

*　　*　　*　　*　　*

Tuesday - Feb 16, 1943 - 10 PM

My Darling -

I'm sitting here just glowing with that internal flame your opening lines of Saturday's letter enkindled again. Oh, precious, how you can find the exact words to do that to me! As I read, I could feel myself coming under the spell of the passion that swept over me in the early days of our love. How can I help loving you, dearest, when a mere letter from you can make me so deliciously happy! My dearly beloved.

I, too, have been giving the "body beautiful" some thought of late; for I, too, want to keep me just as you would have me always, thin and supple and caressable. So last night before taking my bath I spread our knockabout blanket on the dining room floor, put out the lites but kept the radio on for company, and proceeded to do some improvised calisthenics, not strenuous breathtaking muscle builders, but stretching exercises, with emphasis on shoulder, busts, waistline, hips (hip, hip away, I hope) and thighs! Don't misunderstand me, I'm not getting fat! Mom, insisted on weighing me and after supper I tipped a mere 138.

My darling, just keep saving all those pent-up kisses for me,

233

darling. I'm saving all of mine for you. Six more weeks and perhaps we'll really have a run on our accumulation of osculation. Oh, my darlin', I just quiver with delight at the prospect of things to come. Homecoming and my darling in my arms again.

Exquisite ecstasy

Elizabeth

P. S. I shall do calisthenics to Beethoven's seventh! Wotta boon RADIO!

*   *   *   *   *

Friday, Feb 19, 1943 10:30PM

My Dearest -

Got in a tangled mess on one of our wage rate adjustments and so I worked on it till closing time. Official notification that records have been changed to show "Elizabeth N. Doty née Jusewich". So you may now address me as such; but now my initials spell "END". Marcella says it's considered good luck by the Hebrews if your initials spell a word. Could be!

Darling, as I read your letters telling me what you'd like to do to me with me for me, I can just shut my eyes and experience all the delicious feelings your caresses used to invoke. Oh, dearest, I am truly grateful to Fate, to circumstances which brought us two together. I just can't imagine myself married to anyone but you, so glad that I didn't accept anyone till you came along. No matter how long you and I were separated, so long as our letters continued to flow as it were between us, our love for each other would just continue to increase in its intensity. I have so many beautiful memories, and so many inimitable expressions of your love for me, and I am truly thankful.

I love you so very much, dearest, and when I read of your feelings, I find myself so emotionally affected, such a desperate love. You're right, our lives welded to one destiny. 'T will all work out, I know.

Always your wife,

Elizabeth

*   *   *   *   *

My Precious:

Heard Madame Chiang Kai Shek speak this noon. A truly marvelous speaker in every respect. I have never heard any English-speaking person who had a more meticulous enunciation of the language than she, as well as the emotional quality of her voice. — About 5 WAAC officers arrived and caused a flurry of excitement as they walked down the street this morn. Everyone gaping out the classroom windows. Have to admit they looked there [sic] part well. Military, yet definitely feminine.

Two men were flunked out of our barracks today. One crybaby nigger whom no one really liked and one rather slow witted lad from an Oregon coast artillery outfit. They both had about 5 U's already. About 5 or 7 others were warned that they were on the borderline.

Your exercises darling I do wish you would do what I asked you to before. You should join the YWCA and stay down at least two nights a week and get your body in some semblance of condition or tone. The sedative [sic!] life which you lead cannot help but have a deleterious affect [sic] on an organism inherently built for action and muscular life. The flaccid condition of your muscles and general lack of vigor is due to the fact that your body is never given the usage for which it was meant. Never fear your getting unsightly muscles. If you are in complete athletic fitness you would just glow with feminine health and vigor and your lithe muscles and perfect tone, strong and elastic, would mold your body to female beauty, tantalizing tigress.

*　　*　　*　　*　　*

11PM Saturday February 20, 1943

My distant dream

I worship the thought of you always, caught happily in the web of your enchantment. You are the culmination, the composite of all loves and all desires for me. In you I find the comfort, the warm sweetness of mother love, and I lay my head on your naked breasts and remember instinctively the shelter and kindness drawn from woman body. In you I recall the carefree naughtiness and playfulness of childhood, romping in mischievous innocence. You are the realization of the sexual flowering of a boy, his erotic dreams inspired by curiosity, the ultimate pinnacle of his first embarrassed kiss. You are the thrill so long sought in adolescence. You are the conjuration of myriad daydreams of shipwrecks with beautiful girls, orgies in fur-lined secret mansions, dramatic heroic rescues, of living lifetimes of high success and perfect happiness, the woman at his side brave and strong, beautiful and loving and they surmounted all. I used to dream of full bosomed houris, gossamer clad, caressing by the half-dozen, the couch of down and bearskin swallowing erotic locked bacchanites in insatiable delight, rhythmic. But now I close my eyes and feel knowingly the unretainable pleasantness of wrapping my "furry" leg around a smoothie in flannel pajamas with her hair tousled and her sleepy lips searching the darkness for a good nite kiss; and reaching and finding those expressive lips, I feel another token of love pass electrically between us, lips so familiar, lips that know their mate, know they will be kissed each nite always.

To experience this greatest happiness of all, the possession of a beautiful loving wife, is the end for which all past dreams, all past living did mold and prepare me. This was why I felt secretly curious about girls, why I played "post office" with adolescent nonchalance, and why I spent carefully counted quarters taking a high school date to the roller rink, why I learned to dance, to wolf, to drink and loosen maidenly modesty, to find the brothel in carousal, to become studious, to be ambitious, to learn, to be healthy, to be emotional, to live and experience 20 years of life that I might love you as fiercely, deeply, tenderly as I do.

And the rest of my life I want to spend just being your husband, for it is the most beautiful life I could imagine, so full in the rich reward of your wifely love.

And it makes me so happy to hear how my darling is keeping her body so lovable "slim and supple and caressable" while I am away. The eternal beauty of her soul should rightly be kept and represented in the physical beauty of her body.

In the army you can plan or count on nothing which is not liable to change at any moment. What I will be classified as will depend mostly on the requisitions this school receives at the time we graduate. If there are 100 men suited for truck drivers and 200 men top rate clerks and an order comes thru for 250 truck drivers, there are 150 clerks who become truck drivers in a big hurry. That's the way it works despite all the baloney you read in the newspapers. They try to give you what you want or what you are suited for but usually you and the request don't coincide. However, I think I've been pretty fortunate so far. — Got that "S" in Fiscal which I was slightly worried about. That study I sneaked in after KP put me over all right. There were 21 "U"s in our company on that exam. Flunked out 3 more men today.

*　　*　　*　　*　　*

Sunday, Feb 21 1943 - 9:30PM

My Dearly Beloved - Salut d'amour

Such a lonely despondent little girl, that's how I'd describe me this weekend. And why? 'Cause I didn't get a letter from my darlin' yesterday, and now I've been wondering why? And worrying a bit, is everything all right on the army front?

I've pasted all of your "battle" pics into my photo album. Someday we'll get a great deal of pleasure by looking at this pictorial record of our early married life. There certainly has been nothing dull about our marriage so far. To me it has seemed to be a continuous series of climaxes. Each one preceded by a period of doubt and fear of the future, and then the event occurred and somehow it wasn't as bad as we had figured it to be; and thinking of that does make me more encouraged so far as the future is concerned.

*　　*　　*　　*　　*

Tuesday, Feb 23, 1943 - 9:30PM

My Dearest Sweetest Darling:

Dearest, your spelling is TURRIBLE! I hope you get a good stenographer when you become an officer, on a/c your letters will be written in code à la RWD.

Sweet little exerciser! Stiff. is more like it! I've been keeping at them a bit too enthusiastically, I guess, and here's how it's done: about ½ hour before bedtime, I drag out the old blanket and spread it on the dining room rug. Put out lights very modestly and strip, and oh, what a fine feeling to lie in the nude on the blanket and stretch your muscles in a series of movements until your body assumes a rosy hue and becomes bathed in droplets of perspiration. I actually enjoy the odor exuding from me, and what a luxury to step into a warm bath, perfumed with bath oil. And when I get into bed, I just sink into the yielding mattress and opulent pillows to fall sleep so effortlessly, usually with a smile on my face as I think of some very sweet thought about you. A

237

nightly ritual with me. Maybe we can both do it soon TOGETHER?

Darling, I don't think I'd like the "Y", at least not the cool delicious swim. Dearest, I once told you I was like the cat who avoided even a sprinkle of water on its fine silky fur. I'll wait till you can personally sell me on the idea, but I like a warm tepid perfumed bath, and chlorinated cold pools leave me uninterested!

Dearest, I agree with you that we should have a long, happy healthy life. Your concern over my bodily perfection really touches me, but sweet, you're not afraid of me deteriorating before you, or something like that, now are you? Afraid that perhaps before this war ends, I'll be too old for you. That thought is frightening. You don't have that in mind, do you? Don't be angry, but I'd like to know.

Your Saturday letter leaves me breathless and starts this heart of mine working overtime as I read. Dearest it took me a long, long time, and I had reached this conclusion before I met you, that the only happiness, the only real deep, satisfying happiness, lay in being mated to one who could see my way of life, to live and love "fiercely, deeply, tenderly" and work and live and think together, two united forever. This idea of being a career woman seemed a second choice, a sublimation of the real hopes and desires of one frustrated in her quest for a husband who could be a lover and a father of her children. That "father" deal means a lot to me, too, 'cause I want my children to have as fine a heredity as I could possibly give them, my dearest!

*   *   *   *   *

Wednesday, Feb 24, 1943 10PM

My Husband - Robert Dearest -

Oh, darling, your letters show that you are awaiting our anticipated reunion in April with just as much impatience and expectation as I am.

It has been so so long since the 25th of September, even my visit to you in December seems so distantly in the past. The only tangible link between us is through our letters; but so many intangible things, dearest, bind us so firmly to one another. Those five days in Petersburg were truly period of rejuvenation for me. The girls at the office all remarked at the change in me when I returned. My face radiant in spite of 30 odd hours on the train with little sleep. My dearly beloved, you are exactly what the doctor prescribed for me, a tonic that never fails to produce what the French so aptly term "joie de vivre".

*　　*　　*　　*　　*

Saturday - 8:30 a.m. Feb. 27, 1943
Robert dear — [Begun with a ruby red kiss]

. . . . My daily lecture noted, Robert, dearest. Don't you dare lecture me by remote control! I know you do it for my own good, but you remind me so much of my dearest Momma who felt it necessary to supervise my every move and advise me from morning to night on what to do and when to do it, etc. but did that cure me of smoking? No! did it make me drink milk? No! Did it keep me from marrying you? No! You see how hopeless it is, dearest. I don't try to make you "over" in my letters, do I?

Well, to take up the subject of Felicia. Would you like to know what I really think of her letter? The assininity of filling up a whole page with meticulous handwriting just to tell you her "short hasty letter" would be followed "as soon as possible with a more extensive reply to both your letters"! Why the devil didn't she answer your letter right then and there? Instead she says nothing. Boy, some technique! Would you like me to write you such stilted unnatural stuff? I note she hopes to hear from you many more times in the future. Robert, you're heading for trouble if you keep corresponding with that gal. I consider myself a modern, tolerant and understanding wife, but this triangular correspondence deal, I dunno.

[Inter-Office Memorandum] February 27, 1943 About 4:30 p.m.
From: ME
To: YOU

Boy, am I in a rambunctious mood today! Ain't sorry for it either. I overslept this morning and got down to the office on time but with hair uncombed, minus my rings and wrist watch. I almost expected to find me with some other item of my clothing missing, but no, thank heavens! I wrote you a letter first thing this a.m. It probably reflected the mood I was in.

I hurried over to the Federal Bldg to inquire about your tax deferment. I finally got directed to the proper office and then was stopped at the door by a little fellow with a red (?) moustache and a pair of brown shell rimmed glasses which were perched on the tip of his nose, he did look funny. Told him I wanted to know how to go about getting tax deferment for my husband and he said, "Your husband?" as if to doubt the fact that I had one, only he said it as though he were talking to a juvenile. The little so and so! So he disappeared into the room and popped out with 3 forms. Said to send only one in and when I asked about the others he stated very ambiguously that "it's a good thing to have couple extra's around." And with that, he was going to disappear in again with a "Well, that takes care of you," and that got me mad. "No, it doesn't, I've got some more questions to ask you," I replied, and he waved me airily towards a line 4-deep of many people waiting to get into another room. "Well, You've got to get in line," and so I very saucily told him. "I haven't got time to get in line. And don't you go ordering people around like that!" And with that I turned on my heel and walked away. I wanted to call him a bureaucrat but felt that was heaping insult on the poor little guy.

*   *   *   *   *

10PM Saturday February 27, 1943

My beloved wife:

Again my suspicions are confirmed, you are gloriously beautiful. The two pictures which you sent darling hypnotize me with your loveliness and the remembrances they bring to mind. Seeing you seated in the car [Fig 12] I can feel my arm slip around your shoulders and draw you close, leaning for a kiss, so many many kisses and embraces that car enclosed. It was, you might say, the womb of our marriage, the pod from which the seed of our love grew, flowering into marriage. We will never forget the days we spent in it. Those summer nights of love, our honeymoon, our spring trip, all you and I so close under one roof as we should always be. -

Feel as though a great weight has been lifted from my back.

240

Our academic is over! That is cause for a feeling of relief. We were inspected thoroughly this morning by Capt Risick our new Bn commander. He's tough but a good soldier. Really dished out the gigs. Came to MacDonald and says "Let's see your belt buckle" so Mac lifts up his blouse and the captain sees his hat stuffed under his belt. Gives him hell for that and asks to see his undershirt so Mac opens his shirt displaying a brilliant blue sweater which he had on underneath for warmth. Needless to say Mac was gigged. Brown; then Doty. Got off to a good heel clicking start, which he liked I think. Step out says he and then in he starts, clothes all buttoned, ah, overcoat buttoned backwards, fine comb teeth should be facing where you have the large; couldn't find anything wrong (enough for a gig) tho so he takes a scrutinizing look at my footlocker (my darling [Figs 17, 20] smiling up at him makes me jealous), and now out he pops with a bouquet "This man's footlocker is very neat, I like the arrangement. He has taken pains in preparation of his display". (He should have heard me cussing and fuming as I hastily threw it together.) Then he passes on to Mitch and gives him a thorough going over and finally says "This man is right there to". Mitch and I scored this week. Last week we didn't do so good as the Captain (Hoff) remarked gigging us then "Mitchum and Doty will share the honors on this dirty windowsill". Guess we cleared ourselves this week getting complimented by the Bn Com.

I should now reply to some of those 18 precious pages of love my little lovely kitten has sent me. I love you.

Monday - my beautiful, lying in moonlight dreaming erotically of me as I do of her. How wonderful it will be some morning to awaken and feel the bulky warmth of us really together, so sleepily romantic, snuggling deliciously close, my wife x o oxoo x. And your nylon bras "so flattering to the female bosom". Darling you make me quiver with remembrance of your beauty revealed, opulent, tantalizing as your arms stretched slipping your silk slip over your gorgeous hair by the soft light of our cozy bedroom. How I loved to take you in my arms like that and feel their soft firmness against my bare chest. Beloved.

Your musculature is beautiful, female, curving in sinuous delight, seductively graceful; but it is strong, strong arms to crush, strong framed chest to breathe the clean air, strong hips, stomach and thighs to bear and feel the beauty of my love, to expel the creation of our love, mammalian, from your nourishing darkness. You are strong, fierce, tartar, bred from the lines of 100,000 years of sturdy lustful flesh, your bones built for swinging an axe at the wolf's fangs, protectress of the infant suckling at her breast. That is the history of your muscles which delight in naked vigor of sweat, the welcome freshness of a scented bath. To keep the invaluable jewel of health you must polish it daily. We will live and love together darling, retaining as long as possible the flame of youth, relinquishing it gradually as we deteriorate into remembrance of life lived fully, complete in the natural beauty inherent in all living things.

I lay my body, my soul, every atom of my existence, at the altar of YOU in utter adoration, and live in eager anticipation of the ecstasy of your presence. But oh, inexpressible rapture of this religion, to know that you and you alone possess this, adored goddess. My divinity, I worship you, symbol of life, wool warm wife bare legged in her flannel nightie our bed our love.

Robert

*　　*　　*　　*　　*

9:30PM Sunday February 28, 1943
My sweetest delectable honey drop

Golden glitter of liquid love
Distilled from the jonquil's heart.
Supple sweetness, tempting a sticky kiss;
I want so to taste and feel again
Palpable you, clean, fresh smelling, my viscous delight.

I am just settling down to write sweetheart after spending 2½ very laborious hours printing out 24 pages of "Personnel Placement Questionaires". Spent all morning reading your letters of December. So long ago darling. But at that time we knew even less of the future than we know now. It makes me happy to look back and see how our hopes have been satisfied at least as much as this war permits. You and I were both so anxious over this OCS. I'm not out yet, but dearest it seems now more a matter of just waiting for time to drag itself heavily by until the thing is accomplished.

We are both so strongly sexual, welding us so perfectly as man and wife. That is the true foundation of our marriage beloved, our hot passion for each other's glowing sex, the mystic ritual of flesh entering flesh in an orgasm of ecstasy, to bring forth life in a paroxysm of pain. Tho I were to write a thousand years I could never plumb the mystery or describe what goes on within me when I feel

242

the nipple of your breast pucker and swell against my caressing hand, or when tangled in the furry warmth concealed between your woman thighs my fingers feel the slippery smoothness that is designed for our pleasure, and our lips lock in enraptured happiness. Those moments are the peak of living. Surely we must be accomplishing life's purpose as we press our naked bodies together in such orgies of delight, for the whole of our physical and mental being is brought into that pleasure, constructed specifically for it, the male and female functionally designed for mating, and for nourishing and protecting the results of the irresistible pleasure of creating. And from this hub or altar of our sex radiates all the happiness which makes the lifetime union of a man and woman so complete in contentment. It is because we lust and desire the naked beauty of each other so strongly that we are able to build our home, our life, so securely upon it. That is why we feel so happy just watching each other eat, bathe, dress, sleep, work, play; why we take care of each other so fondly when we are sick, why music stirs us so deeply, why our letters are so precious, why we want to succeed, why we want to raise our children healthy, intelligent and teach them the zest for life which we possess and fulfill so eagerly. - You too darling echo my thoughts and feelings so. How glorious to be so similar, to feel and understand each other's love, to experience the same goading desires, the same uncontainable pleasure and share the same dreams and hopes for an entire lifetime.

*   *   *   *   *

10PM Monday March 1, 1943

My dearest darling:

Today has been a very busy one for me. All morning was spent hiking out to the "Crater" (you remember where the Harrison's took us) and back about 6 miles all told. We went there to hear a lecture on the battle [Part of Grant's siege of Richmond, terminating the Civil War] and look over the ground. Then this afternoon we had "Gas" all afternoon but good. Started off with an hour of movies and then two hours field demonstration. They exploded 4 toxic gases and we had to run through the clouds and sniff the odor so that we will be able to detect them in the field. The first was Chloropicrin a lung irritant and a persistent gas. It smells like licorice or anise, heavily sweet. Of course we only got a little of it but enough to identify it and get a little of its lachrymatory effect. Chloropicrin eats the lung tissues when inhaled very much. The

243

next was Lewisite which is a highly persistent vesicant agent. At low concentrations it smells like geraniums definitely. It also is a lung irritant but its main function as a casualty agent is producing blisters on the skin. Then we had a whiff of mustard gas. It too is a commonly used vesicant agent but does not contain arsenic like lewisite. It smells somewhat like horseradish and irritates your throat. They then exploded a tube of Phosgene, also known as cough gas as I found out. It is a lung irritant like Chlorine and Chloropicrin only 9 times more toxic. It smells like new mown hay or ensilage. I will never forget this one for it scared the pants off me. It's deadly stuff, though it doesn't stay in one area for very long. I started off taking a slight whiff which made me know what it smells like. Then another to make sure; this made me gag slightly and I took a breath to clear my throat. That breath immediately reflexed me into a cough, taking a big lungful of air and phosgene. Thought I'd cough my lungs out before I got out of it and continued coughing for about 15 min afterwards. It's lethal stuff and I'll sure reach for my mask instinctively when I smell that again.

*   *   *   *   *

Monday, March 1, 1943 9:30PM

My Dearest Husband -

Oh, Sweetheart, I'll never NEVER write you a letter that might in any way hurt your feelings. I'm afraid I wrote you a bad one last Saturday morning - forgive me, precious, 'cause I don't really mean it, my emotions just get the best of me. I hope you don't write me a scathing reply. Guess I do those things 'cause I love you so much.

Your Friday letter, darling, your words caress me much as your hands upon my body used to do, and incite some of the same pleasurable sensations. Oh, my beloved, you circumvent the enormous distance between us when you can make words work such a magical effect on me. You certainly qualify for the one and only man who could affect me so, with words. I could never doubt your love for me after such a letter! "Leisurely and lovingly" written letters. Oh, how I treasure them!

Oh, how wonderful it will be to share our voluptuously yielding bed with you again, and as you say, to know you are there, by touch, by sound, by smell! Oh, what I'd give for one of your snores, and to feel your "furry" legs with my toes!

So, darling, I leave you with the most loving of thoughts, if a bit saddened at Grandma's passing away. [Fig 14]

*   *   *   *   *

Tuesday March 2, 1943

Darling - I love you!

"We live in the present, we dream of the future, but we learn eternal truths from the past". I quote from Madame Chiang Kai-Shek's speech. I'm listening to her, admiring her precisely perfect English, and beginning to listen intently as her voice rises and falls. I do believe her visit and speech-making here in America will be to China's advantage. We Americans need something tangible to represent China to us, and China has always seemed just a large mass of humanity; now we can think of Madame and so our interest in China increases.

*   *   *   *   *

9:30PM Tuesday March 2, 1943

My dearest sweetheart:

We spent the entire morning field stripping the .30 caliber machine gun. Learned a great deal about it.

Over to the theater [The hideout I had appropriated for my privacy in the evenings] and started practicing. Got going for 45 min when in walks a damn outfit to see some more films. To top this off the screwball lieutenant in charge makes me play a solo for the group. Quite reluctantly, but with simulated good-nature I did and did a putrid job, but I guess my efforts at least were appreciated. So then the two looies horn in on my private spot and we raked the QM School over the coals. One of them was an Infantry officer just transferred here from Fort McPherson and was he disgusted. The other was a good natured guy and I picked up a bit of the instructor's side of the picture from him. Don't think I'd care for it too much.

I agree with you on Felicia's letter. Quite stilted etc. We'll forget the subject.

Missed my shower last night which I think is responsible for my grumpy mood all day. I love you darling so much even if this letter

245

doesn't sound much like it. Just not romantic. One of those nights if I were home when I would just want to snuggle into bed with you and not "pester" you like I used to sometimes.

*   *   *   *   *

9:45PM Thursday March 4, 1943

My darling wife:

I love you so, and as I read your precious letters can just hear your lips echoing those beautiful words. Could just sit here all night reading YOU and looking at your pictures. Have already taken my invigorating cold shower so as to be sure not to miss it and now I may write undisturbed till 11 PM almost. Today has been a very cold one about 20 . Went out for a field exercise this morning 1st thing about 8 AM and we nearly froze. Were out about 1½ mile from our area, learning how to lay hasty mine fields. I got warmed up a bit by being one of the 22 men (a team) who laid a minefield of over 100 mines in a geometrical pattern in 58 seconds and recovered them in 35 seconds. Had following that a 1½ lecture on defense against mechanized attack. Had two more hours this afternoon on .30 cal MG and I learned how to detail strip the bolt.

Both your letter and one from my Pop arrived today telling me about Grandma Mack [Fig 14]. Am so glad I wrote her when I did and your sending her that little gift was very sweet. By far more effective and satisfying to her soul than your or my heaping tons of flowers upon a dispirited body. Nor can I say I feel sad about it. She lived a long and useful life and enjoyed as much health and happiness as we as humans can expect. The time had come when she could look at her children and see a life well done, her body, her life drained into theirs and her deed was done. She is now soil from which life may once more rise eons hence. I can honor her memory far beyond anything that will ever be found in a mercenary, formalized cash and carry church or undertaking parlor. Therefore I have no regret whatsoever at missing her funeral, or any funeral for that matter. In pace recquiescat, as the rest of the world does not. My attitudes on so many things are so strongly divergent from other people's. You, beloved, more than anyone else, understand them or at least appreciate those which you don't condone. That is why you are so inseparably my wife, and the longer we experience life together, the closer our understanding will become and the tighter the bond of love between us.

9:45PM Sunday March 7, 1943

My darling beautiful

    I love you so much. Was going to write a real long letter today but instead got fooling around with a poem and spent quite a while trying to polish it up. The idea is perfect but the development can be so broad that it is hard to choose the correct limits. Also the usual trouble to get any form to the thing instead of just a flow of words and ideas. Well here's the poem.

THREADS

Caught cataclysmic
Wound on a spool of death
Life spins a fragile thread,
Stretched in tortured tautness
To sew the seam of history.
Speeding, bobbin bound,
Shuttled from the whirring rod,
Needled swiftly to Fate's gown;
Nescient of purpose,
We patch the robe of God
- Or hem some cosmic bodice,
A vast, near empty lattice.

*   *   *   *   *

Relentlessly unwinds our thread,
Till the omnipresent spool
Shines bony bare.
Rattling a taunting tune
Death shakes a toothless head . . .
Discarded now the spool,
Some raveled threads remain,
A multitude of moments,
To clothe Eternity.
An ever- changing raiment
Spun from the Earth's great loom,
Infinite in design,
Ineluctably unwinding, our protean doom.

247

Yet lustrous and lovely.
Rose silken dream skein.
Stained, yet nonmalign,
Tattered, but not breaking,
Resilient to defeat, respun
Clean, clear, and diamond strong,
Weaving again a stalwart net,
Another life begun.

*   *   *   *   *

Concealed within this mystic bag of life
The unseen Tailor has a miracle called birth
Crochéted with the needle, Sex,
Into a lace of love.
Within this eddying earth-knot
Exist two kinds of thread -
One metallic, supple, strong
Tense with urgent power:
The other, diaphanous as dew,
Yielding, lithe,
Patterned for temptation
Irresistible in hue.
The two, now twined,
Form Beauty, brilliant,
Breathless in delight
Deathless as the night.
Welding thread
To mated thread,
So yet another spool is spun,
Until the World is done.

Rough, but reasonably good; with a little shuffling to overcome some clumsy rhythms it would be an excellent blending of philosophy and poetry - a difficult accomplishment.

My sweetheart's letters are so satisfying to me even though we echo each other's impatience. It means so much each day to experience a part of your thoughts and feelings, to receive the intense passion of your love, beautiful, serenely cooled by the medium of paper but which we know burns so deeply within us. The impressions and ideas recorded so literally on paper are seized by our imaginations and reconverted into the original rapturous kisses so eagerly desired. And all our little practical doings and quibblings of our home substituted for by mail. I will bring all your letters back with me darling and some day we can compile them into a written record of our love.

There is a constant insatiable hunger within me for your body, your love, your companionship and all the indescribable, subtle moments of the happiness of living with you my wife.

Your husband
Robert

*　　*　　*　　*　　*

Friday - March 5, 1943 10:30PM

My Dearest Husband -

I always get a thrill addressing you as "my husband"; guess I'll always feel that way, too, 'cause the novelty of that has not disappeared yet. Today marks the beginning of my "M week" and I've been quite uncomfortable all day. Always miss you more than ever, too, on days like this.

So, you admit you used to "pester me" at times! My darling, these wintry night's would have so much more appeal for me if I could be a snuggle bug cuddled up close to you, being lulled to sleep by your regular breathing and snoring! You certainly were a fine bed warmer, too. Sleeping alone leaves me cold even with all available blankets heaped on top of me.

*　　*　　*　　*　　*

Sunday, March 7, 1943 - 8:15PM

Dearest -

Oh, back in the "sanctum sanctorum" of our own apartment, now I can really sit down and write you.

P.S. #2 - I love you!

To turn to your Sun letter.

Dearest, your opening lines, pure passion in poetry are like a strong wine, its potency affecting my mind and body, and leaving me intoxicated and exhilarated!

Dearest, I know it was the recognition of our mutual thoughts and feelings that attracted me to you. Other men attracted to me just didn't fit into my way of life. I always feared

249

marrying a man who could not understand the depth and intensity of my emotions, or one who would think that a display of sensuality was improper and that our marriage would result in maladjustment. And finding you, so frank and unequivocal as to your passions yet endowed with romantic ideals, I felt instinctively that Fate had intended for us two to live and love a lifetime of wholesome uninhibited pleasure. Let's never surrender our zest of life, nor let petty things destroy any of our high hopes and ideals.

Dearest, I love you

Always,
Elizabeth

*   *   *   *   *

Monday, March 8, 1943 10:45PM

[Decorated with drawing of a pensive female, resting her head in her hands, elbows on leaves of a calendar.]

Dearest Darling -

Twenty-five days more! In the meantime I watch the calendar dates go by. How I wish I could tear off the whole month of March and catapult us into April right away!

I thought you'd feel that way about Grandma Mack. She got your letter before she died and I think she died happy. I'm glad I went to the funeral though.

Yes, my dearest, I think I understand you pretty well, and dearest there aren't many things I have to merely condone about you. Let's say we understand each other's divergences with loving tolerance. You write in your usually beautiful manner, Robert. I can't exactly hear you saying those things, but I can just see you there writing them. And Robert I've discovered more things about you in your letters and just being with you than I have from hearing you discourse on those things. I'll bet we set a record on the number of letters we have written each other since our marriage. And I'm struck more and more by the fact that our overall outlook on life and philosophy are so much alike.

I'm proud of your 3 bulls eyes, too; I'd love to see you shoot those rifles, dear.

250

*   *   *   *   *

9:50PM Wednesday March 10, 1943

My dearest darling:

Just pages of letters from you today, Sat & Sun both. I love you so.

The afternoon we went out for "Jungle Trail". This turned out to be a very interesting and practical lecture and demonstration on jungle warfare. Learned how to float 200 pounds of equipment on water for 4 hours using only two rifles, a shelter half and tent ropes. How to float a jeep across the river by wrapping it in a tarpaulin! I was the only one in our platoon to get to "sleep" inside one of the new jungle hammocks. This was brought about by my asking the instructor whether the hammock might not become a shroud in the event you were caught in it at a night attack. So he made me get in it and demonstrate how to get in and out etc. It is a hammock with a rubberized roof and walls of mosquito netting. Fastens with zippers. Has a false bottom to keep the insects from biting through to your body. Weighs 2 lbs 4 oz and will support 250 lb man. Came back to our area and had 1½ hr on the MI cal .30 carbine. It is a small weapon looking like a pop gun, weighing 5½ lbs 35½" long and used by most service troops. It is however a very effective weapon for defense purposes. Is gas operated like a Garand rifle and will fire 15 shots as fast as you can pull the trigger. 2000 yards maximum range and highly effective within 2 or 3 hundred yards. - Had movies tonight till 9 PM on Traffic control and Arms and Weapons of the Reichswehr.

*   *   *   *   *

9:45PM Thursday March 11, 1943

My sweetheart:

Am sitting here entranced by the delicate hint of perfume rising from your letter, so sweetly seductive as you are. Have had one of those physically rugged days which make me want to curl up in the loving security of your arms and relax so luxuriously, my comforting mistress. I love you, and in the intensity of my desire for you seem to project myself through space and time towards you my warmsoft, only to fall short into a pool of pastel memory, moonlight caressing your milk white breasts modestly revealed to the breath of a summer night. I remember kissing them, being tied eternally to you by some deep mystic spell, ineluctably enslaved to

251

the beauty of your womanhood and all the fierce joy of living, of possessing, of mating, seething hotly in my blood in the quiet night under the cool stars. We could never have resisted the continuance of those glorious nights of togetherness, having been caught and entranced by the slightest taste of our love, we must we knew, spend a lifetime in satiating our appetency for this irresistible companionship. And darling, in each day of my life the attachment and dependency on the drug of your love grows more acute, more intense, till I could burst with desire for you, but never be surfeited with the radiance of your dawning smile, the mysterious attraction of your eyes, your voice, to coil your luxuriant flowing hair in my hands and playfully run a finger down your forehead over your nose, your graceful neck, between your lush tempting breasts, across the smooth stomach, deeply naveled, into the crinkly good-to-scratch hair above the receptive portal of our love so ecstatically slippery, grasping with keen pitched delight, altar of pain and pleasure. You are my companion constantly in all things, you are my wife, thrifty, wise, councillor, you are my mate, the mother of our future flesh, the spring of our eternity. There is so much I mean when I say simply "I love you".

Spent all day at the field bakery [Fig 23] learning how to bake bread in the field. You put 100 lbs of flour, 3 lbs milk powder, 2½ lbs yeast, 3 lbs sugar, 1 lb salt and 6 gal water (not exact figures). Anyhow you dump them systematically in a trough, observing the temperatures of the air, water and flour. Then you start kneading. You get a mass of dough weighing about 150 lbs. We had 6 men, 3 on each side of the trough. 3 would grab it, lift it up and slap it down 25 times and then the 3 on the other side would go at it and so on for 20 or 30 min. Your hands and arms get so tired you can hardly move them. Best workout I've had in a long time.

*　　*　　*　　*　　*

Wednesday, March 10, 1943 9PM

Darling -

I haven't an idea in my head tonight. I feel I should tell you and forewarn you lest you search this letter in vain. I guess it all started early this morning. I turned off the alarm at 7 AM and snuggled back to bed for 15 minutes and awoke at 8: 30 (8:15 correct time). Outdoors the snow was coming down in a slow, sleepy sort of way, and everything was so quiet, as though all noises had been silenced by the thick blanket of snow.

I dressed hurriedly and taking a deep breath called the office, wondering in what kind of a mood I'd find the Colonel. Well, I forestalled arguments by bluntly telling him I had no alibi and I just overslept and would be down as soon as I had my coffee. So he said, "Ah, throwing yourself on my mercy, eh?" And chuckled; finally got down to the office about 10 AM.

Hurrying home (snow stopped by then), I couldn't help comparing the scenery with that day in Petersburg after a snowfall when the branches of the trees were heavy with snow and the ground was covered dazzling white.

My darling's letter was nestling in the mailbox and I prepared my supper with keen anticipation as I always do when I get your Sunday letter; and I wasn't disappointed! My darling's poem "Threads" has got some fine phrases. The idea is important, without idea or thought, what good is form and how can you have development? Someday you can polish up these "gems" you dashed off during your Army days.

Oh, Robert, I share your insatiable craving for companionship and love as we have known it. You must believe me when I say a part of me has been as though lifeless, stirred only by incidents that recall our happy days together, waiting for you to return and bring it back to that glorious state of "joie de vivre" again. Darling, life just ain't no fun without you; and when you call me a "Sweetest cuddle kitten", I find myself on the verge of tears. Dearest, I await your homecoming so eagerly and expectantly.

Elizabeth

*　　*　　*　　*　　*

Thursday, March 11, 1943 10PM

My Darling -

Your Darling is just finishing her third tall glass of gin and coke. Hope I get pleasantly drunk before I go to bed. Why? I'm just thataway today. Just want to get woozy.

So-so day. I blew up and gave my gals a good talking to about various transgressions, tardiness, excessive lunch periods, abuse of public phone booth privileges, etc, which they didn't like and which left me with a bitter aftertaste. Oh, hell, they deserved it. If they complain to the Colonel, I'll tell him off, too!

I don't like your mention of Felicia. Such a femme fatale! Oh, dear, what I did miss by having such outmoded ideas of fairplay and chastity and innate naivete. I wonder if any of my ex beaus are bemoaning their loss of my "terrific physical attractions and mental", too! [This refers to comments in a letter from my pal Beamish.]

But my husband loves me and says so at least once in every letter, so perhaps being a thrifty frau has its compensations. I never could keep my friendships on a purely platonic basis. Bango! My platonic friend would turn out to have honorable and/or dishonorable intentions on my beautiful body! My latest admirer told me he didn't mind my being such an ambitious idealist even if it did make him very miserable. He thot I was a priceless "gem", his very words!

I'm getting woozy, Robert my love, but the handwriting still looks legible so I'll carry on. You didn't say I was a "priceless gem" did you? I don't remember. Anyway, if you keep mentioning that Felicia gal, I'll get the idea you like them that way and I'll stop being a "thrifty frau". I think this is very silly, don't you? You should see me, dearest. I'm feeling very high, and tomorrow I go for a Red Cross blood donation! Terrible if they turn me down for "alcoholism". How will the Dotys ever live it down? I've been so tense emotionally the past few days, I think the gin cokes will do me good.

*   *   *   *   *

Friday, March 12, 1943 9:30PM

Darling -

So today I am a blood donor! I feel very very patriotic and have made an appointment 10 weeks hence for another donation.

Your Tuesday letter my sweetheart is really the next best thing to having you here beside me. How beautifully and eloquently you describe our love for each other. What a thrill to read again those precious words "I will always love you my glorious wife, so sweet, so loving". 'Twould be a sacrilege to use those

254

words in vain, for I truly believe our love for each other is something "out of this world". My dearest, how gladly all of me echoes back your sentiments, modestly grateful that you said them first.

Our life as a symphony, a beautiful simile, Robert. It'll be a never-ending symphony, too, with the recurrent theme of "I love you forever". The few dissonances that may creep in will only serve to avoid the monotony of an everlasting serenely beautiful melody, sort of like some counterpoint injected into pure harmony.

My beloved husband, I do so love you, and when you speak of caressing me with a veil of lovely memories, I think it's the most beautiful love phrase any man ever wrote a woman. My wonderful one!

Elizabeth

*   *   *   *   *

[On red-bordered IMMEDIATE ACTION stationery]

March 13, 1943 [Saturday]

201 (Doty, Elizabeth N.)
SUBJECT: Daily Report
TO: My Darling Husband

1. In accordance with long-established practice, there is submitted herewith detailed account of events for the period March 12, 1943 to March 13, 1943, inclusive:

a. Oh, heck with the formality, I'll preserve the outward form but I'll write in my usual haphazard characteristic manner, towit: I went to bed like a tired child and slept so soundly and woke up so refreshed this morning, before 7 AM and so I had time to eat a leisurely breakfast. Wore my new suit down, want to "show off" to your folkses tonight.

Robert, your comments about the ballet are most unkind. Do you want me to give you a detailed description. Perhaps I should have sent you the program. Anyway, I thought you were familiar with the numbers presented.

Your statements about the piano <u>hurt</u>! We own the thing jointly and I refuse to part with my half of it. So if you want to sell it, a predicament arises. Would anyone want to buy half the piano, or a half interest in a whole piano? Maybe it'd be simpler to

255

just let the thing remain ornamental until we can both take time off to learn to play. Now, really, Robert, aren't you a bit unreasonable to expect me to take an active interest in music, the arts, and other "cultural" things in addition to my present 48 hours at office, time spent in traveling to and fro, keeping up the apartment, doing my shopping, cleaning, taking care of my clothes, and etc. etc.? Why bring up the idea of a "farce", why talk of "pretense"? I haven't the strength for it, Robert. I'm sorry if you are disappointed. This probably will not seem like a pleasant letter to you either; just a "realistic" account of my day.

I'm sorry I stopped off to get your letter before coming to your folks. It's changed the gala mood I was in when I started over here. It is a blow to get one of your "nasty" letters when you've been expecting one of the kind that warm you inside and leave an after glow of inner happiness.

Disappointed
Elizabeth

*   *   *   *   *

Sunday, March 14, 1943 11PM

Dearest -

I'll bet you're grumpy about my Sat letter, yes? I suppose I'll hear about it come Friday of this week. In the meantime I'm going to pretend it never came.

Oh, sweetheart, I can't wait until I can be with you again. All these little problems that have arisen can be so easily straightened out, not by letter, but sitting down and talking things over as we used to. I think this strain of our first really long separation disposes us to misinterpret our letters, read into them more than the words therein contain. Believe me, Robert, I've gone through a mental agony these past months. Reminds me of that phrase, for men must go to war, and women must wait; and the waiting is just as bad as the war, and war is hell, so there!

I do love you darling, so intensely - my every thought revolves about you.

Always
Elizabeth

256

WARNING - DON'T JUDGE WITHOUT READING AT LEAST TWICE

Monday, March 15, 1943 - 9PM

Oh, My Dearest Darling -

This is a memorable day, the Ides of March, income tax deadline, and a day when the "fog" lifted for me on many things. Incidentally, it has been a foggy day all day, warm, almost sultry, with a constant drizzle - the sort of day when one's spirits just hit rock bottom and no amount of diversion will make them rise.

I thought of us all morning.

- and I kept thinking of us, dearest, thinking how silly I've been to even entertain the thought that there had been any strain in our relations, dearest. Perhaps petty things, but Robert, I might as well 'fess up, your Sat letter expressing yourself on the ballet and piano situation really hurt me very much, and recalled lesser wounds like your scolding me about housework and blouses and that Felicia dame. I don't mind telling you, Robert, these past six months have been quite an emotional strain for me. I've tried to be very brave about it all, but I've been under nervous tension right along and some days I felt like I'd just "snap". Not your fault, dearest. I don't mean to even hint at that. You've been the ideal husband and lover, to the fullest extent possible through the medium of the written word; but there have been so many little things at the office and at home that had to be taken care of, and underneath all that, this constant anxiety about your welfare and the worry about the eventual outcome of this horrible melée that the whole world is in. The only real pleasure during this period has been from your letters, my beloved; and Col. Jensen has been a perfect dear to me.

Your little rebukes and criticisms have become matters of major concern to me, made me feel as though I'd "let you down" somehow. In my own mind, I just couldn't see it. I felt I was directing my time and energies to the most pressing things of the moment, and that when all this was over, there'd be time for the recreational things in life. You see, darling, I don't possess that indomitable will, that store of inexhaustible energy that you possess, Robert, and your letters make me so aware of my inferiority

257

in these respects. I guess my "ego" felt hurt, and the harder I tried to suppress those thoughts, the more deeply rooted they became, and so I built myself quite a case of wounded pride and self-pity. You know the psychology of the thing, dearest. It was also confusing, one day your letter would transport me to the dizzying heights of glorious happiness, and the following day I get a letter which would without warning knock me off the pinnacle, down to abysmal depths. See what I mean, dearest. So if some of my letters have been disappointing to you, so have some of yours to me.

But I realize now that all this misunderstanding has resulted because of misinterpretation of our letters and not because of any basic conflicts between us.

As I started reading your Thu letter telling me of the perfumed letter you got from me, I remembered how I purposely sprayed it for just such a reaction from you, to remind you of the "odor" of other days. Darling, the happiest moments of my life have been spent nestling in your arms, and surrendering all of me as though to consecrate forever the ecstasy of our love. The passionate physical part of our love has been and will be one of the strongest bonds between us, I know. The intellectual side has had its ups and downs, because we both have "minds" of our own, and I'd just as soon have it that way. [What a penetrating insight: the constancy of physical appeal, contrasted with the vagaries of **mental** life.] Intellectual honesty and integrity would prevent me from ever surrendering entirely my independence of thought and action; and by the same token, I would never try to enforce my will upon you as some women do to their husbands, never that; and although I rebel at what I consider unwarranted domineering attitudes on your part, I acknowledge your right to express yourself, and I expect a reciprocal privilege. 'S only fair. - 'nuff of that! To return to your letter.

Dearest, your definition of "I love you" is breathtaking in its intensity and scope. Does it give you that feeling of catharsis, an outlet for your emotions, that I get from reading it? Oh my precious, we both need each other for a full-rounded happy life.

How I'd love to be saying all this to you, sitting on your

knees with my arms around your neck, punctuating my remarks with kisses.

I LOVE YOU
Elizabeth

*   *   *   *   *

10PM Tuesday March 16, 1943

My dearest sweetheart:

Well, about 3 PM we started another rehearsal for this damn parade and pranced around the rest of the aft. Our Bn Commander got a bug up his pants over something and we had to doubletime back to our area and also do an hours drill from 7: 30 to 8:30 PM tonight for punishment.

*   *   *   *   *

9:45PM Thursday, March 18, 1943

My beloved wife

Tonite, as usual, it is late and so am I and also tired. That guard deal kind of knocks you out a bit with all this other stuff. Had 4 interesting hours on the 37 mm anti tank gun this morning. Field stripped the gun and the breach block assembly. It is not an artillery piece, simply a very large, high-powered rifle, penetrating 3½" steel or 2½ ft of cement. It will shoot 7 miles. Weighs 912 lbs, 6½ ft 197 lb barrel, 22" recoil. A good crew of 5 men can get off 20 to 30 rounds per minute, or can in 45 seconds set the gun up fire 6 shots and hitch it to a jeep and move out of hostile fire. So you see it is a very maneuverable weapon.

Enjoyed my beloved's nice thick juicy Monday letter so much today. I do love you darling, deeply and intensely, and a continual flow of our letters is all that has made this separation bearable. We have committed so many beautiful thots to writing, expression of the radiant happiness we feel in our love. Monday you caught many truths in your analyzing pen, but there is one thing you stated which is very erroneous. You say you "don't possess the indomitable will or store of inexhaustible energy" which I do. In that you are wrong. You do, else you could never have equaled and returned in kind the intensity of my love. In that you are indomitable and inexhaustible. There is that same power and strength within you for all other things if you would only assert the courage to use it. Because the vast mass of society is lazy, weak and stupid, you are afraid to

259

use the deep driving energy within you. Afraid to be different from the herd by being strong, intelligent, free in your own world of will. You are afraid not to wash blouses because everyone else does, you are afraid to be aloof to time-wasting gossip, afraid to create your own world, to live without the advice of others. It was the mystic woven spell of our quick-springing love which tapped the well of power within you. You seethe with energy, strength of body and mind, but fear to digress from the insipid path of the multitude. With me you have let loose the bonds of custom, and broken the stifling chain of such reactions which had shackled you in well meant correctness. You have lusted in sensuous abandonment, satisfying the innate craving of your female body for the inexpressible pleasure of the male caress. This was not an instantaneous transition from the correct young Miss to the sensual, seductive woman, beautiful in ecstatic passion. It was a slow breaking down of mental fears and reservations far more than a physical adjustment. Likewise, too, perhaps I sense within you the strength for other things, the inexhaustible, the indomitable, suppressed within you and by my goading, persuading, scolding etc. attempt to free you from the cage of fear, the judgment of the mass humanity.

. . . so good night my beautiful wife, princess of pleasure, glorious with the wholesome happiness of our smiling home.

Your husband loves you
Eternally
Robert

*   *   *   *   *

10:30PM Friday, March 19, 1943

My gentle moonbeam
Whose kiss in thot caresses me.
Lissom cloak of loveliness,
A phantom weight of tenderness
Laid invisibly upon me;
Yet am I ensnared,
Enraptured
In this netted veil,
Eternally imprisoned
By your ethereal beauty.

I love you darling such a warmsoft little love kitten to cuddle and

260

caress. Soon now I'll be able to do instead of dream all these beautiful things which to me means "us".

$$* \quad * \quad * \quad * \quad *$$

[Written on Division Engineer stationary, crossed out and labeled "Chez Nous"]

Wednesday Midnight, March 17, 1943

[Begun with an imprinted kiss]

My Precious Darling -

Your comments on my letters and our reunion, I'll reserve for further amplification tomorrow. I have an idea you're probably right, dear, about our needing each other. I think my letters of Sat & Sun explain the gin binge, etc. I love you, and it's such a fierce possessive love that I react very strongly to things that probably wouldn't phase [sic] someone else. So! You discovered my secret! Getting slightly whoozy does bring out some of my inner thoughts, etc that I try to conceal during my periods of sobriety! Oh, Robert! I never thought you remembered my first real drunk with you. What else did I tell you besides M.S.? You understand why I draw the line on two drinks or so, on account of when I get sufficient alcoholic stimulant, I seem to undergo a personality change. We must go into this subject when we can sit and really discuss it thoroughly.

My dearly beloved, you do bring out the voluptuous sensual side of me as no man ever did, for which I am very grateful. What a drab colorless life it would be to retain that mask of propriety and modesty. So darling, when you get this short note, just think of me as I will be, restraining my eagerness and anticipating with subdued inner delight, the happiness of our reunion, perhaps forever.

Elizabeth

$$* \quad * \quad * \quad * \quad *$$

10:30PM Saturday, March 20, 1943

A whole new battalion of rookies coming in today to start Class 24 after the graduation of Class 17. We are the seniors of the school now. One of the new cadets over in the mess hall was given hell by a KP for banging his tray on the garbage can. The rookie says to him

261

in all seriousness "You can't talk to me like that, I'm one of the O.C.S. cadets here". We sure got a bang out of that and he will too when he hits the earth quite forcefully after his first 14 hour KP as an OCS Cadet.

*   *   *   *   *

10:15PM Sunday, March 21, 1943

To the most beautiful art I ever hope to know. To you my glorious woman, my mate, my song. Sculpture in all poses, balanced, dynamic and in the most appealing medium of warm satin flesh. You are my painting, such delicate brushwork, vital in color; the genre: nude, portrait, abstraction, all in one. You are my poem of life, reaching new depths of expression. You are my dance, lithe grace, rhythmic, sensuously sinuous, captured in a feathered whirl, supple in orgy, vaulting to surfeit, before a backdrop of: a blue couch, a bed soft to roll in, a bathtub, two radios, a kitchen stove; and now we hear the caress of Chopin, the torsion of Tchaikovsky, catapulting moods, tender, sad, gay, powerful, despairing, raging, victorious, possessive, sparkling with intoxication, joyous, serene; and the soft light, diffuse and buoyant, glides from the moon, caught in chords of cloud, peeping like a snowsoft breast from its veil of silk. My precious cuddle kitten, cloaked in foam and lulled by dreams, memories of two love-craving bodies locked to each other in a symphony of shared delight, a vision of flesh wrought in love.

Just thots, darling, of you and us and the ever nearing future. I twitch with impatience for your loveliness, tingling in every muscle to know the feeling of your arms encircling me, and mine crushing your swelling bosom tenderly against my body. I love you my sweetheart, my wife.

*   *   *   *   *

9PM Monday March 22, 1943

My lovable little lioness

Fluff soft, yielding gently to caresses. How I would love to rough your body playfully and then run a smoothing hand over all the tempting squeezable woman curves of your alluring molded figure, vivacious, pulsing with warm life, as I dimple your love beckoning breasts, placing my lips upon their naked beauty tenderly, like a dainty butterfly sipping the honey of a cherry blossom. I love you, my glorious wife and will ravish your entrancing charms, to be absorbed eternally in your radiance. I will bathe in your beauty, warmed by the passion of your love, cleansed of impatience by your caress, and quiver in the ecstasy of your nearness, knowing you for my mate. You are a deep silent palace hidden at the bottom of a green sea, where the seeping sunlight dimly casts a haze, diffuse, upon the languid pleasures of slow, swaying female hips, deliberate, erotic, rotating in sinuous rhythm of prolonged delight, fluidly, skin brushing noiselessly, recumbent on a mat of weightless weave, keen flash reflected from some emerald jewel, shadowed leisurely by ripples across the ocean floor. Oh, may it last forever in the vastness, inaudible delight sensed languidly in peace, with only the silver fishes to behold our sleek-limbed love.

I could love you like this all night, pouring out the intensity of my desire for you in words. After writing like this to you I feel vaguely as if we had possessed each other in some magic spell of love. Darling I love every moment we have spent together, all our discussions, arguments, baths, breakfast, rides in our car, shopping, each little experience I cherish and long to resume once more; but beloved, the craving I feel for the voluptuous glory of your soft flowering female body is beyond expression.

My beloved, what ecstasy awaits us soon. And we must never part until we are dragged from each other's arms by fate. We must live together, dearest, for every moment that we may. Your job, you're leaving with prejudice means nothing. We need each other, we want each other, we married for each other, and we must not allow ourselves to be separated by such a needless thing as your job any longer. You know that darling, so I won't say any more now.

* * * * *

Thursday, March 18, 1943

MY DARLING! I LOVE YOU

Oh, before I forget, I played your andantino on the piano, dearest. [This was a short piece of music I had composed.] You're right, it does have an air of expectancy and does have a haunting melody about it.

You do make out a fine case for your way of life. I've never had any quarrel with that, dearest, provided the necessary routine is still taken care of. It's like "variety being the spice of life", but "monotony being the staff of life"; and when you are mentally and emotionally upset, there is nothing finer than monotony and simple routine tasks to keep you occupied. You speak of a petty stalemate, my office work, home, letters. The fact remains that every moment of our life is unique, distinct, different from every other moment. It's all in the way you look at it, I guess. I refuse to admit that life is monotonous. That accusation comes from escapists who haven't learned how to get simple pleasures from the ordinary routines of life. But here I am getting philosophical and sleepy at the same time. I used to be quite an escapist, darling. Well, I found myself and now I don't try to avoid things as I used to.

Darling, I'm sure we'll never become slaves to shallow triviality. We may have to compromise on what we consider triviality but if we take turns giving in, I'm sure we'll hit a happy medium. If we do come to an impasse, I'm sure our love for each other is deep and strong enough to provide a solution.

Find myself groping for words tonight, which is a small matter because the only really important things I want to tell you are these oft repeated phrases: I love you, I need you, I miss you, I wait for you with such longing and with such anticipation. My every thought, awake or asleep, is of you. I love you. Darling, two weeks from tomorrow. I'm so thrilled at the thought!

Love,
Elizabeth

* * * * *

[Written on stationery from Hotel Linker, LaCrosse, Wisconsin!]
Monday March 22, 1943, 10:15PM
Do you remember our stopping at this
place for a fish dinner? [On our honeymoon]
Darling -
So you liked my "juicy Monday letter". I really blew my top on that, didn't I? I felt very much relieved by telling you just what was on my mind. You see, dearest, I still feel inhibited when writing to you on some subjects, an inhibition that doesn't exist when I talk to you in person. Will have to go into this subject when you're home. Suffice it to say now, that I admit my hesitation to venture into new fields. I definitely need a firm guiding hand. The hand of one I have the utmost confidence in, when I

have to undertake something alien to my way of life. You have been a wonderful influence in that direction, dearest, but you can't hope to do it overnight or in a month or in a year. Dearest, you've got to be patient and understanding. When you get to know me still better, you'll understand better why I am what I am. But no goading or scolding, more subtle tactics, please. Otherwise, my ego rebels but good! Oh, sweetheart, your greeting "My gentle moonbeam, etc." was like a caress, a soft brushing of your lips across my cheek. I love you, darling, with all the affection that has been accumulating these past months.

*   *   *   *   *

8:30PM Tuesday March 23, 1943

My dearest beloved:

Tonite I am officer of the day, my last duty in Co F I hope. I have had my C.Q., K.P. and Guard so this should be the last. On the night you get this there will be only one week between us and total happiness.

Darling, our reunion will even surpass the happiness of our honeymoon. Our marriage was swift, we plunged hopefully with young passion into a new realm of experience. We were goaded somewhat by curiosity, by the attraction of novelty, just how would it feel mentally, physically to lie naked between the same sheets, how would it be to buy furniture, to be intimate in all the details of living, to share all thoughts and feelings? We know now the glorious answers to all those questions and tremble eagerly in remembrance. We are not now two beings about to be united, we are one love separated, painfully in twain. Married life does not mean a gay holiday, it is more like the resumption of the habit of breathing in a suffocated man. We know with certainty the beauty which awaits us, the perfection into which we blend. Our beautiful year together established new cravings and desires within us. We learned the habit of kissing each other every time we felt like it, of watching each other devour our food, of seeing the nakedness of our two bodies, of planning together, talking, playing, working, doing everything together so deeply in love and we can never forget those moments and must look on all moments as incomplete without such things. I want to hear you fuss foolishly over me again, see you squirm into your girdle and fasten your stockings on your shapely legs so wifely before me, to have you on my lap and kiss you dozens

265

of times, to walk down the street proud in possessing you my pretty sweetheart, to admire your curving figure and know I may unveil it, to hear your voice calling to me from another room and I enter and you are there, so real, so sweet, so happy with love-lighted eyes and maybe a dab of toothpaste in the corner of her laughing mouth, hair touseled and little useful feet protruding cutely beneath her baggy nightie; I'll kiss you, fold you in my arms and bounce you on our bed. Sensuously within me burns a fierce flame of lust for the delight your voluptuous female body so capably excites and satisfies. My beloved wife, I feel so intense a craving for this unsurpassable pleasure springing from the precious touch of our nakedness. I want to drink with my eyes the tantalizing lines of your opulent nudity and watch you stretch in seductive grace. I want to stroke you from head to toe, lingering excitedly to absorb the mysterious ecstasy my hand feels at contact with your womanhood. I will kiss you with trembling lips in the valley of your bosom, and feel your nipples crinkle in joy. To cuddle each night into the secure warmth of my mate, restoring each other's vitality in love-locked sleep, peaceful, calm, after a whirling storm of indulgent sensuality. I kiss you forever.

Robert

*   *   *   *   *

Tuesday, March 23, 1943 - 9PM

Darling -

I began this letter listening to Charles B. Hughes, news commentator on WGN, and he's talking from Knoxville, Tenn, discussing the characteristics of the town and the TVA program. Oh, what nostalgic memories it recalled to me, our short stay there last spring [Fig 15]. I still think I would have loved the mountains, dearest, if you had not been so masculine and headstrong. Funny, the very qualities about you that attracted me, I have been opposed to in the main since our marriage. But anyway, that's the train of thought this broadcast got me into. I love you.

The rest of my day - well, the Colonel and I got into a heated discussion about the communistic trend our country is taking. Is he rabid about the Jews. The "curly headed boys" he calls them, and warns of rioting, etc. in this country if the "great middle-class" (with which he identifies himself) is pushed too far by this rise of the proletariat, etc. You can't discuss things dispassionately with him. He gets red in the face, his voice becomes hoarse and he just blusters. Well, I have to tactfully wind up the discussion, otherwise he sulks all day.

In the meantime, you wait at Camp Lee - I wait here in Chicago. Life has most devious ways of making people unhappy, hasn't it? Darling, I know how you feel about our being together while you are in this country. I share your feelings, but dearest, before committing ourselves, let's wait till you find out where you'll be stationed, etc. "Look before you plunge" or something. When you come to Chicago, Robert dear, we'll think this thing out. Don't misunderstand me, my beloved, there is nothing more I'd rather do than cast my lot with you and live a vagabond-like existence, the glorious happiness of sharing a great adventure with you would compensate for any loss of material comforts. But this is war, dearest, and we are not free, none of us, to cater to our own desires. I know we'll figure out the right solution, dearest, but I feel it is only fair to tell you I reserve my opinion until you get here, darling. You understand, don't you? The easy thing to do is to throw up everything and do as we please, the harder thing is to deny ourselves our happiness in the interest of duty or something. Dearest, don't get angry.

Oh, dearest, as I read your letters and recall those inexpressibly ecstatic moments in our married life, all my good resolutions to be "sensible" about everything just dissipate into thin air!

When you get this on Friday, only 7 more days will remain. Wonderful! Now those last days will seem an eternity though.

*   *   *   *   *

Wednesday, March 24, 1943 - 10:30PM

My Dearest Husband -

Your Sunday letter, so filled with sensuous superlatives, and so expressive of your thoughts about us, dearest, was certainly a priceless treasure to find waiting for me tonight. Oh, my passionate lover-husband, how well you convey your thoughts, and how those pen and ink phrases stimulate and "stir the vivid sparks of memory". You speak of trying to "skip the torturing interval", and I can well understand that. This coming week will seem endless in passing, but we must reconcile ourselves patiently, even though a "fierce joy of expectancy" pervades all our thoughts.

While at Mom's I had the unlooked for and unasked for "pleasure" of having an old girlfriend of mine now married and the mother of a three-year old child, drop in for a visit. Boy, wotta brat - got into everything everywhere. I then and there made a resolution that none of our offspring would behave like that! That will be interesting darling, to see if we can mold one of our own into an image of all that is best in us. I'd want him (our first must be a "him") to be very much like his father in appearance, with his father's IQ, but emotionally tempered a bit with some of my conservative and practical ideas, you wouldn't mind that, would you? Our little "she" could be very much like me, only there I'd want her to have some of her father's courageous outlook on life, but I still want her to retain some of my own child-like naiveté. Oh, dear, there I go again.

I get all choked up inside of me and my hand actually trembles as I think of your home coming. I'm reminded, too, of Cleveland; remember how we sat on a suitcase in the railroad station and almost got swamped when the interurban passengers came streaming our way? That was a glorious reunion. My dearest, you've made me very happy by your letters during this separation. If it were possible, I think I could love you all the more because of your devoted daily epistles of love. My darling husband, I do so await your coming.

With all my heart and soul,
Elizabeth

*   *   *   *   *

Thursday, March 25, 1943 10 PM

My Beloved -

It's exactly 6 months ago that you left for the army, dearest. How poignantly I remember that day. We had a restless night, both of us. I remember I was awake even before the alarm rang at 6:30. And how I got breakfast ready in my p.js, a good breakfast because I wanted to give you a good sendoff. I remember dressing nervously, with strange jittery feeling in the pit of my stomach. How your Dad called for us at 7:30, and we drove up to the draft board to find no one there. And then several other selectees came along and a draft board official and how we went upstairs to wait. Then driving to the I.C. Station [Illinois Central Railroad], standing there in the waiting room, filled with selectees, and men in uniform and families to see the boys off. Then at 9:30 or so you had to board the train and how you kissed me, so impulsively and how I didn't want to cry before you, couldn't cry, just felt a dull pain inside of me and I wanted to be alone. Your Dad drove me home and I went straight to bed and slept till 5 PM, dreaming, wishful dreams about you, dearest. How vividly I recall all those details, and then the agonizing days, weeks that followed. I don't think I relaxed until I came down to see you in December, my darling; and now only 8 days remain to be bridged before you will come home triumphant in your officer's uniform, back to my arms again.

Oh, dearest, after reading your letter tonight I did feel as though you had possessed me for a few moments in the "magic spell of love" you speak of. You tell me I'm very modest in my letter writing to you. Darling, my longing for you has been just as intense, but to attempt to describe it in words, I just can't seem to do it. That's why I felt that just "echoing your sentiments" would make you understand, darling. How could I begin to put into words the warm glow that seems to diffuse my entire body as I recall your loving embraces? How to express the heightened joy in being alive that comes upon me after reading your letters? I really feel like a transformed being under this spell of your "pen and ink" embraces, and I seem to become all that you would want me to be as your mate when I am with you, starry-eyed, radiantly beautiful with a strange surge of strength flowing in my veins! I seem to recapture for the moment the naive innocence of childhood as I cast off all carefully instilled inhibitions and just surrender wholeheartedly, unhesitantly, unquestioningly to the pure pleasure of the moment. The joie de vivre - vive l'amour!

*   *   *   *   *

My glorious darling wife:

Today has been a very healthy one, though very tiring. We started out at 8 AM with rifles, lite packs and gas masks and two sandwiches for lunch. We rode first about 12 miles or so and then got off and hiked some 6 miles. By the time we stopped for lunch those two dry G.I. sandwiches tasted as good as a juicy steak. Almost an hour off for lunch and then we entrucked again and rode to within 9 miles of "home", and hiked back. Was a clear warm day and my face and hands are tanned from the sun. Enjoyed it too, but my feet are very tired.

Oh how I long to have you with me tonight, that I might rub my aching toes over the smoothness of your thighs. Deep-rooted ativism, perhaps, of the days when I rode high on your female haunches grasping your furry legs with my hind feet. Darling, we have done these things for millions of years. That is why they are so strong within us, why it would be so futile and foolish to deny them vent. We live today because male and female mated hotly, bucking each other's loins in animal lust eons ago. Every chain of life within us has burst into being in such an orgasm and has delighted in the smell and feel of sex, mysterious deep flowing within the germs of life. The sowing of fertile seed, flesh gouging rhythmically, ecstatically into flesh, plunging life into the womb in spasms of intense sensation. That is how we have been brought to life through the ages and we unite our bodies in this insatiable pleasure from the deepest instinct of our being, the eons spent mouthing and sucking the nipple of a warmsoft breast. These desires are deeply rooted within us. That is why I love to teeth your tempting flesh, to mouth your breasts. How beautiful it is to see you beckoning my entrance. You are like some seething sun awaiting the glow of a comet, in an orgasm of flame, sinuous female, undulating slowly her hips in a rhythm that makes me savage with desire. Beloved, we approach in our embraces and caresses the acme of love, playing with each other's bodies as instruments of pleasure, in the innocent curiosity of children seeking the thrills and novel ecstasies our sex may bring us. We revel in the divine beauty and intensity of love which our bodies and our lives have inherent in them. We have not jumped to this point. Since that nite you sat so lovable and sweet upon my lap in Milwaukee and explained the condition of your female person, so kissable in her baggy wedding nightie; and we both felt a bit relieved that we could work slowly into the sexual perfection we both felt so capable of. From the weeping darling bride who loved her husband so on that trying night in Winona to the wholesomely panting man and wife locked in thrusting joy on a squeaky bed in Petersburg is a long way of happy unforgettable moments of learning to please and satisfy the cravings of each other.

My sweetness, I feel that this will truly be our second honeymoon, and don't ever worry if it starts like our last did. Your "sickness", beloved, is the monthly price we pay to nature for the glorious gift of your beautiful full blossomed sex. The keen satisfaction I will feel at just the common routine of sleeping, eating, living with you would be enough to carry me out of this world in happiness. If you are bleeding from the wound of love, we will find in just the mere fact of our presence a complete happiness till I may tenderly heal your love-aching parts so gently, my woman, my eternal mate. I feel so content, so happy in the thought of our mutual possession. We belong to each other forever.

Robert

*   *   *   *   *

9:30PM Monday March 29, 1943

My darling sweetheart:

Makes me so damn mad to think of the idiocy of higher ups in calling this piddling around officer training. For one solid month they have worried about and stressed nothing but how we'll look at the graduation parade. Damned chicken shit waste of precious time. While the boys in Tunisia get the hell shot out of them because they don't know how to use the weapons they have, these asinine fools bucking for promotion worry about how snappy the men look at eyes right. Sure makes good soldiers but some of these men will never be soldiers in that sense, but every one of them should be hard, tough, know how to kill and live. The calisthenics have been about as vigorous as an old maid's breathing exercises, and the marches have been strolls in the woods and as far as this school is concerned, here not one man has been taught anything about the use of the bayonet [Fig 22], how to use firepower, beaten zones, defiladed areas, machine gun patterns, how to establish and maintain communications in the combat zone, scouting, patrolling, patience, foxholes, living in field conditions under hard physical exertion. We have learned many things but there is so much left completely untouched that its omission is criminal, especially when 50% of our field time has been spent on recruit training stuff. That gripes me, but I've dug out most of that stuff myself and it's the

271

hide of the man that doesn't know these things that's in danger on the other side.

So much in our lives is being condensed into so short a space; for months we chafe helpless apart and then for a few fast flying days express our pent-up love, snatch at each moment to wring from it a kiss, a glance, a touch, avid for love to lay away the memories which nourish us in the aching hours of separation.

My beautiful, I seize your molded, graceful body tenderly and cover you with kisses so passionate in thought, so soon to be translated to the rapturous ecstasy of reality. We approach each other the eternal male and female, magnetic, ready to burst with love, drinking the serene cool waters of pure truth, union in perfection, my oneness, my love

Robert

*   *   *   *   *

Monday, March 29, 1943 7:30PM

My Precious Darling -

Darling, promise me, you'll never expect too much of me too soon. Please! I know your feelings, the scope of your passion and ardor, and I shall try to make you happy to the best of my ability. But love is to be wooed, not forced, and I am one to enjoy being wooed by my virile, irresistible lover-husband! And I promise you, we shall be happy, gloriously happy, dearest, always.

Listening to Sibelius "Valse Triste" as I write this. Oh, Robert, do you remember our playing that record over and over again those summer evenings before our marriage? Our 90-day whirlwind courtship was such a romantic one, with its poignant as well as happy side. We had the courage and devotion to one another to overcome the seemingly unsurmountable obstacles in the way of our marriage then, and I feel confident that we can solve our problems now. I do crave your companionship now even more than I did before our marriage. Even then I had realized that life was dull and drab without you. Oh, what miserable hours those evenings when we didn't see each other, the crisis that arose when I "wouldn't" and you "would". Darling, shall I tell you a secret? I came so close to being a "victim" to your charms, it frightened me. But Fate meant it to be otherwise and so we went through the formalities. But dearest I knew I belonged

272

to you from the moment you kissed me, and your kiss held so much promise of more ecstatic moments! We did enjoy our innocent lovemaking those summer nights, didn't we, darling? And the thrill seemed to increase with every day of our married companionship, as we both discovered that we had but stumbled on the threshold of life's greatest satisfactions. Oh, my dearest, we can truly say "unlimited horizons" lie ahead for our discovery and exploration.

I bow my head before your very forceful and logical presentation of why we should be together. It is perhaps selfish on my part to want to "keep the home fires burning", so that you can return to our established home and pick up where we left off. We shall discuss this further, dearest. I recognize the fact that my main duty is to be with my husband, dearest, and I don't want to shirk that - Never! I know you'll straighten out my fears and apprehensions when you take me into your arms and "plant innumerable kisses hotly over my eager body". Oh, my beloved, - Tues - Wed - Thu - Friday! This will be my last letter then, and I shall greet you next in person. Darling, so happily, eagerly, anticipating our reunion!

Elizabeth

*   *   *   *   *

CHAPTER VIII

Our Greatest Crisis - Surrendering Career and Home for the Uncertain Life of an Army Wife

Synopsis - The storm developed slowly, but persistently. I broached the issue shortly after I began OCS. Indeed, the possibility of having her join me was always one of the guiding motivations in my trying to become an officer; and she had herself given expression to that fond hope within a few days of my induction (her letter of 29 Sept 1942). As the actuality approached, however, she kept coming to the same logical and unequivocally sensible conclusion that, while togetherness was a wonderful dream, the unrelenting uncertainty of my future made the odds of realizing such a dream unacceptably high. She alone would bear that cost, lose the security of the high level job she had struggled for years to attain, abandon the home [Fig 9] she had so lovingly and creatively furnished, and leave behind the support of family and friends. This she would have to exchange for life as a transient, snatching stability momentarily, as opportunity provided. Our arguments, by mail, were long and intense, indeed, on my part, savage. But I did prevail. At first, upon re-reading this drama, I was often overwhelmed with guilt, at how cruelly I pressured her, and accused her. The dilemma, of course, is that we were both absolutely correct in our different viewpoints. Had she not joined me, and I had been blown to bits by being in my office on the ship when the torpedo hit, she would have spent a life of utter misery and remorse (See O'Neill's *Strange Interlude*!). Instead, once I had persuaded her to join me, she did so with full enthusiasm for the adventure that we then shared; accepting the correctness of our decision in braving

274

romantic chaos in lieu of a security that meant an aching heart. As I had so confidently believed, she consistently displayed an uncomplaining resilience and resourcefulness in coping with our somewhat vagabond way of life. For the remainder of our lives we both came to relish this history, that added further to the bond that we shared, in adversities met and overcome. Of course, her acquiescence also fueled her largely justified complaint during our subsequent quarrels that she was always the one to concede, or initiate reconciliation.

She joined me at Fort Warren in Wyoming. Our (my) clearly "irrational" choice bought us, on this occasion, a mere 38 days together, 18 at Fort Warren, 2 on the train to NYC and New York Port of Embarkation, 10 days in Brooklyn, 2 in Baltimore, and 6 in Newport News waiting for convoy before I left for North Africa.

The beginnings can be seen in her diary:

Thu 28 Jan 43 - Robert's letter [I had then been in OCS not quite a month.] looks into the possibility of my joining him upon his commission. Says he thinks he could support me with his pay if he does go overseas.

Sat 20 Feb - Took Lake St L out to Doty's. Sitting & talking about Robert's idea that I should close up the apartment & join him after he graduates. They both think I should proceed cautiously & not throw up the traces, home & job for a will o' the wisp.

Thu 25 Mar - Found a very impassioned letter from Robert. He wants us to be together for as long as possible. What to do? Put furniture in storage and join him, give up my job. Then if he goes overseas, what do I do? It's a problem. Only 8 days till he graduates. Where will he be assigned?

Fri 26 Mar - I dread the thought of having to reach a decision of what to do on Robert's proposal that I join him at his new station.

Tue 30 Mar 43 - phone rang and it was Robert! He got his orders today, to report at Fort Warren, Wyoming for a month's training in refrigeration. Sounded very happy and of course insisted that I take steps to put my affairs in order so I can go with him. Oh, what a problem! So uncertain, where he will go after that month's training, perhaps overseas. I called his folks, talked to Sis, thought it all over, and decided against going; to wait till after that month and see what happens. Give up job and home for a month's happiness and then come back to start all over again. I think Robert should see it my way. Let me remain here and work and plan for our future until his future is more certain.

*　*　*　*　*

[Robert was on leave in Chicago, 3-13 April 1943, enroute to Fort Warren.]

*　*　*　*　*

Mon 19 Apr 43 - Got a 4 page Air Mail ltr from Robert - a glorious letter telling me he'll abide by whatever decision I make. . . . Still feel tummy all upset - Wonder if it is due to working in the apartment - or Junior?

Fri 23 Apr - 4 page letter from Robert telling me to prepare for joining him by end of May. I don't know. I'd like to & yet my common sense says to wait before making a commitment. . . .I called Robert's Dad this aft & told him of the contents of Robert's letter, but I don't think I'll say any more about Robert's request that I join him. That is a problem for us to work out ourselves.

Mon 26 Apr - M - I came home to find 2 letters from Robert. Such beautiful letters, expressing his love & affection to me, & pointing out that if this war will last for years, we should grab at every opportunity to be happy.

*　*　*　*　*

9:30PM Saturday April 24, 1943

Darling

You are the sweetest, most wholesome, most desirable woman on earth. I love you till I could burst with happiness and am just as infatuated with you today as before we were married. Even more so, for it is a far richer wine which intoxicates me now, mellowed by

276

2 years of knowing and possessing your love and your enchanting beauty. Your pictures make me tremble in remembrance of ecstasy taken richly from your parted lips, the soft tussle of your hair, the electric delight of passing an intimate hand over your warm smooth thighs, the slimness of your supple waist so familiar to my grip, the classic contour of your shapely grace yielding seductively to my ravishing caress. My goddess of the eternal female I could enshrine your pictures and worship in daily adoration to you and the full deep beauty of our relationship. We are to each other as the laws are to the cosmos, as natural, as necessary, as perfect as the attraction between stars, as the progression of time or the extension of space. We are as real and beautiful as 10 million salmon shattering the swift stream to spawn in the silver-dripping pools; as fierce and lustful as the tawny thick-maned lion mounting the young cowering lioness, power rippling claws cuffing her hide possessively; as delicate and subtle as the honeybee brushing pollen from the liquid yellow dandelion, softly, the common act, the act of all, potency to fruition, union of flesh in pleasure to create flesh in pain. Turtles never know the miracle they do; but we know all, possess all, are all in each other my life in your flesh, mammalian we cling suckling eagerly the great mother breast of our love. I am entranced by you my lithe little female, my woman mate, my wife. Your pictures mean so much to me and I can sit by the hour just devouring the enticing sight of you and yielding to the flood of memory called up from the gem-glittering halls of our glorious past; and I sweep impatiently on to the future when I may once again press your pictured life-loving body tightly against mine and feel the throb of mated joy pulsate between us, eager love radiant in your eyes, your lovely womanhood quivering almost imperceptibly, expectant of caresses and warm-blooded delight. Your smile as you kiss me is the most beautiful sight there is. I long so for it.

My beloved I am so absorbed in your pictures that I can hardly think of anything even tho your letter too lifted me to the clouds. But the pictures are so real and natural, "unposed". You, so pretty entering the front door [Fig 20]; you, wind-blown in your big bear hug coat; you, so womanish and handsome in the chair, and my eyes have a passion for the risque revelation of your stockinged thigh; you, coquettish, yet wifely, sprawled in supple female grace across our bed. Our bed means so much to us. It is where we play innocently with love, where we abandon ourselves completely too lascivious sensuality, where we philosophize, where we plan, where we cuddle sleepily, kittenish and warm beneath our covers, skins intimate in married bliss. How I wish we were together in it tonite. But tonite we must sleep in lonesomeness relieved only by the beautiful dreams of the happiness we have known and which we know will come again. I must get up at 5 AM to go on the rifle range so, beloved, I must kiss for the thousandth time tonite only this time it is good night. I love you beyond all life my only mate, my woman my whole life is lived but to love you forever.

Robert

*   *   *   *   *

Tuesday, April 27, 1943 9PM

Darling -

Oh, precious darling, when you tell me I'll never take a back seat for anything, I just get all filled up with emotion. My eyes seem to tear up and I have an impulse to have a good cry. Silly! I am so overwhelmed with happiness, so filled with fierce love for you. I hate myself for trying to be sensible, for trying to think of anything but making you happy. But intuitively, I know I would be miserable if I did something that wasn't sensible.

Apropos that, dearest, you wrote something about our marriage not being sensible. I wish to refute that emphatically. It was the most sensible thing either one of us did, finding ourselves mates who can bring us such happiness. I shall never regret marrying you, Robert, for you helped me find the feminine in me, something I had been afraid of before I met you. You've made me realize what ecstatic heights the love of a man and a woman can reach. Similarly, I've known the grief of a woman separated from her mate. Right now I am undergoing an emotional struggle such as I have never thought I'd ever face. Dearest, since I married you, I've been living life. Before that I was only existing. "Strange letter my little girl writes me", must be in your mind by now, my dearest, and I don't know what makes me write all this. It's just in me and I've got to get it out.

*   *   *   *   *

7:30PM Thursday April 29, 1943

My beloved wife:

To begin with I see you accept the fact unreservedly that the

278

war will last at least 3 more years and secondly that we are very lonesome and unhappy apart. We agree and experience this gnawing ache undeniably with mutual intensity. We both want to be together but you don't think the price is worth it, to put it roughly but truly. However, your logic and analysis is quite faulty in many respects. You "wish to refute emphatically that our marriage wasn't sensible". Well, it certainly was not sensible, and you display in that reasoning alone the key error of your argument. You are analyzing the past from the <u>present</u> instead of from the <u>past</u>. Surely you haven't forgotten the trepidation and hesitation with which we entered marriage. You haven't forgotten that we had to borrow money for our honeymoon, that I was making $33 a week and was due to enter the army in perhaps a month. That we had only a dreary room to live in. It cannot be denied that we married in infatuation at the peak of sexual craving, of curiosity, for adventure, from war fever and through kindness and fair play in not letting each other down. Those 5 reasons we can now see formed the entire promulgation of our marriage, for then we did not possess the full rich depth of love which only the intimate moments of constant living together can build. We did not, could not, realize what a beautiful perfect thing we had done, as we do now. But the point is, we did it then. With far less to be sure of, if you will now correctly remember the past, we plunged ahead and seized the fate of our future, rashly acting on the impulse of our love-starved minds and bodies. That is the past from which our present grew. Similarly we are now faced with the same problem reiterated. To be happy for a few uncertain months or to do this sensible thing and languish in the throes of unsatisfied longing, the more poignant in that it could have been avoided for a while.

Do you now put yourself in the proper perspective of August 1941 and view the tortuous curtained future from those days so pregnant with the question of what will happen if and when. I know you do not regret the fact that we were foolishly impulsive then, acted against all advice and the dictates of sensibility. We raised the curtain tremulously but with firm resolution to succeed, and we revealed to ourselves the glorious correctness of our desires and longings. Shall we now hesitate to do the same, armored as we are in the sureness of our undying love, a cushion of cash, and buoyed up by success in marriage, in our jobs, in all we have undertaken? To me there seems but one answer.

*   *   *   *   *

Wed 28 Apr - M - During the day I kept reading Robert's Sat letter, a very ardent declaration of his love, and found such pleasurable comfort in his precious words.

Thu 29 Apr - M - Now at 10pm hurriedly writing to Robert. He is such a precious darling & still insists on my coming out to see him.

Fri 30 Apr - M - 8 page letter from Robert - very eloquently posing again the question of my joining him right after his graduation. [From course on refrigeration and air conditioning at Fort Warren] - Which made me rather angry because I thought we had settled that while he was here. . . . now I'll write a short letter to Robert - I wish he weren't such a 'quick trigger' man.

*   *   *   *   *

10:30PM Monday May 3, 1943

Coupled eternally to time I lay
Watching the radiant weave of galaxies
Silent, wrapped sublime in awe
Drifting thru myriad blades of living grass
Up to the massive majesty of clouds
Up, up into the brilliant nite
To glean the curving edge of space
And roam imprisoning infinity.
There grasped my mind an eager truth,
For I could see the nurturing earth
As more than futile dust;
Thereon the pain of fertile birth
Became the struggling spawn of cosmic lust.

*   *   *   *   *

I built a dream.
It took many months.
It was hard work.
It was good inside to see it grow
Glittering shimmering dream
Lovely and gay, sweet to the sense
As the fragrance of moon-bathed lilies
Studding star-flecked water.

Oh, soft dream, so fragile, so gentle so
Golden dream folded in fur and warm in the sun,
Unspoken longing
Languished in silence
Bliss now come true
This is my moment
This my achievement
My labor's creation, my harbor of desire, my. . .
And I paused to admire what I had done,
As the lover looks before kissing.
I paused to see my art's completion
Savor the ecstasy before possession.
Yes, it is beautiful, it is graceful, it is warmth
It is, it is, it is, DUST
Cruel teeth of the scoffing wind
Strike, shattering the shaft of joy
Plunge pulverized to utter gloom
Devoured by the lean fang of fate.
Oh derision, oh dust dream
Oh the taunting pumice of defeat.
And my mouth is dry with anger
And my eyes are wet with hate
And my soul cries from its hollow
"You built your dream too late."

          *   *   *   *   *

The shimmering portals of the past
Have closed, and thru the dismal hall of now
There comes an eerie whisper, like the sound
Of silver bells beneath the sea deep drowned
And deadened, muffled in despair
The joys that were
Sift ghostly thru the air.

          *   *   *   *   *

<u>My thots, my mood</u>

                         Love
                         R.W.D.

          *   *   *   *   *

Sat, 1 May 1943 - Came home disconsolate, thinking of Robert and myself - whether I should weaken and join him - or whether I should risk his anger by remaining adamant in my refusal.

Wed 5 May - Paid rent tonight - Found 2 letters from Robert - Sat ltr very despondent - Mon ltr a very cynical, disappointment expressive poem - a powerful indictment against fate that destroyed our happiness - Wrote Robert 8 page letter trying to cheer him up.

*   *   *   *   *

[I thought the next pages, written on lined, spiral dictation pad paper, had been lost or destroyed. However, I found them in March 2001 among a batch of letters labeled with the fateful date 14 May 1948, when I had opened one of them, not heretofore received, which I did at that time during a bitter and unsettling quarrel with my beloved. Clearly, I had been reading, in that disquieting circumstance, our tumultuous past, and this letter of 5 May 1943 was certainly part of our desperate quarrel of 1943. I am now surprised that I had the audacity to send it to her for it is unreservedly brutal. Happily, as she wrote several times in later years, she ultimately became enthusiastic about acceding to my pleas, joining me then in adventure, rather than continuing a rigid pursuit of the life of comfort and security that she was staunchly, and logically, defending when I wrote this diatribe.

Despite all these ex post facto arguments, the present document is a vicious attack upon her motivations and her character. It accurately reflects my mood and arguments at that time. My penchant for the vituperative is well illustrated here, and perhaps exemplifies why, in many subsequent quarrels, we "fought our battles" with grim silence. Had such intemperate language pervaded our later life, the effect might well have been irreparable.]

[Deduced to have been written Wednesday 5 May 1943]

To my acquisitive wife -

To whom gold holds more claim than kisses. That fact now stands raw, startlingly plain, undeniably affirmed; for it is in action not words that the real truth is revealed. You may vow adoration to the gates of heaven, but if you live willingly in hell, you are the devil's own. You write eloquently of your love, yet cling avariciously to the stronger attraction of $233.00 a month. It would now be futile of you to deny that this is so, for it has been deliberately enacted in just that manner. "The price was not worth it," and by Midas you didn't think it was.

That is the essential difference in us I feared from the 1st hint of our marriage, and you no doubt remember it quite vividly as it meant so much to you. I never could accept the yoke of cash you wanted, and I never will. Truthfully, I said that happiness could not be bought with any money and that it was entirely independent of worldly wealth. The happiness of a nigger boy with a 10-cent knife and the happiness of a queen with a full length ermine are essentially identical, not analogous, but identical. My happiness was in you, not in our possessions; BUT you must have money, property, security, a wall of bank books to brace your joy in life, and inevitably you built the very foundation of your happiness upon it. You failed, however, to convert me to basing my estimation of achievement on the accumulation of financial treasure. My basis of life always has been and will continue to be the fullness of living, the depth of experience, the richness of memory and the untold wealth of happiness that can lie in each living breath I take.

I fought your rapacious foolish grasping on many instances. I admire thrift, but I detest the outcropping in your actions of that irresistible lure of gold, the desire to save niggardly a dime developing pictures, to fritter away an hour waiting & walking to save a few cents of taxi fare. I must on those & similar occasions have felt instinctively the rift in your love, your soon to be chosen path of financial stability in preference to the undoubted joy yet mundanely unprofitable adventure of our projected reunion.

You have chosen worldly security, the sedentary path, static but safe, as against my plea for quick pulsing joy of dynamic life, facing the fate of the future, intrepid with the knowledge that the present was the most perfect possible.

Tuesday night I tried to phone you to see if your decision still held and tho I was unable to reach you, your following letters verified that the matter was entirely settled in your mind. You had revealed your true self irrevocably by your choice, for despite your insistence on love for me, your preference was demonstrated by your action. That fact is too clear cut to debate, and severs life between us as sharply as the sword of war could have desired. I would never now ask you to join me even if you would, for you would contrive to be miserable despite all happiness as you had been "forced" to come, as your bank book future was threatened.

The emptiness of my efforts is now apparent and has thrown my mind into a chaos of emotion. It would certainly be better to be a joyful ditch digger than to be a miserable king. I am now gleaning this knowledge painfully, the certainty that achievement in social strata is devoid of satisfaction. I have as much desire for my commission as a dog has for a pedigree. But that is not the point.

There seems little need for our carrying on heart tearing letters of longing when we willfully choose to be apart. We have no hope or further desire to be together till the years of war have passed, for it would leave you careening helpless on your feet with only $150 a month allowance to live on till we met again. Your cowardice and lack of confidence in yourself shocked me at first, but I see you are not above any other women (as I had thot you were), just insipidly weak and in love more for security than romance. It is a shame you neglected your mother's advice for that once, and married a man with wealth in his mind and body instead of his pockets.

Tho I continue to be your husband and also your lover (for memory is still extant), I will be dead to you till and if I return from war. Let us seek the anodyne of time, soothing the heat of passion with forgetfulness, smother the flower of memory with an ever lengthening past, lingering to obliteration. If I come back, we may be able to live a future together (provided of course that I could secure it adequately with cash), and if I don't return, consider me dead to you from this moment, as it is the logical time for such a death, relieving us both of the fear which it holds, and permitting us a free mind and free action from now till we resume a dormant love.

*   *   *   *   *

Thu 6 May - Home disconsolate at not finding a letter from Robert - I suppose he's angry at me for my letters - which makes me very miserable because I don't want him to feel that way. - I did some sewing tonight- hose, girdles, etc. - Wrote a 6 page letter to Robert - more or less reminiscing about our pre-marriage days - Can't help thinking of his Mon nite poem and that phrase "you built your dream too late" - Something sinister about it and I don't like it.

Fri 7 May - Bizerte and Tunis fell - The Tunisian campaign is drawing to a close [The portent of this for our future was totally obscure; but perhaps one of the many reasons for my getting transferred to the

Transportation Corps was to bring to the US some of the thousands of AfrikaKorps Kriegsgefangenen from that terminating campaign, e.g., Fig 31.] . . . no letter from Robert - that makes his Tues & Wed letters that I haven't gotten - Mrs H. came to 'console' me - she had noticed no letter in my mail box - Cold comfort to think I'm doing the right thing if Robert's affections are alienated in any measure.

Mon 10 May - Still no ltr from Robert . . . .I came home only half-heartedly expecting a letter - Something tells me that Robert won't write to me for a long time - A man's love ceases when he can't have his own way, it seems - Yet I can't quite believe it - It's too fantastic.

Tue 11 May - I found an 8 page Air Mail letter from Robert - a very bitter, uncomplimentary letter - a denunciation of me as 'acquisitive, cowardly, etc' - which really hurt very much - I went to bed at 7:30 and slept till 9:30 - Got up to write a rather calm letter to Robert, making no attempt to refute any of his accusations, inviting him to write me. . . .Somehow Robert's brutal exposé of his selfishness, and his simulated grief - in reality anger at frustration, leaves me entirely unmoved - When he accuses me of marrying him for security, I find myself laughing ironically. [She sure gives as good as she gets!! - I didn't marry such a glorious woman just for her looks, and the intellectual (but horribly emotional) battle between us is joined with equal armament!]

Wed 12 May - During lunch the Col and I went to the Art Institute & went thru all the exhibition halls on the 2nd floor. Reminded me of some of my art-seeing days with Robert. He was a good companion for "arty things", but as a partner in marriage he doesn't wear well. Somehow I've known that right along, but it does come as a surprise to me to find that his threats of severing us completely (for the duration or longer) does not affect me as it's calculated to do. In fact, I've been thinking of how to rearrange my life so as to make it most comfortable & pleasant for me for the present. - Now I'll write a letter to Robert.

*   *   *   *   *

285

My wife:

Tho my mind is still unbalanced by the wound you have given me, I feel the necessity for writing. I should not write you in the mood that I am in, but it has not left me for days so perhaps it will be better to spill the discordant chaos of my mind before you than to withhold it in equally grievous silence.

Your flat refusal to join me, preferring instead the embrace of false security, has torn with vicious claws the fragile sheen of most cherished memories and dreams. I have as yet been unable to re-cover my composure and deliberate the situation in cold clarity. Perhaps I never will, but it is only fair (or is it?) that I break my si-lence [I had stopped writing her.], tho I do it with reluctance, with a sense of inadequacy, incapability. I am enclosing a letter written Wed, [5 May, above] a bit [!!!] brutal and blunt in its accusations. I have lost some of the bitterness of the mood in which it was writ-ten but still cling morbidly to the intrinsic truth of its statements. It furnishes a picture of my thots for these trying days. Delete the verbal brutality, the bitterness, and you have the hollow haunted sorrow of my present. I do not know what to do. The urge is strong to leave it all by asking for overseas duty immediately. Then there would be no temptation, no necessity for longing, no possibility of further frustration. For years there has been the feeling within me strong, definite, that war would bring the end of my existence. Per-haps the feeling accounts for my intense ideology for the avoid-ance of war and all its futile waste. It certainly accounts for the cynical emotion I feel when you blithely plunge off into years and years of future happiness utterly oblivious to the unmistakable per-ils of the rapid present. I have never spoken to you of this for there was little use in placing this haunting doubt in your mind too. Now with the day drawing ever closer I seem to feel the ragged steel al-ready clutching at the life within my skull. I do not fear except for the suffering it leaves in you and the surety that you will curse in desperation every moment of love unlived, denied. You mentioned "Strange Interlude". You would do well to read it again and be taught by the tragedy portrayed in it. You quote a phrase, but over-look the whole. I write of these thots not to frighten you, merely to reveal the thots of my mind. I wrote you some poetry last Mon. You must not interpret it literally phrase for phrase or try to make logic of it. It is a poem, a captured mood, a swirl of half-truths and emo-tion set down to portray the inexplicable feelings of that moment.

For a while I thought it best that we should leave each other completely, abruptly. Not to write, not to think, not to wonder, not to remember but to forget, blot out, erase all traces of each other from our minds (tho that were impossible) - and when the years of butchery have subsided and we still lived whole and healthy, only then we might resume the warped path of our once intertwining lives. If the day of resumption never came, or if we or circumstances changed, the death would already have been mourned, the sadness drowned, the soul calloused to its pain. That seemed the course indicated by your decision, the logical sequence to this separation we were willfully choosing. If we were not to be together when we had the opportunity, were it not better to obliterate these longings and avoid the inevitable melancholy of frustration.

I still can make no decision. I don't feel capable of it in my present desolate mood, so we will keep up the routine of our existence for the past 7 months, tho now to me it has the mark of self-imposed martyrdom and seems a foolish mockery of agitating unnecessary pain.

You do not like letters of this sort. You would prefer that I prattle the trivia of daily events, but my mind does not dwell in that world right now. The emptiness of each day is better left unnamed and unlinked to the common routine of perfunctory existence. This would not have been written except that your imagination could possibly conceive worse shapes, for [Letter torn here] you have so far seen the workings of my mind correctly in your letters.

I want to express emphatically also that this is not to be taken in any way as a reiteration of the plea that you join me. That decision has been made and will stand despite anything. Don't know when I will write again. Perhaps after this you won't care to hear from me anyhow. It may be in time that I will subside to a state of normal sadness and resume the daily history of my army life to you, but at present something wrought up within me forbids this and stifles innocuous thoughts from my pen, putting instead the tortured whirl of frustration before your eyes. I am sorry for that surely, but it is all the present I have. I close with love for you not only from force of habit, but from some deep compulsion within me which says accept your fate. It is the same force that prevented my severing us completely for the duration of tragedy. Maybe you are stronger in this respect as you are in other sensible things.

Love, your husband
Robert

*   *   *   *   *

I shall try to write tonite, tho my mood is as sullen as when I tore up last nite's attempt. After a few letters like this you won't care for any more; I'll stop writing altogether and we'll be able to call it quits. I am sick in my mind and the poison from your wound has spread like a gangrene through my soul to the point where it will never be removed. You have set me right back where you found me, in a morose cynical misanthropic outlook on this damnable life. Even as I write this my hand twitches with anger to destroy it. Thruout the day my mind is a constant throb of despondent gloom mellowing gradually into bitter sorrow. There is something in what you have done that has completely overthrown my reason. I am not the same. I am sick at heart as tho you had ground me into the dirt and then laughed and mocked my wounded helplessness.

Cut tongues ground in the butcher's mash pot and poor rolls of celluloid crawl helpless on the lush plenitude of hair surrounding the navel of 25 cents a dozen and a dollar to the girl with the cut tongue twained in severance from being rolled on jelly beans purple and orange like one-eyed fish the other being rationed to feed teeth sunk in flesh pots of Egypt where the Sphinx wipes sand from his eye and winks at a sweater girl looping the remnants of one long blond hair in a corybulus of lust kalipygian on a lily stalk utterly balanced in pastel longings for the real thing Johnny does it better because Pluto was discovered in 1933 by a man using abundant halitosis but he discarded it later for a telephone number of 13 digits 3 more than I have toes to tickle the pink plush peregrine protoplasm jelly-like and oozing hard green marbles from the core box tops 10 for the Sphinx's wife and a quarter for the second throw because bananas are not used for that thing every day instead of taking par 5 for that hole full of machine gun bullets whose bayonet stud looks like a movie actress eating peanuts with her nose elephantine and the propinquity of her probocis is startling.

And after that hastily written scramble of free association my mind feels much clearer, like a Freudian catharsis and my pen feels more natural in my hand. I hope it has broken the spell which has kept me silent. You know my literary reasoning better than to be alarmed at such an outburst, or to take it as a judgment of my sanity. I am insane, but only inwardly, and it revolves about one point. A fixation which keeps my emotions constantly aroused and my thots swirling in the Maelstrom of my distraught moods. Do you want letters like this? I know perfectly well you don't. You would prefer that I didn't write at all and you could live in peace and forgetfulness. I still cannot write. I will write you no more till I recover, so don't expect any for a long time. Somehow I still love you, tho very sadly and disappointedly. I am sorry for all this

Robert

*　　*　　*　　*　　*

Diary: Thu 13 May - <u>Phone</u> **call - . . . a nasty 4 page letter from Robert which got me crying. Called Mrs D. Her advice was to forget about writing to Robert for several days and see what happens. She doesn't think he'll do anything drastic. . . . Robt called me collect and we talked for 10 min. He sounded very disconsolate. I said I'd think of joining him.** [Beginning of the resolution, i.e., she surrenders. Oh so happily, she never regretted doing so, and in later months and years was enthusiastic about our adventures together, the deep bond it formed between us in sharing the ever-fluent experiences that were to follow.]

*　　*　　*　　*　　*

11PM Thursday May 13, 1943

My darling:

I do feel happier after talking with you tho not very much assured that you will join me. But a swift rising surge of love for you is welling up within me once more. I feel like one on the verge of death must feel after a reviving transfusion. My beloved one, you did sound so tired and lonesome and I know you have suffered too, tho in my stubbornness I feel you accountable for your own injury, tho I know that I am also very much to blame, and did abuse you. No letter could ask the forgiveness that I seek, but I repent and will try to stem the brutality of my passion-driven pen. The blow from the hand hitherto used only to caress must pain a thousand times as much. I want to have you for my wife at every possible moment of my life and anyone, even you, seeking to obstruct the natural course of my love must bear the brute passion, the fury of my frustration. You, the person seeking to keep us separated, become so completely different and separate from the you, my wife, my eternal love. It was not till now this instant that I realized this fact, for even I at times wondered how I could think such brutal thots, lash you with such bitter words, and still deep down inside love you desperately. This splitting of you within my mind must have been the

289

root of the horrible anguish that has shaken my soul for the past few weeks. Now that this fact has been exposed to my reason, darling, I shall try to avoid it, writing and thinking only of the you I love so dearly. And darling, I do think you should join me. Not only for my sake but for yours as well. For us. You sounded so forlorn, so fate-locked and sorrowful in your powerless longing for the happiness of our marriage. You love deeply my sweetest one, weigh in your heart the value of what you have now and compare it with the joy that we as two together experience. Just that delirious certainty should be enough, but to satisfy the peculiar sense of security so purely feminine within you, I must also resort to more concrete arguments.

*   *   *   *   *

Fri 14 May - Had a talk with Dad Doty this a.m. and he said to ask Robert to submit a concrete proposal, etc, before I take any action. - But I called the Jackson Storage people to send an estimator out this eve. - Jackson says $50 to move and pack furniture and $10 a month for storage. Called Dad Doty and he cautioned me to go slowly. Talked to Mom and decided to send Robert a night letter telling him I was making arrangements to join him June 1st. Went to bed rather high strung and overawed at my great decision.

Mon 24 May - . . . letter from Robert telling me of difficulties in finding an apartment and warning me we may have to room or I shall have to look for quarters. Doesn't bother me very much somehow. I dashed off a short letter to Robert telling him of my disappointment at his folk's lack of cooperation - He admits that they are pinch pennies.

Wed 26 May - . . . busy with my packing of records, clothes and other paraphernalia so that it would be ready when Fritz came - So much of it; I can't understand where it all came from. So I worked until 2AM and then felt how the lack of time made it a much harder job than it was. - No ltr from Robert but perhaps he is very busy - Do so hope that we'll be together for a long time . . . . Wrote Robert a short letter telling him of my progress - Do so hope dentist will be thru with my bridge work by Fri so I can really leave Mon nite. - Feel my decision is the right one in view of

290

Robert's desire that I join him - Wearily to bed again - All curtains down - the house really bare looking.

Thu 27 May - Fritz moved all my stuff over to Mom's, leaving only clothes and odds and ends for Sat moving - No word from Dotys - I'm beginning to hate them - So to Mom's for good supper. - Sis sporting a $225 square diamond ring. Officially engaged! Well, well!

CHAPTER IX
Mediterranean Theater

Synopsis - The Chapter begins with the arrival of Elizabeth at Fort Warren, for what turned out to be but a few novel days of life on an Army Post. Things changed abruptly, and we sped across the country [Fig 28] to New York City and what was to become a life of transience for the next several years. I was soon on my way overseas, Elizabeth staying in our Brooklyn apartment and working at temporary jobs. Upon my return from Algeria with prisoners of war [Fig 31] and being assigned another ship, she returned to a less lonely existence at her parents' home in Chicago. On this second trip my ship paused at Gibraltar, then long at Palermo, Sicily, before taking a load of high octane gas to Naples. In the meantime I kept assaulting my worried wife with a barrage of unsettling letters, describing the turmoil of a society surviving the tide of war, and the effects of the intense loneliness and sexual urges I was experiencing. I was desperate to hear from her, but mail never reached me in the 3 months of these turbulent peregrinations. I visited the front lines in the battle of Cassino. Then, awaiting loading of ammunition for the Anzio invasion, my ship was sunk [Fig 32], my survival depending upon mere luck. After some impatient days in Naples I managed to find an agreeable Colonel who OKed my flying return to the States [Fig 33] and another rapturous rendevous in Brooklyn.

*   *   *   *   *

Tue 1 June 1943 - In Cheyenne at 8:45 - Robert met me at the station - We got my bags, took a bus to the post and carried them for blocks to the guest house. Rustic but clean, a corner room with the wind howling outside. Very nice shower room for us gals down the hall. Robert and I slept in one army cot locked in each other's arms. To bed at 10 or so, setting alarm for 5AM for Robert to get up.

Wed 2 Jun - Had supper with Lt and Mrs Duncan. Danced at Officers Club, then over to the boxing matches at the gym. Fairly interesting - So cold and windy out here I don't know if I'm going to like it. The guest house is fairly comfortable, public showers not bad. Very good meals at the Officers Club and so convenient. It will be fairly interesting to stay here if we can find a place. We can stay 7 days before being asked to find other quarters. [We rented a nearby room for $10/week, and for 18 days enjoyed life on the post.]

Thur 17 Jun - Robt gets Orders to POE - Slept till 10 AM. Beautiful mild clear day. RWD called at 10:30 for me to go out and sun myself. Well, I had breakfast, washed out a few things, dressed and walked into town to buy some buttons for Robert. Picked up his shirt and slacks from cleaners, stopped at bus depot to inquire about busses to Estes Park. Phone call at 4 PM from Bob stating he got his orders, to go to N.Y. Port of Embarkation, Brooklyn, New York. Owah! Said he was going to protest it in view of fact that Post HQ had him scheduled for Vancouver Barracks with a refrigeration company. I met him at the Service Club. Had a few drinks with Lt Gurin and his wife. Then to see the boxing matches, very enjoyable. Sort of relaxing before the hard day before us to pack and wind up things here in Cheyenne.

Fri 18 Jun - We leave Cheyenne - Got up at 7 with Robt. Fixed breakfast for him (trying to eat up as much as possible of our stock of groceries). Then I went into town and returned two books to the Norvegie Public Library. Withdrew $200 from bank. Came "home" to start packing. Called Grace Millay in hope of selling some canned goods to her and found that Francis had gotten orders to go to Shenango, Pa. Robt called to say he had seen Col Cleoster, but was told he had to comply with orders. He came home about 2:30 and we both packed. Left for post about 4:30 and while Robert got his final clearance I went over to the club. We had supper, home, taxi to take our 4 bags which we were going to check through to N.Y. We returned to the Westrup's. Had a final snack and chat with Leonard and Mrs W.

Sat 19 Jun - En route to Chicago - Left Westrup's; lift from Pete (one of Robert's friends) to RR station. Some difficulty getting berth. Breakfast at station. Telegram to Mom and on the train. Got a lower for both of us, good. Quiet trip all told. Took a nap. Ate supper about 7 PM in the diner. Then I put my hair up in curls. Berths were made up and so we went to bed. Two of us in a lower, and Robert insisted on making love to me. Finally fell asleep. Rather comfortable at that. Got up at 7 AM, dressed in summer clothes and waited for the train to get into Chicago. 9:30 AM, Max met us at the station.

Sun 20 Jun - En route to New York - Got us a double bedroom on the Penn 3:30 train. Taxi out to Mom's. So happy to see them and they us. Breakfast. Then a fine chicken dinner. Taking some snapshots [Fig 28] before we left at 2:30 on the L after futile attempts at getting Bob's Dad to put us on the train. Jogging along in our private room. A very comfortable way to travel.

Mon 21 Jun - Arrive in New York - Got in at 10AM. Took subway to St George Hotel, Room for 30.00 a week (owah!) but RWD thinks it's all right. Breakfast at hotel and then going down to look over the NY Port of Embarkation. Huge place where cargo is received and loaded on boats. RWD bought 3 suntan shirts and 2 pair slacks at the QM Sales Office. Back to the hotel. Meeting 2 of his friends who have been here for several weeks. They have been assigned as Cargo Security Officers. Don't know what RWD will get. Hope it's good. Took shower in aft (after some watermelon) and napped till 7 or so. Washed out my seer sucker dress, hose, slip, etc. We dressed and had a delicious crab dinner at a restaurant across from the hotel. About 8:30 then but I decided to go see Loretta Jelenkiewicz [Her cousin]. On the subway to Prospect Ave. Got a nice welcome from her and her husband. Sitting in their small flat very hot and sweltering. They served sandwiches and drinks. Adorable baby (now 9 mos old). We left about midnite. Took trolley back to the hotel. Washing out a few more articles of clothing. To bed finally about 1:30 AM. Falling asleep watching lights of the city and the hum of traffic down below.

Tue 22 Jun - Slept till 9:15 or so. Showered, dressed and had breakfast at Plymouth Cafeteria. RW got a haircut in the hotel. I read NY Times. Then we took subway to the Grand Army Plaza to go apartment hunting, but we got waylayed [sic] at the Brooklyn Public Library and the Museum. About 1 PM Robt decided to report in to the NYPOE and see what his assignment will be. I returned to the hotel. Robt came back at 4 or so very angry at the whole setup. Civilians in soldiers' uniforms, etc. irked him. I took a nap. Went to Prospect Park to hear the Goldman band in a concert. Fairly good. We looked for furnished apartments around the Park. No luck. Guess it'll be up to me to really start looking. I don't care for the St George Hotel a bit.

Thur 24 Jun - Out of St George to 294 Henry St - Robt angrily left this a.m. I determined to get us out of the St. George and lined up in an apartment before the week was out. Went to call Anthony [Another cousin] after breakfast to get address of Renting Council in NY. Stopped at Lanes first and he sent me to 285 Henry St. Liked it very much, one room with kitchenette facilities; also small bedroom, nice bathroom, 2 closets, linens furnished to Oct 1st. Good enough for the time being. Came back to find Robert home. So we both went over and took the apt @ 60.00 a month. Then moved out of St. George (19.70 for 3 days!) Perhaps unwise but we moved to an old rooming house across the street from 285 Henry St, an experience if anything and we will save about $10-$11! Met a very nice gal, Leanna Coleman in apt below us at 285. She's very sweet. Took subway to Times Square, all dimmed out. So we returned to our room and went to bed about 11:30 PM. Boy, has it been hot this week! How I miss Cheyenne! And Chicago!

Fri 25 Jun - Robt and I went out to the Brighton Beach, got wet in Atlantic Ocean, also in pool. Robt rather disgusted with me cause I can't swim. We stayed on the beach till 7 PM. Had a vegetable supper at a Jewish cafeteria around there. Came home about 8:30, both of us rather tired. Robt has dozed off every afternoon this week. Just learning things about this cargo security setup. I guess he's a darling, but he makes me angry with his constant criticism of my shortcomings. My hesitation to do something new and different. I guess we're making progress as it is, but heck, our money sure is going fast and that's no joke. After we get settled in the apt, I'm going job hunting.

Sat 26 Jun - This a.m. we found a "bug" on our bed. Trying to identify it? Started savings account at Brooklyn Savings Bank. Robt will make allotment payable there $200 per mo.

Sun 27 Jun - At Uncle John's today for dinner. [Fig 29] Nice welcome from them. In the eve Loretta & Ed, Jean & Anthony went with us to Coney Island. Walked on the boardwalk, looked at the concessions. The boys drank beer. Took a ride. We left about 9:15. On crowded subway getting home 10:30 or so to our awful room. But fine breeze blowing and so falling asleep. God, what a hole this NY is!

Tues 29 Jun - Orders! - Robt came home before 4:30. He was told today of his assignment. Will leave city and will try to postpone same till after we get settled in our apt Thursday. I felt very much downhearted, but c'est la guerre! Over to library to read a while. I'm trying to figure out my mode of procedure after he leaves. Do so hope he can postpone it for a few days. I'm going to do my best to be lighthearted about this, but partings are not easy for me ever, and certainly not now even tho he will be returning. Letter today from Col. Jensen.

Wed 30 Jun - Robert Prepares to Leave! - Dismal day, cool. I slept late and ate breakfast at drugstore. At library making application for card. Back to sign draft to collect Cheyenne bank a/c. Shopping to use up red points which expire today; also coffee. In aft at TVSO where Mrs Koven gave me pots and pans and dishes and silver to really equip me for cooking. Robt came home at 3:30 with carbine and gas mask. Left to return to port. Baggage arrived from Penn Station. The Franks said we could move in to apt tonite. At least 1 nite in our apt before he leaves. Robt back at 6:30 tired, with musette bag, ammunition, impregnated clothing. We moved our stuff into apt. While Robt packed, I fixed sandwiches and we drank cokes. He had 3 shots today and felt too ill to go out and eat so I ate toast. Unpacked my bags and tried to get settled in apt. The poor darling had chills and fever and stuff. I put extra blankets on bed. Trying to sleep. Alarm set for 4:30 so he can take 6:30 train for Baltimore. Mrs. Coleman says she will go with me to see him off.

Thurs 1 July 1943 - Robert Leaves for Baltimore - We managed to get up at 5:45 AM and I tried to fix breakfast in a makeshift fashion while he dressed and finished packing. Mrs C came at 6:30 and we left at 6:45 or so. Subway to Penn Station. Hoping we get there on time to take 7:30 train. Robert in full battle regalia, helmet, carbine, musette bag, gas mask bag, trench knife. [The latter had been given me by our landlord in Cheyenne, a World War I veteran.] He looked fierce. Seeing him off. Having so-so breakfast at H & H automat with Leanna. Robert called me about 1 PM from Baltimore to tell me they were sailing Sun and for me to join him at Lord Baltimore Hotel tomorrow. Said I would. Why not?

Fri 2 July - I join Robert at Baltimore - Up at 7 AM, breakfast of toast and coffee, dressing haphazardly and leaving house 7:40 or so. Lugging bag to St George subway station. Crowd at Penn Station but I managed to get a seat. Sat next to a Corp Tafkin who was a fair conversationalist, and who carried my bags and bot me doughnuts and coffee in Baltimore. Taxi to hotel. Robert had a nice room, 4.50 single, 6.50 double, Room 1044. I took a bath and got into bed awaiting his arrival from work. He called about 4 or so and said he'd be out soon. The darling came soon and found me refreshed from my aft nap. Says he'll be Cargo Security Officer and Troop Transport Commander on this boat. Has been eating lunch at Holabird QM Depot. His office is close to hotel, HQ of 3rd Service Command. Got milkshakes (made with ice!) at drugstore in hotel. Ret'd to hotel. Robert took apart his carbine and showed me the workings. We tried on gas masks too and I'm taking back the one he got from the POE. We went to bed past midnight. So good to snuggle to my darling.

Sat 3 July - Robert had left about 7. Went out for breakfast. I returned to hotel as I expect a phone call from Robert. Wondering if he is leaving today, tomorrow? He came home at noon. We ate lunch together. At 4 he left to take his baggage on board ship. Will have to be there 8 AM tomorrow, so I'll try to leave on 7:44 AM train for N.Y. We had supper together, came up to our room early. I packed my bag. We went to bed early, holding onto Robert tight and thinking what changes have occurred since our marriage almost two years ago. Tomorrow he leaves, says he'll be back Sept. 1st. God, I pray that this all turns out all right. I get panicky at the thought of being left alone.

Sun 4 July - Robert leaves - He left at 6:30 AM. I checked out shortly. Taxi to station, breakfast, impatiently awaiting train to N.Y. Holiday crowds made me more sad at my loneliness. Back "home" by noon. Out to Uncle John's, chatting with the gals. Subway home by 9. Looking over want ads in NY Times regarding employment opportunities. I think I'll feel much better with a job.

Mon 5 July - Woke up about noon. Leanna called from her Aunt Ruby Geddy's (hotel) to say would I put up Ruby for tonite and I agreed, why not? They came about 1 or so. Got 2.20 seats for "Rosalinda" a Johan Straus musicale (Der Fledermaus) for tonite. Went to Radio City on a guided tour of the studios (55¢, & in Chicago costs nothing). Went up to the observation roof, 70 stories above street (Leanna had tickets for that, otherwise 50¢).

Tues 6 July - AIRMAIL LETTER FM ROBERT - Awoke at 9. Ruby went down to eat breakfast with Leanna. Going to Macy's to shop and look. . . . Leanna came up with letter from Robert mailed from Newport News, Va yesterday, telling me he was enjoying his trip so far and for me to enjoy myself. The dear darling.

*   *   *   *   *

[My letters before leaving on my first voyage:]

3:30PM Mon July 5, 1943

My darling -

This is kind of against regulations, but I know you're wanting to hear what's been happening to me. We sailed from Baltimore at 9 AM yesterday and arrived here about 2AM this morn. I love the ocean so far and my appetite is terrific. The food is fine too and plentiful!

Watched the ship get underway and then went to work. Read all my orders, regulations etc. Went down to inspect the troop quarters and the cargo which would be accessible to them for pilferage. Have accommodations for 353 men. All they have to do is prowl around a little and they are going to discover how easy it would be to help themselves to clothing and food stored right under them. In fact I discovered one bundle of officers shirts size 15 - 35 I'd like to open myself.

Lt Patterson, the gunnery officer, and I are going to hit it off well I'm sure. He's a fine fellow, clean cut, hard-working etc. Like him and he should help make this a good voyage. He and I and the Captain came ashore this morning about 9 AM and by noon I had found where I should be and gotten over here. Landed at Sewell's Point on Norfolk and had to come all the way across the bay here to Hampton Roads. Got all the dope on my setup. Am taking about 7 MP detachments of 32 men each to the other side. They have one officer to each group so that will mean I'll have about 8 officers to do the work and I think I'll let them do it while I relax. Have sure been chasing around today getting arrangements for my PX supplies, medical supplies, etc. The troops I am to take won't come aboard till Thurs or Fri. Don't think I'll write again from here sweetheart, but I will when we get to the other side. Bought a bunch of airmail stamps, shower shoes, soap, mirror, etc. at the PX here.

Most likely will not come ashore again until Wed or Thurs. Hope you are enjoying yourself darling. Sure is hot here and I wish I were out on Coney Island. Have a good time sweetest while I'm gone for I sure am getting the vacation cruise on this deal and tho I miss you already my snugglebug, there is plenty to be happy about. Don't forget you have concerts, museums, the YW, good books, etc. etc. to keep you till I come back. If I'm not back when we plan, I may have had to get prisoners at a different place, but it's fairly certain that things will go as planned.

Love you so much
Robert

*   *   *   *   *

9:15 PM Tuesday July 6, 1943

My beloved -

Feel so lonely, so philosophic and poetic tonite. Have been sitting up forward in one of the open trucks we're carrying as deck cargo and reading poetry. Cool breeze, peaceful, anchored in the middle of the harbor with the land and docks surrounding us dimly distant, an occasional ferry or harbor boat breaking the monotony of motionless ships between dirty water and clouded sky.

Last nite we spent being de-Gaussed, which is a difficult way of saying de-magnetized. A ship that acts as a magnet will set off a type of mine known as a magnetic mine. These mines are detonated when a magnetic needle within them is disturbed by the attraction of the ship. Therefore we were put through this de-Gaussing business. Was quite a sight to watch with a heavy rainstorm coming angrily across the bay and Negro workers chanting rhythmically, weirdly, straining to pull the heavy cables aboard. It was quite a sight to see as so much of this sailing is and I think continually of how I wish you were here to see it too.

Tomorrow we set our compass, take on water and anchor off Hampton Roads to be ready to take on my troops etc. I'll be glad when we finally start across, the sooner to be back to you my sweet one.

My room is too hot and I keep the fan going all the time. Am going to get a cot that I'll be able to sleep on deck on warm nites.

10PM Wed. July 7, 1943

Started to ration water today. It will be on from 7-9 AM and from 4-6 PM each day.

*　　*　　*　　*　　*

7:30 PM Friday July 9, 1943

Sweetest darling -

Our medical supplies (army) came aboard last night and I have the narcotics here in my room waiting to put them in the ship's safe.

Hope my little cuddlekitten is having a good time seeing New York. You should darling. And please beloved don't forget the exercise, the swimming, etc that you promised to do. I hope you're a regular little Amazon when I get back. I love you so much darling and want you as lovely as you are always.

I should come back black from the sun, strong from the sea and so eager for the adventure of your arms. I love you my wife.

*　　*　　*　　*　　*

8:15 AM Saturday July 10, 1943

My lovely one -

Just heard on the radio at breakfast that we are invading Sicily. That's good news but I'm afraid this ship won't go anywhere's near it. Since we were at dock yesterday I was able to get the army to build me a sturdy storeroom for my PX supplies. Lt Patterson [Navy Gunnery Officer] and I are to eat at the Captain's table. He also says that the other army officers we get aboard will have to eat down in the hold with the men so that will give me just that much more prestige (perhaps necessary to subdue some 1st Lt with ideas on how things should be run.) I don't think I'll have any trouble tho for

I'm going to "delegate" most of the authority (i.e., work) to the other officers which should make them very content at being allowed to "run" things their way.

*   *   *   *   *

7:15AM Sunday July 11, 1943

My precious

. . . 335 men (11 officers) are going to be, have been already a headache but I'm thru worrying about it after yesterday. Sure disgusted with the inefficiency of the Hampton Roads PoE.

*   *   *   *   *

Thur 8 July - M - Stage Door Canteen - Slept till about 10 today. After breakfast Leanna and I went shopping for groceries. Went to Public Library and got us some books to read. 2 Russian grammars, Wolf's "Web and the Rock", Cumming's poetry and Saroyan's plays. Got referred to Army Placement Bureau at 165 Bdwy. Don Beyer (the Coast Gurard boy) was there and he said he'd escort me to radio program on CBS "Stage Door Canteen" tonite. We also got tickets for tomorrow to see Cities Service program. Got a lot of advice on things to do to keep busy. Don came by for me at 7:30 and we went down to CBS theater #2 on 45th St 250 West. Enjoyed radio program - Lin Yutang, Anna May Wong & Mary Jane Walsh were the guests for the evening.

Fri 9 July - M - Found letter from Mom, also 2 letters from Robert, the dearest darling. Love Robert very much, so very much.

Mon 12 July - M - Slept till 10:30. Awoke groggy like to find a hot sultry day in full swing. Found Fri & Sat letters from Robert enjoining me to enjoy myself. This immediately pepped me up. . . . To Federal Bldg. Sat for hour or so in War Transfer Unit waiting to get a gencral release. Came home by 5 PM; hot, dusty, tired, hungry. Found another letter from Robert, last one until he gets on the other side. So sweet of him to write.

Tues 13 July - Shopping with Leanna - Today we did visit St Patrick's Cathedral (where I said some prayers for Robert's safe and speedy return and our happiness) and also stopped in N.Y. Public Library.

Wed 14 July - Call from Robert - Awoke at 8:30. Right after

301

breakfast phone call from Robt fm Newport News, Va., stating he'd be there for 10 days or so and asking me to come down right away. Asked me to get laundry fm POE etc. Well, I said I would come Fri. Robt called again to tell me he had a room all ready for me @ 10.00 per week and to come tomorrow, so I said I would.

Thurs 15 July - Arrive at Newport News - Enroute to Washington sat beside a Lt in S.C. and carried on conversation to pass time away. In return he carried my bag over to train I took for Richmond on F R & P Line. Awful, not air-conditioned. Had to stand for hour or so. Marines and sailors everywhere. At Richmond nuisance of transferring from Broad St Station to Main St Station. Had to take taxi across town. Paid 50¢ fare charged and rode with 4 other passengers. Phooey! Robert met me and we had sundae at PX before taking bus to room at Dobson's, 222 Hollywood Ave. Showered up and got grime off my body. Napped all aft. At 6 PM we rode into town, ate at officers mess and then went over on pier and watched some soldiers fishing for crabs. Saw Robert's Liberty ship anchored offshore. Walked around town. Hot and humid. Sitting on front porch talking to the Dobsons. To bed with my darling so sweet.

Fri 16 July - We ferry over to Norfolk - We decided to go to Norfolk. C&O ferry (33¢ one way) about one hours ride. At Norfolk hot and humid but good! Shopped for another seersucker dress and got one for 3.99. Had deviled crab snack before dash for ferry at 6:30. Nice calm trip, watching gulls following ship. At N. News at 8 PM, gobs of ice cream at PX. Discussing my plans after I leave here. Whether to stay in Brooklyn or go back to Chicago. Robert wants me to stay and putter around until he returns. Undecided. Perhaps I can clarify things before he leaves.

Sat 17 July - We swelter in Newport News - RW came home at noon and we decided to go to town. Waited ½ hour for bus. Then had a so-so lunch at restaurant. Hot so we went to movie. Out at 5 or so. Ice cream at PX. Out at pier but so hot. Didn't eat supper because Robt had no tie on and couldn't go into Officer's Mess.

Mon 19 July - Buckroe Beach - Robt thinks we should go out to the Buckroe Beach this aft if he's at liberty. Have a feeling of loneliness and irritation at not doing anything these past two months. Tried to convince Robt I should go back to Chicago, but

302

he is adamant that I stay in N.Y. But I will get a job. We did go to the beach this aft. Very small compared with Coney Island, bathhouse facilities mediocre and filthy, but we got out on the sand. Robert swam out to the pier offshore. I stayed on the sand for a while. Then he insisted I go out to the pier with him and I did, following the ropes and then just floating the rest of the way. Fine sunning ourselves on the pier on clean boards instead of the sand. Stayed there a few hours and then started back for shore. Boy, I swallowed some saltwater, and went under a few times, but it didn't frighten me much. Got back okay, surprising both Robt and me. Had fine meal at Officer's Mess. Came home to wash off saltwater and to treat our sunburn, which both of us got.

Tues 20 July - Old Point Comfort - Ft Monroe - Slept till quite late this morning. Phone call from Robert that he'd be busy all day. . . . Robert came about 5 PM. Preparations afoot for sailing soon. He said Lt Patterson and his wife would like for us to dine with them at the U.S. Hotel Chamberlain at Ft Monroe where they were staying. So I got all dressed up in my black chiffon dress [Fig 30] and we set out for the trolley. Met them on the car. Had a very fine meal (1.00 per) at the hotel. Visited after dark on the veranda overlooking the bay. Walked around a bit to look at the old Fort with its moat filled with water, old gun emplacements. Understand Jefferson Davis was kept a prisoner here for 2 years. Left at 10:30. Mrs. Patterson will return to NY Thursday. We exchanged addresses, etc. Decided I leave tomorrow and get back to town to decide what to do about the apt, a job. Robt wants me to wait till October 1st before going home or anything. I will, if under protest.

*　　*　　*　　*　　*

8:45 AM Saturday July 24, 1943

I must get busy now, get my PX supplies and make an appearance in Capt Stewart's office (I.G.) which I'll bet means they'll want a report of the voyage when I get back. That would make the Intelligence, QMC, TC and IG I'll have to write reports to for this deal.

*　　*　　*　　*　　*

11:30 AM Sunday July 25, 1943

Sweetest wife -

In the afternoon I got the additional PX supplies and had them put aboard. The evening I spent in conference with the chief steward, and getting the refrigeration and ventilation system functioning properly and in drawing up a schedule and list of duties and orders for the troops.

First thing this morning discovered the drinking water was shut off down in the troop quarters which almost gave me a stroke after thinking that had been fixed for a week. After two hours the chief engineer finally found the combination and it's okay now. Then had deodorizers installed in the latrines, and got all the water system checked and functioning properly. Got a detail of army men to give the whole works a final cleanup so that everything is prepared for the troops at 4 PM.

Darling, the chief mate and I rather suspect they <u>may</u> have changed our destination for they wanted to know what heavy lifts we had aboard. I don't see how they could change the destination of all these numerous articles we have without causing a colossal mixup. However, sometimes the army is capable of this so bear that in mind if I'm not back by Oct 1st. I really believe tho that it is still the "express" trip as previously planned, and it looks like we'll have an ideal voyage.

I will be dreaming of you as I watch the water dancing exuberantly before the ship's prow and remember your beauty as the cool breeze whispers the sun into the ruddy rolling sea. Be happy darling and keep living and experiencing all you can while I'm away that when we next meet we both will bring to each other a little deeper understanding of life and its beauty.

*   *   *   *   *

[V-Mail]

Monday August 10, 1943

My beloved wife, my sweetheart.

. . . went below and inspected the EM's chow. Feeding them has been quite a problem but the army cooks have been doing a sweet job. Spent the morning taking inventory of my PX. Opened the PX and supervised the sales from about 12:30 to 1 and from 6:30 to 7 PM. Lay in the sun reading "Les Miserables" from 2-4 PM ("Tom Jones" finished).

. . . went out to watch sunset and get a breath of air before retiring into my stuffy, blacked out room. Usually stick the mute in my horn and practice for about 30 minutes and then read to midnight or talk with someone. Occasionally go down in the engine room to learn what I can about it. There have been many things of interest, flying fish, sponges, the luminescence of the water at nite. The other day I had a startling fright. Was laying [sic] in my cot sunning next to the rail on the boat deck when not over 50 feet away a glistening black hulk rose out of the waves making a loud stertorous noise. My first thot was submarine! But a moment later the object rose from the water, snorted again and dived, shaking the huge tail of a whale, kind of laughingly, before my surprised eyes.

*   *   *   *   *

1PM Sunday August 15, 1943

Beloved

This is, tho a typical North African city, a strange mixture of Arabs and Europeans, palm trees, cactus, crooked streets, ragged filthy beggars, women in sheets that give you a weird look with their one unveiled eye, such a contrast to see following behind her a French doll dressed in form fitting clothes, bare legged, high heels (all wooden soled shoes here). What a gulf of difference between these women.

I'm going up sightseeing tonite but this aft I have to wait for the QM to come and pick up my excess PX supplies. Turned in $1000 to the Finance Officer this morning and I'll soon be rid of this PX headache.

*   *   *   *   *

[The remainder of these V-Mails were typed, all CAPS in radio shack]

1:30AM Monday August 16, 1943

Went to the Red Cross officers club where they serve lemonade and sandwiches. All of a sudden there was a tremendous commotion, and melee of which a line formed clear around the room. We were quite puzzled at first at this strange behavior of these men but soon perceived it to be all due to one simple thing: the Red Cross was going to give out one can of ice cream! We left the ice cream to those who hadn't seen it in months and went in quest of more potent and stranger, concoctions. Found a place which said officers

305

only, so we wandered down into the basement and found about 50 officers, cavalry, tank corps, infantry, Navy etc. crowded into this one little cocktail lounge, piano going full blast. We sat down and the waitress asked us if we would have "Meeky Feen". As that was all of her lingo we could understand we consented to have 2 Mickey Finns brought to us at a cost of 32 francs each. They weren't bad, some cognac and wine deal. I switched over to "vin blanc sec" tho for the next course which was excellent cold and only 10 francs. - Couple mosquitoes flying around in here now which makes me glad I took that atabrine on the way over.

*   *   *   *   *

8PM August 17, 1943

People over here must take the Americans for terrific suckers for they have some of the most preposterous prices on all their merchandise and stick adamantly to that price. For instance one little shop wanted $5 for a 25¢ Chekoslovakian pin and $6 for a pretty green belt which you could have bot in any American dime store. About 5 PM we got disgusted and headed for the tavern we had found the nite before. Their Mickey Finn is made of one shot of cognac, a slug of muscatel and a generous topping of white wine. Discovered the real potency of this stuff drinking as we did on an empty stomach. Must say that I got royally soused and my partner in crime confessed this morning that he didn't remember how we got back to the ship. (Don't suppose you better tell his wife that even tho all we did was get just plain good and drunk and very unexpectedly at that.) I sure remember how I got back on the ship tho. In fact I'll never forget it, for when I came back the ship was gone! It was now 10 PM and you can imagine my sinking feeling being far from sober and stranded. Got into a rowboat with two paddles instead of oars and a bunch of sailors coming back from their nite's escapades. They knew where they were going tho and soon left me to try and get this French kid to paddle me to my ship which he knew nothing about either. After a half-hour of this and getting a bit frantic, I managed to hale a motorboat run by some native and he took me to the ship with no hesitation. Was I glad to get "home"! WOW and how, and I gave the guy a 100 franc note with my profuse thanks. Don't think I'll ever come near getting drunk again while I'm over here, but then I didn't expect to this time. Those Mickey Finns just snuck up on me.

7PM Monday Aug. 23, 1943

My eyes hope for nothing lovelier than the mirrored sight of yours, flaming love, flashing from the silent jewels of your soul, meaning forever, and my hands are strong and eager, keen for the delight of clasping curves hidden in the warmth of silk, like the swift tide bringing sudden coolness, irresistible, to the hot sand. The quenching of a moonthirst, foam melting to starlight in each ephemeral surge as the kiss is brought firmly to moist lips, meaning possession which is to be eternal, to be unity, to be sustained, a separate perfection in the cyclic flux of unseen suns, dreaming of reality only as the ground from which to leap. I say to you love: and you know it to be identity, to be an immortal future, to be the young passion of the sand dunes beneath the silver shadows of the pines, now mellowed to a molten glow of glad fire, intimate, sublime, fertile, nourished in complete beauty, as memory springs ever triumphant from the purity of the past. I love you my wife, tho the precision of the typewriter makes me stammer and fumble as I try to express this deep emotion.

*   *   *   *   *

Wed 21 July - I start for New York - After a hasty packing, so-so breakfast in town, Robert put me on the train and we parted with "see you in New York" about 9:30 AM. Hot trains. Found my connecting train had left and next train to NY was 4 PM, 3/4 hour wait so I had another sandwich and coffee in station. On train to NY met a 1st Lt Air Corps who had ret'd from 18 mos in Africa. Had ice cream and coffee in diner with him. He amused me with anecdotes of his travels. Had roll of currency from each country he visited while in the Air Transport Command, Iran, Egypt, Dakar, Ethiopia, India, Russia, Brazil, etc. etc. Spoke French and we exchanged a few phrases. He was going to be stationed on Long Island and said he'd like to call me sometime. Why not? Lt Woodrow saw me off to my subway. I got "home" about 8:45, hot, tired and dirty.

Friday 23 Jul - . . . . Sent me to the Universal Trade Service at 724 5th Ave where they wanted a gal for 2 weeks, 30.00, 5 days per week from 9:30 to 5:30. Well, I guess it'll be okay. I'm to start

307

Monday and this Mr Blumenthal seems an easygoing fellow, office is small but the bldg is located in a swanky section of town.

Mon 26 Jul - Work 1 - Gee, I sure hated to get up at 7:30 AM for work. Got on wrong BMT train and had to transfer but got down at 9:15. Dinky office and hot and muggy today but on the whole it was all right and when I figure I'm making 6.00 a day of which I would not get loafing, it's OK for two weeks. Learning about the news agency business. Mr Blumenthal, Mr Herrick, the feature writer, Rose Ulric the bookkeeper, they help me understand the average New Yorker. Lunch for 20¢ at Automat, fair. Home about 6:30 to find 5 letters, wotta scoop! Am just thinking of Robert's last letter that their destination might be changed. What if he doesn't get back by Oct 1st? What to do then, go back home or wait? Problem! I am tired after my 1st day at office work after 2 months of loafing and sleeping late.

Wed 28 Jul - A bit cooler today, anyway I felt more disposed to work. Blumenthal gave me my weeks salary of 30.00 today. Herrick asked if I'd be interested in a job with some publishing concern after my two weeks are up. During lunch went over to Central Park Zoo (65th St) and watched the seals being fed. Kind of a grind at the office. Oh well, I need a little brushing up on typing, and shorthand, after my 2 yrs of loafing with Col. Jensen. Letter from Dad Doty appeals to Robert to write, if only for Rich's sake. What to do about him, obviously they don't care to hear from me. Nice long chatty letter from Sis; sounds so sweet. Wish I were home with them instead of in this "hole". Well, I think I'll stick it out another month or so just to see what all happens. Do feel tired. Just returned from library where I got 3 <u>fiction</u> books.

Mon 2 Aug - Crazy sort of existence I'm leading. Constant ache and nervousness, missing Robert more than ever. God grant that he returns to me safely before Oct 1st that we may straighten out this mess. I do want to get settled somewhere. I just don't enjoy this being stranded away from the folks. With Robt it's OK, but alone I don't like it. So lonely.

Fri 6 Aug - M - Last Day at UTPS - Rather cool today, a grateful relief. Very busy all day finishing up things. During lunch I took a long walk around the neighborhood, finding much of interest in the architecture and the mdse display. My last day here, all so unreal, my being here in N.Y.; afraid I might get to like it. I just don't want to feel that way. Perhaps it's the menstruation, but I do feel apprehensive of the future. What will we do when Robert returns? Where will he work? Will I have a home of my own? These thoughts run through my mind.

Sat 7 Aug - M -Stadium - Ezio Pinza - Called Mildred [Patterson, wife of Navy gunnery officer on my ship] and made date for tonite Stadium Concert. Met her and another Navy wife Eileen at 116th. All Russian program with Pinza in arias from "Boris Goudonoff". Fairly good. Made date for Mon nite when La Boheme will be presented. Home by 11, bot Times. Leanna came up re playing bridge. I said no, too tired.

Mon 9 Aug - M - USSS called with referral to Electric Advisers, Inc, 70 Pine St. So I hurried and got dressed and took IRT to Wall Street. There at 10 but not thru being interviewed till 12. Had to fill out more questionnaires and take a dictation test! Hired for a month at $150 a month, hours 9 to 5; 9 to 1 on Sat. so I started right then and there. Sat around most of the aft. Had a little typing to do. Wrote letter to Marie & to Lt Mitchum who wrote in answer to Robt's letter of 6/14. He's at Myrtle Beach, S.C. now. Leanna & I met Mildred Patterson on the subway and out to Lewisohn Stadium to hear Bidu Sayao in "La Boheme" with Smallens conducting & an all Met cast.

Wed 11 Aug - Tomorrow and for balance of week I am to relieve gal who has been taking the place of Mr Beauchamp's secretary; a very swanky carpeted office. And I understand we'll be paid this Friday! Home, eating supper, ironing a few things. Mr Blumenthal called at 8 re supper date next week.

Thurs 12 Aug - AIR RAID 5:30PM - Down to work today to take on my duties as "fill in" for Mr Beauchamp's secretary. Swanky, air-conditioned office, carpeted floors, walnut desks, a brand-new LC Smith "Silent Secretarial" typewriter. I sat and read my French book all morning. A few phone calls came in. I took the messages. Mr B. dictated a short memorandum to me. I wrote it up, and sat and read. Wonderful view of the Brooklyn, Manhattan, and Triboro bridges out the window, but rather monotonous just sitting around.

Mon 16 Aug - To work in Mr Griswold's office, swankier than Beauchamp's, mountain scenery mural on one side of his office, long table, upholstered sofa, chairs, my office, very lovely, too, all air conditioned. Very easy day. Got a bit acquainted with Mr G. His daughter is a Navy wife. Saw a Dutch freighter pass through the East River with front of hull shot away by torpedo. Robert darling, don't let anything hit you!

Wed 18 Aug - Very quiet aft. Getting on my nerves this inactivity with Mr G sitting in his office reading, I in mine doing likewise. Met Mr Blumenthal at 5:30 at Museum of Modern Art. Saw 1½ hr long film "Nazi Propaganda", mass hysteria in Germany in their "adoration" of Hitler, also film of invasion of Poland. Mr B wanted me to dine in his apt. I refused so we were going to eat at the Russian Tea Room but it was crowded so we ate in a hotel dining room. Talked. Parted at 10. He's nice but rather boring.

Fri 20 Aug - I found a Special Delivery Airmail from Robert in the mailbox, which excited me no end! Called Mildred re Robert's letter. She hadn't heard from Hugh as yet. Robert's letter merely states he's in a typical No. African town and says nothing about when he'll return. So happy to hear from him. I feel so relieved to know he's arrived safely.

Sun 29 Aug - Columbia University - Up at 9 a.m. & out at Mildred Patterson's 440 Riverside Drive by 10:15. Surprised at the small dinky room she has there. Went for 11:00 services at Riverside Church, beautiful structure. Coming back we found her bro John David home on furlough from North Ireland, a Sgt in Air Corps. So the 3 of us sight saw Columbia U. campus, Grant's Tomb, Riverside Drive, Morningside Drive, the Hudson River.

Mon 30 Aug - My 2nd Anniversary - Bot some haut sauterne before coming home. The man in the store said this was his 7th anniversary. Congratulatory card and letter from Mom which made me feel good. Started reading Lin Yutang's "A Leaf in the Storm" and was absorbed in it when at 9:15 Mrs Frank knocked on my door to show a Navy officer and his wife the apt. First news that I couldn't stay after Sept 30, coming unexpectedly it made me furious, this invasion of my privacy; I showed it, too. So I had a glass of sauterne. Feel very sad and neglected.

Wed 1 Sept 1943 - M - 4 years ago today Hitler invaded Po-

land - Very quiet at the office, no one in and I did very little. Have almost drunk up my wine. Think I'll finish same and get more.

Thurs 2 Sept - M - Wish I'd hear from Robert. Is he so occupied that he can't write to me? If I don't hear from him regularly, I'm going home Oct 1.

Fri 3 Sept - M - Italy Invaded! - Home to find Vmail from Robert telling me I might expect him Sept 23 or so. Lovely letter. Bothers me that he wants me to <u>swim</u>!! I also got his postal mail from Baltimore, which was supposed to tell me of his safe arrival. The allies invaded Italy early this morning!

Sun 5 Sept - M - Slept til 12:30 to get up to answer phone from Mildred. Went out to her apartment, sat and talked awhile. About 4:15 started out for the Cloisters in Ft Tryon Park. Enjoyed the medieval art and architecture. Bus back to 110th where we toured the Cathedral of Saint John the Divine. Imposing Gothic, like Notre Dame. Supper at M's apt and talking, 8:45 when I left for home.

Wed 8 Sept - Italy Surrenders! - I bot a qt of haut sauterne. Hear news that Italy had surrendered Sept 3, announced today by Gen Eisenhower. Hurried home to find letter fm Sis telling me her wedding day is set for Nov 27th and asking me to be her matron of honor. Mildred didn't come till 7. She got letter fm Hugh dated 8/25 saying it might be the last one and that he expected to see her on her birthday (9/15) which might mean that they'll be home by then.

Sat 11 Sept - Another Day - No Mail - Do wish Robert were here. This tense waiting is driving me nuts or almost that!

Tues 14 Sept - 3rd Officer of Geo S. Woodward calls me at 7 pm - . . . . summoned to phone. Thinking it might be Mildred, I hurried down to find it was the 3rd officer of Robert's ship telling me Robt was in town but could not get ashore till Thursday aft or evening. Incredulously I asked if it was a joke. Gave him my office phone number to call in case I'm not home, etc. Told Mr Frank all about it and asked him to let Robert into apartment. Now I am so excited and dazed by the news!

Wed 15 Sept - Robert comes home! - During lunch bot qt haut sauterne for Robert's homecoming. Came home and Mrs. Frank told me Lt Patterson had called around 5 just to say Robt might come in tonite: if not, then for lunch tomorrow. So I guess I'll stay home. Go back only to pick up my book, etc. So excitedly I am listening to the radio and waiting, hoping he does get in tonite. Wonderful thot! He did! Bronzed and with a moustache and dysentery! Had been to Oran, Mostaganem & Mus al Kebri, Algeria. We had a wonderful time acquainting ourselves with our respective adventures, etc. The darling had to leave at 4 AM for the ship!

Thurs 16 Sept - Robt ill - Robert said something yesterday about wanting me to stay on in NY especially if he gets another 7 week assignment, which makes me wonder what to do. Robert late for supper. [I had to see to the discharge of the 700 Afrikakorps prisoners I had brought.] Came about 7 PM. We listened to music, drank some of Verlain's haut sauterne and felt very happy. Raining outside but I feel very happy with Robert beside me.

Fri 17 Sept - R ill - Up at 8 AM and rushed through breakfast and I off to work and Robert to the ship docked at pier off Brooklyn Bridge. Robert home at 6:15. The poor dear has a bad cold, nose running, sore throat, still has no information as to his "disposition". Tomorrow my last day at the office. Guess I'll stay home while Robert is in town. Look for an apt, etc. if we decide I should stay here.

Sat 18 Sept - R ill - Last Day at Electric Advisers, Inc. - Cold, not much to do at office. Got my final check (14.85), came home to find Robert in bed. I prevailed upon him to go to the dispensary at the army base about his "dysentery" and cold. I slept till 4:30, when he got back with paregoric and nose drops. Is supposed to be on quarters tomorrow. Possibility that he may ship out before the end of the month. So he packed his belongings. Poor dear, he doesn't feel very good.

Sun 19 Sept - Slept till 10:30, Robt went out to get newspaper. Having terrible cramps and diarrhea all day, feverish. Robert and I have agreed that perhaps I should go home for the winter and not see him for a couple trips.

Mon 20 Sept - At 10 AM phone rang, Capt Dinato of the Dispensary calling re Bob's condition. So after breakfast he went down there. They gave him more medicine and told him to stay on his restricted diet. About 3 PM Robt and I left for Macy's to buy a chess game and thot we might go to a show but he became ill and so we came home about 6. Supper. Decided to go to library and get some books on Russia and on chess. Feel rather sad at the way our NY reunion is turning out. Can't decide whether it would be best to go home or not.

Tues 21 Sept - Robert recovered - Tobacco Road - The darling fixed breakfast for me this morning. Feels better and went down to the pier this afternoon. The Capt of the Geo S. Woodward called to say Robert owed him $53 for room and board. To the Ritz Theatre to see "Tobacco Road", very lewd, salacious, unsavory; we didn't care much for the realism that it is supposed to depict. Going to bed about 1:30 AM - my darling is completely recovered!

Wed 22 Sept - R gets 4 days leave - Ah, wonderful to sleep till 10 AM! Then to awake to fix breakfast for us two. Got 4 days leave, and then I suppose he'll ship right out. So I guess I'll be going home October 1st. We played chess till 2 AM. Robert angry at me for something, but I was tired.

Thurs 23 Sept - Slept till 9 or so, fixed breakfast for Robt and he went down to the Army Base. He came home about 1 PM and so I fixed lunch. Took a nap and Robt got mad and slept all aft. Went down to Gimbel's [dept store]. Looked at antiques and art collection of Wm Randolph Hearst on display there. In books section Robt buying "Look Homeward Angel" and books on German. Home by 11, bite to eat. Robt and I had a misunderstanding and we went to sleep in a hurt frame of mind.

Fri 24 Sept - We visit the Cloisters - Radio City - It was about 11:30 before we left the house to go to the Cloisters. I think he liked the peaceful medieval surroundings. Took a picture of me in one of the cloistered courtyards. Radio City NBC studios for the Cities Service concert. Walked to Victory Center on 50th Street and looked at the exhibits. Home again; bite to eat and to bed. My darling so very sweet.

Sat 25 Sept - Metropolitan, Modern Museum, Loretta's - Set out for Metropolitan and spent till 3:30 looking around. Had lunch at cafeteria, then walked to Museum of Modern Art

Sun 26 Sept - M - Call fm Irene and she came out for drink of wine and candy. We went to her home for supper, chess, taking pictures. Took her with us to Brooklyn Academy of Music for "Cavelleria Rusticana" and "Pagliacci", both very good. Home midnight, snack to eat, working crossword puzzle till 2 AM and so to bed.

Mon 27 Sept - M - I discarded stuff preparatory to packing tomorrow. About 2:30 we left the house to pick up films, Robert's glasses and on to pick up ticket permits for "Arsenic and Old Lace". Enjoyed this bit of murder and nonsense very much. Tomorrow I start packing. Robert remarking - wonder where we'll be a year from now?

Tues 28 Sept - M - Robert had to report in at 8 AM and we both had trouble getting up. I went back to bed after he left and slept till 12:30! The Presidential Steamship Co. calling Robert about his bill for room and board. He's been assigned to a ship (Wm S Rosecrans) to go to Sicily and may not be leaving for 10 days yet, which brings up the problem of whether I should stay here with him until he leaves. Robert and I played a game of chess and didn't get to bed till after 1:30 a.m.! Robt thinks I should plan on staying till he leaves, and tomorrow I'll go see Mrs Koven to see if I can get us a room for a few days.

Wed 29 Sept - M - We make moves towards moving - Robert left at 8 AM, I slept till 11. Got us referral to a room in Flatbush @ 10.00 per week with kitchen privileges. Robert came home at 4:30 and we went over to Mrs McDonald's to look at the room. Old house, but we decided to take it. Robert is to get a truck to take our luggage over to the RR Station and I'm going to try to get a ticket on the Trail Blazer for Tuesday. Robt thinks he'll be gone by that time. I hope not. Hope he stays for at least a week.

Thurs 30 Sept - At Mrs McDonald's - Our room is reminiscent of the one we had at Mrs Larsen's [After our marriage, Fig 7]. Went out to delicatessen and got food and fixed sandwiches in the kitchen. Too wet outdoors to look for a restaurant. So to sleep.

Fri 1 Oct 1943 - I sleep away the Day - Malaise - Robert left early in the rain, I slept away till 1:30, waking up every so often to find it still raining. Robert had checked my baggage thru to Chicago, moved his stuff to the ship. He had a snack to eat in the kitchen and then we went out to Flatbush Ave to look for a restaurant. The darling thinks he'll be leaving Sun. morning. I am hoping he'll still be here when I leave for Chicago on Tuesday. Wonderful to have him see me off.

Sat 2 Oct - CHINESE DINNER - Raining when Robert left about 7:30 AM. I got up about 10. Naples was captured from the Germans yesterday.

Sun 3 Oct - MUSIC HALL - Sending Robert off to work. Back to bed till 12:30. To Museum of Modern Art to see exhibit of Alexander Calder's wire and metalwork. So-so dinner in a French restaurant on 53rd Street. Music Hall bill "So Proudly We Hail", heroic tale of nurses on Bataan. . . reading Sunday Times and so to bed. My darling has been so so sweet these last few days.

Mon 4 Oct - Day before we Part - . . . . Robert and I took a walk on Flatbush Ave and bot his valve oil, some cactus needles for me. Robert so happy that he has been able to be with me so long. Will be three weeks tomorrow. I feel jittery at parting from him.

Tues 5 Oct - Robert leaves - I leave for Chicago - The alarm rang at seven but we stayed snuggled in bed till 8. Then I fixed breakfast for us and we leisurely packed his belongings and said our farewells. He left at 9:30; won't be leaving the country till the15th but has to be on board ship from now on. Found my seat (#36) next to window, coach half empty. I ate supper about 7. Tried to sleep during night. Every time I woke up, the train was standing still. About 10 the lights had been put out and the trip was quite uneventful and comfortable, but I think we'll be late. Wonder if Mom will meet me.

Wed 6 Oct - I arrive, 2½ hours late! - Woke up at 8 to find our train 2 hrs behind schedule. Finally got in at 12:25, Mom waiting for me at the gate. Had been there since 9:30 AM, poor dear. Mom and I took L home. Good to be home with Mom and Dad and Sis and Max and Dick. Eating supper and exchanging notes on my experiences. To bed with Sis.

Wed 13 Oct - Rainy Day - Home Loafing - Drizzling this morning and I slept till 11 and really enjoyed it. Looked over our collection of letters this eve. Wrote withdrawal blank on the Brooklyn savings bank for $1,000. Expect to put the money in a Bldg & Savings Loan account here in Chicago. Wondering how my darlin' is, has he left the country already? I can see that the coming weeks will be long and monotonous unless I get myself busy doing something. Pasted all my snapshots in the album. Need a new album.

Wed 20 Oct - The Beamishes & I see "The Student Prince" - A beautiful spring-like day and I had to sleep to 11! Left house at 7PM and took Ogden Ave Street car to the Loop, noticing the numerous neon signs along the way, different from N.Y. where the streets are all dark. Successfully avoided being picked up by some sailors and a <u>civilian</u>!! Met the Beamishes at the Erlanger about 8:10. From the 2nd balcony enjoyed very much the "Student Prince" operetta. Cast fair, scenery, etc wonderful. They drove me home.

Thurs 21 Oct - Fritz is coming home Oct 30th - Awakened by phone call from Sis about 10:30 that she had gotten letter and telegram from Fritz; said he was "washed out" of OCS and would be coming home. Later this eve she told us he called her long distance that he'd be home the 30th and for her to make arrangements for their wedding. I opened a Savings and Loan account (3% interest) for $1000 at the Lawndale Savings & Loan.

Mon 25 Oct - M - Max and I go to U of C - Got up at 9 AM and debated whether to go out or not. Max said yes and so in spite of threatening clouds and coldness we left at 10:30 for the Rosenwald Museum of Science & Industry. Walked to U of C campus and stopped in at the Home Study Dept to ask about Robert's inquiry. They said they mailed a catalog to him in Sept. Got another one and she gave me reading list in German, also said he could get 50% discount on the fee. Stopped in for an hour at the Oriental Institute. Remarkable displays of mummies, statues. Reading some more of my Russian, to bed at 11 exhausted.

Fri 29 Oct - The Day Before the Nuptials - I helped Mom clean house. Really gave it a thoro going over; think I've had enough of this housework and will either get a job next month or go out every day. Mom is rather domineering. This aft Adeline brought 2 smoked hams (totaling 25 lbs) for 10.75, without points. Sis came home after 5 PM with a marriage license. A bit melancholy as I recalled my own preparations for my wedding 26 months ago almost to the day.

Sat 30 Oct - Sis gets married! - Slept till11 - Got wire from Fritz about 12:30 saying he'd be in at 2:30. Sis went to meet him while I helped set the table. They came about 7:30. Sis got a diamond band ($50.00). At "51" club having champagne en route to J.P. Weil in Cicero. At 10 the ceremony was performed, simple but nice.

Mon 1 Nov 1943 - Mom let me sleep till 12:20 and got me up with the announcement that there was a card for me from NY, a blank card with Robert's name, an indication that he got safely across. This makes me happy in the thought that I may hear from him in perhaps a week or so. This aft, inspired by the thought that perhaps in a few weeks I'll be joining my darling. Fritz and Sis stopped in about 7. Somehow they don't look like a honeymoon couple. I think Robert and I had a nicer honeymoon. Oh well neechevo ponamayet [Written in Cyrillic - i.e., "not to be understood"].

*   *   *   *   *

[This series of letters all written aboard the Wm S. Rosecrans]

11:15 PM Wed. October 6, 1943

My beloved darling:

I have kept thinking of you continually, my sweetness, wondering how the train ride was, your home coming etc. I love you so intensely and so deeply, and our glorious togetherness in New York remains with me like a glowing jewel lighting vividly the shades of my memory. Unforgettable happiness! The tangible prophecy of so many years of full, vigorous beauty awaiting - the ineluctable ecstasy of loving you. - and such an endless store of joyful reminiscence and hopeful imaginings to accompany me this trip. Beloved, I thank you for each priceless kiss your lips have expressed to me, the playful, the pleading, the passionate, the greeting, departing, the impatient, the thotful, the impulsive, the teasing, the sleepy, the exuberant, thru all the variety of our lives the versatile meeting of our lips; and each touch a closer welding of two souls. My luscious wife, so lovely, so ever sweet and gentle, I shall never forget New York and its addition of so many days of beauty to our inseparable memories.

This is going to be a fine trip dearest. Everything is working out perfectly. We are now anchored in North River, up where we saw all the ships the day we took the 5th Ave bus to the Cloisters, right near the Washington Bridge. Since we'll be here a couple days, I'm going to sneak ashore and mail this and spend the day at the museum, but since it will cost $1.00 boat fare each way I think I'll only make one trip.

Have taken over the doctor's room on the tween deck [A fateful step had I been there; the first torpedo hit almost in this office.] since we have no doc, and am using it for a study. Perfect privacy. Starting out slowly to get back in shape on the horn. Reading Studs Lonigan, playing and reading chess, a bit of German, a little physical exercise. If Bess gets married while I'm away, give them a good practical wedding gift like a large wardrobe footlocker with built-in alarm clock. I can just hear you, too, orating with the wisdom of experience on the care and treatment of husbands, you darling, I love you.

10:30PM Thurs

And sweetness, would you also go down to U of C and ask them what I can be doing etc., to expedite my 7 years of medical school. I'm sure at least of my ability to carry that desire thru successfully and work it in with being the happiest husband in the world with you - and I bashfully hesitate to also add, father. Makes me feel sort of funny writing that word and having it refer to me. Kind of scares me a little and makes me wonder what it will be like. Does it you too? I love you so much.

*   *   *   *   *

N. Y. Public Library

5:45PM Friday October 8th, 1943

My sweetest one -

Today has been a full one and very enjoyable. Not quite according to plan however because boats back to the ship don't run after 8 PM. That therefore canceled my opera. However, darling, I did find a marvelous new museum [Of NonObjective Painting, later to become the Guggenheim on Fifth Avenue in a Frank Lloyd Wright designed building.] purely by accident, just wandering around. Am enclosing two pics of it and I bot a catalog of their stuff which you can see later. Spent the whole morning there studying the paintings, etc. I met and talked with Baroness Hilla Rebay, the curator (and also painter) and learned a lot about the principles of this school of painting, but it would be too lengthy to reiterate them now. We'll have to go there when I get back.

*　　*　　*　　*　　*

11PM Saturday October 16, 1942 [sic!]

My dearest darling -

Is it a gloomy, rainy October day in Chicago too and you watching the rapid raindrops splatter sharply against the window, dreaming of the first nite we listened to that rain music comfortably together in the car with a strange disturbing feeling beginning to stir deep within us. How much we owe to that nite and that refreshing storm. I love you so passionately, my beloved, and feel so intensely happy with our past; it has been so fresh and free and sparklingly romantic, and I know it always will be so, and I dream of you and our future.

*　　*　　*　　*　　*

9:30PM Friday Oct 29, 1943

I love you always my lovely wife. I do want to be a doctor, a good trumpet player, a poet or composer, travel etc. etc., but far above and beyond all that is the desire just to live with you. This is life's purpose for me most completely fulfilled.

*　　*　　*　　*　　*

9PM Sunday Oct 31st, 1943

My sweetheart -

Am safely across the Atlantic now and hope to get ashore tomorrow and mail all these letters to you. Hope I can find an American Post Office too. Have no idea how long we'll be here or even any assurance that I'll get ashore, but if you get these without any P.S. you'll know that I hit land Nov 1st.

Nothing much I can write about. It was sure a site coming in here. Was foggy and raining all day and just as we start to pull into port the sun burst thru the fog and now it is clear and cold, the stars like crisp jewels and so good too to see the lites of a town again [Hint, since lights are on this can only = noncombatant = Spanish part of Gibraltar peninsula!]. I wonder what you are doing this Sunday afternoon as I am dreaming of you longingly tonite. I love you so,

Robert

*　　*　　*　　*　　*

[Handwritten, until noted otherwise]

319

To my beautiful darling -

Beloved, there is so much of this world that I am seeing, and enjoying each experience - the thot that you must remain at home torments me, so please, dearest, spare yourself nothing, that you may keep apace with the continual broadening of my experience by extending yours also. I know you can't see mountains in Chicago, but you can see and do so many other things that tho you are unable to experience the identical things that I am, you are still getting the tang of living and building a limitless and varied realm of experience which will add subtly to the happiness of both of us.

I love you so vastly, so strangely and thru and above my insatiable thirst for the ecstasy of your lithe body there is the mysterious bond to your mind, your intellect, broad, intelligent, alert, philosophic, feminine. There is the true bridge between us on which our love meets, for tho we nourish each other hotly, intensely in the mutual pleasure of our flesh, even eager joy must end in the mind as memory and be always with us as such. We are gloriously male and female in body but in mind we are an identity and must always strive to be a beautiful and growing identity, a coalescence of ideals and knowledge which gives an eternal and boundless aesthetic happiness.

6PM - That is a brief snatch of my nebulous mystic thots, all that I have said is felt in my mind in one tiny instant and then goes sweeping on and on, calling forth the whole marvelous field of thot, but always the same underlying mood, the same emotions as I have attempted to describe.

Someday tho we must come here beloved, tho I really am not sure as any place could be more beautiful than the headwaters of the Mississippi on our honeymoon. You are physically so perfectly matched to the wild free beauty of nature, primitive, sure, good smelling, strong, clean, vivacious, fiercely capable of passion yet soothing and eternal. I wish you could release yourself from those learned restrictions of your soul which make you fear hardships and high places, thorns and bugs and just let yourself revel in the open purity of animal joy, the sturdy sense of power and conquest flood your warm woman body completely, knowing you are part of this wild awesome glory of mountains and rivers, sky and stars, suck the clean air into your good lungs, feel the tightness of your breasts, and earth fertile beneath planted feet and say "I am a woman of one million years of women, the sea is in my blood and the soil is in my body and the soft bending of the willows is in my hips, and my legs can become spring steel like those of the puma, and my hands caress with soft grace like snow settling on warm fur. My eyes are beautiful with lakes and dark forests and my skin is tough to the sun and the wind, to cold and the bite of pain, but it is the velvet of heaven to my mate. The earth is my body and my body is glorious with the earth, and my mind rules all, my body and the earth, and my mind loves and I live. I live loving and I love living. The beauty that is life, is my life." You are always such to me, my mate, my wife beloved.

Robert

*   *   *   *   *

WESTERN UNION

CABLE - SANSORIGINE - 1943 NOV 2 7:13
EFM MRS ELIZABETH N DOTY
2115 SOUTH TRUMBULL AVE CHGO=
ALL WELL AND SAFE PLEASE DON'T WORRY FONDEST LOVE AND KISSES =ROBERT DOTY

*   *   *   *   *

Tues 2 Nov - I get cablegram from Robert - About 9 PM Max handed me a Western Union Cablegram from Robert, "sans origine" that he was well and safe and not to worry. So sweet & thoughtful of him. Now I'm hoping he'll be back before the 1st of the month.

Mon 8 Nov - I feel awfully down in the dumps. Mom scolds us unceasingly about everything. I know Robert would not want me to take that sort of thing. Oh, well, everything comes to an end. Do so hope I hear from Robert.

Sat 13 Nov - Robert would be angry to know how much I miss him.

Wed 17 Nov - I'm getting disgusted with this present life of mine. I sleep late, get up and have breakfast, help clean up the house, study a little Russian, wait for the mailman to come, no letter from Robert as usual & so, downcast, I listen to the newscasts, studying more Russian; Mother starts scolding about my smoking, wants me to go to bed early, and so I retire to lie awake until

1:30 or 2 before I finally fall asleep into apprehensive dreams of what might happen to Robert.

Fri 19 Nov - M - Phone ringing at 11:30 awakened me. Marie asking me to come about 4 PM as she had to go downtown this aft. So. I looked in the mailbox and there was a V-mail from Robert! Said he hadn't figured on this "stop" and might be delayed. Was apparently a British port, so? Trying to figure out where Robert could be. Perhaps Gibraltar or Malta? But would that be magnificent scenery?

Tue 23 Nov - M - My 28th Birthday - Listening to radio broadcasts that Berlin has really been <u>bombed</u> by over a thousand planes and is in ruins! Perhaps I do have something to rejoice about today! I do feel rather dejected at not hearing anything from Robert and wondering just when he will return to this country.

Thur 25 Nov - Awakened this AM by Max giving me letter from Robert mailed Nov 3 (air mail) consisting of 16 pages. Overjoyed I was reading it when about 10 AM an air mail special mailed Nov 6th came, also 16 pages long. Interesting and beautifully written, but he says he probably won't be back before 1st of the year and is doubtful of what I should do. Really something to be grateful for, these messages of love from Robert. I guess he was at Gibraltar when he mailed them. Got into a tiff with Mom about 8 PM about making coffee for supper. And one thing led to another and we both cried etc. etc. Went to bed 11:30, a very tearful & self-pitying little gal. So the gamut from pleasure galore upon receiving Robert's letters to the sorrow of being frustrated by ma mere - pauvre moi!

Fri 26 Nov - Robert would applaud my drinking cocoa this evening. Played "Les Sylphides" & Schipa's "Grenada" and thought of listening together.

*   *   *   *   *

4PM Friday November 5, 1943

My most adorable sweetheart -
Somehow you and our relation seem so different to me than the similar situation in other people's lives. You're not to me just "the wife" nor do I think there is ever any possibility of your becoming

322

such. We will always be lovers, and the common fact that we are husband and wife will not mar or deflate our love. I'm sure I was afraid of this when I wanted us to take up life with each other without the formality of marriage. I had seen so many husbands whose fire and zest for their wives was quite gone and left only a half bored respect and habitual fondness. I was afraid that that was a part of marriage, but I'm sure that I was wrong. It is a disease of unimaginative minds.

I see now how necessary and glorious our marriage was. It gives us the common experience with the rest of the world of having our quarrels, my being "your old man", the trite, enjoyable, vulgarity of just being married, but then in addition as we rise above this we feel the ecstasy that we are passionately in love, inseparable and indispensable to one another and we feel a wild, free elation at our intoxication and our superiority at maintaining it above the jejune and humdrum fact that we are married. To me you will always be the shapely maiden that I would want to seduce on moonlit sands (I'm still going to do that some day too) or with whom I would get most unreservedly drunk and perform the most sensual & inebriated delights I could imagine, or with whom I would sit entranced listening to Gieseking's dazzling fingers playing Chopin, feel that mysteriously powerful thrill come mutually over our souls, inarticulate with strange emotion, tortured by the inexpressible rhythm, exquisite passions of melody and I can feel deep inside the throb of interwoven chords like the bursting of a galaxy or the fierce trampling of frightened horses, and tears want to express what my tongue cannot; and I squeeze your hand and you know, you understand and shiver at its beauty; and if I were ever to demand respite from the gentle eager passion of young love, or the hot lascivious satisfaction of sensual appetency or the aesthetic ecstasy of art, I can always take my beloved, clasp her, kiss her and spend an evening admiring her intelligence at chess, or philosophy, or daydreams, or just nothing at all but delicious and vivid memories. I do love you so completely.

11:15

Staying with your folks has a great physical and practical advantage, but somehow I don't quite like you to do it. I would prefer you free and independent. Come back to N.Y. and then when I leave again we'll send you off to Florida for the winter. You could get some jerky job down there and have a good time knocking around and keeping warm and healthy. At least don't plan to park with your folks for the duration.

*   *   *   *   *

My beloved -

I decided I'd have to hike to the top of this bloody rock as the English call it. Not knowing the proper route up, I set off haphazardly taking any lane, street or steps that were going up. As I was also pressed for time if I wanted to be back for the 6:30 boat my pace was of necessity quite rapid. My guess work on routes wasn't so good either and twice I wound up in a cul-de-sac and had to retrace my steps, costing me at least ½ mile each time. Finally, sweating breathlessly and dog tired, I reached the top and it certainly was worth the trip. The view was absolutely enchanting, as though I had become a cloud that I might see the earth as it should be seen. The immensity of the panorama and its unceasing variation, the intensity of the coloring, the realization of the force that must have heaved this massive rock over 1000 feet above the sea, the glorious tumult of mountains and brilliant changeless ocean as far as you could see. It was hypnotic and I felt again that awesome sense of the majestic mystery of nature surge thru my mind. I, a tiny, indistinguishable speck upon this towering solidity of insensate stone and yet I surveyed all, made it a part of me, moved and carried it with me. In my mind it will always be vivid and real, that white ribbon of foam gracefully curving along the coast for miles, sharply contrasting the deep blue of the water and tawny sand. I will always see the towns, miniature and dreamlike, sprinkled among the hills, white pauses in the continuous rise and fall of green splotched earth, and always away in the blue mist, dim and distant, the bulge of higher and greater mountains, yet to be explored. And dizzily below specks that you know to be gulls pass from the sunshine into the distinct shadow of the rock upon the water, and ships moving like toys, slowly, with imperceptible motion. You can hardly see a man in the town, just minute dots; yet the cool breeze carries the vague, quivering notes of the bagpipe up to this pinnacle of passivity; and you become aware that you are human, resist the temptation to stay till night to see it all by moonlight, and start reluctantly the long descent.

*   *   *   *   *

My beloved wife -

Well, about sometime after supper, and seeing it was Armistice day, Joe German decided to do some celebrating too. What I expected last night [with full moon] came today and I imagine every day from here on. Don't mind saying either, I was damn scared. That feeling that there is something up overhead with a couple hundred lbs of TNT which might fall on you as it came for the 1st time was kind of shocking. But I was able to fight it down and it certainly was a thrilling sight to see and hear that barrage of gunfire. The whole sky seemed to be alive at times with swirling red and white dots of light, the ship shaking with the sharper burst of the big guns and then shuddering in rapid cadence to the blows of a stick of bombs, and you sigh with relief thinking there's 3 more in the water, 3 that won't hit this ship and then you look up, or strain out into the moonlit distance and someone cuts loose out in some other direction and you think, Christ, they're coming from over there. Was watching a particularly beautiful flower of shrapnel off our stern, thinking that's close enough for some of it to be falling on us when zowie! something glances off my helmet and slaps both of my arms. That too was a bit shocking, but it turned out to be only the aerial that one of our gunners shot down. The radio operator told me it could have been <u>very</u> shocking. - But bombers or no, darling, I keep thinking of you and dreaming of the day when I'll be able to tell you all about it and get a kiss for every shot I heard. I love you so my beloved.

[What I could not describe was that 6 ships were sunk that night, out of a convoy of perhaps as many as 50. Reputedly only 7 German planes, from their Cagliari base in Sardinia. The most spectacular was the ammunition ship that blew up in front of us and one lane to starboard, such a massive explosion that I thot we had been hit! The huge Liberty ship simply disappeared, a dramatic end to a couple dozen lives. An immense cloud ascended a couple thousand feet into the air, in which we thot we saw a German plane seeking obscurity while selecting its target. Actually, the greater danger, as the incident above with the aerial suggests, is the thotlessness of the Navy gunners in directing their fire without regard for the surrounding environment, sending a spray of 20-mm shells across the water!]

*   *   *   *   *

[This section begins a continuous series, amounting to 12 handwritten pages]

1AM Monday November 15, 1943

My dearest sweetheart -

There's nothing at all for you to worry about darling except what to do with your sweet self till I am able to come back to you. Just be thankful like I am that I'm on a clean, well fed ship with nothing to do, which is pretty soft when you figure this is war.

So they dropped us off high and dry in North Africa [Bizerte] this morn, but it seems no one wants us here, we're just paying a social call or something, like at Gibraltar. Hope to get ashore and look the place over tomorrow so I'm writing my safe arrival letter tonite. It's all very puzzling but I quit trying to figure the army out long ago. I just don't want you to start worrying tho that they've taken me off the ship or something. Everything is quite O.K. in that dept.

My impatience to be with you is the only real flaw in this existence. I keep thinking of you continually, trying to picture what you're doing, feeling uneasy because I know your worrying about me. I have no faculty for worrying somehow, but I do feel that you are in as great a danger as I am. You watch your step dodging automobiles, dearest, and as you succeed in doing that so will I too avoid the various possibilities of getting hurt over here. The relative danger is about the same.

*   *   *   *   *

11:30 Monday November 22, 1943

My lovable darling -

Was pouring rain all yesterday in morn and aft, so I waited till noon and then set off with my helmet liner, my trench coat, and pants rolled up. The radio operator, Mitch, and 2nd Engineer, Alex, came with me. As soon as we got outside the boundary of the port area [Now in Palermo, Sicily] we were besieged by kids, not begging, but wanting to beg, borrow or steal or buy <u>cigarettes</u>. Mitch gave one kid a pack and got a whole handful of coins in return. So we strolled along looking over the bomb gutted buildings. The town hasn't been leveled, but it certainly has been pretty well sprinkled with bombs, grass already growing in some of the crater rims and in the rubble of houses. The people have taken up life

326

again and the place seems pretty well populated. We were invited into a little hole in the wall during a particularly heavy shower and I watched the boy there, about 13 years old, making shoes, carefully conserving each tiny nail. The women's shoes he had made were old uppers with a huge sole of cork. Very light but somewhat clumsy I imagine. As we walked on we were hailed from a taxi by the bos'n and one of the ABs ["bosun", sort of the Master Sgt of the deck crew, and "Able-Bodied" seaman] already pretty well oiled. We had to have a drink with them and went into a small wine shop choked with huge barrels. The wine was surprisingly good, not like that junk in North Africa. Had some Malaga, some Muscatel, some Pantelleria, which was particularly sweet and delicious. Made from the small grapes of that island. 1 Lire = 1 cent and the wine costs 50 Lire per liter. I'm going to try to buy you some. Had a good time trying to talk with a good-looking chap who was very friendly to us there. He couldn't speak English but was able to tell us his folks were in San Francisco, Calif and he'd had a brother killed in the Italian army. He was wearing a little black band with a star on it for this. Everyone was delighted when I sang "La Donna e Mobile" in good Italian. We left boisterously with good byes and good wishes and gratias etc. and piled into one of the numerous carriages and the driver drove through one of the market streets, crowded and full of little carts with tangerines, lemons, almonds, etc. with kids and little wizened old ladies, just like Hell's Kitchen back in Chicago at the feast of St Rocco, except not so bounteous. The AB almost started a riot by throwing a pack of cigarettes up for grabs, and when the driver got down to settle the fight, we drove off in his carriage. They sure must think Americans are nuts.

Finally we jolted to a stop and piled out and the driver led the way up an impersonal and shabby apartment building hall, up the steps and we were all admitted to our 1st Italian brothel. Only it wasn't exactly a brothel, just a girl about 20 & one about 30 doing a little business with a picturesque, bald and stooped gink who served as their pimp I guess. He smiled obsequiously and rubbed his hands together like Uriah Heap. About the 1st thing the bos'n did was puke disgustingly all over the tablecloth, but the gink just rolled it up and stuck it away somewhere. It was a poorly lit, low ceilinged room with doors to the rooms made of some brown paper maché stuff and opened by lifting a latch. I used their toilet (?), a small room with a cement basin near the floor with a hole in it. I imagine that is the normal European version of our toilet bowl. In this same room they kept all their pots and cooking utensils and water too I suppose. An American Corporal & a Staff Sgt came in and a violent argument ensued between the corporal and the older girl over the price and various matters so he took the younger one and retired. The sergeant told me this older woman was his Captain's gal friend. I walked into one of the other rooms and looked at the wedding pictures and family portraits, a bottle of benzene for cigarette lighters, numerous holy pictures and a little book in which it appeared the pimp kept his record of the girls' business, apparently 4 girls. So the soldiers left and the girls, figuring we weren't going to buy, started to dress, the older gal telling me in violent Italian what she thot of the soldiers who had left, appealing to me as an officer, etc. She was sure a spitfire and kept reminding me of that gal we saw in that old-time movie at the Modern Art Museum. In the meantime the little AB got sick and the bos'n broke out a bottle of wine and we all had another drink. Then Alex's Polish blood got the better of him and he took the spitfire off to the room and we waited for him. Alex is quite a character. Speaks English with a heavy accent, has a magnificent black beard and wild glittering eyes. He was a veterinarian in Poland and the son of a Polish diplomat. Been in the U.S. since '37 and got married.

10PM same day

Alex interrupted me this noon so I'll continue, or rather try to, where I left off. I know my frankness may be shocking to some people, but I think my darling knows me well enough to understand, to love me for it and actually to expect it. Therefore I am writing the exact truth and depicting my life in Palermo in reality.

I guess I left us in a whore house so perhaps I better get out of there.

Alex finished his session with Rita and came out ready to go. Somehow, my beloved, the intimacy of our life has made me familiar enough with the female body that other women have little mystery or enticement about them. I could look at this woman's flexible hips, her copious bosom, just as casually as I would look at an animal, appreciating its contour and musculature, but not the least excited or curious. I know perfectly well that before my life with you such a "temptation" would have been irresistible or at least quite appetizing, but though familiarity has not bred contempt in me, it certainly has unveiled the mystery of woman and sex so that I may knowingly forego the choicest bit of female flesh with perfect calmness.

Can't quite get all the relations straight over here tho. While Alex was in with the Captain's mistress (for which he gave her 100

Lire) her Italian boyfriend came up with a bouquet of beautiful yellow roses, quite amicably chatted around and then took her out to dinner, I guess (?). We left & jolted down to the docks in our carriage and back to the ship to find everyone quite drunk, 3 fights going on and a jolly good time in general. Had steak for supper, some more wine and somehow didn't get started back to town till almost 7 PM when it was too late to go to the concert. Walked up the totally black, bombed streets hoping we wouldn't run into any stilettos and finally wound up in the Allied officers club. Downstairs they had an empty bar, but upstairs they had a mob of officers, women, a 5 piece band & liquor. Quite wild. Got hold of the 1st Lt who runs the place and he told us all about it. Says all the girls are clean except one undergoing treatment and that they are semipro prostitutes. Same crowd comes each nite. Had a singing waiter with a very good tenor voice only they didn't let him sing enough so far as I was concerned. Drank about 10 rounds of lemon juice and cognac before I discovered that by dumping a glass of Malaga in this concoction it sweetened it to perfection and made an excellent drink. Was quite amazed at my capacity for liquor (even more so after today). The place closed at 9 PM and everyone grabbed till all the girls were gone and then disappeared in small groups. Went back to the ship and what do I find in the mess room but 4 of these gals from up at the officers club, the 1st Eng, 2 British Naval officers etc. etc. How the hell they got them by the Provost Marshall I don't know, but there they were with the victrola going. Was certainly a wild ship that nite with all the ship's officers trying to gang shag these 4 gals and I guess they succeeded quite well too. I don't quite get it, for the girls were neither prostitutes (accepting no money) nor virgins (accepting all males) but then this is Europe. Perhaps that explains it. I went to bed about 12:30 AM wishing very much for the sweet and lovely little girl I know is waiting impatiently for me back in Chicago.

[Next day] we had ourselves driven out to the catacombs which was well worth the trip. They are not as large as I thot they were, but they were in the business from 1599 to 1880 and have a collection of some 15,000 skeletons tacked and stacked along the walls. Run by the Capuchin monks (not monkeys). I think little could display the inane barbarity of religion in general, and Catholicism in particular, more than this immense display of aboriginal superstition. They had two processes it seems, one where they embalmed the body, the other where they soaked it for 1 year till only the skeleton was left. The monk that ushered us thru gave us to understand that the "skeletas" were superior to the "embalmo". It is only the nobility and ecclesiastical that are buried here and the monk had a little joy all of his own showing us "princeps" so & so or "generale" so & so and then chuckling with childish delight and saying in broken English "princé no more" etc. Can certainly appreciate E.A. Poe's "Cask of Amontillado" after that. I bought a bunch of postcards there too so you'll be able to admire the grotesque rows of skeletal bishops tacked up along the wall with their nameplates hung on them. The South American Indians who pickle human heads have got a thing or two to learn from the asinine savagery of Occidental religion.

Also went thru the chapel they have connected with it. A very beautiful wood carved altar and then along each side of the room, I guess you'd call them subaltars or shrines, where they had little nooks dedicated to one or several saints and some relics or souvenirs from said saint. One saint is even fortunate enough to have his bones neatly done up in three wood & glass boxes and jewels studded into his skull. This was done in 1870 when the glorious, edified missionaries of Christianity were bringing the refinements of our religion to the poor superstitious South Sea Islanders or the Chinese etc. What a damn fool world this is!

So you see life for me has been far from dull, and dearest I do hope you are trying to have as much fun and experience as I am. I have been completely "true" to you physically as I always will be spiritually. I doubt too if there will be any senorita winsome enough to disturb my self control and I can never look at a woman and think of her as being a woman without remembering vividly the graceful perfection of your lithe fresh body so intimate with mine, but above all there is the inviolable, eternal bond to your soul which keeps me your husband lovingly forever and makes physical consideration small by comparison. I promise you to be utterly frank, as I am your only lover, and always, my sweetest -

Love
Robert

*　　*　　*　　*　　*

Wed 1 Dec 1943 - Awakened about 9 by doorbell, special airmail from Robert. He was at Gibraltar Nov 1st, Nov 11 they were bombed by Germans (no mention of damage) Nov 15 put in somewhere in No. Africa and Nov 20 finally in Sicily. Still thinks he'll

330

be in after Xmas. So? Got mad at 2 pages of lecturing about exercise and what will happen to me if I don't!

Thur 2 Dec - A pleasant way to be awakened, an airmail letter from Robert, telling me of the "wild and wet" goings-on in Sicily. "Wine, women and song" is really appropriately applied to his sojourn. Very frank description à la R.W.D. in 12 pages! Started and finished reading "Queen of Spades" by Pushkin, in the old Russian orthography & with very adequate vocabulaire. Did some exercises last night before retiring & I do feel rather stiff today. A radiogram from Robert wishing me "Loving birthday greetings. Keep smiling. All my love dearest." Better late than never. I suppose he sent this out on Nov 22 from Sicily & it was delayed in transmission.

Mon 6 Dec - Oh me, oh my - 3 letters from Robert which have really startled me, one telling me to expect him after Jan 15th; the other all about marital fidelity - seems he is very much tempted there in Palermo - this doesn't startle me any. Received a very nice letter from Mrs MacDonald in Brooklyn telling me she would gladly reserve a room for me till the end of December. Now the question of what to do, go back to NY Dec 29th or wait till I hear from Robert.

Wed 8 Dec - Slept late and no wonder seeing as I did not fall asleep till 3:30 AM, just lying in bed and thinking of Robert's letters which I received Monday. Somehow the futility of expecting Robert week after week when he may not be back for several months. His proposal that I take advantage of sexual freedom appals me. Read some of Freud this eve. Decided if RWD thinks I'm "frigid" he can be accused of "satyriasis". Wonder how I'll feel seeing him again?

Thurs 9 Dec - Got up at 12:30, enjoying my "life of Riley". Read some Russian. I have decided to wait till I hear from Robert definitely that he's in this country. Get guilty feeling about not working, but feel that I can afford the dubious pleasure of loafing. Am running out of money and will have to withdraw some, I guess, from our NY bank. To bed early but as usual lay awake for hours just thinking.

Mon 13 Dec - Got up at noon, V mail from Robert, still telling me how to employ my time, fencing, concerts and operas? Read some of my diary notations and felt very sad so stopped soon and crawled into bed.

* * * * *

9:15PM Tuesday November 23, 1943

My beautiful darling

Way up into the mountains in back of the town to the Cathedral of Monreale. It is a magnificent & ornate structure, immense, having the barbaric splendor of Karnak. In fact I marvelled the whole time at the similarity between the ostentatious mysticism of Christianity and the guargantuan glory of Egypt's rituals, 5000 years from Karnak to Monreale. What tyrranic fear of death will be held distorted over the heads of men when archeologists explore the ruins of Monreale and the lay people of 6000 AD gape curiously at the childish mythology portrayed on the walls of this Christian temple. This cathedral and all others are massive interpretations of the groping chimera of religion, a monstrosity of the people's pain sweated out of their hides and dedicated to the perpetuation of their illusion, the gross gaudy fake of immortality.

In 5000 years of thinking the peoples' mind progressed from Osiris to God, from the Lotus to the Cross, from Isis to Mary, from the pyramids to the catacombs, from the glory of Amon Reh to the glory of Jesus Christ, from the weighing of the heart by dog headed Seth to the keys of heaven by winged St Peter, from amulets to rosaries, from intonations in high Egyptian to intonations in Latin, from incense and tapers to better incense and tapers, from the painted splendor of colossal Karnak to the mosaic magnificence of Monreale. Strange isn't it this helpless, hopeless repetition of the foolish misery of mankind, and we feel sorry for the poor dung beetles instinctively following their routine pattern. Man is only a glorified dung beetle monotonously burrowing his slightly more complex life away without once looking the world over to see the foolish cycle of his idiot mistakes. No wonder I'm a misanthrope.

Intensely and eternally I love you.

Robert

* * * * *

9:30PM Sunday Nov. 28, 1943

Dearest . . . .

Sometimes I think you should have a little pesky pants to look

332

after and keep you company while I'm away, but then again I know it's best that you don't. We must wait for that, too, beloved just as we must wait for most of our happiness, till the day when we can be always together. But it is such fun dreaming, picturing you getting big with our child and all my looking after you and worrying and making you take proper care of yourself and then the big question mark, girl or boy? I want both darling, a little girl to be just as sweet as you are and a little boy to grow up into all the things which I cannot. And I know we'll make good intelligent parents and have the smartest toughest kids on earth. Both of us strong and well built and intelligent, I know our flesh will blend perfectly. I'll bet they are nearsighted tho, but all the better, we'll make defense workers out of them and they won't have to go to the next war. I dream about our kids and want them so, but I know it's you more than anything I want and when we are together we will want to enjoy being with each other for a while alone without a squalling 3rd party. But my sweet little one will make such a good healthy mother.

Darling, I keep thinking too about our system of birth control. Perhaps we have the most foolproof, surely the most convenient system and I'll keep buying contraceptives over here (they're rationed to 6 per week), but I think we should do a little experimenting. At least when you reason things out there are plenty of things wrong with our method and much to be offered by the diaphragm deal. I really think we're missing something there, in fact I know we are. You have been set against it and I haven't argued, but now that you have the time dearest I insist you go to either Dr Belding or your own Doc and get measured etc. and buy all the paraphernalia. I won't be satisfied until we have at least tried this and I'm sure once you get the knack of it you will wonder how we could ever have lived two years without it. I wouldn't mention this in a letter only I know it would never occur to you and want you to get it taken care of while there is time. I hope you will do this not only for me, but for yourself. In fact I will really be very angry if you don't. Now I'm mad at you so I'll stop writing.

*   *   *   *   *

[V mail - Found this in her diary]

11:30Pm Thurs. Dec 2

My delicious darling -

Am getting sleepy from the wine I've been drinking so I'll try and write fast. Accomplished a lot today. This afternoon I went to the PX and bot 8 packs of cigarettes for 40¢, some toothpaste, candy etc. Then bought 40 fine postcards for 80¢, all good views of the city. Found a wine shop that I had been looking for and bot a bottle of Crema Mandorla, a liqueur made of almonds and Marsala wine for $1.50 (2 pkg cigarettes), came back with $33.00 left which I hope will last all December. Won another game of chess. Spent an hour with a seniorita this evening and gave her $1.00 for her services which (you'd never guess) was as an Italian teacher. You see I went to the Red Cross and told them I wanted to learn Italian and here's where I was sent. It was very interesting, going to the house (her uncle is an international lawyer) and I did learn a great deal, but $1.00 an hour is too much to pay so I'll try to pick it up elsewhere. My German tho is a great assistance in understanding the structure of the language, but I do get my vocabularies mixed up. Don't forget to write me SS Wm S Rosecrans airmail. I love you my sweetest wife and kiss you dreamily good nite.

Your husband
Robert

*   *   *   *   *

WESTERN UNION

1943 Dec 2 PM7:52

CAF208 WIRELESS=CD AMOFAM VIA MACKAY RADIO
EFM MRS ELIZABETH N DOTY=
2115 TRUMBULL AVE CHGO
=LOVING BIRTHDAY GREETINGS. KEEP SMILING. ALL MY LOVE DEAREST
ROBT W DOTY.

*   *   *   *   *

[Ordinary letter]

8:45PM Saturday, December 4, 1943

There is in me now an incessant and insistent urge to seek sexual relief, slightly similar to the fullness and mild discomfort that awakens the desire to urinate. I suppose quite a bit of it is psychological, tho nonetheless real, but there is also a very definite accompaniment of mild nervousness and restlessness and a tightness in the prostate region. Sordidly descriptive I know, but I believe you share my curiosity and interest in anything which explains and clarifies the actions of living things. So I as a living thing of a sort went out yesterday, mailed my darling's Vmail, got a haircut and had all good intentions of looking up a disreputable, but clean and well built seniorita.

. . . approached by kid about ten years old who wanted to take me to a buona senorita I began doubtfully questioning him Bella (pretty) "Giovane" [This should probably be "giovana?] young, non malattia (not diseased) and finally said "Io guadaro, ma se vostra sorrella non mi piace, Io non compraro." (I look, but, if your sister doesn't please me, I will not buy). So, uncertain but curious I followed him a block or so when he suddenly ducked behind a curtain hanging across the doorway. I likewise ducked, took off my sunglasses and saw 3 women; one their mother I guess, and two women, one slim with a rather irritable face about 33 - 35, the other younger with very pretty eyes (blue) an aquiline nose, hair recently wetted and combed, and as I stood beholding what I had expected, but still disappointed in finding it, she looked at me with an odd pleading sort of look which I guess my licentiousness mistook for passion. I said no about 6 times then suddenly decided what the hell this is what I came for, get it over with. So I nodded impatiently to the younger one and as I followed her through another curtained entrance I made the observation from her figure that she might be pregnant, but I gulped this distasteful realization down hastily, and with firm resolve set about finishing what I had begun. The only furniture in the place was a chair and a very short, none too clean bed. With a sort of desperation I tried to assume my premarital nonchalance in such matters and anticipate the act with this woman instead of the surroundings. So, hastily, so as not to lose my resolution, I removed my cap & field jacket, took out my purse and tossed a paper wrapped rubber on the bed and then noticing that this prospective piece of tail hadn't started to disrobe yet, I started making motions etc. indicative to the Idea that she should shake a leg and get her clothes off. Oh, what a well of ignorance her face appeared to me then, dull, moronic submissiveness; slow, plodding dismay crept furtively into her eyes and she undid something, perceived my horrified staring at her gut, so she sucked it in with an effort. Darling, at that moment I almost fainted. I became palsied with disgust, with repugnance at myself, my intentions, my surroundings. I trembled in fright, my head swam giddily with an overwhelming repulsion and I shuddered as tho I had touched a foul and nasty gob sputum, and I couldn't shake it from me quickly enough. In panic haste I put on my shirt my jacket, even picked up the rubber, foggily considered giving these poor devils 10 or 20 lire for their trouble, but couldn't stay long enough to do even that. I frantically retreated out the curtained entrances into the sunny world, noticing as I passed, the offers of the older woman and the added presence of some baldheaded old man. I walked in rapid confusion down the street, embarrassed, wondering if I had buttoned or unbuttoned my pants, but self-consciously afraid to ascertain their true state on the public street, I was more shaken up then than the night we had the air attack at sea, and felt a need of a good stiff drink to steady my startled mind. I have never experienced anything in the way of emotion or mental mood like I did there. It was a terrible experience, very strange, so I have tried to describe it to you in detail in all its repulsive vividness.

To regain my composure I spent the afternoon walking. Saturday afternoon in the narrow crooked market streets, jammed with barefooted urchins, peddlers, selling their boiled octopus or little fish roasted on a wood fire, or all sorts of dirty looking cheeses, odd, but green and fresh vegetables and herbs, oranges, almonds, strange candies and pastries; little 6-year-old girls holding a loaf of heavy brown bread and yelling "Pane" (bread). A motley assortment of uniforms from the onetime Italian army being worn by the former soldiers, but also by beggars and urchins, a red-faced peasant from the mountains with a raw hide hog skin bagpipe and several people explaining to me in Italian what it was, and all the tiny kids say "'ello" and bigger ones say "Hi Joe" or "officier" and stare. Picture your mother's alley only about 2/3 as wide with 3 or 5 story buildings making a chasm out of it, and twice as filthy and winding thru all these shops and stands and you have an idea of this market section. Not all of Palermo is like this at all and I left this squalor to wander out through a serene and verdant park full of statues and palms and cactus. Traveling on I noticed 3 large red domes of which I had a postcard picture, but had never known where or what it was. It was a Moorish mosque built in 900 A.D. The most beautiful thing is the garden, old and moss covered, sprawling anciently around the restored and repaired mosque. Met a painter in these gardens and I'm going back tomorrow to have my portrait drawn for $2.00.

Came back to the ship very tired, but went out after supper for an Italian lesson at the Air Corps Club, but that was a false alarm for they haven't a teacher yet. Bot a bottle of Crema Mandorla for

$1.50 and one of Pantelleria for 70¢ and came back and stocked them away for our reunion. Have 12 bottles now and still have $33 left! No room to explain. Keep writing dearest [address inserted]. Somehow I am still your "faithful" husband beloved, but you see what perils, I would even say tortures, I have been thru with it. More later dearest; now, I love you as always, forever

Robert

*   *   *   *   *

9PM Monday December 6, 1943

My sweet darling -

Did practically nothing except in the afternoon had my portrait drawn by [name clipped out by censor]. It is by no means a good drawing, but it is a likeness to me so I'm sending it on to you. He drew the face quite lopsided and disproportionate, but I didn't have the heart to tell him so. He showed me writeups with his name in them in old worn out newspapers of Belgium, France and Italy for his watercolor work on the cathedrals around [name cut out]. His old mother was sitting there, crouched and wrinkled looking, so like a big mouse with glasses and knitting needles. He with his skullcap, horn rim glasses, and large featured face, would occasionally hold my portrait away from him & cock his head from side to side, scrutinizing it with the critical and temperamental eye of the great artist he was; and she would get up & look over his shoulder and smile at me over her spectacles and say "very good", and his brother-in-law would look at it and say "um, buono!" and smiled winningly at me. They all called him the professor. I was going to have him copy a photograph of you, but he wanted $3.00 so I didn't think it was worth it. Paid $2.00 & 2 hours of my time to get me drawn, but it was also an experience to observe this Italian family.

The cadet woke me at 7:45 and told me to get dressed if I wanted to go to Tunis with him. So I did hurriedly and without breakfast, cadged an army truck and jostled out to the airport where our plane, a C47, was waiting to go. We climbed in and sat metallically on the cupped aluminum seats, and looked over the bags of mail, the yellow life preservers, out the plastic windows onto the drab, olive wing. There were two Sgts, two nurses, and upon the arrival of a bombardier Lt and the prettiest little girl I have ever seen over here (a Red Cross worker), our passengers were complete and at 8:30 the motors were roaring powerfully, shaking the plane with thundering vibration, which added a bit to that ex-

337

cited feeling we had for the first few moments of the journey. We taxied jerkily onto the runway, and then with terrific noise commenced lumbering hugely over the ground. Objects began passing with startling rapidity and for a moment you felt a slight tenseness of acceleration pushing mysteriously against you, but only for an instant. The plane, lifting with imperceptible effort, leaves the ground into the smooth grace of flight, and you seem to share the plane's lightness, its easiness in the air. Quickly things fall away beneath you, losing all the sordidness and dirt of reality and becoming sort of a dream world spread toylike in immeasurable expansion about you. There is no sense of distance or size, only the pleasantness of seeing colors and shapes blending in natural proportion, but undisturbed by measurement. Miasmic wisps of mist wrap the sprawling sun-bathed city, lifting as it were the coverlets of nite from its back, and pushing them slowly up into the mountains. Strong backed, sturdy mountains standing a motionless watch over the honeycomb of houses, hills nestling the white dwellings up to the blue and silent sea. And passing slowly beneath the long spread of the wing you see a little dollhouse apartment building with one bomb torn corner, crumbling in dainty ruin like a crushed ant nest. Climbing, climbing into the exuberance of morning, into the purity of unseen air, and a vast tumultuous panorama of billowing mountains stretching away into the infinite and hazy distance. What beautiful color effects, such tangible texture and tone, ceaseless variation of shades and subtle contrasts, all woven into a verdant quilt of farmland. The brown velvet of plowed and fertile fields, the soft tufted green foam of pastures, the deeper bushy green of spinach or kale patches, citrus orchards prosperously plotted in neat exactness, the tiny tiles like myriad viriscent polka dots, and each separate plot of land distinctly demarcated from the other, precise green & brown rectangles rolling endlessly over the wrinkled hills. Ribbons of road winding with straight-edged persistence across the rugged trails of the terrain. Careless yellow rivers crinkling in muddily gouging loops thru the irregularly twisting valleys, carving the ageless name of water, sinuously, across this static stoicism of earth & rock. Clouds began to form, fleece flecks rising from the valleys, gathering gaily on the mountainside and then gliding with stately whiteness over the shadow dappled world.

Slowly you realize the mountains are behind you and now a comparatively flat expanse stretches off towards a glitter which is the sea. The plane wheels and heads down, hurriedly over the ground a slight jar, the wheels touch and as the speed decreases, the plane begins to bump along, taxiing past parked planes, a few bombs, a junk heap of wreckage, and everywhere that close & gooey reality of mud. Didn't take long here and started taxiing up to the runway again when **BOOM!** We stop. Well, somehow it seemed ludicrous after all those miles of clean winged speed, but here we were squatting on the very muddy earth with a flat tire. It was 9:30. Got out and looked, of course. So reminiscent of those days when you get a flat tire out on a lonely country highway and you feel so frustrated and impotent standing in the tall grass with the crickets after such recent swiftness; then the swishing zoom of another car windily passing you, fading into helpless quietness leaving only the rustling of leaves & the far off oink of pigs. That is about the same feeling we had here in our stranded condition. Keller & I soon set off through the mud in search of a breakfast for me. At the other end of the field we bummed a ham sandwich from the E.M. mess. Came back to the plane in a hurry only to find the crew just starting on it. Finally, after a bit of chow we left at 2:15. Were fortunate enough to fly over the battleground of Gela where the Sicilian invasion began and could still see the plowing traces of the tanks and the fields pockmarked with craters, a sunken ship, wave-washed near the beach and, up on a hill, the cost, measured in several hundred white crosses neatly tallied in perfect rows.

Then the sea, its ruffled blue, like shining corrugated porcelain, splotched with irregular specks of white from the minute and occasional waves. Now clouds under us, a dazzling whiteness of virgin cotton, carpeting in luxurious softness the brilliant blue of the sea. An island poking its peak above the clouds, and then as we approach, the isle itself, peacefully oblivious to our prying eyes, like some relief map worked out with meticulous reproduction. Fifteen minutes more, a convoy crawling in hopeless slowness far below, the coast and sunken ships, the land and wrecked JU-88s [German planes] lying in fields with the grass now growing around them. The landing this time on steel nets making a strange whirring clatter as we skim over it. A few minutes on the ground then back into the sky, the sun sinking rutilantly into the misty West and the moon already a floating bowl of luminescent silver high in the mauve rose dusk. Twilight fading into moonlight, the eerie chill of a clear, starlit evening settling over the rugged coast, a huge fluffy cloud cloaking the summit of a jutting mountain, like some snowy octopus enveloping with tender tentacles a sharp and silent flower on the floor of the silvery sea. Familiar crags, then wing flung moonwards, circling the crest, gay lights flickering hospitality in the town, sparks spitting from the hot exhaust, weird ghost of propellers whirring in the landing lights, a slight jolt, brakes, and back to the bumpy security of earth, hungry and glad to be near the familiar surroundings of my two weeks' home.

*   *   *   *   *

9:15PM Wed. December 8, 1943

My beloved wife -

Studied Italian for a while and after supper came down & finished "Gas House McGinty". You should look that book up and read it darling, for it gives a very good picture of life. I believe you can get a pretty exacting impression of many aspects of male mentality from this book, a true insight into men's conversation and thots. Farrell is uncannily real in conveying such incidents in all men's lives as frustrated, secret boyhood loves, egotistical grandiose daydreams, the "should have pasted him one" attitude, the more sublime thots which men keep to themselves for fear of being thot queer, the subtle character differences yet similarity of pattern, the groping, shallow emptiness of their narrow-minded lives. Tho you think the conversational language he puts in his characters mouths is outrageous, it is far from even approaching the common lewdity & obscenity of actual male conversation. Right here on this ship the conversation at noon chow has been running for two weeks straight, bantering and punning on Sicilian whores with continual kidding as to who is corn holing whom aboard the ship, the size of the 3rd Engineer's dong, the Capt's blow job, the girl who plays the mouth organ, the number of times they can last, etc. Long ago back at Hotpoint I gave up participation in such monotonous and changeless wit, but I have never ceased to marvel at the intricate ingenuity with which most men spend hours of each day, concocting highly involved vulgarity. Farrell gives a good impression of this, but it is not too exact because he has tamed down the language a good deal so that it isn't too lewd or shocking to a female reader. He has tho preserved some of the poetic forcefulness of this obscene idiom; for instance when a truck driver who is backing a truck into a tight spot brags he "could drive it up a goose's asshole without touching the feathers", and you are struck with the power of this analogy despite its vulgarity. (Here again is the question I touched on this morn, what is vulgarity?) The far-fetched yet commonly understood and readily apparent associations and metaphors used in this obscene slang is remarkable and wholly impossible to duplicate

340

in any other field of language. Knocked up, two months gone, doing homework but no connection yet, in the saddle, riding bare-
back, beating his meat, put the blocks to her, cop a feel, pocket
pool, workin' upstairs, muff diver, putting out (opposite of "giving
in", yet identical in meaning! - Freud calls it the law of opposites, I
believe; the Egyptian word Kos meaning weak or strong. Also English and German word but I can't recall it all. Look it up darling, Chap
III of Int to Psychoanalysis), gash, pussy, snatch, coose, quiff, dipping the stick, polishing his pole, hosing, skin the savage, etc, etc.
Meaningless words and phrases all revolving on a clever sexual key
and bringing a sordid sense of satisfaction to those adept in their
employment and invention. Men will wade for hours thru this interminable maze of metaphor, revelling in their sense of comprehension or in their ability to give the twisted denotation of sexuality to
any common word or phrase. I have known many women and girls
too who were extremely dexterous at that sort of conversation;
where the most innocent wording has a hidden obscene meaning.
You have undoubtedly met such girls. I wish tho, darling, that you
would make an effort to disclose the workings of the female mind
and life. I don't think it has ever been done to any degree of correctness. Joyce attempted a little of it, and Farrell too, but it is impossible for a male author to depict a life he has never lived no
matter how closely he observes it. Could you set down for the female the exact picture of her life as Farrell has done for the male.
The ordinary woman, her girlhood play, thots, actions, her awakening to sex, her attitudes towards it, in their experiences and sensations with men, her daydreams, her daily existence, the female
conversation of the "ladies room", the memories of past actions,
the inner self attitude, the nourishment and defense of the ego,
etc.

There is one great fault in Farrell's writing & that is his continual
reliance & use of the effects of highly contemporary & local language, events etc. Some of this will always be self-explanatory like
Hugo's references to contemporary events, but I think that much
of Farrell's language etc. will be incomprehensible in 50 years. I believe an author should avoid that. There are some, as I say,
self-explanatory events, and universal slang which will always endure, but the use of ephemeral expressions should be avoided.
Even now I know there will be many subtle references in Studs
Lonigan or McGinty which pass right by you unnoticed. In a book in
Farrell's style and as good as it is such usages should be avoided.
Joyce is abstruse but his meaning will always be revealed by a little

thot, but Farrell's obscure phrases will be lost with the generation that uses them.

Beloved, I keep worrying about you worrying about me. I'm afraid you are envisioning me in all sorts of dangers, bombs, burning ships, etc., but I'm sitting here just as snug and safe as I was in N.Y. Don't let your imagination build up in a picture of me on a sinking ship when at the very time I am most likely sitting in a bar having a delicious glass of wine, and anticipating a supper of pork chops and spaghetti. I know sometimes I think about you and automobiles or you and pneumonia and I get brief pangs of fear before I master such foolishness. Your risks and mine are of about the same degree, so darling, we'll concentrate on keeping ourselves well and healthy, and let the other do the same.

*   *   *   *   *

9PM Thursday December 9, 1943

Sweetest darling -

Noticed that one of the local theatres had Gigli in "Ave Maria". I had seen this picture in the states back about 1939. I remember very definitely taking Millie Raymonds, my little Italian spark, to see it and she didn't understand the Italian because she spoke the Firenze (Florentine) dialect instead of the pure Toscano. You see all the provinces of Italy have their own dialect, Siciliano, Milanese, Genoese, Napolitan, etc which can hardly be understood by each other but then they also all speak Tuscano the literary & legal language which is the real Italian.

I waited for some time for the theatre to open & then a mob besieged the box office so I gave an usher 50¢ & he got my 16¢ seat. The theatre was identical in layout to the opera house only not so large or elaborate. - I'm sure the movie I saw in the States was a great deal different from this one. They must rearrange the stuff for the American audience, but I don't see why. This movie was the same stuff we get, the same appeals, & emotions. I enjoyed it thoroly. I enjoyed recognizing the few words and phrases of Italian that I knew, I enjoyed observing the audience, their smoking & spitting, their yells & whistles of "forte!" when the sound would fade off or go on the fritz, the intermission while they changed reels, but above all Gigli. Darling, you must buy all the records he ever made. I got one the other day which I want you to go down to Lyon and Healys tomorrow and listen to "No...Pazzo son, Guardate" from Puccini's Manon Lescaut. Buy us that "Vivo vino spumigiante" from

342

Cavalleria & "Occhi Turchini" & "Ave Maria" & I also want the albums of him in Pagliacci & Cavalleria. No singer has ever lived that compares with him & I've heard most of them. He has the fury & passion of Caruso, the delicacy & control of Crooks or Schipa & his interpretation & expression is perfect.

But that is getting away from the movie. All thru the picture I kept returning to the fact that all Occidental people live for the same things, live the same lives, so identical. This was so apparent in the purely Italian movie. I, an American, or a German, or a Pole, wouldn't have to know a word of Italian to be perfectly at ease seeing this picture, familiar with its atmosphere, comprehend all its plots, human & tragic. I was moved by its sadness, choked back tears of emotion at the beauty of Gigli's singing. It was a time worn plot. Opera star loses his wife & is all broken up over it, licentious nite club girl plays goody goody sister to win his money, but then falls in love with him, but her partner discloses her former intentions & Gigli receiving the news of it just before he sings the 3rd act of La Traviata goes out and sings directly to her sitting in her box. Magnificent scene and singing, god he can sing! But it has a happy ending.

*   *   *   *   *

1PM Monday December 13, 1943

My sweet lovely wife -

Before going to the concert in the aft, we stopped by Mamma's again and her little 3 yr old niece was there. The cutest little blond headed girl I've seen in a long time and I was amazed at the soft paternal feelings she aroused in me.

Oh sweetheart, in her every motion & childish word I could see you as a little girl and see also here the image of beautiful days to come when there would be a little girl so like you as a little one to be with us & be ours and romp gleefully through our home. I used to think our kids should be boys, but now dearest I know how I'd really love to have a sweet little girl, my daughter, what strange thrills of happiness that thot brings. It was doubly amazing tho how my silent thoughts communicated themselves to little Delia. She was a bit bashful, but that soon wore off and she brot me a picture of her uncle in Melrose Park, Illinois. Then she started bringing me all her toys & her bambola (doll) and would point at me and lisp "tu papa!" Or she would back up against the wall, stand on the point of her little shoes and run towards mamma and wave her arms "flying". - Try as Sparks would he couldn't get her to come near him. We got out an accordion and tried to play a little. Too hard to coordinate squeezing and playing for me to get the piano melodies out of it. - And when the shoe of "mia piccola senorita" came undone she would allow no one to fasten it up again but me. How proud I was. When we left, she had to climb about my neck and be kissed several times and squealed loudly when we tried to leave, but we finally ducked away.

That experience made me so confident that I would make a good papa, both in my own heart and in my children's. I am so certain now that I will love and be loved by my children with the same beautiful tenderness with which I love and am loved by my gentle, loving wife.

Came back to the ship to find the officers aboard not only with two women but a 3 piece orchestra from the American Bar as well. I wasn't much attracted to this after the afternoon I had spent with Delia and at the concert, so I stepped into the room of Richard Bsahra our 1st cook and furthered a very interesting acquaintance. He is Syrian and they have an estate in Maine. He is 40, single, used to run a sporting goods store for the Tuxedo Park neighborhood, speaks 7 languages, taught high school French, has 2 bros in the Navy and 3 in the army. Aboard this ship of drunken slobs we both feel a mutual attraction and like the other's sense and intelligence. He was up to see his brother at Foggia the other day and the next time he goes I'm going with him. You and I are also invited to a real Syrian dinner when we hit N.Y. too, dearest.

*　　*　　*　　*　　*

9:30AM Thurs. Dec 16th

Dearest one -

I'll never forget this morning. The cadet woke me at 5:30 AM and said, come see the volcano [Vesuvius], it's spitting fire. So hurriedly I jumped into some clothes, lest this immortal should die before I had seen it, and climbed up onto the bridge into the crisp morning air. The moon was suffused by clouds & just the faint hint of dawn made the rocky shore & islands visible. Perhaps 20 miles away a massive symmetrical cone of darkness rose forbiddingly into the somber sky, and as I looked I felt a shudder of awe run thru me, for from its summit flared the hot fiery bowels of the earth. Huge red tongues of flame burst intermittently amid a shower of sparks, lashing upward from its monstrous maw like some angry

344

demon rising out of hell. Long before the Etruscans people must have worshiped this mystic altar of fire, and I can understand why. Hope I can climb it. Porpoises playing in the harbor, the sky dimpled with silver balloons [antiaircraft], the city sprawling haphazardly around the shore, misty & beckoning, and I long excitedly to put my arm around you and squeeze you happily as we both see this someday. [We did in later years, but without the eruption.] I love you always my sweet wife.

Robert

*   *   *   *   *

Thurs 16 Dec - M - New Britain invaded - Listening to the radio: we've invaded New Britain Island; announcement that 2 weeks ago the Germans sank over a dozen ships at Bari, including 3 cargo ships with 1000 casualties, and Robert tells me not to worry about his safety!

Fri 17 Dec - M - 2 V mail letters from Robert, asking for mail. One demanding that I get me fixed up with a diaphragm - So? - Aft mail brought a pencil sketch drawing of Robert via airmail 12/8. So happy to get it. Wrote 2 4-page letters to Robert enclosing a snapshot of me in each letter. Hope he gets them soon. Newscasts that Allied invasion of the Balkans is to begin. Patton's 7th Army in the lead. Ships from Sicily to take part. Will that involve my darling? [Interesting ploy to mislead Germans: we're preparing for Anzio. They can see something afoot, but we mislead them (??) with the Balkans. I know, from a German colleague, von Mittelstaedt, who participated, that German troops were *subsequently* moved from Balkans to Anzio.]

Sat 18 Dec - M - Met - Rigoletto - Robert's letters so frank and realistic, just like him. Mailman just brot me 3 airmail letters from Robert, one telling of his struggles to be "faithful", another how he had his portrait drawn by that artist; also his trip in a C-47 to Tunis; asking me to please write him. So I wrote 2 long ones and mailed them airmail.

Tues 21 Dec - Xmas Shopping - Home and then going to bed, but lying in bed till 2 or 2:30 thinking of Robert letters and his stories of his struggle to be faithful. Angrily I composed many "mental" letters on the subject.

Thurs 23 Dec - I get fitted with Diaphragm - This eve Fritz drove Sis & me down to Dr Buky's where we spent an hour being educated in the use of the vaginal diaphragm, my anatomy being used to demonstrate for Sis' benefit & vice versa. Paid 5.00 for the darn thing. Must remember that the darn thing is not to be removed till 12 hours after last intercourse.

Sun 26 Dec - Scharnhorst reported sunk today by British. 5 days till 1944, I shall be glad to see this year go by. I've had some happy moments, but the whole of it has been one of much acute agony, and they say the war won't end till 1949!

Mon 27 Dec - Mom let me sleep till almost 2 PM. Read Robert's letter (so long delayed) [that of 28 Nov] with mounting resentment at his frankness. He says he doesn't expect to be back for a couple of months.

Tues 28 Dec - Decided to stop in at the Division office, about getting back on the payroll. So I chatted with Marie Sloane, Maj Hartman, Capt Peterson, Col Nelson - upshot of all I decided to do no further job hunting. Wondering if I'm getting myself into a jam wooing GLD again; anyway, will see it thru & deal with Robert's wrath later.

Thur 30 Dec - I face the coming year with fear and apprehension - 1944 - an enigma?

Fri 31 Dec 1943 - New Year's Eve - Phooey! - Felt no particular consciousness of the fact that the old year was ending & a new one beginning. Just wondering whether RWD has received any of my letters and could his silence indicate he is homeward bound? I'd like to see him before I get bound up in a job or something.

*　　*　　*　　*　　*

12:15AM Saturday Dec 18, '43

Beloved -.

Yesterday (Thurs) all I did was watch for the pilot to come aboard to take us to dock, but in vain. So we had a big 7 handed game of poker and I was unable to avoid losing $11 - Eleven dollars I couldn't really afford to lose and I was very disconsolate and angry with myself. A gambler's regrets to a conscientious husband are really agony. Perhaps too it makes the joy of winning twice as great. But it didn't look like I was ever destined to win. $10.00 I had paid to play poker for a few nites and very much against my better judgment, but with that goading gambler spirit I played again tonite.

346

Didn't take me long to lose $6.00 more as I saw my chips draining away I became despondent and decided to quit; oops almost, and there's a king, stick it out and I won a pot for a change. My luck turned and from $6.00 behind, I've finished $14.00 ahead for the evening, or $4.00 ahead of the game. Whew! There is really an excitement to it.

*   *   *   *   *

Sunday December 19, 1943 11:30 PM

Sweet one -

I was interrupted to lose a game of chess for a change. Then I went up and had phenomenally bad luck at poker. Didn't even win a pot for 1½ hrs and wound up losing $12 for the evening. My luck was so consistently bad that I had very little fun even in playing. The chief engineer won $23.00, but since he lost $87 playing craps in the afternoon, he needed it. I incidentally won $17.00 in that crap game so, tho I am a bit muddled as to where it came from, I still have $44.40 to last till the 1st of the year.

*   *   *   *   *

7:30PM Wednesday Dec. 22, 1943

Darling beloved. -

Tonite, to this frenzied agony of wasted life, I have to add also the curse of my own ungovernable foolishness. Many times before I have felt the curse of gambling, but never as strongly as I do now. When I first started a week or so ago I felt a deep misgiving, a foreboding of a minor disaster, but I am uncontrollable. It was a good way to kill time, too much time. I liked the excitement when I won, didn't mind losing if it was light, what I could afford. But their [sic] was the continual fear of losing too much. It became an exaggerated and possessing fear and the disgust I had of myself when I did lose too heavily was unbearable. Sitting four hours in a still, smoke filled room in a constant fear of losing, in anger at bad luck and failure, yet each night go back for more. I lost $15 last nite and having $20 left today I knew there was only one way to get rid of this damn disease of gambling, to free myself and my mind from this drug and its continual remorse or false joy. I resolved to throw my $20 away and thus to buy my freedom with it. Without money I would be unable to gamble and I purchased my liberty in 4 rolls of the dice losing $5,00 each time with a sort of thankful deliberation. Now I am

347

finished. True, I am thoroly disgusted with myself, but the incubus of fear etc. has been lifted from me and tho my asinine conduct has cost us about $33, we can be happy that it is over. I will have to draw now when we do get ashore, but I promise that money will not be wasted. I can also say that that $33 was almost all cigarette money, because Sicilians smoke and I don't. I'm glad I couldn't gamble those 14 bottles of wine! So dearest, you have another item of foolishness to chalk up to your husband in case we ever need it to balance the score of our "crimes" against each other. I love you so and will see that you never suffer because of my inanities.

Have no idea when I'll get ashore again to mail this so I'll just keep rambling on. As you must know from the hasty P.S. I tacked onto the other letters, I went ashore yesterday. Just had to get in & see if there was any mail from you and I spent the entire day doing just that. It was, I believe, about 10 AM when a limey launch came out bringing one of our navy boys back from the hospital. (He cut the tips of 3 of his fingers off in one of the 20 mms the other day). It took only 5 minutes to change my clothes, grab the letters and go back with them. Took care of some official stuff at the port office & then wandered uptown in search of my APO. Didn't find it till noon and must have walked about 4 miles tho it isn't ½ mile from where I started. Italy appears much more prosperous than Sicily & this town is not as badly damaged as Palermo. They have beggars & slums of course but not anywhere near as many as Sicily. Not one brat tried to bum a cigarette. The shops have a good variety of stock & seemed better kept. I believe the restaurants are open to the soldiers too, which they weren't in Sicily. Some very fine modernistic buildings too, and tho I don't know as they are running or not I saw a whole yard of modern streamlined railroad coaches (interurban, I believe.) And traffic, a constant roaring, rumbling stream of trucks and jeeps. Amazing when you stop to think that they all had to be brot here by ship!

It started to rain, but I got a ride direct from the base P.O. to the pier. It gets dark at 5 PM & it was 4:50 when I applied for a launch to get back to the ship. Had visions of spending a nite getting drenched looking for a place to sleep. I got service tho & after I got the British Naval Lt in charge to decide the argument of the Italians as to which one would take me out, I just stepped into the cabin of the launch and watched the rain bombard the harbor mercilessly. A gray ominous dusk settled rapidly on the water making everything obscure. Only the blustering rain &, outside the breakwater, now the heavy slap of the waves above the muffled chug of the engines.

348

In the gloom and rain I mistook another ship for ours and began to fear that I was lost, but with a sort of desperate certainty I pointed to a ship about 500 yards off & motioned the chief of the crew to go to it. I was right, but now the problem of getting aboard. The Jacob's ladder could just be distinguished dangling over the side. The waves tossed the little launch like a chip & the rain lashed mercilessly down soaking thru my field jacket. The clumsy Italian handling the launch couldn't get it up to the side of the ship properly where I could grab the ladder. I had visions of missing the ladder & and falling in the black slushing water beneath me, down between the ship & the launch. I lunged as the boat lifted on a wave and grabbed the ladder and, holding my feet doubled up beneath me to keep out of the sea, swung with a bang into the side of the ship. The jar knocked my cap loose and I couldn't let go with the two hands necessary to catch it. It was lost in the darkness and the rain. Little did I think when I bot that cap in Petersburg last March that I would lose it in the Mediterranean this December. I came off tho with only a bruised groin from hitting the ship and a thoroughly drenched field jacket.

Just went up & made myself a toasted cheese sandwich & heard that the Chief Eng won back the $195.00 he was out in the crap game. Glad that is no longer an affliction of mine and I'll make no attempts to get my money back.

Looked out at the nite. A few stars hazily twittering thru the scudding clouds. An occasional eerie cloud-cloaked flash of lightning reveals the choppy heaving of the sea, & the ship is creaking & groaning as it sways slightly in the waves. Intermittent depth charges go off with a metallic thud like someone hitting the ship with a huge hammer. Not near as bad as at Gibraltar where the darn things kept almost knocking you out of bed all nite.

*   *   *   *   *

9:15PM Friday, December 24, 1943
My lovely, gentle wife whose glowing image hovers in my mind like the motionless beauty of warm moonlight flooding in constant silence upon the tossed and turbulent sea. The joy of you who shines in me fixedly, inextinguishable, the heavy clouds of my existence vanishing into the tenebrosity of nite, scudding before your brilliance like dry leaves before the clear winds of Autumn. You scatter my sorrows & bring to me that pure & bubbling music of love. You cause in the weedy rocks of my soul a garden, a fantasy of fra-

grance, flowering & fertile, delicate blossoms redolent with desire, the roots firm fixed, clinging in wholesome soil - no longer the stale aridity of sand, barren & shifting, for the magic of your fructuation has congealed life, has conceived happiness, has created a purposeful beauty from the vacant sterility of my casual youth. - Thru all this maze of euphemisms I mean I love you, sweet adorable one, and want to spend my life forever in the full rich happiness of your love.

[In the contemplation of Christmases past] . . . where was I in '36 & '37? Where were you? What were you doing in your suave sophistication as your drunken future husband was feeling up some not overly willing teenager on her back steps. In whose strong arms was your delectable virginity reclining as your lifelong love patted Maria Romano playfully on her broad dago ass and felt thirsty for another drink of gin. What longings did your lips yield in kisses, what hands tingled on your body as my soul throbbed with the thot of Felicia and my fingers toyed with her golden hair? Oh where, oh how, with whom, the crossed, snarled threads of fate, who wove the glorious pattern of our mated interlocking lives, the heavy hand of experience coloring the cloth, strengthening the thread, carving grooves within us that we would fit each other perfectly, knit our bones solidly, bound into each other by the unknown past that created us. What an unending fascination & complexity life holds when we examine its strange workings.

9PM Saturday December 25, 1943

Sweet darling -

Today has definitely been a good day. The announcement of the attack soon to be launched from England was undoubtedly held to give everyone a mental "boost" for Xmas, 2,000 tons of bombs on Calais, Eisenhower and Montgomery commanding the attack from the West, 3,800,000 American soldiers overseas. Sure sounds encouraging. By next Xmas I think the end of the war with Germany should be in sight. In fact I wouldn't be a bit surprised if I spent next Xmas in the Pacific theater.

What I can't stand tho is these simpering speeches about this war ending all wars, and the great big beautiful peace they're going to build to last forever and ever. The world free from oppression. No more war. Who the hell do they think they're kidding? We're still in the middle of this war & they're already announcing the little farcical treaties and guarantees to minor nations that will form the excuse for the next debacle. And they boast about it and say oh look how we have guaranteed the independence of this handful of

Gypsies that they may rot and stew in the lethargy of their national incompetency. Russia, of all nations, a traitor to the bloody but sublime principles in which the Soviet was founded, signing a treaty with Poland & Czechoslovakia. Why the devil do we want Czechs or Poles or Lits, or Croatians. Why not Europeans, then if the greedy state of Italy wants a piece of France, they'll have to fight like mad to get the European Congress to vote for it, and once they have it, so what. Louisiana was granted 100 sq miles of Texas territory, so what. But yet after 8,000,000 lives in the 1st World War and who knows how many in this, they'll still leave Europe a cauldron of petty, narrow, ambitious nations, and a hive of trivial & needless trouble. The futility of it sickens me, but I know one thing darling, that we will make our kids tool & die makers or "key men in essential industries" that they may spend a comfortable & happy wartime at home when their generation rolls inevitably into the gaudy emotionalism of war.

Had a very good meal this noon, turkey, mince pie, etc. We also had a very comical visitation from Santa Claus. The 3rd ass't Eng. is about the most clever comedian on the ship. He's thin & well over 6' 4" and came in with a mop, for a beard, some string for hair & clad in a red bathrobe with a gunnysack on his shoulder. He presented the Captain with a "nite spy glass" (a piece of pipe with a little bulb wired to it) & gave me a long series of pipe joints with a funnel in the end (a bazooka). The 1st Ass't Eng notoriously has 6 flash lights so Santa gave him a short piece of pipe with a bulb in it (another flashlight for him). The Chief Eng received a deck of cards. The 1st Mate got a bottle with a nipple on it (he's an awful drunkard). This is some ship! They were down trying to borrow a bottle of my wine but I refused them.

So we came in this afternoon. One of the 1st things that greeted us was a blast that almost turned us inside out & scared us half to death. Only an Engineer outfit blasting some of the wreckage loose along the waterfront. Some of the rocks fell on our deck tho. Good to hear the winches grumbling overhead again. I'm down, as usual, in my "dungeon". It's a little cool down here these days but not bad. Very nasty outside tonite, cold & raining. The Negro stevedores have their G.I. overcoats on & the raincoat over that. Poor devils. We're by another sunken ship, but it doesn't stink like the last one did. Can hear the "ducks" go droning by in the water next to us. They are sure a useful vehicle over here. A truck with a body like a boat & with a propeller. They crawl in & out of the water by the prow of our ship all day & nite.

I looked up into the southern sky and wondered what that peculiar red light was up there. Then I remembered the volcano. It has been holding its peak in the clouds for the last few days and I didn't recognize it immediately from our new position. Then suddenly the whole sky seemed to burst into huge liquid flame. The clouds & smoke diffused with a fiery glowing red. Hell bubbling up from the seething belly of the earth, splattering its weird molten light, fluorescent, upon the mask of clouds. An unforgettable & indescribable sight, and I watched it as it would fade away to a dull glow, then a minute or so later blossom up in a new fury, throwing a terrifying flower of fire into the sullen sky.

*　　*　　*　　*　　*

8PM Tuesday 28 December 1943

My beloved:

... At 11:30 AM we were eating a good warm meal with a medical unit about 10 miles behind the front. In the States the GI dumps his garbage & coffee into a can or a pit. Here there was a long line of civilians each with two cans, in one can they had the soldiers pour their coffee, & into the other the leavings in their mess kits. I still can't figure out how the civilians get over the front lines & back into their home town.

We heard that 30 German planes had just bombed & strafed the town we were going to. Keller had another moment of indecision at hearing this, but we went on & hoped that if they came back in the afternoon we would be near a deep fox hole. Our truck climbed & climbed jolting up the narrow, precarious road that spiraled thru the mountains. Never realized Italy was so mountainous. It is as rocky & rugged as Spain or Sicily in this part. The road curved so sharply at times that the truck would have to back up & try again to get around it. We had been hearing the roar of the guns since some 20 miles back, but now almost on the lines we could hear them above the roar of the engine. I thot of planes. We would never hear them. I had been prepared to have shells popping around us too, but none came closer than 500 yards all day. (It was, tho, a rather quiet day in this sector I guess.) Otherwise most of the warfare lived up to my expectations. It was amazing to find that good old Camp Lee had been fairly accurate in its training. All along the way I noticed this, and could picture it on the maps just as we had studied it. The railhead, the dumps, the bivouac areas, the convoys, the maintenance echelon; the combat teams, the Bn aid station, the

C.P. (command posts) the camouflaged trucks & the artillery. It made me feel a little confident that I would also know & do the right thing in case of attack. How to take & make use of cover & concealment. Where to expect booby traps, etc.

We now reached the crest over 3,000 ft up & started to descend the sinuous road. Before us lay the most beautiful view, [The Liri Valley] hills jutting in great heaps up from the valleys, and within this vast panorama crept the horror, war! Soon the truck stopped. As far as he dared go now without fear of drawing fire. We got out & the crepitant grumble of artillery could be heard rattling incessantly from mountain to mountain. About 1½ miles off over on a German held hill [Mt Trocchio, in front of clearly visible Monte Cassino and its Abbey] we could see our shells bursting into its side, working methodically up and down. What a hail of death it must have been for any living thing on the hill, yet that mass of insensate rock & dirt lifted its peak out of the dust & seemed to laugh like a dull cow hit with a small boy's pea shooter. Occasionally a puff of black smoke would blossom over the Jerry positions. Aerial shells, bursting & raining shrapnel downward. A fox hole isn't much protection against that. Constantly the rumble of shell fire shook swiftly through the mountains. One battery in particular was making sort of a symphony of noise. It was a battery of 4, firing in slow cadence 1...2....3....4, two minute pause, then again this stiff punch of the 1st gun its heavy shattering echo sssprrufmmmm punctuated by the blast of the 2nd gun & then the two echoes joined in a bass vibrato, etc.

On the way up to the front we had noticed all the bridges blown out & repaired, and an occasional shell hole or tree scarred by shrapnel & gunfire, but here the whole area seemed to have been raked with artillery & there was hardly a tree unscathed. Looking down into that green valley we could see the whole floor of it pimpled with brown craters, so numerous that they looked like holes in a colander. Could stoop down almost anywhere and discover a piece of shrapnel. Brought a couple back with me.

We went down thru a large grove of twisted willow trees, following a telephone wire to the Bn aid station. The American telephone wire is a blackish gray & very hard to detect from a few feet. The German wire is red! Don't know why the efficient Germans should use a red covered wire. Perhaps it's leftover from the African campaign. We found the shell torn, straw floored hut that the medics were using for their home & stayed a while there. While we were there one of the Sgts of A Co came in for treatment of a boil on his arm. He is a tall skinny fellow needing a haircut very badly, but he will most likely get the D.S.C. for his action the other day. His company had been assigned the job of capturing a Jerry held hill. A particularly steep & difficult one. They snuck up to within 100 yds of the enemy at nite & attacked them in the morn. They made their initial success by this surprise, but the Heinies were not easily discouraged & hung tenaciously to their rock hewn fortifications. "A" company kept digging them out with grenades. Advancing. Then they ran out of grenades. This Sgt used <u>rocks</u>! And they continued to advance, the rock landing in the Jerry dugout, he thinking it a grenade, jumped out & is promptly shot. The men don't take many prisoners. The terrain here was so rugged that it sometimes took 20 hours to get a wounded man down to the 1st aid station.

The Germans use Italian labor, blasting these fortifications out of solid rock & then build them up with rocks & railroad ties. They stock them plentifully with food & ammunition & sit there & wait for the Yanks to come. Some of these dugouts have received direct hits with 155s & still hold up, so you can imagine what a job it is to capture one of these hills. Sure have to hand it to the infantry. Too bad some of the gripers about taxes, gas rationing & meat shortages can't get into a combat suit, dig their fox hole home in the gooey mud, live on "C" & "K" rations for weeks & then crawl up thru machine-gun fire, mortars & artillery to take a hill inch by bitter inch. They'd be damn glad to get back to their $90 a week & pay their taxes on it without so much moaning. When I got back I absolutely revelled in the fact that I had a shower & a clean dry bed.

We went up to within perhaps 200 yards of the forward outposts, but as I said things were pretty quiet that day. We wandered back up the hill into the blasted town & on up the road. Stopped & took some pictures of me on an overturned tank, with the valley stretching away behind me, a white puff from a phosphorus shell rising out of the woods. Think the tank at least should show up. Took a whole a roll of pics. Went back to a battery of 155 howitzers & looked the territory over around there. Found a German dugout up on the hill, cases and cases of machine-gun ammunition, an 80-mm mortar & a lot of mortar shells, rusty German rifles, gas masks etc. I took an ammunition pouch off a dead Heinie & a signal rocket for a souvenir of my trip. A couple bodies had been thrown about 50 yards when this German dynamite truck blew up. Could still see the yellow blocks scattered around & the mangled wreckage with the KRUPP nameplate on the radiator.

As it started to get dark we commenced hitch hiking back. Our

354

most interesting ride was a long one with a French officer who spoke English worse than I speak French. I knew how to get where he was going tho & got him there & ourselves 40 miles closer to "home". Got back to the ship about 8 PM and ate everything I could lay my hands on. Showered and dead tired I slept luxuriously till 10 AM this morn.

*　　*　　*　　*　　*

11:15 AM Friday Dec. 31, 1943

Sweetness:

I am now on the last day of this year of separation & loneliness, still lost in the ennui of impossible desires. I feel an appalling sense of loss when I review the past year and see that we were together only about 60 days of the 365, and when I think of this coming year & realize that our time together will be far less than that, I could cry with an agony of despair. Oh that I could believe in the myth of immortality to soothe the wasted hours of this world with hopes of an eternity in the next. This miserable crawling mystery, man. Oh why, oh what, aching with passion, languishing in the subtle grip of a steady continual love, tormented with the unknown, & tortured with the impossible. My sweet beloved, we will live our life with an intensity that will make each hour worth a year, with an art that makes each slight pleasure an overpowering delight. We will live in the abandon of complete sensuality, the most glorious hedonism, yet preserve always our precious health & revel in it. Beneath & beyond this will flow the great power of our intelligence, the ecstatic, boundless joy of a keen aesthetic mind. Let us train now to live this way - but what training do we need? That has always been our way of life & the world has robbed us of it. Would that I could crush the tawdry bubble, earth, in my hand or rather erase the foolish face of mankind from its magnificent area & roam free in the natural sweetness of its forests, knowing only you & your soft-spoken love. The Eden wish of man. -

Dearest, our day will come, we know that, and these long years of separate yearning will fade & mellow as our long life of happiness lengthens. We will be enriched by this sorrow. Read again for me that passage in "The Prophet" that says we can experience joy only to the extent that sorrow carves its chasm in our soul. We drink life from a chalice whose depth is fashioned by sadness & the beauty of which is etched in experience.

355

*   *   *   *   *

6PM Monday January 3, 1944

My darling wife -

I'm going to be very formal in this letter because I don't want to get our plans messed up. I have 3 things to contend with in writing this: 1) the fact that I have heard nothing at all from you for 3 months, 2) the fact that nothing is at all definite as to what is to become of me & 3) censorship. I am writing to prepare you for the eventuality of my home coming around the 1st of February, yet I must also foresee the fact that I might not arrive till April and also the slight chance that I might arrive at Norfolk instead of N.Y.

Now if you are already living in N.Y., everything is simple, you just stay there and wait. But I'm almost certain that you're in Chicago & will want to stay there till you are certain that I am coming.

I have no idea what sort of mail service you have been getting, but you should get this by the 20th of January at the latest. I have been writing you almost every other day for the last two months. You know if those letters are coming regularly & reliably or not. Use your judgment then; if you hear no more from me for 10 days or so after receiving this, you can figure I'm on my way. Since that is not at all reliable, I'll try to send more definite word, but I'm not sure that I'll have the opportunity to do so. I'm going to send a V mail too in case that gets to you sooner. Did you get that cablegram from Gibraltar & the happy birthday cablegram from Sicily okay? I'm going to send you another happy birthday cablegram if I can find out for sure that I'll be home as planned, and if I find out that I won't be back for a few months, I'll send you a cablegram telling you to keep writing to me. That is, if this all gets thru the censor and you know when to expect me & what meaning to place on the cablegrams. This is one hell of a way for a man to have to arrange to meet his wife, but I know of no other way to do it, darling, & I don't want us wasting 2 or 3 days of our precious time while you come from Chicago to N.Y.

*   *   *   *   *

WESTERN UNION - VIA MACKAY RADIO
EFM MRS ELIZABETH N DOTY
2115 SOUTH TRUMBULL AVE CHICAGO ILL
LOVING BIRTHDAY GREETINGS. I WISH WE WERE TOGETHER ON

THIS SPECIAL OCCASION ALL MY BEST WISHES FOR A SPEEDY REUNION. PLEASE DON'T WORRY
ROBT DOTY

[END Diary notes receipt of this 15 Jan 1944, my letter states that I sent it on 7 Jan]

*   *   *   *   *

[The following was written on "onion skin', the evening of the day the Wm S Rosecrans was sunk - perhaps that explains the misdating of year!?? - END must read between the lines here to see that the ship was sunk, which she did, i.e., that the rest of the ship's crew was also put up in Naples, etc., etc.]

7 PM Thursday Jan 6, 1943 [sic]

My lovely darling -

Last nite I wrote you of how safe I was [And this letter must have gone down with the ship, Fig 32!] **& today I am even more so. It is definite that I am coming home now. May get there sooner than I expected and will start my leave right away instead of tinkering around in port.**

So many things I want you to buy me too beloved. I wish you would buy a little portable chess set with holes to plug the men into [This is the kind of chess set I had, where the men would not slide around as the ship rolled, and she, knowing this, must immediately deduce that it has been lost.] **That is something I'll miss this time at sea. Books, too. Darling buy us a copy of "Studs Lonigan" & "Look Homeward, Angel"** [Books she knows perfectly well I had with me], **two marvelous books & you can annotate them for our library like I did "Ulysses". I would also like you to get one of those Valpak deals preferably with zippers, but I may have to wait & get that myself since I imagine the army PXs are the only places that have them. I won't have enough stuff to bring back from over here to worry about getting one here.** [Previous letter had "complained" about how much stuff I was toting and problem of getting it back.] **You might get a couple of good bottles of wine for us to celebrate on also** [Knowing, of course, that I had acquired a <u>case</u> of Pantelleria Moscato].

*   *   *   *   *

9:30PM Sunday January 9, 1944
Guess I saved more stuff than anyone else on the ship, at least as far as value goes. Ever since that attack way back in November, I

357

had my blouse, overcoat, camera & wallet ready to go. Recently I added my pistol to this so that I just slipped into my coat & saved $170 worth of stuff [But, according to plan, wore my helmet rather than fancy hat [Fig 26], having previously encountered erratic (Navy) gunfire. The Sam Browne belt, of course, was irrelevant.]

*   *   *   *   *

11:15PM Monday January 10, 1944

My lovely one -

I'll bet all of this place [Pensione Maurizio, overlooking Bay of Naples] is beautiful in the summertime. It was even beautiful last nite when I opened the tall French windows onto the moonlit bay and heard the water swishing on the rocks below. I'll never forget one nite, too, anchored out in the harbor, the moon peering thru the clouds like a soft lite through a frosted window. Then the fierce wind coming up, sweeping the clouds away, and the stars shone bright & cold, glinting on the lashed whitecaps of the water. The wind screamed steadily thru the rigging, shaking the ship, but the moon hung motionless in its liquid fairy lite. Vesuvius, snowcapped, looked like Fujiyama, and its peak glowed like a red hot coal set on an ice cream cone. Moonlight, snow mountain & a fiery cap of wind-whipped flame - what a strange dream-like sight that was, and I left the letter telling you about it on my desk, pen beside it, and now no eyes will see it in the dark silence of the ocean floor.

That, too, is a strange feeling. I used to sit at nite sometimes & try to imagine what my room, the corridors, the beds etc. would be like underwater, deep beneath cool seas, undisturbed, quiet, rotting slowly in eternal solitude; and now it is so, and I can see in the dim chill lite the tiny creatures of the sea floor invading thotlessly the rooms were once my feet stepped firmly & my voice echoed airily from the walls.

Those that "have" live well I guess. Came back to the hotel & went up to the lounge. Discovered that this must have once been the apartment of Duke Andrea Carafa D'Andria, a Major in the Italian Army & a good Fascist. Anyhow, he must have left here in a hurry for he left everything behind & I browsed thru his gas & light bills, his bankbooks, the receipts for the radio he bot on installments (it's a good one too), his maps of No Africa, his citations for bravery, his letters, his pictures of his wife & horses in the days when there was sunshine & wealth & happiness for them. I browsed thru his library of Italian & German books. Among the German were several novels

358

by Pearl Buck, D. H. Lawrence; even "Gone with the Wind" and I glanced at the frontispiece "Ein Mensch ist in seinen Leben wie Gras, er blühet wie eine Blume auf dem Felde; Wenn der Wind darüber geht, so ist sie nimmer da, und ihre Stätte kennet sie nicht mehr. Psalm 103", and I wondered if Maggiore d'Andria remembered this passage now that the winds of war had swept the flower of his life from these fields wherein I stood.

Then I read parts of a Fascist book called "Un Reveluzione e un capo" (One revolution & one chief or leader) with an introduction by Il Duce [Note, Il Duce and Der Führer, both meaning "The Leader"]. One striking chapter gave very clearly the tenets of Fascism. It pointed out the other revolutions in history & the splits within the revolutionary party & showed how in a democracy there were always different factions, & ideas & leaders working against each other. Fascism gave "Un popolo, un idee, un capo". Another chapter dealt with the role of women in Fascism, raising & educating strong children. They had a great responsibility in the building of this great & secure Italy.

Read parts of two other books which, if they had been written in English & the words German & Italian substituted for English & French, would have been a standard tirade such as you read everyday back home. - One book dealt with the militaristic and threatening growth of the English army, the militaristic attitude of Englishmen in general, their military weddings, royalty, India, the maneuvers held in England practising for an attack on Germany & Italy with a brutal sweep across a neutral country, the English domination of the sea & their preparation to dominate the air. The other was a collection of testimonials, pictures & stories of brutalities & horrors supplied by Italians in concentration camps in France before the swift brilliant action of the Italian armies swept into France & liberated them. It is the same identical bull shit that is slung at all the world to make them fight. I'll bet that 99.9% of the American population never once thot that the Germans & Italians got the same type of news flashes, atrocity stories, pep talks & nationalistic philosophy that they do.

7 PM Tuesday January 11, 1944

Sweetness -

It was all a false alarm, darling, and I am still sitting here in Italy, waiting. Went around & said goodbye to everyone, cashed in my money & toted my small barracks bag of stuff down to the office & then some one changed someone's mind

. . . It will sure burn my blood to have to contribute taxes for the

359

rest of my life to pay GE, Standard Oil, GM, Farben, Krupp, etc for all the factories of theirs we ruined with bombs. In fact, that is the dirtiest part of these damn wars, the international companies that control the politics that starts the war can't lose. No matter which side wins they have factories & interests in that country & to top that off are reimbursed for any damage or loss caused by the war. It's not so bad having to pay for all the Italian, German & French homes & railways destroyed by us, but I hate the idea of paying for GE's factory in Milan. We still owe France money for the small damage of the last war. How long will it take to pay up for this one?

*   *   *   *   *

7:30PM Wed. January 12, 1944

My darling wife -

Took the Red Cross tour of the city which was a good way to kill the afternoon. First stop was at the Cathedral of St Gennaro of course, the patron saint of the city. They didn't have any skulls, but they did have a couple bottles of old Gennaro's blood and the usual immense barbaric altar & church. Anyone who tries to convince me that a Catholic isn't a groveling savage is going to have a hard time after all I've seen over here. You wouldn't think such superstition possible in this supposedly civilized world. And the outrageous irony of it all when you see how a man who comes the closest to being a true Christian since Spinoza is the ridicule of the Christian world. I mean Mahatma Ghandi who advocates the exact philosophy of Christ yet the entire Christian world scoffs & fights on and puts pictures of their boys on altars so that Mumbo Jumbo Jehovah will protect them, and sing innumerable asinine hymns. How I detest mankind and their bestial stupidity!

*   *   *   *   *.

12:30AM Sunday January 16, 1944

Bot a book "Parliamo Tedesco" (We Speak German) which promises to be a great help in my learning of both Italian & German for I find that what I don't know in one language I can get from the other, and it gives me exercises in both languages. While in the shop an Italian asked me to correct a letter for him which he had written in English. I did & we got to talking since he spoke pretty good English & he offered to teach me Italian for nichts, I accepted readily; but was a bit suspicious of his kindliness, eagerness & willingness to oblige so that when I met him after supper I was carrying my gun loaded & ready in my field jacket pocket. It was a needless precaution tho for he is quite sincere, but I was just as glad to be packin' a gat on the way home at midnight.

Went up to his house on the top floor of an apartment bldg (5th floor) in a lower middle class tenant district. 5 rooms all tile floor and could have been very comfortable at one time. They have removed all but the barest essentials of their furniture tho because of the bombings a while back. Just he and his mother live there. He is an accountant for a Naples bank and works 6 days a week from 8:30 AM to 2:30 PM for 60¢ a day. Bread on the black market costs $1.00 a kilo & 4¢ a kilo on the ration of 125 gr a day. Meat is at least $2.00 a lb if you are able to get any. They live mostly on fruits & vegetables. He is a fairly intelligent person having studied in Munich for several years and speaks German quite well & English fair. I keep pumping him all the time to get the truth on how the Italian people look at us, the Germans, etc. & I have succeeded fairly well. Also learned a lot more Italian and was able to use some of it thanking his Mother for her hospitality. At about 11 PM they insisted that I join them for supper (what an atrocious hour they chose to eat supper) and I was unable to refuse tho I felt it unjust that I should eat their scant food. They were fortunate this evening in having some pork liver which his sister had sent from the country & I took some of it fried with onions & some of their precious bread. They made me eat some old pickled carrots (garlic & oil) that weren't bad & wine & nuts & figs. They had very little but they were certainly wholeheartedly generous with it. Showed them my one remaining picture of you & they sympathized with me for being away from home. His mother was very surprised to hear you were "Russian" for she thot the U.S. and Russia were bitter enemies. I straightened them out on that. - I'm to meet him tomorrow and we'll learn some more, I Italian and he American. I would have to meet him just when I am ready to leave instead of when I arrived, but there will be time for each of us to learn some from each other in the short time remaining.

*   *   *   *   *

10AM Wed January 19, 1944

But I didn't finished telling you of my day yesterday. It wasn't much, but I did take a long and difficult hike up the main hill of the city about 750 ft high and from there I got a marvelous view of the sea, the town, the mountains. Somewhat like Gibraltar, only here the city spreads before you like a huge irregular honeycomb, and I thot of how similar these crawling myriad creatures were to a hive of bees, each with his cell & individuality, yet forming such a minute portion of this hive, so infinitesimal in the eye of history. Down thru all the dirty crooked streets, houses jumbled in senseless plotless pattern, & in them, life! Cold miserable life, living in rags & filth, hungry, brutal, the ordinary insipid life, earning money, buying food, scolding children, the life of youth, the life of old age. In these houses as I watched, soldiers with whores, death with the suffering, plans with the dreamer, the bookkeeper coughing, the dirty urchin rolling his hoop; great sprawling life, twisted & vulgar, laughing with a sneer, sobbing with a terrified "why"?; and it was here like this when the seed of my life urged itself from one body to another centuries ago & it will be here still laughing, still vulgar, when the remote flesh which was of our transmission sobs & asks "why"? - In the centuries of the future.

*   *   *   *   *

[Red Cross stationery]

North Africa 8:30PM Thurs Jan 20, 1944

My beloved darling -

So much has happened that I hardly know where to start. It all happened yesterday when I got tired of sitting in Italy & decided something should be done about it. I visited about 6 different HQs all over town & finally found the right man, a Colonel, who had the authority to allow me to fly back. I convinced him that since I had practically no baggage it would be a fine time to fly, and of course I told him how all the other HQs said it was okay with them. So with a little nerve, a little logic, and a good story about my adventures, I procured a ticket to fly across North Africa! [Fig 33] Was I happy, and things have sure moved fast since. Got my orders at 5 PM & with a little hustling was booked to leave this morning & I did as you see.

Said a reluctant goodbye to Luigi & his mama, the only reason I regretted leaving Italy. They certainly were swell folks, and of course I promised to bring you back to visit them when peace came again. I imagine Italy is very pleasant normally.

*   *   *   *   *

9PM Friday January 21, 1944

Sweetheart -

Today has been a full one, very interesting in a strange city and

362

what a city [Algiers]. This is the finest spot I've seen from Gibraltar to Italy. Well dressed school kids with their books, feeder buses, fine looking women coming out of beauty shops, clean streets, parks, railway service for civilians, department stores. It certainly is a metropolis and almost as untouched by the war as N.Y. My arrival here & the first few hours were extremely inconvenient & mixed up, which usually makes you dislike a place, but somehow I've liked xxxx [Algiers] since the moment I got off the bus. It's the nearest thing to the States I've seen and wouldn't even be a bad place to live.

In the aft I took a Cook's tour of the town. We went 1st to a mosque & were allowed to enter, being careful not to step on the prayer mats. This was the most interesting & impressive thing of the day, to gain this 1st hand impression of Islam. I must study more of this religion. The rituals & superstitions are quite similar in nature to those of Christianity. They have some good ideas such as their ablutions, which they must perform before stepping onto the prayer mats in the mosque. The Catholics only sprinkle a little water on their foreheads, but the Mohammedan must wash his face, hands, feet, mouth, armpits & genitals before stepping onto the sanctified ground. (Most of these people should go to the mosque more often.) Their praying is also excellent physical exercise. The muezzin in charge asked the crowd of sightseers, thru the interpreter, if they wouldn't contribute a couple of sticks of gum to his cause. Guess he must need it for his voice.

We visited several Moorish castles & homes & learned some of the bloody history of this city. So much blue tile used in decorations. This tile came from the Dutch who paid their tribute to the Corsairs in tile instead of silver. Then we went up to the fortress on the hill which commanded the town & harbor. Visited the museum there on the Foreign Legion & other French Colonial troops - The walk down tho, was the thing I had really come for & I wasn't disappointed [i.e., the Casbah]. I thot the narrow crooked slums of Italy were rank & squalid, but here must be the nadir of this type of cliff dwelling. I can understand how it is one of the most infamous spots in the world. It is a labyrinth of filth & mystery, Berbers, Negros, French, peering out of dark, furtive holes. The buildings jut awkwardly out over the 8-ft wide "street" making it like a tunnel, and up & down the steps & around the innumerable haphazard corners run barefoot creatures that make a gamin a saint. Strange creepy women in their sheets & their toe nails painted, ragged sneering thugs, grisly looking individuals in turbans & fezes, and some very beautiful babies crawling in the trash outside their door. This place is off limits to all troops & it was only on this tour that I could see it. It is indescribable & I will always remember it vividly.

*　　*　　*　　*　　*

10PM Saturday January 22, 1944

Beloved one -

Did some more flying today. How I love it, seeing the world stretched vast & beautiful beneath, your eyes covering miles at each glance. Immense Africa sprawled in infinite pattern & panorama. Hills bubbling higher and higher above wide mist-covered valleys. The mist hung close to the ground and as it faded off into the distance it looked like a diaphanous sea of pale white jelly and the mountain crests jutting out of it like huge waves of frozen blackness. Muddy lakes, incredibly crooked rivers, the quilted myriad textured rectangles of farmland, herds of grazing sheep looking exactly like dirty gray maggots, and off beyond the haze you could imagine the Sahara, the Congo, the Veld, the diamond diggings; what an enormous & variegated continent Africa!

The flight was very smooth & uneventful. Took much better care of everyone at this destination than at the last one. Got a truck direct to the billeting office & from there to our residence for the duration of our stay here. All the officers are given 5 blankets & a cot in a large bare room. About 20 of us in our "ward", most of them Air Corps officers en route home after their 50 missions. They are a swell bunch of Joes, modest & clean cut lads & they've been thru a lot. Has raised my opinion of the Air Corps quite a lot. The chow is not so hot, but it's no worse than the Camp Lee stuff I used to gripe about. When I first came back to Africa, I thot I would try using Italian on the French waiters in the officers mess. It worked surprisingly well, in fact a couple of them even answered in Italian. It wasn't till the next day that I discovered these "French" waiters to be Italian prisoners! We have them here at this "hotel" too.

Perhaps my flying still isn't over, so I'll hang onto this letter for a day or so. I know you'll want to get this soon, for I'll bet that you are worried that I am in this Roman invasion [Anzio] that started off today. It would have been a good show, but I'm not sorry that I missed it. Also found out that they had announced the Bari raid in the papers back last November. I didn't know that or I would have been worrying about you worrying about me.

*   *   *   *   *

Sat 1 Jan 1944 - So the year started with no mail from Robert. Disconsolately I ate turkey for dinner. Decided to lead a more active life this year, and hope to start tomorrow; a job, more social life, more happiness.

Tues 4 Jan - Job Hunting - Owah! Up at 8 a.m. to eat breakfast with the boys & then preparing to go to the Loop. A very foggy day which really impeded traffic. 1st to the library to return books and to get another Russian grammar and a book on fencing. Walking over to the Civic Opera Bldg; much ado about getting in. MPs posted by elevators, visitors pass, etc. Saw Maj Inskip in the R&U branch on 18th floor & he said he'd refer me to the 6th Service Command if Brodner didn't have anything. V mail from Robert annoyed me with his reference to his daily pastimes in Sicily.

Wed 5 Jan - I Get a Job - Went downtown & stopped in to see that Mike Brodner. He was very noncommital & brusque. I felt very foolish. So I squared my shoulders & walked over to the Loop Agency and got sent out immediately to Royce Publishers. Decided to give it a trial. It's $150 a month & I start at 9:30, so I'll stick at it till I hear more from Robert.

Thur 6 Jan - 1st Day at My New Job - Reported for work & got me put to work right away. A bit trying with three bosses. So I typed up statements all day, writing up letters of demand to clients & preparing statements for Dun & Bradstreet. A bit tiresome, but really very simple. Found an airmail special delivery letter from Robert mailed 12/21. Seems he got to Italy on Dec 16 but lay in the harbor till the 21st. So he's seen the eruption of Mount Vesuvius & lost & won at poker & craps but still had money on hand. If we can save $200 a month consistently, we'll have a nice nest egg after this war is over. Robert's letter encourages me when he says perhaps after Italy he'll be coming home.

Fri 7 Jan - 2nd Day Working - I reread Robert's letter on the L riding to work. The sweet darling. I wonder if he will be coming home after this episode in Italy. Spent the day typing up more statements. Altho cold I walked over to Ontra's for lunch & had my usual Friday lunch of clam chowder, chocolate ice cream and

365

coffee, 34¢ now. Some of the waitresses & the colored waiter recognized me & asked why I hadn't been around, etc.

Mon 10 Jan - Robert visits Pompeii, Casino front - V mail letter from Robert saying that he had visited the Casino front. His airmail letter amplified on that & he described in detail his journey to the front on a hospital train & then in an ambulance truck & his reactions to the action going on 200 yards from the enemy. He also visited Pompeii & describes the sights he saw there of the excavated city.

Tues 11 Jan - Home to find an airmail special delivery letter from RWD covering his experiences Dec 21 to Dec 25th. They docked on Xmas day. Well, he lost $35 gambling in a few days and sounds very contrite about it. Oh, well! He does a lot of reminiscing about Xmases of former years, & vows his undying love for me. Repeats again that if he doesn't shuttle back and forth, he should be home Jan 30. 8PM & we are listening to Pres Roosevelt's address to Congress - (1) New Tax Law to bring in more revenue; (2) Continue Renegotiation Law re war contracts; (3) Cost of Food Law to enable govt to place a floor on farmers' goods and ceiling on consumers' prices to apply to necessities only; (4) National Service Law to outlaw strikes & to draft every able adult for essential services. - Feel like my ego is really deflated while going through the "growing pains" in this new job of mine.

Thur Jan 13 - Home to find a disconsolate letter from Robert written at the end of the year, lamenting our separation. Later this eve I rec'd an airmail special delivery from Robert dated 1/4/44 saying to expect him in 10 days before or after February 1st. To go to NY unless I hear from him to the contrary by cablegram. Excited & agitated at the thought of Robert's return.

Mon 17 Jan - M - I get Reservations for Jan 30 - I didn't fall asleep till 2:30 last nite, thinking sweet romantic thots about our coming reunion. At the office Mr S very busy all day & I broke the news of Robert's arrival to Miss Zimney. She "broke the ice" to him & later told me he'd give me a leave of absence. Wish I knew what RWD wants me to do, stay in NY when he might not return for 6 mos? Reading "Look Homeward, Angel" & I think I see several reasons why RWD wanted me to read it, could almost be an autobiography of his life. Am so thrilled at the thought of Robert's homecoming, my beloved coming back!

Tues 18 Jan - M - While eating breakfast I got an airmail special from RWD which sounded very much like his ship had been sunk & he had lost everything he had, but was safe & awaiting transportation back to the States. I went down to the office a wee bit stunned by this news. Came home to find more mail from Robert, also a pic taken 1/9 showing him "all in one piece". Says he will send further letters in c/o my Uncle John in Brooklyn - so!

Wed 19 Jan - Felt very much better today even tho the thot that I am a "potential" widow frightens me. So hard to restrain my impatience for the 10 days remaining before I start for the East - Can hardly wait till I see Robert again, so starved for love & affection from my darling!

Sat 22 Jan - Found card from Mrs MacDonald saying she had a room for Robert & me & would be expecting us. Getting quite a bit excited that I shall be leaving for New York in a week. Relieved that I have a place to go.

Wed 26 Jan - Robert Calls Me - Stacks of invoices to be written up today & I sat there typing & hating every minute of it. Congress passed bonus for soldiers, but big fight on the soldiers' vote question. 20 min to 2 I got a phone call from Wash DC, Robert just landed from a C-54, having flown all the way from Naples - Route: Naples to Sicily to Algiers - Oran, Casablanca, Maraketch (Morocco) to Dakar - Fortaleza, Brazil to Georgetown, Br Guiana to Puerto Rico to Wash DC. Flying since Jan 20. So, I told him to go to Mrs MacDonald's & I would take the 1st train to join him - Stayed up till 5AM packing my bag.

*　　*　　*　　*　　*

[Excerpts from letter I wrote during flight "home", summarizing some of the events of the recent past.]

GMT 6 PM Tuesday Jan 25, 1944 - - 200 miles off Senegal, 8000 feet

To my bro:

We first pulled into Gibraltar and I wrote you much about this interesting old Fortress and my climb to the top of it. We left the

Rock at last and started in a very slow convoy along the coast of N. Africa. Did you get my letter about the attack we had? It was fine to have lived through that one, but a man would be a fool to wish for another. The Germans, I believe, didn't put a bomb in the water that night, but scored with every one. They say 20 planes came after us and we knew they were coming for we laid down a smokescreen. Only seven planes got thru to the convoy, but they sank six ships and hit another. I will never forget seeing that ship disappear instantaneously [carrying ammunition] off our starboard bow, nor could anyone else; and then when we got hit later, we got the hell off our ship but fast before it pulled a disappearing act - but that comes later.

Wrote you, too, about my plane ride from Palermo to Gela and Tunis. We loaded a full cargo of gasoline and proceeded to Naples. Did the censor pass my descriptions of Vesuvius and Pompeii? Wrote you also about my trip to the front. We were right up about ½ mile from San Vittore, of which you have no doubt read much in the papers. The hill our artillery was pounding that day was Mt Trocchio. I missed the real push in that sector by about 10 days, but I could sure get a familiar picture of the action there from the Stars & Stripes. Had some fine pics, too, of the shell-scarred valley and woods, of San Pietro and of the ruined American tanks along the road. We sent 11 tanks against San Pietro. They never got there, and only 3 came back. I got a good pic of the one which got the farthest. It had received a direct hit from a Jerry 105 and had the turret knocked completely off. (I might add that all of my pics are on the bottom of the Bay of Naples, too). Well, I've written you about all this stuff, even a little about being sunk, but I'll try to tell you more now about the latter.

It was a cold, clear day and the wind had been blowing, a fierce incessant gale for about 24 hrs, sweeping down out of the mountains. It kept blowing our ship out to the open sea because we were empty (if we had still had the gasoline, I wouldn't be writing this). Both anchors couldn't keep us in the harbor, but we never should have been as far out as we were between Capri & Ischia about 10 or 15 mi from the port. I had had an attack of ptomaine from the nite before and was now getting a cold. I got up to drink a cup of tea for lunch and went back to bed with a chill and feeling very sick. At about 1PM a terrific, and I repeat, terrific explosion of unimaginable violence shook the ship. There was no doubt but that the ship had received a death blow. Bombs! was the first thing I thought of and we were really caught with our pants down (especially me without any) and I expected to hear a plane diving in with another at any instant. I jumped out of bed and ran pantsless and shoeless onto the deck to see if we would stay afloat. There was a slight list already. "Fire in #2" someone shouted. Excitement! Rush! I decided I would have time to put on a pair of pants and shoes and the first thing I grabbed was my blouse and overcoat in which I had my camera, my Beretta automatic and my wallet, all set for just such an occasion. I grabbed the wrong pants or I would have saved my mouthpiece too. All this took about 30 seconds and I was sitting on the bench struggling frantically into my shoes when the 2nd one hit even more violent than the 1st. It tore everything right off the walls, sending a brass lamp flying into my hand which cut it rather badly. I could smell all the broken bottles of medicine, hair tonic, etc. strewn over the floor with me. That second explosion took the little that remained of everyone's calm, for we could hear the roar of steam from the ruptured pipes and were afraid the ship's boilers would blow up and finish us all. There was no panic but we were all damn anxious to get our tails in the lifeboats. The deck was littered with wreckage and a ½-inch of sand from the ballast. The heavy steel cross beams in #4 had been bent like wire and the hatch was half full already. The boats were inboard and secured and it seemed to take forever to launch them. Damn undisciplined merchant marine! A Navy boy and I lowered one end of the boat, as I heroically noted my blood coloring the rope slipping roughly thru my hands. We clambered down the nets and into the boats. Could see a huge rent in the side of #2 hold. Was damn glad I hadn't been in my usual spot on #3 tween deck! [Fig 32]- More merchant marine bungling. It was a heavy sea and they damn near capsized the boat by rowing like a bunch of yokels. Luckily, a Limey sub chaser was nearby and picked us up.

We were very fortunate that no man was killed, and we all got off okay. I led a life of luxury for 2 wks after that at the Port Officers' Hotel in Naples. Nothing to do but wait for transportation. By getting sunk prematurely we missed the show south of Rome [Anzio] which we would have been in, but I don't actually regret that. I really startled myself by getting to ride home by air, because I never thot I'd be allowed to.

CHAPTER X
Around the World

   Synopsis - Upon my return from Italy we had 42 days together in Brooklyn before I left on a voyage that was, ultimately, to result in my circling the globe. At the time there was danger of my being assigned permanently overseas, but I secured a ship that was to take a group of Army meteorologists to Egypt, and a cargo of fighter planes to Karachi, India [Figs 34, 35]. The ship was then assigned to the Pacific Theater and proceeded, alone, across the Indian Ocean, into Antarctic seas south of Australia, and across the Pacific to Los Angeles. There, again, I was confronted with possible assignment to overseas duty in the Pacific Theater but, as noted in the next Chapter, succeeded in "escaping" back to NYPOE. In my absence Elizabeth got a job in Chicago interviewing applicants for jobs in the US Civil Service. It was 6 days/week, with overtime, and was thus quite a demanding endeavor.

Thu 27 Jan 1944- Robert calls again - Called Penn RR & made reservations for 3:30 this aft, Informed Sommers & the three gals that Robert was in. They were very sweet about it & I left at 11 with my check for 3 days work. Picked up reservation at station, home packing my bags. Trying to get a taxi, more trouble.

Fri 28 Jan - En Route - Arrival in NY - To NY about 5:30 PM, 7 hrs late. RWD waiting for me. On the subway in the 5 o'clock rush trying to catch up on events since we parted 4 mos ago. At MacDonald's, taking bath, washing hair. Robert getting groceries for our supper, 2 bottles of wine. I tried out my diaphragm for the 1st time. So much to tell me of happenings, the torpedoing outside of Capri, his airplane trip back home. Seems a bit more mature & sober than before he left.

Sat 29 Jan - Up early, to bank getting money, picking up pics he had of burning of his ship. If Robt goes to England, I'll stay here. He got my bags from station. We had a fine supper & indulged in more wine, talk, love.

Mon 31 Jan - Dinner at Lin Fong's - Ate with him, then he left at 7:45. I went back to bed & slept till noon. RWD came at 4:45 with about 170.00 worth of accrued salary, so I took $50.00 of that. We dressed & went to Lin Fong's for a lobster & egg roll dinner. Walking back window shopping & trying to inveigle RWD to go to movie. But no, so we came home & looked over some of his souvenirs & ate a late snack & took a bath & talked etc till after midnite. He put in a claim for over $300.00 for clothes & equipment lost.

Wed 2 Feb 1944 - "Life with Father" - Disappointing - Maybe it was the wine last nite but we were both "huffy" this morning & RWD told me I was a tyrant about making him eat his food. RWD home at 2:30. He did buy a chess set like the one he lost. We played a game which I resigned. Bot 1.10 tickets for "Life with Father" & filled in the time before 8:40 by walking on Broadway. The play was a definite disappointment & our seats in the 2nd balcony were so uncomfortable it really spoiled our evening. A good rule would be to avoid any & all plays that have been on Bdwy 5 years or longer. This & Tobacco Road have been <u>bad</u>.

Thur 3 Feb - "Life of Verdi"and "Dream of Butterfly" - Robert's 1st day of leave. He had to report in for orders & sign out & did so after breakfast. He came back about 2 PM with photos & ration certificates, 32 points for meat. To the movie, Robert getting in for 28¢, me 72¢, "Life of Verdi", which I saw years ago at the Playhouse, & "Madame Butterfly". Good & it was after 10 when we got out.

Fri 4 Feb - Slept late again; leisurely & hearty breakfast, playing 2 games of chess with my darling. Leaving for the Museum of Modern Art, seeing the last half of "Ten Days that Shook the World", story of overthrow of Kerensky government by the Soviets. Then till 5:30 looking at exhibit of Romantic paintings, seeing the beginning of the movie. Robert reading over the poetry he wrote me over the past 2 yrs. & which I collected into a notebook for him.

Sat 5 Feb - Slight tiff with Robt crossing streets against the traffic. So we came home separately. Robt bot 2 bottles of wine, 2 lbs Barracini candy. We've spent about 60.00 so far. Have 125.00 left. Rather sorrowful at the thought of our impending separation.

Sun 6 Feb - Boris Goudonov - Robert read Pushkin's play before we left for the Brooklyn Academy for the opera.

Mon 7 Feb - Museum of Natural History & the Hayden Planeterium. The former no better than our Field Museum; same for the latter. To bed late, rather tired but my darling so passionate & so happy about his leave.

Tue 8 Feb - Carnegie Hall - Brailowsky - We left for the Museum of Non-Objective Painting about noon. Spent several hours looking at Bauer's & Kandinsky's unearthly paintings. Then walked down 5th Ave, stopped at Saint Patrick's Cathedral. Carnegie Hall recital, very good program, Bach, Beethoven sonata 31, Liszt, Debussy, Ravel, Rachmaninoff, then some Chopin. Many encores. Enjoying it all from our 83¢ 2nd balcony seats. To bed at 1:30 AM, so tired but gloriously happy in our days of sightseeing. A little peeved at RWD for being so free & easy with our money.

Sun 13 Feb - M - Loafed around till time to go to Carnegie Hall to hear Yehudi Menuhin in a fine recital featuring Beethoven's "Kreutzer" sonata.

Mon 14 Feb - M - Felt pretty ill all day, nauseated, headache, nose all stuffed up, threw up & felt miserable. Stayed in bed all day. Robert reported to the Army Base, got his claim papers all okayed & was told he'd instruct "rookies" at Kaven Point for a few days before getting his assignment. So he came home about 2:30, fixed me toast & coffee & took care of me. So we had a late supper (8:30), read Russian (& he is really good at it) & played chess & so whiled away the evening.

Tues 22 Feb - . . . . Then we played 2 chess games, both of which I lost. Afraid I lost my temper after the 2nd one & threw his ole chess set on the floor, scattering the men & startling Robert. So, male-like he had to bellow forth his anger, etc. Well, we made up after some tense moments, and now he says I'm very unsportsmanlike & can't take it. Can't see why I'm not entitled to a few tantrums like Robert indulges in. All in all, 'twas a fine holiday for both of us. Tomorrow he finds out about his assignment.

Wed 23 Feb - We finally get Ration books! - Having rec'd Books 3 & 4 for Robert, I recklessly spent 20 points for 2 lbs of steak for our supper. He got home about 4 PM to tell me he got the special assignment to India as the lesser of 2 evils, viz: permanent assignment overseas. So we ate, my 1st real steak since Robert's induction in the army. Afterwards I coaxed him into going to see "Destination Tokyo" - but the 2nd feature, "Sing a Jingle", didn't suit Mr. Doty & he upped & walked out on me. I stayed to the end & walked home the 8 blocks or so at 11:30. Home to find Robert sprawled in bed sleeping & not feeling well. Temperature normal but his throat bothered him. So to bed although I was really angry at his unchivalrous treatment.

Thu 24 Feb - Awakened at 11:30 AM by phone call from Red Cross nurse at Ft Hamilton that Robert was being held for observation at the hospital & not to worry if he did not come home tonite. Went out to Fort Hamilton to visit Robert. Said he had the cyst removed from his throat & now was anxious to get out.

Fri 25 Feb - He's buying his cornet tomorrow & so I have to withdraw money from the bank. Don't like to do it.

Tue 29 Feb - . . . . to the Guggenheim Museum of Nonobjective Painting. Quiet evening, the Baroness gushed & gestured at us for 1½ hrs on these "wonderful paintings of not what you can see or explain but of what the artist feels in the rhythm of nature" & showed us Bauer's sketches of a woman in the impressionistic, expressionistic, Cubist manner. Also saw 15 or so min of films á la "Fantasia", bright colors set to music. Enjoyed that best of all. Had a serious discussion with Robert about our post war future & what to do when he leaves. He persists in being very nonchalant about it all, why shouldn't I?

Thu 2 Mar - Home after 5 PM to hear Robert playing on his newly acquired trumpet. Nice looking deal; with everything including music, it cost him 43.00.

Fri 3 Mar - Going to bed about midnite. I'm just wondering if I'll be "regular" this month. Due March 6th & I'm keeping my fingers crossed. Robert says whatever happens, we'll be happy.

Wed 8 Mar - M - Orders! - Robert called me at 11 AM to tell me he had gotten his assignment, the Nathan B. Forrest [Fig 34], thot he'd be leaving Friday. So I felt emotionally upset but good & really sulked, I guess. To bed wishing these partings didn't have to come. I'll miss him so.

Thur 9 Mar - M - Troops go aboard in the aft, so it looks like he'll be sailing. I have no reservations yet.

Fri 10 Mar - M - Robert leaves - . . . . waited for Robert to come pick up luggage to take to Penn Sta. He finally came at 2:30, & took my stuff. Came back with the army truck at 3:30 to take his things & to give me 3 campaign ribbons (N.A., European, & a new one - Pacific?) & to leave. Said troops were coming aboard at 4 PM & at midnite they were leaving for Hampton Roads, so it looks like he's leaving for good. I got a reservation for Monday on the Trail Blazer. 9 PM & I am missing Robert but good! Have that heavy feeling in my heart. Hope this will be a good trip for Robert.

Mon 13 Mar - I Leave NY for Chgo - Slept till 11, fixed 4 sandwiches to take on train. . . . at 3:30 left for Penn Station. Had an hour to wait & just sat there disconsolately wondering how I'd spend the intervening months before Robt & I would be together again.

Tue 14 Mar - I arrive in Chicago - Awoke at 8 or so to find it gray, damp, drizzling. Didn't go to diner but finished my sandwich & orange. 'Bout this time an MP (six footer & nice Slavic features & build) sat alongside me & we carried on a conversation into Chgo. Train only 28 min late & Mom was there to meet me, to the apparent embarrassment of my MP friend who had expected to eat lunch with me. Good to be back.

Fri 17 Mar - Max & I went to the Douglas Library & got 2 Russian books: "Advanced Russian Reader" by Patrick; "From 2 Aug 1905" [? in Cyrillic, not clear] by Chukrovsky [Cyrillic]; "Of Time & the River" by Wolfe and Maurice Hindus "To Sing with the Angels". Then I decided to bind all of Robert's letters to me in a folder & it will take more time to do it up right. Would be simpler if I copied all on paper of the same size, but I like to preserve the originals. My darling has been gone a week already. Wonder how far he has gone by now?

374

Sun 19 Mar - Decided to get all my letters collected in chronological order & did so.

*   *   *   *   *

[This letter of 19 March 1944 was received in Karachi on 28 April, and was the only news I had of her until letters of 23 & 30 April turned up (after some search!) in Perth, Australia. Thus, this 19 March letter was all I was to know of her for 2½ months!]

Sunday, March 19, 1944 - 10:30P.M.

My Dearest Darling -

Nine days have passed since we parted in New York, and they have gone by quite swiftly for me so far. Somehow those six weeks together don't quite seem real, it's just a precious interlude that seems to live in my mind only. I don't know just how to explain it, but it all seems so far away now that I am back here with the folks. And it is only when I go to bed and in those half-awake moments do I seem to recapture the ecstatic thrills of our nights at the MacDonald's.

But you'll want to know something of what's been happening to me since you left. I think I was more upset emotionally than ever before.

Oh yes, went to Lawndale Bldg Loan & inquired. They still pay 3% interest & we have $5.00 interest on the grand we deposited Oct 21. So I wrote Bkly Bk to send me 1M [$1,000] which I shall deposit here.

Crazy sort of letter, I know, but I'm trying to give you all the news concisely. I do hope you get this, dearest. I've found 3 more of my letters addressed to APO 782 [Italy] returned. I'll write you a weekly letter for the next two months or so, unless I hear otherwise.

I spent the past two evenings going over our correspondence. Have bound all of your letters into one of my brown fibre board binders & I have all the letters I wrote you chronologically arranged in an envelope. I also went thru all our negatives & will have duplicates made of the pictures I don't have in our album (the ones you lost). Will bring the album with me next reunion.

11 o'clock, my precious, and I am the only one awake. The house is still, the fire is dying down & a chill is settling over the

place. It is at times like this that I feel like breaking down & having a good cry. The poignancy of my grief becomes so acute. I know you miss me, darling, and that helps me to bear it more cheerfully than I would otherwise. I know you want me to carry on stoically and I'll try, but as I have written you before, without you I don't seem to have the will to resist the apathetic lethargy that missing you seems to put me into. There just doesn't seem to be any point to anything without you. But I'll try to keep up with my Russian, and I'm getting some books on chess so I can play the game by myself.

Now, my dearest, I must close & hie me off to bed. Do hope I don't toss restlessly for hours as I am apt to do, recalling happier moments & at the same time conjuring up visions of dangers that may beset you. Silly of me, I know, but I can't seem to help it.

Oh, my beloved, I do so await our reunion & eagerly anticipate those loving embraces from your firm strong body. Robert, I do so love you! And there's such a fierce longing for you. How will I bear it when I miss you so already! Dearest, I mail this letter with a kiss & the fervent prayer that you'll be safe & that our reunion may be sooner than we anticipated.

Love always

Elizabeth

*   *   *   *   *

Tues 21 Mar - I go Job Hunting - Went to Civil Serv Com & stayed there till almost 5 PM. Got talked into considering a job as Rating Examiner-Trainee @ 1800 or 2000 pr.a.

Wed 22 Mar - Deposited my $1000 check in the Lawndale Savings Assn. Called Mrs. Crooks again & she had no news. Rather disgusted with the whole thing & the salary is only $1800.00! Course if I don't work, I make no money & even $1800 ($2176 with overtime) is better than that.

Thu 23 Mar - I take the Job - This will at least take me out of the stenographer classification. So I had a physical exam there, blood pressure 130/74, weight 136, eyes 20/30 vision with glasses.

Mon 27 Mar - My First Day - Spent 2 hours filling out forms & getting fingerprinted. Got stacks of stuff to read, then sat by Miss

376

O'Connors desk & listened to her interview various applicants. Miss O'C is the gal who interested me in my present job.

Tue 28 Mar - My 2nd Day - . . . . and I've got laryngitis! Could hardly speak this morning, so I saw Dr. Klein & he sprayed my throat. Saw him twice more during the day & got 2 tablets of something to take this evening. Due to my lack of voice I just sat by Mrs Cordsunian & watched her dispose of 15 or so applicants today. Ate lunch with her & got a few inside tips on the work here, seems the last gal that worked as a recruiter left after 10 days??

Thu 30 Mar - Day #4 - They keep asking if I think I'll like the job, and I tried to avoid committing myself.

Fri 31 Mar - Day #5 - Started out with Miss Eaton explaining different reports. Then we went into applicants supply files section to "learn" how to review application & there we stayed the entire day. Came home to find check from U.S. Finance Officer for $328.40 representing payment for Robert's clothing lost on the Rosecrans. That certainly was quick reimbursement! Wonder where RWD is now?

Thu 13 Apr - I was pretty busy but somehow took it in my stride & didn't mind it. Miss O'Connor, however, really blew up this morning & was red-eyed all day. Guess the pace gets you down after a while. Miss Maier was most solicitous about our lunch periods, etc, guess she's afraid we'll throw up the sponge too. So I stayed my 2 extra hours, eating a sandwich & a candy bar while I worked.

Sat 15 Apr - Came home after a weary day at the office to find a wire undated & with no clue as to its origin, my 1st word from Robert "All my love. All well and safe." Now I wonder if he is in Egypt already?

Mon 17 Apr - Had a pretty busy day, and heard with pleasure that I made several appointments. Getting all het up about not being able to place several Japanese gals at the Social Security Board - oh, well!

* * * * *

[These letters, 23 Apr and 30 Apr 44, #s 6 & 7 in the series she was writing me, I received on 24 May in Perth, Australia. All of her other letters were eventually returned.]

Letter #6

My Precious Darling -

A week ago Saturday I received your cablegram telling me you were well and safe.

Last Friday I came home to find Mom really excited. There was a V-mail from you dated April 8th, your first "safe arrival" letter; and I almost cried as I read it & noted your concern for me, about my job, my getting out to the forest preserves or sand dunes. Darling, don't you spend any time worrying about my welfare. I'll get by. Just take good care of yourself.

Darling, so little happens to me that is exciting. My work has its interesting spots, but it does get irksome, especially being cooped up from 8:30 to 5 (or till 7 when we work overtime) and it's the hours more than anything else that I dislike. But most jobs are on a 48-hour week basis, and working does help to keep me mentally occupied. I find I sleep much better now that I am working.

I've been having some pretty hectic sessions with the dentist. Last Tuesday he opened up an upper molar that was a honey. It hurt from the moment he started drilling & I squirmed & moaned all the while. But he's filled that up & next Tuesday I go for my final visit, unless he discovers new cavities.

I miss you, my precious, so much and I was so relieved and so happy to get that cablegram & your V-mail letter. Keep them coming, my dearest, for they leave me so happy & appeased for the moment. I realize that you may not have the chance to write me with much regularity, but I know you will drop me a note whenever possible. Beloved, I do so hope at least some of my letters do reach you, for I know how you must be wondering about me and what I am doing.

Darling, my heart is so filled with love and joy as I write to you, and I am so grateful to Fate for the happy moments we have spent together thus far, and the happy days that assuredly await us in the future.

Elizabeth

*   *   *   *   *

Letter #7

My Dearly Beloved -

. . . to find a bulky Special Delivery letter from you! Dearest, I have read and reread that letter so many times. So grateful for its message of love and so thankful that you got to Egypt unharmed. I still get a sinking feeling when I think of that attack. Oh, that I could be assured daily that you are well and out of danger! My only consolation is that perhaps our love, our need for one another, will act as a charm to keep us both safe & well till this holocaust ends and we can resume our happy togetherness again! I'm so glad to hear that you've been studying your languages, your music, your chess games; it does help to while away those weary hours, dearest.

Mom had the front apartment vacant for about 2 hours, I guess, when the Bauxes moved out after 10½ yrs residence. The rent is frozen at 20.00 per mo & the OPA won't let Mom raise it. So Mom rented it, but they will do all their own cleaning & redecorating. If there had been hot water heat in the apt, I think I would have liked to rent it myself & put our furniture there instead of paying storage. But just daydreams, I guess, for I don't know what we will want to do after you get out of the Army.

Yesterday, we had quite a flurry of excitement in the office. Miss Rodriguez (I wrote you about her) came around to say goodbye to everyone, as she was leaving, effective May 1st. She claims she had been "grilled" by our Investigations Dept re her 7½ yrs residence in Russia & her outspoken criticism of our office, etc. She claims the Commission is lousy with "fascists" & I wouldn't be surprised, considering the remarks I've heard re the Government's seizure of the Montgomery Ward properties in Chicago. Perhaps you read how the Army had to forcibly evict Sewell Avery from his office? Anyway, that's that.

[In Cyrillic] Do svedaniye (au revoir) tepyer, moi dorogoi muzh. Ya tebya tak lyoublyou. ["So long for now my beloved husband. I love you so".]

Lovingly,
Elizabeth

379

9:30PM Saturday March 11, 1944

To my sweet lonely one -

I'm lying here on the bunk dreaming of you and the past weeks of happiness. How absolutely perfect those days were, and almost 6 weeks together. We were very fortunate, dearest.

Everything so far has gone very well, we are completely & comfortably organized and it hasn't been anywhere near the headache I had anticipated. The officer in charge of the men is from Chicago [Lt Irving Ordower] & he has cooperated fully with me. The mates are fine chaps & the Captain is young & cheerful for a change. Everything indicates a swell voyage. Haven't even rationed water.

I feel like a veteran this time and it makes everything so much easier. I know all the sea terms, I can look at cargo stowage with a practiced eye, I have been sunk & bombed, I have carried troops & PW's; all that experience bears weight and makes my position so much more tenable.

I won't get a chance to write Bill or Luigi, so would you write them a note & tell them, etc. Just write Luigi that you are Mrs. Doty etc. & that your husband was called out in a hurry, that you'd heard about him, etc. His address is Luigi Maione, Via Carlo de Cesare 38, Naples, Italy.

Must get things set for a fire & boat drill now, so I'll be back later, my darling.

9PM Sun

Hastily now, my sweet one, for I do want to get this mailed to let you know that everything is working out okay after the terrible rush in which I left you Friday. I actually felt numb with the sadness of leaving you, but I was soon plunged in work and now it feels like I have been gone for ages, still out on my last trip, and wishing I were coming home.

Oh, how I love you, my precious darling, but I am as used to being separated from you as I ever will be and I have learned a little bit how to "take it" in that respect. The war can't last forever tho, beloved, and we have been far more fortunate than many.

So vividly I kiss you in remembrance of most recent happiness, my lovely wife,

Your husband,
Robert

*　　*　　*　　*　　*

Mid-Atlantic

3PM Thursday, March 16, 1944

My lovable darling -

Have been very faithful in doing my Russian and have written out lessons I & II in Semenoff's already. My writing is coming much easier. There is a Ukrainian on here & I'm going to get some help from him. He has already supplied one word for my Russozisch Wörterverzeichnis "matros" [= sailor, written in Cyrillic] which is another word identical with the German like "kartofel" & "butterbrot".

Wish you would find out how long the process of copyrighting takes. Thinking seriously of copyrighting "Sibelius #1 in E Minor" & "Bomber's Moon". I should try to write some more like that, but when I read the powerful, perfect lines of Wilfred Owen, which combine the steely forcefulness of compact description with the clarity of moral purpose, I realize that my attempts at poetry are hopelessly amateurish.

But all I want from life is your dear love & the presence of your gentle beauty, the soothing ecstasy of your caring hand, the serenity & perfect joy of your kiss, in leisure, thotful & certain, so sure of love & eternal response. I love you beyond the expression of my soul for all my life, my sweet beloved and radiant wife,

Robert

*　　*　　*　　*　　*

10:30PM Monday March 20, 1944

My sweet beautiful darling -

The steward's dept trouble keeps popping up all the time, nastily marring an otherwise smooth trip. If the energy I've spent fighting merchant marine cooks could only have been directed at the enemy!

My Russian is coming fine. I have written 5½ solid notebook pages of Russian & can now write "Ya yeshcyah ne pisal bratu" [In Cyrillic, "I have not yet written my brother"] with comparative ease & clarity. Have been pecking away at poetry with a few decent lines resulting, but no poem.

Slithering, like dry lightning, the rattler glides
Cool bellied over slippery grass and hides
Disguised, a bit of dangerous wood
With glittering, beady eyes.
Written after discussion of snakes with the 3rd Mate, who used to run a side show with them.

But all that is only playing around, I can't seem to make the concentrated effort to make a poem instead of just lines. The furthest I got was with a horror poem about a female ghoul I invented,
"Shahartinya, ghoul of liquid graves
Who roams the world beneath the waves
To rob the silent, watered dead"
It would be as nightmarish as E A Poe, but I change metre every couplet:
Into the dim, dark room she slips
Like quiet murder down a poisoned throat
And the nites at sea when the wind goes mad
And the stars are drowned and the leaks are bad
When hard steel staggers and waves are master
Then to the groan that marks disaster
There comes, unseen, Shahartinya
I should give rhyme & metre up as a bad job for me, because they always peter out. (Wonder where that expression originated ? Alchemy salt petre? Russian peet? [Cyrillic, to drink]. St Peter? sexual, his peter is petered out? A small boy, Peter who couldn't keep up his end of the work? Look it up, dearest, just for fun.) [OED says ca 1850 American mining slang - I wonder if perhaps ultimately related to saltpetre, major ingredient of the explosive used in mining?]

It sounds like I have done a great deal, but really, dearest, I have been goading myself continually for my laziness & lack of initiative. Have read 100 of Shakespeare's sonnets, too, and almost every one of them is a marvel. I particularly like #2 for the manner in which it applies to us. I feel so strongly the truth that the immortality of ourselves finds its expression in our children.

[Sonnet II - Not in the original letter:
 When forty winters shall besiege thy brow,
 And dig deep trenches in thy beauty's field,
 Thy youth's proud livery, so gazed on now,
 Will be a tatter'd weed, of small worth held:
 Then being ask'd where all thy beauty lies,
 Where all the treasure of thy lusty days,
 To say, within thy own deep-sunken eyes,
 Were an all-eating shame and thriftless praise.
 How much more praise deserved thy beauty's use,
 If thou couldst answer 'This fair child of mine
 Shall sum my count and make my old excuse,'
 Proving his beauty by succession thine!

This were to be new made when thou art old,
And see thy blood warm when thou feel'st it cold.]

I have rambled on quite a bit, beloved, but am getting sleepy now, so I kiss you a most tender & wishful good nite and with such fervor that my kisses to you may soon bear permanency and peace, my sweet loving wife. How happy & proud am I to be your husband, forever adoring you as I have learned to in the beautiful years of our love, so deep has become the necessity for you within me, so complete our love.

Robert

[This continues, without pause or space, on the same sheet thruout this series]

I'm so lonely for my darling bed partner, even with her smelly Vicks, window phobia & all. Just as I love you in every conceivable way & for every bit of your character, your mind, your body, so too do I miss you in each of these innumerable fashions, from the explosive ecstasy of your caresses, to the irritating hesitancy of your street crossings. I love you & long for you and everything that is you. And as I say good nite now I remember quite clearly, & long for, the beautiful contentment, satisfaction & happiness that floods thru me as I curl sleepily against your good warm body, my hand certain of the joy of your breasts in the darkness. I know we sleep with a smile and a deep sense of love.

Forever,
Robert

1AM Monday, March 27, 1944

Beloved -

It looks like I am getting back into my old habit of working all nite & sleeping all morning. Finding out why, too, for tho it is easy to set the clock ahead 3 hours, my body still keeps the old time, and this is 10 PM NY time. We changed an hour last nite & I had been getting up at 7:30 each morn, but this morn when I woke up at 7:30 it was 8:30 instead; so I had missed breakfast & stayed in bed till 11 AM for a good Sunday morning's snooze.

0005 AM Saturday April 1, 1944

My lovely sweetheart -

. . . But in gentler thots I recall that ecstasy of so many moments that we have enjoyed, and I become vibrant with desire, and linger long over the delicious memories of our joint & mutual life, so complete with love. I can spend hours on each little incident summoning up the recollection of the subtle movement, of each expressive caress. I remember the hot, sticky nights of Newport News, our damp nakedness delighted by the breeze from a summer shower, listless, in love, wishful for the peace of the future. I can still feel the way you melted into my body with such an aching thankfulness on our reunion in Cleveland; oh, how I knew you loved me, how exuberant I was to be so strongly & firmly your husband. Our marriage was just beginning to be realized in its full depth of meaning & feeling at that time. We were beginning to experience that glorious intangible joy of knowing we were united & eternal, that we were becoming something other than ourselves thru the great power of our mated love. How starved I was for you then, even as I am now.

And this past beautiful month together, beloved, was so full, so crowded with happiness that we surely must have made up for some of those long dreary days of yearning. Yet never once was I surfeited of you or dissatisfied with the continuous ecstasy of having you as my wife, to cook & scold, to pester & to kiss, to drink with, sleep with, every moment together & every moment a paradise. How I smile now when I remember our typical spats, too, with our respective type of temperament, bubbling over with the energy of our love-inflamed minds. Dearest, I know that after this is over we will live year after year in that same type of bliss, and it is that certainty of future happiness that makes this impatient present so irksome, so empty.

I love you, my mate, with all the life, the fire, the senses, the instincts, the intelligence that one million generations of lives have stored within me, and it is all intent upon you, throbbing, living for you alone & for the fascinating years to come when our fires will intertwine like gentle liquid lightning, surging yet soft, hot and powerful, yet soothing & content, so brilliant yet so stable; and forever a swift, inexplicable joy of contact & union, dividing ever into greater joy & more subtle contentment.

I love you so, my wife

Robert

11:30PM Saturday April 1, 1944

My sweet wife -

I guess I feel so dopey because of lack of sleep. I finished writing you early this morning and then went to bed and read for a while. At 3:45 AM I looked at my watch & decided to go to sleep. Felt so good stretching out naked into the clean sheets with a nice cool breeze coming gently thru the port. I had no sooner gotten sound asleep when, at about 4:10 AM, the general alarm takes off with its raucous, frightening ringing. My "expectancies" of the nite before had come to pass. Since I had had the experience when I got sunk of being unable to get my shoes on in a hurry, I had prepared them every nite by unlacing them quite a way down. Didn't bother with underwear, but stuck the blackout deal in the port & got into my glasses, shoes, pants, field jacket & shirt in nothing flat & with my helmet & musette bag made for the bridge. I was more scared this time than before because I knew what could happen, and that getting up in the middle of the nite is no joke. Well, if I was scared before I went out, I sure turned to jelly when I hit the deck. Our section of the convoy was lit up like daylight by a whole string of parachute flares slowly drifting down. Then another stick of five or six, burst into light on our starboard. That's a hell of a feeling to be sitting like a nice big spotlighted barn on the water & not know just what the score is up overhead. It sure felt nice to see big stuff blossoming out up there & it must have been pretty hot for Jerry, too.

It was the usual deal, about like the other one I wrote you about, gunfire, tracers, scanning the sky anxiously, looking for planes. Feel a little better about this one, tho, for I actually saw & identified one of the planes as it flew not more than 100 yards off, directly across our bow. The pilot must have been blinded by his own flares & the gunfire, for he apparently didn't even see us (the flares had just gone out) and he almost ran into us. Well, after the shooting stopped & we had chased them off, we all stayed up till dawn to see if there would be any more excitement. I ate breakfast & went to bed & slept an hour before the alarm rang again and with a lot of depth charges going off. Nothing came of it, tho, but sleep began to look pretty hopeless. When I finally did get to bed this afternoon, I slept right thru chow till 7 PM. Still feel sleepy tho, so I'm going to turn in. It's another clear nite & so perhaps will get it again, so I'm going to be dressed for it.

I love you so my precious one,
Robert

* * * * *

Tue 25 Apr - Woke up reluctantly from my cozy bed & left for work, taking along Robert's letter to read over & over again during my free moments. He does write so beautifully & I refuse to believe that we won't be happy together in the future to come.

385

Had a very busy day interviewing people. Understand I've made 16 appointments so far. Is that good?

Wed 26 Apr - Boy, what a day! Everything seemed to go wrong. I felt like a grievance committee of one as I listened to one complaint after another.

Tue 2 May 1944 - Felt very happy with the afterglow of my darling's letter. Oh, how I wish we were together, everything would be so different. Don't mind working hard if I can look forward to meeting my darling at the end of the day. So I typed this evening, found my work record increases daily. Did 64 1840s tonite. Helps pass away the time & I really don't mind the work.

Wed 3 May - Found another $200 credit to our account in Brooklyn. My total cash assets now $4200, which is pretty good considering we didn't start saving till the middle of 1942. Will make a nice base for our postwar planning.

Mon 8 May - About 9:30 a special delivery letter arrived from Robert dated 4/28 from India giving me a brief but colorful description of his 1st day in Karachi. Says he got my 1st letter on Mar 19th & is happy to know I am comfortably settled at home.

Wed 10 May - So I came home to find a lovely surprise from Robert, to wit: ivory bracelet (elephant design), ivory necklace (same), 3 sandalwood figurines, carved spoon, yellow silk head scarf, dagger in red leather sheath, toothpick. This pkge was mailed May 1st. So happy to receive the souvenirs from my precious one. Oh, I do so love him & how I miss him!

Thu 11 May - Letter re Red Sea-India Voyage - I wore my "good" black dress and my elephant necklace & bracelet. Everyone admired it to my satisfaction. I was quite busy during the day, so many people in today. A 16 page letter from my darling describing his trip through the Red Sea, a real cut up job by the Naval Censor. Wondering what the near future will bring for me & Robert; maybe my elephant necklace & bracelet will be good luck charms for us both.

*　　*　　*　　*　　*

[There now follows a ridiculously mutilated letter, chopped up by an over-eager censor]

In pencil at the top: "Beloved- Got your Mar 19 letter. Please keep writing. Love, R.

My sweet beautiful wife

. . . . Had such a vivid and in a way satisfying dream of you last night. It was strange too in the way it revealed to me the multiplicity of impressions my mind holds of you, each separate & each beloved. Perhaps it is this divisibility of your personality by my mind which enables it to love you so fully. I dreamed of seducing you quite completely in an ecstasy of love, only it wasn't you as my wife, because I was so happy to be in love with both my wife & you. Now, as I think of it, I find that somehow my mind does conceive of you as a number of different people & loves you with equal fervor as each one. I imagine some of my letters must convey that same idea, but I never realized it as being part of my actual mental function to be like that. You see, in my mind, I actually do cherish & remember you as a different person, before we were married, then as another person as a sweet young bride, then my wife in so many different roles & times & places. The memory of you with me in NY is somehow a slightly different person than the memory of you in our home in Chi, etc. Of course, there is no definite distinction, yet this half-fantasy does exist in my mind, so that you are lovingly interwoven into myriad forms & memories & dreams.

The trip is now becoming interesting, darling. Up until a few days ago I was in the old familiar waters of the *Mediterranean* [I will italicize those words that END surmised, and wrote in with red pencil!], but we have now passed through the 94 miles of *Suez Canal* & into the *Red Sea*. To me it will be a memorable experience, this first passage on water thru a desert, but I am very disappointed that I won't get to see *Egypt*———-came straight for *Alexandria* & went right on. . . . *Suez Canal* there are no *locks*, just a straight lane of water about 100 yards wide in most places. At the start we seemed to be surrounded on all sides by lakes, puddles, ponds, etc. in a large uninhabited area. This I guess was part of the————-. Gradually this changed until on the———- side there was only a vast expanse of undulating sand, stretching off into some large & distant mountains of sand & rock. Some very beautiful pastel colorings & shadings, tho, in this dry & sterile expanse ———- side was a bit more interesting and tho almost as sandy was still cultivated in some areas, and along most of the road which accompanied the canal was a line of eucalyptus trees. There were stations & ferry crossings every 10 miles or so, each with its little village, Arabs, camels, gardens, palms, burros, kids, etc. There were tents at various intervals, too, of the *British* troops who guard & service the canal. The canal itself is just an amazingly straight road of water dividing the huge waste-land of sand. . . . There is a large lake about halfway thru, too, which I never knew before.

Lt Ordower got off yesterday & since I had to stay aboard to look after things, I was unable to set foot on *Egypt*.

10:30PM Friday, April 14, 1944

My sweet darling -

This *Red Sea* is certainly a vast place in reality. So startling to find it immense after being used to considering it quite insignifi-cant by its area on a map. Haven't seen land since we left————-. The water is just as blue & monotonous as the At-lantic or Medit. except there is a little more phosphorescence at nite which seems to increase as we continue southward. 1600 miles almost due south, that's a long way.

9:15PM Sunday————————-

My Sweetheart -

Went up on deck & started taking in the sights of————-[Aden]. To the West there was a mass of needle like crags, barren, jutting weirdly from an emerald sea. Looked, I guess, something like the land of Oz; at least it was unearthly. Patches of light sand climbing————- strange sharp fingers of rock added to their—— sterility and made the whole scene glitter its hostility to any form of life. Directly across the bay to the east rose a tremendous moun-tain, far larger than Gibraltar & far more striking in its singularity. To the North was only the flat, glaring vastness of the desert, & to the South the Indian ocean, so that this huge mass of rock, curled up out of the sea & the desert, ruled the entire panorama with its tow-ering solidity of stone.

It didn't take long for the bum boats to get around to us. Don't know as I have ever written you about the bum boats before. They must be in every harbor over here. I know they are at Gibraltar, at Naples & at Suez & they are all alike. Miserable dirty natives in tiny leaky boats who come out to all the ships to trade & sell their wears. Most————- trading is done with cigarettes. In Spain 6 cartons of ciga-rettes gets a beautiful tablecloth, in Naples a few cigarettes will buy an octopus, in Egypt 2 cartons for a Fez and here in———— these natives have cheap knives, woven baskets, wooden spoons, slip-pers, and one lad even got a pair of shorts (made in China) for 4 packages. I borrowed a pack & got a little carved wooden spoon, but most of the other stuff I'll be able to get where we are going for even less than it is here. These natives seem to be sort of a mixture of negro & Arab. They are very dark & have black kinky hair, yet their features are not negroid. They smile continually, showing beautiful white teeth. They are quite thin, yet strong & wiry. I took a couple pictures of them in their boats, so you'll get a better idea from that.

I took the glass & scanned this apparently barren desert where these people live, and discovered it to be quite copiously fringed with palms along the shore. We were so far away it looked like all sand, yet was so flat we couldn't realize how far off it was. With the glass I could just barely make out a walled city out in the desert, which greatly intrigues me, but I'm sure I won't get ashore here to explore it. All I'll need tho is a turban of some sort, for with my tan, beard, shorts & clogs I could pass for a native any day.

Indian Ocean

9:30PM Thurs. April 20, 1944

My sweet darling -

Wish so that you could have been with me this evening to see the remarkable sunset. It looked just like the picture of the Japanese rising sun, with the light & dark bands stretching across the heavens, or like the noonday sun "drawing water". The phenomena [sic] was undoubtedly caused by the reflection of the sun from the Arabian desert, and the sky was streaked with the very distinct bands of lite with a beautiful ruddy glow merging delicately into soft blue & continuing to shade off on up overhead into the metallic darkness of the eastern sky. It was a symphony of pastel shadings & symmetric design.

It was also the sunset of a fairly good day. Worked hard on my Russian all morning, composing this letter [In Russian] to you, which I hope you'll be able to read. My vocabulary is as limited as technique in its proper idiomatic construction, but it should make sense. Spent the afternoon reading Osa Johnson's "I Married Adventure" and acquiring a suntan simultaneously. I like the book & especially get a keen sense of enjoyment somehow in observing how the romance & love of our lives is so closely duplicated in others. All the little male-female relationships, of temperament, character, ambitions, ideals, all are so universal in their fundamentals. Strange that I, so individualistic & anti-social, should take delight in seeing how closely my experiences with love & marriage have followed those of other persons. Perhaps it is that anything reminding me even remotely of you, is sure to fascinate me. I am so in love with you.

While I think of it, darling, would you please look up the saline composition of the plasma of human embryo, chicken embryo, chickens, rabbits, turtles, fresh & saltwater fish, seagulls, lizards & of seawater. I have in mind the possibility of the indication of the period of pre-species emergence from the liquid environment, being found in the saline composition of their blood. The Crerar Library should have some info on that or at least on that theory, because I'm sure I'm not original.

I love you so much, my precious little lookerupper, my sweet wife.

Love
Robert

4PM Wed. April 26, 1944

My beloved

Just as I started to write this the ship began shaking & quivering & I thot Joe was really opening up the engine to bring us in. We're still waiting, tho, but I was rewarded for my trip on deck by seeing a very odd & beautiful sight. The whole sea seemed filled with fishing boats, their clean white sails billowing in the fresh wind as they sailed en masse from the harbor. I counted over 100 of the trim little craft.

Saw some trim craft of a far different sort today too, barracudas! 5 of them, about 3 or 4 ft long swim leisurely just beneath the water, the waves casting rippling shadows over them, so that they looked like grim lances of fluid death. I ran for my .45, took hasty aim & let go. Must have hit or "near missed" one of them, for it jumped a foot out of the water with wicked lashing of its long body. Got in another shot before they completely disappeared, but they didn't come back.

Have just met my first Indian. Some sort of a port official with a whole face full of beard & turban. To say the least, he was quaint, not in appearance, but actions. Admired my fountain pen & wondered if I had another. Asked what we drank in America & if I had an empty bottle. Saw my German & Italian & Russian etc. & said those books weren't allowed in India. Then he picked up Everybody's Trumpet Solos & thumbed thru the music quite puzzled. "This isn't English?" he queried. Guess he had never seen music before.

I, like a Joe Jerk, sat aboard waiting for the Army to come to me as they do in all other ports; but only Indians came, so to hell with the Army here. I'm disgusted, but the boys that did go ashore aren't coming back very enthusiastic about the place. I'm going off bright & early tomorrow and get this in an APO.

390

I love you so, my sweet one, and could cuddle you now in such a delicious, lingering goodnite;

your husband,
Robert.

*   *   *   *   *

Friday, April 28, 1944

My beloved darling -

Yesterday was so full of exciting and interesting events, one of the fullest of my life, yet there is still another ahead of me today, so I will be a little rushed with this. As usual, chronologically.

Started out with my papers & camera with the intention of finding the U. S. Army Port HQ. Well, the Army doesn't run things here, since we are just intruders on neutral soil, so that they raised a hell of a stink about my camera, & do what I could, there was nothing but take it back. Fortunately I did, for on my 2nd trip out, I found the HQ to be only a few hundred yards from our berth, instead of uptown. The Major in charge here is one of the most friendly, efficient & competent men I have seen, so I still have my beard, as well as the freedom of India.

I was in ecstasies yesterday to get a letter from you, my first in all these months overseas. I have read & reread it with the same insatiable thrill with which I am able to kiss you for days on end. It is your Mar 19 letter and I am so happy to know that you are settled comfortably at home. I, too, know that unquenchable loneliness you feel, and the dreamlike character of the beautiful past, the vague, yet certain joy of the future.

Of course you picked up a handsome MP on the train, my darling; you are irresistible and it makes me happy to know that your charm & beauty makes men your servants with such ease.

The grand in the bank sounds good, but here we are getting for 2M what we should be getting for one. Phooey, but it's the best we can do.

Yesterday aft I got a staff car and Lt Greengarten & I took a business & pleasure tour of the town. Got my EM some pay & summer clothes; stopped at the Post Office, & then went out to the QM depot where I bot two pair of limey shorts & a GI cap for $2.00. Had braid sewn on my cap for 1 rupee (about 33 cents). I stopped at the Red Cross & tho they have no conducted tours, the girl told me much of interest. She told me the location of the bathing ghats & the burning ghats, and also told me of the strange religion of the

391

Parsees, who are followers of Zoroaster & worship fire. They leave their dead to be eaten by the buzzards in their Temples of Silence. No white man has ever been known to get into one of these temples, which intrigues me. She says the air corps boys fly over them & scare up the buzzards occasionally.

There are many strange sights, & tho a bit reminiscent of No Africa, it is far more oriental. The signs are written in English, Arabic & Hindustani. The sacred cows are everywhere, cluttering up the streets with indiscriminate apathy. The fakirs are peculiar monstrosities. The 1st one I saw was ambling apelike across the street on all fours. There was another who slid himself along on his hands & buttocks & whose legs had atrophied to skin covered bones from disuse. There is also a naked filthy old bugger living in a hut of sticks and on the sidewalk on one of the main streets.

The people seem to be all a rather homogenous type, with brown skin & eyes, stringy, oily black hair, but Caucasian features. Their clothing, however, defies description in its variety, sort of a sartorial Babel.

In the evening Lt Miller (Navy) & I had a cab which we used from 6 PM to 1 AM for about 13 rupees. Got a much better view of things in our slow-moving buggy, & we also had as a guide a kid who we called "Charlie" who spoke a bit in English. He was a bright kid, the old Muslim driver's assistant, & he kept up a continual chatter. He shined my belt buckle, told us fair prices, etc. We went out to a hotel run by the Army where we could get a fair rate on souvenirs. I bot 3 little sandalwood idols, a carved ivory elephant bracelet & necklace to match, a woven basket & plate, & a pretty yellow silk scarf, all of which cost 21 rupees or about $8.00.

Finally persuaded our cab driver to take us into the "off-limits" native quarters & we ducked our caps in our baskets & sat back & watched the ageless hordes of India as they lived their lives before us. First, we drove thru a rather well to do Hindu section where the people live quite comfortably in 3 story apt bldgs, modern looking & with cool balconies. The cows wandered & the people came & went on bicycles, in carriages & walking, the men dressed in white or gray modifications of European dress, tho some were garbed with gay shirts of green or red polkadotted cloth. The women wore their shawls, their long black hair parted evenly over their caste-marked foreheads, sandals, horn rimmed glasses, etc.

As we got into the poor sections, the homeless people, who are everywhere sleeping on the cold cement sidewalks, increased till the walks were thick with them. Some families just stretched out on the spot with the dogs, others lay down in a thin "bed roll" of linens. Many of the men sat under the street lights playing cards or reading. These people have no homes, no belongings & work for about 1½ rupees a day. They are the myriad, timeless people of the orient, no individuals, only the great patient animal pain of the masses.

We stopped to water the horses & got out to watch a baker at a Hindu hotel. He sat cross legged & erect, his body shiny with sweat, his black eyes glittering & his long stringy hair tied in a quew (?) so that he looked somewhat like a fierce Hindu god. He would take the dough, slap & knead it, dexterously & rapidly, into a pancake shape & then place it in the clay oven which opened directly in front of him. 5 or 6 pieces in, he waited till they cooked a few minutes, then speared them out with a long wire.

We also got some betel nut here & tho we didn't chew it, it smelled quite spicy. It is a concoction of several things, smeared on a green leaf with a red sauce over it. We then proceeded into the native section & down the main market street lit with dirty & barren saloons, and up above, the brothels. We went to a place with a picture of a girl's head advertised outside. Up a worn stairway under Charlie's guidance. We paid 10 rupees for the 4 of us & after looking at the "Delacroix" type pictures from around the walls, we sat down on the red rugged floor & leaned against the cushions. The room was small & over near the balcony crouched the 3 piece orchestra, a lute played with a bow, two hand-beaten drums & an accordion-like affair. A slim woman of about 30 crouched with them, making up betel nut, & one of the musicians kept taking puffs on his hookah for inspiration. The girl was a dark-eyed, olive-skinned beauty with a jewel in the side of her nose. She was about your build only small breasted & dressed in white harem pajamas of silk & a red silk blouse. She was barefooted with painted toenails & had bells around her ankles concealed by the pajamas. We were each given a necklace of the most beautifully redolent flowers I have ever smelled & then were given another which we placed about the girl's neck & got charged for. Then we were given toothpicks with scented puffs of cotton on them to sniff during the performance. The music began & she started to sing & dance a few whirls around the room. Soon we were joined by a company of white suited Hindu boys (looking like interns) out on a spree. They spent their money wildly & got quite a kick out of some of the songs the gal was singing. She kept dancing & they kept giving her money until finally one of them paid enough to win her pleasures & the dance stopped. All in all it was far above the crudity of the American brothel, & her dance was even less suggestive than that of most nightclub entertainers. The strange music, her bells & dancing, the smells of flowers & perfume, certainly give a real impression of the exotic orient which I shall never forget. We went outside & watched a wedding procession led by a brass band, brushed off innumerable filthy little beggars & drove back under the clear stars just as the thin crescent of the moon was sinking into the sandy hills. I will never forget my 1st day here. How I wish it could have been shared with you.

Love,
R.

*　　*　　*　　*　　*

1AM Sunday April 30, 1944

My darling wife -

The main interest of this letter will be the 15 pictures I am sending [e.g., Fig 35], which we took Friday. Haven't even had time to write you of what we did, & this will most likely be the last letter I have a chance to write for several weeks.

The two main events on Friday's program were a mongoose-cobra fight & a Hindu jam session. The pics give a good idea of the "fight". The cobra had been fanged & was a bit sick, the mongoose was well fed & none too ferocious; but it was very interesting anyhow.

The jam session was the deal tho, especially since it was so natural. We were driving home in our gherry when we saw a group of about 100 men in front of a small Hindu temple. They had an old lantern lighting the scene & several of them were chanting a rather melodious tune, while the others would break in with occasional take offs. We sat & listened for several minutes & were invited over to join them. We accepted, & tho a couple old deacons resented our intrusion, most of them gathered around & said "I love you" "You like?" "Good?" etc, & seemed very well pleased that we were interested. They dragged out the orchestra, which consisted of a goat's skin bagpipe, two tom toms, two flutes (which were played like a clarinet & sounded like a high trumpet), and an old gent squatting on the ground beating a large clay vase. This latter gentlemen was the most dexterous & rapid drummer I have ever seen, his hands moving like lightning as he beat out dazzling rhythms. The tom-toms set the tempo and they really had some fine, knocked out conga, bolero & boogie woogie type rhythms. The two trum-

394

pets played high, melodious counterpoint & then one would take a hot lick on a solo, which stood up to Ziggy Elman or James any day. It was all weird, strange, yet so like the natural rhythmic music of a jam session & had the same "physical" appeal. I'd sure like to bring that outfit back to the States, for they'd make a good show.

10 PM Sunday

I'm getting very disgusted with other people's company and think that hereafter I'm going to lone wolf it thru any future vacation spots. I'm going to leave here with a sense of incompleteness, with the feeling that I didn't get right down into the heart of the country & see it & understand. These fools that can think of wasting several hours drinking lousy liquor in a country where there is so much to be seen, disgusts me. It would have been cheaper I think in the long run to have rented my own gherry & gone where I pleased.

It is so lonely everywhere without you, my sweet darling, and I am so weary of this separation, yet it seems useless to hope of our being together for years. I am sad, beloved, and need your sweet loving arms so much. I love you my wife, forever

Robert

*　　*　　*　　*　　*

11:45PM Sunday April 30

It was riding back under the stars & crescent moon that I thot of you with particular vividness & recalled the beauty of our reunion in San Fran, each one of those 70 days a taunting joy. [She immediately perceived the hidden meaning of this. Of course, we had never been in SF and, as she inferred, I was letting her know that I should be in SF w/in 70 days!] I long desperately for those days of blissful happiness, each moment delirious with delight. The remembrance of the ecstasies of the past helps to make those of the future seem so much more certain, and I keep dreaming back, remembering each day, each hour of our past reunions & building from it the keen joy to come. My beloved, I kiss you softly now, & in my mind I feel the vibrant freshness of your love, sparkling on your moist smooth lips, my wife, I love you

R.

*　　*　　*　　*　　*

395

Letter #9 [Not Received]

Sunday, May 14, 1944 - 6P.M.

My Dearest Husband -

This has been such an exciting week for me. I'm so thrilled by your letters and that wonderful package of souvenirs! I love you so, my precious, and am so relieved to hear that you are safely at your destination.

Tuesday May 9. Another "letter" day. I got your letter of April 19th written in Russian! I guess it had been held up by the Censor. [I never thought of that, that the Cyrillic would appear like a secret code to the chap reading these things!] Darling, I read your letter okay and marvel at your accomplishment! Did anyone aid you? I think it's wonderful, seems to be grammatically correct, too. Mom has been "bragging" about your accomplishments & this has given her one more item to talk about.

Wed May 10. More excited when I came home to find a package from you! When I saw what was in it, I really was thrilled! The necklace & bracelet fit me perfectly and they really are exquisite! I put the bracelet up above my elbow just the way the Hindu gals wear them; then I had a few tense moments getting it off. A little cold cream did the trick, however! I think the figurines are adorable. The "letter opener" is really a dagger, isn't it? The silk scarf is so fragile & really lovely. Precious, I do so appreciate these tokens of your love! I noted the package had been mailed May 1st, so the delivery was really quick!

Thursday, May 11. I came home tonite to find a 16-page letter from you (mailed April 27) describing your voyage. This was really cut up by the Naval Censor, but I think I supplied the deleted words & phrases, and the censor apparently got tired, for the last 6 or 8 pages were untouched. Interesting to note that the dagger came from Arabia, the spoon from one of the bum boats. I do envy you the privilege of seeing these strange lands, but I do worry about your safety.

Darling, I think I understand what you mean when you say that you think of me in terms of different persons. For instance, you're not quite the same person I married pre Pearl Harbor. I think the fact that we have been separated for months at a time & the fact that our reunions have occurred in different places helps to create the impression of a different personality. But deep down we're still the same two people who took those solemn vows to love, honor & cherish each other eternally.

I am so overcome with emotion as I think of the various episodes of our married life. How we managed to find happiness just being together under circumstances that were not so hot. I try not to think too much of the future, which is so vague & uncertain, and fall back child-like on my faith in our ability to cope with whatever comes our way provided we are together. I am terrifically interested in getting some hints as to when you might be coming back. The sooner, the happier I'd be. I've acclimated myself after a fashion to living on a from day to day basis, but I still am irked by the inability to take any long end point of view.

You'll be amused by this, I know, but I feel I should tell you. So long as you remain where you are, I'm not as worried about you as I was while you were in Italy. Somehow, the idea of gals who wear jewels in their noses doesn't give me as much anxiety as the senoras in Naples.

I'm so reminded of a year go. 'Twas about this time that I had so much mental agony about the right thing to do [Giving up job and apartment to join me at Ft Warren]. So thankful I did join you when I did, precious, for I would never have forgiven myself if you had gone overseas in July. We have so much to be thankful for, precious, and so don't let this period of separation cause you too much mental torture. We can look forward to a reunion in the near future, and you are not in actual combat; and I assure you my love for you seems to grow more intense with time despite physical separation. Your letters have been so successful in maintaining close contact between us. I've gotten to know so much about you just thru your letters. So grateful for the gift of expression that you possess. You write so vividly, so forcefully.

With all my love, as always
Elizabeth

*   *   *   *   *

Fri 12 May - My 1st Civil Service Exam Junket - Very warm day, 90 or so. I reported at Farragut H.S. at 8:15. So I got my 1st instruction in giving the exam to clerk-steno-typists. Nice bunch

397

of kids, all interested in 146.00 a month. What a far cry from my $10 a week!

Tue 16 May - I Give My 1st Exam - I got up ½ hour earlier & came down to pick up my material & waited for Miss Stewart to pick me up. We got out to Hinsdale 9:30 AM. Right smack we went into the Transcription & I dictated my 1st steno exam. Rating the papers & interviewing 12 or 14 gals for employment at the Chicago Ordnance District.

Thu 18 May - A bit angry at the complaint of discrimination filed by a colored gal mentioning my name. Stayed to work 2 hours after 5 PM to rate papers. Graded 81 tonight. Home to read my darling's letter of 4/28 which contained 15 snapshots he took while in India. Says he will not be able to write me for several weeks & at the end of the letter reminisces about the "70 days we spent in San Fran". This gets me all excited for it would seem that he expects to be back in S.F. about the middle of July.

Tue 23 May - 12 hours today - After work staying till 9:15 rating exam papers & stuff, quite a grind to sit for 4 hours with your eyes glued on papers before you. News that Anzio troops have joined with the Cassino bunch, on the road to Rome! There was such a sweet summer smell in the air as I came home tonite. Reminded me so vividly of the summer evenings Robt & I spent together before we were married.

Thu 25 May - Reluctantly dragging myself to work this morning, still reading my Russian book Tolstoy "Cemyestiye Schastiye". [Written in Cyrillic = "Family Happiness", actually Tolstoy's diatribe against the uncivility of married life!]

Thu 1 June 1944 - I had a very restless nite. Awoke at 2 AM after an unusual dream, an erotic one. Hot today, I wore my brown seersucker & my ivory necklace & bracelet & thought it was striking. Feel downcast at not getting any mail from Robert.

Sun 4 June - Today our armies liberated Rome. Small triumph for the cost involved.

Mon 5 Jun - I got 3 Russian books: Chekov's Humorous Tales, Gogol's "Inspector General", Turgenev's "Father & Son" and a French book of comedies "Lever Rideau". [Raise the Curtain] Home at 7, hearing FDR speak on the capture of Rome. Rec'd 3 letters written in Dec to my Robert, returned undelivered.

Tue 6 June - The Invasion Begins - Awoke at 7 AM to learn that the Allies had landed in France, in Normandy. Later it seems we have established beachheads at Cherbourg. The news seems to be taken by everyone with prayer & grim determination to see it thru. Cool today so I stayed to work till 7 PM, but my mind was not on my work. Mom scolded me for this continuous overtime work because of reheating meals. Listening to the radio newscasts, all regular programs interrupted. Martial music, prayers, etc.

Sat 10 June - The doorbell rang at 8:30 and it was a special from Robert covering the period from May 4 to May 21 when he landed in Australia. Says he expects to be in Frisco in July & will try to get to go back to NY so as to pick me up enroute, but that failing, I am to meet him in Frisco. So excited I can hardly contain myself. 90 days since we parted.

Mon 12 June - Wotta day, hundreds of people coming in for jobs, but I was spared the agony of interviewing by working on my Wash DC appointments, writing my own letters & cleaning up 30 or so appointments. Home at 5:30 to find 3 air mail letters from Robert written from Australia reiterating that he is coming in mid-July. Says he got my April 23 & 30 letters, missing links but at least he knows I've been working.

*　　*　　*　　*　　*

1PM Thursday May 4, 1944

My sweet, beloved wife -

I should have written you earlier than this in this trip, but I have been in a terrible state of lethargy since leaving India. Am recovering slightly now, but there is so much I just haven't the energy or will to do. My last day in port I was quite sick from the dysentery [I was appalled to read of my wholly undisciplined eating of raw fruit in Karachi!!] & rather feared one of those severe attacks, but it went away with a little peragoric & bismuth treatment. Guess I wrote you of my last nite ashore & my bicycle ride. Mailed that letter & a box of souvenirs to you the next day, and at sundown India was just a vague outline of hills. That sunset was a thing of such exotic beauty in the intense quality of its colors. The clouds so soft yet glowing with slow shifting shades of fire against a sky of the most pale, serene blue, the hot orange sun sinking into the deep green waters, casting an eerie, oily reflection on this strange sea. It was a glorious vividness of color, a fitting farewell to this strange, subtle life of India.

Since then we have been coming south, ever south into the beating sun of the equator. Today at noon as I stand on deck my shadow is under the soles of my feet. Altho it is hot, it is not the terrific, unbearable heat that you imagine, for we have a slight breeze & the nites at sea are always cool. The ocean, of course, looks exactly like all other oceans, the vast unbroken monotony of blue, flecked here and there with momentary foam.

Did have an interesting sight this morning when we ran thru a school of thousands of porpoises. They went leaping gaily thru the air, lashing & whipping the water into quite a froth. It was a strange sight to see all these creatures living, lost, in the awesome immensity of this endless ocean. It is hard to imagine mammals living in this trackless waste, in the ceaseless sameness of infinite water - and at nite beneath the dazzling splendor of the moon it seems as tho the whole world must be lost & dead, a vague & distant dream. The only reality is the ship & the throb from its engines, the prow parting the ever-waiting water into bubbling foam, dancing in ethereal swirls, jewels sparkling in the moonlight; while the calm uncertain distance of quietly undulating water glistens, agelessly, like a huge mirror of forever. There is a vast & terrible beauty to the sea, a half-heard song that enchants as it sings eternally a history which you dimly recognize as yours.

9PM Sunday May 14, 1944

My sweet one -

The wind has continued; now blowing I imagine at least 35 or 40 mph, and of course this continued gale for days has started to pile the waves up to a considerable height. It is fascinating to stand up in the bow and watch the ship plunge, shattering into these huge hills of water. Great piled tons of force rush to meet the ship & lift it quivering high out of the water; then we slide breathlessly down to meet the next one, sending masses of foam & spray swirling into the whipping wind. Some particularly giant heaps of water may run 100 feet long and 15 feet high and with maybe 50 feet between crests. It is hard to estimate the size because there are so many waves, all jumbling & tumbling onto each other, but when a couple of them coincide & join, they'll lift the bow of the ship up a good 20 feet & let it fall sharply into an ominous valley, just in time to catch the next wave head on with a resounding thwack & a tremendous charge of spray which the wind whirls away like a fierce snowstorm. It is a beautiful sight to see this power of water, to toss a great ship about like a mere raft. I took a couple pics of it, but I'm afraid the thrill of this great undulating violence will be lost in a still & quiet picture without the whistle of the wind, the swish of the angry water. When the bow dips down, the wheel comes up out of the water & the engine races, shaking the whole ship like a vibrator.

*　　*　　*　　*　　*

1PM Sunday May 21, 1944

My loved one -

Hastily now I'll finish this letter, before a still more hasty day ashore. This looks like a fine country & the people I've met so far are really swell. Lots of fresh fruit, milk, ice cream, etc. It's about like an early November day back home with nice warm sunshine.

Darling, I'm also sending you another letter or essay which I wrote last night. The colored radio operator (the most intelligent man on the ship) gave me a very good criticism on it, saying the details were so numerous & vivid that they overshadowed the moral of the thing, and I think he's quite right; a fault I didn't realize. You most likely recognize my letters in it, which will kind of spoil it, but I'll keep trying on other things. Hope there is some mail for us here, but I suppose not.

*　　*　　*　　*　　*

12:30PM Monday May 22, 1944

My sweet, beloved wife

I am so happy today, & for so many reasons. The anticipation of seeing you is the greatest cause and seems to make every other phase of life so cheerful. Just the thot of seeing you in 40 or 50 days is enough to keep me happy; but the atmosphere here is so cordial & American that you can't help but feel good.

Ate in a place that was, I guess, a fair example of the restaurants & wow, was it primitive! About like a South State St chophouse & I had a little trouble with the language when I asked for some jam or jelly (didn't know jello was "jelly"), but they had neither, but said he'd bring a trifle, which I knew didn't mean a trifle jam by the way he said it. So I was prepared for some kind of marmalade or something. Instead I got a trifle, which is a pudding with cake crumbs. Phooey! [Much later in life she & I learned in Scotland that trifles should not be held in such disdain, can be scrumptuous!]

401

Went up to the officers club & got hilariously inebriated with practically all the ship's officers there. Drank a whole bottle of Chablis & then vermouth & lots of good beer. We had a riot of fun with a bunch of Australian Officers & wound up at a dance. I repeat, the Australians are fine people, in spirit & character so similar to Americans.

*　　*　　*　　*　　*

MAIL!!

1pm Wed. May 24, 1944

My beloved -

I can just feel myself squeezing you, I am so happy, so elated over getting two letters from you just now. Had given it up as hopeless, but then they found our mail mixed up with another outfit's. Got your letter from April 30th & 23rd. Oh precious, I can hardly sit still it makes me feel so good, so close to you, to have these bits of you here with me. It makes me glow all over to know you are safe & well & comfortable, & to be able to picture your life at this instant so clearly & with such certainty. Up to now I knew nothing of what you had done for 2½ months, but now, with these two weeks of letters, I can piece together the picture of your life pretty well.

It seems you are working 6 days a week at some sort of an employment bureau, the State one I imagine, & you are doing interview work which should be interesting, meeting innumerable types of people, rummaging thru their past history & comparing it to the person before you. I don't like the idea of such damned long hours for you, tho, and unless you are making at least $50 a week for those hours, I suggest you quit immediately and get some job that gives you more free time for recreation. In fact, quit for the summer just on general principles, for I want you to learn to swim before I get back. You're a darling.

*　　*　　*　　*　　*

My luscious darling -

We are now headed into the fringes of the Antarctic Sea & the ship has been heaving continually since the moment we left port yesterday. I crave the comfort of our home, the wholesome abundance of our meals, the clean intimacy of our baths, the luxurious passion of our spacious bed, the sweet exhaustion of our love-wrapped slumber. I want you so my wife.

Lovingly
Robert

402

4:15PM Tuesday May 30, 1944

My sweetness -

The storm of the first few days has stopped, and now we are in an uncanny calm, just heavy, lifeless cold. The sky is completely overcast with gloomy, impenetrable clouds, and the sea is like blue gray, molten glass. It heaves lazily in long slow swells, but otherwise the surface is smooth & glistening, a dull oily light, like gunmetal under blue neon. Off in the distance a faint breath stirs the surface so that it looks like lustreless brushed chromium; and always the slow heavy heaving. The only joy is where the prow pushes the white thunder of the foam before it. Whales have been seen. The huge albatross glide & swoop, dipping effortlessly right to the surface of the water, gliding swiftly along, barely inches above the swells but never touching; always gliding, whirling, turning, swooping, poised in the air, their feet tucked snugly into the white feathers, the head turning in jerky bird movements. Quick, beady eyes ever searching the water, long yellow beak splitting the wind as they swoop & turn. There must be 15-18 of them following us.

I think back to 3 years ago today, our life then, the momentous swirl of love ready for our opening, the sweet unseen future poised before us. How beautiful it is to look back over those 3 years & see how the knitting of our lives, the delicious entanglement of our intertwining histories, all springing from the crossings of that 1st day. In the car in the park, the rich, heavy volume of World Literature scintillant with the jeweled thots of all men, the Book of Art & its treasure of what is beautiful; & we, sedulously absorbing all this knowledge, with the refreshing greenness of the park, the vital, exhilarating breath of Spring, the occasional swish of a car past us or of a stroller gay with the holiday sun. We studied, & learned, & I tried desperately not to think of you as a woman, but only as a mind, a keen intelligence wherein rested the understanding and the beauty of all these treasures over which we poured [sic]; and the lives of all these men haunted me & their women & the redness of your speaking lips, the soberness of your smile, the thoughtfulness of your eyes, studious, yet gay, the professional & practiced manner in which you lit a cigarette, the air of maturity instead of frivolity which surrounded you, a successful, brilliant woman, one who could think, one who was wise to the drabness of mankind, but who also felt the vivacious beauties of life, the pervading

403

beauty of the mind. We went for a drink of water. We felt awkward walking together. We were strangers & we knew it. We weren't quite sure of ourselves or of the other. Oh, we had so much to learn. We went over your meticulous notes. I felt in them the contrast of our two characters, one reserved patient, diligent, the other meteoric, impulsive, nomadic. One would take notes & absorb & learn & apply; the other would dream, learn swiftly & seek new dreams. We grew hungry. I liked to talk to you, to parade my knowledge before someone who knew enough to understand it, the age-old braggart, man strutting before the cunning, waiting wiles of woman. But I liked your intelligence, the depth of your culture, the real, earthy quality of your experience, your speech, your manner. You were self-assured, but not contemptuous. You were studious, but not cloistered. You were good company. Perhaps I even looked at your cool, clean woman arms, the supple hands, the neat brushed hair, the sturdy well-formed body; perhaps I did, & thot of you naked on a bed & the suave sophistication of your pleasure seeking studiousness, receptive & exciting, but always reserved, patient, diligent, deliberate, the casual self-possessed adventuress relaxing in the sensations of her body. Oh, how far I was from seeing the snugly little kitten puckering her lips up to mine, sweetly brushing our noses in the darkness, lacing our cold clumsy toes playfully together under the secrecy of the blankets way down in a bed where our feet met and recognized each other; nor did I see the happy little housewife stuffing me mercilessly with bubbling glee on Sunday morning pancakes, the vivacious unpremeditated kiss of a sparkling wife so brimful of gladness to have her husband & breakfast & home, the unkempt hair & ill concealing housecoat, all so radiantly happy, girlish & innocent. Those were things we had yet to learn, which were hidden within us & required the friction of our continual company to grind the clay of formality from our persons to reveal that true joy of our life beneath it.

So long ago, that day in May when the fragrant splendor of Spring stirred its mating insistencies into the abstract day of our study; when love crept into the lives of two people intent on learning the history of man. Lovely Spring, lovely woman, 3 years ago and now here in the leaden bleakness of the viscous sea beneath Australia it seems too beautiful to have dreamed it; yet it is so far away, so nebulous & vague & I want the reassuring warmth of your moistsoft lips to kiss me & tell me it is true. I want the feel of your hand on my face, lightly, the loving caress of your hair laid trustingly & happily on my breast, I kiss your upturned face & know you are my wife forever. I love you so my darling one, always

Robert

7PM Thursday, June 1, 1944

My darling beloved -

The German is a problem. Since I discovered how many words there are in the average vocabulary, I've had to intensify my efforts to acquire one. I've added 400 words to my mind since leaving NY & have now increased the tempo to 25 words a day. I find that whether I memorize 10 or 25 words, there are always a couple I simply can't remember & others which are never forgotten, so it is no greater task to learn 25 words than it was to learn 10, tho I have to spend a little more time at it. But even knowing all the words, it is still difficult to translate & I get all messed up. Sometimes I'll take a word for granted & think I know it, such as "Waldfliegen", which I took to mean "birds of the forest ". Finally, after the "Fliegen" had appeared in a couple other passages & didn't seem to fit, I looked it up & found them to be flies not birds! I knew the German "Vogel" (bird) and the Italian "mosca" (fly) & the German "Flieger" (aviator) and somehow thot I knew all about birds , flies & fliegen, but I didn't. "Eine Fliege" as well as being a fly is also a gunsight, the fluke of an anchor or a light-minded person; just as an English "fly" can be the fly of a tent or the fly of a pr of pants. What a complex thing language is.

Read "The Lives of a Bengal Lancer" by F. Yeats Brown yesterday & it certainly is a marvelous book. Damn Hollywood & their gaudy, trashy romanticism. I certainly would never have read this book based on the movie, but it must be two different things, for the book is excellent. The finest parts of the book were devoted to observations on the religions & philosophy of India. The author struck some deep truths in his treatment of it. The comparisons between the wisdom of the East & of the West are extraordinarily intelligent. "Yoga is a physical as well as mental process. It is written that just as the sweetness of molasses can only be realized by the tongue and can never be explained in a thousand words, so Yoga can be realized only by the senses & never explained by words. You come from a culture that has made a fetish of the brain." Speaking of the phallic carvings on a temple wall: "They idealize Woman without whom we could not be born, nor enjoy. Humanity has been shaped by Her, & thru Her it must be saved. The lingam-yoni is the symbol of the entry of spirit into matter, without which the world could not have been made, and thru whose function it must be sustained." How

405

true, & the ancients' worship of sex is truly a very deep philosophical concept; a far more beautiful worship than the harsh & sterile doctrines of Christianity, altho the Christians made a half hearted attempt to get a female goddess into their religion with the Virgin Mary. "The true object of love is the union of the hearts of the participants. When that is not accomplished, the mating might be that of two corpses." "The true knowledge of Being comes out of the masculine awakening in woman, and the feminine in man, which is manifested on the earth plane as sexual union. In that super-sensual bliss the rock of egoism is riven, and the two become One, and Very God." How that echoes our own thots! Speaking of "positions" (asana) in yoga: "Buddha is generally represented with his right foot on his left thigh & his left foot on his right, in what is known as the lotus seat, which has as definite an effect on the mind as has the Christian "asana" of kneeling in prayer." How absolutely correct. I never realized this very definite connection between body position & mental attitude.

We passed thru Bass Straits between Tasmania & Australia today, and it was good to see land & the scattered humps of the islands. The sky is still choked with sullen gray clouds and the weather chilly. I'll sure be glad to head north.

3:30PM Tuesday June 20, 1944

My sweet beloved -

If I could only harness & direct all the wild, intense energies of my mind, and set them deliberately into the channel of one constant effort. But I am nomadic & I see & feel everything at once, all the great glorious empire of Egypt, rich, oriental, exotic, steeped in its deep mysticism & the countless unremembered atoms of human misery which built & composed it, now forever lost in unimaginable centuries of the past, blown forever into the dry hot sand swirl of the desert. Oh, I see it all, feel it in my blood, feel that living, seething in my mind as in my body, a quick flash from some dim ancestral memory, it is there within me & then is gone.

I am prowling thru the jungle of my own life, ferreting out all the myriad remembrances & impressions stamped so strongly within my person. I remember the smells of the barn, the hen houses, the pigs, the prickly heads of rye, the cool breeze under the shade tree; I feel Indiana is within me, bounteous, rich, it's black loam wholesome in my flesh, the tangy smells of its rolling farmland, the dank woods, the tiny placid lakes with the bull rushes & turtles sunning on the lily pads. It is all within me, all at once, racing thru my mind, beating with my pulse, all the hot, dry summer days

406

in the dusty stubble of the fields, the quick, lush thundershowers & the virgin snow falling among the frozen corn stalks - all of it. It flashes on before I can seize it; in an instant I am somewhere else, in the tumultuous, grimy desperation of the struggling city, feeling the city & its power, its countless people, their heroic, ugly, dirty, patient, callous, useful lives. I feel them & I see them. I feel the might of the country & the grandeur of its amalgamated peoples, built from the flesh of the world like some great sturdy & malleable alloy, wrought into the most remarkable machine the world has ever seen. I look at the quick, strong flood of their lives coming with their tough hands, their lithe muscle & keen hopeful intelligence from the villages of the Ukraine, from the mountainous isle of Sicily, from the rugged slopes of Norway, the green hungry soil of Ireland, the neat seaports of Holland. They come, lusty Lithuanians, hot-headed hard-working Poles, the prudent English, the patient Germans, the sensual carefree Negro, back bent to the dirty job but always giving the world a song; all, various as all the fruits of the earth, and they have dug the riches from the rock, laid the straight steel rails across the new country, manned the countless factories, the cities, towns & farms, the vast wealth of the nation erected by these samples of humankind, assembled from all corners of the earth, welded into one extraordinary nation - and it is mine, it is in me; but before I can get it out, it is gone, fading before some rearing, uncontrollable swell of fresh ideas.

As I lay in the fierce equatorial sun this noon & felt its nourishing warmth beating into my flesh, the stiff breeze whipping the heat away & carrying an occasional brush of cooling spray over me, there came to my mind so many things I wanted to write to you; about the way these vast masses of air keep rushing on day after day, a thick unseen sea of gas whirling nowhere, driving the waves & the great white clouds before it. How strange this fiercely invisible rushing of the thinly strewn atoms, lashing themselves furiously across the unbroken surface of the sea, a blind titanic power. And the sunlight strikes its straight, undeviating course directly thru this seething rush of matter. The light comes, silent, quiet, steady, mysteriously unaffected by the tearing, frantic wind. How strange this bodyless simplicity of light, that it penetrates undisturbed, unblown by the howling bluster of the air.

Oh, so much I thot of & wanted to write you, but now my mind is already tired from this little bit, a trifle vented of its passionate imaginings, but I have still so much to say. Perhaps tomorrow, my sweet one, I will come back & rave to you some more. Always to you, for I love you so, & it is that somehow which drives within me all the deep ineffable dreams racing forever in my mind, & which I am occasionally able to snatch from confusion & give to you. That is it; all my lust to write, to say, to create, is a part of my giving myself to you, making the entire tangle of my soul visible to you & saying "here, my sweet one, it is I". I show you what is within me, what I feel, that you may look upon it, know me & love me. My sweet darling wife. I kiss you with innumerable dreams so fervently, awaiting the glorious realization of all these longings for tender, soft caresses, so full & spontaneous with love,

Robert

*　　*　　*　　*　　*

June 19, 1944

From the great tower, the glorious mountain, straight steel & stone flung precisely upwards, titan shaft threatening the peaceful bellies of the clouds, lithe spire of the myriad glittering windows, stable arrow of man's grandeur, the imprisoning honeycomb of his swarming life. From its high parapets I peer, with dizzying fear of down plunging eyes, the mind unused to soaring; then enchanted, the labyrinth, vast, of intertwining streets, cleaving the chasms of the city. To each horizon, countless soot-gray caves, row on ordered row, roiling anthill proliferate with man. Down among the channels of this hive the little figures creep, dawdle, scurry, each content, battling their way, beetle cars piped slowly along his boulevards. Oh, what glory to behold, instantly this vision, to send the million fingered brain among this whirl of life, to seek & find. Here I'll turn a woman's frowzy head & peer into her restless eyes, or there the wretched hungry fed, both food & subtle lies. I'll watch the kids throw grapefruit rinds, at public buses; and the stenographer, caged in her cubicle, avidly chewing the omnipresent gum, uttering a sophisticated "oh, damn" at each mistake, thinking of Bill.

Flydog, gypsy, spew what shall I write, warming up the brain as the first uncertain catchings of a starting engine. It coughs & hacks & nothing forms. Oh turn it over wildly, faster, spin spin till the thots fly reeling from the giddy centrifuge, till from the inane, inchoate wanderings of the 1st instants the heat will grow and form, taking shape till thots flow from all the dark unwilling snarls of the mind and then, growing to the exuberance of their goal, swarm, swift incessant patterns, quicker than the pen can catch. Oh, don't look

408

back, don't pause; continue, massage the brain with effort, strive, write anything till thots flow with vigor, automatically from the started siphon. Then, as it comes smoothly, seize it, form the energy, the scintillating phrases - into what into, what shall it be? Shall I create a dog, what kind of dog, shaggy airdale, smelly, kinky hair knotted in stiff whorls over brown, fluid eyes. No! Rather man, man upon whose moist pasty skin is hung the distinctive raiment of Scott & Sons, lot #1-774A, draping his awkward human form.

STUMPED, STUMBLE BUM Will an idea come. Will a swift flash from some inner treasure house of thot jar the necessary mechanisms into life, awake from the stupor of indecision, of sterile pencil chewing.

*   *   *   *   *

Tue 13 June - So I met my 17 girls at the Northwestern Station, train late but everything went fine & we got over to the Union Station & wrote in their berth reservations. Got UP timetable at the station, to go to Frisco will take 3½ days; think I'd much rather have Robert comes thru Chicago with a delay enroute. Four years ago Hitler marched into Paris. Now the Nazi counterattack has started, but we seem to be holding our own.

Wed 14 June - I have such a yearning for excitement, such ennui with my job & my present mode of living. Seems like 3 months is all I can take in one place, and it's been that long since I left New York. Counted my money & I have $80 of my salary to show for 3 months work. 'Course it's kept me busily occupied.

Thu 15 June - Japan is bombed! - News that we have invaded Saipan and also bombed Japan. So lonely & disgusted & so impatient for Robert to come back to me.

Sun 25 June - M - I read some Better Homes & Gardens magazines & got very nostalgic looking at ads of beautiful homes & recipes etc.

Tue 27 June - M - TELEGRAM - About 11PM last nite doorbell rang & Sis answered it to get a collect telegram from Robert. "Have arrived today San Pedro may be detained here permanently or temporarily. Will wire as soon as everything is definite love Robert."

Wed 28 June - DEWEY nominated - 98 today but I wasn't so aware of the heat till I got home. Told Maire Robt coming in & I

409

wanted Fri & Sat off & maybe all next week & she said there was talk of taking me out of the clerical unit, & she'd have to take it up with Mr Toon? Came home to find a very long letter from Robert covering his voyage from May 26 to June 27 when he landed in San Pedro. Apparently he had fear of being sent right out from the POE, but must have worked it so he's reporting to New York. Question: How long will he stay in Chicago? Will he want me to accompany him when he leaves? Perhaps he'll stay for 10 days & we can prepare leisurely & perhaps he won't want me to go with him. I guess a phone call would have cleared things. These telegrams are so inadequate. I'm not even excited at the Rep Convention & Dewey's acceptance speech.

Thu 29 June - Mr Toon told me that he heard my husband was coming in & wanted me to know the financial condition of the Commission had improved & the office would take care of its permanent personnel. Well, I guess they'd really like me to remain with the Commission. Home to find telegram from Robert announcing his arrival 7:30 AM at the Dearborn Station.

CHAPTER XI
The United Kingdom

Synopsis - Upon arrival in Los Angeles from my India trip I quickly learned that several of my predecessors were already assigned to duty in the Pacific Theater. Things looked a bit hopeless, for during my absence the Transportation Corps had issued an order forbidding transcontinental travel of its officers to return to their East Coast bases, thus superceding my orders to return to NYPOE. Knowing the foibles of the Army, however, I found an officer willing to accept my original orders, and he issued transportation for me to return to my "home" base. My cleverness did not buy me any apparent grace, for when I wired from Chicago requesting leave in transit, I was promptly informed that I was AWOL and ordered to proceed to NYPOE immediately. Actually, they were glad to have me back, and although I was reprimanded by having a letter attached to my file detailing the incident, and punished by being put on a miserable ship (see below) for the next voyage, in the long run the consequences were very much to my benefit, promotion and shore duty after another two trips.

While awaiting punishment we had 14 days together. Elizabeth then returned to her work with the Civil Service Commission while I went to Ireland and Scotland. At the end of August, 1944, she had her tickets for a 2-week recruiting foray in Bloomington, Indiana for the Commission but, happily, received word from me the day before she was to leave. On that New York reunion we had 23 days together before I left for Avonmouth (Bristol) on a fast ship, and she again returned to Chicago. There she now managed to get back her old position with the Manhattan Project. My letters from the Avonmouth trip seemingly have been lost in the transition that followed, our establishing "permanent" residence in Brooklyn upon my receiving a promotion and shore duty (Chapter XII) with NYPOE.

Fri 30 June 1944 - Robert arrives - Got up at 6:30. My darling's train in at 8 & there he was, moustache, barracks bag & all. He weighs 165 lbs stripped so I guess he won't gain weight on these "cruises". Robt wired N.Y. for a 10 day delay. My darling so tanned & lean & hungry looking - and so sweet about everything. We're quite comfortable in my room. Mom washed out all of his shirts & pants & underwear.

Sun 2 July - Got my 2 weeks leave approved yesterday so I'm all set to leave with Robert on the 3:30 train. The Dotys picked us up at 12 & took our bags. Mad because we had to pay almost 5.00 more for our Roomette. But the train was almost deserted & we had a quiet trip. Worrying about what we'll do for accommodations.

Mon 3 July - Arrive in New York - We got in at 9:30 & immediately called the MacDonald's but they had no vacant rooms so checked in at the Penn, 7.15 room for 5.40. Call fm Robt at noon that he was having a conference with Lt Cols Branstatter & Gillespie. Spent almost all aft trying to get a place for us to stay that would not be so expensive. Robert returned at 6 with 180.00 pay & $26.00 travel pay. We looked at Mrs. Hall's place, no vacancies; & at Miss Yale's for 8.00 & took it.

Tue 4 July - Move to 12 Willow Place - Robt left early, I got up at 10:30 & hurriedly packed everything. I arrived at 12 Willow Place same time as the army truck with our bags. Mrs. Y cleaning up the place & with clean drapes & fresh runners on the dressers it looks clean if a bit bare. Robert says no word as to his disposition yet. Went to the Naples Restaurant for a 1.50 dinner, typical Italian meal, antipasto, etc. [I still remember that this is where I first encountered that great delicacy, prosciutto con meloni!] Stuffed, we rode to Manhattan, took in a newsreel theater, had papaya drinks & picked up our bags at the Penn. Home past 11. Taking quick baths & going to bed in our "new" home. I will feel better when I know what punishment, if any, he gets for his AWOL from L.A.

Thu 6 July - No phone call from Robert so I guess nothing exciting has happened (I hope!). To Macy's where he picked up a German novel, ordered Joyce's "Finnegan's Wake". Arguing re whether I stay here or go to Chi after my 2 wks leave.

Fri 7 July - Talked to Ann Yale, learning quite a bit about the Jehovah's Witnesses. Decided to go hear the Goldman Band playing at Central Park. . . . He's to submit to disciplinary action of his C.O. in lieu of court martial as punishment for his L.A. escapade & this he has done.

Sat 8 July - Robt Gets Assigned - Phila - He called me at 11:30 to say he's got a written reprimand, also assignment to go to Phila Mon 8:30 AM. So he came home & had lunch & we started packing. He left to pick up his orders & stuff. So will still go to the outing tomorrow to Fort Slocum & have an army truck pick us up Mon 5 AM to go to Penn Station & Phila, 6:30 AM train. We ate supper trying to use up all our stuff, but I guess we won't succeed.

Sun 9 July - FORT SLOCUM - Up at 7, really rushing so as to leave by 8 to be at the pier by 9 AM. Made it okay but the ship didn't leave till 11:30, waiting for chairs. Robert almost left me in disgust because of the delay. Nice (?) hot sun on the ship out to this island post. Fine barbecue meal by the water's edge. Then exploring around, resting in the shade of a willow tree. Lovely but the delay in leaving for home was a bore & the damn tub was so slow it was midnite before it got to the Battery. Home finishing packing & setting the alarm for 5 AM. Sunburned & tired to bed.

Mon 10 July - Philadelphia - In the gray of 5 AM we awoke & hurriedly packed stuff to be ready by 5:15 when our army weapons carrier picked us up. Messy dusty ride on the coach to Phila. Met Lt Looney also going to Phila & the boys reported in by phone to the POE. Robt is going to get $7 per diem & our room at the Normandie is $4.

Tue 11 July - Sight seeing - Visited their Free Library & I had trouble getting my darling away from some books on cuneiform, etc. Next we visited the Franklin Institute & that can't begin to compare with our Rosenwald Museum. They charged 25¢ admission too. Next, to the Rodin Museum, nice layout but disappointed in the sculptures displayed, mostly heads of people he knew. Home & dressing to go to the "famous" eating house of

413

Bookbinders - phooey! 79 years in business & their food was icky & it cost us 4.40 to find that out. Saw the Liberty Bell in Independence Hall but the place was closed. Took in a Trans-Lux movie to see the landings on New Britain, official War Dept release.

Wed 12 July - Sightseeing Philadelphia - To the square around Independence Hall to wait for my darling. He came at 1 & we looked at the Liberty Bell & the Hall & the House of Reps etc. Took trolley out to the Art Museum & spent several hours viewing the Stieglitz, Gallatin collections. A quick look at their aquarium & then to town to eat a hearty meal at Horn & Hardart's.

Thu 13 July - Rain - Sightseeing - Movies - To the Atwater Kent Museum showing the development of Philadelphia since 1600. Milkshakes at Loft's & looking for a good movie. Found "Winterset" & "Bill of Divorcement". Enjoyed the double feature & got out at 7 in time for a supper snack at H&H. Home with our books & newspapers to read of the amazing progress of the Russians who have now captured Vilna.

Fri 14 July - I leave Philadelphia - So about 10:30 AM Robert called me to say I'd better get packed as he'd be leaving tonight. Robt thot he might stay in NY a few days before sailing for England & wanted me to return to New York on that possibility. I managed to convince him it would be simpler for him & me if I left for Chicago this aft & so it was decided. Parted at the City Hall subway station & I rode to No Philadelphia to catch the 4:22 train. An individual reclining seat beside a nice soldier boy & the scenery was lovely, seeing a part of Penn I usually don't get to see taking the later train I do. Finally fell asleep for a few hours in the dusty soot-filled coach.

Sat 15 July - Arrive Home - The train got in on time & by 8:45 I was home. Mom pleasantly surprised.

Sun 16 July - ARMY SERVICE FORCES EXHIBIT - Mom & I went down to Grant Park to the Weapons of War show on the lake front. Mom had a $100 bond & I a $25 so we got to ride the "duck" & the jeep. In the hot sun looked at most of the exhibits showing contrast between Nazi, Jap & American equipment. Iggy & Kate came over to say goodbye to Max; poor boy, he leaves tomorrow for induction into the Army, Navy, Marines? Which?

Mon 17 July - Back to Work - Phooey - Said "bonne chance" to Max early this morning, reported to work& felt a bit self-conscious at the "very" warm welcome I got from Maire & Mrs Crooks. So I sat & read circular letters etc practically all day, studying the Starnes-Scrugham Veterans Preference bill.

Tues 18 July - Phooey again! - I guess I really "blew my top" this AM to Miss Hjortsberg regarding the letter I got re my leave & stuff. Now I almost regret having said what I did, but one can never go back, can one? I guess Max has been inducted into the Navy. The Democratic convention will begin tomorrow, much talk as to who will get the vice presidential nomination, pro & con Henry Wallace.

Wed 19 July - We Go to the War Show - At office hearing that Janice Morris is leaving soon for Wash as Caf-5 to be a Caf-7 after training. So I said nothing but my mind is more or less made up that I am going to quit when Robert next comes in & if necessary plan on living in NY. Out to the Lake Front to see the sham battle & movies I had missed Sun. Home at 10:45 to find short letter from Robert saying they left 6 a.m. Sat.

Wed 26 July - Check for 1M from Bklyn Bank so I'll have some $3030.

Thu 27 July - We Start Rating Examiners Classes - Started our instruction on rating exams. Mr Tarbox opened the session with a talk as to the importance of this rating so far as the veterans are concerned & his view of the demobilization to come.

Sun 30 July - WING PARK - Elgin, Ill - Up at 7 AM, hurriedly eating & setting off for the Koteks. We left at 9 for Elgin, Ill. So we ate ravenously of our bountiful lunch, hiked, had our fling at the swings, roasted wieners, read magazines, tried to get a suntan. Missed Robert terribly as I recalled Starved Rock & lately Fort Slocum.

Tue 1 Aug 1944 - Over to the Mart & spent a half-hour or so with the machine accounts unit & I learned what a keypunch machine, sorting, interpreting, verifying & tabulating is; this all in line with my discovering what disabled veterans can do there.

Thu 3 Aug - 98 today - I awoke after a nite of confused dreams

415

concerning my job. Do wish I could take Robert's advice & not take my job too seriously.

Sun 6 Aug - I Visit the Dotys - Up at 11 & after hearty breakfast dressed & left for the Dotys at 12:45. Got there 1:30 or so. Fine dinner spread. Chatted with them all day, no reference to our [political] disagreement. Dad Doty drove me home 10 PM, giving me some peppers, beets, tomatoes & cabbage from their Victory Garden.

Fri 11 Aug - Still hot, around 100 & I really sweltered all day. Met Marie at 6:15, walked to Grant Park to hear Fabian Sevitsky & the Chicago Symphony. Home dirty & tired at 11 PM to find long letter from Robert.

Sat 12 Aug - Went to bed about 11, sleeping in the nude 'neath the bedsheet, such a deliciously sensual feeling. Reread my darling's letter several times.

Mon 14 Aug - 98 - Sweltering Hot - Robert's letter described the seaport town where his ship is anchored & the lovely verdant rolling countryside.

*   *   *   *   *

[This series of letters was written on a deteriorating ship, destined to be sunk as a breakwater at the Normandy beachhead - Clearly this horrible ship was assigned to me as something of a punishment for my "AWOL" behavior.]

9AM Sunday July 16, 1944

My sweet beloved -

It is a very foggy morning as we come up the coast to NY, and the whistle is blowing monotonously every 30 seconds, shaking the whole ship with its racket. We left at 6 AM Saturday morning, so that we could have had Friday nite together. I hope tho that you were able to get a seat, but even if you did, it must have been a rather miserable trip on those dirty, broken down old coaches.

I'm afraid I'm in for just about the filthiest, most disgusting three weeks of my life, & if it takes longer than three weeks, I'll want to jump over. What a stinking, dilapidated old scow this is! [This was a so-called "Hog-Islander", the "Liberty" ship of WWI!] You've never seen more flies than can accumulate on a ship, & the cockroaches are exploring my shoes, books, etc. Found a couple

416

bedbugs in my life jacket, so I let the Chinaman have it who claimed it was his. The room is just above the dry stores locker & at nite the stale, musty smell of old flour & spices, soggy cookies, sugar & steamy damp rice, all seeps up thru the boards. The air is heavy with this annoying mixture of aromas. Makes the blacked out room feel even more stuffy. As soon as I get a cot from the Navy, I'll start sleeping outside. All the linens are yellowed & half clean, & the floors are impossibly filthy with the years of close living, wearing the dirt right into the grain of the wood.

No privacy & no desk, those are the things I find most irritating. Have my books stacked on the bed below me, but there is no place to sit & study or write. I am writing this in the saloon, which will undoubtedly have the disadvantage of numerous interruptions.

The food has been fairly good. At least the Chinese steward department knows its job. My roommate, the radio operator, is not a bad sort either. He is perhaps a bit eccentric about dirt & rules of health, but that should make him a better partner to at least try to keep this hole in some semblance of a sanitary condition. He seems to be a considerate type, so he'll be easy to get along with. Used to play the trumpet, too, & he loves chess. I beat him at two games yesterday and also won 2 out of 3 from one of the engineers. The Navy ensign is a swell guy & the rest of the crew are okay, the usual lively assortment, only some of them don't even speak English at all.

This fog is really thick, can hardly see 100 feet, and there are two or three other ships whistling around us, so we are just creeping ahead. Wouldn't it be something to have a collision, and lay in New York for 3 or 4 weeks under repair.

Darling, I'm in a rather rattled, nervous mood as this letter shows, so I'll just stop here. Those sweet kisses in the City Hall Courtyard of Philadelphia were a far more beautiful leave taking than I could ever hope to write. I am happy only in the thot that this trip should be short & I'll soon be off this nightmare ship; and that my sweet, lovely wife will be waiting so eagerly to give me all the full, wholesome richness of living of which this lonely uncomfortable life deprives me. Till a few months, when again we will have cottage cheese, cool clean sheets & glorious embraces, my beautiful, I love you.

* * * * *

417

My sweet beloved -

This trip is certainly going to be an experience. The only thing good about it is the chow & some of the men. The food is absolutely the best I have ever eaten aboard ship and surpasses most restaurants ashore. The excellence of the food is no doubt due to the sternness & severity of the Captain which, while it has its advantage in the food, makes life at the table, comically silent & gloomy. He is certainly a fool in his use of authority & a highly despicable character. In fact, he is such an ogre in his use of discipline, that he has obtained a degree of notoriety for it by write ups in PM [New York newspaper] & union papers, & by reprimands from the Coast Guard, that now there are no men who will sail under him if they can help it. The Navy tells me that since the Coast Guard called him down, he has acted a bit more like a sane man, but he is still a boor in his use of his power. Everyone aboard hates him, yet they also laugh at him & his inane tantrums of command. He requires all his officers to come to mess attired in full uniform, and he stalks around all day wearing 4 heavy stripes & a high-pressure "scrambled eggs" cap. The poor mates must also be in full uniform while on watch. How different from the other ships I've been on, where all men from the Capt down wore what they pleased. But on this filthy, dilapidated scow, they must wear full uniform! Boy, I'll bet I irk the old Devil, because he can't prescribe the army uniform, since I don't even own a blouse & wear my green pants as I please. I did at least put a tie on to be just a trifle tactful, but I'll keep my cuffs rolled up just enough to irritate him.

That grumpy, foul disposition is somewhat becoming & expected in a wizened old sea dog, but this tyrant is still quite young, so that in him it appears as something monstrous & fantastic. What a lonely, miserable life he must lead, shut up always with the horror that is himself. His presence gives everyone a marked feeling of depression & somber uneasiness. What must such a person be within to have such an effect upon other men? It is sad in some ways, comical to most appearances, yet horrible to the poor creatures who must suffer under his unreasoning authority. The mess boy at supper last nite addressed the chief mate as "chief" asking "What will you have, Chief?". Well, you should have heard the blustering tirade that the Captain bawled forth. Instead of simply telling the mess man not to call the officer "Chief", he launched into a bellowing bullying attack of ridiculous severity that was as unnecessary as it was overdone, like a new shavetail commanding troops for the first time & scared to death they wouldn't know who was boss.

But enough of him. I haven't spoken to him since the 1st day I met him & gave him the cargo papers & he growled "So you finally saw fit to present yourself". I was neither "presenting" myself nor expecting such a boorish & uncordial greeting, so I just laughed at him & walked out.

But outside of the quarters, the Captain, & the bugs, it's a pretty good voyage. All the other men on here are swell fellows. Most of the officers are Belgian & Dutch & the rest are Canadians. It is very interesting to get the opinions & attitudes of these "foreigners" as well as to hear the many tales they have of runs to Murmansk, etc.

. . . Some of those stories in my Simple Russian Reader are very amusing. One by Turgenev was especially good, where God invited all the virtues to a party. He sought two virtues who had never met each other & he introduced them. Charity & Gratitude met for the first time since the world began.

*   *   *   *   *

8PM Thurs. July 20, 1944

My darling wife -

As I take out my little Red Cross calendar card to determine the date, a strange feeling of frustration & hopelessness comes over me. I see there numbered all the long weary days of waiting to be with you. The circled days of March as the clock advanced crossing the Atlantic & the big "T" on the 10th of April when the troops got off in Suez, the hot days up thru the Arabian Sea to India and the long months of May stretching clear across the Indian ocean with a little circle at the end where it was Australia. Long, empty months of waiting. Big vacant June with its days passing forever away, lost in the vastness of the Pacific, lost now forever in the unseen sea of Time, Waiting, Hoping, Anxious. Then, the hasty turmoil of events. Los Angeles, the clatter of a train across the continent. Anxiety. The sweet, brief joy of Chicago, then thru the nite swiftly to New York. Anxiety Hope Love brief hurried Peace then haste to Philadelphia, the hours are winging away like dry sand, clinging without hope to the inevitable parting, and now the empty numbered days stand in their naked, ordered rows of weeks & months, waiting, weeks, & months, alone, unkissed, weeks & months of numbered days again, staring back at me, meaning the sea, meaning this ship, meaning uncertainty & the long numb hours of counting till there will be another hasty, desperate interlude of living, another hour of beauty snatched frantically from the impassive ordered rows of empty numbered days.

*　　*　　*　　*　　*

11PM Friday July 21, 1944

My beloved -

Tonite could be labeled FOG. Thick, heavy fog lies like a pliant net immersing the unknown, unseen expanse of the sea. It seems so tangible, so softly real and dainty, that you could take it in your fingers & mold it into little balls of weightless foam; but you cannot seize it. It rolls & billows gently away, muffling, shrouding everything with its weird soft veil of white. The heaven of clouds has come down to the sea, laying lightly on the waves its slowly coiling mist. Everything is wet, and everything is invisible, obscure, all-enveloped in this giant clinging web of fog. Thru the impenetrable white murk there comes constantly the intermittent intonations of the ships, groping with deep, somber sonority; lost, searching, feeling their way within the swirling obscurity of nite, alone, in slow rhythm emitting their desolate call. The whisper of oncoming waves is ominous, greedy, suppressed & stifled in the thickness of the nite; yet their tumbling crests call forth an ever bubbling luminescence, magic lite within the thickness of the gloom. Inexhaustible these winking flashes, like beautiful souls escaping hurriedly the dank caverns of the tenebrous sea, dazzling jewels ascending from some ancient treasure chest to burst & vanish in an instant glory at the touch of air.

*　　*　　*　　*　　*

8PM Sunday July 23, 1944

My wife -

Last nite I went up to the saloon to continue my letter to you since my roommate would soon be coming down to go to bed; but I had no sooner gotten my 2 cups of cocoa & settled down, when in come the Navy & the mate & engineer just off watch. There was no way to keep from being involved in conversation. It was rather interesting, tho, as I cross-examined them all I could on what little they had observed in Brazil. It sounds like a beautiful, modern &

pleasant country. And, of course, that started my mind to dreaming.

And I like to dream, shifting the background, the scene, to see which most becomes us, which is more adaptable to us, conveniently near at hand. That is why last nite I built lite, airy dreams of sunshine in Brazil. I could see the intense hard years of study in Chicago, our children growing to a hardy age, the eventual success & completion of my years of study & training, perhaps a nomadic year or two of searching, exploring the remote & fascinating corners of the world & then settling in lush, tropical Brazil, bounteous & fertile, the very spot for an intelligent endocrinologist from America to teach in some progressive college and practice his specialty in rare & interesting cases.

So many million things we can do, dearest, but I think our best & most accessible passport to the independence we would like, would be for me to get the MD & PhD which gives one access to almost any field. I know that by the time this war is over I will be already at an age when most men have these degrees & are starting on their careers. I will be beginning my studies! But I know too what feats of study I can perform, and also care very little whether I study 10 years or a lifetime. I would try to hurry & to succeed, and have no doubt but what I would; yet if there should be delays or failures, as long as I had you & the blessed, simple happiness of our home, I would be blissfully happy & content.

And now, sweetheart, it is after midnite. As usual, I left off in the middle of the letter, but I must come back tonite to tell you of the extraordinary phosphorescence in the water. I have looked for this thru the Red Sea, the Arabian Sea, the Indian & Pacific Oceans where it is supposed to be so common, but never have I seen it quite like this. Always before it has been myriad tiny individual flashes & sparks of lite, but tonite it is different. The water, too, this afternoon, was an unusual hue, a very delicate, creamy sort of cobalt blue, a lite glassy powder blue lifting in long lazy swells. The air is quite cold, about 40 I imagine, and for a brief period we ran into fog again. But now the air is cool & crisp & the Milky Way is glittering in a resplendent span across the sky. Here and there out of the blackness of the distant sea will come a sudden lingering glow where the prow of another ship is spewing the luminescent water before it. I first noticed this phenomenon tonite when I looked over the rail & noticed the whole length of the hull aglow with soft iridescent silver. Not individual, ephemeral twinklings, but a complete steady foam before it, the lip of this huge semicircling wave was like a widening halo of molten moonlight, beautiful & delicate in its fading wreath of silver fire. Then I climbed back, stumbling over innumerable unfamiliar pipes, ventilators & cleats till I reached the fantail, and there the sight was breathtaking. As the huge churning wheel would lift up towards the surface, the whole stern of the ship seemed to be lit by a strong submerged lite, and there for yards behind us the bright swirling splendor of our wake stretched out till it slowly subsided into quiet darkness. This strange luminescence of the sea is an awesome sight & its loveliness is like something from a fairy tale. Imagine the whole dark brooding mystery of the sea, vague and ominous, almost invisible in the deep gloom of nite; in fact, only discernible from the black sky as a more intense murkiness, and its unseen undulations there like the quiet breathing of some hidden monster. Then the chill breath of the Arctic stirs thru the nite and suddenly the sea appears, a huge bowl of liquid ebony flecked with myriad ripples of quivering lite, a million little silver tongues laughing at the stars from the inky silence of the sea.

4PM Wed. August 2, 1944

My sweetheart -

I'd better finish this letter now, just in case I get a chance to mail it here, tho I don't think I'll be able to.

There is always something lonely about lying at anchor, waiting, waiting, motionless; till all you can think of is home & how much longer will all this last. The moon is mirrored on the sea, glowing dully thru the thin haze of nite, a yellow sphere heavy over the sleeping land. The great ships rest in massive majesty, sleeping beasts, studding the glassy surface, sullen & resigned on a listless sea.

How many nights of my life, anchored in silence, waiting, wondering, counting the long lonely hours, while a soft breeze from dim hills beckons a better tomorrow. Motionless and waiting, sinking forever into the depths of time. Yet my heart beats fiercely on, a pulse of fire within this mute serenity, eager, seeking across the somber world my sweet and hopeful wife, so far away; and I love you, forever

Robert

*   *   *   *   *

My darling -

Have had a marvelous day seeing this beautiful, green country. The day was warm & bright & all the hills just seemed to sparkle in rolling fields, hedges & forests like a bright, viriscent multishaded jewel. Even the water was like smooth green glass as we came in & as soon as we landed the church bells began to peal in a tinkling carillon which seemed to be a sort of special welcome to this land [Near Belfast, North Ireland]. Just a quaint, little seaport town & somehow all the day everything I kept seeing, from the advertising on the front pages of the newspapers to the people & their pharmacy shops, & snug chimneyed houses & the tide along the waterfront, all in some way reminded me so vividly of Joyce's "Ulysses". He seems to have captured & magically preserved in his book the very essence of the atmosphere here, so that I felt a strange sense of familiarity, as if I knew these people & their manner of living, their seaside, their lovely virgin fields, their mode of cooking, all here actually so akin to his depiction that I am once more deeply impressed with the profound capabilities of literature.

The 1st thing, practically, that we did was to register at the Red Cross & get us a room for the nite. The Navy & I are staying together here where we will always be able to be reached. He is the only other officer, of course, who can stay ashore.

. . . The soft, indistinct evening noises & the sweet breath of heather, the gentle twilight settling on the cozy huts & their rhapsody of flowers, all this beautiful, rolling, fertile land so serene & simple; and I wanted in the most insistent way to have you strolling there beside me that I might slip my hand tenderly around your waist and whisper to you that I love you, and that all this peaceful lovely world is ours, ours with its beauty & its joy, boundless and enduring, soothing, quiet, for always, like an August evening coming over the fresh green land from the blue mist of the sea. Always my love.

*   *   *   *   *

11:15PM Tuesday Aug. 8, '44

My sweetest darling -

. . . Before catching the boat back we had time for a stroll along the seaside among the throngs of vacationers, for this little town is a resort spot & was quite crowded for the "Bank Holiday" as they call it. Like our Labor Day, I guess. The weather has been fine &

423

warm, so that many of the people were in swimming, splashing around in the dirty water among the slippery moss covered rocks, & others laying [sic] out in the grass along the shore or sitting listlessly on the benches or on the seawalls, all looking here for the thrills, the healthfulness, the relaxation, the romance of the seaside; & somehow it all seemed to be so pitifully absent. The water was a bit unclean, the rowboats rickety & expensive, people's clothes a little shabby, refreshments nil, food scarce, and except for the children, all the faces a bit tired and worn, strained & sad, searching for the lost bubble of happiness, that vanished glitter of romance along this drab bit of sea coast with its old empty windowed houses staring gloomily out onto the dull water of the bay; for the sun did not sparkle ceaselessly, even in resort towns on holidays, and when the arteries of life so rich & young writhed bitterly over the fields of unseen France.

*   *   *   *   *

Tue 15 Aug - Dick leaves - Army - Dick [her younger brother] left early this morning & Mom says he called about 10 to say he was inducted into the army!

Mon 21 Aug - My 1st day in Joliet - Got up at 5 AM in the dark & while the folks all slept, fixed me a light breakfast &, still a bit sleepy, left at 5:45 for the Loop. On the L saw quite a sight, a sub & an army freighter going down the river. Got on the Rock Island suburban train at 6:15 & at 6:35 we got started. The train filled with working men. Reported to Mr Clifton, the Manager of USSS, & got me a desk to recruit. But as the day dragged on, I felt discouraged, for I had only 3 people to interview.

Tue 22 Aug - Gee, I hated to get up at 5:15 AM! Mom had breakfast ready for me, which helped. The train ride didn't seem so long somehow, for I began reading Duranty's "USSR". Mr Clifton told me they are having trouble filling the govt Ordnance plant orders & in fact he & the office are being investigated, etc. So I sat & read my book. Two people came in this aft, but no commitment as yet. I really feel dejected about my failure so far. Why no mail from Robert?

Wed 23 Aug - Paris - Marseille - Toulon - Romania Quits Nazis - The last day in Joliet & I sure hated to get up at 5:15. I had only 2 interviews today, making a total of 7 for the 3 days. Boy, I sure

424

hate to return to the office that way. Home 7:30 to hear the good news that Paris, Marseille & Toulon have been liberated by the Maquis & that Romania accepted Russia's armistice terms & will fight against the Nazis.

Thu 24 Aug - A special delivery letter from Robert, last entry 8/14 which states definitely that he is in Ireland. Apparently he had gone ashore 8/6 but returned to the ship & had been waiting to dock a week.

Fri 25 Aug - Robert is coming home - Home to find 2 airmails & a V-mail letter from Robert stating he expects to be in New York on or about Sept 1st & wants me there ready & settled. I tried to get a reservation on the Trail Blazer, no luck. Wrote Mrs Koven, Miss Yale, Mrs MacDonald & Jeanne & Leanna.

*   *   *   *   *

2:30AM Tuesday Aug. 15, 1944

My sweet adorable darling -

One month today since leaving & with it also comes the news of a swift return. Of course, as usual, everything is nebulous, but dearest, you will be absolutely safe in moving to NY soon after you receive this letter. In fact, you should, to be on the safe side, be in NY before Sept 1st so that we will be sure of not wasting any time of our brief & precious days together.

I love you so, my lovely one,

Robert

Darling -

Have been packing all morning & now getting ready to go into town. [Stranraer, on west coast of Scotland] Will sure be glad to get off this deal, but it is a pain dragging all my belongings around. Have an entire suitcase of books & I hope it won't fall apart, for it is a rickety old one I found.

*   *   *   *   *

11:15PM Friday, August 18, 1944

To my darling wife -

Last nite I left the Red Cross about midnite & it was just like an awakening slap in the face when I stepped out into that pitch black, rainy nite. Inside had been so light & I was completely absorbed in delicious thots of you & home right up to the time I stepped out-

425

side; and then suddenly there I was in an utterly strange city [Glasgow], 4 miles from my room, & the nite so black I might just as well have been without eyes. Rain, noises of people's voices, & an occasional flash of a light or the glow of a cigarette. After asking directions from several voices, I groped at last up to a bundle of GI's also waiting for the last streetcar for the next two hours. They were singing lewd tuneful songs. The dull, hollow steel clatter of a helmet dropping to the wet invisible pavement. Futile shouts as a taxi roared by. Finally, two of these double-decker trams came up & I was thoroly confused as to which one to take. Asked a woman & she kindly told me she'd look after me & see that I got off OK. Not only that, she turned out to be a half-drunk scrub woman & became overly solicitous, & then quite indignant when I asked the conductor if he'd make sure I got off at the right stop. When I got off, so did the scrub woman & was woozily determined to see that I got home all right. I espied an Army Captain living in the same house with me, & tried to shake this Thenardieress by walking with him. It didn't work very well, tho, for he was a bit tipsy too, and quite bent on giving a blow by blow description of his picking a gal up at a dance hall & laying her, despite the rain, in the wet, black grass of the park. [Fantasy!]

My troubles were not over either once I got inside the house, for when I had moved in, I had spent only about 5 minutes in the room, so that now as I entered in utter darkness, I became quite confused. Didn't want to wake the Col with whom I'm quartered by turning on the lite, & thot also that I would make my way to my bunk without any difficulty. Slowly I crept over to it in the dark, then when I got my hand on it there was someone in it & different blankets from my bunk. The wrong room! How stupid. I turned to go out, but had not the least idea where the door was! I stood for a moment in this heavy, muffling blackness & tried to collect my sense of direction. I did, & started off only to get inextricably tangled in a table & chair. Had to retreat & grope gently for the wall, knocked over a number of objects on the shelves & then suddenly realized where I was & followed the shelves along to my bunk. It was a very odd & interesting experience, this getting completely lost in the darkness of a room.

*　　*　　*　　*　　*

[From Edinburgh]

426

My sweetest beloved -

. . . . Went down for a well needed brunch. There was quite a line & as I was waiting a neatly dressed Lt of the Air Corps passed me & I instantly thot I recognized him despite his becoming a trifle bald & with heavy sideburns. I kept looking at him and as he went along he sort of hunched his shoulders & straightened himself, Frank Shepherd! He was the only person that motion could have come from. Yet it was too much of a coincidence. It couldn't be. Yet it kept bothering me, until after lunch I went down & checked the register & sure enough there it was, Franklin J. Shepherd in the room directly beneath mine. I left a note for him & will most likely see him tomorrow. He is an Air Corps navigator. The last I heard of him was in 1938 when he won the Golden Gloves [amateur boxing] semi-finals in Chicago. We were roommates & buddies for several gay months back in those years. Remember when we were driving thru Berea, Kentucky I told you I knew a lad from there. It was Frank. I had been thinking of him the other day, about writing a story about him & the fight he got into at a party we went to once, & here I meet him 4000 miles & 5 years from where I left him in Chicago. It is even stranger than that other chance meeting of mine in the Pacific, which I just wrote down the other day. [This was of learning at dawn one morning on the bridge of the ship in mid Pacific that the man at the wheel and I had gone to the same kindergarten! - Somehow this seems never to have made it into my letters from the Forrest.]

. . . It was 3 PM when I came out of the palace, so there was still time for a climb up to the top of an immense group of hills which tower above the city. It was certainly hard work. I met a fellow about 1/8 of the way up who knew the city well. He kept pointing out the entire geography & history of the place. I'm afraid with my long legs I went up the hill a bit too fast for him, & besides, he was a clumsy climber, putting his feet anyplace & therefore continually slipping & going down on his hands & knees. I climbed the whole 820 feet without even getting dust on my pants & only touching the grass or rocks with my fingers in some of the steeper & more precarious places. It was sure terrific exercise, tho, after so many weeks of laying [sic] around, & I arrived at the summit very winded & weak kneed. It was a dramatic scene, the miniature city far below with the castle jutting out of the jumble of houses, and in the far distance an endless patchwork of green & ripe gold, rambling miles off to the sea coast.

My chance companion stuck with me, reminding me a great

deal of Luigi in Naples, a bachelor, about 35, all his teeth out, fairly serious nature, afraid I'd think him a moocher, etc. He is a clerk for G.E. here & gets £4 a week. During a tea, which consisted of sausages & chips (french fries), tea & cake, we discussed the wages & schooling of the country; or rather, I "pumped" him about it. A tool & die maker they said gets about £4, and when I said "Yeh, £4 a day is about what they get in the States", I was immediately corrected. They get that a week here (straight time). A bartender with tips might make £7 (I think union scale in Chi is $50/week) & when I asked what a girl typist got, one of the men at the table said "Sweets" (their word for candy). The compulsory school-age was just raised from 13 to 15 years. That is, they must go until they are 15 years old unless they get a job first. This sounds like even a lower education system than that of the Belgians (but they have a good one), surely the living standard of the middle-class here is far lower than in America.

Raymond, my mountain climbing partner, & I sat in the park a moment before parting. He insisted that I take an old Latin dictionary which he had with him. [I still have it!] I feel so sorry for these barren hopeless men, who have not found the beautiful warmth & contentment of a wife & home. They are dry & fruitless trees, withering in a stale flat land of arid premature senescence. Their lives are so meager, so pitifully useless, their joys so lonely, so sterile, like a stunted dying flower smiling forlornly in a cavern dank & cold, without praise, without caresses or gentleness, without encouragement, without love; seedless & alone. Such a life castrates a man of all the glory of living, the virile, dynamic tender companionship of woman & a proud wholesome home & the immortal happiness of children. Oh, how constantly thankful & joyful I am to be your husband, your mate thru all of life, boundlessly beautiful, serene, complete & richly satisfying always

Robert

*   *   *   *   *

10:30PM Sunday August 20, 1944

My dearest -

. . . Took a bus ride about 6 miles out thru the country & then came back & I said goodbye to Raymond rather thankfully. He's a good sort, but rather empty once he's exhausted his conversation about the city here. His conception of the world, of politics, of labor, of religion was all quite vague, indefinite, in fact hardly even

428

thot of, other than that the world isn't quite what it could be. His conception of art, literature, music, science, etc., nil. Just a poor toiling blob of flesh, a soggy brain, smiling ludicrously in helpless hope for a happy, bounteous life.

I noted one thing here today which was quite striking, which illustrates with tangible clarity the reason for the backwardness of these people. There was near the art gallery a speaker of the Socialist party denouncing the parasitic upper crust of lords & ladies. Next to him was some loud ranting blabber mouth giving everyone the lowdown on the Catholic-Protestant situation. This petty religious nonsense drew a cluster of listeners 4 times as great as that of the Socialist. How precisely that illustrates the blind, wormlike mind of the masses, so grossly eager to raise themselves to a fictitious, childish heaven, or to explain their woes by intangible nonexistent forces of evil, rather than face the truth & reality of living & concern themselves with the bread in their mouths & the preservation of their one & only precious body & life.

Oh, my lovely one, I can hardly wait till that glorious instant when I see your gentle smiling face again, so happy & so in love & I can kiss you ravenously, with the deep hunger which only the lost, separated months of love & longing can bring. I will crush your graceful yielding body to me as a starving tree entangles its parched roots in the joyful nourishing earth, to quaff up the vitality of life.

Love,
Robert

*   *   *   *   *

10:15PM Monday August 21, 1944

My dearest -

. . . Spent several enjoyable hours in the library tonite. Found my S. Alexander's [A Glasgow philosopher] Gifford Lectures here on "Space, Time & Deity". It is a work in two volumes & well written, very original in some points, but I was in a way disappointed with it. Only had time to thumb thru it & read perhaps 50 — 60 pages, but from all I read his doctrine of emergent evolution has little more than an epistemological value. He merely classifies the cosmos into stages of evolution; matter emerging from space time, life from matter, mind from life, etc, and tho he brings out some highly interesting sidelights, his main tenets are little more than ponderous Kantian concepts brot up to date with relativity. One analogy I thot

429

quite good was where he said that Time was the Mind of Space just as Mind was the Time of the Body. That could be carried to some very deep channels with the relationship between the Mind & Time.

I haven't yet found a philosopher who approaches my materialistic or physical theory of thot (not that I've looked very hard). They all seem to look upon thot & the mind as a separate entity; emerged from matter perhaps, but not governed by it.

Before getting into Alexander I was also involved with a book by [Leo Viktor] Frobenius, the great German ethnologist, called "African Genius" in which he was tracing the links between African & European culture thru art & folklore. In his introduction he made some pungent & excellent remarks on the narrowness of modern living & its "newspaper" day to day existence. He said that the feeling & joy of life (Lebensgefühl) would be immensely expanded if men could only look upon themselves & their culture as a vast history of which they were a part, if they could only feel & comprehend this glorious ancient heritage which is their's & which makes them what they are; the forgotten years & eons of striving, of culture, the living of our innumerable ancestors.

*   *   *   *   *

9:30PM Saturday, August 26, 1944
To my lovely waiting wife, so soon to be crushed & kissed sweetly with all the arduous joy of love renewed, refound, replacing two months lost to futile longing. I am so happy, my darling one, to be returning now to all the glorious, ineffable beauty that is you. I come to you so eager with desire, so impatient for the tender soothing comfort of your caress. I have said it all so often, yet my feelings do not change, dearest, how then can I change the words with which I say "I love you".

Oh, darling, words are incapable of conveying the mute invisible throbs of pleasure & possession that seethes thru every nerve & fiber of our being as we lie lithely locked in the mutual eagerness of our living naked flesh, coiled & inextricably entwined in the wonder of our lust & love, my wife, Nor can they match that bubbling, blithe companionship which has the power to touch with its very casualness the most deep & inexplicable emotions of our soul; your sleepy smile, awakened from an afternoon nap, satisfied, refreshed, rested from our bout of love; your frown, concerned at breakfast with my lack of appetite; the dreamy, drowsy plans so hopeful in the darkness before we fall into close curled sleep; the fretful prompting at my lassitude in dressing; the pleading, vexing goads & persuasions with which you send me for a paper; the dainty, sensual way you sip your wine, libidinous glitter in your eyes; your sweetness & hearty lipstick kisses, so warm & full of girlish glee, when you come home, bringing all the sparkling happiness of the earth, to hug me when you find I've fixed our evening meal; the serene & mysterious beauty of your simple act of washing out my socks, so warm nakedly woman bending her graceful shoulders over the basin with devout unthinking wifeliness, attending sweetly to her husband's needs. The thousands of stolen kisses in the kitchen, the rich contentment of the intimacy with which my hands seek the smooth curves and sinews of your soft but sturdy body, treasure your nestled silken breasts, fingers laughing with male glee to feel your sinuous temptation as you walk & sway beside me. All these million little bits of life, so insignificant, so common, yet so completely glorious & eternal, which belong to us, which is us, & for all our life of love. In all these trifling instants of our togetherness there is somehow a beauty so priceless, so inexplicable, so keenly jubilant that we can only burst with speechless ecstasy at the thot of it and hug each other tighter, with kisses more full & lingering & little gasps of inchoate joy that we have this precious lifelong gift of each other. We can indulge ourselves boundlessly to sensuality or tenderness, all is ours in an inseparable bliss, our mated lives mutually possessed, mutually enjoyed. This is the most fascinating, rapturous paradise attainable and we have achieved it in the complete beauty of our marriage.

Oh, my sweet one! Sometimes I know you accuse me of over accentuation of our sexual roles, of our sensual, carnal combination. But beloved, what else in all our life & all our marriage can so faithfully coalesce our joyous unity than can these instants of incomparable communion. Quivering shafts of pleasure that race hotly thru all the pores of our flesh, your lovely naked back arched over my stroking hand, your hair long, clean & resilient, fragrant and soft as the meadow's pliant grass, your lips as fresh & sweet as dew-moistened clover in a field at dawn, firm & full with the keen, turbid pulse of life. Therein comes forth the ripe fecundity of the earth, subtle within your soul, prompting the thrusting glide of your rhythmic hips, sucking eagerly the ecstasy from my trembling loins till I must burst with desire; your body tensed & vibrant, curved & taut like a harp, throbbing, clinging, grasping in fierce female lust each glorious second of my virile movement within your womanwarmth. Your eyes shut, breathless, savoring this wild &

ageless rite, a choked cry of relief as senses burst in passionate sur-render, a dehiscence of delight flooding every nerve & sinew of our being as now, in delicious relaxation, our teeming juices mingle & flow in viscous perfection, bodies blending in indescribable bliss. Oh, only in this wordless rhapsody of mated flesh & soul can the full enchanted beauty of our lives come near to actual expression, only in those intense moments, so mutually experienced, can all the broad complexity of our happiness & love be condensed and con-summated in one vivid symbolic unity.

*   *   *   *   *

1PM Tuesday August 29, 1944

My darling -

I date this Tuesday, tho I am not sure. This voyage is a dateless, disgusting duration. There is not a moment that is not of interminable length, heavy with drear monotony & discomfort. I am so sick from boredom & lassitude, from the stinking, close packed hold of the ship, the foul chilling wind & weather, the constant roll & pitch of this slow lumbering vessel & its continual jiggle, jiggle, jiggle like an old Ford shuddering up a hill, and its filth & utter aridity of anything warm, comfortable or clean. I have a raw sore throat & a room with no port on the tween deck, in which are 5 other officers & an omnipresent haze & stench of cigar & cigarette smoke till the very sheets on which I have to sleep reek with this stale unpleasant smell & air comes over my throat with a rasping irritation in stuffy difficult gasps of unpleasantness. No place to sit down, no place to read or write, my clothes & toilet articles piled in a jumble on the floor, a latrine with two wash basins for 50 men & a shower with only plain cold seawater & no soap. Except for the food & the privilege of going on deck in this miserable North Atlantic weather I might just as well be going back as a prisoner. My brain seems pulverized with the nauseous, barren distastefulness of this existence, till I could vomit at this damnable jiggle, jiggle, jiggle, the dull moist stench of the hold, the rough sunless seas & the waiting, waiting, waiting as we plod slowly back to America & its tantalizing promise of warmth, cleanliness, comfort & love.

*   *   *   *   *

10:30PM Friday Sept. 1, 1944

. . . Have read a great deal of "Ulysses" over again & find the book much more enjoyable now that I am thoroly familiar with what is taking place in it. However, I've changed a few of my opinions & ideas about it. I still believe it to be one of the finest, best written books in the English language, but it is like an opera in a foreign tongue, if you don't know the story, you're rather lost with the thing except for the beauty of the music, in this case the writing; but there is a great deal of "technical harmonic" to be appreciated in this book & for the average reader it is far too abstruse to be appreciated or even understood. Moorish, French, Italian, Latin, Jewish, German, Hindustani, Irish and Old English is a bit too much for any reader, tho the phrases in these languages are not too important in the book. However, the thing is just too recondite for the common reader, even in its more simple sections, for Joyce seems to take a cryptographer's pleasure in garbling the language, the scene sequence, the characters & the whole pattern of the book; till, to the uninitiated, the whole thing is just a hodge-podge of words & fragments. Yet it really is the most closely integrated & realistic book ever written!

. . . Something I wanted to mention, dearest, the slight character differences in us which keep costing us occasional arguments & which, if we continue, could really cause unhappiness. It is so clear to each of us what these things are, and how they operate, & we should therefore be able to iron out our lifestyle quite easily. Here is what happens. I have just an ever so slight disdain for money, perhaps a minute strain of extravagance. You have a minor tendency towards penny pinching & miserliness, a taint of acquisitiveness. Alone, neither of our traits would be harmful to us individually, but together we notice the characteristics of the other & try to convert the other to our way of thinking, & in so doing we overaccentuate our own tendencies in seeking to oppose what we consider a deficiency in the other's character. In other words, I oppose your miserliness by example of my own extravagance, & you seek to compensate for what you consider a failing in me by being extra acquisitive. This sort of thing is rather silly when seen in this lite, but the trouble is when we are actually performing this little tug of war to get the other over the fence, we are blind to what we are really doing. Let us both remember this when we start arguing on a street corner about taking a taxi & let us both remember that we are both thrifty by nature & experience & well versed in the meaning of money. Some of our other arguments have little more foundation, such as my walking out on you in a theater, or falling asleep in the evening, but those things are only normal frictions which we will always have & overlook after they have passed, but anything which seems to grow habitual or threatens to develop into a silent, continual battle of principles we must seek out its cause & by its exposure, end it.

Oh, but darling, I have no fear of our strife ever becoming any more than a stimulating battle of angry wit's, & tho the part of reconciliation has so far fallen almost wholly to you, I am learning, sweetheart and will someday, perhaps, have as sweet a disposition as you; but may I never nag! You are the most adorable, pestiferous nagger & I threaten here and now to halt abruptly the first intimation that we should visit your cousins. I'll stifle you with a thousand kisses.

*   *   *   *   *

Sun 27 Aug - I Begin to Pack - Got all of Doty's stuff in my pullman case. Deciding to go very light myself this time, but guess I'll have to take both cases. If I only knew how long I'd stay, then I could plan for it.

Mon 28 Aug - I Get Myself "Resigned" - I've been invited to come back to the Com if & when I get back. So home to find long letter from Doty telling of his sightseeing (in Scotland - Holyrood Palace?) & again telling me to be in NYC before Sept 1st. Well, I'm resigned as of tomorrow & expect to take the train Wed aft. Just hope I find us a place to stay & that we have a pleasant reunion. I am so thrilled.

Tue 29 Aug - My Last Day at C.S.C. - Home to find wire from Mrs Mac telling me our "old" room will be ready for us. Sent a wire to Mrs Mac re my arrival Friday.

Wed 30 Aug - My 3rd Wedding Anniversary - I stay Home & Loaf - Slept till 11:30, thot of my stupidity in resigning as of August 29th, a whole day before me to be wasted. Ironed a blouse, read my magazine, interested by the modern home designs. Waited for some word from Robert but no letter or wire came. By the end of the evening I was one very sad, lonely little gal. Do wish Robert arrives as planned & that we have a long reunion this time.

Thu 31 Aug - I Leave for New York - Slept til 10. After breakfast the mail came, with it a letter from Marcella stating John Flaherty wanted me to call him at Knoxville, Tenn re a job in

Chicago. So I did <u>collect</u> & learned that about Sept 11 a small office will be opened in the Civic Opera Bldg for Manhattan Engineers Labor Relations. Said he could get me $2300. Told him I was en route to NYC & had resigned my job with Civil Service & he suggested I get in touch with him when I get back. Got me settled in a window seat in the Trail Blazer & everything would have been fine except for my seat partner, a Philadelphia Lawyer who reeked of alcohol & tobacco.

Fri 1 Sept 1944 - I arrive in New York - Got out to MacDonald's about 11:30 & found Mrs Mac expecting me. Still in hopes Robert will come, as he said, on Sept 1st!

Sat 2 Sept - I start waiting for Doty - Do wonder why he doesn't come in. Do you suppose his plans miscarried & he's not coming? Oh -

Sun 3 Sept - Am getting a bit bored with this waiting & if it's his idea of a joke, t'aint funny. Oh, well - maybe he'll come in tomorrow, I hope.

Mon 4 Sept - Disgusted with Waiting - I am truly angry at Robert & I don't think it's funny at all to be twiddling my thumbs here when I could be doing something useful back home. No word from him, no nothing, how long does he think I'm going to wait like this. At 9 PM I am utterly fed up with the whole thing! [Seems I am not the only member of the pair with a short fuse!]

Tue 5 Sept - Robert Arrives! - Robert calling to the MacDonald's. He had come in the convoy from Ireland, gotten a lift from a Red Cross truck to 42nd St and came straight out here. My darling with a moustache again which he'll have to shave off in a day or so. To Penn Station to pick up the 2 bags I had checked thru. While en route we stopped at a Liquor Store to buy a quart of dubonnet & then ran smack into a practice air raid alarm. Took "refuge" in the station & got our bags out before the all clear sounded.

Wed 6 Sep - Day off - Left after 12 for Macy's, to buy all the books Robert wanted: Joyce's "Finnegan's Wake", "Portrait of a Young Man" & "Dubliners", also Proust's "Swann's Way", total $6.69. So then we rode to Radio Music Hall to see "Dragon Seed", including a Music Hall version of Chopin's "Les Sylphides". . . . We both agreed that we had a very satisfying day, a sort of belated celebration of our 3rd Wedding Anniversary.

Thu 7 Sep - Said Mewborn [my C.O. at NYPOE] is now a Major & would like to keep Doty with him. So I am impatient as to what will be the outcome of that. Robert got him a hair cut while I watched - my 1st such experience.

Fri 8 Sep - **Robert gets LEAVE till Mon** - We ate, dropped his shoes off to be half-soled & rode out to the library where he looked up words in Oxford's English Dictionary while I leafed thru 4 issues of Vogue.

Sat 9 Sep - **Museum of Modern Art - Newsreel** - To Museum of Modern Art, seeing 2 OWI documentary films; also Toscanini in "Hymn of the Nations", a fine exhibit of photography, & new paintings. After a snack at The Salvation Army Canteen, we went on to the Radio City newsreel theater to see pictures of liberation of Paris.

Sun 10 Sep - **Metropolitan Museum** - Saw some Russian icons, a chessman exhibit & some modern paintings. Sat in Central Park, walked to Hector's Cafeteria on Bdway where we gorged ourselves. Home early. Having late snack. Dubonnet & to bed at midnite.

Mon 11 Sep - **Robert gets assignment** - Says the SS Rosemont is a reefer (refrigeration ship) & he'll get orders Thu., destination probably Cherbourg. Question now whether to stay here or go home. We went to see Frederic March in "Mark Twain".

Tue 12 Sep - **Rains all Day - We Loaf** - We discussed pro & con the idea of my returning to Chicago or remaining here, as this trip should take only 5 weeks. Problem of how & where to get an apartment. Both of us weary of all this inactivity. We did have a quarrel when Robert said I couldn't wait until I got home to Mommy & I said perhaps he was right. So we fell asleep on this sour note.

Wed 13 Sep - **Rains all Day** - In spite of the torrents coming down, we went shopping & bot fruits & groceries. Spent several hours on the front porch reading. To NY City Center for the ballet. Serenade, music by Tschaikowski - didn't care much for the choreography 2) Scheherazde - delightful 3) Red Poppy - music by Gliere, very good & new to us both. Still not decided as to

436

whether I stay or go home. I think I'd rather go home & come back.

Thu 14 Sep - Hurricane on its Way - Slept till noon. Rain started again this aft & a rising wind. NY alerted for the hurricane scheduled to hit this evening. Robert went on the ship today. The hatches were battened down & extra mooring lines added in view of the approaching storm. Spent some time on the porch watching the wind blow & the water creep up by degrees till it reached the 2nd step of the front porch by 9 PM. Esta was at a movie & came back looking like a drowned rat about 8 PM. Many trees must've been uprooted by the 90 mph wind & the Mac's basement was flooded. A night to remember!

Fri 15 Sep - M - Buy RR Ticket - Evidence of last night's storm was everywhere, trees torn out, broken branches, mud on the sidewalks. Down to Penn Station to buy my ticket for Thu the 21st. Went to the Newsreel Theater. Saw some interesting pictures of Paris, one on Mexico. Interesting to note the "boos" which greeted the reels on Dewey's campaign speechmaking.

Sat 16 Sep - M - Went to Times Square to see the Artkino picture "1812", also 2 other films, one "Moscow Circus". The film broke & we had a half-hour wait, but all in all we enjoyed the feature film. The Russian was deliberate & very understandable.

Sun 17 Sep - M - Robt back about 10:30 to say orders had been received to stop loading. Results of Quebec Conference to push the Pacific Theater? Anyway, we had the day to ourselves & spent most of it loafing in our room.

Mon 18 Sep - M - We Go Sightseeing Lower New York - Robert says the ship is not being loaded today either. Went out to Manhattan, getting off at Chambers St & walking thru Chinatown, the Italian Quarter (where the streets were festooned with the lights for the celebration of St Rocco's feast) & the Washington Square neighborhood & into Greenwich Village where we stopped for a beer & coke.

Tue 19 Sep - Robert gets new assignment - Robert got a new assignment on a C-2 [faster "Victory" ship instead of the older "Liberty"] which is just beginning to load. The darling was gone all day & didn't return till after 6 PM. We stayed in and Robert & I read a bit of Russian. Decided that I remain here until he leaves. - My

437

Photo Section 2

54 - 28 September 1947, Elizabeth and 21-month-old Robert Jr, one of my more successful artistic endeavors. Newly applied wallpaper in background was subsequently decorated with extensive brown crayon scribblings by one of the subjects (17 July 1948), which we were able to conceal with a leftover piece.

55 - The fence RWD built at 3506, to enclose our extra "half lot" of space, and keep Robert Jr within bounds.

56 - More "art". The book, Lalla Rookh, belonged to Robert's great grandfather, and was famous in its time in that the author, Thomas Moore, had received £3000 for his poem even before he began it. But perhaps the lines: "That Prophet ill sustains his holy call,
Who finds not heavens to suit the tastes of all."
are worth it, relevant even now in the minds of suicidal terrorists!

57 - The traditional Doty form of Jack-O-Lantern that RW learned from his father. (See entry 29 October 1948.)

58 - 24 June 1951, mother and 4-month-old Mary Elizabeth.

59 - Spring 1949, the brand new Hudson in front of 3506.

60 - 25 August 1951, in Rocky Mountain National Park, on our way to a new life in Utah.

61 - 25 August 1951, in the mountains, that we never got to visit in 1943 during our brief interlude at Fort Warren, Wyoming.

62 - 4148 South 20th East, Salt Lake City, Utah, the home we bought and lived in from 4 October 1951 to 27 August 1956. Note the fence, and daughter Mary at the window.

63 - Mount Olympus, a view we had from out picture window at 4148.

64 - Christmas 1951, Robert Jr and Mary Beth enjoying our new home. Brothers just have to put up with sisters attacking their horsemen.

65 - Mary Elizabeth aglow after her bath, 25 November 1951.

66 - November 1951, RW testing Sheba's vision. Faraday cage in background, used for electrophysiological experiments.

67 - RW's cat colony on a Utah mountainside behind his lab at the medical school.

68 - The little family in front of Northwood Apartments, University of Michigan, Ann Arbor, where the Dotys resided for 17 months, September 1956 to 23 January 1958.

69 - 2222 Needham Road, Ann Arbor, the home we finally built, and lived in until 2 October 1961. We lost $5,000 on its sale when we left for Rochester.

70 - 96 Grosvenor Road, Rochester, New York, our home from October 1961 until 1 May 1979. The snow conceals the barberry hedge we planted, to keep the dogs out and the children in.

71 - The setting for our final years, the house we built, 1978-79, surrounded by farm and forest near Rochester, New York.

72 - Staking out our newly purchased land, December 1977.

73 - Planting our second Christmas tree, January 1981, as we continued with the landscaping of our palace. The tree now rises a majestic 40 feet.

74 - Squire Doty in his 60th year.

75 - Constant visitors to our "estate", and the subject of much excitement during hunting season.

76 - Bounty of nearby Seneca Lake, a good catch of northern pike, November 1983.

77 - 70-year-old woodchopper preparing for winter.

78 - Yosemite, October 1987. The light for us was not quite as "eloquent" as for Ansel Adams; but we had only two days.

79 - Sabino Canyon, Arizona, March 1967.

80 - Inveterate diarist, recording the events as we clambered about Mount Hood, Oregon, August 1972.

81 - Blackhead, County Clare, Ireland, 11 August 1977 - only ocean between us and America.

82 - Long Meg, England - the megalith that the poet, Wordsworth, commanded "Speak, great Mother!", a mystery of the ages.

83 - 11 September 1965, immersion in Japanese custom, at ryokan (Japanese style inn) near Mt Fuji.

84 - The beauty of Fuji San. No wonder it is held sacred. Photographed in 1969, this time with my new Hasselblad.

85 - Kinkakuji, world famous Japanese "tea house" in Kyoto, that conveys an extraordinary sense of serenity.

86 - In Japan again, Mount Daisetsu San in Hokkaido, 26 October 1981. When we came down from the ski lift, we were surprised that our host, Professor Shigemi Mori awaited us. He had driven 50+ km from Asahikawa, confident that he could find us by asking if any Caucasians had been seen!

87 - Our hotel room in Tbilisi, Soviet Georgia, overlooking the Kura River, 27 May 1973.

88 - View of St Basil's Cathedral and the Kremlin from our room, one of the 6000 (!) in the Hotel Rossiya, Moscow, 20 May 1973.

89 - St Basil's at night. It was built 1554-60 by Ivan the Terrible outside the walls of the Kremlin after defeat of the tatars made such exposure safe.

90 - 3 June 1973, Odessa. High school student honor guard marches past the "Memorial to the Heroes", who died in the prolonged defense of the city from the Nazi horde.

91 - The Taj Mahal, justifiably reputed as the most beautiful building in the world. Built by Shah Jahan, 1632-47 as a memorial to his wife of 19 years. For the last 8 years of his life the Shah beheld the Taj only from a distance of a mile, imprisoned by the son of that wife.

92 - Reception for the International Physiological Congress, New Delhi, 24 October 1974.

93 - Elizabeth relaxing in our "water taxi", Srinigar, Kashmir.

94 - The trials of travel, doing "laundry" in the International Guest House, University of Calcutta, 3 November 1974.

95 - The living room on our houseboat in the Vale of Kashmir, Srinigar, 27 October 1974.

96 - The gods accept the proffered food; temple at Katmandu, Nepal, 7 November 1974.

97 - Elizabeth mounting elephant for journey to our Tiger Tops lodge in the Chitwan Game Preserve, Nepal, 8 November 1974.

98 - Sightseeing for crocodiles on the Rapti River, Chitwan Game Preserve.

99 - Morning fog, searching for tigers, Chitwan Game Preserve.

100 - Ama Dablam, companion of Mt Everest, as photographed from the grounds of the Everest View Hotel at 13,500 ft, 12 November 1974.

101 - Ruins of the "Temple of Neptune", Paestum, Italy, 18 April 1977. The temple, built ca 500 BC, was part of the civilization of Magna Graecia of southern Italy. The words reflect my thoughts when photographing, or contemplating, this beautiful human achievement.

102 - Beauty in the wild, a milkweed pod on our land.

103 - The leaning tower in early morning, Pisa, 12 April 1977.

104 - Two of my research subjects, *Macaca nemestrina,* interested in what the crazy photographer will do next.

105 - Termite nest outside our cottage at Lake Baringo, Kenya, 16 July 1984. The metabolic heat rising from the chimney was so intense as to be uncomfortable to the hand!

106 - Free supper. At dusk the termite queens emerge by the hundreds for their maiden flight and the birds are well aware of the feast this offers.

107 - Implacable and impartial; two of a group of four whose unsuccessful hunt we were privileged to watch. Tired, they chose to rest in front of our vehicle. Amboseli National Park, Kenya, 20 July 1984.

108 - In Mama's shadow; Amboseli, Mount Kilimanjaro obscured in the background.

109 - Elizabeth at 72, 3 January 1988.

110 - Robert at 68, 3 January 1988.

111 - From the stone walls on our land the rock that serves to commemorate Elizabeth's genius and dedication in creating our home.

112 - Elizabeth would have enjoyed this trip, to Yunnan, but it would have been unduly strenuous in her later condition, and did not quite measure up to our previous adventures (above). Here at Woolong Panda Research Center, Sichuan Province, China, the juvenile panda was indifferent to the proceedings and continued to munch its sugar cane; 22 May 2000. The weighty Hasselblad had been abandoned for a Kodak 265 digital camera, downloaded to laptop computer each evening.

55

56

57

58

59

60

61

62

63

64

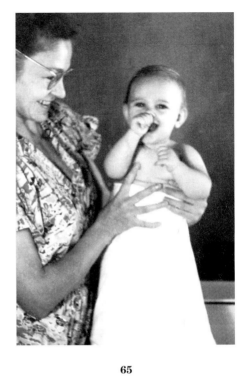

65

66

67

68

69

70

71

73

72

74

77

76

75

79

80

78

83

84

85

86

87

88

89

90

91

92

93

94

95

96

97

98

99

100

101

Hands of worship,
Which wrought indurate stone,
Graceful, to catch the sun's kiss;
Ancestral they to mine,
Flesh of vanished flesh?

102

104

106

105

107

108

109

110

IN LOVING MEMORY OF
ELIZABETH NATALIE DOTY,
NÉE RADZUN-JUSEWICH
23 NOV 1915 – 18 APR 1999
MAY THE BEAUTY OF HER GARDEN FOREVER
REFLECT THE BEAUTY OF HER LIFE

111

112

darling & I can be so happy & we are so in love. Sometimes I wonder why I persist in putting real or imagined obstacles in the way of our being together as much as possible in these times.

Wed 20 Sep - I call Flaherty re job - I got up this morning with the resolution that I call Flaherty & find out if that $2300 job was still open. Placed my collect call after breakfast & got him about 1:30 PM. Said to mail him a Form 57 when I return to Chicago. We went to Lin Fong's on Flatbush to have lobster with egg sauce and chow mein. Walking home both stuffed. Had dubonnet & candy, wrote letters. Canceled reservation for tomorrow and got one for next Thursday. To bed about 1 AM, but what do we care about time when we're together on a reunion like this?

Thu 21 Sep - I pick up my Reservation - Again I sleep till noon while RWD leaves for work at 7:30 AM. . . . Stayed in & did nothing but read and loaf till bedtime. Sometimes I get angry at Robert's ability to fall asleep before I feel like retiring. [!! See first sentence!]

Sun 24 Sep - We Pack Up - Robert home about 10:30 & after breakfast & reading the news, we got our stuff all packed. Sad to think we'll have to part in a few days.

Mon 25 Sep - Mix up in getting the Army truck to take my 2 bags to Penn Station & when we parted we didn't know if he'd be back. But he called about noon & said he'd be home. Robert fell asleep while I was setting my hair. Went to bed about 11:30 a wee bit piqued at Robert for falling asleep so early in the evening & just ignoring me.

Wed 27 Sep - Robert has Day off - Yom Kippur today so the town seemed deserted. We visited the Museum of Modern Art & saw 1923 movie, Wm Hart in "Wild Bill Hickok". Then Robert had to make a phone call to check on where his ship was anchored, & where the convoy conference would take place. That done, we spent an hour or so at the Guggenheim non-objective Museum.

Thu 28 Sep - I Leave for Chicago - Parted without much show of emotion altho I felt like crying.

*　　*　　*　　*　　*

Armed Service Forces, United States Engineer Office

Wednesday, 11 October 1944 [Note start of "Army style" dating.]
Dear Robert -

It's almost two weeks since our last reunion ended in Brooklyn, but it seems such a long, long time already. I started missing you the moment we parted in Penn station. Guess I came as close to having a good cry right there in public as I ever have, and it was with a sinking feeling in my stomach that I sat there those two interminably long hours before train time. I remember worrying about you, whether you got caught in the rain, whether you'd make it all right to the ship, and, then again I worried as to how we'd work it for our next reunion. It was with an indefinably sad feeling that I got on the train & watched the landscape go buy.

My train trip was fairly comfortable until we got to Harrisburg, where they changed the Diesel engine & we got the coal burning locomotive put on. Then, I swear, I couldn't have gotten more seasick on a boat. The train rocked and lurched and bumped; it was all I could do to eat my evening meal in the diner.

Train was on time. As I came into the station I looked for Mom & couldn't see her. Instead, a tall hunk of Navy blue stepped forward to meet me, and it was my big bro Max! He is as big as a "destroyer" and took me over, bag & baggage. He got into Chicago Tuesday before I arrived (Friday) and didn't have to report back to Great Lakes till Thursday of the following week.

I unpacked my bags (& Mom got busy laundering almost all of my washables) & stowed everything away; then took a bath & got to bed about 2 PM. Oh, darling, was it a delicious feeling to sink into the soft mattress after that night on the train & those weeks of Victory bed discomfort!

Maybe I should tell you about my job. It seems that I am back in my grade of Clerk Caf-6 salaried $2300 per annum. As you probably know, the Manhattan District is a hush-hush thing & functions more or less independently of the Corps of Engineers. I think I'll like it, right now we're still on temporary setup & won't begin to function until a Capt Stagg gets here from New York. We were on the 54 hour week all last week, but as of this past Monday we returned to the 48-hour week.

I had to have a medical certificate filled out for this Civil

Service appointment & went to see Dr. Buky, who fitted me with the diaphragm. I am hale & hearty, my blood pressure is down to 110 (??! Can it be always about 130) & I'm up to 141 lbs! She gave me a cursory vaginal exam, but couldn't tell whether I'm enceinte or not. I'm due to be that way today or tomorrow, so we'll see. Mom's been kidding me about practicing up on my sewing techniques so I can make my own "layette" when & if necessary.

*   *   *   *   *

Saturday 10PM - 14 October 1944

My Dearest -

. . . Precious, its 17 days since we parted, and now I'm beginning to get impatient for news from you. I'm emotionally upset after our partings, and I do have my melancholy moments, especially when menstruating. I do get such a longing for you, dear, and I do feel neglected when I ache all over and you're not around to "bully" me into forgetting my physical discomfort. I do get so sentimental & romantic when you're away, guess I exaggerate your good points & minimize your failings; and I feel like such a smug, proudly possessive wife. I try to imagine what you are doing & what experiences you are undergoing. Where are you & are you in danger, & when will you be coming back, etc., etc.; & then I get such an irrepressible desire to have you back here with me as soon as possible.

*   *   *   *   *

[Typewritten]

Wednesday, 18 October 1944

Dear Darling:

Oh, what a joy to come home last night and find a letter from you! I was a little surprised, however, to learn that you are in England, did you get your signals mixed up, or did you just kid me that you were going to France? Now I have a growing apprehension that you might be in the south of England where those damn Nazis have been sending their robot bombs; and I do worry for your safety, dearest.

443

Encouraged by the middling success I've had with my first blouses, I started on a short-sleeved tailored blouse in white rayon satin. Cut it out Monday night and last nite got half-through putting it together. Have hopes of making my third blouse before you get back to the states, for I'd love to have you see my handiwork in this respect.

It's been interesting to spend a whole evening just sewing, for I've been listening to the campaign speeches on the radio, and that has been more fun than listening to Bob Hope. Harold Ickes really dubbed Dewey rightly when he called him the "Chocolate Soldier" in his speech Monday night and refuted all of his "falsifications" one by one. Then right after him Dewey spoke from St. Louis, and he repeated again his statements that have been refuted (repetition makes even lies seem plausible, I guess) and tried to discredit the Roosevelt foreign policy by stating that bickering at home means bickering abroad, etc. I can't get used to his dramatic way of talking!

. . . . Now you've gotten me started thinking about your homecoming may be? I can't go to New York this time (that's for sure) and I don't want you to go AWOL again, darling...... promise me you won't do anything RASH! If we can't see each other this time, I think we should accept it philosophically and look forward to the next trip. Robert, dearest, I shall be very angry if you endanger your status in the Army in any way......... and I do want you to get your promotion, precious........ SOooooooooooooooooo

I enjoyed your letter very much, it's a shame you have to pick such awful roommates. I know how annoying it is to live with a messy person in a small room. Haven't I been doing that with my dear sister Bess?

I'm sorry to disappoint you about becoming a papa this time..... I don't think so, and frankly I'm a little disappointed — but perhaps it's for the best. I had my menses in the normal time and all..... Better luck next time!

* * * * *

[Handwritten]

444

My Precious -

Oh, dearest, I am such a lonely little girl without you. I guess that keeping busy at something as much as possible is all that keeps me from going to pieces when I look back at those two long years that we've been separated, & try to hazard a guess as to the length of time that must elapse before this war ends & we can begin to look forward to a constant reunion. The best opinion is that the war with Japan will go on for 18 mos or 2 years after Germany is defeated & that brings us into 1946 already; and how much longer would it be before you will be coming home? But I try not to dwell too much on thots like this, & I kid myself along by thinking of each day gone as bringing us that much closer to the day when we'll be reunited for good. Oh, I do love you, Robert, for you are always present in my thoughts, my daydreams; and I do have my memories of such sweet moments together.

Today while sewing I listened to Marian Anderson on the RCA program, & heard Toscanini play Beethoven's 1st & 8th, and I was reminded of our Sundays at 1001 Mayfield when we reveled in long drawn out dinners & good music! How distant that all seems, & the tears come to my eyes & my heart seems more burdened with sadness, and I wonder if we'll ever be able to recapture the thrills of our meals together, our delightful bedroom scenes. I think yes, for I feel that these months of separation have only served to deepen my love for you, and I gained an understanding of the suffering every woman must endure without her mate, and I just want to make up for all lost time that has been denied us. My love for you has been strengthened, idealized and has become more than the romantic passion that first drew me to you. I know you feel the same way, my beloved. It is that love for you and the implicit faith that it can survive the time & distance that separate us that gives me the incentive to endure whatever discomfort & loneliness the future may bring.

But I mustn't give you the impression that I am very moody or depressed, for I don't permit myself that. I have my job, I'm cultivating my former art at dressmaking, and I'm reading books, magazines & newspapers & taking a keen interest in current events. I'm starting a scrapbook of ideas for our "Home, Sweet Home" & planning & plotting for our postwar future.

Dearest, I hope the future will bring us as much luck & happiness as the past, and I do love you with all my heart and soul.

Always yours,
Elizabeth

*   *   *   *   *

Thu 2 Nov - Ugh - Wotta Day! - The War Dept business gets on my nerves. Oppenheimer [He was the chief scientist in production of the atomic bomb.] spent the whole day making personal phone calls, using our office facilities & getting me to type up application forms for him. Lt Govero also got on my nerves. Boy, today I could have quit with no compunction.

*   *   *   *   *

5 November 1944

My Precious One -

This past week brought me three letters from you, your letters of 10/15 & 10/23 arrived Monday, & yesterday your letter of 10/19 came, explaining how you got off the ship & went to London.

I feel so nervous & all keyed up, & I know that is due in part to this damn political campaign. Boy, how I hate these Deweyites & their lies about dangers from Communism & the foreign-born if FDR is re-elected! The President has been in fine form, making dignified speeches as befits the office of Chief Executive. But Dewey has been hysterical in his role of "Prosecuting Attorney" & his running mate, Bricker, is a rabble rouser! The heck of it is we won't know the final results for weeks afterwards, as some state has set the deadline for soldiers' votes as Dec. 16! In any event, I've made up my mind to open a bottle of dubonnet, win or lose, Tues nite!

Darling, I've written you weekly, but you've been in my mind & heart every moment since you left. Hurry back.

Love
Betty

446

$$*\quad*\quad*\quad*\quad*$$

Tue 7 Nov - M - Election Day - Slept till 7:30 AM. After breakfast went to vote, straight Democratic! Got to work about ½ hr late. Found out Lt Govero voted for Thomas, a Socialist.

Wed 8 Nov - M - FDR Re-elected! - When I got up, Dad had already gotten the Chicago Sun whose headline read: "Oh what a Beautiful Morning - It's FDR Again!" And so it was. The standing now FDR leading in 35 states with 415 votes; Dewey in only 13 states.

Thu 9 Nov - M - Robert called at 10:30 PM from New York. Says he'll try to get leave & might be in Sun a.m. So excited to hear from him, now I'll be in agony until I know he's coming.

Fri 10 Nov - M - Robert gets promoted! - Finally home & finding a very long letter describing Robert's trip home, his contacts with German & Russian prisoners of war enroute on the ship, but no word as yet (7:30 PM). Wire (collect) arrived 8 PM as follows: "Permanent shore job pending for a newly promoted first lieutenant, rank as of Nov 2. Love, Robert".

Sat 11 Nov - Waited nervously all day for some word from Robert but none came. About 8 PM phone call from Robert calling from New York to say the assignment on Staten Isl looks permanent & for me to get to NY by Sat. I tried to argue with Robert, pointing out Capt Stagg's absence, Lt Govero's absence & the classified nature of my job, but we ended up by my telling him I'd write him.

Sun 12 Nov - Spec Del letter today outlining his promotion details & his assignment on Staten Island. Robert's folks came over this evening & we discussed things. They caution me to move slowly.

$$*\quad*\quad*\quad*\quad*$$

[Another crisis over her job!]

Sunday, 12 November [1944]

Robert dearest -

We did have a "noisy" session via long distance last nite & you certainly sounded "high, wide & handsome"; which picqued me a bit; for after your enigmatic wire of Friday I didn't know whether you'd be coming to Chicago or not. For all I knew you might be en route to the West coast or something. I had waited nervously all Saturday for word from you, & it just irked me when you sounded so happy and hilarious when you called.

But briefly, here is my predicament: Capt Stagg left Wed for a 3 week assignment in the East. I talked to him Fri about time off if you came in to Chgo & he said I could take all my accrued leave (3 days now). I may talk to him Mon at NY & will try to tactfully explain the situation. However, Lt Flaherty at Oak Ridge, Tenn is the guy I'll be "letting down" & I don't like to explain things after giving him my assurances that I'd be status quo in Chicago. Will ask for transfer to New York if possible, but as your letter said, it's highly improbable. I shall write you tomorrow immediately after I have an idea as to when I can get away, but <u>please</u> be patient & please be sure that we have a place to stay when I get in to NY, for it's a bogey here trying to get hotel rooms for our visiting officers.

Fly in the appointment is the fact that Lt Govero left Fri to get married & will be honeymooning till next Fri. That leaves only Millie Smith, who doesn't take shorthand & doesn't type much. Please try to understand that I'll do my best to do as you wish, but <u>don't call</u> daily just to hurry me up, for I don't want to impose on Mrs Galinsky's good nature re phone calls. This job of mine is one of those "classified" things. Phooey!

You're right that I'm reluctant to leave my folks alone. Mom is very much broken up that I won't be home for Thanksgiving (also my birthday, please note) & we had so planned on having you here for dinner today.

Crazy sort of letter, but I thot I better write you that I am trying to arrive at the right solution. In any event, dearest, don't let your "silver bars" get the best of your judgment & don't do anything rash, darling.

If you find out that this thing is not permanent, I warn you, I'm not going to lose face by coming back to Chicago to get another job. I shall be a lady of leisure & just sew me oodles of things, for I've discovered I like it. Brings out the creative side of

me. Incidentally, sewed me a white satin dickey today while trying to soothe my troubled mind.

The foregoing may not reveal it, but I love you so, darling, &
am impatient to be with you again & I sincerely hope that good
fortune is really smiling at us & that this will all work out as we
hope.

In the meantime, darling, be good & understanding & you'll
be hearing from me soon as I have something definite to report.

So lovingly
Betty

*   *   *   *   *

NOTICE: I may be on my way when you get this -
or a telegram may be - so don't call me, dearest -
Dearest -

I didn't write you Wed. for I had talked to you that evening
& I was so happy to hear you had a place for us to live & I returned downstairs to start making plans as to what I'd take, etc.

Thursday was an impatient day for me, as I waited for word
as to whether they'd OK my transfer down in "Dogpatch". [Oak
Ridge, site of the U_{238} gaseous diffusion plant for the A bomb material.] Had occasion to talk long distance to Flaherty & he wasn't
too unfriendly re my "walk out" here. Thu nite I really began
packing & I included the items you mentioned in your letters (except books & letters, no can do for space & from your diagram
we seem to have only one chest of drawers).

But today I really became irritated at the unavoidable red
tape in getting my transfer effected. Called Sgt Harris here at
Area, & Govero talked to Dogpatch & they all say it's going thru,
but nothing can be done to give me T/Rs until T/Os are received.
So, darling, there is a possibility that I won't be able to leave tomorrow as we planned. However, don't get all hot & bothered
for you'll only aggravate my own impatience at this delay & it
may be that I'll be able to leave tomorrow.

Don't you fret & rant & rave, pal, for it's worth waiting a
day or two to get $50 - $60 worth of transportation & I'd like to
make $200 a month for 5 or 6 months yet; after that? I don't care,

449

but dearest, please understand that I can't back out of this as it stands & I know it will work out OK.

Lovingly & expectantly

Elizabeth

P.S. Love you so, darlin' - It's so hard to be realistic at this time.

*   *   *   *   *

[A series of 9 or so letters of mine, noted in her diary, for the period October-November 1944 were probably lost, owing to her moving from Chicago to Brooklyn to join me. These would have been of the trip to Bristol on the Antinous, with return on a Navy ship carrying Russian "slave labor" POWs! She notes in her diary that I had visited London, and I distinctly remember the trip to "Wooky Hole", a paleolithic site in Wales, with ravens circling about the eerie place.]

CHAPTER XII
Shore Duty in Brooklyn

Synopsis - This 10-month interlude was such a welcome return to the year of domesticity we had enjoyed between our marriage and my leaving for the army two very long years ago. My duties were relatively light, although often of long hours (24 hours as duty officer, etc) and unpredictable. They involved training new officers, meeting incoming ships, inspecting outgoing ships, writing letters of commendation or promotion, even standing orders in German for POWs. By and large it was often boring and exasperating, but it kept me with my darling. We lived in a basement apartment in a Brooklyn row house [Figs 39-41]. She worked in Manhattan, and suffered the usual vagaries of weather and the New York subway system. We took frequent advantage of the cultural opportunities of the city, within the constraints of our thrift. (We never did get to the Metropolitan Opera.) Living on her income and putting all of mine into the bank, we continued accumulation of a sizable sum for our postwar life. The diary is reticent on many events, such as the bombing of Nagasaki, but most particularly as to our decision to start our family. It can be inferred, however, that this endeavor had been going on for some time, and was ultimately successful on the day of Roosevelt's death. The timing proved to be perfect, for her work with the Manhattan Project, culminating in the bombing of Hiroshima, could be terminated, as was the war, just as her pregnancy dictated that she should return to Chicago for the final months and delivery.

Sat 18 Nov - I Leave for New York - . . . in the office when at 4:45 Harris called to say my T.O. came thru & did I want to leave tonite? I said I did & so he got me a 10 PM Penn berth. Dad,

451

Mom, & Rich came along to see me off. Mom cried a bit. Felt a bit sad leaving them.

Sun 19 Nov - I arrive - 2 hours + late - . . . didn't get in till 7:30 PM. Robert met me & hustled me off pronto. Got out to our apartment & I really was very much pleased, for altho it's nothing fancy, it is livable & quite different. So I had a makeshift supper & got myself astounded by 3 different perfumes, a rayon Jersey, lounging pajamas & a nightgown. The sweet darling even had dubonnet wine.

Mon 20 Nov - Day No 1 - NY Office - Got up reluctantly at 6:30 AM. Robert rushed off at 7, I left after 7:30. Personnel had me make out more security questionnaires. Home in a downpour & without buying any food. Robert duty officer at BAB.

Wed 22 Nov - Back to work & did I have a lot of it! . . . trying to figure out our budget. Money just seems to flow thru our fingers.

Thu 23 Nov - My 29th Birthday - Thanksgiving - Got up for work as usual, had to wait over 15 min for subway & didn't get in till after 8:30. Maj Hill came in today & we were very busy with plans for the special recruitment program for "Y". Home fixing spaghetti for us, Doty had had a busy day, too.

Tue 28 Nov - Madhouse - All Day - Dear Robert left me this morning & I won't see him till Wed nite. Usual hectic get-a-way; so, so mad at the crowds on the subways! . . . sent a M.O. for the 14.30 Robert owed for the Antinous food bill. After work went to see 40 min showing of a War Dept film "Dec 7th", heartbreaking to see all the havoc wrought at Pearl Harbor that day almost 3 years ago!

Fri 1 Dec 1944 - Maj Hill announced that I had been transferred at my Caf-6 grade, which made me very happy of course, $30 more a month is not to be sneezed at.

Sat 2 Dec - Doty gets 282.50 (?) now & is going to arrange to send it all to the Bklyn Bk & we'll try to live on my salary hereafter.

Mon 4 Dec - Guggenheim Museum - . . . the eve lecture by Baroness Rebay at the Museum of Nonobjective Painting. The Baroness was not any different from her other lectures & the movies were the same with 2 exceptions.

Thu 7 Dec - M - Pearl Harbor 3rd Anniversary - Busier than ole heck at the office continuously. Robert bought a small radio for 39.00 & came up to the office about 4:40. So Capt. Stagg got to meet him.

Fri 8 Dec - M - Mailed out all our Xmas cards & also sent out Xmas pkgs.

Sat 9 Dec - M - Robert & I took in the News Theater at Rockefeller Center. Saw the huge Statue of Liberty created in Times Square for the 6th War Bond Drive.

Sun 10 Dec - It could have been a fine day. We went to "Carmen Jones" matinee performance. Only RWD wanted to go to the Museum of Modern Art which was crowded & we were hungry, and then we stopped at an automat which also was crowded & he left me. So we came home separately, and in a huff. He's fixing supper & burned my electric iron cord & I am furious. Gosh, I wish I was home with the folks.

Mon 11 Dec - So we made up a bit last nite. Robt starting on his instructing job & left me at 7:40 AM.

Thu 14 Dec - Robert on duty tonite - After a leftover supper I called Robert expecting to find him alone. Instead Lt Platt answered & when I talked to Robert he said the whole office was working tonite and that he might have to work tomorrow night.

Sun 24 Dec - Tomorrow Xmas, my 1st away from home.

Mon 25 Dec - "Peter the Great" - "The Golem" - Slept till 11, leisurely breakfast & then kidding around till 2 PM when we left for Union Square to see Russian movie based on story by Tolstoi, stupendous mass movements; & the other a bilingual (French & Yiddish). Home about seven to eat our lamb chops which were not too good. News that OPA is putting all meats & canned vegs on rationing list.

Thu 28 Dec - Robert reading Dos Passos & apparently enjoying it very much. We had a couple tall drinks & didn't get to bed till 1 AM. This going to bed late, will it never cease?

Sat 30 Dec - Crowded trains & I was very much disgusted by the time I got home. Found a letter from Dick which made me cry & sob on Robert's shoulder. Written Dec. 27: their training cut 2 weeks short & they were given orders, Dick had 4 days home, 4 days traveling. He had to report to Ft Meade by noon Sunday. Poor kid! He was bitter at this development. Says antitank is a suicide outfit & he's in it. I sobbed hysterically for a long while.

Quieted down to write ltr to Dick & Mom. Listened to radio with my darling. - Sad.

[On the final page of the diary is the following, densely written, copy of a MacLeish poem, so tellingly appropriate - and an echo of my efforts in my letters to capture the magic essence of our love:]

2/21/44 Bklyn

Unfinished History

We have loved each other in this time 20 years
And with such love as few men have in them even for
One or for the marriage month or the hearing of

Three nights cast in the street but it will leave them:
We have been lovers the 20th year now:
Our bed has been made in many houses and evenings:

The apple tree moves at the window in this hour:
There were palms rattled the night thru in one
In one there were red tiles and the sea's hours:

We have made our bed in the changes of many months - and
    the
Light of the day is still overlong in the windows
Till night shall bring us the lamp and one another:

Those that have seen her have no thought what she is:
Her face is clear in the sun as a palmful of water:
Only by nite & in love are the dark winds on it...

I wrote this poem that day when I thot
Since we have loved we two so long together
Shall we have done together - all love gone?

Or how then will it change with us when the breath
Is no more able for such joy & the blood is
Thin in the throat & the time not come for death?

Archibald MacLeish

Mon 1 Jan 1945 - So to work in a dreary drizzling gray morning, streets deserted, no express subway this morning. Maj Hill already in the office. . . . Washed out quite a bit of clothes. Listening to the radio, sipping dubonnet wine. Feel a bit uneasy at the beginning of another year, what will this year bring forth, more sorrow, or hope for final victory?

Wed 10 Jan - Robert is 25 today - Left office about 2:30 PM to go to the Brooklyn Chapter of the Amer Red Cross. Robert joined me about 3 PM & so we went thru processing. Both of us have "O" type blood & so our donation was in whole blood; others not "O" type give for plasma.

Mon 15 Jan - We Hear Serkin at Carnegie - Made my way home in an icky mood, but after our quick supper of leftover chicken we both felt enthused & left early for Carnegie Hall. Serkin played sonata by Beethoven beautifully, also Smetana Czech dances, Brahms, Chopin, but his Bach variations were a bore. [!]

Wed 17 Jan - WARSAW CAPTURED - Lazy Day - RWD on Duty - Home to a supper by myself. Very cheering to hear the Russians captured Warsaw after 5 yrs 4 mos slavery under the Nazis & that they are upon Cracow.

Thu 18 Jan - We Try to Shop - Called RWD this morn to tell him Mom sent us 140 red stamps, but he was annoyed at my call. Decided to meet at the Cabin Grill Restaurant. About 7 PM started shopping. Bought only a white tailored slip & 2 pr hose. Crowded & prices so high. We got angry at one another & separated to go home by ourselves. Angry because Doty bought photoflood lamp outfit for 3.00.

Fri 19 Jan - Robert coming home at 6:30 PM with a large bagful of groceries & meat, and he got rid of 60 red points.

Sat 20 Jan - News from the Eastern Front exceedingly good. We went up town to the Rockefeller Center newsreel theater. Bought our NY Times, home at 11 PM.

Sun 21 Jan - RWD helped to give the apt a good cleaning & we

455

had a luscious steak for dinner, listening to the Philharmonic. Washed & ironed several blouses & slips. Relaxed by reading the newspaper. Ate late, listened to the radio, to bed at midnite.

Thu 25 Jan - Subway Delay - Zero weather - Left at 8 AM but didn't get to the office till 9:50! The damn subway crawled & stalled & I stood in the crowded car trying to control my mounting indignation. . . . I do feel so woebegone today, so homesick & tired & ill, my sinus headache making me all the more irritated with everything. Robert on duty today & I won't see him till tomorrow evening.

Fri 26 Jan - Still Cold - but Milder - Got up okay in spite of Robert's absence, managed to get to work on time. Robert wanted to buy ballet tickets, but I demurred as we have already spent over $18 for amusement this month. Home, finding Robert fixing supper.

Tue 30 Jan - M - So RWD & I left for our respective jobs this AM without our usual parting kiss.

Sun 4 Feb - North half of Manila is ours - Up at 11:30. Had a good breakfast by myself. Trouble getting Doty up but we got to Mad Sq Gardens by 2:30 to see Sonja Heine's ice show. A bit tedious but okay, I guess - more people! Home, eating, mopping floors, drinking gin & dubonnet. Feel very blue and moody.

Tue 13 Feb - Brailowsky - Tired little gal with a bad head cold. Tonight a quick spaghetti supper & off for Carnegie Hall for a piano concert by Brailowsky. He was good but the concert didn't end till after 11 for he gave several encores. [Such different perceptions! I have very fond memories of this in that Brailowsky, in such warm contrast to the arrogant Rubinstein, gave encore after encore, stopping only when the management turned off the lights to let the help go home.] I felt very much nettled by the long subway ride & crept into bed right away.

Fri 16 Feb - We see "The Tempest" - Still have my bad cold & have been miserable with sniffles. Troubles today: the damn gas refrigerator on the blink giving off offensive odor. We complained to Malone & had to keep the window open in order to breathe. Robert had gone shopping at the commissary so we had fresh liver. Left to see Shakespeare's "The Tempest". Good but nothing spectacular. We got home after midnite & both were rather touchy & tired. The house is a mess, dirt & dust all over & I think we've been too much on the go lately.

Sat 17 Feb - Home to find that Mr Malone's brother-in-law had been fixing the refrigerator, & the place was covered with soot! So Robert & I cleaned the place till 10. I washed clothes till after 11. Dad wrote Dick sent letter from France dated Feb 3!

Tue 20 Feb - Angry at Robert for his refusal to take my wishes seriously, especially as concerns the bed which he manages somehow to mess up but good!

Wed 28 Feb - Robert called at 5 to say he'd be late coming home, after 8. We have a little mouse that scurries overhead, I killed a spider tonight, too.

Thu 1 Mar 1945 - So? I lose another Boss? - About 4 PM Maj Hill got a call from Col Nelson. In 10 days he's to report to Oak Ridge. He was really mad & swore. I can't blame his anger for he brought his family up from Wash only 2 months ago. Robert coming home late. Says he was ordered out to Staten Island & the Lt [whom he replaces] ordered to pick out a ship. Thinks the whole CSO deal may be scrapped soon. I tell Robt it's because of his uncooperative unsocial attitude.

Fri 2 Mar - Movies - Surrealist films - Maj Hill in a dilemma all day trying to figure out a way to sidestep this "Deputy Director" job. I called Robert at S.I.T. & he told me he was quite busy but liked his work. Went to 5th Ave Playhouse to see "Poet's Blood" & "Lot in Sodom", 2 surrealist films & a 1915 Charlie Chaplin film satirizing "Carmen". Unique films & we found them most interesting. Home 1 AM & Robert angry 'cause I was tired.

Mon 5 Mar - letter from Dick giving me some definite news. He's in the 103rd Div, 7th Army. Robert went to the commissary this eve. Late supper consequently. Slight tiff about Brahms 1st Symphony which I didn't like. Surprised how angry I got at Robert this evening. [This must be the first episode in a long and painful series of arguments over my playing music in our home. This marriage-threatening division persisted sporadically until, ca 1980-90 {!}, I finally surrendered and desisted from any such effort. It was always particularly puzzling to me, given the attraction we found in music during our courtship.]

Tue 13 Mar - Ballet Russe - Enjoyable - Ballet program at the

NY City Center, found ourselves in good seats, 2nd balcony a few rows back.

Wed 14 Mar - Ants Invade my Kitchen! - [Notice the "my" kitchen, i.e., not "our" - woman's domain!] Sleepy as we got up this a.m., and no wonder for it was after 1 AM before we got to bed. Robert all enthused by his new project of writing up in German "Standing Rules" to be posted on all ships which will be bringing back 100,000 German prisoners. Only he has no knowledge of Military German.

Fri 16 Mar - The 7th Army takes Bitche - 8:30 PM listening to Beethoven Concerto played by Heifetz, waiting for Robert to come home. Thinking about Dick's V-mail stating he had gotten back from the line. Hasn't been getting any of the 16 letters I've written him since Jan 1? The news that the 7th Army is in full swing along the Rhine makes me almost afraid to think that my bro, whom they call the "Repple Depot Kid" is in it. News that McAuliffe ("nuts" guy at Bastogne) is now C.O. of the 103rd Div. RWD home at 8:45, tired & hungry & mad at the subway again. Soothed my darling & we went to bed at 11:30 PM.

Sun 18 Mar - Ballet Russe - Early matinee performance at City Center. Delicious martinis till bedtime. Reading The Times, much was of 7th Army.

Mon 19 Mar - Robert on duty tomorrow and may not get Wed afternoon off. Seems he has to escort some Capt fm Wash all over Staten Island Wednesday. Nuts!

Wed 21 Mar - I buy a trench coat - 23.79! - Letter from Max enclosing 5 snapshots Dick sent, one showing him at the 57 [?sic] mm anti-tank gun. Mom knows he's at the front & Max writes that she worries about the war pretty much.

Thu 22 Mar - M - I initiated my trench coat today amid comments . . . Got told by Maj Hill that he's going to get me a soapbox since I make at least two speeches per day - humph! . . . Robert washed the dishes, for I have that all pooped out feeling.

Sun 25 Mar - M - Museums - RWD let me sleep till 1:30 PM. We left after 3 PM for the Guggenheim Kandinsky exhibit; very interesting to see how his work progressed thru the years. Thence to Mondrian exhibit (awful simplicity) at the Museum of Modern Art.

Wed 4 Apr - Home to find Doty already home & cutting up string beans with my one & only pair of shears. Off to the library. Doty's eyes gleaming as he picked out German books & chess & stuff. I got two Russian books, 2 novels & a book on the Ballet. Home 7:30, taking bath while Doty washed dishes. Picked up prints today, fairly good on the whole. The indoor shots will serve as reminders of our abode here at 1168 Brooklyn.

Sat 7 Apr - Got angry at Robert when he refused to co-operate in cleaning up the apt. Ended up with my mopping the floors. I'm getting fed up with this routine.

Tue 10 Apr - We both fell asleep about 9 PM, second day in a row for us. What is wrong with two sleepy guys like us.

Thu 12 Apr - Pres Roosevelt Dies! - Was to meet Robert about 6 PM & I got down to 34th St about 5:45 PM, & walking to the restaurant where we were to meet, I passed the Chapel of St Francis of Assissi, and for the 1st time I was prompted to go in. So I did & said a general prayer for the welfare of all of us, that the war would end soon etc. Well, Robt met me & we ate, went shopping at Gimbel's & Macy's & bot Sla, moth killer. About 7:30 PM we walked out to see Extras on the newsstands to the effect that the President was dead. Well, we couldn't believe it & in a stunned fashion we stopped our shopping & went on to our newsreel theater, to see some interesting war pictures. Home 10:30 PM, listening to radio learned that FDR had died in the aft at Warm Springs, Ga, but the news was not released till 5:45 PM, the time I stopped in for my prayer in church. Feel a great personal loss somehow. [The evidence is quite strong that, in addition to the coincidence of her prayer, that evening also marked her impregnation with Robt Jr! See her notation to this effect as per 19 April!! - Calculations do not fully support that, but neither do they preclude it. He was born 27 Dec, 361st day of the year. If deduct 280 days ususal pregnancy = 22 March, when she was menstruating; mid cycle of the following period would thus have been ca 4 April, a nite when at least I was not recorded as falling asleep early! - What is most remarkable is the general absence in this detailed history of our life of any hint that throughout these months we had decided to begin realizing our hope for children - next to the decision to marry, the most important decision of our lives!!]

Sat 14 Apr - FDR MEMORIAL SERVICES - We went to NY

City Center to see a fine performance of "La Bohème", beautiful music & unusual settings. Home late, snack & to bed 1 AM.

Sun 15 Apr - Metropolitan - Slept till noon, hurried for our 1st visit to the Met to see the Ballet Theatre, Les Sylphides, Peter & the Wolf, Harvest Time, a new pastoral ballet by Nijinska. Home, having chicken supper. Shampooed my hair while Doty did dishes. More tributes & Memorials to FDR.

Mon 16 Apr - PRES TRUMAN'S FIRST SPEECH - We heard it this eve, & couldn't help noticing the difference between his plain Midwestern speech and the polished eloquence of FDR. Letter from Dick. Says his Lt got court-martialed & wasn't there to censor their mail. Seems the Lt had been looting.

Thu 19 Apr - Chinatown - Shopping - Newsreel - Still not menstruating & I'm beginning to think maybe it did happen 4/12. We walked to Chinatown to have a big meal. Then on to newsreel theater to see the funeral pictures of FDR's last rites. I think most of the audience cried. Robert & I did.

Fri 20 Apr - 29th day & still no signs. I wonder if it is the real McCoy. I think Robert is resigned. Hope I start menstruating.

Sat 21 Apr - Ballet Theatre tonight - News that the Russians are in Berlin battling fanatic resistance. Rain as I left the office & home soaked. Had forgotten we had tickets for the Ballet tonite but we made it all right. Saw all new to us: Petrouchka (good), Undertow (strange, a new ballet), Argentita & some native dances & Princess Aurora - brilliant & with Toumanova dancing.

Sun 22 Apr - Home all Day - Up at noon. After breakfast nagging RWD into doing some work on the apt while I washed and set my hair. Ironed several blouses & washed some clothes. Robert did dishes. Guess I am really enceinte.

Mon 23 Apr - Funny, I can't believe I'm pregnant.

Tue 24 Apr - Feel vaguely uncomfortable throughout my abdominal region. Frightening prospect of becoming big & ungainly looking. Robert assures me it won't happen for some time. [As though I were an authority on pregnancy!] Hope I can get Robert to write some letters also. He finished his first attempt at nonobjective art via colored wax crayons.

Wed 25 Apr - The United Nations Conference Begins - Heard

460

opening session of the United Nations Conference, Pres Truman reading (badly) his welcoming speech; Gov Warren, Mayor of San Francisco & Stettinius making much better speeches. Am going to follow this closely.

Thu 26 Apr - Robert took the aft off & I joined him at 5:15 at the bookstore close by. So he bought Wolf's "You Can't Go Home Again" and D.H. Lawrence's "The Rainbow". Ate supper at Child's and it is startling how little meat restaurants have on their menus, our beef stew was mostly carrots, celery & rice. Went to Rockefeller Newsreel Theater to see some Nazi concentration camps we've overrun, including Artkino release on Maidenek. Inhuman, unbelievable if it wasn't there before your eyes. Piles of human bones & skulls, partly decayed bodies etc.

Sat 28 Apr - False Peace Rumors - Bought Robert box of Barracini candy finally. Newspapers with headlines re rumors that Germany offered to surrender unconditionally to us and Great Britain, but not Russia. Then all evening the radio was full of news that surrender to all 3 had occurred. This finally denied when Pres Truman got on the air to say Eisenhower said all this was unfounded.

Sun 29 Apr - Slept till noon, after breakfast straightened up things & left at 2 PM for the Museum & Library. Got 3 books on prenatal care.

Mon 30 Apr - Felt very full & went to bed for an hour or so. Trouble with Robert who can't understand my reluctance to be as intimate as before. I suppose I should go see a doctor here soon. Wondering if I can take that trip back home as planned. I do have these vague fears & I can't seem to do anything about it.

Tue 1 May 1945 - Report that Hitler is dead - Listening to newscasts that Hitler reported to be dead in Berlin & that Admiral Donetz is his successor.

Fri 4 May - I guess the end is near for about 1,000,000 men surrendered in Italy & Austria yesterday & today Doenitz surrendered his forces in Denmark & Holland & perhaps Norway. Am keeping after Robert to do something about arranging for me to go see the medics at Governor's Island. Want to be sure I'm enceinte before I write the folks.

Mon 7 May - V-E Day? - About 9:30 AM the news got around

461

that the Nazis had surrendered unconditionally. Maj Hill, Capt Smith, Miriam & I left for a walk to Wall St, all the while torn bits of paper, ticker tape, streamers & confetti pouring out of the skyscraper buildings. Lacking official confirmation, we were skeptical of the news. Anyway, met Robert at the Cloisters, a small eating place on 55th East, & then to the 55th St Playhouse to see "Alexander Nevsky", Russ film on defeat of Teutonic knights by Prince Alexander in 1242. Very stirring spectacle with music by Prokofiev. Also saw French film "Amphitryon", story of Jupiter's descent to Thebes to seduce one Grecian matron, Alcamenes, wife of Amphitryon. Very delightful. Home midnite with no incidents altho 500,000 were in Times Square celebrating.

Tue 8 May - VE Day Official - At 9 AM Pres Truman made his radio proclamation that VE Day was here. Business as usual for us. Maj Hill left by plane for Oak Ridge at noon.

Thu 10 May - Army announces its Point System - Robert called to tell me the Army has no facilities for Officers' wives & suggested we go to the City Maternity Center where they refer you to a doctor according to your purse & desires. . . . 85 points needed for a discharge, Robert has only 49.

Sat 12 May - Angry 'cause Robert fell asleep on me again. So the apartment isn't going to get house cleaned tonite!

Sun 13 May - Slept till noon, Robert had gotten up earlier, bot newspaper & mopped up the floors.

Thu 17 May - To A&S in Bklyn to buy me 2 hats @ 3.99 each. RWD angry at me re shopping & home in a huff. But I think I like my hats.

Fri 18 May - Slight drizzle but we went uptown to the Maternity Center Assn; Suggested we go to a Dr Graber, an OB specialist on Park Ave, $5.00 per visit.

Sun 20 May - Miriam Concert - Cocktail Party - Rushing to Town Hall for 2:30 curtain. Jewish chorus for 1¼ hours; then Miriam's group. We stayed for her concerto & then went on to Lt Platt's apt on 82nd & Central Park West. Everyone from Robert's office there w/ their wives. Much drink, RWD very high & happy. Home midnite, hungry & high.

Tue 22 May - We Go to see Dr Graber - So I managed to break the news re my enceinte to Capt Smith and later to Maj Hill. Got off at 2 & on to Dr. Graber's at 521 Park Ave. He assured me I was pregnant & should start thinking up names. Also said I shouldn't plan on going home till after the 3rd menstrual period in July, also said I should make my hospital reservation as soon as possible. Robert fixed beef stew. I napped a bit, ate, feel as tho this is something unreal, this being sure I am going to have a baby Jan 1 or 2.

Wed 23 May - Miriam all excited to hear the news that I am pregnant. Tried to restrict myself to 6 cigs but smoked 11 all told, hard to cut down quickly.

Thu 31 May - Othello - Met RWD at Paddy's Clam House on 34th. "Othello" proved to be very dramatic & interesting altho a bit long. We didn't get out till after 11:30. Paul Robeson very good; also Joseph Ferrar as Iago & Uta Hagen as Desdemona. Home 12:30 or so, nauseated on subway.

Mon 4 June - Came home to find a 4-page letter from Rich, from Innsbruck, Austria. Thanks us for writing him regularly & sending him packages. Gives me a pretty awful picture of actual combat with the Nazis, & says he's eager to get to the CBI to start fighting the Japs. Pretty grim letter & quite an insight into the impact of war on our still adolescent GIs. Robt promises to "straighten" him out in a letter re this Pacific warfare.

Thu 14 June - Visit II to Dr Graber - Maternity Clothes - On to Guggenheim Museum, air-conditioned place to rest. At Dr. Graber's at 3 PM. Everything normal, my blood pressure 124. Stopped at Museum of Modern Art seeing modern home model exhibit. At newsreel theater at 5 seeing 2 hour show, for program changed at 6 PM. Technicolor films of "Iwo Jima".

Tue 19 June - Eisenhower Day - Xciting Day for New York. Maj H brought his 10-year- old son in, & from 11 AM on till 2:30 we devoted our time to waiting, watching & getting over our excitement. At A.B. Dick's 2nd floor air conditioned offices watching Eisenhower drive by in open car standing with upraised arm. Heard Mayor La Guardia present Medal of Honor to Ike at City Hall & Eisenhower's speech of acceptance.

Sat 23 June - Robert not speaking to me today. At 9:30 put on his new uniform & left without a word - Wonder what's up?

463

Sun 24 June - Stony silence entre nous. I shampooed my hair & napped intermittently between nibbling at food. I read newspapers, Doty his book on New Hebrides aborigines & so passed the day, a hot, humid scorcher.

Mon 25 June - Robert & I made up after supper; I took the initiative as usual. Silly for us both to be upset over something that occurs in everyone's experience.

Fri 29 June - Watched the Queen Elizabeth slowly sail up the Hudson, dwarfing everything about her. She majestically moved along, her upper structures filled with khaki clad figures, 15,000 8th Air Force troops aboard.

Mon 9 July - Dr Graber alarms me - To Dr. Graber's for my check up. I weigh 142¼, a gain of 4¼ lbs. Should gain only ½ lb a week. Told Doc about the brownish tinged discharge I've been having & he told me that means the placenta is separating from the womb. Ordered me to bed for 4 or 5 days & prescribed vitamin E. I argued with him on this. Came home early. I got into bed as per doc's orders.

Tue 10 July - I Stay Home #1 - Robert called & spoke to Maj Hill, telling him of my predicament & that I'd be away for several days. Rather tiring this staying in bed.

Thu 12 July - Home #3 - Slept till 1:30 PM. Weary of 3 days in bed. Decided to go back to work tomorrow.

Fri 13 July - Back to the office - Scolded by everybody for coming back so soon. Instructing Miss Alford all morning & most of the aft. She made a few errors, not being versed in military correspondence. Noticed my discharge beginning anew as the day progressed.

Mon 16 July - Dr Graber says I'm OK - To work & teaching Alford more stuff about the office. Left for Doc Graber's 1:45 appt to find RWD did get the aft off & had come to meet me. Doc assured me I was better, my basal metabolism was slowed down of late - guess that's why I gained weight. To continue medication, to rest, get in bed whenever the stains appear. So we went to the Museum of Modern Art. Saw "Anna Christie" with Garbo.

Fri 20 July - I find my average salary on 48 hour week is $66.50! Gee, that hurts to give up all that dough as I must in the next couple weeks. Robert thinks I should ask for maternal leave instead

464

of an outright resignation. The Queen Elizabeth came into NY with the entire 44th Div on board.

Sat 21 July - Robert visits the QUEEN ELIZABETH - Robert took about 40 officers on a tour of the Queen Elizabeth this aft & was very much impressed with the size of the ship. Went to the Union Sq to see a British movie "Thunder Rock" (very thought provoking) and a Soviet film "The Ural Front", showing industry being set up in the Ural Region in 1941. Had a herring salad at midnite at the Biltmore cafeteria. Home 2 a.m.

Wed 25 July - Received check from GE for $10.00, semi-annual dividend of 2%.

Tue 31 July - The Major left for Frisco via airplane re recruiting. Talked to him about my leaving & again he said he wanted to leave it up to me as to when I wanted to leave. Gosh, I'm getting big through the waist!

Thu 2 Aug - Town Hall Meeting - . . . . Arrived at Town Hall for the broadcast. Kaltenborn as guest moderator, subject: How Can America & Russia Live in Peace. Fairly interesting broadcast but 1½ hours of sitting in a stuffy auditorium wasn't pleasant.

Sun 5 Aug - Slept till 2:30 PM. After something to eat we napped again till 6 PM. Spaghetti supper, Robert mopped the floors, cussing all the time. I defrosted refrigerator, washed & set my hair. It was a beautiful day outdoors but we stayed in & slept.

Mon 6 Aug - Our Secret is Out! The Atomic Bomb! - While out during lunch I glimpsed newspaper headline about an atomic Bomb having been dropped on Japan & immediately I thought of our Manhattan District work. Later this aft this was confirmed as later copies of newspapers carried full stories about Gen'l Groves & Manhattan Project & some of our contractors. Exciting! Radio newscasts full of stories about the atomic bomb. Kaltenborn says Japan may fold up in 3 mos.

Tue 7 Aug - Miss Alford finally giving vent to what must have been on her mind for some time when she said she wished Maj Hill had told her this outfit was going to fold up before she gave up her other job, etc.

Wed 8 Aug - Russia declares war on Japan! - Mid-afternoon announcement that Russia had declared war on Japan, to bring a speedier end to the War. This coming on top of the atomic bomb ought to bring an end to the war - soon, I hope. Much comment on this event on radio. Kaltenborn now says war should end in 3 weeks. Mon he said 3 mos. Robert starting to read Capek's R.U.R. which I read last night.

Fri 10 Aug - Home Today - Surrender offer - Decided to stay home, so I slept till almost 1 PM. As I ate breakfast I listened to the radio, much commotion re Japan's surrender note, with the proviso that the Emperor retain his status quo. Can't help feeling relieved at thought that Rich & Max & Fritz will not have to fight. Hope I can last out till the 18th. My reluctance to go down to work increases daily.

Sun 12 Aug - Reading the Times, no news re V-J Day yet. This whole deal so unreal. Robert wondering if he should go to sea; when will he get out? Many problems re conversion, unemployment, demobilization. Hope next week brings definite news.

Mon 13 Aug - A Day of Waiting - We both felt rather downcast at the lack of definite news; everyone beginning to feel that maybe the Japs were playing a trick on us.

Tue 14 Aug - Japan accepts Surrender Terms - At 7:30 AM we heard the radio announcement that Japan had surrendered, supposedly a Swiss broadcast at 1:30 AM. But as the day went on & there was no official confirmation, we began to doubt it & worry. Definitely the whole office had peace jitters. At 7 PM we heard the news that Pres Truman & Mr Atlee (Br) had announced receipt of Japan's acceptance of our surrender terms. Everyone whooping it up in the neighborhood. RWD got quart Madeira & port wine & we drank a toast to peace in our lifetime. Feel relieved but not unduly exhilarated.

Wed 15 Aug - Robert says his Major told him he could have a ship after I leave, so now he's impatient to get out to sea again.

Sat 18 Aug - MY LAST DAY - Miss A not down today. Miriam, Mel & Ruth Ladell took me to lunch at Aetna's. Rhoda, Anita, Yetta & Betty Sosler pitched in for a gift, Balelaika cologne & a bed jacket. So I had quite an aft saying goodbye to everybody. The Major said he wants to take me to lunch & I said I'd leave the last week of August. I'm to take my sick & annual leave and then ask for maternity leave. Good feeling to part with everyone altho

466

I couldn't help feeling I was shutting the door on one phase of my life to await a strange new experience.

Fri 24 Aug - Got quite a scare when I got some severe abdominal cramps. Had noticed stains this morning & this frightened me so I just lay in bed & waited for Robert to come home, about an hour. He called Dr. Graber at Rye, NY who was interested in knowing whether the pains were coming with any regularity & if I was bleeding profusely, neither was the case so I just stayed in bed. Robert doesn't take too kindly to my not feeling well. He was quite annoyed with my staying in bed.

Sat 25 Aug - I Stay in Bed - Phooey - So I took yesterday's warning to heart & stayed in bed. Robert home about 3 PM. Disconsolate that I was in bed. But this idea of being ill gripes me. But the doc said for me to stay in bed.

Mon 27 Aug - Dr Graber - De Gaulle - . . . . As we walked out at 1:15 the reason for the crowds appeared! Gen Charles deGaulle drove by in an open touring car with Mayor LaGuardia - so I saw another celebrity. To Doc Graber's & being told I cannot travel unless I stop "spotting" for at least 2 weeks. So it's to bed again, I guess. Robert not too happy at my "bed sentence" but I guess there's nothing I can do about it. I weighed 152 lbs today! 8 lb gain.

Tue 28 Aug - A Day in Bed - Robert was good enough today to wash out 2 housecoats, a dress, slip & my nightie. Poor dear, he doesn't like this kind of life any better that I do. He hates the petty stuff at the office & feels as I do that we're just stagnating here in this ole burg.

Thu 30 Aug - Our 4th Anniversary - Today I slept till almost 2 PM. Hot, humid, and unpleasantly warm day. The folks upstairs gave us a fine bottle of white dessert wine for our anniversary. Robert went to the Library to get more books. So we observed our 4th anniversary together. God grant we may both be civilians in Chgo by the next one.

Sat 1 Sept 1945 - Japan Officially Surrenders - Went to old film "Resurrection" (based on Tolstoy's story) also "Day of Glory" a film w/ Toumanova & Gregory Peck I saw about a year ago. Home about midnite, hearing broadcast frm Tokyo Bay re signing of surrender.

Tue 4 Sept - Met the folks at the office & on to Longchamps for drinks, RWD joining us at 5:45. 3 rounds & we took off for a Spanish place called Jailai in the Village. Capt Smith, Maj Hill, Sam, Miriam, Nina Alford, RWD & I. So we sat around a long table the 7 of us & had paella (rice colored w/ saffron, clams, shrimp, chicken, and little sausages, & vegetables), w/ Chilean Rhine wine to drink. Good. Capt Smith was paying the check & it was well over $20 all told. Gifts: black leather purse from Saks Fifth Ave, 2 pr hose (Nina) & framed Manhattan District Shoulder Patch & Meritorious Service for me as souvenirs. Home a little high about 10:30 PM.

Thu 6 Sept - Robert says Richard's regiment is due to arrive in Boston on 9/9 on the Sea Owl. So he should be in Chicago a week from that time. Just hope Max stays in Chicago long enough so we can all be together for a "reunion".

Tue 11 Sept - I Get Tickets - Farewell to Office - Left at 9:45 for Bank & withdrew 200.00 (Bal now only 3M). Parted w/ office gang promising cards etc. We packed the bulk of our stuff & didn't go to bed till 1 AM.

Sat 15 Sept - We Leave for Chicago - Everything fine & fairly pleasant trip except that it did lurch & rumble during the night & I hugged a pillow to my stomach to keep Junior from getting all bounced up.

Sun 16 Sept - Nous Arrivons! - Got off train & nobody was there to meet us! Mom Doty & Rich came along soon & we found that Sis' car had stalled. Dick home since Thurs nite, Max on furlough. Wonderful to find the whole family home. Dinner at Mom's, then supper at the Doty's. Robert will be able to use his Dad's car.

Wed 19 Sept - "Queer" Sort of Day - Robert says he enrolled in U of C home study course, 3 courses, English, German & College Algebra, at a cost of $50. Apparently he spent a couple hours at the Dotys & his father must have had some caustic remarks to make about his going to school. Felt all "in" today & for some unexplainable reason feel very sad & downcast. We stayed in tonight, Robert looking over his textbooks & syllabi. With 3 courses, English, German & Algebra, he should be pretty busy for the next 3 or 4 months. Says will require one year in residence for his bachelor's degree. Mom wonders if we'll be able to get along with Robert going to school after his discharge.

Mon 24 Sept - Robert leaves for New York - We parted at 2:20 or so after many kisses. Dreary day, the Dotys drove me home. After supper Max, Bess & I went to see "Wuthering Heights" (old classic I'd seen years ago). Writing a letter to Robert.

CHAPTER XIII
Pregnancy, Birth and the Azores

Synopsis - For Elizabeth these were another three months of waiting and loneliness, now compounded by the inevitably increasing discomfort of pregnancy and the unknowns of giving birth. It was, of course, wise that she was with her family, mother to advise on pregnancy, sister to be of help; yet it was a long and boring time. She discovered her talent and delight in sewing, and this gave a most welcome outlet, especially since most of it was making things for the baby. In the meantime, I was having a grand tour, albeit beset with a number of responsibilities, as well as my constant concern for her, and my hope, not to be realized, of returning to be present when she gave birth. As it turned out, that little drama could scarcely have been worse, save for the triumphant outcome. Caught in a "once in a century" North Atlantic storm, I was "marooned" in the Azores at Christmas with 676 troops aboard and no fuel to get home. Elizabeth had become only too well aware of the many, well-reported, casualties that storm had produced, and my absence, after a false notice of my arrival, was not reassuring. While I coped with the challenges in the Azores, she gave birth to Robert Jr in the early morning of 27 December 1945.

Monday 24 Sept '45

My Dearest Darling -

Dearest, am beginning to miss you already and I know it will get more poignant, this loneliness for you, Robert. Being with the folks will keep me distracted to a certain extent, but there's nothing like being together, no matter under what surroundings.

Oh, dearest, I'll be so happy when we are reunited for good, for each one of our partings have been moments of sorrow for me. Guess I'll never get used to them. Don't think I can write a coherent letter tonight, for I am emotionally upset. I guess the best way to describe how I feel is to compare my feelings with what I experienced when as a little girl I was put to bed by myself and in the dark. I would feel so lonely and frightened and I would fall asleep only after much sobbing and flowing of tears. And that's how I feel tonight, a little frightened to face the future without you and longing for the comfort of your mere presence. Just writing this makes me feel a bit closer to you, my beloved.

Well, precious I'll get busy on the baby's layette later this week. Think I'll start checking off the days on the calendar till the baby comes and until I see you again. I know you'll have plenty to keep you occupied, your work, your studies, so don't worry about me. I'm sure I'll be as happy here at the folks as I'd be anywhere without you.

With all my love & waiting for your letter,
Elizabeth

*   *   *   *   *

Tuesday, 25 Sept '45 9:30pm

Dearest Darling -

Well, Max is leaving for San Diego on the 10 PM plane. Sorry to see Max leave, for he and I have the most in common in the family.

Just three years ago that you left to enter the Army. Even the weather was the same as it was that day, dark overcast skies, a slight drizzle, and a generally melancholy atmosphere. I slept till almost noon today and awoke, not refreshed and rested, but as though from a drugged sleep. I remember having some strange dreams during the night, and remember reminding myself not to snuggle next to Bess as I was wont to do when you were my bed partner, my precious. Oh, how good to lie close to you and run my hand over your smooth stomach!! Mustn't think too much of those joys right now though.

Everybody tells me I'm going to have a boy baby. Seems that male babies are much more active than females & certainly ours has been a whopper. So, darling, here's hoping!

All my love, precious, always
Elizabeth

471

*   *   *   *   *

27 Sept 1945 11:30pm

Sweetheart -

It must've been sad to come back to an apartment bare of many of its former furnishings. But I'm glad you had a place to go to and bathe & rest up. Perhaps you'll have an opportunity to take in some opera & other events before you ship out.

This evening I almost finished a pink sacque with white trim. Did the finishing by hand & it takes time, but I want to get it off my mind [accompanied by a little drawing].

"Ours" is getting bigger & rowdier every day it seems. Keeps me from falling asleep with its movements. I'll bet it takes after you in that respect!

Hope there'll be a letter from you tomorrow morning. It makes the whole day that much brighter for me, my darling. Goodnight, my love

Always
Your Elizabeth

*   *   *   *   *

5PM Saturday 29 Sept 45
[A Father's Paean to His Mate]

My lovely one -

I've been so lonely for you, so utterly, unbearably lonely, and thinking always of the other darling that will soon belong to us. This I'm afraid will be our cruelest separation, for there is no time in our life when we belong together more than we do now. But it will be for the best perhaps, tho I do have to fight down sometimes the doubts I have as to the necessity of our being apart. I know you are better off at home where you'll have someone to look after you. I know I will accomplish much more schoolwork than if I were with you. And I also realize that the agony of our loneliness has and will make our love & desire for each other that much greater; but all of this logic does not alter the intense fact that I long constantly for your precious nearness. There is a vacuum in life which nothing but your presence fills, the mere fact of being with you has become almost as necessary as breathing.

It is strange how a change of space seems to alter all perspective of time, for it seems like months since I have kissed you, so, so

472

far away. It seems as if I have been in this barren house week after week without you, weeks without a glimpse of you, without hearing the sweet persuasion of your voice or feeling your warmth soft & safe beside me in the dark. And darling, how can I ever tell you how I feel about our little one. At first it was something strange and secret, an intruder, an unknown, an unexperienced thing which crept into our life so silently and slowly. It was a change, something to be suspected, feared. But then it grew, and had to be cared for, given way to, and protected. And then it moved and was alive. It was full and warm and round, and seemed so sturdy, wholesome in the ripeness of your womb. And now, my wifemate, I love you and what is so strangely ours, with a love more deep and inexpressible than I had ever dreamt of. It is the most marvelous thing of our lives, this child which squirms so sturdily within you. Our deed, our love, made tangible, given awareness, and made fruitful forever.

Each day will be a barb of impatience and longing until I can return to you and our love. And my sweetness, you have always with you the beloved token of our oneness, and I am continually with you in that. Perhaps it is painful to be a woman, yet I can see too in you the joy, and pride, and fulfillment of being woman, and it must be deeply satisfying. You have such a glowing contentment and certitude about you, my tender one, that no matter how lonely and sad you feel, you have this presence and greatness within you to bring you a quiet, all conquering happiness. You are magnificent in creation.

I love you so completely, my dearest, and now tho sad at your absence, I am overwhelmed with joy thinking of you as my wife, and of the beauty of your motherhood.

Robert

*   *   *   *   *

Mon. 1 Oct '45 - 3:30pm

My Dearest -

Darling, your Sat letter is precious. How beautifully you express your feelings about our "little one". I'm so happy that you do feel that way about its coming, for I know it has disrupted that pleasant routine of living together that we experienced in New York. I finished the kimono Sat evening and put blue feather stitch trim around the edges, the collar & cuffs - and if I do say

473

so, it's a well-made garment, with so much hand detail work on it.

The housing situation is fierce here in Chicago from what I hear, & I wonder just where & how we'll find us a place to live when you get out of the Army.

*   *   *   *   *

0030AM Tues. 2 Oct 45

My sweet darling -

. . . . Got 4 letters from my beloved this morning. I'd give anything to be there watching you sew those dainty little things for our darling. I did a little work for "ours" today too. Went to the library and looked over about 3000 names. Have decided on Ian Julian Doty. I think that is a beautiful combination of names. Especially Ian (eeyan) - it also has the advantage of being short, not at all "sissified", and having no stupid nicknames connected with it (e.g., I like the name "Alaric", but he'd be known as "Al"). You might object to Julian (I like mostly because it is so phonetically perfect with the musical Ian), but Ian goes with anything. Here are some other names I liked: Bruce, Edgar, Eric, Glenn, Brett, Brian, Regan, and Frayne. The last in particular. If we have two boys, I think one of them should be Frayne.

It'll be hard for me to argue by mail, particularly when it is you that's having the baby, but please don't name him junior.

We shouldn't build ourselves up so much for a boy either, my loveliness, for I think there would be nothing sweeter than a little girl with all her mother's smiles & tenderness. Oh, to be with you to watch & see it grow, our love.

I don't know what those sacks are you're sewing, but I'll bet the baby has more clothes than you have if you keep going at that rate for the next three months. I want to thank your Mom & Bess both for being so sweet to you, and not letting you do any heavy work.

. . . I'm glad that we have those pictures of the place where our darling began life, and we can always look at those pictures and know of these eventful days. I love you so continually and for always, my beautiful, wholesome wife

Robert

*   *   *   *   *

My lovable one -

The train was due into Boston at 11:15 PM and made it on time; but then to my dismay I could get no hotel accommodations. Was utterly lost in this town. Its streets are as great a hodgepodge as those of Bristol. With no hotel, my only solution was to try to find the ship & hope the night mate could fix me up with a bunk. Took a cab out to Simpson's Dry Dock in East Boston. I was very fortunate in finding the Transport Services Officer aboard & awake so I moved right in & took over Capt Fishbein's bunk in the room.

. . . Spent the rest of the day checking the property book, PX Inventory etc. & having the Corporal type these lists so that I could assume responsibility & send a copy to the officer I relieved. Moved the PX & Special Service Supplies back into the mental ward where it could be double locked, as they had broken into the locker in #2 TD & stolen the punching bag & boxing gloves. Went over some of the repairs to be accomplished with the Bethlehem Steel job superintendent & got a few other items accomplished. I let the Sgt Major go home to Akron, Ohio tonite since we're to go in drydock tomorrow & won't need a CQ aboard.

I love you, again and for always.
Robert

*   *   *   *   *

THE UNIVERSITY CLUB

40 TRINITY PLACE

BOSTON 16, MASS.

1:30AM Friday 5 October 45

My dearest beloved -

I did have a marvelous experience tonite. I went out to the Boston Opera House where the Ballet Russe is playing. I got there at 9 PM for a performance which was supposed to start at 8:30. Decided that I might as well go in immediately, tho, since I was there, rather than buy tickets for tomorrow & have to come back.

475

So I got the cheapest seat $1.20 in the 2nd balcony. Went inside & asked one of the girl ushers where the 2nd balcony stair was & she said follow me & took me in & seated me in the 4th row on the main floor! Don't tell anyone I took you here she said, but that wasn't necessary, I was completely appreciative of the favor. And darling, it was an entirely new experience to see ballet from the 4th row rather than from the 2nd balcony. We certainly must do that the next time (& may it be soon) that we go together. You get the individual perspective from there, seeing the expressions & truer personalities & grace of the dancer, their labored breathing, & unequaled litheness. Ballet is so sensual from the 4th row. I couldn't suppress a shiver of delicious remembrance of your body when seeing so close strong hands grasp the soft & intimate flesh of a woman's thigh and turn her with a firm, possessive delicacy. I remember your beauty so vividly, so familiarly pliant & receptive to my seeking hands. I will worship you always.

Got in at the end of Swan Lake. The next number, however, was something I shall never forget; a truly great experience in art. This Michael Kidd will even surpass Massine as a choreographer & dancer, and the music, too, was outstanding. You must see "On Stage!" if at all possible (my poor gravid darling) when it comes to Chicago. It is a perfect example of great art, having comedy, pathos, action, story, drama, philosophical comment and sheer emotional beauty, all skillfully played into its few unforgettable minutes. There is no describing it, you have to see it, and you could see it again & again, enjoying it more each time. I applauded for at least 10 curtain calls and it took the house down. The greatest ballet since Petrouchka.

*   *   *   *   *

4:30PM Monday 8 Oct 45

My sweet -

All my men came back today & they seem like a fairly live & intelligent bunch. The TSO, Lieut. John Lomax, has moved into the gunnery officer's quarters so that I now have a private room.

Have had another new experience too, seeing cars held up for a mile along the road while the bridge went up to let our ship pass thru. We passed the heavy cruiser, Canberra, pulling in as we moved down the river.

*   *   *   *   *

My sweet darling -

Looks like sailing has been postponed until Thursday. Was talking to the Chief Eng & he says it will take 9 or 10 days to get from here to New Orleans because we have to buck the Gulf Stream all the way & also because we are so light [ballast removed to make room for grain we will load] that only 2/3 of our wheel is in the water.

*   *   *   *   *

Monday, 8 October '45 - 9:30pm

Beloved -

What a red letter day for me! In the morning mail your Thursday letter came - also the picture card folder from Plymouth. . . . Dressing to go to Field's for our afternoon sewing lesson. The doorbell rang and there was a package for me, from Boston! Precious, you are spoiling me giving me my birthday present in advance like this, and such a striking gift! It's lovely, sweetheart, but my waist is about 10" too wide for it right now, and what if it never gets back to my normal 26"?

Wonderful that you got to visit Plymouth, for I can understand your interest in seeing the place where your ancestor landed in these USA, especially after you'd seen the town in England from where he sailed!

Don't worry about our "Baby". It's having a fine time knocking about inside.

*   *   *   *   *

Wednesday, 10 Oct '45 - 9:30pm

My Darling -

Re Ironsides, I, too, remember contributing money towards its restoration. It must have been very interesting to go on board & see its "insides". Sailing ships have always had a fascination for me & years ago I collected prints of them. Had about 8 framed prints which I bought with a little money I managed to save from my weekly carfare & lunch allowance.

You've been having a lot of new experiences, and I'm glad. You were so bored with the status quo so long in New York. Wish I were with you to participate actively in your sightseeing.

477

*   *   *   *   *

10:30PM Friday, 12 October 1945

My sweet, beloved wife -

It seems, & it is, so long ago that I kissed you & heard your tender whispers, saw the gentle beauty of your loving face, and I ache with all the blissful memories of the past & the delirious hopes for the future, suspended here now in a vacant sterile present. So much has happened that the few days since I left you have been stretched into months, as if the rapid sequence of events obscured the faster the precious memories of our togetherness. The train trip from Chicago to N.Y., the vacant apartment, the moving & train trip to Boston, the ship, the hotel, the trip to Plymouth, the 3 different docks in Boston and now the sea, all these happenings have added their weight to time so that it has sunk quickly into the past, making ever more remote the full loveliness of your embrace, the delicate joy of your caress.

It is so desperately long since I have even heard from you, my precious, and I am burning with impatience to get to New Orleans, hoping there to find a letter from you, or to be able to call you.

Have my men very comfortably quartered on the boat deck. The Navy is off entirely so we've taken over those quarters & all in all my EMs are now as well bunked as I am.

*   *   *   *   *

7:30PM Sunday 14 Oct 45

My precious wife -

It is a warm, moonlit nite down here off the coast of South Carolina. Compared to your secluded life in chill Chicago, it must make you very envious of your roving, carefree male. I think so often of that, my beloved, and wish so strongly that I had you with me to enjoy this wonderful life - but you are having a wonderful life, far more thrilling and adventuresome than this, the life you are living and creating at home, the life that is the essence of our living. I compare my own lean & agile body to what must be the burdensome bigness of yours now as you carry & nourish our love, and I feel ashamed that I cannot help you, that I cannot share & ease the precious task that your capable womb prescribes for you. Yet you bear our tumid fruitfulness so aptly, so proudly, with your pliant womanstomach always lovely in its smoothness & strength, the sweet, delicious flesh that irresistibly enticed my seed, now so stal-

478

wart and invincible in nurturing it. - I love you so fiercely my beautiful, life-giving mate, and my loneliness for you is like the loneliness
of a song aching to be sung, but waiting, futile & motionless, till it is
voiced & given to joyous life, made glorious by the certain talent of
the singer. I exist without you, but I do not live, nor sing, I merely
wait: until your presence allows fulfillment of my only purpose, to
love you. And it is only I that am alone, you are so utterly intimate
and inseparable with the very reality of our love. You are now the
matrix of our existence, the crucible in which our boundless delight
in each other is being blended and formed to our mutual image, I
and our tender ecstasy are continually with you, beating tangibly in
the cradle of your flesh. Always in your body has occurred the
whole fact of our love. You have drawn me to you with the lush
temptation of your loveliness and received me within you, the deed
of our ecstasy always deep within your warmth; and now it is the
same, our love is with you & within you, - and so it must be, for ever
you are woman, love's immortal instrument.

*   *   *   *   *

Fri., 10/19/45 - 10:45PM

Dearest Darling -

Am going to take another chance at writing you in New Orleans. My future letters I shall address to the FPO in NY.

The big news for today has to do with my visit to Dr.
Proud. Vital statistics: I weighed 157 but Doc says I have a total
of 25 pounds to gain. In the 9 more weeks or so I have to go, I
probably won't gain much; most women don't.

He took pelvic measurements & I guess all is well. He told
me that baby is still quite small, no danger of multiple birth (no
twins this time!). He let me listen to the baby's heart beats thru
his stethoscope - and darling, that was really a thrill! They were
faint but I thought much more rapid than my own heart beats.

So I'm supposed to get more exercise walking, in order to get
my muscles in better tone. So far my abdominal muscles are
good, but as the baby's size increases, they may drop. So I'm to
take walks in small doses, couple times a day, etc.

My precious, I've been very happy today, thinking of our
baby, wondering if it'll be a "he" or "she", what it'll look like,

479

how big it'll be, and trying to visualize our future life with Baby present.

Am hoping I hear from you soon. This past week has seemed interminably long with no letters from you; and the weeks & perhaps months before I see you again seem like an eternity.

Sweetest thoughts of you, as I close,

Lovingly,
Betty

*   *   *   *   *

Sat., 20 Oct 45 - 10:45PM

My Precious Darling -

So happy to get your airmail special delivery letter this morning! You mailed it yesterday afternoon and it arrived this morning at 9 AM.

Read your account of your "voyage" to N.O. with much interest, and I'm glad you have the opportunity to see so much of the USA. Very happy, too, that you find the crew cooperative & congenial. You mention "EMs", and I'm wondering how <u>many</u> you have with you.

I'm tempted to start crossing off the days till Xmas, and the big event, now only 9 weeks off! I do hope I'll be brave thru it all. I'm afraid I'll cry & call alternately for "Robert" and "Mom", the two people closest to me!

*   *   *   *   *

11PM Tuesday 16 Oct 45

My sweetheart -

We are in the Gulf of Mexico with a stiff breeze flecking the moonspattered water with glittering froth. It is clear & cool, and as lovely as only the sea can be, great mysterious Lifemother squeezing the earth in her tender, yet mighty arms.

It has been only three weeks since I hugged my little round one. Oh, if I could only see how much rounder you've gotten in those three weeks, if I could only put my hand upon you & feel the vigorous miracle you are performing, to feel that sweet life dance within you, already kicking its heels with the joy of being alive, the life that you have given to it. You are a wife to be adored and a

480

mother to be worshiped. How can I ever love you enough to equal the feeling I have towards you, my beloved mate? It is so awesome this creation of life. All that I have left from our basement in Brooklyn is a faint red scar from a blister I received tying up the last packages to be sent from there, but you have growing daily within the lovely fornix of your flesh the hot gift I gave you, the togetherness & love of that experience. That fraction of our life dwelt out in Brooklyn still exists & goes on with you. You are bringing the most divine ecstasy & passion of life to glorious fruition, making visible & proud the full ardor of our intimate flesh, the vibrant lustjoy of our mating. Oh, our intense closeness, the flame of pleasure in each caress, the orgies of possessiveness translated now into a vivid, sensual thing of life that can itself enjoy and act & love, spreading thus forever the wild delight of our moments, the hot flash of our living; scintillating down the halls of the future. It is the womanliness of you that has made this possible, the serene & omnipotent feminine that accepts the tranquility that follows passion, the soft & silent months of waiting. You have taken the more gentle urgings of our fervent delight & sheltered them in the dark & primitive warmth of your motherwomb. You have created by your love, a new love, a new soul that enters our life & goes beyond it. You have touched the secret of the universe and brought forth its mystery, life. And I revel deliriously in my little part, that I, your husband, held your hand, and kissed you as you unlocked eternity.

I love you beyond all expression
Robert

*   *   *   *   *

11:50 AM Thurs 18 Oct 45

My dearest one -

At 11 AM this morn we began to get into the outer fringe of Mississippi mud. Up ahead you could see this vast area of yellow green & then as we approached it there was rather an abrupt demarcation between the deep blue of the ocean & this sandy green water. Shortly after that we sighted land, the art of navigation having brot us across this trackless gulph to the exact point we wanted. [Arrow pointing to "gulph"] (been reading too many old maps? - Strange the way I spelt "gulf" the way I'd seen it on the maps at Plymouth.) In about an hour we came to the mouth of the Mississippi, the water now being a yellow brown mud. And of all places to find a school of porpoises playing right at the mouth of the river, invisible in the muddy waters until they leap gracefully into the air, sometimes coming out of the water completely in a powerful clean jump. Three of them followed the bow for a few miles, but left as we entered the river channel. The strangest thing about coming up the river was that it started out with a width of not over 200 yards & gradually increased till it is now a full mile wide. That was because we entered one of its many mouths & are now up where the stream is still consolidated. It looks somewhat like the Suez Canal except for the vegetation & the bends of the river. It is over 90 miles up the river to New Orleans & the country is all dissected by the delta into swamps & forest. Along the river bank there is a continual line of driftwood & bleached logs, long legged white birds, blackbirds & an occasional herd of cattle. Off in the distance could be seen huge tongues of flame lashing the air, old oil or gas wells burning, & they make a weird sight in this desolate country. Hundreds of wasps swarmed aboard too, so that I lost no time in putting my screens in. We entered the channel at 12:30 PM & have now just dropped anchor outside New Orleans this instant, so you can get some idea of the distance we've had to come. It has been a clear nite with a full moon playing on the eerie swamplands. The mud of the great river is now a glistening pathway of dark silver, delicate & romantic, till I ache with loneliness for your beloved nearness.

I also polished off the final touches on my German lesson & greater accomplishment, solved the two Math problems that had been holding me up for 3 days. My most fervent hope for tomorrow is that I get a letter from you my most beautiful & lovable wife.

I love you so -
your husband
Robert

*   *   *   *   *

4 PM Sunday 21 Oct 45

I have just finished talking with the most lovely woman in the world, her voice as lush and soothing as the morning sun, lily-cool and clean. Never have you sounded so utterly feminine and dear, as only a woman full & blossoming with child could be. My delightful darling, our baby which you are creating is also having its effect on you, making you more radiantly beautiful than ever before. Previously I have loved you with complete impetuosness, living a glorious passion in you & with you, you were everything; and now this

482

miracle of miracles the wholly beloved made even more so. I am so enraptured by you, my womanmate that I feel almost as tho I didn't exist separately anymore, but dwell only within you, my breath echoing only because of the sheer loveliness of you, woman, creatrix. - I am so utterly happy to have talked with you, and yet so intensely lonely at being unable to be with one so irresistibly lovable. I will hear the ineffable sweetness of your voice whispering quietly to me for months across the barren sea, a thrilling & never to be forgotten music.

Robert

*   *   *   *   *

Sunday, 21 Oct '45 10:30PM

Precious Darling -

So, so happy today! It was so good to hear your voice this aft. I felt just a wee bit guilty limiting our conversation to 3 minutes; but dearest, you must not spend your money on phone calls. I'd rather you splurged on some good Creole cooking while in New Orleans.

I do hope you track down the 5 letters I've written to you c/o Lykes Bros, N.O., & the letters I sent c/o FPO NY eventually catch up with you, for I have given you therein a faithful account of my doings from day to day since we parted.

The 2 weeks ending 12 October Sis & I attended a series of six lectures given every other aft at Field's by a representative of the McCall Pattern Co. Learned a lot about sewing & fitting I didn't know before, and it did get me out of the house for a change of scene.

I made six baby garments and decided that would be enough for a starter. You dress the baby in a shirt & diaper most of the time anyway & I have 4 shirts & 4 doz diapers on hand. Also made myself a short hospital nightgown of a light blue dimity trimmed with blue ribbon.

Don't worry about the "Baby" & me. We're doing fine, and it's only a matter of time before we'll be together again for good. I am very happy now & know greater happiness is in store for me & all of us.

Lovingly,
Betty

483

9AM Wed. 24 Oct 45

My sweetest, most beloved darling -

It is either feast or famine, and I have been literally feasting on the ten letters I got from you last nite and the six this morning. Where on earth they've been for the other four days we were here, I'll never know. In fact, I got so disgusted yesterday that I wrote myself a postcard & mailed it, determined if I didn't get the thing in two days to take it up with the Postmaster of N.O. But now I'm happy, and oh, so glad to hear from my precious one. I read them in the order in which you'd written them, and the last one was the very best, telling me all the facts about you and our baby, your listening to its marvelously tiny heart! What wouldn't I have given to hear that. And everything seems to be going smoothly with you, as smoothly as such a huge project can go. I wish I was there to rub your back & in some way make the carrying of that immense burden more comfortable for you. It must be so heavy and I can tell it bothers you for you say one day you are comfortable only when sitting down, and the very next day you say you are comfortable only when lying or standing.

And you sound so utterly feminine, sewing baby things. I sense so strongly the difference between our two worlds, of home & children & peaceful, patient endeavor, so contrasted to my world of change & wandering, of tormenting lusts and the abstract achievement of erudition.

Our worlds are vastly sejunct, yet somehow they merge into the strong & sturdy unit of ourselves, a family, from the love & dwelling of male & female, the coalescence of two worlds, two opposing forces. And somehow, tho we are so separate, there is a part in each of us given ineluctably into the other's world, so that my lust is tempered with tenderness, and your placidity goaded to adventure.

You must not envy me my travels now, the apparent eventfulness of my life as compared with the stationary calmness of yours. The events taking place within your very self are far greater, more powerful & more thrilling than anything I will ever be able to experience. I can never achieve what you are now doing, the conception, nourishment & creation of a new life, the bearing of a new, vivacious love into the world, far more glorious than the most magnificent symphony or painting ever possible.

To feel the vigorous little kicks of the life within your swollen

484

womb was a more awesome experience for me than any I have ever had. You are now the center of the greatest excitement and happiness in my life, and it is I, not you, who is being deprived of adventure.

The evening so far has been very profitably spent learning how to develop film. The Special Services NCO is leaving & therefore didn't want to lug all the photography equip he's accumulated, so he sold it to the Chief Radio Operator & my Sgt Major. So I'm horning in also & was very surprised to find actually how simple & inexpensive it is. We've been making a mistake in not going further into photography & I hereby set my $200 in the Brooklyn bank aside for buying a better camera & other equipment. Especially with the baby to photograph it will be a priceless record of our lives & well worth the money.

*   *   *   *   *

Fri., 26 Oct '45 - 10:30PM

Dearest Darling -
. . . . I must answer Re "Ian Julian". The reaction is absolutely, positively negative! I just can't see its mystic appeal. It'll probably be a girl, but if it's a boy, I want to name him all the favorite names with me, Robert, William & Richard. Why not three names, giving him more of a choice? The order is not important? Maybe you'll be back in time to thrash it out with me in person!

Feel rather uncomfortable "front & back" and throughout the crotch & thighs. Guess the baby is settling downward.

*   *   *   *   *

11:30PM Saturday 27 Oct 45

My sweet beloved.
Today has been a very momentous one in our photographic history. In fact, I have just spent the past 7½ hours, since 4PM, developing & printing film for the first time. My success was not quite proportionate to the amount of time put into it, but I did prove one thing to myself that I can print pictures, with a wholly makeshift device, as well or even better than they are printed in a professional camera shop.

I got my darling's Tuesday letter today with the piece of housecoat in it and it looks very colorful & gay. You certainly have taken to sewing, and I can hardly wait to see all the dainty things you've made. I only hope you've lost the theory of making things about two sizes too large in case you should begin to grow again or something. That terrifically silly theory has ruined several otherwise good-looking pieces of clothing for you, from your wedding negligee to those blouses you made last year. Please don't expend any more "tailor made" effort on producing a bag-like fit! You can be very trim when you want to be, especially since nature built you that way, so don't waste your beauty any more than you'd waste our bankbook figure.

10PM Sunday 28 Oct

That's a shame about the baby bed, but really nothing to worry about. We'll be able to keep our little one in an orange crate for a couple months till it grows big enough to rate a bed. What a dear little thing it's going to be snuggled in all its soft gentle blankets & the sweet pretty clothes its mother has made. I just want to hug you so when I think of it. And so our child is starting off very early in his career being uncooperative at bedtime! It must be a family trait. I'll bet it's kicking must really be terrific by now, for it was sure vigorous before.

9AM Monday

They've started loading the grain & the air is now permeated with dust and chaff. Reminds me of threshing time in Plymouth [Indiana, as a teenager].

*   *   *   *   *

Tues., 30 Oct '45 11PM

Darling -

I got your bulky letter of Sat, Sun, & Mon 9AM with poetry & photos inclosed. Comments follow re letter: 1) - Glad you've acquired a new hobby, but darlin', don't invest too much money into it right now. I know absolutely nothing about photography, but it sounds as tho you're doing fine. The prints are good, too, but I'm rather fussy about my borders, so in the future, would you try to make them come out in even sizes? You see, they don't look neat when I put them into our photo album (which I did, by the way, this eve, to make sure I don't misplace them.)

Your comments re my sewing are most unkind - and in quite a sarcastic vein. I must admit the truth thereof, however. I don't

486

plan to make them 2 sizes too large, I just didn't know enough about pattern alteration in the earlier days. Right now, in sewing my housecoat, for instance, I couldn't fit it too well because of my oversize condition, and lingerie patterns, in "small, medium, large" sizes only.

The baby has been quite a nuisance in making me most uncomfortable & I'll be very happy to be delivered of my burden.

*   *   *   *   *

LETTER #1

FRI 11/9 - Bess & I left for Dr. Proud's about 12:15 PM, using the "L". . . . weight 160, a gain of 2 lbs, my blood pressure still 108, better low than high, and after he listened to the baby's heart, he said it was on the "boy side" - so maybe it will be a Junior. I asked him about the procedure in the event I had a premature delivery. He told me to call him in the event the "bag of waters" should break & he'd tell me about the labor pains spacing & if I had to go to the hospital to go in street clothes with only my toothbrush, comb, makeup, etc. The hospital will supply all the gowns & baby clothes while I'm in there. Now all I have to worry about is the means of getting me to the hospital.

SUN 11/11 - I'm looking forward to your first letter from overseas. I always feel apprehensive when you leave for an overseas voyage. Oh, how I wish you could be back at the right moment, when the Baby comes! Mom marvels at my state of good health & good appetite & ability to get around & sew. She says most women have swollen ankles & are nauseated & feel ill when they reach this stage!

Precious, I spend so much time daydreaming of the future when we'll be together & have our own place & the Baby - and I do miss you so, darling. Take good care of yourself, no unnecessary risks of any kind, darling, for I'm waiting for you so longingly and lovingly, my husband

Betty

*   *   *   *   *

My sweet wife -

This I believe will be my last letter to you until Antwerp.

Got your Monday letter. I like that diaphanous nightgown stuff (divinity?). I think all of your nite wear should be transparent enough to reveal the lush temptation beneath it, (that is if you insist on anything at all). The flannel thing must be comfortable but the collar pattern looks like a gay '90s pair of overall suspenders.

I am glad you are taking pains to get the proper exercise, especially in your legs because I didn't like the early appearance of those varicose veins. You should have your Sis massage you thoroly each day & work out both of you.

About real estate, I don't think it'll make much difference to us what kind of market it is. It seems obvious that we are going to make very little money on our "capital" by appreciation or interest. Most all of our wealth will come from pure earnings or wages & if we buy or build a house, we're not doing it to make money, but to get a place to live with the least expense.

Dearest, write me <u>four</u> letters to that Belgian address, & only four, so that I'll know when I've gotten all of them. It will take us 3 weeks to get there, so that you will be almost a month or perhaps more without mail from me. But you have nothing to worry about now except your own sweet self and our happy little one within you. - I love you so completely, my glorious wife & mate, and will soon be with you to help care for the precious offspring of that love.

Always -
Robert

*   *   *   *   *

My darling one -

Strange that I should have written you yesterday of my prospects of mailing this letter within three weeks, for now it will most likely be Saturday morning (!). This ship certainly is a Rube Goldberg. It's a rather long story tho, so I'll tell it thoroly. The old chief was fired the day before we left New Orleans & our departure from there was delayed two hours waiting for the new chief to get his gear aboard (and his crutches, as the first chief said in reference to this new guy's age). They fired the former chief mainly because he was drunk all the time, but also because he raised so much hell about how much water & oil he needed. He took 700 more barrels of oil at Chalmette Slip than he was supposed to (we took almost 10,000 barrels there because we were near empty). Then to get more grain on the ship they made the chief pump 600 tons of freshwater overboard, leaving just about 250 tons for the trip. The chief called everyone in Lykes Bros office he could think of an s.o.b. for that & they finally took him off. Now he is fully vindicated. The boilers are on the blink & we are using 40 tons of water a day! And instead of burning the normal 170 barrels of oil a day we are using 250 barrels! Therefore, there is nothing to do but head for the nearest port as we'd never make Antwerp at that rate. These ships have an evaporator which can make about 12 tons of water a day from sea water, but that's not enough for the JB! (A normal ship uses about 10 to 20 tons a day & seldom uses the evaporator).

So, of all the places, we had to be near Norfolk when this happens & at 4 PM this aft (Thurs) we turned around & headed for that —- of creation. Will arrive there sometime Saturday. Don't know what they'll do there. If the marine underwriters will allow it, they might load the ship up with another 600 tons of water, but that will bring her below her marks & I don't think that'll be allowed in peacetime. (The plimsoll mark on the ship [diagram of it] for Summer, Winter, Freshwater & North Atlantic, etc. See my training manual on stevedoring.) The other alternative is a repair job of at least five days or maybe even discharge the cargo & send JB to the boneyard. If it's just a matter of water, I'll be able to make my Dec 28th date with my dearest motherwife, but if they fool around much longer that dream will have to be postponed. It may work out okay yet, so I'm not cursing my fate for a while.

*   *   *   *   *

Norfolk
9PM Saturday 10 November 1945

My dearest beloved -

I never realized how deeply I've come to feel New York as "home" until tonite. Our favorite station WQXR came on to stir memories that are recent and most sweetly homelike; memories that center in N.Y. Its familiar programs transported me back to the quiet evenings with you, to the whole New York episode, which in retrospect is a marvelous experience. That great thronging city worked a subtle change in us, implanting its dynamic spirit of cosmopolitan life. New York has become our intellectual home, and we will also never forget that it cradled the hours of intensely lovely passion which brought our marriage to its instinctive consummation. Those rapturous moments of pure carnal ecstasy seem now so intolerably remote. As I stretch delightfully within the narrow confines of my bed at nite, I am convulsed with pangs of desire for the lush fullness of your warmsatin thighs, the pulsing softness of your womanflesh. But as I turn so freely, so lightly twisting my strength with feline slowness, I recall how your supple loveliness is now bulging, taut with the seething fecundity of our mating. I visualize the awesome bigness of your burden, its vigorous, fretful strugglings for freedom within you, its selfish occupancy of your luxuriant womb, exerting its effort merely to securing its parasitic comfort, devouring your food, your warmth, even the very space of your body. I sense your restless tenseness, your annoying feeling of clumsiness & helplessness, your impatient desire to capably eject this visitor into the world, to love it & control it, having nourished it & created it from an inchoate urge, from a fierce moment of overpowering lust, from a mysterious longing of love, you, creatrix, fashioning from the womanly mystery of your body a strong and living Life. I cannot forget you and the magnificent doings that are yours.

*   *   *   *   *

Mon, 12 Nov '45 - 10PM

Dearest -

So happily surprised this AM to receive your letter from Norfolk. I must admit I was <u>really</u> surprised, for I thought you'd be in mid-ocean by now.

Too bad about the ship water condition. Hope it doesn't delay you too much, but then perhaps it might be better if you didn't come back till the Baby was here.

So you're in Norfolk. I'll bet it recalls a lot of memories to be back there after a lapse of 2 years or so. I'll never forget the Officers' Mess & the salad of pineapple & cheese chunks served in wooden bowls! Or our visit to Old Point Comfort, the ferry ride, the flowers on Hollywood Ave. Oh, dear, now I'm getting nostalgia.

MON 11/19 - I finally got my gold inlay put into the molar Doc Z has been working on. Worried tho when he called attention to the fact that most of my molars are loose. You don't think they'll just fall out, do you? I'm so afraid I'll lose teeth bearing our Baby. I do drink milk & take calcium capsules.

* * * * *

LETTER #3

MON 11/26 -Thirteen days since you sailed and you should be getting into Antwerp in a week or so.

I start "idealizing" you when you're away like this, Robert, and I get so lonely for you, especially days when I feel so utterly "blah". I miss your comforting presence. It's no fun being with child because even at your best, you're uncomfortable, but when you don't feel too well, it's misery for there's nothing you can do about it. I can't wait until this burden inside me is delivered. I feel so bulky and clumsy, slow, lethargic. No man can begin to appreciate a woman's feelings at a time like this. If men had to bear children, they wouldn't periodically try to liquidate mankind by making war. Makes me even more bitter at humanity now that I have experienced 8 months of pregnancy and know firsthand what your mother and my mother and all mothers go thru to bring forth new life!

Of course, I'll feel amply rewarded when our Baby comes and a new experience, that of parenthood, opens up for us. But you must promise to be a good father to our child, Robert. You furnished the spark that started its existence, but I had to feed nourish and bear it all these long months. You mustn't be envious if I do feel great love and affection for the fruit of my womb. My love for you will never decrease, in fact I think I'll love you all the more when the Baby comes. Right now, I want you here to help me thru the remaining weeks before Baby arrives and the weeks afterwards, when I will have to recover my strength. Maybe you will be back soon, dearest.

* * * * *

Off the Isle of Wight

4:20 AM (Greenwich time) Tuesday, 27 Nov 1945

My beloved one -

I have certainly forsaken you the past week or so, having been completely immersed in my schoolwork. Have been working every nite to about 5 or 6 AM on my German. Have been going at a very trying pace, altho the results don't appear particularly imposing. Am enclosing a copy of a typical lesson & if you read over some of it you'll see what I'm up against. Here is an illustration. Translate into German: "She is always running around with these bricks of pressed brown coal." "Es wird ihr immer mit diesen, aus Braunkohle gepresten Bricketts herumgelaufen." The big problem in that sentence is that the English is in the passive voice (the object of the action represented as the subject), but the verb is intransitive (it doesn't "act upon" anything). In German an intransitive verb cannot be passive, so you have to put it back somewhat by saying literally "It is <u>to her</u> in running around". That problem takes a while to figure out. Then there is the deal about the coal, which I instinctively wrote out in German "with these out of brown coal pressed bricks", but it took me half an hour to check if that was correct, inserting the prepositional phrase & past participle <u>before</u> the noun they modified which was already in a prepositional phrase.

Perhaps 90% of the time I can just dash it off correctly, having the "feel" of the language pretty well, but because 10% of the time I'm wrong, I must check everything, & that is where the work comes in. However, I have been forced at last to master all these grammatical terms, Indicative, Subjunctive, & Conditional Modes, Passive & Active Voice, transitive & intransitive verbs etc., etc., which I had previously glossed over rather than understood. It is surprising how this "digging" has improved my command of the language. In fact, I can get most of the German news broadcasts with good comprehension now. I have only 200 pages of a novel to read hastily & write a 1000 word summary of, type it up & then I have half of the course completed. I'll bet I've spent about 2 solid days just typing that stuff too, for it will amount to about <u>75</u> pages!!

So I have worked hard & the only consolation I have for my slow progress is that I have jumped into 3rd year college German and kept my head above water (learning how to swim in the process). The extra effort has perhaps saved me at least a year of German study.

*   *   *   *   *

At Anchorage off Downs, England
00:08 AM Wednesday 28 Nov 45

My sweetheart -

It is very pleasant to be in Europe as far as the radio is concerned. Listened to "Pagliacci" tonite. The reception was a little fuzzy at times & I thot the radio must be wearing out because we're not over 75 miles from London. Then at the end of the program what comes but "Govoreet Moskva!" [written in Cyrillic]. And so I've been listening to Moscow all evening, trying to catch on to the pronunciation etc., but mostly enjoying their music. Heard a ½ hr German news program with 90% comprehension, and last nite I listened for a ½ hr to a Hindustani program sent to Indian troops in the Mediterranean Theater. What a wild, blood tingling music those people have. It has the quick dancing rudity of a campfire & whirling tartars, and if you listen to it for any length of time, you feel the wild carousel of its flickering melodies work into the hidden remembrances of your body.

West Schelde River off Flushing, Walcheren Island, Holland

5:30AM Thursday 29 Nov

. . . . Little one dreaming dimly in the soft waters of the womb, what lost shadows roam imperceptibly in your yet untrammeled blood, what jungled memories pervade subtly the mildwarm flame of your life-thirsting flesh? Do you hear the howls of the ages in your quiet sleeping brain, the screams of the million nites, the hunted & the hunter, the fear, the lust, the dance of spring, the moon upon water, the dry sun on the dead, the spears, the dust, wolves, yurts, fires, songs, rape & rain, horses & the endless plains or the great whisper of the forests - is this breath of men not in your blood, in the secret tunnels of your mind? You are a child of Men and the breast of a mother is eternally sweet & tempting, suckling man into his mystery, giving him the taste of woman flesh which he can never forget & must always long for & return to, just as he returns to the quiet surety of the mothering earth.

*   *   *   *   *

Thu 6 Dec - Letter from RWD saying they arrived at Antwerp. Didn't know how long they'd stay there or anything but says he'll be back soon forever. Worrying as to where we'll live after Robert gets back. Oh, this housing shortage! But I can't do anything till he returns.

Fri 7 Dec - 163? I Must Watch my Weight - I've gained more weight & so I've resolved to start dieting tomorrow for I don't want to gain too much more.

Mon 10 Dec - Robert writes from Antwerp & then 3 letters from Paris where he'd gone on a 3 day pass, transportation, lodging &

meals for free. Says it's a marvelous city & he's enjoying all his sightseeing. Doubts he will be back by 12/28 as planned. He's gotten my 1st two letters already. This afternoon mended some of my summer blouses, patched up Mom's slipcovers, reread all of Robert's letters. Glad that he took time out to write me while in Paris trying to sightsee this city in such a short time.

*   *   *   *   *

Antwerp - 9:15PM Friday 30 Nov 45

My sweet beloved -

Am very sleepy, not having slept since 11 PM last nite, but I'll try to hastily write a few impressions of this place. The weather is very damp & foggy & the trip up the Scheldt was like moving thru an ocean of gray dim land. The fields are green, but the stark barren trees sticking their bony fingers thru the mist gives the utterly flat landscape a naked & desolate coldness. However, cows munch placidly along the banks & the roofs of the houses peek up over the dike, and here & there a ribbon of canal threads its glassy way into the haze of the horizon.

We docked comparatively near the center of town, but it still takes two trolley cars to get to the center. I was certainly surprised to find this place a prosperous thriving city, wholly different from the meager, worn appearance of England or the ruined atmosphere of Italy. The people, of course, have that ruddy, weather beaten appearance, but on the whole they are at least fully & warmly dressed & many of them quite stylishly. But in the store windows is where you see instantly all the difference, the fact that they have prosperity here. Radios, vacuum cleaners, candy, fancy pastries, every nameable kind of clothing, jewelry, perfumes, umbrellas, corkscrews (!), delicious ice cream etc. etc. And there are many civilian cars trafficking the streets, including many Buicks & Chevrolets, etc.

*   *   *   *   *

[American Red Cross Stationery]

Paris
6:30PM Sunday 2nd December 1945

My sweet beloved -

The "we" I speak of is John & I. He's rather a pain in some re-

494

spects, not being overly imaginative or adventuresome, but he is at least "manageable" & all in all much better I suppose then being all alone (though I wonder!).

This is, even from the little I've seen of it, a marvelous city & I promise right now to bring you here some day. I do feel guilty splurging recklessly around the world to my heart's delight while you sit home quietly & uncomfortably creating our future happiness.

*   *   *   *   *

Paris
11:55PM Monday 3 December 1945

My dearest sweetheart -

. . . But Paris is really about the most wonderful city I've seen. It has the beautiful boulevards & parkways of Chicago, innumerable historical spots & buildings of outstanding architecture, & a spirited atmosphere of culture & gaiety that I've never seen or felt the likes of before. It is so interesting for me, too, seeing at last the places I have been familiar with for years, from reading Hugo, Dumas, Dickens, etc, such as Rue St Honoré, Rue St Denis, Montparnasse, Montmartre, Vendome, St Sulpice. And at last I realize what a great artist Proust was. Coming across Northern France I felt strangely as tho I had been there before, as tho I knew each stone, each labyrinthine town & ruddy peasant face & then I remembered Swann's Way & the meticulous descriptions of Cambray, the uncanny capturing of this ancient, simple atmosphere & the skillful contrasting of it to the carefree intellectualism of Paris.

*   *   *   *   *

Antwerp, Belgium
1PM Wed. 5 Dec. 45

My beloved wife -

Just got back from Paris and found your Nov. 27th letter waiting for me, my precious. It makes me feel so much better to know that you are well & healthy with our baby. You are bearing our little one with a proud & splendid strength, my darling, & I hope constantly that I will be able to get back in time to lend my pittance of assistance to you, but mostly to witness the beauty and sweetness of your courage. You are a marvelous wife. - And while you have been painfully creating, I have been thoroly enjoying all the advantages of my mobility.

I have come to realize how fine your French is in comparison with some people's, a 32-year old High School teacher's for instance who took college French & can't speak or read as much of it as I can. This guy John is an insipid soul, but as I say, he's harmless at least. His mouth waters when he sees a luscious looking female, but his Sunday School personality chokes it down & comes out with a benevolently beaming & very forceful "son of a biscuit!", or some such gilded euphemism. He's about as sharp & passionate as my Quaker grandmother.

To the Louvre. It was a remarkable place even tho many of the works of the collection are not up yet. Saw the originals of Venus d' Milo & the winged Victory of Samothrace, strikingly displayed; and I don't know why but the originals looked far more impressive than the copies we have seen. Of course, there was the overpublicized "Mona Lisa" & her wan smile. I fail to see anything very outstanding in that picture. There were, tho, some magnificent paintings by Rubens, & Delacroix's "Liberty Leading the Insurgents" (?). There was Manet's "Olympia" & several delicately splendid Renoir's. All in all the part of the collection on display now is no better than the Metropolitan or the Art Institute, but I was not disappointed, for there were many fine paintings I had never seen & the interior of the Louvre itself, with its resplendent 18th Century paneling & gilded, muraled ceilings was well worth the trip. Also saw several historical items, the crown of Napoleon which he took from the Pope's hand to crown himself, as the Pope in his eyes was not great enough to crown him, etc.

Then we went by the St Germain church over the Pont Neuf thru the Latin Quarter & the Luxembourg Gardens to the Pantheon. Hugo, Zola, Mirabeau, Bertrand, etc, etc, all the great men of France are buried there. The place is the same, almost identical, style as the capital in Washington, and is really a memorial to France's heroes. The huge murals on the walls depict the history of France since the times of Attila and Clovis. Puvis du Chavonnes painted 4 of the tremendous sets depicting the life of St Genevieve, the patron Saint of Paris. She died in the year 512 AD. Later on we were to visit the Sacre Coeur Cathedral built on the highest hill of Paris where St Genevieve kept her watch.

We drove by the Concierge which is the prison that held Marie Antoinette & Petain, past a building built by the Romans in 52 BC during Caesar's occupation & which is still standing in fair condition.

We went thru the ghetto & past Victor Hugo's rooms in the Place des Vosges and then to the monument in the Place de la Bastille. It was now about 5 PM & a smoky dusk was falling on the city. As we drove up the broad boulevards & into the narrow winding streets up to Montmartre, the panorama of hurrying crowds flitting thru the foggy evening seemed to be the vivid heart blood of Paris, the zestful indomitable "now". And then as we rose high on the summit of this hill, we could see the Paris "eternal" winking its first lights thru the wraith of evening, the city jumbling its way beneath us, a twisting honeycomb of chaos towards the Seine, land blessed with fame & history, with the passionate struggle of men toward freedom & beauty. It is only from a hill that the true glory of a city can be contemplated & this commanding hill of Montmartre is appropriately crowned with one of the most beautiful edifices in the world, the Sacre Coeur Cathedral. It was built between 1875 & 1924 & its graceful, huge, delicate cupolas are still white & pure as alabaster, curving lightly into the high sky. And around and below this magnificent church is the Bohemian section, the former artist colony of Montmartre. The damp nite wind made it bitterly cold up there & I can well understand how Mimi's little hands were like ice.

*   *   *   *   *

3:30PM Friday 7 Dec 45

Darling -

Just this minute received the form letter I'd made up when back in Brooklyn to inform officers of their promotion. This one was addressed to me (!) and Mewborn had crossed out the "excellent services. . . . "& written in "superior". I love you, - am going uptown to mail this now & expect to sail Monday.

Your adoring husband,
Captain Doty

*   *   *   *   *

Fri 14 Dec - Our assets as of today, including our bonds, are about $8200.

Sun 16 Dec - A Quiet Day at Home - Helped with housework. Bored & rather tired. Mom & I played cards (rummy) till Bess came home at 11:30. Got into a tiff with Mom over nothing. Cried & went to bed at 1 AM or so to fall asleep right away.

Mon 17 Dec - Received 3 letters from Robert telling me of his

497

sightseeing in Paris & the perfumes, bra, etc. he bought me. Also in Dec 7 letter tells me he is a Captain - $50 more per month! He expected to sail Dec 10 & be in the USA by Dec 27 or so, but not sure of getting leave. Made me very happy to get all this mail from my darling.

Mon 24 Dec - Christmas Eve - I am a bit worried about Robert, for big battleships & cruisers have been coming into NY battered & damaged by this severe Atlantic storm.

Tue 25 Dec - "White" Christmas but not too gay - Uneasy thinking of the Atlantic storms and difficulties Robert may encounter in his voyage.

Wed 26 Dec - Robert's ship arrives [An Erroneous Posting!] - Dad Doty called to say Trib listed Robert's ship as arriving today in NY, so now I'm sweating out a call from him. To bed at 12 or so. About 2AM I awoke with a warm sensation & as I got out of bed I felt a gush of waters, which wouldn't stop. So I thot my bag of waters broke & awoke Mom. She was not sure what to do, but Sis & she went to the L station to call Dr. Proud who told them to get me to the hospital. So she tried to get a cab; called the Doty's but got no answer although it rang for 10 min. So she called Pa Kotek & he came about 3:15. Got to the hospital at 3:45 or so & signed in. Little did I suspect what was in store for me.

Thu 27 Dec - Junior - 5:40 - 7 lb 1½ oz - 19" - Got an enema & that started my labor pains but good. I was soon writhing in agony in the labor room & the intern (Dr Cruse) called Dr. Proud & into the delivery room. He came at 5:30 & at 5:40 the baby was here. Much to the amazement of everyone, I guess, for they didn't expect a primapara to give birth so quickly. So here I am in Ward 435, Norwegian Amer Hosp trying to gather myself together. Everyone assures me I'm very lucky to have had my baby so "easily"; I still think it is the most agonizing and humiliating experience to lie there in the throes of expelling the baby. The ether wasn't sufficient to deaden sensations, and you have to bear down & it is a terrific strain. I could feel the baby coming out, almost see it thru the medium of sensation. I had an incision & the stitches are annoying. Everything on a 4-hour schedule, bed pans, temperatures, baby feeding. Bess knew of the baby's coming as she waited on the 5th flr, & Dr. Proud showed her the

498

baby. I first saw my baby at 5:30 PM. He's small & red & was most inactive. No one came to see me tonite. Felt rather sad.

Fri 28 Dec - I Begin to Get Acquainted w/ Baby - Felt lots better today. My uterus is contracting & that hurts & I can't sit up but I'm getting to love my baby. He looks prettier every time I see him and I've had to try to nurse for 4 times today. He has my nose & ears. So tiny! He's had his eyes open & they're so blue. Mom came to see me tonight & paid the hospital bill ($70 flat rate for 10 days) & brought me cigs & cosmetics. Said Bess called Dad Doty & told him she couldn't get them by phone & he sort of laughed it off. Huh! RWD was sent a wire by his Dad telling him he's a father. Wonder just why we haven't heard from Robert - if his ship is in? Baby is so good, never cries when he's brought to me & he's so sweet. I think he looks just like me, nose, ears & lips.

Sat 29 Dec - Dr. Proud was in to see us & I asked him to have the baby circumcised before we leave the hospital. My breasts are beginning to fill out & I certainly hope I'll be able to nurse the Baby. Mom came out to see me this evening, no news from Robert. Do wish I'd hear from Robert - can't understand why we haven't so far.

Sun 30 Dec - Quite a Day - My breasts were full & painful & I used a breast shield to get the Baby to empty them. No news from Robert. Dad Doty wrote me saying he was going to check with NY re delivery of telegram to RWD. Rather disgusted with things as I went to sleep. Being awakened at 1:30 AM & 5:30 AM to nurse the Baby sure interferes with my rest.

Mon 31 Dec 1945 - New Year's Eve - A much better day for me except that now I'm worried about Baby. Dr. Proud says he's lost weight & I've got to make him drain my breasts each time he nurses, using the breast shield if necessary. Seems 15 min is all he should nurse as more doesn't do him much good & it'll make my nipples sore. Good meals all day & I napped during the aft. If only some word from Robert would reach me. Mother came with good news: airmail spec delivery from Robert covering period 12/13 to 12/22 and which explains things - terrible storm blew them off their course & 12/22 they were near the Azores where they hoped to get more oil, coal & food. He didn't think they'd get to NY till Jan 5 or later. So the notice Dad Doty saw in the Trib was wrong. Baby nursed w/o nipple shield on the left breast, at 9:30 PM. So I was in very good spirits as the year went out & the new one came in. Wotta year!

*   *   *   *   *

10PM Saturday 8 Dec. 1945

My sweet wife -

Nothing of particular importance happened last nite so I didn't write. There's a gang of 20 Belgiques in here to clean up the holds, set the bunks up etc. & my leniency with the men is really paying off, for now that there is work to do they are really pitching in. All the grain will be out of the ship by 3 AM this morn, & we move to the ballast docks at 6 AM. Should be all set up & take troops Monday & sail that nite. That would get us to the States on the 26th or 27th.

I got a jeep & went out to Camp Top Hat, the only place where I could get Captain's bars. My 1st official signature as Captain went for the jeep trip ticket. When a Major called me Captain, I almost turned around behind me to see who he was speaking to! After being called Lt for 2½ yrs it's rather startling to be called another name; but pleasant. The $50 a month raise is, however, the finest part.

*   *   *   *   *

12 N Tuesday 11 December [1945]

My beloved -

. . . . I have been very busy the last couple days trying to get this stinking grain cleaned out of the ship & getting this damn Belgique labor to do a decent job of it. We were all scheduled to sail yesterday, but the Belgies screwed off at 7:20 PM the night before instead of working all nite as they were supposed to, & as a result the ship wasn't ready yesterday. They brot a few troops aboard, but the IG made them take them off again. So we worked all day to 9 PM trying to show the laborers what was to be done. They'd mop all day with the same pail of filthy water if you didn't yell at them every 10 minutes to change the water & quit spreading the dirt around.

6:30PM

Beloved -

Got caught right in the middle of this with embarkation. We

have 676 troops in all. Only 19 officers, so we put M/Sgts & KPs in the other of the 61 officer quarters. Have an excellent group of officers & the CO of Troops is not only the same rank as I, but a swell egg on top of it, so that everything is running smoothly. Most of the details for officers that I had prepared have been filled by volunteers, so that the work will probably be done very efficiently.

✻   ✻   ✻   ✻   ✻

11:10AM Friday 14 Dec

You can see about how busy I am by the amount of time I'm left in peace to write to you. Had no sooner started yesterday when my medic came up about water chlorination. So I straightened that out with the Chief Engineer & the Doc & then it was time to open the PX. Sold to the supply Sgt of each of the 5 units rather than to the individual men & that way sold over $900 worth of cigarettes & candy to 676 men in about 2 hours. But it took me half the nite to count the money & roll up the quarters, etc. Had over $100 in quarters & halves.

9AM Monday 17 Dec 45

My darling wife -

If I can hold fast to my bed long enough, I'll try to describe the marvels of the storm we're having. After all this time at sea I am finally seeing a genuine storm. It is an experience I have awaited with eagerness, but I bitterly regret that it should happen now when of all times I am most excitedly impatient to get home to my beloved one. It began Saturday nite & by Sunday morning the wind was blowing a fierce, steady 60 mph. During the course of the day the barometer kept falling phenomenally until it was far below anything the Skipper had ever seen in 47 years at sea. It reached 27.9 at 6 PM. We took several 35 degree rolls & lost a life raft on one of them, but no seas were coming aboard. We are so light that we ride over the top of them, otherwise just about all the gear on the foredeck would have been torn off. But being light has the grave disadvantage that the wheel keeps coming out of the water, & also the force of the wind on the exposed hull makes it almost impossible to steer or make any headway. However, it is a thrilling sight to see the amazing power of the waves creeping with slow mountainous majesty upon the ship and lifting its great hulk effortlessly into the sky till the bow points over 30 degrees above the horizon & then drops giddily into the yawning hollow of water, before the next titanic swell. The wind, sometimes lashing the ocean & the ship

501

at 70 mph, viciously swirls this stinging spray from each tenaciously driven ripple till the air is filled & fogged with snowy, driving mist & the entire surface of the ocean is lathering like a huge boiling cauldron. It is a truly indescribable sight, terrifying in its feral immensity, gloriously beautiful in the wild majesty of its power. The storm finally got too much for the ship last nite. We were making no headway, & steering into it was almost impossible so that the Captain had to turn tail & run before the storm. We are now being hurtled along thru this churning chaos before the giant push of the gale. We are heading SSE, and where we'll end up before it blows out, no one can say. I only wish that you could see this ocean and its amazing & unearthly vestiture of storm. This morning I stood just outside my room and, sheltered somewhat from the gale & spray, watched the teeming seas, tumbling after us. Leisurely, in giant, cumbrous swells, these foam-tumbling, mist-spewing mountains would move upon us, sinuously arising & subsiding like some huge, ravening beast unable to direct its quivering hulk towards a steady goal. They travel slowly, lifting a thundering white boiling crest into the gale & then fading eerily away to rise again, finally overtaking the ship from the stern, looming fearsomely above it, high seething tons of careening ocean, ready to smash the dizzily staggering toy-ship; but with unfailing gallantry the stern seems to lift itself upon the back of the frothing monster & slip unharmed into the wet, weltering froth of the hollowed sea. Often this 420 ft. ship fits its entire length easily between two wave crests. The larger seas run at least half a block long and about the height of your folks' house. That is a terrific mass of water to see thundering after a ship. - More later, for I must now go on my daily 10 AM inspection of the troop areas.

4:30PM Tues 18 Dec

My sweetheart -

The troops have been aboard for one week now & our destination is still NY, although we are at present heading towards Portugal! For about 12 hours last nite we were able to hold our course at WSW or SW, but after a couple 40 degree rolls this morning we had to go back to following the wind, which is now blowing us ESE! However, the gale is slackening & although some of the seas are still gigantic, the storm is moderating & the barometer coming up slowly (about 29.1 now). We lost pressure on the hydraulic steering system & had to steer from the stern last nite, but got that fixed this morning.

502

Darling -

I am frantically remorseful now that I ever let myself go to sea again & allow my plans with you, my sweet one, to get all mixed up, snarled again in contingencies in this gloriously crucial period of our lives. Paris, Antwerp, Azores, New Orleans, all these months of adventure & education are not worth one instant's togetherness with you at this time. I am wholly confident of your magnificent capability, my lovely one, but I feel intensely the awesome need we have of each other in these trying hours of your creation, of our sharing the consummation of our divinely vital undertaking. I feel a twofold impatience, one, that I am being cheated of one of life's deepest & most marvelous experiences & 2, that I am forsaking you, leaving the whole of an already immense burden upon you alone; that I am powerless to fulfill even my puny role in the birth of our child. I long desperately to be with you.

But the mighty fate of the sea has held us apart. Only now are we learning the true immensity of the storm in which we were involved. Its radius was 1000 miles which means that it covered almost the entire Atlantic. The USS cruiser "Augusta" was damaged so badly that she had to turn back to Southampton with her load of troops & the carrier, "Wasp" was also damaged. So it was, at least, no ordinary event which intruded into our plans, but its novelty does not lessen its undesirability.

Went up to the Chart Room to study up on the Azores. Got the Pilots Guide to African Coastal waters & read all the facts and figures & located everything on the fine hydrographic office charts we have. [Sketchy map drawn] Then the Skipper came in & started explaining some of the difficulties we'll have going in there. We are going to the island of Fayal (8 miles in diameter) on which is located the Principal port, Horta. We've been unable to get a sight today, so we don't know just where we are & therefore can't tell just when we'll arrive, so that in radioing ahead tonite we won't be able to say when we need a pilot. Will set our course soon on the radio beam direction finder at Horta & on another island 50 miles to the West. It should be a pretty sight, the island of Pico only a few miles from Fayal having an active volcano peak about 1½ miles high. We must get 3000 barrels of fuel, 5 tons of coal (for the galley), water &, we hope, more food.

Sweetheart -

We are now coming about 4 miles off the Western point of Fayal & the mountain of Pico is also visible jutting thru a gentle wreath of clouds. The skies are overcast & the ship is rolling lazily & deeply in the long ground swells. The land looms, an enchanted isle, soaring steep out of the sea into the soft, clinging mists. Islands are always a place of mystery, a place alone, a haven, a retreat, a wondrous pause in the desolate monotony of the watery wastes of ocean. They hold a steady & reassuring face into the brutal lashings of the storm, a promise of safety and of firm & restful earth; yet they are a nowhere, a lost & lonely plot of forgotten rock & soil flung inadvertently upon the wild surface of the desert sea, spots that only wanderers touch.

Since the Azores are the main refueling point for the ATC mail planes, I think you should get this letter in about 4 days. It will be some company to you until I can be with you. You must remember that I am with you in thot always, to give you courage & assurance, to soothe your discomfort, to protect you from all wants & needs, cherish you tenderly as my wife, no matter how many earthly miles may separate us. I can sense the vigor of our child within you & the bright pain it will cause to you as it rends your lovely body to launch itself from its sweet nourishing prison into the difficult freedom of the world. It will be strong of mind & body as ourselves, possessing your gentleness & my passion; it will be the most beautiful thing of our lives & a living joy unto itself. The course of our life runs on, & I will now probably see you next as a sweet & loving mother.

Your husband,
Robert

*　　*　　*　　*　　*

END Diary - 1946

Tue 1 Jan 1946 - Sleepily started this 1st day of the year. Baby nurses very nicely so long as I use the nipple shield. My milk is quite yellowish in color which they tell me indicates richness. I do hope I can nurse the Baby. I scribbled two postcards to Robert & asked Mom to mail them in an envelope airmail to NY. Do so hope he'll be in soon & can come into Chicago for a short visit.

Thu 3 Jan - Baby is Circumcised - Baby nursed well at 9:30, but they took him away after 15 min to have him circumcised; I had

504

to sign a request for that. Then he was groggy & wouldn't nurse much at the 1:30 & 5:30 feedings; but he's getting a formula. Hurt like the dickens when the nurse removed the sutures, and I've had a burning aching pain there since. Mom brot Baby's clothes this eve.

Fri 4 Jan - I Stay up & walk around a bit - Dr. Proud stopped in to see me this AM. Asked him about Baby's weight loss & he thot it was about 6 oz., but that I had nothing to worry about. Sat in the rocker for a while this aft. Just noticed Baby was born exactly 40 weeks from my last menstrual period & on the date I would be menstruating. Mom brot letter fm RWD written from Azores where he was spending Xmas.

Sat 5 Jan - Baby Comes Home Today - 6 lbs-9 oz - Had a demonstration on how to bathe Baby, etc. Mom came about 2 PM. The Baby got all dressed up & the same nurse who wheeled me up to the delivery room & was in attendance there wheeled me out to the car where Fritz & Bess were waiting. So about 3:30 PM Baby came home. - Sis & Mom had fixed the bassinet up with blue lining & a white skirt. He slept, the little darling, all the time. Very sick little gal & I spent as much time as I could in bed. Baby doesn't seem to care too much for his bottle, but he's nursing pretty good at my breasts.

Tue 8 Jan - Another day of caring for the Baby, and trying to get a nap in between feedings & changing his diapers. Oh, that itching, aching feeling in the vaginal region. Mom has been giving me warm water douches which give me temporary relief. Took a nap for a couple hours this aft. Woke up to find a long letter from Robert written from the Azores, chafing at the idea of delay because of lack of fuel there in the islands.

Wed 9 Jan - Baby weighs 8 lbs clothed, clothes 3/4 lb - This a.m. radio announcement that the Josiah Bartlett had come into New York. A bit excited. He called Long Distance on Galinski's phone about 6 PM & Bess talked to him. He has some idea of buying his Dad's car & driving me & Baby to NY & getting a shore job, which is a screwy idea. Baby seems to be hungry all the time. He nurses for about 15 min & the breast is dry. Wondering when (or if) RWD will be able to come in. Western Union strike in NY so he can't wire. I wrote Robert airmail letter bringing him up to date on events & telling him how grateful I am to my folks for their aid at this time. Baby had fretful night. His umbilical cord came off at 2:30 & he cried & cried.

Thu 10 Jan - Robert's Birthday - Formula Trouble - Baby seems to have a stopped up nose & his little left eye is still running. He took about 1 oz. each of his formula twice today & each time threw up all of it, necessitating a complete change of clothes & bedding. Mom washed clothes & Baby's things today. Little sleep last nite & no chance to sleep today; guess I got about 1 hour sleep this aft. Baby crying off & on, hungry or in pain? Baby fussed till midnight after his 10 PM feeding, but then slept till 2:30 am, awoke 5:15, sleep at 6, fuss at 7am. Motherhood certainly has its cares and responsibilities.

*   *   *   *   *

9AM Monday 24 Dec. 45

My sweetheart -

Tis the day before Christmas, the sea is refreshingly calm & sunlit, and we are making full speed for Ponta Delgado on San Miguel, the easternmost of the Azores. We should arrive there at noon, get our oil & depart tonite for the States. It is a 10 day run from here to NY, if we have good weather the rest of the way.

Now to tell you of Fayal Island. We sailed almost completely around the 8x7 mile volcanic island about 3 to 4 miles offshore, so that I had a good chance to observe it. The farmlands were so accurately laid out that you could almost call it "agricultural architecture". Atop the hills, too, were many old Dutch windmills, & I later learned that they came with the 1st settlers of the islands, the Flemish, back in 1500. The islands, I believe, were discovered in 1470, and Columbus stopped here for provisions on his voyages.

. . . Two doctors came aboard from the Health Dept. They told us that the U.S. cruiser "Portland" had been in two days ahead of us & had had 4 dead & 45 injured from the storm. Another ship had also been 20 days getting from Gibraltar to here!

*   *   *   *   *

506

Merry Christmas - to my beloved wife -

I have been so completely occupied with the terrific problem of getting 676 troops ashore for Xmas that I've hardly had time to think.

Pulled into Ponta Delgado at 11 AM yesterday & they have absolutely no fuel, the last of that having gone to the cruiser Portland. We have only 2200 bbl & burn 240 bbls a day which, if we hit rough weather, couldn't even get us to Bermuda. In that situation I could do nothing else but take the heavy responsibility of letting these GIs loose. Had to secure permission from the Portuguese Brigadier Commandant of the Island thru the American consul & make arrangements with the civil police to patrol with my MPs, get their money exchanged, worry about pro stations [prophylaxis] & arrange for transportation. We can only allow 160 ashore at a time since the treaty we have with Portugal does not permit a massed landing of uniformed troops. Everything is going fairly smoothly. I saw to the placing of 30 MPs with the Civilian Police this morn and have met a Czech refugee who is a professor of languages & he is fixing the boys up on all the inside wholesale prices & showing us around. He speaks 17 languages & is a typical professor type, spry, gray headed, goatee, etc. I speak to him mostly in German, although his English is also excellent.

. . . And not so long from now daddy can tell his sweetest little one the picturesque story of Christmas in the Azores, Christmas 3000 miles from my darling motherwife.

I love you forever

Your husband
Robert

*   *   *   *   *

9PM Friday 28 December 1945

Ponta Delgado, S. Miguel, Azores

To my wife, whom I love more than all the world. There is something tugging inside of me tonite, an enormous restlessness as if my whole soul would break free and span the tortuous distance that separates us, to be with you in your hour of need. I am fiercely bewildered at my helplessness, tho perhaps even at your side I might feel more helpless yet. But my complete isolation from you at this time, the most awesomely critical of our lives, is frantically pounding my mind with anxieties & hopes, until I am afire with impatience. And I am sad & tired and want only the sweet knowledge of your kisses, the squeeze of your dainty hand, the strange ecstasy of our new & coming life. My mind cannot grasp the immensity of this change within our love, the curious & exquisite intrusion that has come from nowhere, from the oblivious ecstasy of our joy in each other. I am lost and alone, a wanderer, while you carry the beloved happiness of our oneness so vitally with you, so tender & precious, keeping sweet vigilance & care close to the marvelous beauty of our intimacy.

*　　*　　*　　*　　*

I took the MPs ashore Monday nite to get them acquainted with the town & then Christmas Day the fun really started. The entire pass system broke down because the officers, to put it in GI talk, fucked off, and took no charge of their groups of men whatever. Then getting one shift aboard & another ashore was also very complicated. But the worst part was the combination of facts which made it Xmas day ashore for the 1st time for only 3 hours after a terrific & discouraging voyage & no stores open except cafes. Result: one drunken army. However, the majority did behave very well. We had 3 men in jail & about 25 who should have been, but whom their buddies carried back aboard ship. I think we got most of the culprits & put them on the shit list. Those from the jail were made into a permanent scrub detail for the deck for duration of the voyage. Among the strangest papers in my voyage file this time will be a receipt for windows in the city jail here which was paid for by one of the drunken celebrants. They had put him in a cell but left it unlocked & he came out tearing up the police station. It took 6 cops to get him back in. At least we weren't the only ones, for the civil police arrested 13 citizens the same day. Had a man break restriction yesterday & go ashore in civilian clothes. Rather than go to the trouble of court martialing him, we hit upon the ingenious idea of locking him up for the duration for psychopathic observation. So we are now making use of the mental ward.

After the exhibition Xmas day, I restricted the ship for a day & reorganized a more foolproof pass system. The last two days things have gone very quietly ashore. The troops now have from noon till 8 PM, a different shift going each day & the passes are numbered & assigned & then collected at 8 PM as they come aboard, so we know if any are missing.

I must tell you of one of the key figures in my story and adventure, my friend Filip Rich. He is 54 years old & very athletic, being a tireless walker, & claims he goes swimming every morning. He has a goatee which reminds me of Sigmund Freud. He is a Czechoslovakian refugee (a Jew), & has had a son killed in a concentration camp & his daughter was held in Belsen. It is very pathetic to find a man in his old age so completely cut off from the happy fruitfulness of life. He is a distinguished looking & intelligent man & his fundamental profession is teaching languages. He speaks and writes fluently Czech, Polish, Russian, German, French, Italian, Rumanian, Bulgarian, Spanish, Portuguese, Arabic, & English, the most recently acquired of seventeen languages he can speak readily, tho a little clumsily.

He walked our legs off the other day on a tour of the town. The streets are very narrow & have black & white tile sidewalks about one foot wide on each side. About 50% of the people go barefoot all the time, & children are as rife as cobblestones. The poverty & squalor of the majority of homes is pitiful. They do, however, keep the streets clean & somehow have not fallen victims of the war. The WC in most homes is a stone outhouse in the courtyard & it reeks with seeming centuries of foulness. The house interiors are cool & damp & very scantily furnished. In general, heat is not necessary in this climate.

We took a ride out thru the country this aft. The entire road (barely wide enough for the bus to pass an oxcart) was closely lined all the way with these rudely painted stone dens in which 200,000 human beings live on the island. The road was a slough of red yellow mud swarming with mongrel dogs & barefoot dirty, half naked children. The passing of the bus was a big event & it drew all the sorrowful, dim eyes to the one window of the den to peer out with open mouth, registering a dull, animal surprise. The slovenly sunken cheeked women hold children to their tubercular chests, shielding them from the drizzle in a corner of their tattered shawl. And the men would look back from their plodding oxcarts & stare & sometimes wave. It was a depressing sight to behold this bovine squalor of humanity, yet even here was something great in the very animal vitality that kept them living & breeding, battling thru a muddled, dreary life, century after century, the Drudge, the Nameless, the pulp of history on whom Fate leaves a brutish stamp. How many thousands have coiled in the chill mists of the island winters, how many Pedros gone to a dreary grave to leave their heritage of misery upon their spawn, to run barefoot in the mud & beat the

oxen with a nimble cane? - (Echoes of Thos Grey, but it was spontaneous & unintended).

Above all this merciless confinement to life, I could see the
gaudy weatherbeaten churches which dot the island, holding it
thus in an invisible & mighty web of ignorance. In Horta I wandered
into the church on Sunday afternoon. There on the left sat perhaps
50 little girls, their bright straw hats gaily bobbing in vehement
chatter. On the right an equal number of boys wriggling with perpetual impatience, till the black cloaked priest tinkled a little bell for
silence. Then, smiling benevolently, he began his Sunday lesson to
the children. He cajoled them, and made then laugh & then turned
seriously to drive home a point. Oh, a man the children loved & a
man who loved children, all of them so diminutive & helpless in the
huge vacancy of the empty church, the colorful, mystic, spacious,
silent, all absorbing church, which engulfed them in ageless, huge
stone walls, & bowed them in awe before its elegance & its mystery.
Who is to blame the jovial priest or the now attentive, now laughing
children; yet in each word, in each candle, in each tiny heart impressed by the majesty of the tortured crucifix, there lurked an invidious poison, a sleek, intangible drug that slips somehow thus
into the dull minds of men & leaves them dry, deformed, asleep.

How thankful, too, I was, as a I rode thus muddily thru poverty
& crudity, to think that my sweet wife need not bear a child into
such a life, that she need not weep to think her little one might be a
girl & thus foredoomed to double misery, that she can feed & wash
our child & see it grow straight & bright-eyed into a more satisfying
world. Such thots brot joy, but also a deep feeling of compassion, a
keen, sudden knowledge that tho you bear a child into a more comfortable life, it is still with the same pain as the peon's wife, the
same motheragony & hope & into the same life of marriage, birth &
death; forever, cycle upon breathing, laughing, suffering cycle;
who must eventually know the sweating glee of mating, the tearing cry of birth, & the hushed, choked sob of death. We are inevitably human. We are indomitably virile, magnificent & unending
moments of precious life.

To you, who are at this moment bringing forth a new, distinct &
ardent life, must go the worship of all mankind. Fountain of life & of
pleasure, you, my wife, my woman, my nurturess of miracles, my
fertile one whose flesh has made this stuff of the world, you are to
me the very essence of life, its exquisite energy, its eternal passion.
I adore you with every particle of my being, surrendering to the
inevitableness of you & of your beautiful fruition, as to the vast &

majestic tide of life itself, to the love & joy that bubbles in each second of my blood. We have mated the fresh breath of our mouths & the passionate sweetness of our flesh. We are now one, a vital entity, forever.

What a strange & a worshipful fulfillment from the destiny that first caused our eyes to fall upon the other, what bounteously happy years from those beginnings to this triumphal climax; and oh, what a wondrously beautiful lifetime is opening up before us. I can only say, as I always will, that I love you

Robert

*　　*　　*　　*　　*

2:30PM Saturday 29 Dec 45

My sweetheart -

I received a reply to my TWX to CG NYPE from no less than the CG ASF! saying that a tanker was being diverted here. Then a couple hours later we got word that the tanker was definitely coming & low & behold this damned island had <u>500 tons</u> of reserve fuel that they were saving for an <u>emergency</u>, which they then released to us. As tho we weren't an emergency.

Am having the troops rounded up by 5 PM & am now going ashore to spend my last 100 Escudos. I may (if I have a couple more drinks) buy you a Thorens cigarette lighter, but I do wish you would give up smoking with the baby. There is somehow to me an unwholesome feeling in seeing a mother smoking.

I can hardly contain my impatience to get back to you my beloved, to you and to what I am almost certain will be the sweetest, prettiest little baby girl that has ever been born, a darling as adorable as her mother. Oh, how I love you, my wife, my soft, kissable squeezetight

Always
Robert

*　　*　　*　　*　　*

2:30PM Wed 9 Jan 46

My sweet, glorious motherwife

I got Dad's telegram of Dec 27th about 10 minutes after we docked. At first it was just a tremendous, inexpressible wave of relief that went thru me, and then a flood of joy & triumph. I cannot hastily express the really ineffable happiness that I feel towards

511

you, the infinite love and tenderness of this strange new emotion of fatherhood.

I am still beset by the duties of T Comdr, for the troops have only just now started to debark. I called the office & found that Mewborn has taken Branstatter's place & wants me back in the office. Perhaps we should buy my pop's car & come to live in NY sans subway rides.

*   *   *   *   *

8:30AM Thurs 10 Jan 45 [Still haven't changed years]
My beloved -

. . . I called you & got a very peculiar sensation of fear when I heard the assurance to the operator that the person answering was Mrs. Doty. The voice sounded so peculiar! My first frightened question would have been "Darling, has childbirth somehow changed your voice?" when Bess cut in & explained. I'm concerned over the fact that you're still so weak after two weeks & really won't believe everything is alright until I see you & our little darling with my own eyes. I got your letter, and am so thankful that the event overtook you so suddenly & was over so quickly, - and you wanted it to happen while I was away! I will never know why, nor cease regretting that I wasn't there with you - and secretly within me, too, I'm somehow elated that it is a boy. Tho I know I would have felt even more tenderly towards a baby girl, still it must be the ancient rites of mankind that make me feel a rather wild sense of triumph at the firstborn being a son. And I know that you are proud of it, too, my beloved one.

Don't know what I'll say when I see Mewborn today & he asks me to take a shore job again (as I believe he will). If you are too weak to join me, I certainly don't want it & then, if you can come, there is the problem of getting an apartment & a car. However, I'll try to beg the question & get leave to come home & discuss it with you; but from indications so far, I think I'd be better off on the ship for another trip at least.

Your loving husband,
Robert

P.S. - I still don't approve of "junior" as a name. Let's call him anything but that. Please darling.

*   *   *   *   *

512

CHAPTER XIV
The Last Voyage, Father Comes Home

Synopsis - Motherhood now became Elizabeth's occupation, and her passion. Naturally, she looked to her mother for guidance. All was proceeding smoothly, but in the harried 4½ days I was able to spend with my beloved and our 3-week old son I was appalled at Elizabeth's being so wholly dependent upon her mother's judgment. With total lack of tact, of course, I intruded my not overly informed opinions; and it didn't take much to arouse her mother's readily available ire. My poor darling was caught in the middle, knowing her debt to her mother and her mother's experience, yet also recognizing the tyrannical capabilities of her parent. Thus began the in-law problem which, with my unrestrained vehemence, I aggravated in my letters to her, wholly ignoring the fact that, ultimately, we would be best served by living with her parents until that happy day when we might move to our own home. She had an in-law prejudice of her own, in the aloofness my parents had displayed when she needed help in closing our apartment, their deafness when she called on the night of her delivery seeking transportation to the hospital, and their joining me in criticizing her for calling the baby "Junior".

Our letters thus took on an occasionally contentious tone as the long-awaited release from our loneliness approached. I was to have several weeks of tedious duty ashore before finally setting off, with a converted hospital ship [Fig 46], to bring back war brides and children from England, then to account for all the property under my responsibility and, at last, get terminal leave from the army.

Sat 12 Jan - Robert arrives! - Baby threw up his formula and was very irritable all aft. I tried to sleep w/ no success. Robert came about 5:30 w/ his folks. They stayed too long for me, for we had just begun supper. So finally they left & RWD & I had supper. Baby slept beautifully after his sleepless afternoon. Robert brot perfumes, liquor, brass vase, beautiful hankies, lots of coins & pictures from Paris, Antwerp & the Azores. So good to have my husband with me again. He's as sweet as ever and so thrilled at being a poppa! 'Course he has ideas on bringing up Baby but what gets me is his objection to the name of Junior. I refuse to budge, however.

Sun 13 Jan - Robert had an opportunity to observe a typical day in Junior's life, from his bath to his afternoon tantrums. Baby acting up with cramps and too many bowel movements. Robert will call Dr. Proud tomorrow to ask about that & his formula, etc. Do wish I could get more sleep.

Mon 14 Jan - Robert & Mom at Odds - It all started at breakfast when Robert didn't come when called & stalked off to see his Dad at Hotpoint re job etc. He was gone all aft & really accomplished a lot. Called Dr. Proud, continue formula, kaopectate for cramps, argyrol for eyes, baking soda for nose. I guess RWD doesn't care for Mom's kind of cooking. Trouble w/ Baby. Up at 1:30. He threw up formula, cramps, to sleep 3:30, up at 5 & he didn't go to sleep till 8:15! Robert walked the floor with him & that got Mom angry because she feels left out in the cold. And Robert says he is disgusted at my looking to Mom for advice & assistance regarding Baby - & I think he's acting like a child & could be agreeable for these few days. So it goes & I am in the middle! Owah!

Tue 15 Jan - Another Day of Mom vs RWD - Robert greeted me with the remark that Mom was on strike this morn for she wouldn't look after Baby. Then he bolted out of the house w/o breakfast. Brot back pint of Mead's cod liver oil & argyrol. Robert returned from his folks about midnight as I was nursing Baby. Brot his baby book along. We had quite a discussion before retiring. He told his folks I was angry at his Dad's not taking me to the hospital. I guess they rehashed a lot of things about me, and Robert thinks I've been to blame for much misunderstanding, that I care as much for them as he does about my Mom.

Wed 16 Jan - Mom bathed the Baby while Robt & I had our breakfast. Robt drove out to the U of C to see what his chances are for entering upon his discharge this Sept. Says his folks say I can come live with them if conditions are too crowded here at home. Don't think I'd be any happier there. Robert started filling out application for U of C. We retired early knowing that Baby would keep us up all nite. Robt is a full-fledged poppa, having changed Baby's diapers, fed him milk & water & walked the floor with him during the night.

Thu 17 Jan - Robert leaves - when will I see him again? - Well, the nightmare of having Mom & Robert at daggers points ended when his folks picked him up at 1PM, his train leaving 1:30. Bitter aftertaste left when Mom began her tirade against him this aft, refusing to bathe Baby or even get out of bed. So Bess & I gave Baby his bath, perhaps a bungled up job, but he got wet & oiled. Washed out some of his clothes, too, for Mom hasn't done any of his laundry for 2 days. Do wish things would straighten out, Robert get out of service, find us a place to live & let us have a life of our own. Robert says he may not be back till discharge 6 mos later.

Sat 19 Jan - Baby very good all day, sleeping most of the time, and waking up at 3 and 4 hour intervals for food. Am so wrapped up in my Baby & so happy that he's been so good today. To bed early, but doing a lot of thinking before I fell asleep.

Sun 20 Jan - Baby a bit crabby this morning, but has been very good since his bath. Fall more & more in love with my Baby every day & he is beginning to fill out nicely. Why haven't I heard from RWD? Is he angry with us?

Mon 21 Jan - 750,000 steel workers strike - Can't understand what's wrong with Baby. He falls asleep nursing at the breast, then wakes up 1½ hours later hungry. So there goes our schedule! Letter from RWD saying the J.B. is being decommissioned & they want him in a shore job. He's stalling things so he can take Army test in lieu of U of C entrance exam in 2 weeks or so.

*　　*　　*　　*　　*

10:30PM Friday 18 Jan 46

My beloved one -

They're trying to rush me into a shore job, but I'm not at all anxious for it.

Went to the I & E Branch at the Port & got all the info on this Army General Educational Development Exam which I can take in lieu of the U of C entrance exam. They say it's really a tough exam, so I'm going to start reviewing Math, History, dates, etc.

Have bot a can opener for some canned salmon & chicken I've got stowed away & if I get some crackers & a bottle of milk, should be able to make a decent breakfast on the hungry JB.

Please try to sleep & rest as much as possible, darling, until the hours of attending to our baby grow less exacting. He is the most marvelously lovable baby I have ever seen, just as you are the most adorable woman in the world, my wife,

Your husband
Robert

* * * * *

Noon Tuesday 22 Jan

My darling wife -

I cannot explain my infidelity in not sending you this letter sooner. I am very penitent about it & will try to make it up by writing every day this week. The 3 replacements for my EM are utterly worthless, so the only man I have is McElwee (whom I got promoted to Corporal in record time). Spent all yesterday morning packing supplies in the inadequate crates they sent us. Then I talked the Shipyards people into giving us stevedores to get the stuff off. But the only winches working on the ship were in #2 so all the stuff had to be carried out there. Then they had no cargo nets, so we had to improvise a sling. To top everything off, they got half the junk on the quay & the rest of it's sitting on the hatch square all in the rain & then they knocked the gang off to go on another job! In an hour or so I was able to talk someone into allowing them to come back & finish the job. By 4 PM we arrived at the Army Base with a truckload of very miscellaneous junk. Have spent all this morning getting the equipment from the ground level up to the 3rd floor & this afternoon if I get some men, it will be separated & ready to turn in tomorrow!

Spoke to Mewborn this morning & he insists that I have to take a shore job here for a month or so because of 1) there are no ships

516

for me to go on; 2) I'm the only one who can replace Drury who is
being discharged.

* * * * *

Wednesday, 23 Jan '46 - 7:30PM

Dearest -

Baby was up at midnight, 2 am, 5:15 am, & 7 am. He nurses
just so long, falls asleep, & I can't budge him. Apparently he's
still hungry & gets up 2 hours later. I gave him the bottle at 7 AM
& he drank 3 oz., & promptly threw up part of it.

He's so strong and wiry. You should see him kick me in the
stomach when I'm doing the honors with a diaper! He literally
crawls out of his diaper at times, for I find it down by his ankles.
He'll be a strong, supple baby, I think. Tomorrow he'll be 4
weeks old, darling, and how attached I am to the little one already.

Just got your letter, Robert. Glad to get it for I was beginning to wonder at the delay in hearing from you. Considering the
unfavorable circumstances, the pics are surprisingly good.

What you say about my mother. Her behavior towards
Baby & me has been very proper in every respect since you left.
In fact, Mom & I have managed to get along always. She's mellowed in her feelings towards you since you left & admits that
outside of your "lack of tact" you have a lot of good qualities, ambition, industry, resourcefulness, etc. Darling, don't worry
about Baby & me. We'll get along with Grandma until you come
back & take us away to a nice home of our own.

Robert, dearest, you must not fret too much over a situation
that can't be otherwise. I'm still a pretty miserable gal & appreciate not having the burdens of a household to cope with, taking
care of a newborn baby is not a mean task either. Baby & I don't
argue with mother. I think I can drive home a point in other
ways, so we don't clash.

Lovingly
Betty

* * * * *

517

Sweetheart -

Have been buying milk & cookies & eating breakfast aboard the ship, and of course the lunch at the Base is an unbeatable bargain. Trying to make my money last & it's not the easiest thing to do in this town.

Went to the Bklyn library last nite & got a Physical Science Survey book & a similar one on Biology. Have just completed my U of C application & want to record my "Write a statement descriptive of your purpose in undertaking a college course" in case they lose this application I won't have to spend an hour dreaming up another "statement".

"My eventual purpose is the attainment of sufficient technical knowledge (and formal, academic recognition thereof) to teach on a college level and/or carry on research work in some branch of Biological Science. Heretofore I have studied whatever my fancy led me to. Such a style of learning has been pleasant, but undisciplined and, perhaps, unprofitable. I now desire to organize and concentrate the entire effort of my learning upon a definite, practicable goal; to prepare myself for a lifetime avocation." [Note colloquial use of "avocation"!] As always, it sounds rather stilted, but I couldn't think of anything better.

Still rather wondering if you & baby couldn't join me in a few weeks. Found out that the Army pays transportation home of the dependents despite our having taken advantage of it once.

I love you my precious wife, & I love our little one, as darling as his mother.

Robert

*   *   *   *   *

2PM Saturday 26 Jan 46

My beloved wife -

. . . I feel like an imprisoned animal, no exercise, no proper meals, no love nor sex; nothing but 4 dirty narrow walls and a porthole looking out onto the bleak waterfront & the distant jungle of Manhattan. Yet the immediate future seems even worse, to move out to Fort Hamilton & share a dingy room with two cigar smoking baseball fans will be no remedy. I prefer my solitude & inconvenience.

Have read another 450 page survey of Physical Science and after I practice working a few problems in it, I'll feel competently equipped to pass that phase of the exam. Have a 700 page book on Animal Biology & all these History things to go thru next week.

My finances are fast disappearing. Have only $17.50 left, yet I'm going to try not to draw any money from the bank.

*　　*　　*　　*　　*

Tue 29 Jan - Quite a sad, lonesome letter from Robert written Sat, bemoaning the fact that for months he has had no love or sex and has been lonely, frustrated, unable to accomplish anything. He's sending 2 bedding rolls, mess gear & blankets to his folks for storage. Strange that they didn't have room to store anything of ours when I was breaking up the apt. Wrote Robert long letter today trying to boost his morale. Boy, nobody ever does anything to cheer me up. Seems like all my life I've been comforting other people, but when I have to face something, I do it alone. At times I want to "go to pieces" and carry on, but my common sense makes me realize how futile that would be & so I act practically.

*　　*　　*　　*　　*

Tues., 29 Jan '46

Robert -

. . . I hope your letter of Sat, 26 Jan., was inspired solely by the aftereffects of that gruesome combination of cheese, crackers & beer rather than by the state of your physical & mental well-being! Darling! You really get me worried when you write in that vein of sad lonely frustration, and yet I, too, have been separated from my beloved mate, denied the love and sex life you complain of. I, too, experienced that overpowering ennui those months before Baby came - Oct, Nov, Dec - physically uncomfortable, my activities circumscribed to the house & short walks in the neighborhood & the visits to the doctor, and my mind a sort of vacuum, unable to work up any interest or enthusiasm in anything for long. I deliberately forced myself to remain occupied with menial household tasks & with sewing. I doubt if I could have accomplished as much sewing in that 3 months under normal circumstances, but I felt that gnawing inside of me & found an outlet for it in my sewing, stitch by stitch, seam by seam.

519

Hush - re that U of C correspondence deal. I think you've done very well with your German considering the duties you had to perform besides studying. Don't force yourself to study for a while, you had a harrowing experience, the storm, the mix up in the Azores, your worry about Baby & me. All's well now and I'm sure you will regain your former élan vitale.

Get off that ship. Ft Hamilton may have its good points, the library, gym and club facilities; and you may bunk with someone you'll like. I never thought I'd enjoy my stay at the hospital maternity <u>ward</u> (your mother wanted me to take a <u>private</u> room but I didn't think it worth $30 more to be alone).

Re finances: please don't buy a camera or other equipment <u>yet</u>, wait until the postwar stuff (or GI surpluses) are on the market PULEEZE! Try to "husband" your money, dearest, for we'll sure need it if inflation really gets underway or that bogey of a depression comes.

Re sending stuff to your folks to store - have you asked them if they have the room? They couldn't take in even so little as your good suit & 2 overcoats when I was closing up the apartment.

Cheer up, precious. Baby & I love you & soon, I know, we'll be together for always.

Beth

*   *   *   *   *

Wed 30 Jan - Letter from Robert not too happy, bemoaning finances living in NY. His attitude towards my Mom (probably justifiable) pains me. A slight altercation bet Mom & Dad resulted in a long loud abusive harangue from Mom. Got me all upset but I managed to get Mom quieted after an hour or so. Paid her $60 for Feb, increase of $20 on a/c Baby. Bess & Fritz at movie. Thankful for I'd hate to have Fritz in on a family quarrel.

Thu 31 Jan 1946 - Baby 5 weeks old - Another angrily written biting letter from Robert which really aroused conflicting emotions within me. RWD does get me all upset & that may account for my flabby breasts. I've composed (mentally) half dozen mean letters & started 3 to him, but I guess I'll write a nice chatty letter. Bess thinks Robt is justified in his attitude towards Mom &

says Fritz feels likewise only won't express himself. Did write a nice letter. Perhaps this will blow over.

*   *   *   *   *

Mon - 28 Jan '46 - 7:30PM

Darling -

I am ready to ship "Jr." to you or take him back to the hospital! Such temper tantrums; he screws up his little face, gets red as a beet, kicks his little legs and waves his tiny hands like he was signaling violently and lets forth such lusty yells! Has Mom & me scared half to death. You pick him up & all becomes calm, for a little while. And the way he attacks my breasts when I start to nurse him! Boy, oh boy, a chip off the Doty block, believe you me. Don't know why he acts up like that during the day, for he's pretty good during the night, just awakening for his feedings.

*   *   *   *   *

Noon Monday 28 Jan 46

My darling -

Have just received your Friday letter with all its fresh, vivid news of our lovemite. He is a continuously marvelous event in our lives, and I wish I could share each precious moment of him with you. You must make every effort to get sufficient rest tho, beloved, for as you say it's not the physical harm it does, but the damage to your incomparable disposition that must be considered. You must never become nervous & fretful.

*   *   *   *   *

1PM Tuesday 29 Jan 46

My beloved wife -

Just received your Tues & Wed letters of last week. First of all I'll answer your questions. 1) I did let my folks know that I had a strong dislike for my mother-in-law. Was there any reason I shouldn't have? I'm sure such mutual dislike was more than obvious to my parents, they being on the receiving end of it for me when I'm not there. I hope they will be as thoro at despising a person as I am. Your mother's stupid avarice is too patent for my taste, & I certainly hope she gets a good bellyfull of the Koteks, whose wealthy inten-

521

tions she has made so much of. (Don't take that to mean that I wish your Sis any bad luck, but I'm afraid your old lady instilled in her a bit too much hope for generous in-laws.) You needn't defend my cause either, for I have no worth that a person of your mother's type would ever be capable of recognizing, and it bothers me not the least that she & 100 million other vicious, superstitious, bigoted, greedy, human blathermouths are immune to wisdom or the perception that there are other values in life, other than money & personal aggrandizement. What I am particularly bitter about is your servile submission to her ideas, (sometimes even to her ideals). That a keenly intelligent, modern woman should be unable to give her own child a teaspoon of medicine without the permission & advice of her mother, is a thing I can neither understand nor tolerate. The sooner I can remove you & the baby from such cockeyed domination, the better off you'll both be.

*   *   *   *   *

Thursday 31 Jan 46

Darling -

    . . . . I received more evidence of my "outstanding contribution to the Atomic Bomb Project" in the mail today, a certificate signed by the Secretary of War; also a bronze "A" pin. Someday I'll frame that certificate & hang it on a wall. Gee, I enjoyed my work, and to think that I'm reduced to all these thankless tasks of changing diapers, and standing by to answer cries for food & attention from that little parasite who has so dominated my life for over 10 months! Even my husband bullies me with threats, more than once, won't even let me name the little one after the man I love! I think if my husband was a mother, I'd let him name the baby anything he wanted, even Ian Julian! But then I'm a very submissive, docile sort of creature & have always agreed with Wm S. who said "a rose by any other name - " would still be a rose, n'est-ce pas?

    Bobby & I would be so much happier if our daddy & husband would write us nice, cheerful letters. We miss him so and look forward to his letters daily & then he scolds & rants & raves. We know everything will solve itself in due time. Why get so excited?

522

We're so busy taking care of ourselves, we'll have to close now. Goodnight, with lots of love

Betty & Bobby

*   *   *   *   *

11:45PM Tues 29 Jan 46

My sweet darling -

Am very excited tonite (& you'll probably be too, for different reasons) over the prospects of getting a new camera [Fig 43]. It will cost $90 (including case) which, while it is a lot of money, is really less than what I thot I'd pay for what I wanted. I'm getting a Perfex #55 with a coated f2.8 lens (the coating makes it equal to about an f2). The reason for the cheaper price is understandable in that the others are imported cameras subject to considerable tariff, and also this camera is not as finely machined as the German cameras. However, the most important thing, the lens, does seem to be wholly reliable & of 1st quality, and tho I'm still a little skeptical of the other parts, I'm sure they are sufficiently accurate & serviceable for my purposes.

Went out to Ft Hamilton to see about quarters & find the only thing they have are plain barracks with <u>double</u> bunks no less. How lovely. I certainly will stay on the JB until she sails.

*   *   *   *   *

9:30PM Friday 2/1/46

Darling -

So delighted when I read your letter of Tuesday telling me of your enthusiasm about that camera (tho I must admit $90 is a steep price for a picture taker, but it will be a lifetime investment) and I certainly think your technique in taking self photos [Fig 47] has improved considerably! Those pics of the ship are very distinct & interesting. Those of you are the most flattering in a long time. You've got photogenic possibilities, my sweet!

Big event, that dissolving suture dissolved today as I was bathing, no more sticking into me, hurrah!

Sweet, I do love you, though you exasperate me sometimes but good! Take care of yourself & and write us <u>nice</u> letters, yes?

Lovingly
Beth

523

*   *   *   *   *

10PM Thursday 31 Jan 46

My darling wife:

Spent 2½ hr taking the English part of the GED test. Found out, too, why U of C accepts this exam. Altho it's an Army test it says "copyright University of Chicago"!

*   *   *   *   *

10:30PM Friday 1st Feb 46

My darling wife -

Got your Tuesday letter this noon & was a little taken back by your strong insistence that I not buy the camera yet. It was pretty bad in view of the latest developments in that dept! But sweet one, I don't see too much advantage in waiting. As far as prices go, they won't come down for a couple years & as I explained to you, I didn't do too badly on the price. There is another reason too. I want to send you the old camera that you can start taking pictures (patiently) of the baby right away. I also want to be an expert with this new camera when I come home so we don't have to waste two months of the baby's growth while I learn how to take pictures all over again.

My sweetheart's letter was very analytical this time, the way I like them. To tell the truth, I know you've been excelling my letters by far the past few weeks. I enjoy letters from you so much, each one a little grenade of joy that I break open & let explode its happiness upon me for a few minutes each day, - an intimate packet of YOU, of your thots & your life.

I was a little wondrous at one of yours the other day, "Loving regards from Baby & me".

*   *   *   *   *

5:45PM Saturday 2 Feb 46

My beloved one -

. . . There's been a strong wind blowing all day & we sure had a time of it. I'd been taking pictures of the "East Point Victory" as she came into the basin. Heard the pilot yell from her bridge "Let go the port anchor", so I had my camera trained on her waiting for a good shot as the anchor hit the water. All of a sudden she started drifting rapidly before the wind & I followed her from the bow of our ship to the stern as fast as I could walk. The pilot on her was now screaming

524

to let go with any anchor, but they apparently weren't ready for that eventuality, & in a few seconds the bow of the "East Point Victory" was cutting into the after gunwale of the "JB". Was getting fine pictures of it when I came to the end of the roll & had to go up & change film. She left about an 8 inch dent in the gunwale & a few notches on one of the gun tubs. 'Twas all very exciting, my first collision.

*   *   *   *   *

[A *very* revealing letter]

7:30PM Mon, 4 Feb [1946]

Darling -

You're forgiven for your extra<u>vagance</u> (notice the makeup of that word) in the camera department. It's probably just as well you got it, but I <u>implore</u> you not to be too free with your purchases, Robert. It makes me feel like Cinderella here at home skimping & stuff to read of your nonchalant purchase of a camera (not an absolute necessity, you must agree) for $90. I keep thinking of the lean years to come & feel we must stow away what we can while we can. Not to be considered a lecture or severe rebuke, but a sincere statement of my feelings on the subject. <u>Finance</u> with us has always been a "touchy" subject, and I'm afraid it will get worse as our income decreases, as it will after you get out of the Army. (Mental observation: you probably won't think this one "a little grenade of joy . . . to explode in happiness", but it's the way I feel).

You know I almost developed a wholesome dislike for you when you were away on your last trip and I was confined to home in my uncomfortable physical condition. I'd get your letters describing in luscious detail your $3.50 dinner at Antoine's in New Orleans, and your 1000 franc purchases in Antwerp & Paris & stuff, and I did so envy your ability to travel & go & come as you please & enjoy what you wanted in the way of food or amusement. I think you understand what I mean, and then facing the "unknown" when Baby was born, I felt so terribly alone and neglected! And I was so hurt when your folks were displeased that I had named our baby after you and then you also complained!

525

Lots more I could say along these lines, but the foregoing will at least give you a hint of the inner conflicts within me; when you "swooped" in on us, and high-handedly disagreed with this and that. I've always tried to conceal my feelings, especially tried not to hurt you, knowing how sensitive you are, but I feel I should tell you of my thoughts so you can understand my perhaps subconscious manifestations of same, i.e., that "aloof formality" of ending my letter with "loving regards".

It's now 8:15 PM and I've had to pause to go look after Bobby. Must tell you of his facial expressions. The "smile" consists of his drawing his under lip in & turning up the corners of his upper lip, very "cute" and then he makes funny noises & "dribbles". This has its desired effect & stops effectively any nasty ideas one may have about baby being a big nuisance.

So glad you find time to write to me every nite, Robert, even if some of your letters aren't altogether pleasing to me. I promise hereafter to devote most of my letter to Baby and me, and leave out all those unpleasant things that are really trifles compared to the love we bear each other & which has been strengthened threefold by Baby's arrival. Loving him and caressing him, I feel I'm loving you,

Betty

*   *   *   *   *

Tues 5 Feb '46 10:30PM

Darling -

Got your letter of Sat-Sun today. Very exciting, reading your account of that collision. Were you ever in any real danger? I can just picture you now, camera in hand, intrepid, shooting pictures, while the two ships were colliding! You sure do have all sorts of unusual experiences, don't you? And here I am, tied to Baby's kimono strings! Too bad we can't work that "Turnabout" deal (remember Thorne Smith's nonsense novel?) and change places for a while.

You mention recalling & longing for those "lazy, sensuous Sundays" we used to spend at 1001 Mayfield. I wonder if we'll ever have the freedom we then enjoyed. With a little one around, our time will never be our own. We'll have to plan everything to fit into Baby's schedule. But there will be compensations, the joy of seeing our son literally grow inch by inch & pound by pound under our very eyes. He weighed 10 lbs for sure this AM before his bath.

*   *   *   *   *

Noon Monday 4 Feb 46

Precious one -

It's either feast or famine, just got 3 letters from you and am bubbling over with happiness. You are right, I should send you more cheering letters, yet perhaps it wouldn't be me unless I had a few arguments to air. - Sounds like our little son is entering the world as a personality. Strange, how there are always such clashes of individualism even between a 5 weeks old baby & its mother. Let him tantrum til he's purple as long as there is nothing wrong with him. If it stops the instant he's picked up, you're pretty sure that the lack of attention was the only trouble. Maybe he'll work off that double chin if he cries enough, tho I'm so proud of his weighing 9½ lbs already. He owes it all to his mother's nourishing sweetness. - Was so pleased & relieved at your enthusiastic reaction to my buying the camera. I was almost afraid to open the letters, fearing a rather strong lecture on economy etc. might be forthcoming after what you wrote the other day about not buying one yet. (I guess the "yet" was your strongest objection.) Of course, accompanying my announcement with some good pictures must have helped too!

*   *   *   *   *

Mon., 11 Feb '46 - 8PM

My Dearest -

Relieved to receive your letter of 7 Feb this AM about 11 when I was nursing Baby; and then yours of 9 Feb arrived via airmail this aft.

Ah, your Sat letter starts out with a note of normalcy: my darling, patting himself on the back, and tossing the usual egotistical bouquets at himself! So you learn math too fast & therefore forget it just as quickly! I used to enjoy Math, what little I had of it in high school, used to love geometry, in fact.

Re throwing the baking soda away & then retrieving it. I hope it teaches you a lesson. I warn you, if you throw anything of

527

mine away when we resume our domestic life, I'll do something drastic! I seem to remember many incidents when that occurred & I took it meekly, but nevermore! (I just couldn't resist this comment.)

Don't blame anyone but you for holing yourself up in the cabin studying "gd algebra". You've been doing it of your own choice. Before you do anything re the U of C application, let me in on it. Don't want you shelling out dough for a course when you may not be out of the Army in time to start Sept semester; could be, too, that future applications will be accepted only from veterans & you may not be considered till you <u>are a veteran</u>.

I've got more worries, too. Hope you and I don't have the troubles Bess & Fritz are having. Bess won't go live at The K's & they can't find any place & Dick is coming home on furlo. It ain't funny. Now if we really economize & have enough dough to buy a place <u>outright</u> (which will take more than the $7000 which we have, and I don't intend to cash our <u>bonds</u>, they're for Junior's education & stuff), we might be able to get us a place to live.

*   *   *   *   *

11PM Sunday 10 Feb 46

My darling -

. . . . He's certain to love us. Strange how children cling to their parents so instinctively when they are young. There was a little girl on the streetcar the other day snuggling up to her immense, brutally ugly mother so trustingly & lovingly & asking her questions in Spanish. The great, truculent woman seemingly ignored her, but when the time came for them to leave, she whisked her little one off the car with skillful, tender might & the two of them trudged off into the bleak, dirty jungle of Brooklyn to their dark pauper's lair, lovingly hand in hand.

I wish I could preserve somehow the amazing polyglot character of this section of Brooklyn, the raucously individual atoms of life who ride the Crosstown streetcar, ride along the barren, beaten bricks of the waterfront, between shabby, cheerless rows of stores like Mohmul Mazoom's wholesale spice shop, El Mundo Lunch, Sol's dusty windows of secondhand clothes, past gaunt empty lots aglow with glittering fragments of shattered glass & jagged cruel cement, the burned black branches of a naked Christmas tree be-

528

tween rusted twists of wire. Thru here in clattering dingy cars ride the people of the earth, yard workers with lime-covered overalls, seamen with scraggly beards, welders & stevedores & nite watchmen; the sheiks & bimbos of the slums with their hair oozing in oil; big Italian whores with their faces comically pudgy & harsh in gaudy rouge; ex pugs, their glassy stare wandering between slouching hat brim & turned up coat collar, noses bent pulpily back into their jaundiced face; scrawny Negro scrubwomen going painfully to work; loud mouthed Irish sandhogs; the timekeeper & the stenographer, reading of the latest, thrilling sadist rape; voluble Italians & sharp-eyed Syrians, old quiet Jews & carefree niggers; barbers, countermen, truckers, bartenders, bums, foundry men, store clerks, waitresses & kids; nowhere is the human type so variegated as on the Crosstown car.

. . . Remember that fellow Harry whom I knew before we were married? I used to think he was somewhat mentally unbalanced, but now I know he was only a normal specimen of the mass boob of NY, big shot, bright lites, crowds, tips, tinsel, wiseguy & just swirling in imaginary money on $15 @ wk.

So I spent an interesting hour at the Newsreel & here I am back in my hole again & ready for more algebra. Have really been studying this jejune jumble of the alphabet, because I would like very much to pass that exam & I know it will be very tough for my unmathematical inclinations.

*　　*　　*　　*　　*

9:15AM Wed 13 Feb 46

Beloved darling -

. . . . Mewborn announced to me that I would take over the supervision of these war bride ships. However, he did promise me a ship in a month or so after I made it very definite that I wanted to get out of here. Perhaps the new work will be a little more interesting, visiting these various luxury liners, etc. At least it's something new & different.

*　　*　　*　　*　　*

Friday, 15 Feb '46 9PM

My Beloved -

The "squawler" is at it again as I begin to write you, and I despair of arriving at a solution. He's fairly good during the day, and isn't too bad during the night, but the evenings! Until he's finally exhausted by 10 or 11 PM, he is a "holy terror". If I had to be away from him for a few hours, I shudder to think of the consequences! He'd have everybody tearing their hair out!

The big news about me is that I started menstruating again, and all the old symptoms and aches are with me. Only 2 days off from my computations based on my last menstrual period (Mar 22, '45). [An absolutely remarkable biological clock!!! - What's this about nursing a child forestalls fertility!??]

Supervision (?) of war brides ships sounds very interesting, but just what would your duties consist of? That ship you've been promised, will it be a "war brides" ship? You might pick up some ideas re child care, for I understand they are literally floating nurseries.

*   *   *   *   *

SUN - 17 Feb '46 9PM

Darling -

. . . Yesterday we gave the baby a rattle, placing it in his tiny fist. Well, he waved it about, shaking it, all purely spontaneous; & of course managed to hit himself in the head a few times. But he doesn't know enough yet to cry, just looks startled. Decided to put it away for a while as he doesn't show any interest in the rattle or his stuffed toys; just holds them when placed in his hand.

Now for some scolding:

SLEEP - you forget about a 28-30 hour day & allot at least 8 of the existing 24 hours to sleep. If you don't, you're going to end up with some sort of complex, the result of frustration in the matter of sleep and rest. I'm serious, Robert, when I ask you to get the proper amount of rest, for aren't we (Baby & I) dependent on you for our future welfare?

STUDYING - I feel that you put in entirely too much time on studying for those exams. Math is not your forte, so why bang your head against a stone wall. Know your limitations and put forth your endeavors where you can succeed.

EATING - I do wish you'd eat as many meals as you can at the base or some army mess, then I'd feel that you were getting something resembling a well-balanced meal. Knowing your most unorthodox tastes when you eat a la carte, I believe you're inviting digestive upsets every time you eat elsewhere.

*   *   *   *   *

10PM Monday 18 Feb 1946

My beloved wife -

Just opened and read your three letters from Wed, Thurs & Fri of last week.

Re your letters: Was very surprised even shocked to hear that you are menstruating so soon. I thot it was 3 months after the birth. And the same discomforts; my poor sweetheart deserved a longer vacation from nature's torments than that, & to have the same troubles as before. It worries me to think of your having to tend to the baby when you're not feeling well. He certainly is a nuisance with his irregular hours. Speaking of squawling, I went into the nursery on the Vulcania today where there must have been 40 kids penned up, 75% of them crying. If you'd had your eyes shut you'd have sworn, at the sound of the place, that you had walked into the monkey house at the zoo. What a din; & typical simian screeching!

*   *   *   *   *

Noon Saturday 23 Feb 46

My beautiful beloved -

. . . Had a marvelous dinner on the Algonquin. They had a sad case on that ship of a good-looking, intelligent gal whose husband had wired her that he had divorced her, remarried, & would take no responsibility for her. That must be a terrible blow to receive. (The Red Cross hadn't told her yet.) There seem to be one or two cases of that sort in each shipment. Then, too, it works the other way around. The woman being the bum, that is, merely using her husband as a means to get to the US. There were some of those on the Vance. In fact, they were brazen enough there not even to be the least surreptitious about it, two whores necking a couple drunken, dirty looking crewmen right at the head of the gangplank on the ship. They had the first really bad trouble of that nature on the Vance & it would sure be a hot potato if the press got hold of it. The Major was pretty perturbed over it. Some promiscuity undoubtedly takes place on every ship, but certainly not as publicly as on the Vance.

531

Schlingerman has been after me to go see Maurice Evans in Hamlet, so I got tickets for Tuesday eve. Called him to tell him & he insisted that I come over to his house last nite. His wife has already left for Minnesota. I like Rae & appreciate his fine mind & judgment, yet even with him I had the feeling that I was wasting my time, that I should be back at the ship studying, completing those courses, etc. Books are really my only friends, they are the most versatile, the most intelligent & highly profitable; they are faithful regardless of my position or money, they are completely submissive to my convenience, they are deathless & always reflect the same deep beauty. The variety of their wisdom is infinite, and so long as I have sight & mind, they will be my intimate & invaluable companions above all except you. You are more beautiful & tender, more lovely & satisfying than anything I have found in life & I love you immeasurably forever.

Robert

* * * * *

8:30AM Tuesday

Beloved -

Am too sullen & angry to write anything. Every time I think of spending a month & half in this rotten situation because some stupid bastard wants me to do an even more stupid job, I could crack the first person I see square in the face. I don't think I can stand Ft Hamilton, it is filthy, cold, full of stale odors & trash; no place to write or study. Came back to the barracks after trying to do Math in the din of one of those inane uproars called a "Dance". Such things I could barely tolerate as an enlisted man, & now that I'm not compelled to, am afraid that my patience is already exhausted. Yet it turns me white with anger to think of having to waste $60.00 a month to gain a little comfort & privacy. Add to that the $20.00 a month sea pay I'm losing and the situation is seen to be not only gallingly uncomfortable, but damnably & needlessly expensive. This comes of doing good work & becoming ingratiated to a person because your ability has in the past led to certain advantages for you. I would most likely have been better off never to have spoken a decent or intelligent word about this GD office & then I could go my way in untroubled peace.

I love you my precious wife & am burning with impatience to be with you, free & unfettered by the whims of a selfish overlord, released from the senseless gnashings of this machinized Army maw.

It has struck me with renewed force how utterly I detest every-thing connected with Army life, and the thot of life with you in our own sweet home is absolutely paradisical. I can scarcely wait for that dear day of liberty & the return to your love & to the blessed joy of our baby. I love you intensely, always & forever.

Robert

*   *   *   *   *

11:15 PM Thurs 28 Feb 46

My beloved darling -

    . . . Wholeheartedly agree with you that you shouldn't clutter up our photo album with those lousy pictures. Re humdrum civilian life: never could stand it, but guarantee you it will never be hum-drum. Our precious pest will see to that & we also have school, pho-tography, music, fencing, a car, etc. etc. to keep us intensely & pleasantly occupied; to say nothing of the rapturous delight in each other. And oh, what a typical woman you are, not more than two months removed from the torture of childbirth & you're already starting to hint towards another one! Nature is the most marvelous psychiatrist & hypnotist there is to be able to cause that. You are such a sweetheart.

*   *   *   *   *

9:30AM Sunday 3 March 46

My dearest beloved -

    Nearsightedness is certainly unhandy &, of course, possessing a guilty feeling adds to your embarrassment as well. Was drowsing away about 8:30 this morn when an old dignified & generalish look-ing officer sauntered onto my sun porch in a "tour of inspection" gait. He was thotfully smoking a cigar & had another officer tagging behind him. He looked intently at my locker & then asked me if I were going over or getting out. I took him to be the CO of the Post on an Informal inspection. Knowing I was not supposed to be in this barracks, I popped out a hesitant "Sir?" to gain time to think up a good answer. Well, after a few more questions putting me on the spot, he stepped a little closer & what is he but some damn inquisi-tive & inconsiderate Captain just moseying around to take a look at the post from the sun porch windows! If I were only able to see!

    Shouldn't tell you this, but put $100 in the bank yesterday so that the cost of my camera is reimbursed. However, I fully intend to

533

take that money to buy the other equipment I'll need, such as an enlarger, a tripod, flash gun & perhaps a photometer. But at least my frugality is paying off.

. . . Went up to visit my old friend Wilby who is ass't TComdr on the Washington. Had dinner aboard & then we talked till about 9 PM. He was on the Athos II, the trooper that was in Horta when we were at Ponta Delgado & so he told me his story of that storm. We certainly had an easy time of it compared to them. Their galley range broke loose & broke out all the bulkheads, fixtures, & tables in the dining hall. The portable refrigerators broke loose & made mud out of the potatoes, eggs & oranges in them. The setee in his room came out & crushed his leg, & fractured three vertebrae of his chaplain. The office was completely demolished by loose desks & a field safe. They had a fire in the PX, the portholes in the lower deck were smashed in, the area filled with water & the pumps stopped up. Several men broke their legs, a paint locker worked loose & ruined all the belongings of 20 or so officers berthed near it. Their main trouble was the engine which couldn't function properly when the ship was pitching, so they had to lie helpless in the trough of the sea. They got the engine going once & water came down the funnel & burned out a rheostat and that stopped it again. The water in the bilges came within 12" of the boilers. I guess that was one of the worst North Atlantic storms & we must just have been fortunate on the JB.

*　　*　　*　　*　　*

Tues - 26 Feb 46 - 9:45 PM

Darling -

"Life has become rugged" - sez you. Want to change places with me? Would you like to be on 24-hr duty with our precious infant, charged with feeding, bathing, diaper changing, laundry, amusement, etc. of 12 lbs (11 lb. 14 oz exactly) of strong, wiry, healthy human being? He wears us both out, Mom & me, and my right arm, especially, actually aches from the dozens of times a day that I go thru the motions of picking him out of his crib, onto the table, off the table, into the crib, etc. etc.; and try holding him in your arms for 20 min or so when he's feeding, your arm sort of suspended in mid-air!

So you've met another old acquaintance! So what? If I know you, you'll never have any of these interesting people over to our home & I'll have to be stuck with Bobby and our other children (?!?) and never have any choice but to become an old stick-in-the-mud!

You don't know how I welcome an opportunity to get away from home & Bobby for a little while. Look forward so to my next sewing lectures at Field's tomorrow! Mom is such a good sport to let me get away for the 3 hours or so. What'll I do when we get a place of our own?

You wanted to know the state of our assets. Practically unchanged from last reckoning, roughly $7500 cash; and if I didn't want a <u>home</u> badly I could think of ways to spend it all but quick.

*   *   *   *   *

Sun., 3 March 1946 - 7 p.m.

Dear Husband of Mine:

. . . . Re not wanting to live a day in my "mother's house" - well, it's not only her house, but Dad's too - and know what, I don't expect you to live here. Go on live with your folks. You left them once at an earlier age and before you had developed all these extreme likes and dislikes. Wanna bet? In a week, you'd be swearing that you wouldn't live at their home an hour! Remember, my sweet, they've been especially nice to you of late only because you've been a "returning hero", etc. Would you prefer to bunk with your bro in preference to your wife? Seriously, tho, I think you should find <u>us</u> a place to live right quick upon your discharge. I'm tired of trotting over to Jackson's [Storage] with $8 every month!

Re changing your name when you become a civilian - you do that, my sweet, and I'll change mine, too! By court decree: separate maintenance and the right to resume my maiden name, if those two can be decreed at the same time. Ain't kidding, either. I think there has been much too much ado about Baby's name, and frankly, I never expected such reaction on your part! If you make such a fuss about such a minor thing, what about major differences that might occur concerning his education, training, clothing, etc.? As for two non-identical people, boy, Bobby is a chip off the old block if I ever saw one! He gets to look more like you every day and he certainly has your temperament! Why is it

535

that a sweet, patient creature always gets linked up with the exact opposite? But, I'll fool you two: I can get tough, too, when sufficiently riled up!

You contradict yourself so, my sweet. You take such vigorous exception to my naming Baby, yet later in your letter you speak of valuing the "warmth and pure devotion " that I have given you. You have an odd way of reciprocating it my dear! How can you worship someone, yet say such biting things and threaten me with all sorts of action that I find distasteful. I wish you'd give some thot in the time remaining before your return to Chicago as to just how much you do love me, just how much you are willing to compromise to make me happy in our marriage; for I frankly fear that someday you will hurt me so that it will kill all the unreserved sweetness and devotion that I have given so far to our marriage.

Re your letter of 2/23: Glad you're reconciled to living at Fort Hamilton, and "Y". You'll probably go there for a really vigorous work out, I suppose, after reading my letter; and why do I inwardly wince at the thought of perhaps hurting or angering you by such frank statements as in the foregoing paragraph? Do you feel that way when you say or do things that you know pain me deeply? Can it be that I love you more? I've been doing a lot of thinking . . .

Guess this is all for now. Almost 8:45 PM and I've been typing slowly but steadily, getting a lot of things off my chest. Feel fine physically now (except for being sleepy all the time) but I am disturbed mentally about so many things, actually have nightmares about it. And your letters are so disquieting, if we truly love each other, I know we can solve any problems Life can pose, but we'll have to make concessions. What do you think?

Beth

*　　*　　*　　*　　*

8PM Wed 7 Mar 46

My sweetest wife -

. . . Of course tonite, after your Sunday letter, my naive dreams of pleasure are abruptly reduced to more serious wonderment. You call into question the very fact that we love each other, throwing

536

some rather ponderous doubts about with amazing unconcern. Your ever ready threat of separation with its usual emphasis that you mean it particularly challenges me. You make this statement in argument too frequently to vividly realize its full implications, & I am therefore inclined to overlook it as a typically feminine attack. Yet I want to point it out to you & also the fact that in my greatest anger I have never dared make such a statement. Because of our seldom seeing each other our love has had a tendency, in fact has been forced, to become symbolical in nature in order to bring it into the realm of reality. It has become a goal, an abstract symbol of our desires that will be realized at some indefinite, future time. In such an abstract state our love is exceptionally prone to become two distinct & different hopes. Unshaped by daily intimacy & attrition, it grows tangentially along the course of our individual wishes until, in its intangible state, it reaches two varying & sometimes conflicting conceptions as to just what & how that love is.

You tend to symbolize our love as serene security, the practical emphasis. You love with a deep, sacrificial, mothering type of love, steady, possessive & assured. I, however, prance lustily along a different conception of it, more exotic & romantic. My love is passionate, sensual, wildly inflammable. It is idealistic & dreamily ecstatic. When we are together, our ideas of love frequently clash, but they combine & hold us to a center. When we are apart, we diverge into the unreality of what we each want in the other.

However, that analysis does not fully explain the vigor with which you attack my nature, what perhaps you might call my eccentricity of mood. I believe there are deeper factors operating in this schism. The trauma of motherhood has worked an indefinable psychological change in you. You have assumed towards me a rather aggressive attitude of independence which you never displayed when you were, actually, with your own good job etc., far more independent of me than now. It is probably a defense mechanism within yourself attempting to compensate by this display (no matter how mild) for the greater dependency upon me which you subconsciously feel, and whether you can sense it or not, there is also an inevitable transference of your love for me to the baby; in a manner following the path of least resistance, where it cannot impress its full desire upon me, it turns to the more pliant personality of the infant, there to vent its less inhibited or obstructed desire upon the child.

You also correctly discern your envy of my freedom whilst you were burdened with the great gravid results of my pleasure. I fully understand & sympathize, yet can do nothing to change it. You are fully justified, but helpless.

And then there must now undoubtedly lurk in you a feeling of your vast superiority over me in the creation of our beloved baby. You can lay violent claim to the greater share, in fact he is almost wholly you're doing and there will be nothing I can ever do to alter this.

All these things are the normal & natural psychological readjustments in our relationship, which the production of our lovable little darling inevitably cost. It is perhaps for the best that it takes such patent form & outlets in such things as your giving my name to the baby. And it is my natural reaction to resent this transference. This is all in the course of life & love.

But there seems to me to be a more unnatural & dangerous force operating within you, seeking to call my love into question. "I wish you would give some thot in the time remaining before you return to Chicago as to just how much you do love me . . ." That expression is not wholly the result of your suffering with the baby. I believe such weighty doubts as this arise from the more insidious association with your mother & your home. You are receding under its influence into the imperceptible wish to return to the mother-guided girl life that you experienced so securely & simply in this same home for so great a part of your life. You would yield to your mother's dominance once more to regain the carefree happiness of girlhood. Her dominance offers the familiar, which appeals strongly to your more conservative nature. It simplifies so many of the trivial inconveniences of life. It is a haven, a retreat, in which you feel you could avoid the volatility of and aggressiveness of my nature. I feel your return to your home has been the most unfortunate happening in our marriage, for it has changed you, drawn you away from me, given you a false haven in which you believe you could find a former peace. "You can't go home again", and one should never try.

I have a wholehearted liking & respect for your father, but it is not his qualities or nature that seem to be influencing you. Rather it is the insinuating, cunning, self-pitying, cleverly ingratiating personality of your mother that is so softly infiltrating into the untainted sweetness of your being. You argue that you lived with her for 26 years without ill effects, but there was a considerable difference; then you were hers. Her guile in that circumstance was innocuous & venal. In this case it is vicious & bitterly subversive. Her right of influence over you is pitted directly against mine. Her motherhood over you is in the past, your husband is your present & your future, as ineluctably as maturity follows youth.

In all this argument I am not trying to absolve myself from the caustic criticism that I have occasionally been guilty of. But I do want to bring to light some of the latent factors that would seem to be making inroads on our precious love. I do not accept your alarming attitude. I am wholly amenable to your frankness, but believe the import you draw from it here tends to be quite too drastic. In any event there is one certainty, our affection must not deteriorate, by correspondence as it were. We seem to oscillate between love & annoyance with comical consistency, in exact tune with the time it takes an indicting letter to reach one & be curtly answered by the other. Your strong letters always seem to find me in a loving & beatific mood & never fail to abruptly reverse it.

Having now had about 5 pages of "my say", I'd ought to switch to something more serene. It does pain me to think of hurting you by sharp remarks, but I'm unlike you in my attitude towards anger. I accept anger as a normal & unavoidable part of domestic relations (of course not to excess) & am therefore not so reluctant to anger you. My anger, tho more vehement, is not near so serious as you imply, nor so permanent in <u>effect</u> as yours.

But enough. Have devoted almost 3 hours to this & have now moved about a ½ mile over to Barracks 600 which has a lounge.

I share your anxiety over our finding a place to live, but I promise we'll have a place of our own at the first possible instant even if it's only a tent.

I do love you my sweet one, despite your querulous letter, and am overwhelmed with impatience to get back & start on the problems that confront us. There is no room in my mind for doubt, but only the beautiful certainty that we are, have been & always will be, one of the most happy & fortunate couples on earth. With our keen minds & sturdy bodies we have fashioned a beautiful love, a joyous baby, & have a future ahead of us unparalleled in its possibilities for contentment, satisfaction, security, & the entire lusty fulfillment of our varying desires. I love you always, my wife

Robert

*   *   *   *   *

Dear Darling -

Received your lengthy reply to my letter (also lengthy) of last Sunday; but I've had an exceptionally busy day today & am hardly in the mood to make rebuttal to some of your statements, or even to comment on it, except to say that you certainly had your "say". I'll bet you even enjoyed writing that detailed analysis of what makes me "tic" when you "toc".

*   *   *   *   *

MON - 11 Mar 46 - 10:30 pm

Dearest -

I'm a very, very busy gal these days. Just finished scribbling 2 postals to our Senators in Wash DC urging them to support the subsidies (to small producers of bldg materials) and the ceiling on used homes, features of the Patman Housing Bill. The H.R. defeated them, our only hope is the Senate.

Received your Thu & Fri letters. Re Algebra exam, if you read the reverse side of that slip of paper, you noticed (or did you?) that your percentile rank of 98+ indicated that out of 100 average students taking such exam, 98+ get grades <u>lower</u> than yours. That sounds good to me!

He's such a sweetheart. I picked him up today to change his diaper & he began to laugh, and laugh. It warms you inside, makes me glow with pride for both you & me to look at him. He's such a perfect product of our love, Robert. He gets better every day, too, but he still wants a feeding in the wee hours of the morning, 3:30 AM yesterday & then 6:30 AM; this after his usual 10:30 feeding. Love you, sweetheart, & I do sympathize with you in your present job; such awful hours! Better luck's a comin! I know

Lovingly
Beth

*   *   *   *   *

My Darling -

Precious, your Mon latter is so sweet, my Darling at his "lovingest best". I'm sure it's the eloquence of your romancing by letter that has endeared you so to me, for we have been apart more than together. I'm so happy you feel the way you do about our baby, and please don't ever think that because I love him, I love you less - rather you both draw on heretofore untapped reservoirs of love & devotion

Always
Beth

*   *   *   *   *

12:45PM Wed 13th March 46

My sweetheart -

. . . You may call me an extremist, etc., but I happily note that you are just like me. Once you've undertaken something, you just can't rest until it's finished and perfected. You throw yourself into that sewing business as if your life depended on it, and I love you for your impetuous enthusiasm. Do wish, however, that you would soon graduate from the housecoat-nightgown field and be able to make yourself some real snappy, custom styled tailored dresses etc. You should wear the most perfectly fitted clothes in the world for the beauty of your body was designed for it.

I see you too have forebodings of another war. The thot has haunted me for some time, but I haven't mentioned it, thinking perhaps you were too busy to have given anxiety to it. Never has there been greater evidence of the correctness of the attitude of misanthropic people like myself that Man is a dangerously ill-educated beast and his floundering at morals & ethics the merest hypocrisy. I certainly think the political & economic maneuvering going on thruout the world is one of the most deplorable & dangerous situations in history. There is a vast criminality of thot in the meager hearts of men or the world could not so viciously support this. The flagrantly invidious propaganda of our prostitute press is matched in catastrophic foolishness only by the Russian mania for expansion. I certainly do not wholly approve of Russia's actions or methods (tho perhaps some are justifiable & sincere), but the ghastly spectacle of the inflammatory distortion of this country's public mind to the will of our financial Kings arouses in me an ugly detestation of the mass-stupids, who can see only what is in front of their noses. It is truly alarming, the tremendous pressure of hate & distrust that is being deliberately built up brick by subtle brick. No newspaper seems to dare mention two sides of a picture. The Russians are pressing in all directions, extending domination of Eastern Europe, eyeing the Dardanelles & Arabian oil, the temptation of Manchuria; but who cares or dares point out the British troops in Greece, in Java, the British throttle grip upon Egypt, India, Palestine, Malaya, the French war in IndoChina, the equal presence of US Troops in China trying analogously with the Russians to pry open the door for their own economic steal, & bar it to the other. We have the Panama Canal, why could anyone ever want the Dardanelles, etc.

* * * * *

Fri - 3/15/46 - 10 pm

Darling -

We have an adorable baby, but I sure wish I were twins so as to take care of him & get ½ the things at least accomplished that I want to. He was 11 weeks old yesterday & he weighed 13 lb. 3 oz. this morning. It is gratifying to get some intelligent reaction from him after so many weeks of just caring for him with no recognition from him. Mom says seeing that you & I are his parents, he should be quite a child, smart but stubborn & spoiled! And she tells me what a precocious but "bratty" little girl I used to be, walked at 9 mos & could talk at 12! Says I used to pester her to death with all sorts of questions about everything about me. And when Mom runs out of tales, Dad takes over. They seem to be reliving the early years of their marriage & parenthood with Bobby going thru the various stages of babyhood. You know my Mom is quick-tempered & sharp tongued, but where Bobby is concerned, never a harsh word. She just adores him, ditto my Dad. And I recall my childhood days & I can't remember my Mom being cross with any of us. She was always so proud of all of us & was always doing something for us, cooking, sewing, mending, knitting.

You write in such glowing terms of the future & our happiness. I heartily echo those sentiments, but practically speaking I'm all confused & unable to visualize just how all those perplex-

542

ing problems of housing, your job & my adjustment to being a mother-housewife on my own will all work out; & am so fearful that you are going to undertake to do too much at one time: job, school, etc. etc. Don't try to explain, dearest. We'll just have to stumble along & hope it's the right way.

*　　*　　*　　*　　*

[Typewritten]

Sunday - Mar. 17 46 - 9 p.m.

Dearest:

. . . Cute little brat, knows what he wants when he wants it, and gets it (like his father). We have a nursing session whenever he wants it, and there's no mistaking his demands for food. He opens up his mouth and yells if I ignore his crankiness, and his subtle smacking of lips and sucking of fingers. And if I have him in my arms, he turns towards my bosom and actually gropes with his hands for the breast. If Mom has him in her arms, he just squirms and acts up, and when I take him, he buries his head in my bosom. Wotta guy! When he's all thru, he rather contemptuously (or so it seems) lets go of the nipple, and if I put it in his mouth again, he actually wrinkles up his nose and pushes it out with his tongue.

*　　*　　*　　*　　*

3:15PM Sunday 17 Mar 46

My darling wife -

The Y [YMCA] closes at 11 PM, but I'm never finished at that time & they allow me to stay there & leave thru the gym where the door locks as I close it. Last nite, however, they locked the gym & of course all the other doors. I was locked in! Explored several possibilities & finally found a door leading down into the furnace room & thence to freedom. But there was no way of closing the door to the furnace room, it had to be latched from inside the Y, and in fact it wouldn't even remain shut unless it were latched. Fearful of leaving this door standing open & being blamed if anyone broke in, & certainly branded as careless even if anyone didn't, I had to exercise my ingenuity. How would you latch a door from the outside when

543

the latch is on the inside? Remembering my Conan Doyle, I went back to the barracks for a piece of thread. Doubled the thread over the latch stud, closed the door, pulled the thread, slipping the latch into position & loosed the thread from the stud so that they'd never know the difference. It was almost fun playing detective story.

*   *   *   *   *

11PM Wed 27 March 1946

My sweet beloved -

. . . I did succeed in getting myself assigned to the USAT Jarrett M. Huddleston [Fig 46] as assistant Trans Comdr. It was getting late in the afternoon, but I took a ride up there to see what was going on. Was afraid the personnel aboard would resent my coming, for they are all Lts & the former TComdr, a 1st Lt, is now reduced to Sales Commissary officer. I also mess up their situation by displacing the Trans Service Officer from his private room. But they all accepted it as inevitable army & apparently with no hard feelings towards me.

Am pleased with my assignment, particularly in having a private room & shower.

Where will I live when I come to Chicago? Don't know that either, but am sure it will be solved when the time comes the same as, given a bit more time, the housing of us together will also be solved.

I love you sweetheart, always

Robert

*   *   *   *   *

10:30PM Thurs 28 Mar 46

My sweet wife -

It has been a sparkling warm Spring day & I have lived the life of a General for a few hours. Reported to Col Nelson's office at 9:30 & about 10 AM we went down to the General's boat. However it had nothing to do with the General. Merely a Colonel & a Navy Captain who have just come to NY to head the giant Army/Navy Procurement something or other. This Col Nelson, a rather young & definitely hefty Swede, Regular Army, is head of NYPE Supplies & Facilities Division & had the job of orienting these other big shots to New York Harbor. I supposedly knew the harbor & was therefore detailed to the party & a Lt O'Brien & his wife, friends of Col Nelson also

544

came. Then leisurely cruised up the glittering Hudson to the Washington Bridge, back down the Jersey side, Caven Point Terminal, then around into Kill van Kull up to Bayonne Bridge (between Staten Island & Jersey) then along Staten Island over to the Narrows & Gravesend Bay, back up the Brooklyn Coast into East River past the Navy Yard & back to the Battery & to BABT. The weather was perfect & so was the $250,000 yacht. It had formerly been owned by the president of Ronsen cigarette lighters Corp and has been kept immaculate, the paragon of the expression "ship shape". We had lunch about 1 PM while cruising leisurely about Gravesend Bay. The cuisine (it really was "cuisine") was marvelous.

Besides the ever interesting & magnificent panorama of New York Harbor we were also fortunate enough to pass right next to the immense carrier "Midway" coming back from North Atlantic maneuvers. Then too there were the great carriers & battleships in Brooklyn Navy Yard and Bayonne. These O'Brien people were strictly society hustlers, Army style, particularly subtle & smooth with the Colonels. Mrs. O'Brien thot I should have saved some film to take a picture of the group! That is the last thing I want, to collect a mass of stupid snapshots of people I will never see again.

No letter from you today, my beloved one. I most likely owe that lack to our precious little tyrant's demanding another all nite session of subservience. I hope he will soon grow to leave his sweet mother the luxuriance of her slumber, he is too readily like his father in demanding of her warm body its infinite delight at any hour. We love & adore you & would possess you, always, with impatient ecstasy

Robert

*   *   *   *   *

9:30AM Saturday 30 Mar 46

My dearest -

Have so much to write of, yet also must get up to the ship. - Got a jeep the 1st thing yesterday morn. (Found out that Danny Nolan, the screwball Irishman you met at Lt Platt's party, is working in the motor pool now. Called him up and told him I was Major Farrish in Colonel Olson's office and wanted him to know that Maj General Ross would bring his helicopter with him when he took over command of the Port & that the motor pool should make plans where to keep it. Danny said a few thunderstruck "yes sirs", very anxious to please the Major, Colonel & General, but when I nonchalantly said

545

"Of course, you people know all about the maintenance of helicopters", his reply was so bewildered that I couldn't contain my laughter & gave it all away. So now I can get what I want from the motor pool!)

Picked up the greater part of my belongings at Ft Hamilton & moved them onto the ship. Reviewed the physical set up of the ship & noted several things which should be changed.

* * * * *

Friday, 29 March 46 - 10 pm

Darling -

The clock has just finished striking ten. I fed Bobby & he's asleep & now for a quick letter to you. Have your letter of 27 March at hand, also the photos you sent. They're beautiful, your enlargements! Really good enough to frame!

How thrilling to be invited to the General's yacht! I only hope it wasn't for some nasty ole job or reprimand! You be sure & let me know all about it, what the yacht is like & why the General has to have one; as a taxpayer I'm interested in these details. Might even write my Congressman about it, seeing as I "broke the ice" with our Senators. Re your running for Congress, I am half serious about it. Kinda like the idea of having a _personal_ representative in Wash DC to introduce my pet legislation.

Re your living in Chicago after discharge: you will _hurt_ Dad's & Mom's feelings if you don't come here right away, but we'll see.

* * * * *

10PM Sunday 31 March 1946

My sweet beloved -

. . . We will carry 326 women & 150 children or pregnant women. Will have a staff of 1 TComdr & Asst, a doctor, 7 nurses, 4 Red Cross workers, 1 TSO, 1 Sales Commissary Off, 1 Chaplain, 1 WAC officer + 6 enlisted women & 12 EMs. The crew numbers about 150. The ship is a regular Liberty ship hull & engine, etc, except that all the decks and superstructure have been built into a passenger ship form. The Army officers and Ship's officers live on the Bridge Deck. On the boat deck is the Nurse, WAC, & Red Cross quarters, a large hospital area with two complete operating rooms, lobbies, etc, a 2

546

chair dental surgery, and in the forward frame a room to accomodate about 50 passengers. On A deck is the Officers mess & pantry. The Starboard side is devoted to two lounges & a nursery, and there are quarters for about 100 persons fore and aft. "B" deck is "below decks" (tween deck on normal Liberty). On it are the galley, crew's quarters & mess, passengers mess, mothers with babies mess, playroom, offices, dispensary & pharmacy and quarters for perhaps 100 passengers. On "C" deck there are another 100 or so passengers and a lot of storage space. "D" deck is down on the floor plates & is devoted to storage space. There was a large commercial type laundry on "C" deck, which is now being closed off & the former ward offices in the various areas about the ship are being converted to laundries with 1 tub & two ironing boards each.

*   *   *   *   *

8PM Tuesday 2 April 46

My sweet wife -

. . . Took a 5th Ave bus ride up to the Metropolitan Museum. There was a veritable fleet of $15,000, chauffeured Cadillacs parked there & had to use the side entrance. Inquired what was up, & what had I done but stumbled into the 75th Anniversary of the place almost on the hour of the ceremony, & General Eisenhower was guest speaker!! So I took a brief look around the rearranged Egyptian exhibit & then went back to boldly place myself in a point of vantage in front of a group of dried, old socialites, members of the Museum. O'Dwyer & Spellman were also there. Eisenhower's speech was just like the newsreels of him, his emphatic reading of a manuscript that someone had done an admirable job of writing for him. However, his personality was certainly cordial & obviously pleasant. Tho I often disagree with him, I like & admire the man, & he is a just & liberal character, particularly for a General. His real self came out quite obviously in a few instances when he abandoned his manuscript reading to relate events that were what he had actually contributed to the "speech". Then his thots & his delivery of them were clear & profound. He made some humorous remarks about "Mr Mauldin & his friends" which I failed to catch because I was watching the methods of the press photographers.

*   *   *   *   *

My lovely one -

. . . Was very disgruntled & discouraged this morning over the way physical things seem to be obstructing my desires on the ship & over the poor showing I've made on these correspondence courses. But I received news which brought my spirits & my confidence up to their usual peak, reaffirmed my genius. My grades finally arrived from USAFI. At first glance my heart fell, for I saw mere 76, 86, 81, 74, and immediately decided I hadn't heard from U of C because I had failed. And then there was a column II which showed percentiles for college freshman & sophomores which read 99, 99, 99, 98, and which I took to mean the average score that most students got on the exam. But happily I was wrong. The 99's were my score (!!), so that in the entire series of examinations I rank on the pinnacle. Am very much gratified over the results of my efforts. Now I wonder if USAFI has let U of C know about them. When I call you, you can tell me, & if U of C hasn't received these grades, I'll forward them.

*　　*　　*　　*　　*

Thurs 4 April 1946 - Robert calls to say he's sailing - I sewed another night gown for Mom, using flat fell seams instead of French. This evening about 9 PM after I had just fed Bobby & put him to bed, Robert called fm NY collect. Said they were sailing at 11 PM w/o the Major & Robert would be Transport Cdr as the Major couldn't be found. Going to Southhampton & would return in a month. Went to bed rather peeved at Robert. He earns $50 more per month & yet manages to spend it all on himself in spite of my pointed hints that we should try to save more. RWD says I insulted the Dotys, hence they don't come over.
Fri 5 Apr - After lunch I went to pay our storage bill & w/draw $100 from Lawndale Bank. Mom says she will buy Bobby a high chair for his 4th month birthday.

*　　*　　*　　*　　*

My beloved wife -

Am still rather thunderstruck at finding myself so suddenly Trans Comdr. It is a heavy responsibility I was not overly desirous to accept. Have full confidence in my ability to do the job, but it will mean working considerably harder & more conscientiously then I usually care to. However, I must also admit that despite the work & responsibility involved, I am secretly pleased to be in the top position, gratifying my natural yen for fame, power, etc.

It will be a strange psychological change to switch abruptly over to civilian life where I am one of the unnumbered millions, my station in life becoming vague & obscure as contrasted to my present position of command, rank etc., so patent & assured. I know my character is resilient enough to accept a more lowly & uncertain position gladly & my self-confidence will be unjarred; but I do believe this "loss of station" is a great factor in many men's choosing a military career, thus displaying their attainment in society before all their fellow men.

My most valued congratulations on getting the "promotion" came from my EM, who were wholeheartedly overjoyed at the news. Have had almost no contact with them as yet, so was very pleasantly surprised to find myself so well liked in such a short time.

Robert

*   *   *   *   *

Tues 16 Apr - Almost afraid to open letter fm U of C addressed to Robert; but I did, and he's been accepted for admission. Also, if he can take their General Education Test, he'll be eligible for admission on the divisional level in the Summer quarter. But when will he be back from England? Sewed another house dress for Mom this aft.

Sun 21 Apr - Bobby's First Outing - 74 - Lots of excitement as we took him out, 1st in backyard & then for a 3/4 hour airing by me in his carriage.

Thurs 25 Apr - M - I Buy Bobby a High Chair - This aft I took a walk to Goldblatt's & bought Bobby a Thayer convertible high chair with "toilet" facilities. Cost 13.95, but worth the money.

Fri 26 Apr - M - Robert writes of his trip across the Atlantic. He landed in Southhampton England on 4/18 & will bring back 471 war brides & children. Said he'll try to get to visit London before returning. Only one indirect reference to Bobby in his letter, his "conception" a year ago.

*   *   *   *   *

1st day at sea
10:15PM Friday 5 April 46

My sweetest darling -

Was so rushed this morning that I was utterly unable to write you the farewell letter I had intended. Had two EM who hadn't reported aboard, as well as the Sales Commissary Officer, and it took me a morning of phone calls to round them up & make sure we got them. Also got the WACs some seersucker work dresses, for they didn't have any. Ten minutes before sailing, our last personnel arrived! Then we had to make up the next of kin list & send it ashore with the tugs. Wanted to hold an orientation meeting at the 1st possible instant, so at 1 PM we had it. I explained the ins & outs of seasickness to the girls before they could begin to feel it, and believe they will hold up much better now, at least no one is sick yet.

This afternoon I moved into the Transport Comdr suite. It's sure a fine life. Have a spacious room with adjoining shower & an office with a large desk, a couch & a safe. Even have a telephone in the room. Quite a deal to graduate into from the old "JB" [Fig 42].

11 PM Sunday 7 April 46

The Captain & I decided to turn thumbs down on a dance that had been planned for ships officers & the nurses & WACs. They pulled a few sour faces at the news & I really hated to do it, but is much simpler to allow them to form their acquaintances slowly & quietly than to further things by an "official" dance, etc. (sort of fan the flames). There are too many complications that can set in when you permit yourself to be the least bit lenient.

3:45AM Monday 15 April

My sweetheart -

Received an answer to my radiogram today which seems to indicate that we will have almost no time for shore leave in Southhampton. We are also getting 80 infants! Had set up for 20. Then there are 33 children, 107 mothers, 6 pregnant women (+ probably a dozen more who are afraid to admit it) and 245 childless women, a total of 471 persons. Have the berthing plan pretty well set up & my standing orders are about ready for publication.

8:15AM Thursday 18 April 46

My sweet lovable wife -

We are just pulling into the Solent between the Isle of Wight & Portsmouth and will be in Southampton in about 2 hours. Don't know what our schedule is here, for tho I've been trying since last

550

nite, have been unable to reach them on the radio-telephone. Yesterday I was awakened at 10 AM with a story that really got me going. My WAC officer (the only one of the girls quartered alone) had awakened at 4 AM to find a Negro looking down at her. He ran as soon as she spoke. She thot it was her room steward, but when she went to identify him this morning, she wasn't sure enough to make it stick. Am rather worried now to have a maniac of that type aboard & not know who he is. He should certainly be locked up.

Postcard of New Polygon Hotel - Southampton, England

9PM Friday 19 April '46

My sweetheart - Ate lunch here today & that's about the sum of my sightseeing. Have been so busy that my brain feels like it had been thru a wringer. Sailing tomorrow morn with my 470 brides & babies. I love my own the most.

Robert

9PM Friday 19 April 46-Southampton

My beloved one -

It has been a very hectic 24 hours. Was very much disappointed, too, that I was unable to get to London. We docked at 9:30 last nite, and it was 12:30 before we were finished berthing the people (on our berthing plan that is, using the passenger list). Then was up until 3 AM with other details.

Got up at 8 AM & had a hasty breakfast. Then after considerable argument, I finally talked the motor pool out of a car to take myself & the others who had had to stay & work last nite, out on a tour of Southampton & and environs. We got underway about 10 AM and went out to Winchester to an old & uninteresting cathedral. It was Good Friday & Services were going on in the Cathedral. To me they seemed just like children playing some silly game in utter seriousness. They were all dressed up in musty purple capes & carrying a hooked cross in a procession about the church, chanting as they went. They chanted "God bless Princess Elizabeth", and then all choir boys & adherents in the procession gravely repeated it in clumsy rhythm, striding slowly, slowly solemn, intently serious. "God bless all our deacons" intoned nasally, the blackened cross swaying, the dirty cloaks softly swishing as they paraded slowly, slowly in valiant earnestness about the empty church. They call it the "Atomic Age".

Got back to the ship in plenty of time for embarkation, which came off as scheduled. Ran them aboard very smoothly in about an hour, but then the trouble started as usual, for couldn't get them organized fast enough for the first meal. So messing was a mess tonite.

However, it should be okay tomorrow. My WAC officer is working on it now. She is the best officer I have, and particularly valuable in contrast to that other Missouri farmer designated to assist me. My enlisted men, too, have certainly out shown the officers for both quality & quantity of work. Officers think the world owes them a good time first of all & then, if they're in the mood, they'll do a little work.

Sail 8 AM tomorrow, but the only hurry I'm in is to get back to read your sweet letters once more. It makes me very lonesome seeing all these babies here & I want to see my own little family so much. Loving you -

Robert

*   *   *   *   *

1AM 24 April 46 Wed.

My sweet wife -

Last nite there had been a lot of commotion, laughter, clapping etc. down in B deck square. I investigated & found only the crew having some good clean fun & three gals quite away from them watching the show. Against my better judgment, I resolved not to be despotic & to let the fun continue. So tonite my leniency paid off. We had an affair down on B deck square that looked like a wild dime-a-dance hall out in Stickney. About 30 crewmen & a dozen babes having a jitterbug session. I took 3 names, called the Chief Officer & Master at Arms & broke it up. One of the names was a phony, but the other two reported to the Captain's office, & after warning them, we let them go. I'm looking for the wiseguy with a phony name, however. Took the loudspeaker out of the square there immediately, & am going to put it specifically off-limits to passengers. You can't afford to be kindhearted, for that old saying about give an inch & they'll take a mile is certainly true.

So all that excitement wound up, I went down at 11:30 to take a last look about before turning in. I suddenly espied the character we have been shadowing for the last 3 days. He came out of his quarters & walked directly down the passage toward the passengers' quarters. I watched him long enough to be sure of his intent & then as he went thru the mess hall door, I grabbed one of my EM as a witness & assistant & trailed him. Miscalculated on the time, however, for a watertight door had blocked his route & he was just going through it as we opened the mess hall door. We stepped back, but he had been alarmed & soon came sauntering back thru the mess hall door. We arrested him there, for I was dead certain he was

552

the man we wanted & should be locked up at the earliest possible moment even tho we had failed to catch him red-handed. Perhaps I didn't write you of how a Negro entered my WAC officer's quarters at 4 AM. Then the incident was repeated, a similar person entering the room of one of the nurses at 1AM. The nurse was certain she recognized the person & the following nite saw him in the passageway at 2:30 a.m. I met him at 11 PM two nites ago & scared him off to his quarters, trying not to arouse his suspicions that he was under surveillance. Then tonite.

The Captain is afraid of getting in trouble for jailing him without sufficient evidence, but I'm insisting he be locked up, for I'm almost dead certain he is the prowler & a potential rapist. The nurse identified him, he also fits Lt Hammond's description tho she can't positively identify him, & he has been seen twice previously stalking about at odd hours of the nite. He had no excuse whatever for being where I caught him tonite.

So must sleep now & try to think out a speech to these passengers to straighten them out on this question of discipline.

I love you, always -
Robert

*   *   *   *   *

Sat, 4 May '46 - 10 pm

Dear Robert Darling:

So glad to hear your vibrant voice again. Was so excited after talking to you that I couldn't sleep till 12:30 AM or so, altho I retired about 10 PM & Bobby was asleep. My heart kept pounding so & I was so conscious of it, and my mind was so alert & filled with lots of the problems & decisions we have to make when you "come back to face the music", as you put it.

Am glad you're coming back as you say by 20 May. Don't think you'll regret missing a trip to Panama, not when you see your little son, such a "pint-sized" copy of his father! You'll have to spend an entire day with us & see what we go thru in a normal day in "baby's life". Are your muscles strong? Can you stand the strain of a lively, squirming 16-pounder who wants to bounce up & down every time he's picked out of his crib? How's your patience? Can you coax & scold him for about an hour until cod liver oil, fruit juice & cereal are inside Baby's tummy? How's

553

your grip on things? Can you hold a naked, slippery little guy who kicks and splashes and lunges out of the water as you try to hold him with one arm & wash with the other?

Big news today, too! Rich's airmail arrived this AM (it's his 20th birthday) stating we can expect him on 20 May! Mom's so happy she can hardly restrain herself.

So, darling, it looks like you and Rich will both be home at the same time. I'm really happy, deliriously so, dear, to think that finally we'll be able to do something about our post-war plans. Somehow I feel that our good luck so far will come to our assistance & we'll be able to get settled before the fall; but do think of possible solutions to the problems we'll face.

Hope you'll understand the brevity of my letter. It's late & I've got to get to bed. Write me of your progress in getting demobilized, darling -

> Lovingly
> Beth

*   *   *   *   *

Mon 6 May 1946 - 9 pm

Darling -

. . . Bobby has all of us at his constant beck and call, and we don't mind it a bit. Mom & Dad are so much taken up with him, I know they'll miss him terribly when we leave. They've been so grand to both of us, and I feel that you should be appreciative of the help they've given us and be generous in overlooking their shortcomings.

Very little else to write, except to tell you that I am so glad that in a few weeks we'll be together and can both plan and do something about our future. I've been so alone, Robert, since our parting last Sept and have had some pretty deep moods of despondency as I'd contemplate the months ahead and know I could do nothing but mark time until your return. Have missed your loving caresses, too, Robert, and I am a creature who needs affection and attention in order to bring out the best in me. 'nuff said!

Write me as much as you can, dear, each day if possible to speed the days until you return

> Lovingly
> Beth

＊　　＊　　＊　　＊　　＊

6PM Monday 6 May 46

My sweet darling -

. . . . Will probably be home in two weeks. Haven't the least idea of where to stay. Mean what I said about going to your mother's house. Am sure I could never stand it. Will probably have to get a room until we can find a place to live. I am so anxious to see you & our little darling, but find myself now looking with even more impatience & longing towards the day when we can be by ourselves, when we have a home again. It will be an even more beautiful home now with the precious joy of our baby. I love you both so dearly

Robert

＊　　＊　　＊　　＊　　＊

1:30 <u>AM</u> Wed. 8 May 1946

My sweetest beloved -

The big news tonite is that I leave for Fort Sheridan with 3 days travel time on Monday, 13 May. It is not wholly definite yet, but that is what they told me it would be in all probability. Also got your enthusiastic letter, & it makes me just seethe with impatience to get home to you & to our little squirmer. You are both so lovable. Our dreams of the last 3½ years are now about to come true, and I'm sure it will be even more wonderful than we have ever anticipated. If we can only find a place to live!!

This getting out is taking place with such swiftness that I find myself a little startled and at present am in a deep dark quandary over where to live. From here I feel there is not a roof in all Chicago to put over our heads. And am also worried about where to live until I find us a place. Your brother's coming home rules out your mother's house more emphatically than ever, & I know I couldn't stand my folks for long. Have never felt so like a homeless vagabond in my lIfe.

I love you my precious wife & am so anxious to live with you, forever -

Robert

＊　　＊　　＊　　＊　　＊

555

My sweetheart -

Am quite disgusted over this getting out of the Army. Have spent most of the day battling the inane pill counters of the Medical Corps trying to get clearance from them on the "Josiah Bartlett". But nothing would suffice for them other than I sit down & do a full day's work that one of their clerks should do. Imagine being unable to get out of the Army until going thru a damn rigarmarole of that sort. Yet there was nothing else I could do, and it has probably delayed me for a few days as well, even tho I have worked until just now posting my Property Turn-in Slips to the account. I guess such a stupid deal is a fitting termination to my Army career, it makes me so furiously glad to be leaving.

Yet I am also fearful of arriving homeless in Chicago. Am seriously considering not seeing anyone there until I have found a place to live. We have been apart so long & have dreamt of our reunion in such beautiful fantasies, that any distorting compromise would now be tragic. I cannot picture life at your folks as being a beautiful thing. Perhaps it would be better were I not to see you until we had a place to go to & live alone, hold our blessed reunion in the setting it so well deserves. My mind has no answer for that disturbing problem, but my mood is turbulent & uncertain; going "home" is not as pleasant as it should be.

. . . I am so excited at the prospect of seeing him, yet I shrink from the thot of being a mere onlooker in his life until we are alone together. Each time I think of living at your folks', I shudder & wish I were out in Japan with 10 years of Army life ahead. I cannot face my position as a 2nd best there & I will not. You must understand sweetheart, if I wait a few weeks to find us a home before seeing you. It will be much simpler that way. I love you, my wife, so intensely

Robert

*   *   *   *   *

NOTE: To be read when cool, calm & collected

Wed - 8 May '46 - 8:30 pm

Dear Robert -

Worrying is a mighty poor substitute for thinking, but when thinking puts you in a cul-de-sac, the only recourse is to worry or even pray. And I'm doing a lot of all three, thinking, worrying, praying.

Your letter of 6 May came this morning and again I am all upset. You're anxious to see Bobby and me, yet you say you'll never enter "your mother's house". Just where do you propose to see us, out on the sidewalk? I'm a bit (perhaps more than that) angered at your attitude. Think you should have gotten over the whole thing by now. As for finding a room (I presume for yourself) that will be like looking for a needle in a hay stack, & besides you have to think of our finances. I don't think you should let your personal feelings & prejudices penalize our slowly built up funds. I'm writing all this dispassionately and hope you will consider it similarly.

Fritz has left their name & address at 20 or more apartment buildings in hopes of finding an apt. No success thus far & they've been hunting feverishly for several months. I feel that we should be <u>together</u>, planning & searching for a home, & I can think of no better base of operations than right here in my folks' place, where Bobby can be cared for when we're away.

Do so want you to be with baby & me so you can watch his daily life & really get to know our son. If you don't come directly here, Robert, who knows how long it will be before we are reunited, & in our own place; and it'll be a loss of face if you do have to or decide to come here later. Do so want you beside me again, Robert, as a kind, patient, understanding, loving husband and father of my child.

If, as you have so often professed in your letters, you do love us both so dearly, Robert, I'm sure you'll do nothing to hurt us or the ones we love in any way. I'm very sensitive (perhaps overly so) about good relations between you and my family, and your proper attitude towards them will endear you even more to me.

'Tis a letter written by a gal with much on her mind. If I didn't think you cared about my feelings, I wouldn't write this but would steel myself against the unpleasantness that your disregard of my wishes would bring. As it is, I'm sure you'll come back, an affable son-in-law, and the affectionate, eager husband & father, yes?

<u>Very</u> sincerely
Beth

557

Besides: how you will you take pics of Bobby if you're not with us? Huh?

*   *   *   *   *

Midnite Friday 10 May 46

My beloved -

I know I wrote you a very poor letter last nite, and I'm in about the same mood tonite. The entire day has been spent in the throes of medical supply accounting. If they knew I was on 3 other ships with their damn supplies, I probably wouldn't get out of the army for another month. And trouble always multiplies. These people have made a fool clerk of me & forced me to account for property for which I had no accountability, setting up a bunch of papers which have no logical meaning whatsoever, yet which will keep a dozen people at work for a day or two. Their crowning achievement, however, has been to delay my discharge two days & by so doing have held me in the Army just 24 hours long enough for me to become involved in another stupidity of similar vein. The Water Division is now going to make each officer "reconstruct" an account of his property for them!! After 9/10 of the officers are discharged and the entire war gone by without an account being kept, some officious numbskull has discovered a rule that will waste untold reams of paper and hours of labor upon a futile, meaningless effort to clean up old files. How I detest pencil pushers, and the regular army variety in particular.

So I will not leave for Chicago Monday, nor Tues, etc. Am almost finished with the Medics, but have no idea how long this Water Div inanity will hold me up.

But I am still also considering not seeing you until we have a place to live. Can think of nothing in life I have dreaded more than the thot of going "home" to you at your mother's house. Am sure it would be a very disappointing & disillusioning experience for all.

I sent you that letter of my father's that you could see his side of the picture. Don't agree in the least with his ideas about how happy I would be as an icebox salesman, but otherwise think the letter OK. I suspect you will try to blame him for my defection at your mother's house, but he really had no influence on my feelings in that respect. He merely confirmed them.

Wish getting out of the Army were as simple as getting in.

*   *   *   *   *

My darling -

Received your Wed letter. I knew you would feel that way about my not wanting to live with you at your folks. Yet how will you feel when I clash with your mother; as I inevitably will. There seems to be no solution, and as I say, it sort of takes the joy out of coming home. That too, of course, increases my liking for your mother no end. I'm not a person to forget & forgive, because I've seen how futile that was in my folks' home. Where there is a clash of personalities, there can be no peace or pleasantness & the few moments of happiness that do come occasionally are more than overshadowed by the almost continual feeling of hatred & ill will. Can't bring myself to say anything encouraging; much as I would like to, but I feel so utterly discouraged over this coming home business. I have a beautiful wife & child who I am burning with desire to see & be with, yet I can have them only in hell. I feel so helpless against this strange fate.

Love
Robert

*   *   *   *   *

Monday, 13 May '46 - 9 pm

Dear Robert -

This will be a hasty letter to tell you how disappointed I am that you will be delayed in arriving. Am afraid that if you delay seeing Bobby & me until you find us a house, your little son will be old enough to ask me "who is that man, Mommy?"

I'm not blaming your father or you for your attitude towards my "mater". She's not well and is very high strung & now this trouble with her teeth. One must make allowances, Robert. You've never been a mother, & so you'll never understand the possessiveness, the worry, the affection a mother feels for her children & her concern for their welfare; and please don't ever think anybody influences me. I give in to people (even you) on too many occasions merely because I dislike unpleasantness & I can compromise and make the best of a great many seemingly untenable positions. But someday I shall blow my top & really let off a lot of steam, for I'm fed up with being in the middle all the time.

How would you feel if you were me & had a recalcitrant hus-

559

band who threatened not to see you because he didn't like your folks? I've always met you half way or better on a lot of occasions, Robert.

You can go off & try to change your mood with picture taking, and I? I grit my teeth & light another cigarette; for I never could run away from things, nor can I now. Bobby's been crankier than ever yesterday & today - teething? Or just a reaction to my unsettled state? We won't have a happy home ever, Robert, if you persist in wanting your way always.

This is a mean letter, I guess, but I feel you should know that my existence has been anything but idyllic; constant catering to Bobby, being so confined to home, & then worrying about our problems. Oh, to roll back the clock to 10 years ago when my biggest worry was what to wear when my best beau called!

YUP -

Betty

*   *   *   *   *

Thu 16 May - Letter from Robert written Mon says he expects to leave for Chgo this Friday. Wonder if he'll come here or to his folks? Feel not elated over his return, but relieved & yet a bit apprehensive of possible repercussions. Telegram fm Robert he'd arrive Sat on Trail Blazer but would have to go to Sheridan the same day.

Fri 17 May - Bobby Starts on Carrots - Museum of Modern Art picture comes - Pic we admired in NY at the Museum of Modern Art came today. Guess RWD paid $10 for it. Decided to clean house today, vacuumed & dusted in view of RWD's arrival this weekend.

Sat 18 May - RWD Home - RWD called about 9 AM. His folks met him at the station. Difficult persuading him to stop by before proceeding to Sheridan. His Dad & Richard came with him & they stayed 2 hrs, watching Bobby. He called fm Sheridan in the aft to say he'd be able to leave Sun aft & his folks would pick him up & drive him here. A bit excited, wondering if our previous conflicts would continue.

CHAPTER XV
Hausfrau, Night Fireman, Undergraduate

Synopsis - The pace of our lives never slackened, although it now underwent a dramatic change in style. The transition to civilian life was by no means as unendingly delightful as we had so eagerly anticipated in our letters and our daydreams. By the fourth day after my return from the army, however, we had purchased a home [Fig 49]. While this provided us great relief, that we were not to be thwarted in our postwar dreams by the abysmal lack of available housing, it also began a three-month period of frustration until we could actually move in. The house, on Chicago's "Southside" (Marquette Park section), with reasonable transportation link to her parents' home and the University of Chicago, was a 5-room brick bungalow, with the added feature of a lot 38 ft wide rather than the usual 25, and with a two-car brick garage; but sadly in need of repair and refurbishing.

Our 3-month wait for possession was made doubly frustrating by the crowded condition under which we lived with our infant son at her parents' home [Fig 4], constantly threatened with a disruptive clash between Elizabeth's mother and my impatient self. I did, of course, finally accept the logic of our position, and despite my vehemently expressed protestations in Chapter XIV joined her, as submissively as I could manage, in the bosom of her family. Poor Elizabeth needed all her considerable diplomatic skills to keep things on an even keel. In addition to these cross currents of personality, there were several other aggravating features. First, we were not as lucky in obtaining an affordable car in the constricted postwar market as we had been in finding a house. Our very used Graham Paige [Fig 50] no longer had a company to support the repair it was constantly in need of. Then there was my job. Because of my "seniority" and army service, my former employer, Hotpoint, (a division of General Electric) was lenient as to what position I might assume. I "chose" the job of fireman on the third shift, 23:30-07:30, which was ideal for my beginning full time study at the University of Chicago. Twice a night I had to remove the clinkers from the furnace and shovel 4 tons of coal into the automatic hopper, otherwise I simply watched the steam pressure and did my homework.

The workaholic nature of the two of us became fully evident once we had moved into 3506. We learned all the skills of painting, papering, making curtains, sanding floors, and feeding the coal-fired furnace. Elizabeth assumed her role as homemaker with unparalleled zeal: laundry, vacuuming, mopping, tending the baby, baking, shopping, the constant routine of meals and dishwashing; and, so it seemed, devising an endless list of things that needed my attention. I often failed to measure up to what she thought should be my end of the bargain, busy as I was with a double agenda of work and school. This led to several tests of our emotional stability. She was also frequently, and understandably, dismayed by the almost total lack of social or recreational life that this period demanded. I was too busy for that, and thus she had recourse almost solely to her family; her mother and father also providing much needed advice and assistance to the still amateur parents and home owners. She acquired an ardent devotion to gardening, indoors and out, affording some relief to her strong instinct for accomplishment.

Our letters to each other having ceased, her diary is the only record of this phase of our lives. It is, of course, replete with the quotidian, so that only the more salient events are preserved herewith, along with passages that illumine the general nature of our activities.

The Chapter ends with my obtaining a Bachelor of Science degree in Physiology.

Sun 19 May 1946 - RWD Arrives - Waited impatiently for RWD. He arrived at 6 PM with his Dad, bringing facial tissues & Hershey bars for me. We started unpacking, but Fritz & Bess came about 8:30 PM & so we had to stop & visit. They stayed until 10 PM, & so to bed. Apprehensive as to how RWD will like staying here.

Mon 20 May - RWD up early & getting his Dad's car to go see about certificate of eligibility for educational benefits from VA. Also went to FHA & Better Business Bureau, some RE offices re purchase of home. Stowed away his clothing today & I think we'll be comfortable; if only RWD doesn't clash with Mom.

Tue 21 May - RWD at U of C making arrangements for exam June 17, start school June 24. Looked at many houses (just fm outside) and thought they were out of line, price, location, etc. Angry at RWD for some of his foolish stubborn attitude. Mom takes offense so easily and I'm so nervous over it.

Wed 22 May - We Look for Homes - RWD looking for used cars & having no luck. So we looked at 5 or 6 places. Disgusted w/ prices, locations, etc. One place for 11,500 appeals to us, 2nd house fm corner & nice appearance from outside. [This is what we bought!] Had a big blow up with RWD tonite re lites, etc. & told him for Bobby's sake we've got to soft pedal our own feelings. [Perhaps this was the time I erroneously put a PHOTOFLOOD lamp in the bathroom to replace the 25 W bulb so I could see better to shave!?]

Thu 23 May - We Buy a House - An exciting day. Dad Doty picked us up at 10:30 AM. The place isn't our dream house. The woodwork & floors are dark (oak); it needs redecorating but the structure is basically good (1928, 5-room bungalow) and the 38 ft lot, the covered porch & the brick 2 car garage interested me. So favorably impressed we picked up Dad & Mom & Bobby and gave it a second look-see; and they were enthusiastic, so we signed a contract this aft, paying $600 earnest money w/ Dad Doty present. A bit worried about getting the Smiths (tenants) evicted in 90 days. OPA notice is to be served today so as to expedite things. Also apprehensive of the $5400 judgment notes we signed so as to qualify for enough equity for OPA purposes.

Fri 24 May - Some question re his earning enough money to qualify for GI loan as our monthly payments would be $43 on a $5000 mortgage. Now I'm even more apprehensive, but RWD says not to worry.

Sat 25 May - M - Getting more misgivings about getting into our house within 90 days. What if the tenants refuse to move? What if

563

the bank refuses our loan application? Worrying if RWD is trying to do too much with school & work & a house?

Sun 26 May - M - Robert out all day with his Dad trying to buy us a car. Came back disgusted at the junk on the market & the prices so high! Bobby is getting 4 upper teeth soon, cries, can't eat or sleep & so I'm all upset, too.

Mon 27 May - M - Bobby 5 mos Old - Teething - We Buy a Car, '39 Graham, 4 dr - About noon Robert left to start looking for a car. When he came back about 6 PM he'd found a '39 Graham for $752 that he thot was the best buy he'd seen. Was a bit reluctant about it, but we decided to take a look. So his Dad drove us out there & frankly the body looks pretty good. They said they'd make several minor repairs & give us a warranty (which is backed up by the OPA). So RWD put $40 deposit on it. New cars will not be plentiful for some time to come & we do need a car.

Tue 28 May - M - OPA Eviction Notice - RWD starts on his job - RWD picked up copy of the OPA eviction notice. He left for Hotpoint at 3, starts 3:45 PM & works till 12:15 as a Millwright Helper, 90¢/hr plus 10% bonus for 2nd shift & will get a 25% bonus monthly. This till the fireman job opens up. Did a little sewing on my plaid gingham dress.

Wed 29 May - M - RWD Picks up the Car - RWD left about noon to pick up the car & when he returned at 3 PM was hopping mad & rueful of his bargain. The joint had made no repairs & offered him $160.14 discount to take the car as is w/o warranty, and he took it. Is afraid the motor is shot & that we won't come out ahead. I got up at 12:30 AM to fix him some soup. Worried about the house deal.

Thu 30 May - Bobby out all aft - After dinner RWD & I took him for a stroll in Douglas Park. RWD & I took a ride in our car & looked the neighborhood at 66th & St. Louis over. Think it will be okay. If only everything works out all right. His Dad thinks he got a pretty good buy on the car, but RWD is pessimistic.

Fri 31 May - The Car Doesn't Run! - Rain pouring all day, dark, cold, dreary day; and our car doesn't run. RWD called several garages & they estimate $150 for all the necessary repairs. But he's going to wait for the title before doing anything. Fixed RWD soup & a snack for him upon his return from work. Beginning to worry whether we can get possession of our house in 90 days; a longer delay would be the pay-off after the deal re the car.

Sat 1 Jun 1946 - RWD working away on his Math to way past midnite; has trouble with college algebra.

Sun 2 Jun - Bobby sits by himself very nicely. Is such a sweet darling. So happy that his father loves him & plays with him.

Mon 3 Jun - Dear Robert plugging away on his Math. Difficult this Correspodence Course. Sewing on my gingham dress. Bought Bobby his 1st pair of kid shoes (1.69), a safety strap (1.18) & 2 pair of training pants. A baby sure costs money.

Tue 4 Jun - Feel very downhearted at the delay in our getting settled in our house & with all the things we need. Can't blame RWD for he's trying his best.

Wed 5 Jun - Re car: Hotpoint Garage can't find Graham parts & so our car still stands in front of the house. Definitely a mistake in buying it.

Thu 6 Jun - We Look at Ranges, Refrig - We're to get a range (used in the experimental laboratory) for 99.00 (usually 180.00). He's trying to get a fireman's job at the Cicero plant, but it seems he has to take the 3rd shift which doesn't suit either one of us. He got his paycheck for 3 days work, $23.76. I kidded him about the amt of money he makes & that really got him upset. Finished another yellow percale tailored housedress & it looks pretty pert.

Fri 7 Jun - OPA notice re Eviction - We Buy a Range - Had a spat w/ Robert early this morning, 1:30 AM when he wanted windows wide open in the bedroom & I objected because of the draft, Bobby's sake. So he proceeded to sleep in the car! RWD slept most of the morning as his sleep in the car wasn't too comfortable.

Sat 8 Jun - We Sign Mortgage Papers - RWD came home about 8:15 AM after working 15¼ hours! A rush to get bathed & dressed when his father & Rich came to push our Graham to Graham dealer on Lawndale Ave. About 11:30 we left to sign trust deed installment note, 20 years, $43.80 with prepayments on taxes. We have the privilege of prepayment on principal on 30 days written notice. Saw appraisal report on our bldg and it shows valuation of house 8100 (replacement price 10,750); garage 1000 & land 2000, total 11,100.

Sun 9 Jun - RWD studying for his U of C placement test. Bobby kept us awake, from 12 to 3 AM by crying intermittently & refusing to go to sleep.

Mon 10 Jun - Robert working days as a fireman. Left for work at 7 AM.

Fri 14 Jun - Robert at the VA this AM re his certificate of eligibility, but couldn't wait for his turn. Took the exam at U of C. Thought he didn't do so well in the Soc Science exam. Mom indisposed (as usual) so I was busy w/ supper & dishes & Bobby's fussing (guess it's his teeth). Such a life! I am a virtual prisoner in the house. Mom's assistance to me has been nil & I have to clean house & care for Bobby & live in constant dread of Mom's & Robert's dislikes for one another! Oh, me!

Mon 17 Jun - Mom on a rampage again about RWD & he senses it acutely.

Wed 19 Jun - RWD came home w/ the car, a bit disgusted at the bill, $220.50 & everything not fixed yet. Tells me he's going to work nites starting Sun 11:30 pm & will have Fri & Sat off.

Fri 21 Jun - RWD having trouble starting car again. The garage sent a man out, had battery charged, but it needed a new coil. Bot slipcovers for the car for $14. Paycheck for 32 hours work 30.72 which amts to 96¢ per hour, not too bad for the fireman job.

Sat 22 Jun - M - RWD enrolls at U of C! - RWD gone at 8 AM & didn't return till 6 PM. Registered for a physiology course, chemistry & introductory psychology, $130 for that. VA account. Will try to complete his German & Math via home study.

Sun 23 Jun - RWD leaving for work at 11:30 PM.

Mon 24 Jun - M -Max Comes Home! - No school for Doty until Wed when his 1st class starts, so he slept a bit after his work all night. Said it wasn't too bad as he could rest in between shoveling coal. About 5:45 PM, after I had fed Bobby, I noticed a sailor coming down the alley, Max in full uniform, home at last! He had come in from Shanghai to San Diego on Tues, 3 days enroute via Santa Fe. So we had quite a bit of excitement as we all sat around

& listened to his tales about his life in the Navy. Max looks good, weighs 200 lbs., and is glad to be a civilian again. RWD bot car insurance today, 32.50.

Wed 26 Jun - M - RWD off to school & didn't return till 5 PM. Quite a schedule, as he will be going to school M-W-F full schedule & a lab on Tuesdays. So he ate & to sleep at 5:45 PM & he'll be up at 11 PM to go to work till 7:30 AM.

Thu 27 Jun - Six Months Old Today! - Bobby gets 1st Immunization Shots - A very hot day. RWD didn't get much sleep as he got up at noon to fix the car lights & we had to leave for the Doc's at 2 PM. Bobby enjoyed so much his ride in the car. Looked about with wonder as we rode. Gave him 1st injection of diptheria, whooping cough & tetanus & Bobby yelled.

Fri 28 Jun - We are no financial wizards - The Bank called us Wed to conclude our deal as of Sat. W/o thinking we agreed. Now we find that we lose all our interest for our Bldg Loan accounts, some $70 or so! But rather than postpone it, we decided to let it go at that.

Sat 29 Jun - We Close our R.E. Deal - OPA dies tomorrow - Max went w/ RWD & me to the Mutual Bank to close our deal. So we paid out in cash $5493.37, now we owe $5000.

Sun 30 Jun - We Go Visit the Smiths - About 2:30 PM we drove out to the Smiths but found only the Grandmother home. Asked to have the the Smiths call us. Mrs. S. called about 6 PM, wishy-washy on their buying a place for themselves & Robert told her we'd take legal action to gain possession soon as possible. The OPA dies at midnite - then what? The deluge? Still very hot & my nerves stretched so taut.

Mon 1 July 1946 - Ma had 2 teeth pulled, old crank, scolding me on the slightest provocation. RWD is to see (Lt) Irv Ordower this aft re eviction of our tenants. [Ordower and his weather Company had been my "passengers" on Nathan B. Forrest, dropping them off in Alexandria, Egypt] RWD came home at almost 7 PM, really tired. School till 2 PM, conference w/ Irv & Ben Ordower. He served Mr & Mrs Smith & talked to them. They had put a deposit on a house, but it would be more than 30 days before they can move. They're so nice, it's hard to feel they're just stringing us along. Collected our 1st rent. So to bed for Doty.

Wed 3 Jul - Richie comes Home! - The "conquering hero" all 204 lbs of him, our little Rich. He's as charming & spoiled as ever. I went to bed at midnite, Mom went to bed at 3:30 AM or so. Well, at last we're all home & the service flag came down!

Thu 4 Jul - Bobby's 1st Fourth - RWD doing his homework all morning and aft. He had to work tonight. We sat on the back porch with Bobby, who stared with wide eyes watching the flares, sparklers, rockets, etc. go off. No firecrackers.

Fri 5 Jul - With OPA dead, prices are soaring. Round steak, which sold @ 45¢/lb last Sat at National's sells for 1.20/lb today. Meanwhile, Congress piddles around, doing nothing! RWD in school, doing homework till 9 PM when he went to sleep. Little Bobby getting cuter & smarter every day. All he wants to do is stand & jump & do knee bends. Rather disgusted with the dull life I am leading these days.

Sat 6 Jul - Hot day & I feel so bored with my existence. So much more work w/ Max & Rich home & Mom fussing over Rich as tho he were a baby. RWD gone all day at school in the lab. Back at 5 PM & now busy w/ homework. Lots of companionship in that! Bobby a little fusser and I acted up after supper and demanded RWD take us for a ride. So out to Frejlach's for milkshakes. Bobby tasted a bit on RWD's spoon & licked his lips over & over again.

Tue 9 Jul - Almost 99 - Bobby has us alarmed - Bobby was feverish last nite when RWD was leaving. At 3 AM he awoke just hot as can be all over. Alarmed, I awakened Mom & we tried giving him water, limewater & chamomile tea. This AM RWD alarmed me by diagnosing 102 & poliomyelitis & called Dr. Belding. Dr B's associate, Dr Meyer, came out 10 AM & looked Bobby over. Nothing wrong. Prescribed aspirin (½ tablet 3x/day); 3.00 for his visit. RWD getting more sleep today but so cross. Between the two Dotys [Notice this, Baby is a Doty when she's irritated!] I'm really fenced in. Feel the drain on my strength nursing Bobby as he refuses to take any other food.

Thu 11 Jul - Mom had her last 3 teeth pulled this morning & was in bed all day. Bobby a little fusser & I spent most of the day caring for him. Feel really down in the dumps. We're so crowded here I can't call a nook my own & all the circumstances make me feel so frustrated. RWD slept about 8 hours today before going to work & apparently felt the better for it.

Sat 13 Jul - This eve RWD & I drove out to Frejlach's for ice cream, then drove to the old neighborhood & I showed Robert the house where I was born at 2144 W Coulter.

Mon 15 Jul - Bobby is eating again! - A very dull existence I lead these days. If it weren't for Bobby, I'd call it quits. RWD no companion at all, spends so much time at school, at work, most unappreciative of my never-ending tasks.

Thu 18 Jul - 99.9 F! - Hottest since 24 July 1934 - Mrs Smith phoned re receipt of water bill & I talked to her about vacating the premises; vague as usual. Disgusted at the prospect of spending another month here in my "home, sweet home". Gets worse since the boys are home.

Fri 19 Jul - Still hot, Bobby, a little fusser, & refusing his cod liver oil & other food. Do think it's partly due to his teething. Clean house today and resent Mother's implications that I don't do my share of it. Can't get out of the house for even a few hours. RWD busy with his school studies. Terrific grind taking Chem & physiology (2 lab courses) & psychology & trying to finish his Math & German home study courses.

Sun 21 Jul - M - Hell of a day. Dad set up Bobby's crib in the LR & Mom raised a squawk. Now she's mad at all of us. Grandma not talking to any of us "Dotys" tonight.

Sat 27 Jul - M - We visit the Smiths - Rec'd OPA cert of eviction & so decided to see the Smiths. Mr. & Mrs. S were very nice, thought they'd get out by 8/15. Looking the place over again I find the kitchen rather small compared to Mom's. The LR & DR I like. It'll be nice after living in cramped quarters.

Tue 30 Jul 46 - 1st Payment on Mortgage - RWD home early & going to sleep right away. So I have little companionship from him. And as soon as Bobby goes to sleep, 8:30 or so, I retire also. Have no ambition or inclination to do anything, altho I do a lot of daydreaming about our house & when we do finally get into it.

Mon 5 Aug - RWD angry at me this AM for not indulging in romancing with him & left w/o breakfast & didn't return till after 5 PM.

Tue 6 Aug - I Buy a Dinette Set - Doty not coming home till 4

PM & went straight to bed w/o talking or eating. Sometimes I hate him!

Wed 7 Aug - RWD home for breakfast & played w/ Bobby. He suggested I get in touch w/ Mrs S re the electric service. So I called her & she said they were going to sign mortgage papers tonite. RWD came home for supper & went to sleep about 5:30 PM. Not much sleep for him before he had to get up to go to work, which he did most reluctantly.

Sun 11 Aug - RWD working on his chemistry until 6 PM. Then to sleep & going to work 2:30 AM, as he had told the Hotpoint people he would.

Tue 20 Aug - M - Angered by RWD's refusal to eat margarine this AM & he left w/o breakfast. This whole situation is driving me into a morbid mental state. Resent the feeling that I'm an outsider & being constantly told I'd better move. Went to National's this aft. Bot couple dozen cans baby food & home. Found no butter for RWD. RWD home at 6 PM. Had been in the Lab all this time. So hurriedly he ate & to bed. And to bed myself early. To dream of the day when I have my own place & everything in its own place.

Sun 25 Aug - RWD busy all day studying. Final exams coming up next week & he has to turn in his notebooks in Chemistry & Physiology. So he went to bed at 8 PM. Then Bobby started acting up. Slept all eve, but 11 PM started crying & last till 2 AM, when I took him into bed with me.

Mon 26 Aug - My poor darling had to go to work with 4 hours sleep & had an exam at school. RWD home 3 PM, having supper, & to bed. Doesn't have to go to school tomorrow, but will study for his final exams.

Tue 27 Aug - Bobby is 8 months old - 7 teeth - Had to take Bobby to bed with me last night at 1 AM in order to shut him up. He likes to sleep with me. RWD studying at the Toman Library & in the Park. Home 4:30 PM, eating, & to bed. Fixing RWD's lunch & to bed; but awakened at 11 PM & seeing Robt off.

Thu 29 Aug - 2nd Payment on our Mortgage - Dear Bobby woke up at 1:30 AM & not wanting to take him into bed w/ me, I tried to put him to sleep by rocking & singing to him. But he kept on yelling & at 3 AM I gave in, so we slept till 8 AM. RWD home for breakfast. He played w/ Bobby till 10, when I got up. Still no word fm our tenants & Robert thinks we'll have to file suit as they won't be out for 3 weeks or so yet. I fervently hope not, as conditions at home are unbearable. Mom cross as a bear & so <u>crude & rude!</u>

Fri 30 Aug - Our Fifth Anniversary - RWD's last day at school & final exam in physiology. He came home at 4:30 PM. After supper we picked Bess & Fritz up at their house & drove out to Froelich's for ice cream, and home by 9:30 PM. Thus we celebrated our 5th wedding anniversary.

Sat 31 Aug - We Buy an Easy Washer - We Visit our Tenants - RWD talked to Ben Ordower this AM re filing eviction proceedings.

Sun 1 Sep 46 - Robert Walks Out on Us - After a nite of fussing w/ Bobby & having him sleep in our bed, RWD blew up about 9:30 AM, called me "stupid, ignorant, etc." and said he was leaving. Told him to go & he did. Valpak of clothes & all his books, camera. The Doty's called to ask us for dinner & so got the news. Insisted Bobby & I come & so we did. Had a nice dinner. Bobby got a white creeper suit, 2 pr socks, a toy, a silver spoon. Sympathy from the Doty's.

Mon 2 Sep - More People Call on Us! - RWD called me last nite to say he made a mistake in directing his remarks to me, but I told him I wanted a personal apology from him to my whole family, & hung up on him. Wondering just what Doty is doing. Where he is, etc. A darned shame he couldn't keep his temper under control until we moved out. Now I am really in a quandary.

Tue 3 Sep - Bobby sits up by himself! - The little guy refuses to sleep in his crib & I had him in bed with me all night. Mr. Smith called this eve to say they ordered their movers for Fri aft & we could plan on Sat for our moving. Oh, that Doty guy! I could shoot him for blowing up so close to our moving date!

Wed 4 Sep - We Can Get our Refrigerator! - Doty called me early this AM to find out what Smith had to say. So I told him to go see his Dad. Called Dad Doty at 11 & RWD was there. So we decided RWD should come here this aft & we would do some shopping. He came at 2. We took Bobby along. At Spiegel's buying ironing board & other HH items. At Sears getting paint &

571

putty & clothesline, etc. RWD has been sleeping in the car parked in forest preserves, the jerk!

Thu 5 Sep - Easy Washer Arrives - It came! Put it in basement & will have the Movers take it to the house. RWD over in the aft & I gave him some of the boxes stored in the basement to take out to the house. Says it looks like they're really moving. I spent the day beginning my packing. More things scattered all over the house! I really monopolized closet space with my clothes and stuff & the basement with HH items!

Fri 6 Sep - More Packing! The Smiths Leave - Packing all day, and Bobby acted up so; wanted to be near all the time & wouldn't go to sleep. Fell out of his hi-chair but luckily it was converted to a low chair! So I guess I'll have to have his safety strap on him always. RWD stopped by for another load of stuff this AM & went out to the house to wait for the Hotpoint refrigerator. The Smiths moved out this aft; lots of cleaning to be done. RWD washed down the pantry tonite. The baby fussing so I went home at 10 PM.

Sat 7 Sep - RWD paints pantry, washes closet - We Move into our House [Fig 49] - Robt at the house until noon, when he came out for baby & me. So we finally moved. Mom in tears, me ditto. Stove not connected, so used gas stove in basement to cook our sketchy supper. Working till 2 AM. I got almost all my dishes washed & put them in the linen closet, RWD washes & paints closet.

Tue 10 Sep - Odds & Ends Only Today - Our Coal Arrives, 97.40 - 8 tons Pocahantas small nut came, 97.40 w/ hiking charge. The electricians worked some more on range wiring, so I continued to cook downstairs. RWD & I unpacked the books, other boxes, & cartons, & he took a lot of the stuff up to the attic. Straightened and unwrapped furniture so we have more room in the LR & DR. RWD to sleep about 4 PM & I had my hands full cleaning up the kitchen, caring for Bobby, & then looking thru my collection of color schemes & home decorating stuff.

Wed 11 Sep - RWD fixes Bath Rm Window - Cleans Ceiling in Bobby's Room - Electric Range Installed - Grand to have a kitchen stove & I think I'll like it. After RWD went to sleep at 5

PM, I washed my range, ironed rest of my kitchen curtains & hung them up. So the place looks more livable.

Sat 14 Sep - M - I got acquainted with my Easy washer when I washed 3 days clothes for Bobby, & socks & undies for Robt & me. It's wonderful & I'm glad I got it! Bobby cried himself to sleep (in 15 or so min) 3x today & has been sleeping since 7:30 PM this eve. We cleaned wallpaper, ceiling & woodwork in our room & it looks nicer. Tired, but feeling good. Robt bought light green enamel for kitchen; a saw; fixed a doorknob, put up a pulley clothesline. Is cleaning basement now.

Mon 16 Sep - RWD out all Day - We Order Venetian Blinds - RWD leaving early & returning 5 PM or so. Reserved a "steamer" for Fri & will try to remove the awful wall covering in the living room. Washed Bobby's clothes, changed bed linens, cooked chicken cacciatore, scrubbed down stove in basement, & that's about all I accomplished altho I was busy all the time. Taking care of Bobby is quite a job, feeding, changing diapers, washing him. Does he crawl! Boy, oh boy!

Tue 17 Sep - Big Wash Day for Me! From 9:30 to 2:30 pm! - Bobby up at 7:30 & nursed, so when Robt & Bess came at 8 I was up fixing breakfast. Had all sorts of towels, sheets, and Robt's clothes & kept hanging them out to dry as fast as my Easy washer got them done. I do like the machine, especially the Spindrier. Robt wanting to go to bed. He drove Bess home, ate & retired after 4 PM. He never gets enough sleep.

Wed 18 Sep - I iron clothes - RWD washes Calcimine off DR ceiling - So little progress. Took Robt all day to wash that ceiling! Bobby quite a fusser today; must be the smallpox vacc. Now Robt has to have the car fixed again! Damn! Doesn't seem like we'll get too much done before Robt has to go back to school. I want him to take a vacation, but he's stubborn.

Fri 20 Sep - We Steam Celutex off LR, hall & chisel DR walls - RWD coming home with steamer & started on hall at 9:30. Perhaps it was a mistake to attempt the DR walls, as they were covered with wallpaper, paint, celutex, spackle & more paint. So we steamed & chiseled & by 5 PM had only 1 wall done, so went to work on LR. That came off surprisingly well. But RWD worked to 11 PM (no sleep for 24 hours!) & we were both so tired! Don't

573

know what to do re DR walls. Guess we'll keep the steamer & try tomorrow. So much dirt, trash, dust, fm all our chiseling!

Sat 21 Sep - Worked on DR walls till 4 PM & had only 2 completed, so quit. We'll paper them as is. RWD got white flat paint for ceilings, but now we have to fix sash cord in all the LR windows. I want RWD to take a week off from work before school starts. RWD started washing calcimine off LR ceiling. Made him quit around 11 PM. Took our baths.

Sun 22 Sep - Robt washes LR ceiling - patches plaster - Gosh, it'll be good to be rid of calcimine. Took Robert all day to wash the LR ceiling clean. He patched some of the cracks in the plaster.

Mon 23 Sep - Robt paints LR ceiling 1st coat - We get Bobby a Playard - Robert started painting LR ceiling & it took him till 2:30 PM. Looked at some wallpapers, but the two I liked RWD didn't. Just saw Robt off to work & now at 11:30 we'll go to sleep.

Tue 24 Sep - We Select Wallpaper - RWD Paints Hall & LR Ceiling 2nd Coat - So Robt painted hall ceiling & 2nd coat on LR ceiling & very tired went to sleep at 5 PM. Trouble w/ Bobby in getting him to stay in his playard; yells & wants to be with us. I took some more wallpaper off LR walls.

Wed 25 Sep - Another Busy Day - I wash clothes - RWD paints DR ceiling, patches - Indefatigable Doty starting to patch plaster cracks early, then washed DR ceiling once more & painted 1st coat. Spent rest of aft patching, knocking out more loose wall of DR. I had quite a time w/ Bobby who fussed & cried but I had to get my washing done.

Thu 26 Sep - I wash down woodwork - Hall & DR - RWD paints DR ceiling - gets some sleep - The DR a mess, so I scraped off wallpaper & brushed down walls, took out our heavy paper pads & swept up all the dirt. My right arm is about ready to fall off.

Fri 27 Sep - Bobby 9 mos old today - Bess & Mom over - We Start Wallpapering DR - RWD was sanding down walls when Mom came unexpectedly. Good thing she did, as her pointers re papering were most useful. I almost went hysterical while Robert struggled to hang his 1st piece of wallpaper on DR wall! Mom helped, & it came up OK. We finished our 3rd wall about midnite. Went to sleep exhausted.

Sat 28 Sep - We Wallpaper LR till 5AM ! - Early this morning Robt started wallpapering. I measured & cut & trimmed while Robt hung. More paste mixing & pasting!

Sun 29 Sep - We Finish Hall Papering - At 10 AM Bunny wouldn't stay in bed any longer & so I got up. Let Robt sleep till 2:30 PM. Decided to finish the hall & about 3:30 we started, using the razor, small scissors, the floor for measuring, a whisk broom for pasting & a large one for smoothing. At 8 PM had finished.

Tue 1 Oct 46 - Robt starts U of C Autumn Semester - [Comparative Anatomy, Quantitative Analysis, Analytic Geometry (Halmos), Physics (Enrico Fermi)] His boss called & said he needed Doty tonite. I managed to steel wool the LR & hall baseboards. Fixed supper for RWD by 4:30 PM when he returned fm school. So he ate & to bed.

Wed 2 Oct - I paint baseboards w/ seal coat - RWD home 7:55; quick breakfast & off to school 8:10. Back 1:30 PM w/ microscope fm school. So Robt ate lunch & off to work at 3 PM. I put this stain seal coat on the baseboards and hall, LR & DR. Awful smelly stuff & I got a headache doing it. Worked for about 3½ hours doing my "painting".

Thu 3 Oct - Flat paint on Baseboard - Another hectic day. RWD home last night about midnite & up at 7:20 AM to be at school 8:30. Didn't return until 4 PM. Mom Doty called re things. Thinks Robert is looking bad. How about me?

Fri 4 Oct - Robert starts sanding floors - RWD at school till noon. When he came, it was w/ sander & small hand sander, floor sealer, lacquer, varnish, etc. Got started sanding about 2:30 PM & by 11 had only given LR & hall the rough going over. To bed rather disgusted that sanding takes so much time. RWD angry at me on account of that same thing again.

Sat 5 Oct - Finishes LR & DR - Seals both - Dad over to help - Angrily RWD set to work on DR this AM. Had to go to school for 11 class. When he returned at 4 PM, Dad had just arrived. So Dad helped him w/scraping of corners & dusting of floors. RWD finished sealing the floors about 9:30 PM & Bobby & I went along when we drove Dad home.

Sun 6 Oct - BRs sealed - LR varnished & 1 BR - Robt picked Dad up about 9:45 & they set to work right away. Rubbed down LR & hall while Robt sanded BR #1. Then he started on BR #2 & Dad dusted & sealed BR #1. Dad varnished LR & hall before he left, Robt driving him home 7pm. Finished sealing BR #2 at 10:30 PM & varnished BR#1.

Fri 11 Oct - We spent over $1000 last month for refrigerator, washer, coal, payment on mortgage, paints, etc.

Sun 13 Oct - Very angry at Robert today. He "studied" upstairs while I washed Bobby's clothes & straightened up the house.

Mon 14 Oct - Bobby & I Go Shopping - RWD home 4:30 PM. Is going to work tonite & is sleeping now. Bobby playing in his playard. Pres Truman just announced over the radio that price controls will be removed from livestock, feed & meat in hopes of ensuring meat supply.

Tue 15 Oct - RWD not going to sleep until 10:30 PM, 24 hrs sans sleep!

Wed 16 Oct - It Gets Colder, We Stay Indoors - Typical AM, not getting out of bed till 9:30 AM (shame on me for letting RWD fix own breakfast). Then after our breakfasts Bobby to nap & I to straighten house & wash his laundry. Bobby played quite happily in his playard while I waxed floor in his room.

Fri 18 Oct - RWD home almost 6:30. I was quite nervous & really let off steam. Poor RWD! Guess I do let my temper get the best of me. Mom, Bess & Fritz surprised me by dropping in about 8:30.

Wed 23 Oct - RWD using streetcar to go to school & leaving at 7:30 AM, not home till 7 PM. I ironed his 3 shirts. RWD paid $15 for car repairs.

Thu 24 Oct - Washed kitchen door inside & out; also porch door from inside, sure needs coat of paint, our porch. Angry at dirty walls in hall to basement & I started washing same down, to discover they're calcimined! Must get them painted as it's horrible! Not much done, but still towards our aim, a comfortable, clean, livable home.

Tue 29 Oct - I Go Shopping w/ Bobby - Have gotten into the habit of daily mopping kitchen floor so Bobby doesn't get too dirty crawling around. RWD tired after no sleep since last night, but hung up my two floral prints in bedroom.

Fri 8 Nov - M - RWD disgusted at the "D" he got on his Biology Notebook. Is working on another section, overdue. So much work involved in this school business.

Tue 12 Nov - M - Robert tense after no sleep since last nite. Some words, but to bed finally, both of us.

Fri 22 Nov - RWD and I Have a Spat - I washed clothes & it took me quite a while. Scrubbed kitchen floor again & waxed it. Baked a mince meat pie for RWD this afternoon. Bobby fussed again & I think he's teething. RWD having trouble with his homework again. We had a spat re window opening in BR & he packed himself off upstairs.

Sat 23 Nov - My 31st Birthday - Max over 6:30. Rich & Jean 8:30. Robt opened bottle champagne & we really had a nice evening. Robt was such a perfect host I was pleasantly surprised.

Mon 25 Nov - Bobby beginning to walk a bit better & keeps me on alert keeping him out of mischief. So broke these days, I worry about having enough money for the milkman, etc. RWD home early fm school. Angry because I wouldn't "humor" him & sulked. We had a heart to heart talk re our shortcomings. I baked a mince meat pie for him (also coffeecake) & he refused to eat it [Food really is not the way to a man's heart! - she never could believe this], saying he didn't care for "substitutes".

Thu 28 Nov - AT THE FOLKS [Thanksgiving] - Reconciliation w/ RWD. Fri 29 Nov - RWD very good natured today. He decided to do something about my kitchen table & painted first-coat of white paint. Figure we'll paint it before putting on the inlaid linoleum top. This evening I sewed up a pair of curtains for my basement laundry window. RWD tackling physics tonite.

Mon 2 Dec 1946 - M - Robt home 4PM, going to work at 11 PM. The darling has painted my small kitchen table & glued on linoleum & it will be ready for use in a few days.

Thu 5 Dec - M - Bobby takes 7 steps by himself - I finished my curtains today & hung them up. But they're skimpy & will do only till I get something better. Being as broke as we are, that may not be for quite a while. This eve he took 7 tiny steps by himself, tempted by a piece of chocolate in Robert's hand.

Fri 6 Dec - M - So broke RWD will have to shop tomorrow when he gets his paycheck.

Thu 12 Dec - Frankly, I'm worried at the state of our finances. His GI checks are past due 3rd month now & we've been drawing money out of the bank. Only $200 remains in the local acct & even that may have to go. He would be going to school at a time like this! And with Xmas coming on, too!

Thu 19 Dec - Bobby Really Begins to Walk - Robert had his chemistry exam today & didn't leave till noon, working on his titration curves and last-minute attempt to finish them. I had my laundry almost finished before he left. RWD studied for his Bio Sci exam scheduled for tomorrow. Doesn't think he did so well in Chemistry. If he passes all his subjects, he should be satisfied. Will take only 3 subjects next semester. Hate being cooped up like this.

Fri 20 Dec - RWD thru w/ school - Robert home 3 PM. Says he'll get a "C" in Math, but not much better in his other courses. RWD & I had another one of our spats this eve. He just can't take any criticism.

Sun 22 Dec - Slept late. RWD didn't start washing down bathroom till almost noon & had to stop half-way thru at 2:30 as he had to go to work at 3. I had taken down all my curtains & managed to wash, tint yellow, starch, dry & was hanging them when Robert came home 12:30 AM. Finished, hung up curtains & shade in pantry before retiring at 1:30 AM.

Mon 23 Dec - RWD painted bathroom ceiling & trim white, working continuously from 5 PM or so until 1:30 AM. Frankly, I don't like his work & I think he's too slow. To bed 3 AM or so.

Tue 24 Dec - Robert working tonight - Xmas Eve - Bess, Fritz, Rickey over - After breakfast RWD went to get bread, eggs, a holly Xmas wreath (which we hung on our front door). Had him paint quarter rounds in our bedroom which had been nicked when he sanded floors. I used Bruce floor cleaner on floors in hall, LR, DR, and our BR, vacuumed, dusted, wiped blinds in our BR, hung up my newly tinted yellow curtains (nice looking). I think RWD darkened the turquoise blue paint & started one wall with it. Simply furious. It will look dingy.

Wed 25 Dec - A Wonderful Xmas Day - RWD home 8 AM fm

working all nite & surprised Bobby w/ a toy & me w/ a pr blue fuzzy slippers!

Thu 26 Dec - Robert Finishes Bathroom - We got up around 10:30, both of us refreshed after a good night's rest, although Bobby was a fusser & I had to take him in bed about 6 AM. Robert painting bathroom & really worked, putting the two-tone blue paint on walls. Had trouble mixing the lighter shade of blue. Also difficult getting clean lines around trim.

Fri 27 Dec - Bobby's 1st Birthday - RWD finished the bathtub today, started on kitchen. Washing kitchen ceiling, but as usual, time to go to bed before we got started. Tore oilcloth off kitchen walls, more unexpected work!

Sun 29 Dec - We Paint Kitchen 1st Coat White - Robt to work 7 AM. Lots of snow. Robt shoveling same, eating. We lit Bobby's one candle & started on cake. About 5 PM Robt started painting kitchen. I helped paint lower walls & woodwork. This going on until 1:30 AM. God, will I be glad when it's done. All undercoat on. Tomorrow the green paint & ceiling.

Tue 31 Dec 46 - New Year's Eve - When midnite & the New Year came, we were still busily working, and we didn't stop till 3 AM. Both of us so tired, and Robert has to go back to school Jan 2nd.

Wed 1 Jan 1947 - Bobby weighs 26 lbs clothed - The new year found us busy w/ our kitchen. Lots of snow & Robert had to shovel same. I had a lot of washing to do, but we both got busy on the kitchen, Bobby confined in playpen in middle of the room. Hope this year will bring us more happiness & a less hectic existence than last year.

Fri 3 Jan - Winter Qr of School Starts - Do wish Robt's GI check for 3 mos. subsistence would come. Sure could use the money. 23.83/week fm Hotpoint doesn't go far & we've only 125.00 in the Bank.

Wed 8 Jan - Robt got up about 4 AM & worked on his Bio Sci assignment due today.

Wed 15 Jan - RW & I had another squabble last nite over open or shut BR window, but as usual I effected a reconciliation. Slept w/ Bobby till 11 AM. Didn't want to leave him alone, so I changed bed linens, dusted, vacuumed & cleaned inside of windows in

579

LR, DR, & our BR, mopped kitchen floor, etc. until 1:30 PM when I tucked him in bed & started my laundry.

Wed 29 Jan - Robert & I had "words" this AM & I was angry at him all day. Had big wash (since Sun) to do & dear Bobby carried on while awake. I waxed venetian blinds in kitchen & bath tonight. RWD upstairs till 2:30 AM. I got busy on darning his socks this evening.

Sat 8 Feb - RW really fixes the car! - RW slept till 11. In the meantime I was getting laundry done. Then while he finally broke car battery, I "pressure" cooked chop suey & made up lunch for Sat - Sun as he decided to spend the night at work in view of no streetcar service (to speak of) on Sun mornings. So I was alone until Sun aft. Bobby is getting to be a real problem child, pulls out everything & punishment does no good. He pulled my blue mixing bowl full of flour off table, luckily no breakage, but flour all over floor!

Mon 10 Feb - A sombre Monday - I managed to get house cleaned & laundry done, when RW came home w/ rented battery for car. I felt hurt that he didn't remember to bring me cigs & told him so. Then he got mad & went to bed in a huff. RW left for work 11 PM.

Thu 13 Feb - Took Bobby down with me when I went to pick up my laundry & he likes to be in the basement. RW had him outside walking for ½ hour before he left for work 2nd shift. RW came home 11 PM. Another spat w/ RWD tonite & I shed tears aplenty.

Fri 14 Feb - Bobby fussed 4AM & so to bed w/ us. RW sweet as pie today after last night's nightmare.

Sat 15 Feb - M - Socially Isolated, and how! - RW off to work early shift. General housecleaning, dusting, vacuuming, Bobby my little helper. RW home, looking (or at least acting) very tired. He left car in front & I was sure we'd go out this evening. He said he had a lot of homework, but instead at 7 PM he went to sleep! Angry, I should say! I had hurriedly baked gingerbread & cinnamon rolls, hurried with dishes, planning to go see the folks. So I spent Sat nite fixing up his OD pants, pressing them & other items. To bed 11:30, & RW getting up to study.

Sun 16 Feb - M - So I was cool to "dear" RW today. Felt really hurt at his utter disregard for my wishes. Had a big wash to do this AM. Had to rush as always, getting house straightened, fixing lunch & his sandwiches. He finally left for work at 3 PM & I got busy on my kitchen, more dishes & junk to clean up.

Fri 21 Feb - RW home early & after a bit of lunch we drove to the War Surplus Store on 26th St where I bought a WAC "all season" coat with blanket interlining for 10.00. RW & I are still very polite, but correctly aloof & confine our conversations to general subjects, the house and Bobby.

Sun 23 Feb - RW off to work early today. I got up to see him off. We're still very much aloof in our dealings with one another.

Tue 25 Feb - Slept till 10 AM & I know RW was mad at this. He doesn't talk to me & I don't talk to him as I get no reply when I do. Angry at him when he put the car away upon return fm school today, and I got ready to go vote & put Bobby in bedroom w/ RW. Returned to find Bobby crying & RW glaring at me. So now he's mad at me!?! Well, he slept till 7:30 or so when I awakened him for supper. Am getting awfully bored with his attitude of indifference and his ignoring of me. This is going to come to a crisis, and soon.

Thu 27 Feb - Bobby 14 months old - The Koteks Visit Us - RW home fairly early today & we went shopping for groceries. Bobby enjoyed his outing & pushed the cart for me. This eve 6 PM the K's came (after Doty & I had a "tearful" on my part session about our way of life - never again!)

Fri 28 Feb - I Do Up Kitchen, Bath, Ptry Curtains - A very busy day for me. I had the laundry to do and house to clean. Doty didn't come home until 4:30, and then gobbled some pie & milk & wouldn't eat the supper I was warming up! (Could kill him for acting like that!) Bobby & I went down & washed, tinted & starched the remaining curtains & after I fed Bobby his supper & tucked him into bed, I ironed & hung up the curtains. This kept me busy until 11. Then I retired, leaving Doty still upstairs studying. When I awoke at 2 AM, he was still upstairs. Such a life I lead these days! If Bobby were only older, we'd leave!

Sat 1 Mar 1947 - Bobby gets a Sled Ride - We Visit the Folks & Max - Doty to work at 7 AM (I didn't get up). Doty home 4 PM to eat & then take Bobby for a sled ride, then to shovel snow. We drove over to the folks a little after 7.

Sun 2 Mar - Another Sled Ride for Bobby - Busy with laundry & sweeping up the basement, then making Doty's lunch, heating up beef stew & sending him off to work. After I cleaned up the kitchen, Bobby & I went to sleep fm 5 to 7pm. Read news & listened to radio until Doty came home at midnight. Maybe I'm wrong, but I believe Doty is trying to "make up". He'll have to make all the overtures from now on.

Mon 3 Mar - The furnace went out & I had to rekindle it about 11 PM. This "loveless" life we lead certainly is an empty hollow of what our marriage could be.

Tue 4 Mar - Set alarm for 7:30 AM and Bobby & I both got up to await arrival of Bess & Ricky, but RW didn't come with them until 9:30 AM! The louse, had trouble with his car (so he says) & couldn't pick Bess up till 9. RW had closeted himself upstairs upon return fm school, but came down for his share of the steak dinner.

Wed 5 Mar - Doty not home till 6:45 PM. Said he'd been working on a Biology report! Huh! This evening I got him to sandpaper bath stool & put coat of paint on it.

Thu 6 Mar - We Go Shopping - Snafu - A busy, crowded place & I didn't like the way he was looking after Bobby, & I said for us to go, meaning Spiegel's. But no, RW angrily drove us home, neither of us saying a word till we got home. I was furious! He played phonograph records for hours. My iron cord broke this eve, but he doesn't know how to fix it. So it goes. He made a lot of hot water & suggested I take a bath. Very considerate of him.

Fri 7 Mar - Reconciliation - Why not? - Waited for RWD till 6:15 PM. He had shopped & also brot home an extension gate, proposing to put it across Bobby's door, which I promptly vetoed. We thawed out this eve discussing hot water heaters & gas heat for house. Then in bed I decided to be the more adult of us two & make another bid for harmony. The darling took me up but quick.

Fri 21 Mar - Robert off to school at 7 AM for 4-hour exam session starting 7:30 AM. Shampooed Dining Room rug today. Baked 2 coffeecakes & mince pie. After supper Robt went upstairs to start enlarging and printing pictures. I joined him after putting Bobby to sleep & we stayed there till 12:30 AM. To bed, only at 3:30 AM Bobby awoke & carried on. So I took him to bed with us, but he didn't sleep & no one else did.

Sat 5 Apr 1947 - Our Basement is Flooded! - Woke before 8 AM & found streets flooded. Check of basement showed at least 3 ft of water w/ things floating around. Seems conduits just couldn't carry off 4" rain. First time in 23 years this has occurred to such an extent the neighbors tell us. RW to school. Back at 1 PM for lunch & at 2:30 to work. Furnace out. My laundry marooned in basement, no hot water. I kept the oven on WARM to take chill off. By 10 PM about 6" have drained away. Worried about my washing machine which is about half tipped over. Afraid to wade in the water because of inundated wall outlets.

Sun 6 Apr - At the Folks - the flood's over - RW over past 7 PM. He started cleaning basement (there'd been a foot of water in basement this AM, but it had drained by 4 PM). Home to a warm house. The basement must have been a mess. He finished hosing it down. I scrubbed my washing machine down. Such a smell.

Mon 7 Apr - M - Big job of the day was washing by hand Bobby's clothes & other necessities & hanging them outdoors. Feel all blah about life in general & sick about the washer and the damage to walls of basement, wood buckled & all my paper cartons gone.

Tue 8 Apr - M - We Continue Work on Basement - RW home 6 PM. After supper he took motor off wash machine & put it in oven to bake after cleaning it.

Thu 17 Apr - RW had to go down to Traffic Court & pay out $7.00 for the speeding ticket he got.

Sun 20 Apr - Dad comes to our rescue - RW to work 7 AM. Dad over at 9 AM & got busy on the toilet. Had to remove the fixture, turn it upside-down to get the plastic bracket Bobby had thrown into it. Then Dad removed the hot water pipes fm our boiler, patched up hole; bricked up hole in coal shed; and fixed the washing machine switch.

Mon 21 Apr - Bobby's 13th tooth out - RW not home till 9:30 PM. Thinks he passed the 3 hour German exam he took this evening.

Wed 23 Apr - We Work Outdoors, 76.8 - I tried to clean up garage, but Bobby kept going out into alley. Oh, what a job! More stones, glass, tin cans & dried weeds & I was tired after 1½ hour, but it is a beginning. Must clean out under porch & get RW to put up screens, gates & fix his light & water in garage.

Sat 26 Apr - RW working early & then going to the U of C to pick up his embalmed cat (anatomy classwork).

Sun 27 Apr - Bobby 16 mos old - A bath & waiting for RW who came home at midnight. Depressed at my lack of social life these days.

Mon 5 May - M - Bobby & I Weed our Lawn - Bobby & I went outdoors to work on our "lawns" again. I pulled out dandelions & crabgrass in front & then started working towards the back. Bobby a pest, as he keeps running away from me. We do need a fence on the east side.

Tue 6 May - M - Wash Clothes - More Weeding - My mind is so full of ideas of things that should be done in & out of the house, but RW continues to be occupied with his studies & I am unable to do anything about it.

Fri 23 May - RW & I Quarrel - More trouble w/ Bobby, he's so active & doesn't mind scoldings one bit. Really got all het up when RW took my oak laundry bench upstairs to put his enlarger on it. I scrubbed it up & found it so useful & then he has to take it! So mad I didn't go up to watch him print 2 rolls of Bobby's pics. He slept upstairs. Bad nite w/ Bobby again.

Sun 25 May - Waited up for Robert, but he went upstairs to sleep.

Fri 30 May - M - RW Cuts Down Last Tree - I Bake, Cut Grass - I got busy on baking while RW cut down the "tree of heaven" near our BR window. After dinner I asked RW to wash down bath & kitchen as he had promised. Guess he was tired, because he gave the bathroom a casual going over & started dabbing our kitchen ceiling (looking for the dirty spots) & I protested & we had words & he stomped out to finish cutting up the tree. I was furious & threatened to go to my folks w/ Bobby. Afterwards I did Bobby's laundry & Bobby & I cut back & front lawn.

Sat 31 May - M - RW to school today. He put in Bobby's window screen & started staking out his fence [Fig 55]. Waited up for RW who came home in a thunderstorm.

Sun 1 Jun 1947- Wax Linoleum - Hang Curtains - I Wash Kitchen Walls - After Bobby to bed & RW upstairs to "study", I scrubbed linoleum & waxed it. Now the kitchen is cleaned till Sept or so, but so much more work to be done.

Thu 5 Jun - Clean Curtains, Closets & LR - RW tells me we need 2 more tires for car. Angry at him for not taking us shopping this aft. He played the radio upstairs all eve "studying". Feel all in & tired & nervous & just sick of being a nursemaid to this bungalow.

Mon 9 Jun - Wash Day - Temp in 90s - RW going to work 2nd shift today & apparently will work Thu-Fri-Sat all summer, leaving Sunday's free.

Fri 13 Jun - Everything Goes Wrong - RW's exam in physics. Wrong posts delivered for fence. Robert had to go to work 2nd shift. RW came home at midnight, took offense at my criticism of the fence posts, & went upstairs to sleep.

Sun 15 Jun - Father's Day - We Visit Both Fathers - I washed clothes & hung them in basement, RW doing dishes & making bed for 1st time in <u>years</u>!

Mon 16 Jun - The Fence is Torn Down - Robert ordered 18 5½" cedar posts. He worked like a trooper getting that old fence down. It was hard to get the posts out. Had to take $100 out of bank for posts (11.00) & to pay my insurance premium & water bill & milk bill to come, car insurance (42.50) also due the 25th! RW upstairs like a hermit.

Tue 17 Jun - Rains all Day - Go to Library - Really angry at RW today for not wanting to drive me to Mom's w/ Bobby so I could go to dentist. He couldn't do much re fence because of the rain, yet he puttered around till 3:30 or so & then went up to read in bed. Managed to get him to take us to library where I got six books on gardening, fascinating material I hope to put to use in our garden. Bobby fusses so about sleep & keeps waking up. RW is angry at me when I go to Bobby. I am all upset.

Thu 19 Jun - Cut Grass - Weed & Prune - The fence is taking shape with the 2x4s in place the length of it [Fig 55]. RW to work 3 PM. Waiting for RW to come home.

Wed 25 Jun - M - RW upstairs studying. I feel so tired & is such a hopeless job trying to keep the house spic & span. Do so enjoy my cut flowers of rambler roses & weigelas & a few red peonies. Love flowers!

Sun 29 Jun - The Koteks Move In Next Door - Noticed the K's moving van parked in alley. Fritz & his bro unloading their furniture. Bess came out about 2 pm, fed Ricky here. I washed out her baby's diapers in the afternoon.

Tue 1 Jul 1947 - Grandma Visits Bess & Me - Surprised when Mom rang the doorbell at 10:30. She'd been over visiting Bess already. So while she minded Bobby, I did my laundry, also 2 lines of Bess' diapers.

Fri 4 Jul - RW Paints Fence - I Mow Lawns, Water - Bobby fussed 1:30 AM until 3 AM & continued fussing all day. Afraid we spanked him rather freely, but he got into the paint while RW was painting fence & had tantrums over every little thing. RW finished fence painting 8 or so. Altercation over how I'm bringing up Bobby. RW upstairs sulking.

Sat 5 Jul - Another Painful Incident w/ RWD - RWD "resting" upstairs all day, supposedly studying. While at Mom's, RW spanked Bobby for wetting & Mom raised a scene, wanting to strike RW. So we left hurriedly, drove home in silence. RW retired upstairs. It does make me angry when he strikes Bobby for such a thing! Losing respect for him.

Sun 6 Jul - The Dotys Over - So he sulked upstairs all day, just coming down for meals. His folks came out 5:30 PM, bringing home grown beans, cabbage & turnips; also a ham bone & a lb of dried lima beans. While they were here, Bill Beamish called & RW invited him for dinner tomorrow nite. I really let off steam re RW's failings to his folks, also his earning power, lack of appreciation for my position, etc.

Mon 7 Jul - The Beamish Jr's over - Cussing RW & his damn foolishness all day as I hurried w/ washing, baking, straightening the house & preparing the meal. They came at 6:15. Floozy Diane, a hideous 4-yr-old boy who coughed incessantly, her 3 wk old daughter & Bill, as wide almost as he is tall. So we ate dinner & visited after a fashion. The child was so incorrigible about 9 pm we drove them home to 4000 North on Sheridan Rd where they live doubled up in a 2 room furnished apt. Told RW off re inviting such riff raff to our home.

Tue 8 Jul - I Loaf Today - RW not home till 7. Angry at him for withdrawing more money fm Bank. In fact, I'm getting to detest him.

Thu 10 Jul - RW continues dour & sullen. I've been reading a lot about flowers & gardening in the evenings & have compiled a list of the kinds I'd like to raise in our backyard, but RW sullenly refuses to dig up the yard.

Sat 12 Jul - RW worked till 5 PM & so we had a nice day to ourselves. Made plans to go see the folks w/ Bess & Fritz this evening, leaving RW sitting in the LR "studying". Came home 11:30 PM with Bobby half asleep. The dope was upstairs & I didn't bother talking to him. He's gotten so he doesn't do anything but dig his nose into his books.

Sun 13 Jul - The Dotys have a verbal Row - A Very Hot Humid Day - Angry at RW for sleeping till noon & sitting about "studying" all day & when I reproached him for that and his general attitude of neglect towards me, Bobby and the house, he adopted his usual morose, sullen attitude & suggested we get a divorce & and what was my price? Everything, I said, & he demurred, & general incriminations followed, in the heat of a hot summer day. This evening we drove out to Evergreen Park for milkshakes & Bobby enjoyed sitting & eating at the counter. My precious baby that his idiotic father can't appreciate.

Mon 14 Jul - Bastille Day - Our Daily Double Continues - RW home 6:30 PM & our biting repartees began when he refused to go to Sears to get gardening implements. Said it wasn't necessary as he wasn't going to live in it that long. He continues insulting me & Bobby &, frankly, the situation is becoming unbearable.

Tue 15 Jul - Reconciliation effected last nite between RW & me; as usual, I made the 1st move. RW is too stubborn to admit he's wrong. So peace reigns supreme again in our little household.

Wed 16 Jul - Another scorcher. I spent most of the AM & afternoon cleaning, defrosting refrigerator, scrubbing bathroom, dusting, vacuuming & washing a few odds & ends. Also got in some weeding, crabgrass time is here again. RW's operation on a dog in his physiology class makes it necessary for him to be at school 6 AM, & so he went to bed early.

Sat 19 Jul - M - Wash Clothes - RW had to go to school this evening to look at his dog, but he did chop down the mulberry tree growing among our roses. More reading re flowers this evening.

Mon 21 Jul - M - Gardening Enthusiast - Bobby Gets a Trike! - I dug up the daffodils about the mock orange bush in center of yard & that was quite a job. Bot an automatic sprinkler for garden. At Spiegel's found a small tricycle for Bobby. He was so delighted when he saw it. Now if he can only learn to ride it w/o injuring himself. Had to let Bobby cry it out again tonite.

Tue 22 Jul - M - Clean House, Wash, Pies, Iron - Spent fm midnite to 1 AM writing up index cards on flowers I'd like to plant in our perennial border. RW studying for an exam tomorrow. He does so enjoy his neurophysiology courses.

Fri 25 Jul - Water the Lawns - I waited up for Robert & he agreed on my choice of shrubs: pepper bush, forsythia, Tatarian honeysuckle, hydrangea, Japanese Quince, Weigela florida.

Sun 27 Jul - Bobby 19 months old - Up at 10. RW took Bobby in front for "bike" lesson before dinner & to the park for some "swinging" after lunch. Angry w/ Robert for not doing more about the house this weekend. But he had to study for an exam tomorrow.

Mon 28 Jul - We Dig More in Garden - My sweet baby was good today, ate fairly well, napped 2 hrs, giving me time to wash the porch trim a bit. Washed clothes today, scrubbed bathroom, weeded in garden & played w/ Bobby. This eve RW dug a strip along the garage & I transplanted some iris, & some of the flowers growing along the fence.

Thu 7 Aug 1947 - RW & I Quarrel - Made the error of telling Robert when he came home at nite about the Gibson-Staley reunion this coming Sun & he was all for going & I thot not, hot weather, polio danger, etc. So we quarreled, as is usual when we don't agree.

Sun 10 Aug - The Annual Reunion at Plymouth - Left house at 10:30 & got there 1 PM after hectic hot ride w/ Bobby fussing. But we enjoyed our visit there. The picnic lunch at the cottage on Pretty Lake was pretty good (I brot 2 pies). Brot along boiled water, OJ, & milk for Bobby so he wouldn't have to change to raw milk & well water. About 4:30 left to look over Van Vactor's farm. Bobby was interested in the chickens, dogs, cats, but not the cows or hogs. So it wasn't too bad, very tired, however.

Sat 30 Aug - Our 6th Wedding Anniversary - Dad over, Fixes BR wall switches - Bobby took a long 2½ hour nap this aft & so gave me a chance to hang out my big laundry. RW home at 5, supper. Then Dad washed up & we opened one of our precious champagne bottles and we 3 drank it. Got some beer & over to the folks. Mom fixed corned beef sandwiches, the Kotek's came over, too & so we had a little celebration.

Mon 22 Sep - I fix up Bobby's Room - RW finished wallpapering - Trouble putting up our "Swedish modern" plaid in our room. RW cussed & carried on as he worked. Somehow when the house is upset as it is during redecorating, you keep going around in circles & nothing gets accomplished. Just cooking meals (3 a day) for us three keeps me on the go. RW varnished window frames in our BR & I do think it makes quite an improvement.

Mon 29 Sep - A very busy day - Washed Bobby's clothes, took down yesterday's wash & swept up basement. RW so messy when firing! I started on LR. Washed inside windows & frames, blinds, hung drapes, vacuumed LR & DR & cleaned upholstery. RW angry when I wouldn't let him take screens down from inside (after I cleaned LR & DR, & the BRs are all cleaned too!). So up in a huff upstairs. I followed, changed linens & mopped the floors, so dirty after summer w/ windows open. Mopped hall stairs. After supper Bobby & RW upstairs to print pics & I washed pantry & kitchen floors & waxed them. After dishes, ironed some starched items. At 11 finally to rest & read. So my days go.

Tue 30 Sep - Screens Down - I Bake - RW home about 11:30 AM. I didn't expect him so soon. In spite of my vigorous protests, he proceeded to remove the screens from inside & I was furious! I hate him for his stubbornness. Lunch & RW off to work.

Fri 3 Oct - M - RW caulking this aft - Slept till 10. Quickly straightened house & washed some of Bobby's clothes. Was hanging same when Robt home 12:30 with caulking compound and gun. RW upstairs printing pics w/ Bobby. Have been very happily surprised at Robert's industry about the house this past month.

Mon 13 Oct - RW so busy with his studying trying to catch up on a lot of reading & he's no company at all. So I listened to radio programs & read. Am so engrossed in my gardening. I read for information in hopes of really having a garden some day. [Hopes that were to be fully realized.]

Sat 25 Oct - RW Takes Med Exam - Exam for entrance to med school scheduled for 6 hrs this AM, so RW took his lunch for work & didn't come home till 1 AM.

Tue 28 Oct - M - We Plant Shrubs - Put in the following shrubs: 1) pink Tartarian honeysuckle; 2) Red twig Dogwood; 3) Deutzia, Pride of Rochester; 4) American Cranberry Bush; 5) Blue Althea; 6) Hydrangea, P.G; 7) Hansen Cherry Bush.

Fri 31 Oct - M - We Go Shopping - Five more Plants arrive - Upstairs w/ RWD reading some of his books on the menstrual cycle, etc., trés interesante. He's studying French in hopes of passing the exemption examination this coming Monday. A real feat if he does.

Mon 3 Nov - Start on Kitchen Drapes - Washed clothes, straightened house, brooded on RW's remark (how sincere?) that he hadn't looked upon me with any desire for the past two months. [???] RW took his French exam today, home 10 PM. A most ideal "reconciliation" affected this evening, after sips of his delightful heart warming cordial. Then RW back upstairs to study far into the nite.

Fri 7 Nov - Bobby is such a problem these days when he is cooped up indoors. This gloomy weather gets me on edge & I'm cross w/ him. RW has been sweet as a darling since our reconciliation & that helps make things bearable. I do wish Mom lived closer to us. I would so enjoy seeing her more often.

Sat 15 Nov - I do wish Robert didn't work Sat nights. I feel so lonely & neglected on this night when others are in the social whirl. [Shades of the "Charlie" days!]

Sun 23 Nov - M - My 32nd Birthday - As a result of which RW let me sleep till noon. I washed accumulated laundry while Bobby slept; RW "studying". I stayed up a while reading & suffering as I usually do on my menstrual days.

Fri 5 Dec 1947 - We Entertain the Gordons - My Sewing Machine Arrives - I vacuumed my rugs & straightened the rooms, cleaned up my pantry, waxed the kitchen floor, baked 2 apple pies. Put Bobby to nap & went downstairs to do my wash when I heard a loud thud & ran up to find Bobby had fallen out of his crib. Wash done, I mopped the basement floor. Got spaghetti done & table set & us all washed & combed when our guests came at 7:15. RW & Bud [One of my classmates, later an MD.] study in basement while Lillian & I sat in LR & talked.

Sun 14 Dec - We Visit the Folks, altho Late - RW let me sleep till 11. He & Bobby were playing in bright sunlit LR. Suggested riding out to see the folks & RW agreed; but first he had to fix the windshield wiper which took till 6 PM. Then he very leisurely supped & dressed. I got tired of waiting, bundled up Bobby & me & walked out intending to take streetcar if RW didn't follow up with the car, only he caught up with us & we did get on our way finally.

Wed 17 Dec - M - Hemorrhage - RWD home early from school with news he'd been offered a lab assistant or fellowship ($2400 p/a) fm Dr Hutchens, head of Physiology Dept. I went down & did a quick wash of Bobby's things while RW played w/ Bobby. About 7:30 PM I began flowing so freely, hemorrhaging & feeling so weak & faint. Called Mom. She said to lie down & be quiet.

Thu 18 Dec - M - RW Stays Home - Robert stayed home fm school today & I stayed in bed till 2PM. Bobby had fussed during the nite & I'd gotten up to take him in bed w/ me & RW went upstairs to sleep. RW entertained Bobby, gave him a bath & put him to bed. I talked to Robert about my severe flow yesterday, which has practically stopped today, & he thinks the wine & all the hot coffee I drank during the day was responsible, but that I should be examined by Dr. & take some vitamins, etc.

Fri 19 Dec - M - AUTO ACCIDENT! - RW to school for final exam & last day of quarter. Left house at 6 PM & were driving north on Cicero Ave when **BOOM!** a car going South jumped into our lane & hit our left side so we turned completely around & landed just short of embankment. Our car a mess, his worse. Called Dad Doty & he came out. More delays while police wrote up report, till car was towed away. Home at 9, feel bruised &

shaken up. [Happily, she was holding Bobby in her arms, otherwise he might have been thrown around. It was probably only because of my skill that we didn't turn over. The canal crossing there was a bit tricky, and the other guy missed the cue, even jumping an 18-inch concrete center barrier to hit us!]

Sat 20 Dec - M - The Day After - We slept till 11. Just couldn't go to sleep last nite. Miracle we weren't killed. My neck is so stiff, my head hurts, my whole body aches, & I have trouble swallowing. RW wrote letter to Chgo Motor Club, checked w/garage. Think our car can't be repaired. RW left for work 2:30 to go by streetcar.

Mon 22 Dec - My Aches Get Worse - I See Doctor - So stiff I can hardly get out of bed at 11 AM. So after talking to Ben Ordower, the atty, RW decided I should go see Dr Buky & we rushed with lunch, so we could leave w/ RW.

Sat 27 Dec - Bobby 2 yrs old - Over at the K's, Max over - Our sweet baby fussed during the nite & I had to rock him to sleep. RW & I did the week's wash & what a mess it was! 2 hours, I washing, RW hanging. Max over just as RW was leaving for work. Waited up for RW who tells me he'll work tomorrow in boiler room.

Tue 30 Dec - Another late arising - After RW off to work I started washing down kitchen walls & woodwork, but got half done (and no ceiling) when I got tired & Bobby was sleepy. Disgusted w/ RW for his neglectful attitude re house.

Wed 31 Dec - New Years Eve - RW went to work for just 4 hours today. I vacuumed rugs, changed bed linens, scrubbed bath & kitchen floors & waxed floor lightly. Waiting for RW to come home, darning socks, etc. He came about 9. RW took pics of both Ricky & Bobby under the Xmas tree. Fritz brot beer. Bess brot popping corn & cookies. So we popped corn, drank beer, ate cheese & crackers & then coffee & applesauce cake till 12:45 AM. Bobby became quite overwrought & I had to calm him down by rocking him. All in all a rather satisfactory New Year's Eve. We sat up with Xmas tree till 3 AM.

Fri 2 Jan 1948 - Wash clothes - Slept till 11. RW salary for last week was 72.00. This week's will be much less.

Mon 5 Jan - More Pics - RW not home till 6:15 PM. This eve upstairs printing pics again till after midnite. RW says he had a very nice chat with Mr Gerard re doing research work for the Navy. Do wish we could get our car fixed well & soon. It's such an inconvenience not having it, for shopping & a lot of other things.

Tue 6 Jan - Mr Hansen of Chgo Motor Club comes - Mr Hansen called to "investigate" the accident. After short talk w/ him I sent him away & called Ben Ordower. He told me to send him packing the next time he calls.

Sat 10 Jan - RW's 28th Birthday - Dr Hora Visits Bobby - RW to school today and to shop for groceries before going to work. Alarmed when I noticed a rash on Bobby's chest & neck & Bess' report that Ricky was ill too. So I called Dr Hora. I literally sweated out the rest of the day. Doc out at 10 PM. Said Bobby had congestion in upper respiratory tract & he prescribed a sulfa drug, a cough syrup & nose drops. RW's 28th birthday not such a happy one at that.

Sun 11 Jan - We Get the Car, NG - Bobby at his Worst - Bobby slept 8 hours straight & it was 9 when he awoke. RW dressed him & started feeding him. I got up at 11! At 12:30 RW went to get the car & when he came back, he had Fritz look it over too. Looks nice on outside, but the inside is not so hot & they didn't do too good a job on a lot of things, so back it goes tomorrow. Baked a layer cake this eve w/ RW's help. We lit candles for supper.

Mon 12 Jan - RW home late. I'm afraid that guy who fixed his car is giving him the runaround re fixing the several minor things on our car. Wrote Ordower letter inclosing paid bill fm Repair Shop for 552.50. Sure hope we come out of this accident OK, at least get fully reimbursed for our expenses.

Sat 24 Jan - That Car! - RW returned late sans car which had refused to budge, so left it in Sears parking lot! This upset me so!

Wed 28 Jan - Angry at RW for not shopping & I was all out of cigarettes. Spent evening writing cards for copies of seed catalogs and reading some of the library books RW brought me. I do wish Robert didn't work on Weds or Saturdays. I get so tired of being cooped up on those days.

Sat 31 Jan - RW & I had quite a spat when he returned fm shopping trip & broke another vacuum bottle. [??] So I let him finish making his lunch.

Mon 23 Feb - Atty Ordower called to say he "settled" our case for $1500, $1000 net for us.

Tue 24 Feb - RW telling me he's thinking of quitting Hotpoint & trying to get work at school while studying for his Masters. So he's been talking to Dr. Gerard & Dr. Hutchens. Thinks he'll definitely turn down M.D. idea (now that he's been accepted for admission to Med School) & instead will work towards Ph.D. in Physiology. I'm just a wee bit worried about finances, but I guess we'll manage OK.

Fri 5 Mar 1948 - M - RW downstairs studying. All this excitement now that graduation is only 2 weeks away. He's thinking of quitting Hotpoint first of April & lining up lab jobs at school. Perhaps with the increased VA subsistence allowance, we'll be able to manage. But his program at school is an overwhelming one, with nite classes & I'll really be on my own for the next 6 months.

Wed 10 Mar - Irv Ordower brings the Check - He & RW left at 2:45 for the Bank to deposit $1000 in our a/c & $500 for the Attys fees. Bal now $3350.

Wed 17 Mar - I am Regusted! - Bobby was especially naughty today, & I can't help feeling it's due to his not being well. RW home today studying for his calculus exam tomorrow. Got RW's suit all ready for his "graduation" & that's about all. Spent the evening reading gardening books & drinking 2 glasses of wine. My nerves all on edge, cooped up w/ Bobby for over a week & he's so full of mischief & bad temper.

Fri 19 Mar - RW gets BS today - We Start Spring Cleaning - Scrubbed down porch door & porch, cleaned debris fm under porch steps. Managed to bake a layer cake for RW, who came home 6 PM w/ lots of groceries. This eve I washed out clothes (for Bobby mostly) & ironed, straightened up pantry a bit, wiping off shelves & throwing out odds & ends. RW tired fm his exam, studying & asleep as I write this 11:30 PM.

CHAPTER XVI
PhD, Postdoctoral Study, Mary Elizabeth

Synopsis - It was almost 3 years between completion of my undergraduate studies and the birth of our second child, Mary Elizabeth, whose name had already been chosen in Elizabeth's letter of 28 October 1942! Elizabeth had had a debilitating miscarriage in October of 1948, so Mary Elizabeth's coming 28 months later was doubly welcome.

Elizabeth had experienced not only the usual discomforts of pregnancy, but throughout October and November of 1950 we were engaged in the most enduring quarrel of our lives. In such times we maintained a peculiarly disciplined animosity, interacting both socially and domestically in a reasonably normal fashion, yet each miserably aware of the situation between us, and unable to reduce the other to surrender. The horribly protracted course of this domestic standoff was no doubt partly attributable to the stress of pregnancy as well as the continued tension between us over my all night immersion in my experiments. However, there was for Elizabeth an additional strain of having an ugly divorce threatened between her parents. Happily, both her parents and ourselves eventually accommodated to the reality that love is not extinguished by disagreement.

It bears emphasis that our quarreling was by no means as commonplace as the frequency (**all** cases) with which it is noted herein. Aside from the lengthy episode just discussed, there were in these 1000 days but 30 on which contentious words were exchanged between us. In other words, while this was a time of great stress, as I struggled to establish a career and she dedicated herself with uncommon skill and fervor to establishing and maintaining her hard won home, we both reveled in our deep love and success, in the bounty of our domestic life and the quick delight in the astonishing precociousness of our growing son.

Being exclusively from her diary the record, of course, is quite one-sided. Following our decision that Medical School would be much too prolonged, I became a "Teaching Assistant" in the Dept of Physiology and, with additional support from Prof Gerard's funds from the Office of Naval Research, I was able to exchange my "blue collar" career for one in academia. I did use my previously acquired machinist skills, however, to mill a multichannel respirometer with which I could stimulate dissected frog nerves and record both their electrical action potentials and the amount of oxygen they used in producing them. This led to my Masters Thesis: "The Separate Inhibition of Resting and Active Oxygen Consumption in Frog Nerve", which Gerard and I subsequently published in the American Journal of Physiology.

The road seemed clear for my PhD research, for Gerard had assembled a talented team of neurochemists to analyze the metabolic basis of synaptic activity in the rat spinal cord. The experiments, presumably, were already up and running. However, fellow graduate student, Howard Jenerick, and I spent 6 months proving that the blood substitutes, being used to perfuse the spinal cord with carefully measured metabolites, could not possibly have supported synaptic transmission! Thus, I was left "late" and hanging. My solution, however, turned out to be a happy, if difficult one; specifying the pattern of neuronal input that triggered the act of swallowing. My PhD thesis, "Effect of Stimulus Pattern on Reflex Deglutition" found favorable review with Warren McCulloch at the Illinois Neuropsychiatric Institute, University of Illinois College of Medicine, and I obtained an NIH Fellowship to work with him. This saw no respite in my all night experiments on swallowing; and I began another series of experiments on recovery of vision in kittens suffering lesions of their central visual system neonatally.

My Postdoctoral Fellowship forestalled for another year the necessity of our leaving the comfort of the home to which we had devoted so many laborious hours of "repair". But the threat of moving lingered, for I must find a job. It was while Elizabeth was in the hospital with Mary that we finally decided that it was the

University of Utah for us, and from then on the family question was, could we sell our house in time.

Wed 24 Mar 1948 - The Closets are Done - RW starting to paint hall. I laundered all my drapes, scatter rugs & accumulated laundry. Fixing dinner & getting RW off to work & finishing stairs up to landing which RW couldn't paint. Bobby spilled cereals on all my flowerpots & killed 2 more rose seedlings. Needless to say he got spanked but good!

Sun 28 Mar - M - Bobby Enjoys his Easter - We Visit the Folks - Bobby & RW looking for colored eggs this AM & Bobby's delight in that & his Easter basket was wonderful to see. Quarreled w/ RW for his "easy" attitude of loafing, while I washed clothes, straightened house, made dinner, etc. But we made up & left for folks about 4 PM. Brot over our lamb cake. RW & I looked over Bobby's pics, hundreds of them, & I sorted them by month with a view of pasting them in a scrapbook someday.

Mon 5 Apr - The Folks Sell House! - This eve Rich called to say that folks left w/ people to sign contract for sale of house for $12,500! Really floored me coming so sudden. Feel it's a good thing, for the neighborhood is degenerating & they'll never get that much money for it again. So to bed rather excited. My roses came today!

Thu 8 Apr - Waited for RW till 8 PM to come home & then he brot album of "La Boheme" w/ Gigli which cost $7.00! Furious, but what can I do. Got him to write his Aunt Winifred a letter.

Sun 18 Apr - Bobby falls down Basement Steps - The Folks Buy a 2 Flat in Cicero - Bobby & I in yard. He was riding bike & tumbled down basement steps. Nasty bump on forehead & RW & I had words but good! He put the hose reel together & because it took him an hour carried on like a baby & I flared up, and so it went. In meantime calls fm Max re their progress in house hunting in Cicero. Decided on a 2 flat (5 rooms) for 17,750! So they signed a contract and gave them a $1000 note. Haste again!

Sun 25 Apr - At Brookfield Zoo - To Brookfield Zoo & made the rounds, Bobby seeming to enjoy it very much. Saw the baby hippopotamus. I noticed w/ interest the shrubs & trees in bloom, forsythia, cherries, quinces, honeysuckles; never paid attention

597

to them before. RW so lazy, going to sleep & leaving me to water our lawns, & w/ Bobby "kibitzing" that is a chore. Did get him to play w/ Bobby this evening & I settled down to catch up on my diary notations and to try to listen to Theater Guild drama on radio.

Sat 1 May 1948 - Irritated by RW's absorption w/ his studies these days. He takes no interest in the house or his family.

Sun 2 May - Rushed w/ housework & dinner and then RW didn't like the pot roast, too greasy for him! I was furious.

Tue 4 May - RW home 6 PM. After supper he went out for a haircut & then to his books again. Had thought he'd take care of Bobby so I could sew those bathroom terrycloth drapes, but no. So another evening gone by, for Bobby not to bed till almost 10:30 PM. I'm so bored of this.

Thu 6 May - RW home for supper and then going to bank to w/ draw $40; still no income fm U of C. He took Bobby along w/ him & they returned w/ some toys for Bobby, an atomizer & a wastebasket for me. RW upstairs & I went up there to talk to him, but got the usual stony reception, so down to bed en seul again.

Fri 7 May - At the Folks - Mother over earlier - RW sleeping late & it was 10:30 when Mom surprised us w/ a visit. RW left for school soon, rude as ever in not being friendly. So we went & had a nice visit, only the K's didn't pick us up till 12 & we had planned on going home by 10:30! So home to find RW in bed, said he didn't think we were coming home.

Sat 8 May - I Have it out w/ RW - The jerk didn't get up till 11:30. Angered but good at Doty when I reminded him of the ashes downstairs & he told me to shut up. So he left for school. I straightened up the house. RW home at 6:30 & I got a lot of grievances aired, but as usual got no response, just a lot of stony staring silence.

Sun 9 May - Mother's Day - We had a good breakfast & I said to RW I wanted to go see the folks re Mother's Day & also to observe Rich's 22nd birthday. He wanted to go to the Rosenwald Museum & get to folks around 6 PM. I demurred & said we'd go with Bess & Fritz, which we did. Exasperated, I told him we weren't coming back. Left him in his usual sulky mood. Had a good time at folks & the time went by quickly. Discussed my difficulties w/ RW with the folks & Dad said he thought things weren't as bad as they sounded. So we came home w/ Bess & Fritz about 9:30 PM. To my surprise he met us at the door. Apparently he had spent the day reading our letters to one another during the war. He hadn't eaten since breakfast, so I warmed up the spaghetti fm yesterday & he ate it. To bed our separate ways.

Mon 10 May - Listening to radio & amusing Bobby until RW came home at 9 PM. He received check for 66.67 for his Physiology instruction.

Tue 11 May - Grumpy RW decided to dissect his frog & while he did that, I did the painting of flowerpots I've wanted to do for weeks. Bobby to bed. RW upstairs studying. I went up there to make up my shopping list for tomorrow, but got no response from him. So to bed en seul again.

Wed 12 May - I straightened things up, put Bobby to bed & waited for RW to come home, which he did about 11 PM. Took a bath and went upstairs w/o saying a word to me.

Thu 13 May - RW home at 6 PM. Rather grumpy. He got paid his $100 for the Navy research work & gave me $50; keeping $50 for himself w/ comment that he's not going to deposit any more money in the bank.

Sat 15 May - RW & I Make Up - RW cuts grass - We Visit the Dotys - RW sleeping till 11:30 & then going shopping for 25 lb flour & other odds & ends w/ Bobby while I changed bed linens & did up the laundry. He off to school. RW cut grass when he came home. Nice evening & I suggested to RW we visit his folks. Bot a lb box candy as a belated "Mother's Day" gift & took it over there. We got home at 11:30. Sat up to 2 AM discussing the present state of our marriage & we decided to both give in more so as to make a go of it. So here we go again!

Sun 16 May - M - We Visit my Folks - RW varnishing the front storm-screen door & doing other odds & ends. We stayed up till quite late reading & listening to the radio. RW trying to study. I feeling very miserable as I usually do the first day & so sat up.

Sat 22 May - M - At Carnival - We Wash Windows & Frames - RW home & after supper he washed the screens in garage while I started on West windows. By now 8 PM. Hurriedly dressing & taking Bobby to church carnival. Once on merry-go-round was enough for Bobby. We sat up reading & discussing schizophrenia article in one of RW's magazines.

Sun 23 May - At Museum - Jackson Park - Dotys over short visit - Quarrel w/ RW re screens this AM, but we made up. Went to Museum about 1:30 PM. Bobby seemed to enjoy the exhibits. Unfortunately he tripped on a step & cut his lip & was very quiet afterwards. Fell asleep enroute chez nous. RW put up screens while I watered my backyard.

Wed 2 Jun 1948 - Home at folks & Mom throwing a hysterical fit over house & their RUIN! She quieted down & we left; but I do feel so sorry for Dad, & Max too. Bobby carrying on today but good, such a cry-baby. Guess he's teething badly as he wants to bite me always [Suggesting that he wasn't weaned yet!??].

Fri 4 Jun - Another 90 scorcher - RW home 8 PM, now he's upstairs studying for PhD admittance exams tomorrow.

Thu 1 Jul 1948 - RW & I Have a ROW but good! - Found RW in midst of preparing creamed egg supper. Bobby had been munching on food all aft & refused to eat & RW hit the ceiling. Shoved me from Bobby & I threw his slide rule at him, cutting his lips. But we talked it out later.

Mon 12 Jul - Josephine gave Bobby a toy rake, hoe, & shovel, & he said "Thank you, Josephine" so nicely! RW not home till 10 PM. Listening to Barkley deliver keynote address at opening of Dem convention this evening.

Tue 13 Jul - Frank Shepherd over - This eve got a phone call fm Robt's friend, Frank Shepherd of Kentucky, who is in Chgo to get lined up for law school after his BA fm Harvard. He came out to the house about 8:30 & we sat around talking, drinking beer. Then RW opened a bottle champagne & we sat on back porch till 1 AM.

Sat 17 Jul - Wotta Day! - Bobby began the day by writing w/brown crayon on our bedroom wallpaper, about a foot square. Sick over that. RW home late & he had had trouble w/his instrument at school.

Sun 18 Jul - Frank Shepherd Out - Shepherd came about 1 PM w/ a red & blue large dump truck for Bobby. I had RW serve martinis while I prepared dinner. Shepherd made several moves to leave, but somehow didn't go until after 10 PM. Then RW upstairs trying to study. I made up his lunch sandwiches & joined him upstairs to read my gardening books & smoke & talk till almost midnight. We both agreed Shepherd had been a nice visitor.

Fri 23 Jul - Listening to Wallace Party Convention - Listening to key note speech by Chairman of the Independent Party. A very radical one. 10 PM & no RW yet. Cold out & we're all shut up in the house & I have the jitters. Gee, I wish RW were home more.

Sat 24 Jul 1948 - Bobby & I at U of C w/ RW - RW home about 7 PM & after supper we all drove with him to his lab & we watched him put his respirometer thru its paces. If it doesn't produce results soon, his Masters degree may be held up. Bobby had a frog to watch & saw some guinea pigs in their cages & fell asleep on way home. And tonite we tried for our second offspring.

Fri 20 Aug - Doing Venetian Blinds - Got Better Homes & Garden mag today, also catalog fm Interstate Nurseries & now I'm all enthused about getting more tulips & daffodils & colored irises. RW not home till 11 PM tonight. I am alone so much. If I didn't like reading & my plants.

Tue 24 Aug - M - Hotter! 98 - So Bobby & Ricky got into the tub again. They spill so much water & soak the yard so that I finally took away the hose & they were mad! RW home for spaghetti supper & then took Bobby to park to play in sandpile until it got dark. I started menstruating today & every step I took was sheer misery. And Bobby seems to take advantage of the situation and misbehaves but good!

Sat 28 Aug - M - We Get a Cat? - About 1:30 AM, while having snacks, a kitten meowed at our door. Pretty thing, but so skinny. We fed it & hope it stays as it's a female.

Mon 30 Aug - Our 7th Wedding Anniversary - But no fuss nor bother. RW not home till 10 PM. The cat still around & not quite so fearful. Bobby treats it quite nicely, too. So passed my 7th wedding anniversary.

Thu 2 Sep 1948 - Another Busy Day - Pruned the Rose of Sharon & lilacs. RW home 5:45. Just sat around & read this evening. Bobby to bed early. RW & I sat up reading till quite late. Another attempt to get our next baby started tonite.

Tue 14 Sep - Sleeping till 11 & RW and Bobby left for the Sand Dunes w/o me! Furious, because it was cool & windy & they weren't dressed too well. The "guys" returned at 6:30 PM after I had supper & had finished straightening pantry. Bobby looked very tired & a bit sunburned. I'll never forgive Doty if Bobby comes down with a cold. They brought back a lot of sand for the yard, so I suppose I should forgive them. So bored with myself today.

Fri 17 Sep - RW late in getting up, so I asked him to go shopping for me while I did the laundry. So he took Bobby & bought the groceries. Mailed M.O. for 72 tulip bulbs. Also 17 trumpet daffodils & 17 red cup daffodils. Surprisingly enough RW didn't object.

Wed 22 Sep - Guess I may be pregnant as it's the 29th day since my last menstrual period & my breasts seem to be fuller.

Sat 2 Oct 1948 - Oh this School, School, School - RW called to say he wouldn't be home till 8. So Bobby & I had supper by ourselves. RW home exhausted after running his experiment.

Sun 3 Oct - We Visit the Folks - The BR Wallpaper Fixed - Managed to get RW to paste over the crayon marked wallpaper in our BR. Coaxed RW into driving us out to see the folks at 5 PM. Still much dissension among the folks re the house. Mom doesn't like it & can't wait to get out. Dad feels like throwing in the sponge.

Mon 4 Oct - Wash Clothes - Outing to Library - RW got up 4:30 AM to leave early for school so he could run an experiment before his aft classes.

Fri 8 Oct - This evening so angry at RW for refusing to take us to see the folks. We were all dressed up & ready to go, too.

Sat 9 Oct - I pot up Paper Whites - I Finish Blue PJs for Bobby - Little Bobby really has an appetite these days. He plays independently for long periods of time, too. Today he played w/ his mechanical train, read a story to his stuffed toys. RW dosed Fluffy w/ worm capsules, but the little thing was so hungry. RW not home till 9 PM tonite. Such a dull Saturday.

Wed 13 Oct - M? - This evening I got severe cramps & started getting a brownish tinge, just like with Bobby [Referring to her "spotting" in early pregnancy with Bobby in New York, for which she took several days of rest following obstetrician's orders. Her afternoon of gardening on this occasion may have been the trigger for the forthcoming abortion??]

Thu 14 Oct - M - We Go to Dentist Again - Got home at 7 PM & found RW starting supper. Gosh, I felt punk & more of this brownish tinge appearing. Could hardly stand. Felt just like my whole insides were coming out.

Sat 16 Oct - M - RW Helps Me - RW off to school late & back again as he couldn't go on with his experiment. RW helped me change bed linens & to dust and straighten things. Could hardly stand. I felt so punk, as I do when I start menstruating. RW went marketting again this aft. I started our laundry & RW hung them up for me. Really starting to flow, a red blood discharge now, and such an ache when I try to stand up; and my back aches so.

Sun 17 Oct - M - Dotys over - So I slept till 12:15 today. I think it irked RW when I got up groggy like. RW going out to the garage to give storm sash another coat of paint. RW mixed a chocolate cake & we baked it in time for the Dotys. They came bringing ice cream. Gosh, I feel punk today. My dear mother-in-law thinks I may be starting the menopause ???? [! strange!]

Mon 18 Oct - Miscarriage - RW home early & we got to the folks about 7 PM. About 9 PM I went into the bathroom & something came out. RW recovered it & he thinks it's a very young beginning of a foetus. So I was pregnant!

Tue 19 Oct - RW Stays Home - RW stayed home fm school today. Called Dr Hora who said I should stay in bed for several days & then come in to see him. I stayed in bed & lounged around, flowed quite a bit. Feel all pooped out, cumulative effects of the past week. Seems the biggest concern now is to prevent hemorrhage & catching cold.

Wed 20 Oct - M - Bess Takes Bobby for the Day - Bess came at 11 & took Bobby w/ her for the day after straightening up the house for me. How good of her. I can't understand why I should feel so punk. Still flowing freely & I guess it's the loss of blood that makes me feel so utterly energy less. RW has been doing the supper dishes & putting Bobby to sleep, etc.

Fri 22 Oct - We Go See Dr Hora - Felt awful to have Mom & Bess do the laundry (& there was a lot of it) while I took care of the kids. I seem to have stopped flowing & I told Mom I thot we'd go see the Doc tonite. He thinks I had a miscarriage & prescribed sulfanilamide tablets & warm boric acid douches plus Lextron (liver-stomach concentrate) tablets for secondary anemia. A lab analysis of the "thing" will cost us $6. Medicines & stuff $8 already. Where will it end? I'm a very sick girl, I guess, for I get so tired from the slightest exertion.

Mon 25 Oct - Mom Irons My Laundry - Mom came over this AM & ironed 2 weeks starched laundry.

Tue 26 Oct - Robert has been exceptionally understanding & kind to me these past days. Doing the supper dishes & tending to Bobby so I can rest, for which I've been most grateful.

Thu 28 Oct - 1st Penicillin Shot - Gee, I love my Bobby! And it pains me so these days when I can't minister to his every whim, which RW says is good! Spent the rest of the day raking leaves. Tonite went w/ RW to get penicillin, more sulfa & w/ syringe needles it costs over $5.00. I was pregnant & to avoid complications fm inflammation of the womb, I must take penicillin intramuscularly.

Fri 29 Oct - 2nd Penicillin - Terrific how tired I get after changing bed linen and on one bed! My temp hovers at 99 - 99.2, the sulfa nauseates me. The baby irritates me. I have no interest in anything but my own feeling of malaise, this after more than 2 weeks of this! RW bot a large pumpkin & spent more than an hour carving out a very scary face, lit up with a red lite & placed it in our front windows [Fig 57]. More for his benefit than our little boy's, I think. Another penicillin shot tonite, & less pain felt than the 1st.

Mon 1 Nov 1948 - RW brot home 3 books on gynecology & I spent the entire evening looking at them re my own problems. Bobby got a haircut from his Daddy tonite.

Tue 2 Nov - Election Day - I Sit up to 3 am, Close Race - Finally arrived Election Day, Dewey, Truman, Wallace & 6 other Pres candidates. RW voted on way to school. Bess & I went about noon to vote for Truman. RW in school till 1:30 AM. I sat up till 3 AM listening to CBS election returns. Whole Dem slate elected in Ill, very close race bet Truman & Dewey. Poor Wallace didn't make much of a showing.

Wed 3 Nov - Truman & the Democrats Win - Slept till 10:15 AM. RW awakened me then to tell me Dewey had just conceded the election to Truman! 304 electoral votes for Truman. The entire Dem state & County slate elected. All the polls & newspapers wrong.

Fri 19 Nov - M - Did get laundry done, basement mopped & a thoro cleaning of LR & DR; also bath, kitchen & Bobby's room, before RW arrived at 6 PM laden w/ groceries. My home has been sadly neglected these past weeks and I do feel guilty. Bobby has a fixation about trains bothering him, thanks to Grandma's constant complaints re her place.

Sun 21 Nov - RW at School till 3:30am - Takes big cat to school - I cut out Bobby's snowsuit - Late brunch & RW off to school to run a long azide experiment. So alone w/ Bobby. I started on new snowsuit for him.

Tue 23 Nov - I am <u>33</u> today! Gave my bedroom a good going over w/vacuum & mopped floors. This evening got interested in the draperies for my bedroom. Put in headings by hand & pinned in top pleats. Fussed around with material re valence and slipcover for boudoir chair. Finally quit about 1 AM. RW so busy with his schoolwork these days.

Sun 28 Nov - RW & I see "Hamlet" - We drove the folks & Bobby home to Cicero & off to see Olivier's movie version of "Hamlet". Marvelous! 2½ hours of rapt attention as that classic tragedy ran its course. Home 6 PM & having supper at Mom's.

Thu 2 Dec 1948 - Washed clothes today, not too much, but w/ starching & mopping entire basement floor, it was an all aft job. Sewed some more on Bobby's jacket, but starting at 10 PM (when the little darling fell asleep) doesn't give me much time before midnite, and RW is so incorrigibly romantic these days.

Sat 11 Dec - M - Dr Gerard's Party - Charades!? - 6:15pm dinner at the Quadrangle Club at U of C where Dr & Mrs Gerard were having all the Navy Research group to a dinner. Hors d'oeuvres & sherry, than a fine meal of filet mignon. Over at the Gerard's green frame house having drinks & then 2½ hrs or so of stupid charades. Left at midnite. So I met the bunch. They may have degrees, but not much polish or culture. Bobby was in Bess' care all evening.

Fri 17 Dec - We Visit the Boyarskys - 9 pm when we arrived. Mrs Boyarsky Sr there from NY to see her son Lou get his PhD this aft. So we left at midnite. RW drove Max home as it was 1 am.

Sun 26 Dec - We Entertain Bob Tschirgi - RW & I tried out our new chess set, staying up till 2:30 AM, so I was most reluctant to get up this AM. Did so at 11. Putting ham in to roast, fixing sweet potatoes, straightening beds before I had breakfast. At 1:30 PM Mr T arrived, sans some gift for Bobby or hostess. RW really was the perfect host w/ sherry & then port. I spent most of my time in the kitchen w/ food & dishes. Oyster stew for supper. Bobby most friendly w/ our guest, had him running his train, reading him stories. Bobby to bed 9:15. Then w/ port & conversation until 12:15 AM when RW gave Mr T a left to streetcar. I think Tschirgi was very much impressed with our home & hospitality. Perhaps he can do RW some good.

Mon 27 Dec - Bobby is three Years Old! - Late in arising again! My temp seems normal, but my back aches & I am so tired. Had planned on washing laundry but RW decided to fix leaky lavatory pipes & put in new washers in hot water faucets. RW downstairs w/ his books, so I had to entertain myself.

Fri 31 Dec - Ring out the Old - At Bess' tonite - RW home. Dr. Perkins called him re Instructorship next quarter. Bess called us at 9 PM & I got RW dressed & over we went. Lots to drink & eat. Fritz rather high. We didn't get to leave until 2:30 AM or so & RW didn't like it. [In pencil following this are brief notations for Jan 1, 2, 3, & 4 - until got new diary. — Also 4 pages of closely detailed notes on garden plantings - and Xmas card addresses.]

Mon 3 Jan 1949 - RW all excited about the physiologists' meeting in Detroit this coming March. Deadline on abstract of his paper today & I helped him type some of his notes. We had planned on going to the Loop today to get RW a suit, but he came home too late.

Tue 4 Jan - Reading some of the abstracts of scientific papers at last mtg of the physiologists this eve in between my nursery catalogs.

Thu 6 Jan - The tree comes down tonite - I Finish with Dentist

- I was glad I went, for this was my last visit. This eve RW retired to his basement study & I started undressing the tree w/ Bobby's assistance. Took all evening & I was tired! I'm getting very angry at RW's lack of interest in house affairs.

Mon 10 Jan - M - Robert is 29 years old today! - But we made no fuss about it. I washed clothes today & decided to start on curtains & drapes, starting w/ Bobby's room & bath. Gosh, I will miss Bess when she moves away. It's been very nice to be able to go over there whenever the mood came upon you.

Tue 11 Jan - M - Rich Brings a Dog - This evening Rich called, wanting to know if we wanted a female puppy. Impulsively I said yes, so he brot it over via street car in his jacket. The pup is huge (2 mos old?!!), a brown & white terrier, not housebroken but very energetic & friendly. We gave Ginger a bath. Let it sleep by radiator as it whined downstairs. RW says we're letting ourselves in for trouble, but it will do Bobby a lot of good. He's so afraid of dogs right now.

Wed 12 Jan - M - After putting dog & cat in basement, off to the library we went. Got 2 books on dog care, a book on house plants. I spent the evening looking over my flower catalogs and reading book on houseplants. Do want to get some fine plants; feel I have passed the stage where just any growing thing will do. Trying to housebreak the dog is beginning to get me down.

Thu 13 Jan - M - Max Baby Sits - We Go to Surrealist Movie - RW & I left for Mandel Hall at U of C & the surrealist technicolor movie "Dreams Money Can Buy". Beautiful color photography. Reminded me of the films we saw in NY, more logical, however. Alexander Calder had a "dream" showing off some of his handiwork & that was interesting.

Fri 14 Jan - It persists in wetting on the slightest provocation & doesn't seem to understand why we put it out. Fluffy is very much taken up w/ it. They play together very nicely & share one another's beds & food.

Sun 16 Jan - Howard & Helen Jenerick over - Much flurry & ado on my part, put up LR drapes this aft. The J's came & we entertained them w/ supper, records, chess.

Tue 18 Jan - He refused to clean up after Ginger this AM & I went about that distasteful task before breakfasting.

607

Sat 22 Jan - I sat around looking thru my clippings on gardening while RW studied. We didn't retire till 3 AM in the morning. "Ginger" is cute, but a nuisance. If only the car would start!

Mon 24 Jan - "Ginger" leaves our Household - Robt took the pup w/ him this AM & frankly I was relieved to be rid of it; cute, but such a mess & trouble. Scrubbed up floors, washed the laundry.

Wed 26 Jan - <u>We Pick up our New Hudson!</u> [Fig 59] RW off to Loop this AM with bills to pay, $26 on his 75.00 suit; 2 mos phone bill; the electric bills; $50 to Fair for my suit & Xmas gifts; a M.O. to Peter Henderson Co for 2 copies of "Enjoy Your House Plants" & seeds. He withdrew $2600 fm Bank, leaving a measly $700. I ironed today. So about 8 PM we drove to the Hudson dealer on 103rd St to pick up our platinum gray Super Six 4 dr sedan w/ 400.00 worth of accessories (radio, heater, overdrive, air foam seats, electric clock), 2752.00 & $150 for our Graham.

Thu 10 Feb 1949 - Robert working so hard on his Master's thesis, reading literature, taking notes, typing; he's been leaving for school about noon & that disrupts my household day as I sleep later & can't get started till after he leaves. Poor Bobby, his Daddy has been neglecting him since he got involved in this M.S. degree by March thing.

Sun 13 Feb - At Field Museum - A snowy-sleety day, but RW wanted to take Bobby to the Field Museum, so we went, returning in time for supper. Bobby did enjoy the stuffed animal exhibit. He "showed" us the glass exhibits <u>so</u> enthusiastically.

Wed 16 Feb - To Dinner with the Perkins [Physiology faculty] - Helping RW with draft of his thesis & again he was late leaving for school. Said he'd be home 6:30. So I was all dressed (in my suit & yellow blouse) when he came & hurriedly dressed. Left Bobby with Bess. The Perkins live in an old frame "mansion" near U of C, tastefully furnished with Oriental rugs & antiques, & we met the P's child, 5 yr Molly. A buffet supper, & coffee in LR. Much talk & listening to LP records. Nice in the usual restrained manner of university people. Home 12:30, & picking up our son who had had a fine time at Bess'.

Sat 19 Feb - RW going to Chinatown tonite with the whole physiology bunch to honor Dr. Gerard with a Chinese dinner. In the meantime, I had one anxious little boy on my hands all evening wanting to know where his "Dada" was.

Thu 24 Feb - I got started on the thesis and typed about 12 pages with a new ribbon in machine and the low typing table, the results are pretty good. Robert worked on his graphs. And, of course, our little man kept getting in our hair & cried when ordered to play in his room.

Fri 25 Feb - RW working feverishly on his graphs & I helped type in the legends. He left for school 4PM to get them in for photostating & to get my 12 pages of typing approved. [The person in charge of acceptance of physical quality of theses, Kate Turabian, had written "the bible" for such academic pursuits, and was remarkably talented at spotting the least error or erasure or misspelling within innumerable pages of text. She had her own team of typists who could meet her stringent standards, and she was quite suspicious as to whether END could measure up to her requirements. However, it all passed her most careful scrutiny.] Saddened to find our little black fantail goldfish dead this AM. We dropped it in toilet drain and told Bobby it was going out to the river. This evening I typed on RW's thesis still 2:30 a.m. Decided tomorrow we finish it or else. Am so tired of books, paper & junk all over dining room. Surprised to find that I can still type with good speed & accuracy.

Sat 26 Feb - M - After supper to work on the Masters Thesis & stayed with it until 4:30 AM. 50 pages of text including 4 Tables etc. So tired.

Tue 1 Mar 1949 - M - Dr. Hutchens (the head of the Dept) was quite miffed when Robt handed him the thesis. Seems RW has to take an oral exam too as a preliminary to getting the M.S. degree. Question is: can it all be done in time? So RW is hurt & perplexed and I can sympathize with him.

Mon 7 Mar - BLUE MONDAY - RW's day to take final exam re Master's degree. Bobby & I were surprised to see him home at 2:30 PM. Seems he didn't do so well at the exam & then Dean Mullen decided he couldn't get the degree this quarter because sufficient notice hadn't been given, etc. So RW glumly said he felt like going back into the Army!

Tue 8 Mar - MAYBE RW WILL GET HIS M.S. - RW a bit more

cheerful this eve. Seems the faculty took a vote among themselves & decided rules could be waived, so perhaps he'll get the degree.

Fri 18 Mar - RW gets his Master's - RW home about 6 PM with groceries, and his Master's degree. This evening after Bobby was tucked in for the night, we sat around in the LR till 2 AM drinking martinis & talking.

Tue 22 Mar - LR & DR clean up - RW has been so good about cleaning things these past two days.

Sun 27 Mar - M - Have the Folks Sold their House? - A couple put $1000 deposit on their house. So now Mom is all excited & nervous about that.

Sat 9 Apr 1949 - Dad over early this AM to paint the kitchen. Hadn't expected him, but we got underway OK. The green paint RW bot was too dark, so we lightened it w/ white enamel. RW in school all day. Quite downcast because things aren't going as he'd like them to at school.

Mon 18 Apr - M - RW leaves for Detroit - Dad to stay w/ us. - Sleepless nite w/ Bobby fussing with a running nose & slight fever & so I was too sleepy to see RW off. He had a sore throat, too. I feel punk myself. So washed clothes today. Straightened up house. Shifted azalea into 5" pot. Dad came fm work 5 PM & we were at supper when Howard's [Jenerick] wife called to say he'd called her fm Detroit 4 pm. So they got there safely.

Tue 19 Apr - M - Bobby keeps asking for his Daddy. Hope I get a card or something from him.

Wed 20 Apr - M - First letter from RW from Detroit & not too happy, thinks it's a waste of time & money this Convention.

Sat 23 Apr - Airmail fm RW jubilant over his speech yesterday. RW home about 5 AM & we three tried to sleep in our bed.

Sat 21 May - RW takes PhD Prelim exam - RW taking written exam this AM. Came back 2:30 just exhausted from lack of sleep & the ordeal.

Sat 28 May - The Folks Think They've Found a House - RW took his Ph.D. oral exam this AM. He passed, tho not w/outstanding glory.

Wed 15 Jun - That Dreadful Evening - ugh - Don't think I'll ever forget this day. Hot, humid & I busy ironing curtains & cleaning house. Shopping & fixing supper. Rich [Doty] & his g.f.

Kate, 6:30 or so. Meal OK, but I was so irritated by their attitude & RW's attitude & their picture taking in the attic, excluding Bobby & me, that about 10:30 I blew up and ordered them out. RW angrily trying to eject me (down the stairs?) & then packing to leave home, I in tears, etc. Bobby happily asleep thru it all. We made up, but the hurt remains.

Thu 16 Jun - Mom & I in on RE Closing - Silence between RW & me tonight.

Fri 17 Jun - Bobby & I visit Mrs Balderson - Home about 6 PM with a terrific headache. Went to bed & RW fixed supper for Bobby & himself. Slept till 9. Ate eggs & toast. Silence bet Doty & myself.

Sat 18 Jun - I Go Home to Mother - RW at school till 3 or 4. I was happily busy w/ my housework. He comes home, ate & announced that he "wouldn't see me for a couple days". About 5 PM but would come back for me Mon "if I still wanted to go to the Sand Dunes Mon". So about 6 PM Bobby & I packed overnite bag & left for the folks by st car & L. Sobbed out my pitiful story to Mom & Dad & of course they told us to stay & sympathized w/ me. Mom gave up her bed to Bobby & me.

Sun 19 Jun - Rich & I visit my House - About 2:30 we drove to my house & found RW in LR going over our strong box. I picked up some clothes & we left, for I was afraid of another quarrel.

Tue 21 Jun - Washing Clothes - The day passes by fine, but when evening comes, the folks want to go to sleep early & time seems to stand still. Frankly, I don't care for their house nor the location. The neighbors are too close & the corner ones especially noisy but good, with their TV going till midnite. Bobby seems to be enjoying the novelty of his visit & has been behaving very nicely so far as sleeping & eating go. He does like his grandparents!

Wed 22 Jun - Bess over visiting - We visit my House - Bess & I entered my house. Found signs of RW's continued habitation. Watered plants, fed goldfish, took my magazines & left. Gosh, it made me feel homesick to view my house again! Wish that GD fool would make a move towards reconciliation!

Thu 23 Jun - Washing Clothes again - Rather boresome this being a visitor in my parents' home. No word fm RW & I don't expect him to. I am getting impatient to be back in my own home.

Fri 24 Jun - We Spend Entire Day w/ Bess - Mom & I took LaGrange Road bus about noon for Brookfield. Bess expecting us for lunch. So we had a bite of supper there too. Bess' place is cute.

Sat 25 Jun - I Return to the Doty Domocile - Unpleasantness bet Mom & Dad. We decided to go home about 6 PM. RW not home till 7. So we had a long talk about things after Bobby went to bed. He'd seen Ordower who told him we had no grounds for divorce. I guess RW was very much hurt by my action & was afraid to come after us. Gosh, it's good to be mistress in my own home again!

Sun 26 Jun - Getting readjusted. RW to school for a few hours. I inspected my garden. Weeded a bit. Carnations are just lovely, so spicy. After supper we drove to Forest Preserves, milkshakes, home.

Thu 30 Jun - RW spending so much time at school & at home studying. He's to take a comprehensive reading exam in French one of these days. Tonite I tried to help him study vocabulary.

Sun 3 Jul 1949 - Persuaded him to drive us over to see folks. He dropped us off & drove off to get gas. Picked us up in ½ hour or so. Refuses to go in & visit.

Mon 4 Jul - The Glorious Fourth - RW busy computing results on his nerve metabolism experiments. Bobby lighting his sparklers & the few fireworks we had.

Tue 12 Jul - Another Exemption? - I expected RW to drive to see the folks, but he doggedly refused & we quarreled. So Bobby & I left him to himself. This eve, we took walk to the park & swings. We made up tonite. I know he gets terribly upset every time we have a disagreement, but always I have to be the one to make up.

Wed 13 Jul - Got RW to drive us out to the folks about 8 PM. He sat in car till 9 while Bobby & I visited. Home & while RW read Bobby his bedtime story, I ironed today's laundry.

Thu 14 Jul - RW home "studying". This evening we drove with RW to school, where he started an experiment on a rat. Interesting to watch his technique. Unfortunately, the poor thing expired in the middle of it. So for Bobby's sake RW "sewed" it up.

Tue 2 Aug 1949 - M - I am Sick! - Laundry out okay, but my headache & nausea persisted & I finally took to bed. RW not home till 6 PM & he had to fix his own supper. I took a small dose of baking soda which resulted in violent vomiting. So RW had to put Bobby to bed. RW took his comprehensive French exam today & it was a cinch, he says.

Tue 9 Aug - Library - RW some German books. It seems now he must pass a comprehensive German exam in addition to the French.

Fri 12 Aug - We Leave for Plymouth - At Lee's & Edna's 7:30 and they'd been waiting for us for supper. Got Fluffy settled in a cage in the barn. [Our cat had come along.]

Sat 13 Aug - Visiting Martha Jane - Mary Helen - Toured the farm a bit. Bobby hunted eggs in the pullets house. Bobby & Richard got along nicely. We went to look at 2 of the houses Lee is helping build. Taking pictures of us and of them.

Sun 14 Aug - Gibson-Staley Reunion - Got there noon & lots of people there already, including Doty clan. Pretty nice time, altho I felt overwhelmed in crowd of strangers. Late supper at Lena & Russell's.

Mon 15 Aug - We Come Home from Plymouth - 1 3/4 hours via US 30. Left 11:30 laden w/ tomatoes, string beans, sweet corn, pieces of yellow shrub rose (Father Hugo's rose?); double white & red shrub roses & a fleshy looking ivy from Edna. They were so nice to us. We do hope they'll be able to come and visit with us before the year is out.

Thu 18 Aug - Working in Garden - Edged Lawn East - Had Fluffy & kittens in yard in their box & Bobby managed to get himself & everything soaked. This a.m. he spilled half of my Mitsuki perfume on the kittens. Fluffy wouldn't have anything to do with them for a while.

Tue 30 Aug - Our 8th Wedding Anniversary - This evening got RW to drive us & 2 qts root beer over to the folks. All of them home. Their TV fixed & we watched the programs for hour or so. Left at 9:30 because Bobby was acting up. First time RW has visited the folks since our spat in June.

Sun 4 Sep - RW doing some more painting on East side of gutters. Tried to talk RW into going to see Bess, but he absolutely refused.

Mon 5 Sep - LABOR DAY - Overcast skies and RW decided to go to school today, so he dropped Bobby & me off at folks. Worried at Dad's continued concern w/ Bohack's. [This is the first allusion to what was to be his subsequent paranoia over a highly unlikely affair between Elizabeth's Mother & Mr Bohack!!]

Sat 10 Sep - I Help RW Paint - E basement & garage windows - RW painting eaves on E side. I decided to help & painted basement windows E side & then 3 east garage windows. Bobby also painted, his bathroom stool & an old kitchen chair in yard.

Sun 11 Sep - Wanted RW to drive us over to folks w/ kittens, but he stonily refused & angered me very much. He fooled around with his books upstairs.

Mon 12 Sep - I really blow up at RW today - I washed laundry & hung it in basement. After supper I again approached RW about going to see my folks and again that unreasoning stony silence, refusal! So I blasted away at his attitude, to no avail, however. RW upstairs in attic. Wish I had another baby to take care of. Find time hanging on my hands, I've even taken up mending again.

Fri 16 Sep - RW saying his arms ached from the scraping & painting & so about 1 PM we left for the Zoo. Bobby showed fear of the animals. RW's storytelling, no doubt. Stopped to see Bess & Fritz for half-hour or so. RW and I had violent words again. He's so moody and depressed & I've been so jittery lately.

Sat 17 Sep - M - Curses - again! [i.e., she is menstruating, when she had hoped that she was pregnant] - RW starting to paint at noon. A lovely warm day. I helped him paint front door & E window while he worked on the other front windows. Is Bobby to be an only child? It would seem so, here I am menstruating again. RW put Bobby to bed & is napping with him. Don't know why, but I don't believe I've ever been so lonely & depressed in my life. Sans ambition or desire to do anything. The days go by all right, but the evenings seem to drag, & I hate to go to bed.

Fri 23 Sep - Robert working on the west dormers of attic, just scraping & preparing for painting. RW bought a piece of tin &

proceeded to make a huge (coffin like) sandbox for Fluffy & kittens. Gave it a coat of black asphalt paint, handles on it, quite a feat. Very angry at RW who was <u>too tired</u> this evening!

Sat 24 Sep - RW & Bobby visit the Dotys - RW painting & I washed Bobby's laundry & was quite happy till 1:30 or so when RW announced he was going to visit his folks w/ Bobby. They came home 6 PM. Decided to overlook this aft & we had a pretty nice evening reading various mags. Watching kittens frolic in kitchen at midnite. To bed 12:30 AM or so; and we had a reconciliation.

Sun 2 Oct 1949 - Shock over news that Claire Haber (RW friend U of C) killed herself yesterday. [She was a fellow grad student, working w/ Tschirgi on the same Gerard project that Howard Jenerick and I were struggling with. Reason for suicide unknown, and very strange, IV injection of KCl in public park latrine! Tschirgi had to testify at the inquest. After we failed to confirm the Haber-Tschirgi results, Jenerick and I found altered notebooks of Claire's, and always wondered whether they had some relation to her suicide.]

Fri 21 Oct - We See "Red Shoes" - Old Heidelberg - Bobby had helped me pack his overnight bag. Dropped him off at folks."Red Shoes", Technicolor movie re ballet, 8:30 to 10:45 PM. Enjoyable & different. At Old Heidelberg where Bill Beamish is playing w/ a band. Martinis & a sandwich during the 2 intermissions we visited w/ him. Home 1:30 a.m. Our baby spending the nite w/ folks.

Wed 7 Dec 1949 - M - Snow - We Go Marketting - Bobby in buggy & with snow in our faces, we walked to Jewel's for groceries. Talked myself out of buying more plants. I sat up reading new book on gynecology till 1 AM.

Sun 11 Dec - Going Away "Party" at Boyarsky's - Dropped Bobby off at folks 3 PM. Lots of people there, Jenericks. Salami sandwiches, drinks, potato pancakes for supper when only Postls & we were left. Home 9pm.

Mon 12 Dec - At Bess' with Folks - Waited up for RW to come home fm his chess club mtg where he won 5 straight games. The Temple U offer was $3400 as Physiology Instructor.

Wed 14 Dec - RW & I Go Downtown - "Rigoletto" at Annex - I ordered 4 tons coal, had to take 2 tons Pocah egg at 16.50/ton.

This cold weather really uses up coal. So we took Bobby over to Mom's (after flying visit to Sears' Santa for Bobby's sake). Off to loop. RW paid MLR for my coat. Rushing to see Italian opera "Rigoletto", very good!

Sun 18 Dec - We Put Up Our Tree - Tom & Jerry's at the Kay Frank's - This am bot 10' tree, 3.00, balsam. Home & RW wired it. I decorated it bet dinner & supper. Bobby to Mom's 8 PM. At Frank's, meeting lots of people. Dr. Gerard there, John Hutchens, Mrs Perkins, Hesses, etc. Home 10:30.

Mon 19 Dec - Coal Delivered - I Send our Xmas cards - RW dropped us off at folks while he went to Chess Club mtg. RW angered me by not calling for us till 11:30 PM! Bobby crabby & sleepy & I furious!

Mon 26 Dec - M - Turkey Dinner at Folks - RW dropped Bobby & me off 12:30 & he went on to school to run two more rat spinal cord experiments. I felt miserable, cramps, etc. I lay down after dinner. Bobby & Ricky shooting their "smoke" guns. Watching TV. We had birthday cake w/ candles about 8 PM. RW didn't show up until 9:30 PM & Mom gave him a hot turkey dinner.

Sat 31 Dec - New Year's Eve - Only the Koteks Come - Busy straightening house, baking. Baths, making cheese & sardine canapes, setting DR table w/ candles buffet style & waiting. At 9:15 I called Mom & she nonchalantly informed me they weren't coming. Called Orlowska's next door & they declined. About 10 Bess, Fritz & Ricky came & we did have a good time. Most of the canapes were eaten. They drank beer. At midnite RW opened bottle of champagne. Bobby & Ricky played nicely till 12:30 or so when Bobby just went to sleep. They left 2:30 a.m.

Sun 1 Jan 1950 - Paper White Narcissus Blooms - The Doty's Visit us this aft - RW working on his report on rat spinal cord experiments while I read newspaper, Rex Pearce's new catalog. This till midnite after I did up accumulated laundry (no starching).

Mon 2 Jan - RW Finishes Report - At Folks - RW writing his report [This was the end of the 6 months work that was to be my "sure fire" PhD thesis, only to prove prior work had been erroneous; must start some-

616

thing new!] After meatball dinner I typed up his 5 pp report. RW off to his chess club, dropping us off at folks 7 PM.

Fri 6 Jan - In Loop - Symphony Concert - RW to school early & got groceries enroute home. To Orchestra Hall 2:15 for gallery seats (50¢ ea) to hear Eugene Ormandy conduct Chgo Symphony w/ Istomin as piano soloist, Beethoven's "Emperor Concerto"; Egmont Overture, Ravel's Rhapsodie Espagnole & Resphigi's "Pines of Rome". Very beautiful performance. Home 5:30, supper, & heating house before calling for Bobby.

Mon 9 Jan - Tonite RW didn't go to that chess club. Is busy studying for his new experiments on dog, how nervous activity can be inhibited, particularly in the vagus nerve.

Tue 10 Jan - RW is 30 Today - Busy day after loafing yesterday. Washed clothes. Hurried upstairs to bake: 1) mince pie with glazed fruit added; 2) apple pie; 3) orange spongecake in tube pan. To library getting scads of books as usual.

Fri 13 Jan - Set off for the North Side [Lincoln Park Zoo]. Rain down to a drizzle & we visited the Lion House to watch them fed. Saw the monkeys & gorillas, Bushman eating; 5 baby gorillas so playful & messy in their food habits.

Mon 23 Jan - M - We Visit Josephine - Did accumulated laundry. Gave Bobby 10 - 15 min lesson on roller skating. 4 PM over to visit with Josephine. Bobby enjoyed TV. RW & I sat up to 1:30 AM discussing his hope for fellowship at Rockefeller Research Inst in NY & what it would mean, selling our house, furniture, etc, etc. I couldn't go to sleep till 3 AM.

Tue 24 Jan - At Mom's - Told Mom of RW's New York plans. But this eve RW says Dr. Gerard told him they might want him to stay as an instructor for a year or so. He's to talk to Dr. Hutchens.

Wed 25 Jan - RW home 7 PM He talked to Hutchens. Appt at U of C very vague & RW thinks he'll apply for a fellowship in meantime. I'm making mental notes as to our removal from Chgo already.

Mon 30 Jan - SNOW - RW studying & I ironed from 7 PM to 9:30. Dr. Gerard won't be in tomorrow & he's to take over the class lecture. Still up in the air re RW's job. To sleep 2AM.

Sat 4 Feb 1950 - At Folks - RW off to research all day. Mom

617

and I sat up till 1:30 AM when RW called for me. Had been busy on his research all this time! To bed 2:45 AM.

Sun 5 Feb - Mom's Birthday - Gilbert Ling over [Gilbert was a Chinese Postdoctoral Fellow in Gerard's lab, and was famous for having demonstrated intracellular recordings with capillary microelectrodes that he pulled by hand.] - RW & I had words this AM over nothing, so I got dressed & rode over to Mom's 2:30. Found Bobby happily romping about. About 6 PM RW & Ling came & they joined us. We left for home 7 PM. Ling had a lb box Dutch Mill bonbonieres for me. Told Bobby story at bedtime. We looked at pics. Made oyster stew 11 PM. At midnite he left. A rather interesting person & we enjoyed having him out.

Sat 11 Feb - RW off to school at 10, didn't return till 3 AM. Bobby to bed about 10. I sat up and read, then played with the cats until 1 AM. Still no RW, so to bed.

Sun 12 Feb - M - Manteno - At 11 Ray Kjelberg phoned he'd be over at 1 PM . RW took Bobby over to folks. At 1:30 we left in Ray's Plymouth. At Manteno [State Psychiatric Hospital perhaps 50 miles from Chicago] to see cat experiment, but one had failed earlier & Jerry Letvin & Prof Dell didn't want to do another. Instead, we dined on <u>raw</u> (practically) roast beef at Letvin's house. [This was another of Jerry Lettvin's wonderful inventions, pasteurized beef; it remains red and succulent, yet safe!] Very informal sort of thing. Back in Letvin's lab & RW thot his experiment ideal. He's working on similar work as RW on his dog. Home 7:30. Ray [A med student then, subsequently a Harvard neurosurgeon] had to study & didn't come in. Jerry Letvin a MD, U of I nite staff physician at Manteno, daytime neurophysiological research. We're invited to come again.

Wed 15 Feb - M - Washing - RW in school doing an experiment today and didn't get home he tells me until 4:30 AM.

Sun 19 Feb - The Franks over w/ Kiddies - About 5 PM the Franks [Karl Frank subsequently lost the race with John Eccles for Nobel Prize for pioneer work on neurophysiology of the spinal cord.] came w/ Geraldine, Eric & Catherine. Spent most of our time in the kitchen. Bobby didn't seem to hit it off with Eric (about 4½, who goes to nursery school), but the older girl (2nd grade) enjoyed Bobby's story books. In fact, took a little one home w/ her.

Thu 23 Feb - We Go to the Library - The Federation Placement Bureau sent RW a half-dozen listings of job openings & I noticed one for $7500 at Kirksville Osteopathy College. RW all hepped up about that Kirkville job.

Sun 26 Feb - We Write Kirksville - RW deciding to phrase a letter to Kirksville re job & we spent a couple hours getting it typed up & then discarded it as being too patronizing [i.e., re Osteopathy].

Mon 27 Feb - We Get Ltr off to Kirksville - Before RW left we typed up a nice formal letter of application for the Kirksville, Mo job. RW tempted by the $7500 salary. Dr. Gerard seems to think RW would have the qualifications as a neurophysiologist.

Sun 5 Mar 1950 - The New Cat - Garfield Azalea Show - After that we drove out to U of C where we visited the guinea pigs, cats, white rats. RW took with us the young cat which had been given chloralose & was still convulsing. Pretty thing, but so thin. RW gave me an audiometer test, guess my hearing is normal. Showed me his stimulating machine.

Mon 6 Mar - The New Cat - Amazing how it recovered. Last nite was convulsing & too weak to stand up. We let it sleep by radiator. This AM it could walk & ate a bit of meat & drank lots of milk. Mitzi & Tcheri hiss at it angrily & that cows the little thing. Bobby & I went marketing. He walked home all the way fm Jewel's. Bot him a toy wristwatch, "Pinocchio" and a jigsaw puzzle of US cut on State lines.

Tue 7 Mar - Wash Day - RW rec'd ltr fm QMC at Lawrence, Mass re job there @ 4600, research.

Wed 8 Mar - Letter fm Kirksville asking for salary estimate fm RW. He tried to compose reply, but I didn't like what he wrote, so decided to wait before replying.

Thu 9 Mar - RW busy all evening writing up exam questions for his lab class.

Mon 13 Mar - M - Painful Menstruation - Mom visits us - Gee, I felt all dragged out this AM. About 5 PM I started really flowing and a huge clot came out. Similar to the "miscarriage" thing. So I rested for hour or so. Makeshift supper as I was flowing so & didn't want to move about much. RW casually sympathetic, but I felt pretty sick.

Tue 14 Mar - M - Feeling Better - Up at 11. RW off to school leaving Bobby to dress himself. RW busily reading up for paper due Thu on the kidney. Fine company he is, always studying & talking to himself.

Fri 17 Mar - About midnite RW ready to have his paper written up on kidney & CNS Carbohydrate Metabolism [for a course I was taking], so I began typing. We worked until 5 AM. RW reading his report to me.

Mon 20 Mar - We got reply fm Kirksville today offering RW 4000 — 4200 w/possibility more money 2nd year. RW talked to Dr. Gerard at school & he thought RW should get more than that in view of his maturity & experience. We'll sleep on it & see.

Tue 21 Mar - <u>No</u> to Kirksville - Iron - We sat down & wrote a very brief letter saying NO to Kirksville. So now I hope RW can figure out some way to stay in Chgo. Typed several letters re his job seeking. That typewriter is coming in handy.

Fri 24 Mar - RW out at U of Illinois - Ray Kjelberg called for RW & they rode out to the U of Ill to look at the lab. RW hoped to meet Dr McCulloch, but he wasn't there.

Sat 1 Apr 1950 - RW at home, so I suggested we go to see "Cinderella". Bobby liked it. He was so excited at the sights about him, popcorn & lots of children. We left when he didn't care for 2nd feature. Bobby naughty w/ the cat so off to bed w/ him. Reading 2 books of house plans this eve, one on Solar houses. RW studying his German papers. [I read 1500 pages of German articles for my PhD thesis.]

Tue 4 Apr - Busy Day - RW leaving early to see Dr McCulloch at U of Ill today. RW "zombie" like again today. [This long-continuing episode was undoubtedly triggered by her being sexually uninterested consequent to being desperately fatigued at the end of the day from her incessant housecleaning. As she notes, indirectly, this was a recurring problem, and persisted for many years. Happily, essentially all we did to each other in these painful episodes was to signal our continuing displeasure by silence or sullen remarks.] Busy with supper, gave Bobby his bath tonight & RW read him another of "Pooh" stories. I slept w/Bobby tonight, RW all keyed up and jittery. One of his extra mean moods.

Wed 5 Apr - Bobby & I upholster 2 chairs - RW's experiment didn't "go" again, perhaps that's the frustration that brought on another of those emotional (on my part) and cold-blooded sadism on his about 1 AM. I had waited up for him to retire & then he started again and this "let's quit, it's all a mistake" etc. I cried myself into a terrific headache again, the injustice of his attitude & Bobby's welfare worries me. I'm sure having my Gethsemane this Wed before Easter.

Thu 6 Apr - M - I Get a Gardenia Plant - Mom over - "It" off early. Of course, I didn't tell Mom about RW. She'd only fuss & cry & pity me. I gave Bobby his bath & read him a story tonight. "It" busy with his "work", trying to type some data for McCulloch for the research fellowship deal. Talks about renting a room & leaving us.

Fri 7 Apr - M - "Good" Friday - "It" leaving for school to run an experiment. I really felt blue. We colored 2 doz eggs for Easter, Bobby watching with bright eyes. Then got busy & ironed for over an hour. Getting ready to put Bobby to bed when RW walked in at 10 PM. So he read Bobby a story when Bobby asked him to. Feeling all pooped out, cramps & heavy flow. RW silent as a Sphinx. Getting more data ready for McCulloch.

Sat 8 Apr - M - "It" off w/o word to me this AM, presumably to see McCulloch. Hemorrhaging & feeling all washed out. "It" came home for supper. Mom Doty had called for us to come out tonite & we left about 7:30 PM. Bobby got a token Easter candy gift & a dozen balloons fm Grandpa Doty. We had root beer & conversation. Left 11:30. [Note how we both concealed our festering quarrel from the rest of the world.] Home & putting Bobby to bed. I fixed the picnic ham for baking tomorrow. Studded it with cloves & brown sugar.

Sun 9 Apr - M - Bobby looked for colored eggs which RW had placed about the house & found an Easter basket behind a chair. We had an early dinner of baked ham. RW drove us to Mom's about 2:30, but refused to come in with us. I told him to pick us up at 8. He drove away in a huff. Didn't show up for us till 10:30! RW & I got into a discussion with an old familiar ring. As usual I got emotionally upset. Drank several glasses of wine & really got a bit high.

Tue 11 Apr - We Go Marketing - Iron - This eve he started to type his application for USPHS [US Public Health Service] fellowship. I insisted on helping & together we got it finished by 12:30 AM so he thanked me for my assistance. Told him it was to save him from having an apoplectic stroke. [From my fits of frustration at making typing errors.]

Thu 13 Apr - Tcheri has 4 kittens - Surprised to hear meows fm under Bobby's bed. Tcheri had had three kittens already, had a 4th in box by kitchen radiator! RW happily surprised to find kittens when he came home. Washed hair tonite; RW giving Bobby his bath & reading him story. We watched the kittens tonite, deciding we'd keep male & female for us.

Fri 14 Apr - RW Shops for me - I Wash Clothes - RW home till noon, & I suggested he get groceries for me before going on to school, which he did & then fussed 'cause he'd be late for something or another. Bobby stayed up till about 10. Wanted to wait up for his "daddy". RW bathing tonite after remark "you'd changed bed sheets today?" No attempt on either side towards truce in this "cold" aspect of our relations.

Mon 17 Apr - We Visit Lincoln Park Zoo - Reconciliation - Awoke about 5 AM fm simply horrid nightmare, drenched w/perspiration. Out of habit turned to RW for comfort &, surprisingly, he seemed happy to do so. Fell asleep till 10 or so. RW suggested outing to Starved Rock, but skies overcast & I suggested the Zoo instead. So to Lincoln Park & I got to see the Spring Flower Show. RW can be sweet & I know he suffers horribly when we're on the outs.

Wed 19 Apr - RW at school late - I sew - RW not due for supper (has class meeting in the evening) so I sewed on my beige satin blouse. RW not home till 2 AM.

Thu 20 Apr - We Go Marketing w/ RW - Library - He took us to A&P for groceries & then hurried to school for his "office hour" for student consultation. Then to library to get Bobby books, me, RW all enthused about Jamaica & getting 4 books on that. He received an offer fm new university there. Feel I need a spring-summer outfit.

Wed 17 May - Cut Grass - Water - Water - RW had gone w/ Bobby to do the weekly marketing. This evening I became angered when he told me he <u>read (for pleasure)</u> all aft and I struggle so to keep the outdoors neat & growing! Spent evening pricking out petunias. I've put my large geraniums in the open ground to do as they will. Planted little seedlings in 2½" flower pots. Played with kittens. They are so cute now.

Wed 24 May - Nightmare episode - I decided to go at 3:30 & RW dropped us off. Bess very much on edge today & harangued at Bobby so I quarreled with her. Should have left right then & there, for an hour later she spanked Bobby for "hurting" Ricky & I intervened & in the scuffle Dad got involved & Bess swore she didn't want to have anything to do with any of us, only Mom. Fritz took them home right away. Bobby & I got home via bus at 8:30 PM.

Thu 25 May - Hear Dr McCulloch Lecture - RW's cold very bad. He cut lawns for me. We dropped Bobby off at folks 7 PM & on to U of C. Dr M, with grayish beard, gave a very well delivered talk on "Neuroses".

Sat 27 May - M - At the Franks - RW working on his schoolwork in DR while I went about dusting, vacuuming, changing bed linens, getting weekly housecleaning done. Dropped Bobby off at folks about 8 PM and to the Franks. Guests included the Gerard's, Perkinses, Davis, Wilsons, Tschirgi. "Entertainment" an oral counting game, Picture "charades". Bourbon was served, I drank plain ginger ale. So we stayed till 1 AM Enjoyed ourselves after a hectic fashion.

Wed 31 May - M - RW initiated into Sigma Xi, a scientific research frat tonite & not home till 10:10 PM. Got Bobby ready for bed. Reading him one chapter of Dr Doolittle. RW home in time to read the 2nd.

Sat 3 Jun 1950 - Picnic Palos Park - Dotys - RW & Bobby built me another rose trellis for "Summer Snow". Upstairs studying while I changed bed linens, dusted the house. About 6 PM we drove out to Swallow Cliff in Palos Park where med student picnic going. The Perkines w/ Mollie there. Left at 8 w/ Perkinses and drove out to Oak Park to visit w/ Dotys until almost 11.

Fri 9 Jun - House Clean - Garden - Much Revue About Nothing - Dropped Bobby off at folks 7:30 for the night. On to Mandel Hall to see faculty revue. Rather good for an amateur production. Gerard, Mullin & fmly much in evidence in this 2 hour re-vue.

Mon 12 Jun - Wash Day - Cut Lawns - Iron - I typed another 4 pages of our Ph.D. thesis. RW really slipped up on the 6:30 PM Dr Luckhardt farewell dinner today for which he paid 2.50! Remembered it at 6:40 PM after finishing supper! [Absent minded Professor already!] So upstairs struggling on thesis. Trouble getting Bobby to fall asleep tonite & no reason that I could see but a "witch" dream he had last night.

Fri 16 Jun - Wash Day - Telegram over phone fm Natl Inst of Health "Fellowship Approved pending appropriation fiscal year 51, Letter follows."

Sun 25 Jun - Visiting the Dotys - Thought I was beginning to menstruate, but no, so maybe I am that way?

Thu 29 Jun - Gardening Day - RW gone fm his attic (I asked him why the retirement last nite & got no answer!) when we got up at 11. RW betook himself up in attic right after supper & that's all we heard of him. Why does he act like that? Never really been a companion to me, nor is he much of a father to Bobby. It's really lonely existence I lead, left to my own devices all day & evening. If it weren't for Bobby & my gardening hobby.

Sat 1 Jul 1950 - Busy Day For Me - We all slept 10:30, RW not going anywhere today. After eating, I hurried to get laundry out on line. RW cut my hair a bit; gave Bobby a haircut. RW read to Bobby. News of the Korean situation not encouraging. I went up & typed RW's draft of thesis until 12:30, then bath. Drank wine & talked till 2AM. RW retired w/ me.

Sun 2 Jul - At Folks - I wonder if I am going to have a baby.

Mon 10 Jul - RW Home - Laundering - Watering - Ironing - RW studying literature so as to prepare for writing his "Discussion" of Ph.D. thesis. Did get him to cut back lawn. I cut front. The Korean situation doesn't seem to be improving. They're going to draft 20,000 men right away. RW listens to every newscast. He threatens to volunteer his services to the Army soon as he gets his Ph.D. Owah! And me expecting.

Tue 11 Jul - Watering, Watering - Atrocities being reported. Late news that Pakistan offers troops for use by UN. RW says that means we have Moslem support. Wondering if I am pregnant. Today is the 21st day. Should know for sure by this weekend. Then to select a doctor.

Wed 12 Jul - Wotta Day - Bobby Cracks His Forehead - RW & Bobby observing fireflies. [This was part of an experiment for a class {Eckhard Hess} in which Joe Hind and I, as lab partners, were measuring interval between flashes as function of ambient temperature.] About 8:30 PM Bobby came up on porch. Next thing we heard was a loud cry. Bobby had hit his forehead on stone threshold & did it bleed! Stopped the bleeding. Decided it needed professional treatment. Wed nite being doctors' nite off, we took him to Holy Cross Hospital where an intern & sister treated him. Put 2 clamps across the cut, adhesive taped it in place. Fee $2.00. Bobby behaved beautifully at hospital. Not a sound from him, just as brave as can be.

Sat 15 Jul - 51 - Wash - Clean House - Bobby gave us quite a time with his worries about a "hole in his head" when he bumped his forehead. Thought he was bleeding, etc. Typed some more of RW's thesis. Listening to more news of US withdrawals and Red breakthrough in Korea. Apparently our reinforcements are slow in coming. Not feeling too chipper about the prospect of a World War III coming so soon.

Thu 20 Jul - 56 - Went up to start on RW's thesis & we didn't stop till 1 AM. RW upstairs busy on graphs for his thesis. Worried by news that Reserves are being called up, by Navy, Marines, Air Corps, & some Army. Wonder what the future holds for us all?

Sun 23 Jul - 59 - Bobby at Folks - We Type Thesis - I slept till 12:30 PM. Upstairs to type his Ph.D. thesis. More trouble trying to get everything just so, leaving space for Figures, typing in legends; typing up tables. Picked up Bobby 8:30. After we put him to sleep upstairs on cot (he saw a crocodile under his bed; it wet him w/ water & wrestled w/ him) we kept on typing. Got 25 pp done. This by midnite. RW has to give early lecture tomorrow.

Tue 25 Jul - 61 - Typing Thesis - The Joe Hinds over - RW off early. Has to lecture all this week. Joe Hind, in RW's class in Psych, & his wife over about 8. The men folk observed fireflies and their habits in backyard until real dark. Then on porch talking till after 10. Served beer & coke.

Thu 27 Jul - 63 - RW gave 3 copies of his thesis to Dr Hutchens to read & criticism was made that it's too technical. He has 2 weeks before the deadline Aug 11th.

Tue 1 Aug 1950 - 68 - Bath & Kitchen Washed Down - RW not going to school today & I was amazed at his industry. Washed down walls of bath & kitchen (I helped), cut grass, opened several DR & LR windows which had been painted shut.

Wed 2 Aug - 69 - 136½ - At U of C - Begin Prenatal Clinic - At Lying In by 9:30 AM Blood specimen taken, said it looked as tho I was six weeks pregnant, uterus is tipped, which might account for spotting before Bobby's birth.

Sat 12 Aug - 79 - In Plymouth - Quite a scurry this AM getting bags packed and house prepared for our weekend visit. Left 10:15 AM. Little traffic & we were at Mary Helen's by 12:15. They asked us to stay for supper, so we did. Bobby & Richard hit it off very nicely.

Sun 13 Aug - 80 - The Reunion - At Reunion, usual bunch. The Dotys in force there. I had little to do w/ them. RW went in for a swim. Bobby waded in the water w/ the children. So we drove back to Lee's to watch cows getting milked.

Wed 16 Aug - 83 - Second visit to U of C Clinic - 10am appt, so we dropped Bobby off at Mom's. RW drove me to Lying In. Then quite a cursory exam. Blood type O, RH positive, weight 137.9, blood pressure 130/78.

Sat 19 Aug - 86 - Bobby is Better - No temp when he got up. RW trying to write paper for a psych class. Bobby still fussing,. His father spent all evening playing "soldiers" with him. Gave him bath and to bed. Retired after baths. RW in a romantic mood tonite.

Mon 28 Aug - 95 - Laundry - Family Spat! - RW off early & not back till around midnite, running an experiment. About 6 PM Mom called hysterically that Dad hit her. Max walked in then. I called later & he said he made Dad leave, that Mom's eye was swollen & they'd see a doctor tomorrow.

Tue 29 Aug - 96 - Dentist - U of Ill - Dad over - Slept till 11. Exhausted by my troubled mental state over family strife. We didn't get to dentist till almost 2. Doc only treated Bobby's teeth. Prepared mine for filling w/ silver. At U of Ill Neuropsychiatric

Institute where we talked to Dr Stein. RW will report Sat for work on his postdoctoral fellowship. I started preparing dinner when Dad walked in. So we talked it over & decided he could stay with us temporarily at least. So we made Dad comfortable on Army cot upstairs. I called Mom about 10. She'd seen Doctor & Janinski (atty) & he's started a separate maintenance action. Wotta mess!

Wed 30 Aug - 97 - Our Ninth Wedding Anniversary - Still in bed at 11 when Mom came by. RW & Bobby up already. Mom's eye really a shiner. Cried & tried to justify her position in this domestic crisis. RW left for school, to do another experiment. Almost 10. RW not home yet.

Thu 31 Aug - 98 - Talked to Mom on phone & she says definitely no reconciliation. So are we to be saddled w/ Dad forever? This eve RW & I had a long gabfest & he's convinced Dad is irrational, but not psychotically so.

Fri 1 Sep 1950 - 99 - RW gets his PhD degree - Chinatown - RW drove me to Rockefeller Chapel. Exercises started 3 PM & lasted till 4:45 PM. Interesting to me, as it was my first attendance, but really rather dull. RW got his "hood" with his diploma which he can store away. So we drove to Mee Hong's basement restaurant for a "9 course" Chinese dinner @1.25.

Sat 2 Sep - 100 - Dentist - Dad out all nite - RW off to U of I to report in. I had words w/ Dad when I told him he'd have to find a permanent place to stay; so he left saying we were all against him & he was being turned out into the street.

Sun 3 Sep - 101 - I am Frustrated! - Mom & Max over at Bess' today & I tried to prevail on RW to drive out there this aft, but he adamantly refused. He can be so stubborn! Dad came about 3 PM, saying he'd found himself a place to stay starting next Saturday. Of course, we told him he could stay. RW busy with his speech for Columbus. Got Bobby to bed. Still early, but I feel lost, bewildered, confused. I wonder just how Mom & Dad will settle their separation.

Mon 4 Sep - 102 - RW deciding to go to U of C to do an experiment, so I decided to do my laundry. Bobby & I dressed & went over to visit Mom. Home by 9 PM to find Tcherina w/kittens, four by time RW came home at midnite. RW deciding to take them to U of I to remove occipital lobes fm 2.

Tue 5 Sep - 103 - Busy Day - RW home late & brot extra gray kitten also operated on. Kittens unconscious, body cold. To bed 2AM w/ only one kitten really conscious. But 4:30 AM awakened by kittens mewing. Fed them.

Wed 6 Sep - 104 - Wt 141? - Hospital - Shopping - RW drove me to Lying In. Left Bobby at Mom's 9:30. After waiting till 11:30, told that Dr Lorincz was in the Army. Met RW at Billings library. Our kittens seem pretty much back to normal. All three of the operated ones, and to think we thought they'd die that 1st nite.

Sat 9 Sep - 107 - RW gives me a Toni - RW cut my hair & gave me a Toni wave, his first & rather clumsy attempt at it. Started at 9 & finished at 1 AM.

Sun 10 Sep - 108 - Drove Dad & luggage over to Uncle Iggy's bungalow. [Uncle Iggy was Marinya Jusewich's brother.] Dad will stay there. Dad very bitter towards Mom & everybody, I guess. Frankly, I'm relieved to have him gone. [The nubbin of this is that Dad Jusewich accused Mom Jusewich of having had an affair, an unequivocally ridiculous accusation!] After putting Bobby to bed, RW upstairs writing his speech to be given in Columbus. I typed some of it for him.

Wed 13 Sep - 111 - We Get to Columbus, 330 miles - Left Bobby w/ Mom 9am, ditto Tcherina & kittens. RW hit US 30 in his stride. Surprised at size of Ohio State & how lovely the campus is. Scouting for place to stay, finally settling for twin bedroom in a large old home. RW memorizing his speech for tomorrow. Finally to sleep 11:30. Wondering if Bobby is OK.

Thu 14 Sep - 112 - Alarm at 7:45. Dressing & over to Pomerene Hall for breakfast, then to Botany & Zoology Bldg to listen to papers on central nervous system. I sat & listened to the speeches. Tschirgi gave good "off the cuff" talk; then RW. Ran out of time, but gave fairly decent delivery. Talking to Jacobsons from Rochester re U of Rochester & Dr Adolph. Walked thru OSU flower gardens, beautiful roses. Peeked in their greenhouses. "Home" for bath & clothes change. In Lounge meeting Dr. Gerard. Dr Perkins there.

Fri 15 Sep - 113 - The Am Physiological Soc Banquet - Sitting in on papers all AM, Dr. Gerard chairman of session. Interesting movie by Macht of Cincinnati on decorticate & decerebrate cats. Dr. Adolph of Rochester met us on lawn & we sat & talked, $4000 a yr research & instructing w/ no promise of advancement for years. Hurrying to Neil House Mezzanine where we each got a martini. Talking to Dr Halstead, [George] Bishop. Dr Mayerson of Tulane talked to RW about job at La State, New Orleans. Sounds interesting.

Sat 16 Sep - 114 - The Last Day at Columbus - Dr. Gerard, Jenericks, Tschirgi, Karl Frank, Taylor & Mike Davis, we all ate together & Dr. Gerard picked up the checks. We drove Frank to airport & wasted an hour or so. RW all set on seeing his "cataract" falls & insisted on taking off US40 onto side roads. So we didn't get to Shelbyville till 6. Had supper at a cafeteria there, not bad. But in deciding to go to Martinsville we got on R44 & what a road, narrow, winding, crushed stone only in some places, a nightmare & it took us an hour to travel 30 miles. Finally ended up in a nondescript tourist home on R37 out of Martinsville, 3.00 a nite.

Sun 17 Sep - 115 - Turkey Run - Left Martinsville tourist home after the old lady showed us her 2 young cats. Then to visit Grassyfork Goldfish Hatchery, huge place w/ lovely evergreen landscaping. Interesting. Then on to Cataract Falls over miles of gravel road, dirty, dusty, bumpy. Finally found the cataract & it was a different site. Reached Turkey Run State Park about 4:30 PM. Reserved a cabin for tonite, 5.35 per person including 3 meals. Wonder how things are back home?

Mon 18 Sep - 116 - Home Again - Met up w/ Bloomfield & bride (B a med student at U of C) in the dining room and RW offered to drive them home this aft as they'd come up by train. At 9 we left for a hike along one of the trails, which got me down a bit walking along narrow ledge. But the climax of it all was when RW lost the trail & we found ourselves up on top of this hill with apparently no way back but to climb down as best we could. I still get a sinking stomach as I think of how dangerous it was, but we made it with shaking knees afterwards. Bobby hadn't even asked for us this past week. RW gave him a bath. Told him about our trip (with maps).

Tue 26 Sep - 124 - I Wash Draperies - RW not home till 7 PM. I was angry as I had left clothesline & poles for him to take down! He just doesn't give a damn!

Thu 28 Sep - 126 - Busy Day - So Tired - Up 9:30 & really stayed busy all day. Fussed a bit with houseplants, re potting some, discarding others. Swept up porch & mopped floor. Put up bathroom drapes, cleaned blind, washed bath & kitchen floors. Ironed 4 shirts, 2 dresses, blouses etc. Angry when RW showed up at 7 for supper. He criticized my new version of spaghetti, so I didn't talk to him all evening. I gave Bobby his bath, but he insisted RW read him his stories.

Fri 29 Sep - 127 - 7 tons Coal, 115.00 - My garden is a mess. Do have some lovely 'mums blooming, bronze, pink, yellow & red bronze budding. RW home 6:15 PM today, but right after supper up in attic with Bobby, so he's not much of a companion.

Sat 30 Sep - 128 - Dad over - I am upset - I really am miffed, RW just up and played w/ Bobby in attic all morning, no effort to start on housecleaning or any outdoor work. Then about noon Dad came over & hadn't been here 5 min when he started to rave about Mom's supposed misbehavior 38 years ago. I just burst into tears & of course Dad left shortly. I do wish he'd stay away if that's all he has on his mind. Managed to get the "vegetating" RW to drive me to 5&10, A&P & Hi Low to shop for week groceries. So we had supper. RW put Bobby to bath & bed while I relaxed with mending & then reading. To bed without any more words between RW & me.

Sun 1 Oct 1950 - 129 - RW just sat around & read of all things "Lady Chatterly's Lover" by D.H. Lawrence. Gosh, I despise his lack of any interest in the house or his lack of regard for my wishes in that respect. So to bed very embittered at the whole affair.

Wed 4 Oct - 132 - I Sew House Dress - RW as usual deep in a magazine after putting Bobby to bed. Lots of companionship there! Coolish today, in fact near freezing temperatures for tonight & I asked RW to bring in potted plants I had out in yard.

Fri 6 Oct - 134 - Laundering all Day - Those d—n kittens get around the kitchen & leave nasty evidence! So tired I could cry. White Lady, Mentor Boy blooming; also wh, red & pink dble begonias.

Sat 7 Oct - 135 - Ironing - Dr Gerard's 50th Birthday - Almost 10:30 when I got up. I ironed 3 of my blouses, 4 of RW's shirts, 5 of my housedresses. Still at it at 2pm when RW came home. Don't know how, but he & Bobby agreed to get my groceries & I continued ironing. At Quadrangle Club before 7 PM. "Banquet" of ham & other meager fare for about 50 people. Seeing "All Quiet on Western Front" at local movie house & not home till 12:30 AM. Bobby spent nite w/ Mom.

Sun 8 Oct - 136 - I Sew Light Green Blouse - RW picked Bobby up at Mom's at 9 AM. Then w/o a word RW upstairs practically all day playing war w/ Bobby. The house a mess & all the "Spring" cleaning yet to be done & he wastes time like that. I cried bitter tears into 2 or more handkerchiefs & then had to lie down for hour or so to recover my composure. Then fixing dinner RW grumbled at Swiss steak! I kept quiet. Another thing that I don't like is his idea of keeping the five kittens down in basement since I complained of their messing kitchen. The poor things there in the dark. I haven't the inclination to go up & down the stairs to feed them or look after them.

Mon 9 Oct - 137 - Another Dismal Day - Just can't do any housework. I get dizzy & nauseated every time I stoop or kneel. My midsection seems to be so bloated or something. I noticed some brownish discharge yesterday. Is this going to be another miscarriage? RW came home, again w/o a word of greeting to me. We ate silently. I silently washed dishes. RW reading & otherwise acting the part of Lord & Master of the house.

Tue 10 Oct - 138 - Dentist - at Mom's - Had it out w/RW last night & about all I got out of it was a severe case of convulsive sobs and tears. Notice I've been "spotting" & I guess that's why I've been feeling so depressed & irritable. So relations "thawed" a bit between us because I acted as though nothing had happened; but I do feel very hurt at RW's attitude of disinterestedness.

Wed 11 Oct - 139 - Guess RW is peeved at the fact that I didn't even look at the kittens all day. I have enough to do w/o worrying about 5 kittens.

Thu 12 Oct - 149 - We were all thru when RW came home at 6:30. So I served him & went into the DR to cut out long-sleeved & short-sleeved blouses. I guess that miffed RW, or the fact that I hadn't fed the kittens, because he gave Bobby his bath and took himself and books upstairs. The dishes & table stood uncleared until I hobbled out to clean up. I do feel so tired at the end of a day. That pressing down feeling especially frightens me & I have cramps in my buttocks. I wonder what I should do, ignore RW or just throw in the sponge?

Fri 13 Oct - 141 - I Finish Peach Blouse - Angry at RW for not getting up to fix fire as Bobby bounced out of bed and it was cold in the house. Then RW remarked I didn't know how to cook when Bobby objected that his cream of wheat wasn't "like daddy makes it". So I suggested he get his meals out. So we ate in our customary silence. I washed the dishes while he fooled around with his kittens (in basement). Reread my Diary of 1945 poignantly.

Sun 22 Oct - 150 - So after Bobby was safely tucked into bed, I told RW I wanted to talk to him. As usual I got very emotionally upset, he seemed a bit disconcerted when I told him I would talk to Max about moving in with them unless RW did something to lighten the burden of the house. He said he'd do the laundry weekly and clean house once a week. Thought I shouldn't think of a separation until the "baby" is past the diaper stage. Nothing really settled, but I suppose I shall wait.

Mon 23 Oct - 151 - Mom over - a Busy Day - We Do Laundry - After supper got RW to come down and help with laundry. He put up lines & hung most of the clothes up. We finished in 1½ hours. He's taking his white shirts to laundry. Having a glass of vermouth before retiring.

Tue 24 Oct - 152 - All of us in Loop - So home. I started making pancakes for supper. RW queered my enthusiasm by his "what again?" So they fixed their own meals. I sewed on my maternity dress & when I went to bed it was finished, buttons & buttonholes & all. Needless to say stiff silence bet RW & me again!

Fri 27 Oct - 155 - Walk to 63rd & Kedzie - Home 3 PM & RW home too. But not a word fm him. He did go to A&P to get bulk of groceries on my list. He suggested a movie & although my feet were aching (varicose veins) I agreed and we drove to an outdoor movie to see a silly grade B picture & "Destination Moon" which was interesting; but outdoor movies, never again. Home 11 PM. All of us to bed silently.

Sat 28 Oct - 156 - I am Bored, Depressed, Apathetic - His promise "to clean house once a week" apparently forgotten, RW left at 10:30 AM to return 5:30, no word as to where, why or when. RW put Bobby thru his nightly routine (bath, story) & then settled down with a book. I have never been so bored, so disgusted at my inability to get things done. The house is a dirty mess. I have no interest in my garden, the kittens, plants or radio.

Sun 29 Oct - 157 - RW and Bobby go to Lake Geneva - Getting breakfast when RW announced he & Bobby were going to Lake Geneva. Of course, I remonstrated & got tearful about Bobby going w/o me, but RW told me I was insane & walked out with him. So I had me another emotional jag & when I regained a bit of self-control, I got busy and cut out three dress patterns, resting after each one. I am terribly upset and my whole inside seem to be heaving & weaving. Another example of how much my opinions count with RWD! They came home at 9:30, altho I thot they'd stay overnite. This situation is intolerable, but I just can't see how to get out of it. If only Mom & Dad's affairs were all settled! I'm so upset I feel like I'm going out of my mind.

Mon 30 Oct - 158 - Decided to do laundry. RW in garage with his kittens, so I started washing. Put up line in yard & started hanging with absolutely no help fm RW. When I remonstrated, I got the reply "when you change your attitude". Phooey. Debated whether I should call J & G for advice [attorneys for whom she had worked]. All day job w/ laundry. I also washed out scatter rugs. Tired. Washed up sink full of dishes. Fixed supper & as usual we were thru before RW came home. Amused to see him scouring out bathroom sink. I just can't get everything done these days.

Fri 3 Nov - 162 - Asked if I wanted to go to library & so we three went. I got 2 books on sewing which might prove interesting. RW fixed big radio this eve. I sewed on bodice of red check dress.

Sun 5 Nov - 164 - Another Boring Day - Slept w/ Bobby last nite; no comment fm RW. RW & Bobby fussing w/ kittens & taking photographs of them [e.g., Fig 56]. Fixed steak for our dinner, letting RW fry his the way he likes it & Bobby got me into tears when he complained that his wasn't fixed the way "Daddy's" was. RW reading in bed with one of his photographic reflectors, so I let him read in solitary splendor, retiring w/ Bobby again.

Thu 9 Nov - 168 - RW didn't show up until 7, w/o a word of explanation. RW opened checking acct at Marquette Natl Bk, jointly with me.

Mon 13 Nov - 172 - At Mom's - Awakened 7:30 by RW's alarm. Sun shining & I felt good & expansive, so I joined RW in bed & coaxed him up to fix fire. Dozed off for hr to find Bobby up & RW off to barbers. Anyway, he drove us to Mom's about noon. Midnite now & RW still busy with his studies, a book worm but good.

Sat 18 Nov - 177 - RW did laundry all by himself, bleaching white things in Linco solution in tub. He also changed bed linens.

Mon 20 Nov - 179 - Mom over - We just sat and talked while I sorted out basket of laundry RW had brot up. I must admit clothes look white after his bleaching. RW had retired early, groaning with his cold. When I asked him about the boiler, he said he'd build a fire in the morning. So I got mad & asked him what his intentions were that he'd neglected to tend to the fire even. Nothing settled, as usual, & I just had to blow my nose & wipe my tears. He agreed to do some household work. How frustrating to have to put up with such unrelenting attitudes!

Tue 21 Nov - 180 - Birthday card fm Dad - RW off at 11. Feeling rather tired after my emotional outbursts at 3 AM w/RW, but I wiped down range & refrigerator, scrubbed bathroom fixtures & floor, dusted blinds & hung up drapes. So much work to be done in this house. Will see if RW lives up to his promise to help me clean up.

Wed 22 Nov - 181 - We Clean Front Bedroom!? - Sleeping late; why not, when we don't retire till 2 or so? He decided not to go to school & I suggested we clean BR. In due time he got around to it & did only what he felt like, vacuumed walls, molding, blinds & floors. Says he'll clean this spring. So I washed all bric brac, cleaned windows, polished furniture. He turned rug over & set furniture to rights. I ironed drapes & scarves & I must admit it looks much better. He gave Bobby a bath & then lay down himself, all tuckered out from big day's work! Rec'd Birthday card from Mom, too. I don't suppose there'll be anything from RW.

Thu 23 Nov - 182 - I am 35 today - RW drove Bobby & me to Mom's at 2PM. Mom had half turkey in oven & we set table for 5:15. RW just walked in as we all sat down. RW never even said "happy birthday" to me today.

Fri 24 Nov - 183 - RW says he'll type his deglutition paper himself in school. I said nothing. Went back to sleep w/ RW. Bobby crowds me too much.

Sat 25 Nov - 184 - Bobby's Room "Cleaned" - A busy day. RW off to do marketing when I got up at 11. So after eating I went down & started laundry. RW came in time to start hanging first batch. Lots of clothes, including Baby things I sewed. Upstairs listening to English version of Mozart's "Magic Flute" when he got a phone call fm Dr Cole of U of Calif Agric College at Davis re interview for job there. Agreed to meet him tomorrow at noon.

Sun 26 Nov - 185 - In Loop - Dr Cole - Macbeth - RW brot up laundry. I sorted it while they cleared snow off walks. At 11 we dropped Bobby off at Mom's. Got down to Sherman House at noon & Dr Cole of Davis, Calif met us in lobby. Talking about job openings there in school of animal husbandry. Joined by Dr. Hughes & all in all we spent 2 hrs discussing job, housing, climate. RW said he'd think about it. So to World Playhouse to see Orson Welles in "Macbeth", a very moving, if a bit over done version; also "Birth of a Ballet".

Mon 27 Nov - 186 - Cleaning Pantry - RW says he will type his paper on deglutition himself using typewriter at Illinois. I offered to do it, for a consideration, so he should not feel obligated. No reply. At least my mental attitude has improved. I'm not upset emotionally anymore.

Tue 28 Nov - 187 - We Clean DR China Cabinet - I decided to wash all china & glassware in DR. Did so; waxed the cabinet, then dusted the venetian blinds, cleaned DR windows, straightened plants in windows, vacuumed DR rug & it was time to start supper! And was I tired! Fixed Swiss steak for us, fried round steak for RW when he came home at 6:30 (the louse!) So in the d—n kitchen till 8 getting things cleaned up.

Wed 29 Nov - 188 - At U of C - Up 9:30 & hurrying to drop Bobby off at Mom's by 10:30 so RW could see Gerard at 11. I went to the Billings Library to wait for him. He appeared 11:45 to say Gerard would take us to lunch. So at Quadrangle Club. RW objected later to my "chitchat" during lunch. Anyway, saw Dr. Lane for a few minutes. He's pleased with my weight gain so far. Suggested I get Multicebrin vitamin pills (4.86 for 100). So, meeting RW at Abbott. He was in w/ Karl. We saw Tschirgi, Willey & didn't get started home till 4:30. Thinking about Gerard's remarks that RW could wrangle a good salary at Utah or even Davis. Frankly I don't know what to think with the Korean-China situation the way it is.

Fri 1 Dec 1950 - 190 - I Sew Baby Quilt - RW off very early today as Dr. Davenport of U of Utah to see him this AM. So I had to get up early, too, at Bobby's insistence.

Thu 7 Dec - 196 - RW & I on much more amiable terms. This AM I was in such a mood for affection, the inevitable occurred. Feel as tho a heavy burden were lifted from me [And I am sure from me as well. As I had suspected during the depressing transcription of this bitter episode, I felt that this was the heart of the matter, aggravated by her fanatical approach to cleaning house.]

Wed 13 Dec - 202 - RW finishes his "paper" - This evening I helped him proofread it again & wrote letter of transmittal.

Fri 15 Dec - 204 - RW staying in school late - He left at 11 & didn't return till 1:30 AM. News from Korea bad. Pres Truman made a speech tonite. National emergency declaration, expansion of defense production, military personnel, etc. etc.

Thu 21 Dec - 210 - U of Utah offer comes - Mom over - Tree Set Up - Slept till noon. Awakened by Mom ringing back doorbell. She brought over some Xmas cards & I addressed several for her. Bobby printed 2 cards. Excitement over two letters, definite offer of 4500.00 & asst professorship at U of Utah which RW would like to accept; and an intriguing offer of 2 possible jobs 6400 & 7600 at Navy Air Center in Phila as director of research. So I convinced RW he should at least inquire further. To bed 3 AM again.

Mon 25 Dec - 214 - Bobby bounced out of bed 8:30 and was so overjoyed to find his mechanical pencil, blackboard, 8 small model planes, Erector set, etc. RW gave me my gift, a terry cloth bathrobe which I certainly could use. RW leaving for school to do an experiment & so we were alone all day. Bobby played with his toys, the blackboard came in for a lot of attention; also the planes.

Thu 28 Dec - 217 - We Start Stamps - Felt tired all day, My legs bothering me. RW not leaving for school till after lunch. Bobby sorted all the German stamps. He got so he can recognize "Deutches Reich". RW not home till 2:30 AM or something. I couldn't sleep and so I had stayed up till 1:30 or so myself. Miserable sort of existence this waiting for the baby to arrive.

Mon 1 Jan 1951 - 221 - RW at School All Day - RW home about midnite & he got interested in the stamps & we both worked on his and Bobby's book till 1:30 AM. Having snack to eat, and so very late again retiring. Bad news fm Korea. This year is starting badly. How will it end?

Tue 2 Jan - 222 - RW decided to talk to Gerard about this Navy offer, afterwards to fill out application for it & write U of Utah reason for delay in his decision. So this took all morning. I typed up his letters. Bobby is feverish and fretting. I kept dosing him with aspirin. Managed to finish sorting stamps. This eve RW brot his enlarger down and analyzed film of action potentials on his cat's brain.

Tue 16 Jan - 236 - We Take Mom out for the Day - Picked up Mom 1 PM, to library first, then on to Field Museum by 3. Chinatown to Tai Dong's (where Gilbert had taken the U of C bunch) & Mom loved it! Then to see Technicolor movie "King Solomon's Mines" (really marvelous). So not taking Mom home till 10:30. Tucked Bobby into bed, hoping he'd sleep off this exciting day. But middle of night RW had to go sleep with him.

Fri 19 Jan - 239 - Mom called about noon to say she'd received a long letter fm Dad & could we come over. So we drove over there about 2 PM & I read the lengthy ltr, printed in Polish, in which

Dad reiterated his accusations. This eve RW & I did laundry; I washing, RW hanging.

Wed 31 Jan - 251 - We Go to Garfield Pk Conservatory - Deserted & we slowly browsed thru; cyclamens, cinerarias, poinsettias, begonias. The bromeliads I saw were lovely! RW, Bobby & I fooling around with our stamps.

Wed 7 Feb - 258 - We Pay Hospital Bill, 201.00 - At U of C to see Dr Riesen in Psych Bldg at 11. RW discussed his cat-kitten research w/ him. At Lying In waiting fm 1:30 to 3 before I could see Dr. Lane. While waiting, we talked to Ray Kjelberg & a couple other med students. My blood count okay. I fessed up I'd been taking feosol tablets right along.

Fri 9 Feb - 260 - We cash War Bonds - Dr Gerard's, Quadrangle Club - He & Bobby went to Marquette Bank & cashed our savings bonds (950.00 and a 75.00 interest gain). Dinner w/ Physiology students & faculty. Then out to Gerard's & we looked at color photos taken by Mrs G of Vermont & Nassau thru 3 dimension viewing specs. RW played a chess game. Gerard talked vaguely OSRD research at U of C that RW might be interested in. Home midnite. Snack, looking at Newfoundland stamps.

Sat 10 Feb - 261 - Dad & Mom Reconciled? - RW picking Bobby up at Mom's. Lunch & off to school. Dad over 3 PM. We talked about him & Mom, & I tried to straighten him out on his attitude. He wanted me to call Mom on phone, which I did. Upshot of it all was that she said he could come over & talk to her (Max away at movies). Called Mom at 6:30 & she said Dad was there; she was fixing supper for him! That he wants to make up & had given her 20.00 to buy herself a birthday gift. Later she called to say Dad told her he'd do anything for reconciliation. She sounded very happy. RW did dishes; put Bobby to bath & bed.

Sun 18 Feb - 269 - Dinner at Folks - To folks at 1:30. Dad very gay w/ few drinks in him. Dad brot out his old squeezebox & played. The boys (Ricky & Bobby) took turns trying to play it. I wasn't feeling too chipper, so we left at 5 PM. We soaked more U.S. stamps & sorted them. 11PM & I'm beginning to get my contractions. Owah & I w/ only 4 hours sleep last nite. RW & I discussed stocks & our desire to buy GM perhaps. He filled out his 1950 Income tax return.

Wed 21 Feb - 272 - Lying In, 154½ - We got up at 10. RW & Bobby went down to paint portholes & name "U.S.S.Utah" on the ship. Watered plants, etc. We left Bobby at Mom's at 1 & on to U of I for 2 PM seminar. RW made a 10 min report on work he is doing. We left after Scheibel's report. At U of C 3 or so. Saw Dr Dufour who assured me all was well.

Sat 24 Feb - 275 - I Try to Catch up on Sleep - RW had to be in school at noon & was gone when I awoke. RW home 7 PM. He did dishes after supper & I ironed 2 blouses and my maternity slip, sitting at ironing board. RW & Bobby played chess before Bobby went to bed. He does so enjoy his battleship & plays w/ it all day. 10:30 PM & I'm feeling uncomfortable. This has been a most uncomfortable pregnancy! Sat up till 2:30 w/ RW looking over stamps etc. I didn't fall sleep till 6.

Tue 27 Feb - 278 - Watchful Waiting - RW stayed home today. I went back to bed after brunch & somehow slept till 6 PM. In meantime RW & Bobby had vacuumed porch, cleaned under porch, vacuumed basement & attic. Pains off & on since I got up, but so far most irregular (11 PM). Do wish the baby would come & I could get it over with. These last 2 weeks have been a total loss for both RW & me; all these false alarms & no sleep for me.

Wed 28 Feb - 279 - The Baby is Born! - Awoke 6 AM with pains which persisted & seemed to gradually become more severe. Ate breakfast & awoke RW 9 AM to eat in case we had to go. Got Bobby up, too, & by this time I'd have to sit down when a pain came along. At 10 or so we really had to leave, dropping Bobby off at Mom's w/ his play ship. At hospital before 11 & we sat in car for a while as I smoked a cigarette & timed my pains. Still apprehensive it might be a false alarm. Finally inside & at register desk. (Forgot to mention had twinge of blood show at home which prompted me to go to hospital). Upstairs to 5th floor to get prepared for labor. Unpleasant intern examined me. Had met Dr. Lane in hallway & he greeted me. He had another "labor" going on at same time. By now it was noon & my pains were 8 - 10 min apart, but getting severe. Enema & they started more rapidly. Nurse remarked my cervix was thin & baby could come quickly.

In separate room w/ bedpan & RW beside me for an hour or so of increasingly more severe pain. About 1 PM Dr. Lane examined me & ordered a hypo & then all hell broke loose. They came at 3 - 2 - 1 minute intervals. Finally I could feel the baby's head. 3 interns beside me & they hurriedly (& guiltily, as tho late) gave me the saddle block. At 2 PM into Birth Room; 2:02 cries of baby, a girl, 7 lbs. 10 oz, 20" long. I think I'll never forget the details of her birth.

Thu 1 Mar 1951 - Had practically no sensation in my legs for hours yesterday, but back to normal today; & pain pills! They do the trick when you get those excruciating pains! Didn't get to see my baby till 2 PM today. Dr. Lane stopped in to see me & I told him bitterly he had failed in his promise of a painless birth. "All's well that ends well" was his sober reply. Baby sucks vigorously, think she resembles me, but oh, such long dark lashes! Called Mom. RW came to see me this eve w/ candy, mags, etc. He's a darling. Had gone down to buy GM stock, got 5000 VA life insurance, etc. He's having rugs picked up for cleaning & will start painting ceilings & molding in hall, LR, DR while I'm away.

Fri 2 Mar - III - Dr. Lane prescribed a cough syrup for me to relieve congestion in my throat. Really hurts deep down in stitches area when I cough. RW came tonite w/ news that his Am J Physiol paper had been returned for condensation & revision, too long! He had taken Mom & Bobby shopping today, then gone to school to do a dog experiment. Typical day at hospital: 6 AM, temp & pulse readings; babies in for 1st feeding & ravenously; sleep or try to; 8 AM breakfast, sponge bath, shower (but we never did go); 10:30 babies in, rest till lunch at 12; 2 PM babies in, sleep, try to read, doctor in; 5 PM supper; 6 PM babies again; 7:30 to 9 visiting hours; 10 PM babies in; 11 PM to sleep after pills, etc.

Sat 3 Mar - IV - Woke up during nite w/ pain & had to ring nite nurse for pain pills. Milk hasn't come into breasts yet, but my baby is really learning how to suckle. She's so much quieter than Bobby, falls asleep after nursing. The nursery feeds babies at 2-3 AM & we are not bothered w/ 2 AM feeding. RW over at 8. Navy finally notified him he qualified only for GS-9 rating, so Phila is out. He got a roll of DR wallpaper & paint & will start on DR. He goes to nursery every time he visits me & takes a look at our daughter. I really believe he's very much pleased w/ her. He's been so sweet coming out to see me nightly. Stops in to see Bobby daily, too. My sweet darling!

Sun 4 Mar - V - Wotta Day - Dr. Lane removed my outer stitches (3? only). Felt practically no pain whatsoever, marvelous. Every time I nurse Baby I get painful uterine contractions. Gads! RW over at 8 PM. Said he'd taken Bobby home this aft & given him bath & haircut. Is having trouble covering dark molding with white paint. To sleep 11; up 12:30 with such sharp pains. Had to ask ole frozen face nite nurse for pain pills again.

Mon 5 Mar - VI - We Get Gifts - Felt pretty miserable all day. Pains in uterus & vaginal canal. RW had stayed home & worked on his AJP paper while waiting for rugs pick up. Hopes to have decorating started tomorrow & finished by Fri aft when we have to leave hospital. I walked to nursery window w/ RW to look at Baby & had to return to bed in about 2 min time. Just can't stand! Complained to Dr. Lane that I felt terrible today. Have lumps in my breasts (says baby doesn't empty them). Tonight a treat, heat lap treatment for our sore "bottoms".

Wed 7 Mar - VIII - RW having trouble w/ paint job. Broker bot 20 shares GM's stock at 50 & he mailed him the $1000 + commission. Getting rather bored & tired of this hospital life. Food begins to pall on you; you worry if babies are getting proper care & I do miss Robert and Bobby.

Thu 8 Mar - IX - Went to pediatrics lecture & managed (to my surprise) to sit with not too great discomfort thru the 40 min talk. We can start babies on solids almost immediately & start them on cereal, veg, fruit & meat, anything we wish. RW over at U of C to watch an experiment & so visited me from 4:30 to 5. Says house is in terrible shape & maybe I should go to Mom for a few days. I dunno. Talked to Bobby & he was thrilled that we were coming home.

Fri 9 Mar - X - HOMECOMING - 7/7 3/4, 143 - After lunch we went to bath demonstration in lecture room & I feel I really learned a few tricks. After 2 PM nursing we hurried to get into our street clothes. RW came w/ baby clothes. I was weighed. RW paid rest of hospital bill, 31.65! (So it cost 75+201+31.65 to have our baby). Downstairs Mom & Bobby were waiting. Into car & at

Mom's till 9 PM. RW had windows open airing house after painting ceilings & fireplace. Home in a tearful state. I ached all over it seemed & everything was an effort! House all upset, furniture in BRs & on porch. Crawled into bed &, fortified w/ Empirin tablets, I prepared for the night. Baby very good so far.

CHAPTER XVII
The Move to Utah

Synopsis - This short Chapter forms a fitting ending, successful completion of the postwar struggle: a home, doctoral degree, new baby; and now a great transition, to another State, 1500 miles from family, to a newly built house, and the beginning of an academic career. The transition, of course, was somewhat hectic. Elizabeth took the normal time to recover from the horrendous trauma of giving birth, and was then plunged into the psychological trauma of selling the house over which we had labored so long and mightily. That was followed by the inevitable, although more tractable, trauma of moving, and trying to find a suitable home in unfamiliar surroundings. These stresses were met and happily resolved. The scene closes with a picture of domestic perfection, playing with the children on the living room rug [Fig 64], our years of turmoil finally translated into the long anticipated bliss, or at least as close to it as human beings allow themselves to come.

Sat 10 Mar - I Sleep Practically All Day - Waist 34" !? - 7/9 - Awoke 8. Baby up only at 1 & 5AM & then fell asleep nicely. What a contrast to Bobby when he was her age! RW fixed breakfast and supper. I got up to eat. Unable to sit for any length of time & so back to bed. We gave Mary Beth her sponge bath. RW joined me in bed to read till midnite. I keep nite lite on & so he slept w/ Bobby again.
Sun 11 Mar - The Koteks over - Mom - Mom took a bag full of laundry to be starched & ironed. RW started putting new wallpaper on W wall of DR.
Mon 12 Mar - 8 lbs - Grandpa & Grandma Doty over - Slept till 10. Men folks up already. Fed Baby 3 meals of cereal today. RW

putting LR & DR to order. Coaxed him into wiping floors & baseboard (how well, I don't know). I got up & fixed breaded pork tenderloin for us. Poor Bobby, I must get well so I can feed him properly. Poor RW busy doing dishes, then helping w/ bath. Then diapers, then douching me.

Tue 13 Mar - Navel Cord Comes Off - Baby Fusses - Mom over - Baby good during nite, up 3:30 & then 7:30 AM! RW working on letters to Davenport & plan re getting grant fm Cerebral Palsy Research Fund. I typed 3/4 hour. My back ached & I was a mess! Severe pains, 4 pills in 4 hours & blotto! Baby awake 3:30, then 4 AM; 4:30 AM & I have lamp on my sore bottom.

Thu 15 Mar - Grandma & Bobby Wash Clothes - The little darling had eaten so much cereal & peaches that when she nursed at the breast it just overflowed, so she needed a bath. My breasts are really so full, only one was enough. Mom & Bobby did some laundry to save RW job of washing diapers tonite. Poor dear, he's been up past midnite doing laundry every night this week. He didn't get home till 7:30.

Sat 17 Mar - Baby Fusses But Good! - 8 3/4 - RW home & busy all day. He & Bobby went to get groceries, then downstairs doing laundry, including DR chair seat covers, throw rugs. I managed to nap a bit, woke up to find bath & kitchen floors mopped. He had vacuumed my room earlier, now he was giving basement stairs & basement a cleanup. The darling has been so good at doing things about the house.

Sun 25 Mar - At Folks - Our First Outing - 10 lbs? - Bobby had gotten up to look for the eggs RW hid last nite & in turn had hidden some for RW to find! RW proofreading his revised paper for Am J Physiol.

Wed 28 Mar - I clean windows - Tend to Plants - Baby 4 weeks old today - In between tending to Baby I moved plants fm our bedroom window to DR windows. Cleaned inside of BR windows, DR, bath & kitchen. RW brot home some obstetrical books & I read a bit about saddle block and normal pregnancy and delivery.

Sun 1 Apr 1951 - April Fool's Day for Bobby - Bobby already playing April fool's jokes on his daddy & mama off & on during day; got so excited he didn't want to eat. RW making notes on lecture he's going to make week from Wed. Baby asleep 2:30 AM, & exhausted me, too!

Wed 11 Apr - 6 weeks old today - Mom over - Gen MacArthur relieved of his command as of 1am by Truman. RW taking care of Baby all evening, little fusser. I cut out pair trousers for little girl out of khaki shirt.

Thu 12 Apr - Mom over - I Straighten Pantry - 12/4? - I sewed up a sacque for Baby fm odds & ends of flannel. RW thought it looked very strange, too wide or something. All he's done is sit & sort his collection of stamps. Doesn't do a damn thing. Find myself all worked out just carrying for the little one, making meals & keeping the house in some sort of order. Sometimes I wonder if it's worth it.

Fri 13 Apr - 1st Postpartum Visit, 143 - Dr. Lane examined me internally, womb is tipped up towards left. He touched cervix w/ silver nitrate in view of vaginal discharge & told me to use vinegar douche 3X wk & to come in to see him before we leave town [i.e. before we move to Utah]. On way home my bottom started aching but good, could hardly stand all evening.

Fri 20 Apr - Mom over - Daffodils blooming - 12/10 - RW staying home today getting attic & basement & garage cleared of junk. Sold paper, rags, cardboard, old iron, old stove to junkman for 1.40. Returned empty bottles & got wine from liquor store.

Mon 23 Apr - Mom over - RW not home till midnite. My tenderness thru abdomen & perineal region increases & I was in quite a state of self-pity. So I complained of being stuck in the house all the time, etc. Baby had been a bit of a fusser, too, & that really got on my nerves. Mostly, I am perturbed over my inability to pitch in & do a good day's housework, to get the place cleaned up for when we put it up for sale.

Wed 25 Apr - 8 weeks - 13/0 - My pains in lower abdomen continue. By 4:30 PM I decided to call Dr. Lane. So he reassured my symptoms were quite normal, etc. I might be getting ready to menstruate.

Thu 26 Apr - Mom over - MacArthur in Chgo - 13/4 - RW miffed as he didn't get to leave early for school. Ran into MacArthur parade fm Airport to Loop. Mom & I had a big "altercation" w/ Bobby when he refused to obey either one of us. I'm in no physical condition to cope w/ him these days. I read book on Obstetrics & Gynecology by Adair. My "pressure" symptoms in the pelvic area continue & the varicose veins in legs are acting up. Yet I hesitate to go to hospital tomorrow. This might be a temporary condition. Will try a heat pad tonite. RW home 10. So I took my bath & vinegar douche & now 12:15 (early) am going to bed to see if I can get myself to feel better. RW & Baby fussing together. Wish I could get house straightened up.

Sun 29 Apr - Mom & Dad over - RW leaves for Cleveland - 13/7? - Bobby a bath & to bed, Baby a good girl all day, but not going to sleep till 1:30; at which time I took quick bath. My feet ache, but the other aches are sublimated to other considerations. Even ran Smokey [cat with neonatal extirpation of "visual" cortex] 10x in his psychological test.

Wed 2 May 1951 - RW Comes Home - Baby 9 weeks old - Letter fm RW saying he might try to come home tonite. I started pinning DR drapes this eve; at it when RW called 10 PM fm Englewood Station, so he was home 11 PM. RW brot Bobby a small chemistry set.

Mon 7 May - Mom over - Busy Day - RW home 7. He looked at 2 houses & is convinced we should get $16,000 for ours. So this eve washed kitchen down. I did blinds & some of the woodwork. We got thru 1 AM.

Tue 8 May - Bobby Bad Boy - Bobby dropped ½ gal milk carrying it in this AM, broken glass allover porch steps. Later in day he messed up garage but good w/ Georgie, throwing sand at one another. Also wrote on front porch w/ chalk. Oh my! Mom did all my ironing. I waxed LR, DR furniture, scratch remover on dark woodwork. So much more work to be done. RW brot 3 more kittens home after operating.

Wed 9 May - Mom over - Baby 10 weeks old today - Mom over at noon, so while she took care of Baby I did laundry. Straightened up open part of basement, mopped floors, dusted. Cleaned out loose mortar fm fruit cellar room, mopped basement floor. Worked like a dog. RW home 6 & told me I was psychotic for doing all this work!?! Anyway, stairs to attic & basement are washed. He painted back screen door gray. After supper I felt punk; too much bending & stuff, I guess. RW took kittens to school, Tcherina wouldn't nurse them. I'm angry at him. I work like a fool & he relaxes & after I do the work, he says he was just getting ready to do it, hah!

Fri 11 May - 2nd visit to Hospital - 136 - 14/8 - So after RW straightened garage (sand spilled by Bobby), we left. At Lying In 2:15; RW off to see the boys in Physiology & didn't come back for me tell 4:30. I waited till 3:30 to see Dr. Lane. So it seems the cervix erosion is not serious, another application silver nitrate. The other aches are due to nerves injured or blood vessels not uniting after episiotomy wound has healed. Guess I was his last patient, because we talked a bit; said he'd been in Salt Lake City & thot it the cleanest City he'd been in; that we'd really live there instead of existing as in Chgo. I waxed kitchen floor. We did laundry; RW painted screen door one more coat. The ad inserted in Trib for Sun.

Sun 13 May - Our ad gets 2 responses only - Mother's Day - We got only 2 calls and 1 fm RE firm re our Sun Trib ad. Mother's Day, or our price the reason?

Mon 14 May - So we got a few more calls re ad today, but nobody came out to see us. RW inserted ad in Sun Herald for this Thu, only 1.30 for 4 lines, left out price this time. Feeling very tense & after the children were asleep & I had a hot bath, RW & I tried to resume our former intimacies, but I guess I'm not ready yet. Hurts. But the former pain seems to have disappeared & the vaginal discharge has lessened. So I guess my visit Friday was really worth while.

Thu 17 May - Our 1st Customers re House - Mom over - 7 PM our 1st people came & RW showed them thru house. The man was very much interested, but the old gal demurred; another old gal came over to look, too.

Sun 20 May - M - Awoke to find myself flowing & felt miserable all day. Several phone calls re Southtown Economist ad, but only one man out to see house. RW pretty much disgusted that we haven't sold house yet. Told him I thought we should wait till 1st of June before placing w/ RE agents. So here I am at midnite drinking martini sans olive & trying to figure out what to do. Sale of house, our move to SLCity really has me pretty much upset.

Mon 21 May - M - Mom over - 15/0 - A very busy day for me - Few phone calls re ad. RW left for school to do an experiment, not home yet 1 AM. Mom over just as RW was giving Bobby a good spanking for riding bike out into street. Had 3 RE agents today. They assured me they could get $16,000, so? Poor Bobby had to stay home all day; his buttocks are black & blue fm spanking.

Wed 23 May - M - Mom over - 1st offer for House $15,500 - Phone call this a.m. that Mr Clancy (husband of woman out yesterday) would be out & RW said we'd take 16,000 & when Mr. C. came, he offered 15,500 & RW refused it - so that ended that. I'm beginning to think we'll have to call in the RE boys. Feeling rather disgusted and out of sorts. Gad, I'm anxious to get this house deal all straightened out.

Tue 29 May - We Leave for Lake Geneva [Wisconsin] - Visit Bess - RW up very early, cut grass, took kittens to school. Finally leaving at 1, flat tire. At Geneva [where Doty parents now lived] by 5:45. Dad showed me his garden. Baby behaving very nicely.

Wed 30 May - Motor Boating on Lake Geneva - RW & Bobby off for boat ride. Exhilarating to be in Rich's big boat. Lake is large & you really can get around. We ogled the big estate homes on water's edge, wonderful! Bobby just loves the water & had a "floating" feeling when he got into bed. Baby put up a bit of a fuss & RW & I couldn't get to sleep till 2:30 AM. Be glad to be home.

Sun 3 Jun - Mom & Dad over - 16/0 - RW wrote a letter of recommendation for Frank Shepherd re admission to Kentucky Bar. Drafting formal application for research funds from Cerebral Palsy Fund.

Wed 6 Jun - 14 weeks old - That RWD! To think we could have sold the house 2 wks ago! I transplanted some white mums along fence to replace those I'd given to Mom & Dad (& now I find Mom gave them away to their neighbors!) Boy! maybe it will be good to be away from the family! RW working on correcting galley proofs of his paper on reflex deglutition.

Sat 9 Jun - First Prospect & Brought by RE - 16/8 - Embarrassing in a way; 10:30 AM agent w/ 4 adults & child coming to look at our house. Had them look at outside basement while we tidied up beds. He called back later to say they were interested. RW told them we'd take 16M clear. Bobby stayed up to wait for his father. We played "Petrouchka", "Peter & the Wolf", Grieg's A Minor. I sewed on blouse & managed to get it all finished. Bummer wide awake till 1 AM. 2 AM, RW has finished running his cats.

Mon 11 Jun - 1st GM dividend 20.00 - RW stayed home all day, not leaving for school till 8 PM. We had a number of phone calls & a RE agent come out to look at the place. RW to school w/ Mimi to do a unilateral removal of her visual cortex. Brot her home midnite w/ comment he did a very neat job.

Tue 12 Jun - Mom over - Don't know why but I'm so impatient to pull out of Chicago, maybe there is a streak of adventure in me at that. Oh, for a lucky break to sell the house before the end of June so I can relax and do as I please. This constant waiting & expectancy is getting me down.

Fri 15 Jun - Max over - Chadwick & Strauss had their man out this aft & he gave us quite a spiel. Wanted 15 day exclusive. Turned him down on that. RW leaving for school 3 PM to do a dog. Max over 6:30. We discussed stocks & bonds & business in general. At it when RW came home at 10. His dog didn't last, so we sat up & talked of this & that; our bum luck in unloading this house. Max finally left at 12:30 AM after bottle of beer. I had had 2 glasses of wine & felt really romantic. RW obliged.

Sun 24 Jun - "Il Trovatore", "I Pagliacci" - Had RW drive Bobby, Baby & me to Mom's 1:30 PM. So we went to the operas, enjoyed them both immensely. Not just opera films on stage, but with background scenes to interpret the story with English narration & subtitles. Il Trovatore dramatic and enjoyable. Pagliacci a real climax! Wonderful catharsis for bottled up emotions. Home. Sewed a bit, talked. Romancing w/ my darling.

Wed 4 Jul 1951 - Real Estate Deals, Phooey! - 18 weeks old - At 2 sharp Delaney showed up, then Mr Master, wife & 6 mos old boy, to be joined by 3 Clancey's (construction people). So they toured the house thoroly. Delaney & Master sat down to talk terms etc & it developed Master didn't have the money for down payment even. So they all left at 4:30 PM. Nuts! So I sewed. Got red striped seersucker pretty much finished. RW helped Bobby light some sparklers. He'd been shooting caps as his way of celebrating the 4th!

Thu 5 Jul - We Give Delaney an exclusive - Schechel showed up asking for 10 day exclusive. Called RW & he agreed. They want to have an open house this Sun & I reluctantly agreed. With RW away till very late it's hard to do much in the evenings as I have two babies to put to bed.

Sat 7 Jul - Scheibels out this evening - Dr [Arnold] Scheibel & wife [Madge] out from Evanston 8:30 & stayed till 2 AM. Showed them our house & grounds. They watched RW put kittens thru their discrimination tests. We drank remaining bottle of champagne, sandwiches & milk. Baby & Bobby behaved nicely.

Wed 18 Jul - M - Baby 20 wks old, 18 lbs, loss wt? - Up 9:30 AM when Moeller called to say Talman appraiser gave $10,000 mtge on house; he'd be over 2PM w/ $1000 check as earnest money. He had $500 cash & we gave him receipt, will throw in range & refrigerator.

Thu 19 Jul - M - The Boyntons sign contract - Daughter apparently liked house okay. We got cashier's check for $1500. We signed contract. Moeller brot some beer & we sat on back porch & talked.

Tue 24 Jul - Didn't go to sleep till 3 AM. RW leaving 11:30 for school to sit in on human brain operation, subject prone to epileptic seizures, excision of areas producing same on stimulation, using RW's stimulator. Moeller & party stopped by to say their mtge application approved & they were going to sign it today.

Thu 26 Jul - A-Buggying - Hot, sticky, humid but good! Baby feeling the heat, too. RW off to school, planning to return late. Special Delivery airmail from Dr Davenport telling RW faculty housing (not very elegant) would be available & no need to make trip next week. Buggying to Kedzie & 63rd. Ice cream bar for Bobby as reward for watching Baby while I shopped in stores. Home. This evening finished my rayon suit, buttons, seams. We typed letters to Dr Davenport, Dr Farber re CP Research funds.

Fri 27 Jul - Baby gets Crib - We see Jose Ferrar in "Cyrano" - A fine performance and most entertaining. Out 10 & home 30 min later to pick up our 2 darlings from Grandma. So, eating at

650

home, washing supper dishes, now relaxing over martinis w/ RW.

Sun 29 Jul - "Joan of Arc" w/ Max - At Folks - We took Bobby & Max w/ us to "Joan of Arc". Interesting, could have moved a bit faster. Back at 10:30, picked up our darling daughter & home to eat a bit. Didn't get to bed till 1:30 AM, after reading last wks Newsweek. RW boning up on Joan of Arc in Guizot's "History of France".

Wed 1 Aug 1951 - Baby 22 wks old - We Start to Pack - Slept till noon again. Mess of laundry, including 5 starched dresses. RW sent in notices to all our mags re change of address. I got a lot of Army barracks bags & stuff I'm going to wash out preparatory to our moving. It's 3 AM. I got jacket all finished except for finishing & buttonholes; so much to do & so little time to do it in.

Sun 5 Aug - Opera Films, Faust, Carmen, Don Pasquale - Slept till noon. RW ran his cats & about 3 PM out at Mom's. RW off to operate on Merchelle's kittens. He returned 6:30 & we took off to our Opera movies. "Faust" rather good, Opera by Gounod. Baby had been very good, cared for by Grandpa.

Mon 6 Aug - RW & I Start Packing - RW busy with his cats. Fluffy's yellow male kitten thriving, eyes open. He's "Tigger" and Merchelle's black striped male kitten still alive & improving. He's "Jigger". M still in garage & nurses kittens nicely. I spent several hours mounting photos of Bobby and Baby. Then packed all photos in box, threw out old mags, recipes, etc. RW emptied 2 drawers of his chest, packing clothes in barracks bags. He has attic stuff pretty well underway, too. To bed 3 AM RW and I.

Fri 10 Aug - Bobby & RW in Loop - They left at 10, visited stock broker's office & RW placed order for 100 shares Utah-Idaho Sugar @ 3; 50 sh Belden Mfg @ 18.00. Up on top Board of Trade Bldg for a view of city. I was busy with laundry. Did manage to sew up another sundress for Baby. RW packed good china glassware in barrel; also my pottery in bushel basket. Then, instead of doing more, he read. We got into a misunderstanding when he & I disagreed about sightseeing mountains etc. on our trip to Utah. So to bed w/o speaking.

Sun 12 Aug - I Wash Drapes etc all day - So Mr D is very aloof. Left for his lab & didn't return till midnite. I laundered baby's diapers, BR & DR drapes & other odds & ends, including 3 scatter rugs. My pulley broke & I really had a time of it.

Mon 13 Aug - Another Working Day - RW home 7ish. Grisette est morte! Seems she hemorrhaged badly when he operated on her today. RW shows no inclination to pack or do anything to help me get things set & is only 9 days to the 22nd. I feel like crying. Feel so tired & so unjustly treated. He starts these things & then we're both miserable.

Tue 14 Aug - Mom over - Robert packs - RW deciding to stay home after our reconciliation last nite. So RW packed records, one crate of books. Got Bobby's toys sorted out & packed. Photographs, lamp bases, etc. I cleaned out desk drawers & emptied out shelves of clothes closets. Mopped bath, kitchen & porch floors. Baby a sweetheart.

Fri 17 Aug - M - RE Deal Closed - $9959 - RW getting busy with the basement, throwing out junk & starting to pack. Our mortgage almost $4,000, so we got check for almost $10,000. Stopped at a tavern & RW treated to drinks. The Boyntons are to come Sun at 4 PM to look at stuff we'd like to sell, porch furniture, lawnmower.

Sun 19 Aug - M - The Boyntons Buy our Odds & Ends, 50.00 - Mr Moeller over w/ Tess & Rodney Boynton & RW showed them the lawnmower, rake, spade, etc, which we wanted to leave behind. Surprisingly, they did give us 50.00 for same, no profit in it for us, but it does simplify storage problem. Gave away the balance of houseplants.

Tue 21 Aug - Busy Packing - M Day Minus 1 - RW & Bobby off to school w/ cats which will be airfreighted to Utah later. RW busy packing things in his lab. I had been busy vacuuming the rugs. After supper RW fixed his top carrier on car, using cot spring & lashing on footlocker, tire, etc. Keep thinking 5 yrs ago moving into this house, 10 years ago getting ready to get married.

Wed 22 Aug - M Day - We Move! - Up at 7 AM. RW took Baby to Mom's. The movers over after 9 AM. Josephine gave me a Mexican Boy pottery with an aloe, a book "Imitation of Christ". About 1:30 PM I had RW drive me to Mom's. Movers didn't finish till 2:30. Our furniture will only run 5100 lbs, not 7200 as originally figured. So 9 PM, Baby & Bobby bathed we're sitting around visiting. RW wants to start early tomorrow.

Thu 23 Aug - Iowa - 430 miles to Corning - Somehow we got up 5:30 & had hearty breakfast w/ folks, red eyed from little sleep. Baby fussed during nite. We left, our car really loaded down. Got to Bess' w/ Mom about 8 AM. Fed Baby there. Bess gave me Ricky's 1st red corduroy pants for Baby as it was cool out. So we left Chicago & its environs. Took it easy at first, but RW opened her up as we hit the road. Big thrill crossing muddy Mississippi at Moline, Ill - Muscatine, Ia, a dirty river town. We had lunch & bot Baby more Kleinert's diapers & a plastic bib. Rolling hills of Iowa. Milkshakes at Oscaloosa. On to Corning, Ia to RW's Aunt Teed [my stepmother's sister, whom I had once visited ca 15 years previously] & Mike. Got there around suppertime & they took us to a Church supper under canvas. Bobby got to ride a pony. They're very nice people. Teed so much like RW's mother. They put us up in twin beds, Bobby on Army cot. Baby in her bassinet. So tired, we really slept!

Fri 24 Aug - Nebraska - Raining when we got up, so our visit to Wayne's farm off as we'd get stuck in mud. Up & down hills of Iowa, crossed over toll bridge into Nebraska & saw more of it than we care to again, long sweeping rolling hills & lots of barren flatland. Stopped at Lincoln for lunch. Nice capitol bldg. At McCook for the nite in a modern tourist home, basement room w/ dble & single bed & own shower, 5.00.

Sat 25 Aug - Colorado - Rocky Mt National Park - RW really had the road to himself. Getting up high, too, & it reminded us of Cheyenne, flat barren land w/ low clouds overhead. The scene changed as we got into Colorado. In Greeley about noon & we shopped at Super Market for groceries & had a picnic lunch on the roadside. Got to Estes Pk 3 or so, RW got a reservation at Bear Lake Lodge. I really had my heart in my mouth when RW started his mountain driving. We have a 2 bed cabin w/ lights, steam heat, hot & cold running water, 2 meals at Lodge. We hiked around the Lake before supper. RW took a few pics [Figs 60. 61]. All of us rather tired. RW & Bobby going on Chuck wagon breakfast at 6 AM tomorrow.

Sun 26 Aug - Colorado - We cross the mountains - Their

breakfast hike on horseback started 6 AM & they didn't return till 10:45! Worried; they <u>merely</u> went up one side of mountain & down another! I breakfasted at Lodge w/ Baby who fussed all the time. So hurriedly getting underway at 11. Descent to Estes Park where we got more diapers for Baby. Then US 34 winding thru Rockies. Scenic, splendid, spectacular & <u>so</u> scary for me! Finally getting to US 40, but even there more mountainous country. We stopped on a high meadow for lunch on Greeley, Colo supplies. Kept on driving until we got to Craig, Colo. Just 2 mi out we got a flat. RW changed tire 6 PM. In town taking a large motel with kitchen, bath & upstairs room, 8.00. I washed a few things before retiring. Even little Bum slept nicely.

Mon 27 Aug - Salt Lake City, Mid Aft - Up early, 6:30. RW off to get milk & we breakfasted on bananas, milk & cheese sandwiches. On our way at 8. Drove thru country like Cheyenne for a while. Crossed another mountain pass in Wasatch mountains in Utah. Utah more barren, mesa-like country, greener as we approached SLC. RW, being difficult, took road thru Emigration Canyon to get to University quicker. We got lost trying to find Cancer Research wing. Found it & met Dr. & Mrs. Davenport. Visited w/ them in office for a while. Mix up about our Stadium Village place, RW taking care of details. We got into a Lunt Motel w/ kitchen, nice bath, 2 BRs @ 7.00 per day! So we are set for a while. Supper at <u>home</u>.

Tue 28 Aug - Baby 6 mos old today! - I Do Laundry - We Look at Houses - RW & Bobby off to unload our car top. I bathed Baby, me, did all our dirty laundry; messes of it, but it dried nicely in screened back porch & large closet. 2 PM going w/ RE man to look at 4-5 houses, narrow lots, no basement to speak of & 3rd BR a <u>porch</u>! Baby beginning to eat her cereal; so off schedule during trip, would only nurse.

Wed 29 Aug - Our Furniture Arrives - I iron today - The driver came to motel. RW went w/ him to pay cash 543.00 for moving; also to put furniture in storage. RW & Bobby 2 PM off w/ van to unload boxes & furniture we'll use in Stadium Village. RW came to say we could move into our apt. Till 8 setting up beds & moving furniture around. It'll be a tight squeeze, but I think we'll manage, a BR for our furn; a ½ room for our nursery & Bobby's playroom & chest; cot in LR, kitchen. Shower stall surprisingly clean. RW & Bobby and Baby asleep, 11:40 PM & I just finished laundry & dishes.

Thu 30 Aug - Our 10th Anniversary - 1566 Delta St, Apt 3, Stadium Village - Baby cuts a tooth! - Leisurely breakfasting and getting ready to vacate Lunt's Motel. I put up curtains of a sort on all the windows, beginning to look like a home. It will do, but it's pretty much of a makeshift affair. What will the next 10 years bring?

Fri 31 Aug - We Look for Houses w/ Mr Chavré - RW looking thru newspaper for owner listings. Prices seem to be about that in Chicago.

Sat 1 Sep 1951 - House Hunting - RW off early to lab to talk to Dr. Davenport re research funds. Out to look at houses advertised by owners. Most of them a disappointment in price or layout. Really getting to know the town driving about. Came home to find note from Chavré that he's found us a "wonderful" home we'll see tomorrow.

Sun 2 Sep - HOUSE HUNTING - Coming to conclusion old homes not for us in view of resale probabilities. Something about a new home that gets you. I did up a bit of wash before retiring.

Mon 3 Sep - We Go House Hunting again - "Bum" fussed during nite. Up to lab for hour & I typed RW's reply to Dr. Farber re research grant. He'll have a new, light lab room for his research. Up in the mountains in the County looking at new homes. Bobby all excited about going to school.

Wed 5 Sep - The Cats arrive - House Hunting - Stopped at lab to look at cats. Tcherina seems to be the only one to recognize us. After we fed them, they seemed normal. Tigger is a fluffy yellow one.

Thu 6 Sep - Dr Stein Baby Sits - We Go to Borison's - RW took Bobby to Wasatch School to enroll him. The bus will pick him up & bring him back. So I did laundry, straightened up. Unexpectedly I got guests for lunch. RW brot home Dr Stein of Ill, his son Allan, 4, Don MacKay (Britisher RW went to Cleveland with) & Ross Dugan, the neurosurgeon at Ill [all from McCulloch lab]. We were invited to Borison's for buffet supper. Dr. Stein volunteered to stay w/ children. So we got dressed and RW picked him

655

up & Allan; the latter fell asleep on cot. We left at 8, back by 10. The Borison's had a lot of people from Columbia U there, also a Dr Goodman who is head of Pharmacology here & who is rather overbearing.

Fri 7 Sep - Bobby's 1st day Kindergarten - Up 8:30, RW off to Physiology sessions [Fall meeting of Amer Physiological Soc being held at Utah]. I bathed Baby, did laundry. We put Bobby on bus 12:35. Waited fm 3:30 on to see Bobby get off bus. Seems quite enthusiastic about school and I'm glad.

Sun 9 Sep - Tschirgi & Taylor [From U of Chicago Physiology Dept] for Dinner - House Hunting - Bobby went to the LDS Sunday School at Institute of Religion at 9. RW off to pick up T & T & locate them in a motel & bring them back for a spaghetti dinner, which they ate w/ relish. We got out of entertaining them all day by announcing we were going house hunting, so dropped them at their motel at 2:30 PM. Looked at houses, new ones, mostly. The light airy feeling of a new home appeals to me.

Tue 18 Sep - We Try to Buy in Holladay - Reluctantly up 9 AM, RW off to lab to run his cats. We looked again at our Prince stone 5½ room house w/ 2 car attached garage. The decorating very trite, but the location, on top of a hill w/ wonderful view of Mt Olympus & valley, 140'x120' lot (½ acre) appealed to me [Figs 62, 63]. Decided to submit written offer. Chavré to let us know tonite. At 9 he came out to say he talked to owner-builder & he wants his 21,500 for it. But he'll work on it, so we'll see.

Wed 19 Sep - We Buy House for 20,000! - RW home at noon with Chavré to say Sutherland would take $20,000 for it & redecorate the LR & Bedrooms. So new contract drawn up. We will assume owner's FHA loan & save loan expenses that way. Chavré is to give us names of 2 dealers we can buy range & refrig at 25% discount. Nightly we're teaching Bobby "rummy", he seems to like it.

Wed 26 Sep - RW calls Dr Bosma re Baby - Mary Beth seemed okay in morning, but as the day progressed she squirmed & fussed and then just cried, nothing would soothe her. RW went out to call Dr Borison re name of pediatrician. Dr B suggested he call Dr Bosma (head of pediatrics here in U of U) & he came out to house (professional courtesy) & gave Mary Beth a thoro exam.

Her throat just brick red, virus infection. He prescribed aureomycin & aspirin & I began at 10:30 PM when her rectal temp was 102.4! 101.6 at 12:30 AM.

Sat 29 Sep - We Go Look at House - Baby much better today. I continue medicine & she manages to avoid most of it. Did a really big wash today. Stopped 1st at lab to see RW's new cat Sheba. She is a silverish cat [Fig 66], very lovely. Tigger is just adorable, Cherina the black panther type. The rooms will look nice. The jerk hasn't cleared the lot of all the rubble as yet.

Mon 1 Oct 1951 - We Close the RE Deal - At 3 PM paying $9500 more (total 10M) & assuming Sutherland's mtge of 10M. Kept back $200 until he grades, replaces brick. Chavré there. Says he's going moose hunting for a month, so we won't see him for a while. Drove out to house this eve with load of stuff & looked at wallpaper. I shudder to think of the work involved before everything is set. So much to be landscaped, too.

Tue 2 Oct - The Rains Come! - No different than Chicago when it pours. Wonder why they don't put any gutters on their houses? I'll be glad to get out of Stadium Village. Not having my washing machine is really a headache. Now that we've signed the papers, paid the money, we're beginning to have qualms about the house. Perfectly normal reaction, tho, I guess.

Wed 3 Oct - Poor Bobby, he's going to miss going to school. Holladay has no kindergarten & he can't be in 1st grade until he's 6! I am mad! Back home he could start 1st grade in Feb! We drove out to house this eve. What a mess! Mud all over the place, dirty inside, cold, cheerless

Thu 4 Oct - We Move! - Mud all over sidewalk, driveway. RW back to Stadium Village & to buy hose & shovel. The movers came & they squawked about mud. Baby crying, Bobby in everything. Screws for piano missing, etc.; everything dusty & needing attention. Range & refrig connected up before we came. Anyway, by nightfall we had beds up & some dishes put away. Windows dirty, mud, dust everywhere. No streetlights out here. Very quiet after dark. I suppose it'll be okay when we get settled.

Fri 5 Oct - RW had gotten stuck in mud when he ran off driveway yesterday. So today he really fixed it with wooden stakes to outline edges. Wonderful to have my washing machine again. So many things to wash, too. Venetian blind man out this aft.

Sat 6 Oct - Bedrooms straightened up - As usual RW off to lab to run his cats. Brot back Turka's 2 kittens for extra nourishment (she'd been neglecting them), but they died. Today got bedrooms wiped down, rugs laid; also hall mopped up.

Sun 7 Oct - We Work All Day - RW & Bobby off to lab this AM & not back till 1:30 PM. After dinner, after laundry, we worked on LR picture window, scraping paint and scrubbing! What a job! Getting real bitter at Chavré re house. House itself okay, but we should have insisted on cleanup job. After supper mopped LR floor, laid our 2 rugs, set furniture up. Scrubbed tile sills all about the house & that is an improvement. So tired my arms, my shoulders. Baby a fusser, Bobby falling all over things.

Mon 8 Oct - M - Kids - Hornets - Phooey! - Bright sunshine, so I took Baby out on driveway in swing & w/Bobby amusing her I tried to wash outside the basement windows. What a mess the grounds are, bricks, rubble, clay! Hornets buzzing around & one got in kitchen. In killing it I killed my little houseplant seedlings. Owah! RW angry because I want furniture rearranged.

Tue 9 Oct - M - Order Blinds - Then Sutherland stopped by & I gave him list of complaints. Peeling cement plaster on foundation, doors, dishwasher, debris. Tonite decided to clean up basement. Hosed down same after good sweeping. So we were at it until midnite, but it'll be cleaner.

Wed 10 Oct - M - It Rains! - I went down to do up a really big wash. Hadn't washed yesterday & ME had wet 3 bedsheets for us! Sutherland was expected to come & fix doors, but didn't. Bobby having a wonderful time playing w/kids. Have to watch them, they started a bonfire w/ dry weeds! Busy moving furniture in LR to my taste. RW had to admit it was better than he had set it up. Unpacked barrel of dishes & tried to use dishwasher to do them up.

Thu 11 Oct - M - We Go Shopping Downtown - Home at six to find Mrs. Davenport had left 3 potted red geraniums on our back porch! RW painting name & address on our rural mailbox.

Tue 16 Oct - Busy Day - RW off to school early. He got his re-

658

search funds certified to U & so made out list of purchases. Not home till after 6.

Sun 21 Oct - Slept till 11 AM Baby & I. It had been snowing this AM & Mt Olympus was white [Fig 63]. RW & Bobby off to lab. We'd taken some indoor pics of Baby & they developed the roll of film before returning at 4:30 PM. Had stopped at a farm & gotten 10 lbs. of potatoes for 2.00, jug cider & some golden delicious apples. We measured LR windows, kitchen windows re getting drapery material.

Fri 2 Nov 1951 - Baby finished the night sleeping w/ us. Re fence, $700 for link fence installed; $350 for materials alone. I suggested Rosa Multiflora, but RW vetoes it. He makes me sick at times wanting his way <u>all</u> the time! Today I really feel blue & neglected and lonely. Really feel isolated and incommunicado these cold days. Sent pics of Baby to folks in letter.

Sat 3 Nov - Busy day changing bed linens, big laundry. RW home at 2. We shopped in Holladay. Wanted him to drive me to Safeway, altercation when he protested "chauffeuring" me around. So we don't have enough groceries for week. However, this eve he dried mess of prints of Baby & house. So we made up before the day was over. Old silliness gets me so mad I'm ready to sack & go home to Mama, only Bobby and the Baby have to be considered.

Sun 4 Nov - At Lab - So we watched RW run his cats & feed the bunch. Leafed thru catalogs & BH&G re nursery stock. I do believe we should wait till spring for our major planting. "Bum" as usual not going to sleep till after 10 PM. Even then she awoke 2AM for diaper change & nursing.

Mon 5 Nov - My 4 Fr Budded Lilacs Come! - Mailman brot my lilac shrublings: so I'm soaking them in tub downstairs.

Thu 15 Nov - We Buy Lumber for Fence - Got cedar post four corners, red oil stain, creosote. 83.90 worth! The fence will cost $200!

Fri 16 Nov - Lumber Comes - Traverse Rods - Bobby played in very nicely. He's numbering pages of his coloring book, cutting out objects, pasting them on paper & printing name under said object! Also plays records. Baby quite a little girl, yells for attention so strong. She'll be walking soon w/o holding on. Lumber

659

came about 5 PM, lengths not right etc. RW will have to do sawing. This eve Bobby & RW made up one section of fence in basement. RW finally got water to stop leaking fm his hose outlet pipe.

Thu 22 Nov - No Turkey for us - I Sew on Drapes - RW off to feed his cats, while I straightened up. Baked a layer cake for our "dinner". Put candles on it as my birthday cake. Baby's eyes opened wide when candles were lit! She cried when Bobby blew them out for me. Want to write folks before retiring. Such a drab Thanksgiving Day!

Fri 23 Nov - I am 36 Today! - Busy with odds & ends as usual, laundry. I keep poor Bobby in to keep Baby amused while I get my house work done. Surprised pleasantly to get birthday greeting card fm Mom Doty. I did manage to finish the 1st half of the LR pic window draw drapes. We hung them up and I was mortified to see the stretched last panel droop so, the bottoms are uneven. I measured and tore each length separately! In sewing they stretched.

Sun 25 Nov - At Lab - Taking Pictures - RW going out to take pics of house and snow-covered mts. Bobby out wading in snow w/ his boots & getting all wet and dirty. Light lunch & leaving for lab at 2. Found the Davenports there & we chatted w/ Mrs D while she injected her mice. Watching RW run his cats. Fixing supper, retiring to our LR now that our picture window has drapes. We need more lamps, tables. Baby playing on rug. RW playing piano records, 9 PM & I'm sleepy.

Mon 26 Nov - I Finish Big Draw Drapes - This eve I sewed up hem of pic window draw drapes, pressed them a bit & we hung them up for good. They do look impressive; a BH&G LR RW says.

Fri 7 Dec - M - Pearl Harbor 10 years ago today! - Somehow Mary slept thru the night (or perhaps she cried & we didn't hear her). She fell out of bed this AM after I nursed her! RW shoveled driveway & off to lab 9:30. Laundry today. Just blah & lay down w/ kids for rest. RW and Bobby out to drive in 3 more fence posts.

Sun 9 Dec - M - We Go to Lab - 22 lbs? - Bobby & RW working on gate near irrigation this AM, got posts in for driveway. After our dinner, we all rode w/ RW to lab. He had to clean cats' cages. Only ran Alaric & Sabu II. Alaric is getting real perky & he is a beautiful cat! Mary crawls all over LR & from room to room!

Mon 10 Dec - Bobby loses tooth - Xmas Package from Folks! - Morning glory blooms! A deep red, lovely; took it as a good omen. Baby behaved nicely all day, ate her food even! I even found time to play piano, becoming acquainted with the keyboard. My hands feel tight after pounding away, tho.

Tue 11 Dec - This aft I tried to make some chocolate fudge and it wouldn't harden! Tried a batch of honey cookies & they burned to a crisp! Guess I have to alter recipes for this "high altitude". RW home later than usual and I worried. The roads have been icy & snow covered. Mary Beth stands up in her high chair and yells for attention! Cute as a button, but oh what a little pest.

Tue 18 Dec - Glad to get 3 letters today. Played some more major chords on piano. Bobby really plays with his plastic horsemen all over the LR. Bobby printed a longish letter to Grandma again. Big news on radio that the Reds have given the UN forces a list of UN prisoners they hold, many names being broadcast all evening.

Fri 21 Dec - The Sun Shines! - Bobby & Mary tearing apart old copies of Life, I practising chords on the piano. Surprisingly well in playing w/ right or left hand, but coordination! So Bobby started picking up torn papers into wastebasket w/ Mary right beside him also putting papers into basket!

Tue 25 Dec - Bobby Overjoyed by Toys ! - We slept late, but Bobby up at 8; of course, he found the brown plastic soldiers, machine guns, tank, etc. set up around tree! What a happy boy! Mary got her doll fm us & this was greeted with extreme fear & flight. RW off to school, returning at 4:30. After supper RW playing w/ Bobby. Mary wanting her brother's toys & grabbing for them every chance. RW taking photoflood pics tonight [Fig 64].

Thu 27 Dec - Bobby 6 yrs old - Mary 10 mos old - Woke up to find Auntie Bess' "Alice in Wonderland" story book & coloring books on his bed. I gave him his box of Circus Stationery in the aft & he started a "thank you" note to Grandma, but wrote so badly with his pen he got discouraged. After supper we lit candles

661

on Bobby's birthday cake. Mary's little eyes just popped. Bobby blew them out w/ one blow. Then RW gave him his pop-pistol & is he good at shooting men off horses! After that a haircut, a bath & then we all played Pirates & Travelers. Bobby won & of course that made him happy. He said seriously "you give me all these things & there is nothing I can give you". He had a fine birthday!

Fri 28 Dec - Mary fell out of highchair before breakfast, then bumped her chin on playpen bars. BH&G and Country Gentlemen mags came & just chock full of nursery ads. RW hung up our front gate before leaving for lab this AM. This evening RW & Bobby played with pop gun, shooting down one another's soldiers & horses.

Sat 29 Dec - Busy Day - We slept till 11. RW off to lab already. Did laundry with Mary in her swing in basement. RW & Bobby sawing up more lumber for fence. In LR children playing on rug, Xmas tree lit up. RW read Bobby his "Alice in Wonderland" story book. I spent evening looking over mags for nursery ads. We'll need a surprising amount of stuff to "landscape" our grounds.

Sun 30 Dec - Bobby loses another upper incisor - The Davenports over, <u>phlegmatic</u> - I tidied up, bathed my darling daughter on a sun drenched table by kitchen window [e.g., Fig 65]. RW worked on fence [Fig 62] until after 4 when the D's came. So we showed them thru the house, Bobby exhibited his toys. We ate: raw oysters & beer; oyster stew. Retired to LR for small talk. They left at 8, to RW & my relief, for the time had been dragging. Dishwasher came in handy to do up my good dishes. We three played Travelers & Pirates, Bobby won again & did he love it!

Mon 31 Dec - New Year's Eve - About 12" snow on ground, sun shining. RW shoveled walk and driveway before going to lab. Made up batch of fudge, but it won't harden. Babies asleep, Bobby with his tooth under pillow. What a quiet way to spend New Year's Eve.

In the back of the Diary are several lists, including the following:

HOBBIES

Stamps   Gardening
Music   Sewing
Photography   Cooking
Chess   Decorating

MAGAZINES

Life   Better Homes & Gardens
Newsweek   Flower Grower
Scientific American   Country Gentleman
J Neurophysiol   Stamp Exchange

CHAPTER XVIII
Epilogue

We spent five happy years in Utah, surrounded by industrious and caring Mormon neighbors. Lovely daughter, Cheryl, arrived midway in that idyllic interlude. Elizabeth delighted in her garden, and we used our irrigation water to grow not only peas and corn but the start of a productive orchard and bed of asparagus. We were astonished to see, upon our return to the scene several years later, that the present owners had replaced with a sea of grass our small efforts at self-sufficiency.

When Horace Davenport became head of the Department of Physiology at the University of Michigan in Ann Arbor, we uprooted ourselves again and trekked back across the country. Finding an affordable house to our liking, and purse, in this lovely town proved unexpectedly difficult, and we spent 17 frustrating months in cramped University housing [Fig 68] before moving into the home we finally had built [Fig 69]. Again, it was planting, sewing drapes, selecting furnishings to make us content with our surroundings; and to the joy of us all baby Richard was born. Elizabeth was nearly 43. We bought her a station wagon with power steering and automatic shift, so at last she learned to drive, with never so much as a scratched fender in the ensuing 35 years.

It was almost as though we had just settled in, when we decided to move again. Actually, it had been five years in Michigan, and my career was progressing nicely. I was called to the University of Rochester as a full professor, a bit of an achievement just 10 years after receiving my doctorate. The move at first was highly traumatic, for Michigan was in a mild depression and there were no buyers for the home that had so pleased us. But in Rochester it was all worth the while. We were able to afford a mi-

664

nor mansion [Fig 70], albeit in great need of refurbishing. We spent the next two years painting and papering, applying the skills Elizabeth and I had learned so well with our Chicago house.

Our yen for travel began to be amply fulfilled. With the children we sooner or later visited, and often revisited, all the lower 48 states plus Hawaii, the Canadian Rockies, Expositions at New York, Montréal and Vancouver. Then in 1965 I was finally able to begin introducing Elizabeth to the fascination with foreign sites and customs that I had experienced during the war. Ultimately we visited most of the scenes of my wartime experience, Italy [Figs 101, 103], Great Britain [Figs 81, 82], and India. It began, however, with Japan in 1965 [Figs 83-86] at the International Physiological Congress. We returned in 1981, as guests of the government thanks to one of my very successful postdoctoral fellows, Professor Yukihiko Kayama. We lived a couple of weeks in Osaka while Kayama and I did a series of experiments; then traveled on our own throughout Honshu and Hokkaido [Fig 86], and on to wonderful adventures in Taiwan. One of our most memorable trips was India, the unforgettable Taj Mahal, Fatapur Sikri, a week on a houseboat in the Vale of Kashmir and the Garden of the Shalimar at Srinigar, the fabulous Chandra temples at Khuajaraho, then Varanasi and the Ganges, Calcutta; Katmandu, Nepal, riding elephants on photographic tiger hunts in the Rapti River preserve beneath Annapurna, and finally, the incredible experience of Everest, Ama Dablam, the vast spread of the Himalaya from our hotel window at 13,500 ft [Figs 91-100]!

We spent a month in Mexico, touring widely between my University duties. Another summer we went to Paris, and then drove 1400 miles throughout thc United Kingdom, London, Stonehenge, Aberystwyth, Long Meg [Fig 82], Hadrian's Wall, rooming in a castle outside Edinburgh, Loch Lomond, Dublin, Galway [Fig 81] and the cliffs of Mohar. We always liked to drive, save in Japan where we couldn't reliably read the signs. One great trip started in Rotterdam, then along the Rhine to Basel, the Eiger and Jungfrau at Grindelwald, in a snowstorm to Grenoble, along the Riviera, Ventimiglia, La Spezia, the Carazza marble mountains of the Appenines, Etruscan tombs, Rome, where our Netherlands car became a target of opportunity despite my care in having a car to conceal our luggage in the trunk. I arrived in Naples for the second time in my life with only the clothes on my back. The hotel clerk was not perturbed by our absence of baggage when we told him that it had been stolen while we visited the Museo di Civilizatione Romana. It was an adventure; and there was Pompeii, a lovely hotel in Sorrento, where we got the idea of using much decorative tile in our new home. On to Amalfi, and the majestic temple at Paestum [Fig 101]. We and a German couple were able to visit it, despite it being closed on Mondays, simply by finding a hole in the fence. Then we proceeded up central Italy to St Pietro Vecchio ("old", and only ruins, "Nuovo" being the appellation of the modern town), where I could show Elizabeth the area of combat I had visited in January 1944. We shed a tear at the amphitheater of crosses adjacent to the rebuilt monastery at Monte Cassino, the cemetery for the Polish dead that, with so many others, had so valiantly striven to break the "Winter Line".

On another occasion we drove from Frankfurt to Budapest via Vienna, and then through the Austrian Alps and Bavaria to Göttingen, and the Hartz mountains, from which we viewed that insult to human freedom, the barbed wire and machine guns keeping the East Germans from the temptations of the West. We had already experienced the strange horror of Lenin's handiwork on an extensive trip to the Soviet Union in 1973 [Figs 87-90]. Our knowledge of Russian made the subtle controls, and lies, starkly apparent. Actually, knowledge of Russian was not necessary to perceive the fallaciousness of the system. Upon our arrival on a Saturday night at the Hotel Rossiya, the largest in the world, they had "run out of" beer! The washstand drain was repaired with wrapped rags. But the Uspenski Sobor, the gold-plated cathedral of the Tzars within the Kremlin was magnificent. We saw Napoleon's sled and many wonders of Moscow, including heart warming hospitality of our Russian hosts. Then on to meetings at Rostov na Donu, to Tbilisi [Fig 87] in Georgia where we were elegantly toured, and rented a little Zhiguli (Fiat) to drive back and forth to Yerevan. The last miles there were on a deserted 4-lane divided highway, from which elderly women swept the stones with a bundle of sticks. We were diverted to Odessa because Intourist didn't have enough guests for the hotel there. The high school children, with machine guns, goose stepped along the waterfront [Fig 90], still in memory of the heros who had held out for months against the German hordes; and all the while, secretively, American grain was being unloaded at the port, as our forbidden camera documented. We finally reached our destination, Vilnius, Lithuania, where we had hoped to visit the birthplace of Elizabeth's parents. A steely "nel'zya!" (forbidden), however, met our every plea.

Our last great trip was to Kenya [Figs 105-108], where we did the usual wonderful tourist things of visiting Abedares, Samburu, Lakes Baringo and Nakuru, the Masa Mara and Amboseli beneath Mt Kilimanjaro. We rented a Suzuki jeep and explored the vast country of Tsavo East and West, all amply rewarded by the sight of great herds of elephant, water buffalo, lions, weaver birds and their ingenious nests; and ending on the shores of the cerulean Indian Ocean south of Mombassa.

In the meantime, back in Rochester, after the children were all on to college (or the army with Robert Jr), we departed our "mansion" after 20 years, and built another on 90 acres of forest and farmland [Fig 71, and Frontispiece] a 15-minute drive south of the city. Elizabeth was in her glory, designing a garden as large and diverse as she could imagine [Fig 71, 73]. The rock garden in spring is breathtaking, as is the nearly a kilometer of daffodils she planted, threading through the hedgerow and along the garden borders; and then the iris, peonies, lilacs, roses, potentilla, lilies, poppies, columbine, phlox, rose of Sharon, chrysanthemums, and numerous viburnums - and the orchard, some 40 trees that yearly overwhelm us with cherries, peaches, pears and apples, and an extensive vineyard. With our honey bees and yearly venison, plus a ¼ acre garden we became almost self-sufficient with food, Elizabeth one year, for instance, making 72 quarts of tomato sauce; and we made our own maple syrup!

We celebrated a full 20 years of that euphoric state before Elizabeth died, almost by an act of will. She had two uncomfortable years, gradually being worn down physically though not in spirit. Macular degeneration deprived her of easy reading, and congestive heart failure began severely to confine her activities. On the day she died she expressed for the first time a desperate impatience with her physically imprisoned state, and that evening, quite unexpectedly to us all, her tired heart simply stopped. From the hedgerows we took a serene and stately rock [Fig 111], now inscribed:

Elizabeth Natalie Doty, née Radzun-Jusewich
23 November 1915 - 18 April 1999
May the beauty of her garden forever reflect the beauty
that was her life.

It reposes beneath the butterfly bush, illuminated by a burst of daffodils each spring. For each day since, I am urged to weep disconsolately for her absence; yet my sorrow is coupled with a sense of triumph, for no life could have been more fulfilling than that we shared. Thus, I cannot mourn, as I am forever blessed with memories of an incomparable togetherness. Life offers nothing to surpass it.

CHAPTER XIX
Analyses and Comment

With an awesome inventiveness Evolution has wrought a system of utter ingenuity for the reproduction of humankind. The driving force to revision of the common mammalian/primate pattern of sexual relations has been the dramatic near doubling of the size of the human brain in the course of a mere 40,000 generations, roughly 1 million years, from *Homo erectus* to *H. neanderthalensis* and *H. sapiens*. What fomented this explosive brain growth must be left for future debate; but the basic problem created by this unparalleled expansion was that the size of the brain at birth contended with the size of the pelvic aperture through which it must pass. The "solution" was to restrain the brain's prenatal size, and allow it to attain its uniquely enormous volume among mammals (in relation to body size) by growing throughout the long years of childhood. Even so, the "minimum" allowable head size at birth comes at a cost of considerable trauma to the mother (see above!); and the offspring enters the world with but a minimum of its ultimate mental equipment, helpless for many years.

Survival of such an initially incapacitated mother and an infant demanding years of nourishment and instruction prior to achieving quasi-independence must surely benefit from male protection and assistance. But how to retain such interest from a male, so free to roam? Everyone knows the answer. The human male evolved into a creature of continual sexual rut, and the human female co-evolved to accommodate it, concealing ovulation while remaining sexually receptive throughout most of her cycle, thus promoting a large measure of nonreproductive sexual activity.

Of course, society, and the lack of other constraints upon

this simple pairing, have contrived astonishing variations on this elemental theme; yet it remains the emotional and practical bedrock from which human sexual relations proceed. In the course of this evolution the brain and mind of human male and female have become as distinctly different as have their bodies. It is estimated that the genetic "distance" between mankind and chimpanzees is but 2% of their total genome; whereas between human male and female it is a stunning 3%! This difference translates not only into the numerous differences in anatomy and hormonal milieu of male and female, but is reflected in the basic organization of the brain and the attendant vagaries of behavior. Individual variation, of course, is enormous, and schooled by custom and experience; yet for millennia the general differences in male and female intellectual skills and predilections have been too obvious to be denied. Current psychological research (e.g., Kimura, 2000; Dobbs & Dobbs, 2000; Potts & Short, 1999) thoroughly affirms and analyzes these inherent cognitive differences, which contribute so greatly to the richness of human experience, and to much of marital strife.

The million years of disparate roles for male and female have subtly imprinted corresponding cognitive styles - male spatial skill derived from wandering in the hunt, female linguistic and social aptitude from cooperative child rearing by women in the band, sisters, mothers, grandmothers, obliviously fostering survival of the genes they held in common.

It is survival through successful reproduction that has also molded the distinctly different male and female sexual perceptions; attitudes deeply organized by Evolution that, a priori, seem quite antithetical to the condition of marriage. The male, forever prey to sexual excitement, would have a world of women, spreading his genes afar; but woman, allowed but a few costly attempts at perpetuating her genetic endowment, needs but the one, the very best male from whom, if she is skillful and lucky, she can extract not only the necessary sperm but years-long service in the care and survival of herself and offspring. Surprisingly, these seemingly contradictory modes of attaining genetic survival are beautifully and effectively blended in the arrangement of monogamous pair-bonding, where the woman has her male support and the male not only relief from his incessant sexual longings but assurance that the children upon whom he will bestow years of care and protection are, indeed, his messengers into the genetic future.

The arrangement is far from perfect. The human male with his incessant sexual urge, driven physiologically by continuous production of semen and psychologically by a high titer of testosterone, is not always attuned in sexual eagerness with the female, who has her own even more complex physiological and accompanying hormonal/psychological states to contend with. This potential asymmetry in desire offers a common, but not insuperable, hazard to the stability of the reproductive male/female bond, otherwise so artfully crafted by eons of success.

Society, however, has not done particularly well in understanding this arrangement, nor the keen satisfaction in life with which it blesses those so bonded, as they acknowledge, and live by, an atavism deeply carved into the essence of being human. Throughout recorded history, and no doubt long before, male strength and desire often made women trophies of war, the rape of the Sabines, the field of the virgins, where the Muscovites assembled the yearly tribute of their daughters to the tatars; the harem, or the houris of heaven. Much of Christianity has been diverted by poor St Augustine's revolt against his autonomic nervous system and a pathological worship of celibacy as the highest of human conditions. With the loosening grip of this mythology in modern times, the escape from family arranged marriage, and relief from other impediments to joyful fulfillment of the sexual roles that Evolution has so strongly fostered, the scene is set for marriage to become the lifelong delight that Elizabeth and I experienced. Clearly, as evidenced in the high rate of divorce, and a sad variety of other societal ills, the path is neither simple nor assured; but we have herewith presented a paradigmatic example that it can be attained; and have illustrated as well the threats which abound along the way.

671

Sex, Intimacy, and Quarrels

As can be seen in Chapter III, in its early stages our court-ship was already sexually contentious. Neither of us had the slightest insight into the above discussed roles that Evolution had assigned us. Nothing in the "marriage manual" that we read, to become informed on sexual procedures, had any hint of the great divide in sexual proclivities that awaited us. The phrase,"not tonight, dear", would at first have meant nothing; but almost any long-married couple immediately comprehends it, the urgent male met with female reluctance. The differences in our sexual expectations were inevitably to become on occasion a matter of deep discord between Elizabeth and myself, as it must between almost any married couple. But this was neither anticipated nor understood, and required many painful episodes before we ultimately learned, to a reasonable degree, how to re-solve the tension between us in this regard. It bears emphasis that this struggle existed between two people intensely, and per-manently, in love with each other, a fact to which the foregoing Chapters massively attest. It was also never a case of simple fe-male disinterest. Quite the contrary, Elizabeth found our physi-cal union to be as precious an affirmation of our love as did I, an expression of ineffable beauty that bound us together in an al-most mystical bliss.

This struggle between precipitate male and equally ardent but rational female began almost immediately, and wove contin-ually throughout our courtship, e.g.:

25 Jun 41 "Then he kissed me, more intimately than ever be-fore; and I told him 'because I love you'. And then that horrid bugaboo again. So I told him of my ideals in retaining my virgin-ity; and we seriously discussed marriage . . ."

This, less than a month after our first "date". And so it contin-ued:

6 Jul 41 "Lord! What can I do when every cell of me craves him, yet craven-like I put obstacles in the way?" **11 Jul 41** "Bob is so

672

passionate, and I know it's difficult for him to hold himself in check. He's remarked about my restraint. Hope he never doubts the sincerity of my affection for him."

But then, with my continuing return to the subject:

27 Jul 41 "Bob wants to get married right away . . . Is it purely for sex convenience that he wants to marry me?" And: **2 Aug 41** "Moonlight, Bob looking as handsome as a Greek god on Mt Olympus. I never wanted to surrender as much as I did then, but sanity intervened and I demurred. And he told me he thot I was afraid he wouldn't marry me and was holding that back as a come on. Well, maybe I am."

In other words, she was on the one hand equally passionate, yet on the other had the clear-headed female's appraisal of the multiple possibilities and irretrievable consequences of sexual engagement.

14 Aug 41 "Odd, but I find myself curious and eager to enter into sex relations with Bob. Can I do it safely and with no loss of face with him? If I could be sure, I would have no hesitation. It would make him happy and gratify my own desire."

Note how we were both aware of the intricate motivations of our respective positions, she as to my urgency, I as to the possibility that she might be using that urgency to her own ends; and we each could only at that time estimate the level of sincerity in the other. Life, even in love, seems to abound with endless alternatives. In the actual fact of marriage, however, these nuances of suspected motivation by either of us essentially disappeared. She might thwart my desire on occasions when she was angry over my behavior, for instance, but I would interpret this as anger, not as a deliberate machination on her part to use sexual attraction as a means to attain her goal. Similarly, when I was demanding while she was reluctant, the argument was never that I was simply seeking sexual gratification.

Indeed, one of the most precious, and unanticipated joys of

marriage we found to be simple intimacy. Orgiastic moments provided the elemental cement, the bond of unrestrained rapture between us; but such moments are relatively brief. It was the ever-present delight of simple touch, a caress in the morning, an impulsive kiss while doing dishes, or as I wrote from the Antarctic Sea with ecstatic recollection:

30 May 44 - "sweetly brushing our noses in the darkness, lacing our cold clumsy toes playfully together under the secrecy of the blankets way down in a bed where our feet meet and recognize each other".

These are the unceasing rewards of marriage, a sweetly reassuring intimacy otherwise unknown save between mother and child.

Evolution provided this state of incomparable happiness to effect reproduction, and indeed it does. However, given the price it extracts from the woman, as well as the present propulsion of the world to a "standing room only" condition, couples with even a modicum of common sense will perceive that the happiness offered by monogamy is profoundly enhanced by contraception. One need only recall the situation with Queen Victoria of England, as joyously married to her beloved Albert as were Elizabeth and I. Yet the Queen, mother ultimately of 9 children, most born without anesthesia, was to write how childbirth was the "shadow-side of marriage", and that she at such moments felt like a cow or dog, "when our poor nature becomes very animal and unecstatic." Of course, her fecundity was partly promoted by having wet nurses for the children; yet it is plain to see how such constant consequence might color the delight of intercourse with her mate. Although Elizabeth and I ultimately had four children, each was a deliberate choice. We certainly did not wish children until the stability of our marriage was well-established, as was our financial situation. This was long before "the pill", and the choice of reliable procedure was the condom or the diaphragm. The former was by far the most natural but, of course, the male would always complain of lessened sensation; Elizabeth professed never to understand how analogous it was to the sense of touch through a surgical glove, sufficient, but attenuated. In any event, with this dissatisfaction I peremptorily "ordered" her (28 Nov 43) to get fitted for the diaphragm. I am now appalled at the demanding tone of my request, yet it must be admitted that the tone was prompted by her reluctance. Though she rather protested, she did comply; and we "experimented", as I put it. I no longer remember any of the details, but within a year or two we returned to our initial practice; the cold calculation of the mechanics prior to the act undoubtedly being a dissuading factor.

Although we rigorously practiced contraception, motherhood was an early and enduring desire of hers, until our family achieved the "ideal" outcome, a boy, a girl, another girl, and a boy. I remain awesomely astonished how, after suffering all the discomforts of pregnancy and the flesh-rending pangs of childbirth, she was so eager to "try again". Does one need better evidence of how the deft hand of Evolution has crafted the female mind!?

As adumbrated in our courtship, the sexual bond between us was both the fundamental source of our delight in each other, and the cause of occasionally serious strife between us. There were times when my advances were refused, from my point of view unreasonably so, and I would "sulk", as she put it. This, of course, was nonhelpful, and angered her, dispelling on subsequent days whatever romantic inclination she might otherwise have had. In other words, a vicious circle was triggered, and it was not easy for us to extricate ourselves from it. For the most part, she was correct in her appraisal that it was she who most often repaired the situation, a conclusion we both fervently, but oh so clumsily, desired. The precipitating factor was almost always more complicated than mere disagreement on an evening's activities. For instance, I shared her pride and exultation in our having, at last, attained a lovely home, but failed to live up to her expectations of what seemed to me redundant housecleaning, gradually building up her resentment. Or over a period of weeks she would justifiably come to feel neglected, as I devoted most of my time and energy to study or research. Or she might anger me by some trivial criticism, of "spoiling" our son, etc. Whatever, the dampening of romance by such happenings could unleash a dismal period of stubborn aloofness in both of us, from which it proved so difficult to escape.

Despite the depth of our quarrels, however, for the most part we almost surrealistically at such times continued the normal rhythm of our domestic life, shopping, visiting family, etc, suggesting that neither of us really perceived the rift as irreparable, certainly not desirable. On no occasion did I ever even consider physical assault, a not uncommon male response to frustration. Female choice is paramount, and should be unassailable. Sooner or later we would both collapse, with an enormous sense of relief as sweet irresistible sex rescued us from our dreadful impasse. The renewal of that bond, sacred to us both, left us overjoyed at the reaffirmation of our love. As she one time wrote, we should never argue by mail, for it lacks the possibility of rapturous reconciliation.

Money

As children of the Great Depression, we were both well-imbued with thrift. Elizabeth was a bit more cautious than myself, sometimes extending our frugality to cases of trivial expense. This occasioned a few brief arguments, but never anything serious. I attribute her "overreaction" first to the fact of being woman and thus instinctively more concerned with security; but also because the Depression had been even more devastating to her family than to mine, her father having lost his well-paying job of many years, and it was only the savings that the family had accumulated that kept them from losing their home.

There were (rare) occasions when I was the more thrifty, one of the more memorable being my lecture to her just before our marriage. Her family had urged her to get a "trousseau" for her wedding, an idea that appealed to her, and two days before the wedding she purchased a moderately expensive dress. I protested this unnecessary expenditure, given our very slim financial resources as we approached married life. She was peeved, and gave no firm hint that she accepted my criticism. However, she returned the dress the next day.

Most such transgressions on our mutual thrift were mine. We were always very careful with our money. While I was in the army most of my pay went to the bank, as did hers. Consequently we were able to realize our hopes of obtaining both a home and an education for me; although our fiscal situation was at times sorely strained. It saddens me now to read in her diaries of that postwar period how she thought I might criticize her "extravagance" in spending a few of our scarce dollars on plantings for the garden; yet it was just such sensibility, and common sense, that kept us from ever being financially threatened. Other than our mortgage, and $20 I borrowed for our honeymoon, we never paid a cent for borrowed money.

Any major purchase always involved careful discussion between us as to its necessity, and agreement on the details of the item, e.g., color, size, etc. For instance, we decided to forego the expense of changing from coal to gas heat, much as we disliked the former; but we did see an electric hot water heater as both affordable and a significant convenience. Elizabeth consistently insisted on purchasing items of high quality, whenever the price/quality ratio indicated value. As reflected in our $10 wedding ring, we both felt even moderately expensive jewelry to represent a foolhardy waste of money. And our marriage had begun with frugality, foregoing the nonsense of a wedding celebration, an outlay whose absurdity Erasmus had warned against already in 1526, although we knew nothing of Erasmus.

We did have one very serious quarrel re finances. This was the Crisis detailed in Chapter VIII. While there were threads other than money in this trying episode, a very major factor in her reluctance to join my army life was that it would mean losing the income from her War Department job. This was significant money, and the choice was the more bitter since she had just gotten the raise and advancement that she had been striving to obtain for more than a year. This "extravagance" in losing this income was certainly not offset by my increased pay as an army officer. In the actual fact she did opt, as I so strongly urged, for this extravagance, and happily so. In the ensuing years she was able to earn, and bank, significant sums from other work, so that the penalty was not as great as first perceived; and the wonderful reward of our togetherness was priceless.

In sum: common sense, flexibility, a pervasive thriftiness, and full consensus between us as to what we should and should not buy, kept our marriage free of argument over money. Fundamentally, we never needed prompting, one from the other, that our desires simply should not exceed our income.

In-laws

That there should be a certain asperity between a husband and his wife's mother is almost proverbial. The relation between mother and daughter, again, is strongly prompted by the care of Evolution that the genes continue. Modern science has established the remarkable fact that mothers pass their mitochondrial genes directly and unaltered to their daughters. This is true also in the case of sons. They have their mother's mitochondrial genes, but of course that is an end of it, for male children cannot pass their mitochondria to their descendants. Be that as it may, the stronger bond is that mothers in all societies fervently attend and assist their daughters when the latter give birth. This empathy is strong, and men rail against it at their peril.

Bonding in the other direction, of a son towards his mother, may be a much more intrusive relation should it be strong. A wife inevitably takes pride in her home, and how she pursues the rights and duties of maintaining a household. The son's mother can seldom resist suggestions for improvement (for her son's sake!), and the wife reflexly interprets such advice as criticism. If the son supports the mother, resentment is inevitable.

In the case of Elizabeth and myself the latter situation was essentially defanged. I had long had a strained relation with my family, an attitude freely communicated to Elizabeth. The temper of the relations with my parents fluctuated, however, and there was a period when her resentment of them carried much farther than did mine (at that time). The story is complicated, but can be discerned in Chapters VIII and XIV. The first occurred when my parents gave her essentially no help during the stressful closing of our apartment when she agreed to join me in Wyoming. In this I fully shared her anger. In the other instance, after birth of our son, I was more ambivalent, since I was at the peak of my furor over my mother-in-law. Throughout the years, however, my parents were, basically, a minor issue, in which Elizabeth and I shared a dutiful relation to them.

The closeness between Elizabeth, as the eldest child, and her mother was a deeper matter. Early on I formed a moderate antipathy toward her mother, in that the woman, quite naturally, questioned whether I was a desirable suitor for her daughter. This was certainly a legitimate concern, in that I was only a low paid factory hand, and was 4 years junior to her Elizabeth. This appraisal I could have tolerated, but what made it contentious was the comparison given with her sister's beau who, putatively, came from a family with more substantial means. In any event, it was a bad start. I suppose it is also correct to phrase it that I was jealous of Elizabeth's ready willingness to retire to the comfort of her parents' home during the peregrinations of my army career, even though the logic of her doing so was perfectly clear to me. My overwrought hostility toward her mother forms a major theme of Chapter XIV. Despite my protestations there was nothing logical to do other than accept the Jusewich hospitality for my wife, son and myself, for 3 long and crowded months. I fear that I was often the boorish son-in-law as we struggled with our frustration. It was a nightmare for Elizabeth, beholden to her domineering and temperamental mother, keeping the ire of her husband in check, and tending to a very demanding infant son. It was a fearful test of tact, and endurance, and it speaks volumes as to the stability of her character. In the long run I did come to appreciate the generous help of both her mother and father as we acquired the skills of home ownership and, although there still were times when her mother and I clashed, we developed a mutual respect. Our move to Utah, of course, removed us from such family tensions, and Elizabeth was just as happy to have it so.

Obviously, there is no set solution to the in-law problem,

save that man and wife must be forever clear as to where their first loyalty lies, to each other. The quarrels it may instill between them must be settled on that principle, on recognizing the nature of these family relations, and not permitting constant provocation and argument to ensue. It would also be helpful, as typified in the cases just discussed, to recognize that emotions may slowly fluctuate with time and circumstance, the antipathies need not be permanent, though they may for a time be severe.

Domains of Dominance

In all societies there tends to be a gender-based division of labor. In many instances this distribution of responsibilities probably draws upon genetically influenced characteristics of the two sexes, but there is also a strong cultural overlay. Elizabeth and I seem to fit the typical pattern of Western culture, in which woman is mistress of the home, primary cook, seamstress, and flower gardener. The man, on the other hand, tends to things requiring greater strength, construction, transportation, and farming.

The most important difference in our roles, other than as mother and father, surely lay in duties of household maintenance. While I took pride in our home, Elizabeth was something of a fanatic in seeing that things met her very exacting standards, of cleanliness, order, and beauty. This was true from our very first married days, although it was somewhat constrained when it was only the 3-room apartment and we both worked 6 days/week. Once we had our own house and she had constant responsibility for it, her enthusiasm far exceeded my own, and led to several quarrels between us. She was never sparing of herself; indeed, one of my main complaints was that she not infrequently overworked herself with mopping, washing, polishing, cutting grass, etc. My role was to do the "heavy work", keep up the furnace, dig in the garden, put up the storm windows, make repairs, etc. She could be a veritable tyrant in extracting such labors from me (admittedly often to my reluctance), and she was free with her criticisms of my performance. One can readily see her frequent remarks disparaging both my commitment and my talent; and, of course, this did little to improve my enthusiasm for her commands. Occasionally, however, I was delighted to be her slave and enjoyed the togetherness of purpose that it exemplified. Yet more often I felt unfairly abused as being uncooperative; or I might vigorously protest that she was making an error, e.g., putting up storm windows too early. Such instances aggravated us both, and sometimes led to serious quarrels.

However, in all these matters of the house and its appearance, of how we dressed the children, of what we ate and how it was cooked, she was unquestionably "in charge". I might complain or advise, and we were, in the vast majority of such matters, in complete agreement. However, it was also always clear that she had complete veto power were my taste or procedure not to her liking.

I, of course, had my areas of responsibility, mostly the car, but also in construction, as in building the fence, painting the exterior trim and, of course, my studies. Again, we always discussed matters of any import, but it was recognized that the final decision devolved upon me.

All these matters were implicit, happening naturally, without our specifically discussing who was responsible for what. The order of things seemed to be simply a "given" of the married state; but it is also of utmost importance that the expectations somehow were mutually understood. Perhaps it is because we were both workaholics, perfectionists, and had a deep sense of responsibility, and unity of purpose, that things fell so easily into place.

Children

I have already remarked on the deep-seated impulse towards motherhood that possessed Elizabeth. Yet she and I were equally in agreement that such event take place only when we were sure that our marriage was stable, that we had adequate income, surroundings and future prospects to assure the full welfare of our offspring. Contraception is an enormous blessing, both to the state of marriage, and to the children whose purpose it is to protect. Planned parenthood should be among the highest goals of humankind.

Little need be said about a mother's incessant care and concern for her infant. When possible, of course, some respite is most welcome, from father, grandmother or whomever; but the mother's devotion is unyielding. As things progress to childhood, however, a father becomes more useful, participating avidly in the education of the little mind. Here a tension at times develops between the mother's protective instincts and the father's more bold or demanding interactions with the child. Ultimately, with us as seemingly with most couples, a gentle arrangement developed where I became the figure of discipline and Elizabeth the dispenser of comfort and security. This was never a starkly divided duty. She too could spank the misbehaving loved one, and usually agreed with the need for my occasional sternness. Sometimes, however, there was disagreement, and emotional arguments ensued, as to how to deal with the errant child, or the nature of the consequent punishment.

One point of persistent aggravation was the desire of the young child to sleep with its parents. I now perceive how natural this is, again an ingrained consequence of Evolution, where the dangers of the night best keep the young fearful and close to the safety of their parents. This innate fear is further reinforced by nightmares, so that the child, grappling with phantoms, is strongly impelled towards the security of its parents' bed. Sadly, this viewpoint was foreign to me at the time, and I was generally quite intolerant of this behavior, much to Elizabeth's ire at my attempted thwarting of her mothering instincts. We went through this with all the children, and while I gradually learned to expect and endure this behavior, my patience never matched hers, and it was a lingering source of argument.

This competition between child and husband for the mother's attention brings about a subtle, but inescapable change in the marital relation. As mother, the wife must then divide the love and loyalties heretofore bestowed solely upon the husband. I no longer remember how Elizabeth and I worked this out. I believe that we did clearly recognize the fact, and understanding the origin and nature of one's emotions is vastly useful in controlling them. However, I think I remember entertaining some vague sense of loss, that the glorious unity, ours when we were but unto each other alone, was somehow diluted when it came to be shared with the intruders, children. It was not resentment, but perhaps nostalgia for what had been. The mother, of course, may recognize, and even explain this fact to the impatient father; but, basically, she is puzzled by his sense of loss, two loves for her are not in the least incompatible. Indeed, to her they are reinforcing. Most of this change between the spouses passes without note, yet it is real, and in some instances may perturb marital peace.

We both took boundless delight in watching the progress of the children. From the earliest moment, when they had sufficient understanding, they were put to bed by one of us, usually myself, reading them a bedtime story. While such was not necessarily the intent, I believe this habit did urge the children towards literacy, for they all quickly acquired an interest in books, and learned to read at an early age.

Health

Good health is an invaluable possession. Both Elizabeth and I were continually alert to preserving it, not only each for himself but each for the sake of the other. At the time of our marriage and while I was in the army I was something of an exercise zealot; but with the subsequent pressures of academic life "workouts" became too time consuming. I continued, however, to take such opportunities as might arise, such as eschewing use of the "up" elevator to reach my 6th floor office.

Despite my repeated exhortations and dire predictions I could only briefly convert Elizabeth to my point of view (e.g., her letter **23 Feb 43:**

"I drag out the old blanket and spread it on the dining room rug. Put out lights very modestly and strip, and oh, what a fine feeling to lie in the nude on the blanket and stretch your muscles in a series of movements until your body assumes a rosy hue and becomes bathed in droplets of perspiration.")

However, she rebelled against my consistent propaganda (her letter **27 Feb 43:**

"My daily lecture noted, Robert, dearest. Don't you dare lecture me by remote control! I know you do it for my own good, but you remind me so much of my dearest Momma who felt it necessary to supervise my every move and advise me from morning to night on what to do and when to do it, etc., but did that cure me of smoking? No! did it make me drink milk? No! Did it keep me from marrying you? No! You see how hopeless it is, dearest".)

She simply was never fond of exercise for the sake of exercise. She claimed empathy with the cat, that so conspicuously luxuriates in its laziness yet remains lithe and agile. In any event, we both remained fit and in excellent health, mine still maintained at 82, where hers began to fail at about that age.

There is no ready explanation for our good fortune in that regard, just a combination of good genes and common sense. Throughout our life we maintained the same weight that we had the day we were married. We ate moderately but always diversely. Neither of us liked greasy or fat foods, yet we paid no attention to avoiding high calorie items. Despite her enjoyment of laziness, Elizabeth spent very few moments lounging about. Both of us were energetic and quick moving, and this may be what allowed us to maintain our physique despite our relative indifference to diet and exercise. We always congratulated ourselves on remaining physically attractive to each other. She frequently maintained that it was her smoking that kept her from getting fat. That is likely to be a myth. Luckily she was always moderate in that nasty habit, but equally resistant to my remonstrances, and later to those of her children as well, that she abandon the addiction. In addition to the one about not getting fat, she had a time-worn excuse: one reason she was attracted to me was that I smoked the same brand of cigarettes that she did. I, of course, gladly gave up the habit some time before going in the army, terminating a foolishness of some 4 years standing. As a physiologist, at the time had I known that tobacco smoke inhibits ciliary action in the respiratory passages, I would have been far more peremptory in my pleadings. Yet it can also be said that nicotine contributed significantly to her enjoyment of life, from about age 14 to 78, when she had a bronchial bleed and ceased immediately. The inevitable emphysema from this often deadly pleasure did complicate her final years. So, too, did some degree of osteoporosis, that might have been ameliorated by less cat-like behavior, or fewer pregnancies.

Religion/Philosophy of Life

The gift of intellect comes with the knowledge of mortality. Early in the existence of *H. sapiens,* and perhaps also *H. neanderthalensis,* the question of mortality was undoubtedly often rendered ambiguous by encountering, in vivid dreams, those who were long dead. This, heightened by Evolution's intense prompting to live, and the baffling mystery of death, fostered the belief that the dead somehow, somewhere lived on. The pervasive and tenacious nature of this idea is evidenced globally, from the handaxe entombed with the fetally positioned, prehistoric corpse, to the elaborate care seen in Egypt's Valley of the Kings or China's vast clay armies at Xian for Qin Shi Huang Din's command in the afterlife. There has thus been built an elaborate folly, otherwise called religion, that continues to ensnare and confuse human thought, omnipresent throughout the world. The pathological nature of this affliction can most readily be appreciated by the vicious consequences attendant to different versions of these imaginings, from the Punic Wars (the Romans, thankfully, ridding the world of yet another Semitic invention, the child-sacrifice demanding god, Ba'al), from the battle of Tours to the Crusades to the present confrontation between Islamic extremists and whomever they disagree with. The 30-Year War, Torquemada, Cromwell, Northern Ireland, Kosovo, small milestones of slaughter for belief.

The foregoing paragraph recapitulates a thesis often visited in my letters. Here it but serves as reminder of the overwhelming power of religious ideas to kindle deep emotion. Were husband and wife to contend for different fantasies, a peaceful marriage seems an unlikely outcome. Of course, given the flexibility of the human mind, it is possible to sequester incompatible thoughts one from the other, something of what the psychiatrists call an "encapsulated paranoia". If the critical subject matter is rigorously avoided by the parties, such a marriage may survive; but it remains endangered, and is basically flawed. In other words, it seems logical in the emotion laden realm of religion that man and wife have corresponding beliefs and philosophies.

It must be admitted that part of the strong intellectual attraction Elizabeth and I had for each other was that we had each worked through the conventional beliefs of our respective religious upbringings and found them simply incredible. We, no more than any other human being, possessed unassailable insight into the nature of reality and our place within it; but we accepted this mystery for what it was, and were prepared to live our lives unburdened with the trappings of superstition. Our success is evident. We never diverged in the least on our view of life, moral responsibility, or even on political outlook. In other words, we were deeply compatible in our expectations from life and our reactions to it.

When the children were teenagers, we did for a few years attend the Unitarian Church. This was a deliberate action to expose the children to the culture in which we most happily lived; and by this formality to insure, to some degree, that our unorthodoxy not leave some corner of morality unattended. We all enjoyed for a while this interchange with our like-minded peers, but ultimately there was a certain redundancy. The termination came when the Unitarian community opposed the war in Vietnam, which we strongly supported, although not the manner in which it was being prosecuted. The Unitarian contact had served its purpose, however, for the children had at least then seen how most of the nation spent Sunday mornings. If there were proselytizing, it remained ineffective, for the children have followed their parents in leading honest, moral lives without benefit of

686

"the word of God" spoken by self-professed intermediaries of often dubious quality and fallible intent.

Conclusions

Sexual attraction is paramount for marriage in most instances, a compelling foundation wrought by eons of evolution. However, the subtly but divisively differing perceptions, desires and consequences attendant thereto for male versus female must also be recognized, and accommodated by each, otherwise marriage becomes a scene of perpetual sexual strife. Nor is sex alone sufficient for primates so generously endowed with mind. Intellectual compatibility, in outlook and ambition, are equally essential, along with a good dose of common sense. From the above example of marriage, and its lifelong success, it can also be deduced that two people intensely in love can, nevertheless, engage in prolonged and nasty quarrels. This sad fact must probably be anticipated for most enduring human relationships, the price somehow we seem to pay for being vividly human. Yet love can still prevail, is deeply reinforced by memories shared, and by the sense of being a couple, a unity, forever bonded against the assaults of a world indifferent if not hostile.

REFERENCES

Aureli F, De Waal FBM (2000) *Natural conflict resolution.* University of California Press, Berkeley, California, 409 pp

Burgess EW, Wallin P, Shultz GD (1954) *Courtship, engagement, and marriage.* Lippincott, Philadelphia, 444 pp

Dabbs JM, Dabbs MG (2000) *Heroes, rogues, and lovers: testosterone and behavior.* McGraw Hill, New York, 284 pp

Doty RW (1951) Influence of stimulus pattern on reflex deglutition. *American Journal of Physiology 166:* 142-158

Doty RW (1998) The five mysteries of the mind, and their consequences. *Neuropsychologia 36:* 1069-1076

Doty RW (2001) Robert W. Doty. In: Squire LR (ed) *The history of neuroscience in autobiography, vol 3.* Academic Press, San Diego, pp 214-244

Doty RW, Bosma JF (1956) An electromyographic analysis of reflex deglutition. *J Neurophysiol 19:* 44-60

Doty RW, Gerard RW (1950) Nerve conduction without increased oxygen consumption: action of azide and fluoroacetate. *American Journal of Physiology 162:* 458-468

Kimura D (2000) *Sex and cognition.* MIT Press, Cambridge, Massachusetts, 217 pp

Potts M, Short R (1999) *Ever since Adam and Eve - The evolution of human sexuality.* Cambridge University Press, Cambridge, 358 pp

POST SCRIPTUM

More on the Possible Pressure of Evolution toward Monogamy

Shortly after inspecting the proofs of this volume I encountered an intriguing set of facts and hypotheses concerning human reproduction, the possible relation between duration of pair bonding and ultimate fertility (Robillard *et al.* 2002, 2003). These data offer a singular convergence, from quite another direction, with the thoughts set forth at the beginning of Chapter XIX, Analyses and Comment. An overview of this felicitous discovery in relation to the previous discussion thus seems instructive and appropriate.

The basic fact, as noted previously, is the extraordinary size of the human brain. This is commonly expressed as the "encephalization quotient", i.e., relation between brain and body size. For man, this ratio is, roughly, a spectacular four times that of the great apes (Jerison 1973). In Chapter XIX the discussion concerned the penalty paid by the mother in birthing this large-brained infant. The data now to be discussed, however, concern instead another feature of large brains, their excessive demand for energy. Brain is an expensive tissue, in adult human beings requiring some 20 watts, *constantly*; consciousness being lost within a few seconds of lapse in oxygen supply. While only 2% of the body weight, the brain uses 20% of the oxygen supplied by the blood, and in young children this ranges as high as 50% (Sokoloff 1989)!

The evolutionary problem is to supply such prodigious nourishment to the extraordinarily large human brain *in utero,* some 60% of the nutritional requirements of the late-term fetus. It is probably this demand that makes human gestation unusual.

Contrary to the placental/uterus relations in other species, tissue of the uterus in the human female is deeply invaded in later stages of gestation. This has the hazardous effect of intimately exposing the mother to antigens of the fetus that are, of course, half derived from the father. It is now hypothesized that the perilous condition of eclampsia (Greek, "to shine forth") arises consequent to this immunological exposure (Robillard et al. 2003). Eclampsia is characterized by severe epileptic convulsions, that prior to modern medicine afflicted roughly 1% of women in their first pregnancy, and was fatal in a third of them. It is now recognized that a less threatening, yet also hazardous condition, "pre-eclampsia" (high blood pressure and other problems), is associated with pregnancy in a most revealing way (Robillard et al. 2002). Pre-eclampsia is far more common when pregnancy ensues shortly after couples begin sexual relations, occurring in 40-45% of cases with less than 4 months cohabitation, 25% at 5-8 months, 15% at 9-12 months, and 3% thereafter. This must be viewed against the fact that human pregnancy is not readily achieved. In animals, undergoing annual periods of estrus, pregnancy results essentially 100% of the time, but for the human female, lacking estrus and repeatedly cycling, pregnancy requires on average perhaps 100 acts of intercourse, with some 15% of pregnancies being terminated by miscarriage. In other words, there is commonly a sustained exposure of the female to the semen and the antigens therein of her male consort before successful pregnancy occurs. Taking that fact together with the diminution in occurrence of pre-eclampsia with duration of sexual relations, the suggestion is obvious that somehow there is a gradual accommodation to male antigens via semen, that is then protective of the female's exposure to the corresponding paternal antigens in her fetus, gradually reducing her susceptibility to eclampsia/pre-eclampsia. In strong affirmation of this thesis, it is found that a woman, having born a child with one father, and being spared pre-eclampsia in subsequent births in that relation, returns to a renewed risk of pre-eclampsia if her fetus is fathered by a new partner.

Thus, one sees a concatenation of circumstances that, in the course of evolving a brain of unique size, would have disposed the human female, and her reproductive success, to benefit substantially from accepting impregnation from but a single male. The interlocking logic of evolutionary steps thus unfolds: 1) the necessity for the unusual invasion of the uterus for the fetus to acquire sufficient nourishment for a larger brain, 2) leading to exposure of the mother to the foreign antigens of the father via the fetus, 3) loss of estrus and concealment of fertility, thus reducing the "efficiency" of impregnation and requiring an extended period of sexual activity, 4) from which the father's antigens are gradually sampled and accommodated to, 5) thus reducing the risk of the mother's exposure to the fetus. In all, it bespeaks an arrangement now well-evidenced in relations between human male and female, an enduring sexual relation between the pair, maximizing reproductive success. Evolution appears to have given advantage to monogamy.

REFERENCES

Jerison HJ (1973) *Evolution of the brain and intelligence.* Academic Press, New York, 482 pp

Robillard P-Y, Chaline J, Chaouat G, Hulsey TC (2003) Preeclampsia/eclampsia and the evolution of the human brain. *Current Anthropology 44*: 130-134

Robillard P-Y, Dekker GA, Hulsey TC (2002) Evolutionary adaptations to pre-eclampsia/eclampsia in humans: low fecundability rate, loss of oestrus, prohibitions of incest and systematic polyandry. *Amer J Reproductive Immunol 47*: 104-111

Sokoloff L (1989) Circulation and energy metabolism of the brain. In: Siegel GJ, Agranoff BW, Albers RW, Molinoff PB (eds) *Basic neurochemistry - molecular, cellular and medical aspects.* Raven, New York, pp. 565-590